MICROECONOMICS
Principles and Policy
First Canadian Edition

William J. Baumol

New York University and Princeton University

Alan S. Blinder

Princeton University

Marc Lavoie

University of Ottawa

Mario Seccareccia

University of Ottawa

NELSON / EDUCATION

NELSON EDUCATION

Microeconomics: Principles and Policy, First Canadian Edition

by William J. Baumol, Alan S. Blinder, Marc Lavoie, and Mario Seccareccia

**Associate Vice President,
Editorial Director:**
Evelyn Veitch

Editor-in-Chief:
Anne Williams

Executive Marketing Manager:
Dave Ward

Developmental Editor:
My Editor Inc.

**Photo Researchers and
Permissions Coordinators:**
Bhisham Kinha, Indu Arora

**Senior Content Production
Manager:**
Natalia Denesiuk Harris

Production Service:
Lachina Publishing Services

Copy Editor:
June Trusty

Proofreader:
Lachina Publishing Services

Indexer:
Lachina Publishing Services

Manufacturing Manager:
Joanne McNeil

Design Director:
Ken Phipps

Managing Designer:
Katherine Strain

Interior Design:
Lisa Albonetti

Cover Image and Design:
Jennifer Leung

Compositor:
Lachina Publishing Services

Printer:
Courier

**Library and Archives Canada
Cataloguing in Publication Data**

Microeconomics : Principles and Policy / William J. Baumol ... [et al.]. — 1st Canadian ed.

Includes bibliographical references and index.

ISBN 978-0-17-625254-0

1. Microeconomics—Textbooks.
I. Baumol, William J.

HB172.M52 2008   338.5
C2008-905671-X

ISBN-13: 978-0-17-625254-0
ISBN-10: 0-17-625254-1

ABOUT THE AUTHORS

■ WILLIAM J. BAUMOL

William J. Baumol was born in New York City and received his BSS at the College of the City of New York and his Ph.D. at the University of London.

He is professor of economics at New York University, and senior research economist and professor emeritus at Princeton University. He is a frequent consultant to the management of major firms in a wide variety of industries in the United States and other countries, as well as to a number of governmental agencies. In several fields, including the telecommunications and electric utility industries, current regulatory policy is based on his explicit recommendations. Among his many contributions to economics are research on the theory of the firm, the contestability of markets, the economics of the arts and other services—the "cost disease of the services" is often referred to as "Baumol's disease"—and economic growth, entrepreneurship, and innovation. In addition to economics, he taught a course in wood sculpture at Princeton for about 20 years.

He has been president of the American Economic Association and three other professional societies. He is an elected member of the National Academy of Sciences, created by the U.S. Congress, and of the American Philosophical Society, founded by Benjamin Franklin. He is also on the board of trustees of the National Council on Economic Education and of the Theater Development Fund. He is the recipient of ten honorary degrees.

Baumol is the author of more than 35 books and hundreds of journal and newspaper articles. His writings have been translated into more than a dozen languages.

■ ALAN S. BLINDER

Alan S. Blinder was born in New York City and attended Princeton University, where one of his teachers was William Baumol. After earning a master's degree at the London School of Economics and a Ph.D. at MIT, Blinder returned to Princeton, where he has taught since 1971. He is currently the Gordon S. Rentschler Memorial Professor of Economics and co-director of Princeton's Center for Economic Policy Studies, which he founded.

In January 1993, Blinder went to Washington as part of President Clinton's first Council of Economic Advisers. Then, from June 1994 through January 1996, he served as vice chairman of the Federal Reserve Board. He thus played a role in formulating both the fiscal and monetary policies of the 1990s, topics discussed extensively in this book. Blinder is a partner in the Promontory Financial Group, a leading consulting and advisory company serving the financial industry. In that capacity, he has consulted for a number of the country's largest financial institutions.

For more than ten years, Blinder wrote newspaper and magazine columns on economic policy, and his op-ed pieces still appear periodically in various newspapers. He also appears frequently on CNN and CNBC, and is a regular commentator on PBS's "Nightly Business Report."

Blinder has been vice president of the American Economic Association and is a member of both the American Philosophical Society and the American Academy of Arts and Sciences. He has two grown sons, two grandsons, and lives in Princeton with his wife, where he plays tennis as often as he can.

MARC LAVOIE

Marc Lavoie was born in Ottawa, Ontario. He attended Carleton University as an undergraduate and then moved on to the University of Paris I (Panthéon-Sorbonne) to do his master's studies and earn a Ph.D. He then returned to Canada in 1979 and joined the University of Ottawa, where he has taught ever since and where he is now full professor of economics.

Lavoie is the author and co-author or co-editor of eight books (two of which are on the economics of ice hockey), and has published over 50 book chapters and 100 articles in refereed journals. Besides sports economics, his main expertise is in pricing theories, monetary economics, and growth theories.

He has been named visiting professor at several French universities—Bordeaux, Nice, Rennes, Dijon, Limoges, Paris 1, Paris 13, and Lille—as well as at Curtin University in Perth, Australia. He has also been invited to give lectures at summer universities in Berlin, Dunkerque, and Kansas City.

Lavoie was a member of the Canadian national fencing team (in sabre) from 1973 to 1984, and took part in the Summer Olympic Games in Montreal (1976) and Los Angeles (1984). He won the Canadian national senior fencing championships seven times, in 1975–1979 and 1985–1986. He has three sons, plays soccer once a week in the summer months, and often plays tennis with his spouse.

MARIO SECCARECCIA

Mario Seccareccia was born in Galluccio, Caserta, Italy, and moved to Montreal at the age of seven. He attended McGill University, where he completed his Ph.D. Since 1978, he has been teaching at the University of Ottawa, where he is full professor of economics.

Seccareccia has authored or co-edited six books or monographs and has published some 70 articles or chapters of books. He is also editor of the New York-based *International Journal of Political Economy*. His principal research interests are in the areas of monetary economics, labour economics, and history of economic thought.

Since 1988, he has taught economics regularly at the Labour College of Canada and, over the years, has been a consultant economist to a number of trade unions, including direct involvement in collective bargaining via the Association of Professors of the University of Ottawa. He has also been appointed visiting professor of economics at the Université de Paris-Sud and the Université de Bourgogne in France.

He has one daughter and two sons and, when time permits, enjoys squash, swimming, and bicycling along the Rideau Canal.

BRIEF CONTENTS

TABLE OF CONTENTS

■ PART III   MARKETS AND THE PRICE SYSTEM   209

CHAPTER 10 THE FIRM AND THE INDUSTRY UNDER PERFECT COMPETITION   211

CHAPTER 11 MONOPOLY   231

PART IV   THE VIRTUES AND LIMITATIONS OF MARKETS   311

CHAPTER 14 THE CASE FOR THE MARKET SYSTEM I: THE PRICE MECHANISM   313

BONUS CHAPTERS: POVERTY, INEQUALITY, AND DISCRIMINATION
INTERNATIONAL TRADE AND COMPARATIVE ADVANTAGE

DOWNLOAD THESE BONUS CHAPTERS OF SPECIAL TOPICS AT www. baumolmicro1e.nelson.com

PREFACE

Seemingly defying the scarcity principle, students and teachers alike are struck by the abundance of first-year textbooks in economics. How is our book different from the others? When we were asked to write the Canadian edition of the Baumol and Blinder textbook, we quickly discovered why the latter has remained so popular over the last 30 years. William Baumol and Alan Blinder can be compared to Alfred Marshall, the author of the first truly comprehensive and successful textbook on the principles of economics: They enjoy applying economic theory, and they use algebra or formalisation only when it is absolutely necessary, not as a deterrent to students' understanding. More than a hundred years ago, Marshall thought that these were appropriate rules to follow when doing economic analysis; we are convinced that these are still good rules to follow in a principles of economics textbook.

The purpose of Baumol and Blinder is not to overwhelm students with a series of techniques, formulas, and diagrams; rather, they seek to have a conversation with their readers, encouraging them to think for themselves and to enjoy all of the facets of economic reasoning. Both Baumol and Blinder have been highly involved with policy making and economic counselling. Their textbook reflects this, constantly dealing with policy-oriented questions and issues, which should appeal to a vast majority of students interested in socially relevant questions about the real world. We have done our best to maintain and even strengthen this strong policy approach in the Canadian version.

Another feature of the Baumol and Blinder textbook that we find commendable is its eclectic approach. While being enthusiastic admirers of the capitalist system, Baumol and Blinder are not afraid to emphasize the fact that most markets do not function according to the standards of perfect competition. Unfettered markets, with no government intervention, often entail letting a few enterprises corner the marketplace. As a result, they pay more attention to the analysis of monopolistic competition than do most rival textbooks. Their analysis goes far beyond the standard introduction of imperfections and externalities in some otherwise ideal market setting. For them, the main accomplishment of the market system is not its static efficiency, which is traditionally emphasized in many competing textbooks, but, rather, its historically unprecedented record of innovation and growth. The same kind of healthy skepticism transpires at the aggregate level when dealing with the macroeconomic problems of growth, employment, and inflation. Baumol and Blinder decline to assume the existence of perfect competition when dealing with all of these issues and point emphatically to the relevance of government intervention. Once again, we did our best to pursue this eclectic approach.

A further strength of the Baumol and Blinder approach that we sought to apply to the Canadian context is their emphasis on the institutional features of the economy. While economics students at an advanced level of study often know little about institutional details, we believe that knowledge of the institutions and structure of the economy helps you to understand how the economic system actually works, at both the microeconomic and the macroeconomic levels. The emphasis on institutions and policy issues thus involved a sizable amount of work on our part to find their relevant equivalents within a Canadian setting. In some instances, this required a considerable number of changes and, at times, a total rewrite.

For a long time, we have considered writing a first-year textbook that would reflect our philosophy of economics and offer students some elements of an alternative vision, so we were truly excited to be offered the opportunity by Nelson Education Ltd. to do this first Canadian edition of the Baumol and Blinder textbook. As mentioned before, Baumol and Blinder are well aware that economics can provide only a framework for thinking out issues, and that the answers economists put forth depend on the assumptions being entertained. This is also our view. Pluralism, not dogmatism, should rule.

Great effort therefore went into exploring the plurality of opinions that constitute the intellectual landscape of contemporary economics.

In keeping with this pluralistic bent, our efforts to present economics as a social science are quite clear in the very first chapter of the book, where we offer definitions of economics that are broader and that go beyond the usual "study of scarcity." Chapter 1 also provides a list of issues on which Canadian economists tend to agree and another on which they disagree. We extend the discussion to include the reasons that explain controversies among economists, which we relate to the new view of research in science and to political winds.

■ FEATURES OF THE FIRST CANADIAN EDITION

Readers of Baumol and Blinder may wish to know the major changes that we introduced, beyond the Canadianization of institutional features and the extension of Chapter 1. Here is a list of the main changes introduced.

In Chapter 2, we have made an effort not only to describe the distinctiveness of the Canadian economy, such as its degree of openness to foreign trade, but we have also spent time discussing comparative economic systems and where the Canadian economy fits within that framework.

While a number of well-established concepts in economics regarding scarcity and choice are found in Chapter 3, a more elaborate discussion of the principle of comparative advantage has been included.

Chapter 4, which covers supply and demand analysis, provides a balanced appraisal of the rent control and agricultural supply management programs that have been set up in Canada, pointing out that freely competitive market mechanisms are powerful indeed, while most markets are neither free nor fully competitive. An appendix to the chapter also presents the simple algebra of market equilibrium, a feature that was requested by many reviewers.

We provided an additional example of apparent "irrational" behaviour in Chapter 5, and also created an appendix on "lexicographic" ordering in consumer choice, which seems to explain the behaviour of some environment-friendly citizens. Chapter 7 also has additional material in the appendix that deals with the fixed-coefficient Leontief technology, the importance of which has been reemphasized lately.

Chapter 6 introduces a few important concepts that were not in the original Baumol and Blinder edition, such as the implications of differing income elasticities in distinguishing between normal and inferior goods. The concept of point elasticity is also discussed in this chapter.

Chapter 8, devoted to marginal analysis, contains two noteworthy additions: the example of a production decision when a firm is facing constant marginal costs, and the results of a survey conducted among economics graduates on a real-life profit-maximizing problem.

In discussing the financial structure of firms in Chapter 9, a distinction is made between limited liability and income trusts, since the latter were so much in the news in 2006. We also had to take a special look at the evolution of Nortel's stock because of the fortunes and debacles made with it on the stock market.

In Chapter 10, a numerical example has been added to illustrate the similarities and the differences in the consequences of a pollution tax and of a pollution subsidy, an example that is made use of again when discussing Pigovian taxes in Chapter 14.

The discussion of cartels has been moved to Chapter 11, on monopolies, thus making room for a more extensive discussion of imperfect competition in Chapter 12. As in various other instances throughout the book, the National Hockey League has been used to illustrate economic concepts—this time, the concept of cartelized behaviour and, at other times, concepts such as externalities, sales maximization, and bilateral monopoly.

Chapter 12 probably has the most extensive additions that relate to economic theory. We have introduced a large section dealing with well-documented features of oligopolistic industries, such as excess capacity, constant marginal costs, markup pricing, and average cost pricing. This section extends the discussion on alternative models of oligopolistic firms provided by Baumol and Blinder, based on the celebrated sales-maximizing firm and the kinked demand curve. Ironically, our additions are partially based on research and surveys performed by Blinder himself, who finds that these features are quite common among firms. We also have an extensive section on sticky prices, also based on work by Blinder, as well as on a survey conducted by Bank of Canada researchers. This chapter now ties in nicely with Chapter 14, which deals with the regulation of monopolies or large corporations that face constant or decreasing marginal costs. It also links up with Chapter 16, which provides the dynamic efficiency case for the market system, based on the ability of firms to raise funds for expansion. Chapter 16 features new interesting material on Canadian inventors and their inventions, as well as a controversial section on whether Canada is a laggard in the innovation race.

Chapter 13 was substantially revised to discuss the particularities of the regulatory system in Canada and the nature of competition policy. An important section discussing the link between industrial competition and foreign ownership was added.

In addition to adapting the analysis to numerous Canadian examples that describe the role of prices in achieving a more efficient allocation of resources, an analysis of deadweight loss in the discussion of consumer's and producer's surplus completes Chapter 14.

In the chapter dealing with the shortcomings of the market system, Chapter 15, considerable information has been provided about the Canadian health care system, as an example of "Baumol's disease": the cost disease of the services. More attention has been devoted to Pigovian taxes and to the implications of Coasian transaction costs. There is also a short, but illuminating, discussion of global warming, so that all students will have some contact with externalities and pollution issues, even if their instructors are unable to cover Chapter 17, which deals with environmental and energy issues. Chapter 17 also includes an appraisal of the all-important Kyoto Protocol for the Canadian economy, as well as a new graph featuring the workings of pollution or greenhouse gas emissions permits. In addition, the chapter highlights the role of oligopolistic forces in determining the prices of depletable resources such as oil and uranium.

As one would expect, the chapter on taxation, Chapter 18, required almost a total rewrite to reflect Canadian institutions. But we also attempted to provide students with a better comprehension of the incidence of excise taxes, as well as the incidence of the corporate income tax under different assumptions regarding the structure of the industry.

Chapter 19 discusses the thorny issue of income distribution and introduces lots of new examples, both Canadian and international, on the nature of rents and profit. On the other hand, Chapter 20 discusses labour income and its determination. This covers many labour market issues, particularly on the role of trade unions, with special discussion of the history and structure of the Canadian trade union movement.

Some instructors may wonder where the chapters on poverty and inequality and on international trade and comparative advantage are. As space in the textbook was stretched to the limit, both chapters have been posted as downloadable bonus chapters on the book's website: www.baumolmicro1e.nelson.com.

WALK THROUGH THE FEATURES . . .

The first Canadian edition of *Microeconomics: Principles and Policy* is written in a way that doesn't overwhelm students. With a straightforward approach, the text provides the necessities required for optimal learning and encourages students to think for themselves. With a good balance of theory to application, *Microeconomics* achieves the right level of rigour and detail and presents complicated concepts in an uncomplicated manner.

Issue-Driven Principles

To bring economics into the student's everyday living, chapters open with a real-life economic "puzzle" or issue to launch the material covered in the chapter. This chapter-opening economic problem is returned to within the body of the chapter to illustrate how it can be addressed with the theoretical tools and concepts being presented.

Policy Debate

Microeconomics: Principles and Policy is known for being one the most policy-driven texts on the market. Policy Debate boxes within the chapters are bound to spark discussion in the classroom!

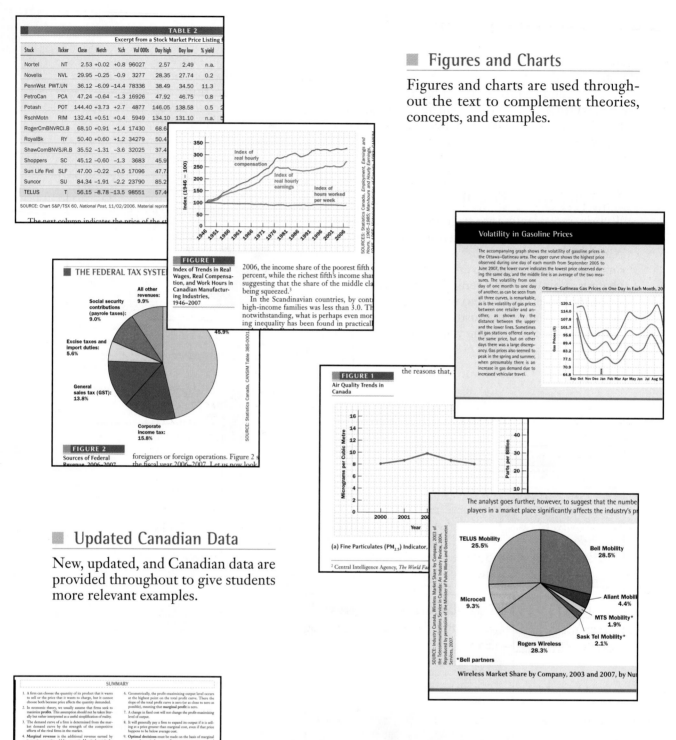

Figures and Charts

Figures and charts are used throughout the text to complement theories, concepts, and examples.

Updated Canadian Data

New, updated, and Canadian data are provided throughout to give students more relevant examples.

Chapter Summaries

Each chapter ends with a summary, list of key terms, and questions and problems to help students complete their homework and prepare for exams.

Bonus chapters: Independent study chapters that are more applied, and non-technical, are located on the text's website to make "on your own" use by the students more productive. Visit the website at www.baumolmicro1e.nelson.com.

SUPPLEMENTS

Instructor's Complete Resource CD

Instructor supplements are available on the Instructor's Resource CD for easy access:

- Instructor's Manual: The Instructor's Manual contains resources designed to streamline and maximize the effectiveness of your course preparation. Every chapter includes detailed chapter outlines, teaching tips and suggestions, answers to end-of-chapter questions in the main text, questions for classroom discussion, and suggested in-class activities.
- Computerized Test Bank: The ExamView® computerized test bank consists of more than 200 questions per chapter, including true/false, multiple-choice, and short-answer questions that assess students' critical-thinking skills.
- Test Bank: Word files extracted from the ExamView® computerized test bank are also available to instructors for easy access to questions.
- PowerPoint® Lecture Slides: A comprehensive and user-friendly lecture presentation for use in the classroom. This presentation covers the chapter objectives and points and is accompanied by graphs and tables from the main text.
- PowerPoint® Graphs and Figures: These art and graphic resource slides provide the instructor with all of the tables and figures from the main text.

TurningPoint® Kit: Nelson Education Ltd. is now pleased to offer instructors book-specific JoinIn™ content for Response Systems, allowing you to transform your classroom and assess your students' progress with instant in-class quizzes and polls. Our exclusive agreement to offer TurningPoint® software lets you pose book-specific questions and display students' answers seamlessly within the Microsoft® PowerPoint® slides of your own lecture, in conjunction with the "clicker" hardware of your choice. Contact your local Nelson representative to learn more.

Aplia: Available bundled with the text or as a digital solution, Aplia is fully updated for the first Canadian edition. The comprehensive, interactive online problem sets, analyses, tutorials, experiments, and critical-thinking exercises give students hands-on application without adding to instructors' workloads. Based on discovery learning, Aplia requires students to take an active role in the learning process—helping them improve their economic understanding and ability to relate to the economic concepts presented. Instructors can assign homework that is automatically graded and recorded.

Baumol website: For assist students in preparing for exams, the text-specific website contains Test Yourself questions and links to various economics websites. www.baumolmicro1e.nelson.com

IN GRATITUDE

We are pleased to acknowledge our indebtedness to three research assistants, Jung-Hoon Kim, Peng Wang, and Jun Zhao. Without their help in collecting data and controlling numerous details relating to the table of contents and the glossary, this book would not have so easily come to fruition. We would also wish to thank in alphabetical order: Geoffrey Ewen of Glendon College for his helpful comments on the history of trade unions in Canada; Ram Acharya of Industry Canada for providing us with information on industrial concentration in Canada; and Armine Yalnizyan of the Progressive Economics Forum for her insights on the public health care system in Canada. A note of thanks must also go to Dean François Houle of the University of Ottawa's Faculty of Social Sciences for his special support of our six-month sabbatical leave during the winter–spring semester of 2007.

This first Canadian edition also benefited from the input of numerous reviewers who read and contributed relevant and valuable comments on portions of the manuscript:

Eveline Adomait, *University of Guelph*

Morris Altman, *University of Saskatchewan*

David Gray, *University of Ottawa*

Jorgen Hansen, *Concordia University*

Ying Kong, *York University*

Eva Lau, *University of Waterloo*

Rob Moir, *University of New Brunswick*

Neil Ridler, *University of New Brunswick*

Herbert Schuetze, *University of Victoria*

Xueda Song, *York University*

Maurice Tugwell, *Acadia University*

Brian VanBlarcom, *Acadia University*

Finally, we are grateful to Anthony Rezek, who originally contacted us, as well as publisher, Rod Banister at Nelson Education Ltd., and Katherine Goodes at My Editor Inc. Indeed, the expert support provided by Katherine Goodes and by June Trusty (the latter for her patient editorial work) was crucial throughout the long process of bringing this book to press. Last but not least, we must thank our wives, Camille Lafortune and Giovanna Mazza, whose patience during our long struggle to complete the book was essential.

Marc Lavoie
Mario Seccareccia

GETTING ACQUAINTED WITH ECONOMICS

Welcome to economics! Some other students may have warned you that "Econ is boring." Don't believe them—or at least, don't believe them too much. It is true that studying economics is hardly pure fun. But a first course in economics can be an eye-opening experience. There is a vast and important world out there—the economic world—and this book is designed to help you understand it.

Have you ever wondered whether jobs will be plentiful or scarce when you graduate? Or why a university or college education becomes more and more expensive? Should the government be suspicious of big firms? Why can't pollution be eliminated? How did the Canadian economy manage to grow so rapidly in the second half of the1990s while Japan's economy stagnated? If any of these questions have piqued your curiosity, read on. You may find economics to be more interesting than you had thought!

The four chapters of Part I introduce you to both the subject matter of economics and some of the methods that economists use to study their subject.

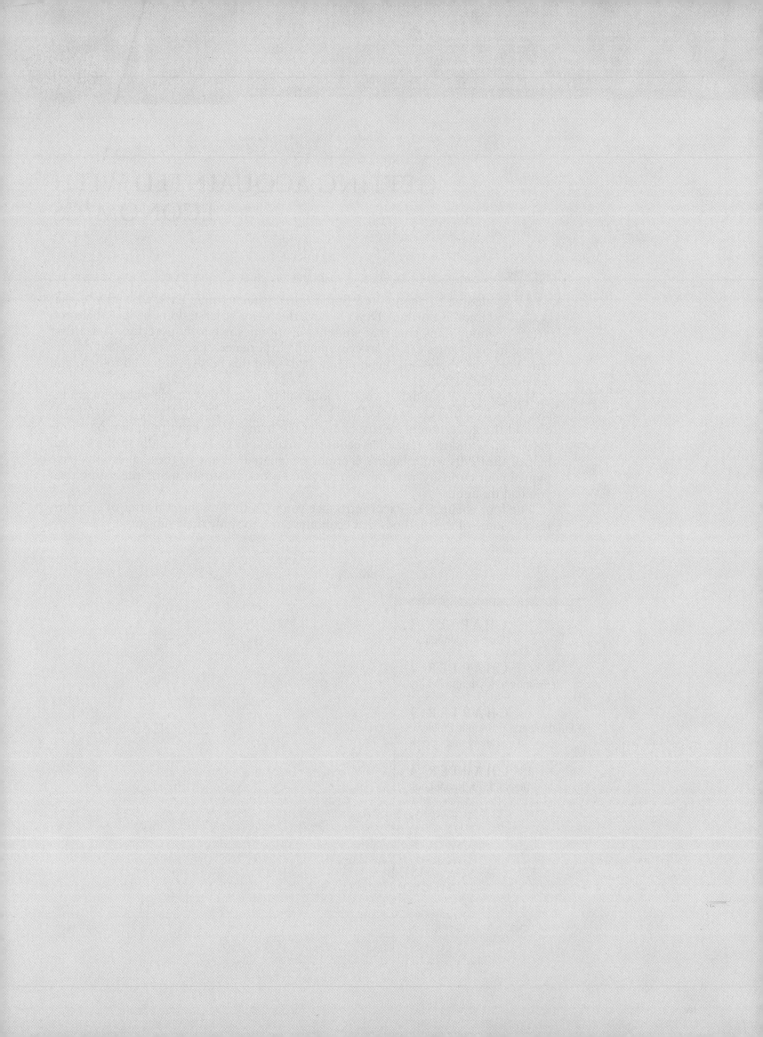

WHAT IS ECONOM

*The purpose of studying economics is not to acquire a set of ready made answers to econ
questions, but to avoid being deceived by economi*

JOAN ROBINSON (1903–1983), PROMINENT 20TH-CENTURY ECONOMIST, UNIVERSITY (
CAMBRIDGE, U.K., 195

Economics is a broad-ranging discipline, both in the questions it asks and the methods it uses to seek answers. Many of the world's most pressing problems are economic in nature. The first part of this chapter tells you how economists have defined their field through time. The second part briefly introduces the tools that economists use—tools you are likely to find useful in your career, personal life, and role as an informed citizen, long after this course is over. The third part will help you understand why economists disagree, or seemingly disagree, on a range of issues.

CONTENTS

...nomics is a discipline that can tackle nearly every issue of public relevance and ...c concern. Reflecting its wide focus and strategic position in the social sciences, ...nomists work in diverse milieus and are engaged in both quantitative and policy ...search. You find them employed in the financial and nonfinancial business sectors, ...the many agencies and departments of government, and numerous international agencies, as well as in organizations that transcend the traditional private/public divide, such as trade union and cooperative nonprofit associations.

Much like the domain in which economists work, students will discover in this book that the subject is incredibly vast and varied and that economics finds application in wide areas pertaining to individual and group behaviour. Its subject matter, however, cannot so easily be delineated and it has changed somewhat historically as the discipline has become professionalized and has embraced more sophisticated tools of analysis. Defining what economics is can be such a controversial task that some would rather say, "Economics is what economists do"!

Definitions of Economics

The origin of economics as a distinct discipline goes back to the eighteenth century. With the opening of markets to trade and commerce, early economic writers began to pose a question that remains crucial to social scientists and policy makers to this day: What makes nations grow and become wealthy? For Adam Smith (1723–1790), the father of classical economics, "political economy" was, therefore, concerned with what were "the causes of the wealth of nations." However, once certain nations did achieve economic growth and markets widened, the question of the distribution of output quickly came to occupy centre stage. Therefore, by the early nineteenth century, the scope of economic analysis began to expand somewhat with David Ricardo (1772–1823), for whom the principal problem of economics was to discover the mechanisms or "laws which regulate the distribution of the produce of the earth." Indeed, by the time one gets to the mid-nineteenth century, under Karl Marx (1818–1883), these two aspects converged and economics became simply the study of the "laws of motion of capitalism"—the study of how economies grow and stagnate as they undergo the social stresses and strains that accompany tremendous historical transformations.

Reflecting the major developments in economics since the 1870s, especially as it evolved as a professional discipline, the domain of economics has widened to include practically all aspects of social phenomena. Nowadays, economists are involved in researching market behaviour relating to traditional issues of pricing, production, exchange, consumption, and distribution, but they are also engaged in addressing less traditional questions of, say, why certain students choose to pursue a college or university degree or why high-level athletes take performance-enhancing drugs even though they know this may shorten their lives. For this reason, we rather like the definition proposed by Alfred Marshall (1842–1924), according to whom **economics** is the "study of mankind in the ordinary business of life" and for whom what distinguishes economists from noneconomists are the analytical tools and methods used to explain diverse aspects of social phenomena. This is why, to such celebrated twentieth-century economists as John Maynard Keynes (1883–1946), economics was seen merely as "a method rather than a doctrine, an apparatus of the mind, a technique of thinking" as it is applied to the study of human behaviour. This opinion is shared by Gary Becker (1930–), who is famous for having extended economics to the analysis of crime, illegal drugs, addiction, discrimination, fertility, marriage, and divorce, and according to whom what "distinguishes economics as a discipline from other disciplines in the social sciences is not its subject matter but its approach." Historically, numerous analytical tools and devices have been developed by economists to understand society in its

Economics is a method of analyzing individual and social behaviour, especially as it relates to market phenomena.

Galbraith on Galbraith

Jamie Galbraith, a professor at the University of Texas in Austin and also the son of Canadian-born economist John Kenneth Galbraith (see the feature "A Canadian-Born Economist Who Wrote a String of Bestsellers" on page 14), made the following comment on the definition of economics when he delivered the inaugural John Kenneth Galbraith Lecture at the annual meeting of the Canadian Economics Association in Halifax in June 2007. Clearly, Galbraith does not buy the definition of economics—the study of choice among scarcity—that is currently endorsed by a large majority of economists.

Our economics should teach the great thinkers, notably Smith, Marx, Keynes, Veblen and Schumpeter—and John Kenneth

Galbraith. We need not reinvent the field; nor should w[...] it. Economics over the sweep of history is not ma[...] scarcity (which technology overcomes) nor about choice[...] generally neither free nor the defining characteristic of f[...] Rather, economics is about value, distribution, growth, st[...] tion, evolution, and limits. The great ideas in these areas, a[...] history in which they were embedded, are fundamental[...] should be taught, not as dogma but rather as a sequen[...] explorations.

SOURCE: Jamie Galbraith, *The Abiding Economics of John Kenneth Galbra[...]* Retrieved from http://progecon.wordpress.com/2007/06/04/the-inaugural-joh[...] kenneth-galbraith-lecture

"ordinary business of life." In the next section, we will begin to explore some key constituents of contemporary economists' box of tools.

Before discussing these tools, however, there is one important subset of what constitutes the domain occupied by economics that is of special importance to most contemporary economists. Lionel Robbins (1898–1984) in his famous *Essay on the Nature and Significance of Economic Science*, originally published in 1932, defined economics as "a science which studies human behaviour as a relationship between ends and scarce means which have alternative uses." He later summed this up by saying that economics is the study of "behaviour conditioned by scarcity." Hence, among most present-day economists, scarcity is the focus of analysis. There is recognition that scarcity is a binding constraint on human activity that imposes trade-offs and forces individuals to make choices in allocating resources among alternative ends. Indeed, numerous concepts that will be presented in the following chapters flow from recognition of what is called the *scarcity principle*.

Microeconomics versus Macroeconomics

The variety of definitions that can be applied to the economics discipline has been reflected over the last 50 years or so by a division into two subdisciplines: microeconomics and macroeconomics.

Microeconomics   The issue of scarcity, which has become a defining characteristic of modern economics, is at the core of microeconomics. The definition provided by Lionel Robbins, but also the concerns of David Ricardo regarding the mechanisms that regulate the distribution of income, are at the heart of microeconomics. Microeconomists deal with questions related to individual agents—consumers, individual firms, agencies, governments—or to particular industries. In each and every case, such individuals must make hard choices. What should be produced? What quantity of resources should be allocated to a given activity or to a given consumption good? How much time should be allocated to a given project? Who should get the resources or the final products?

For all of these questions, prices play a key role, as they reflect the degree of scarcity. Things that are relatively scarce should carry a high price. If some of the materials that you are using to build a house are scarce, they should be expensive, and hence their high price should induce you to use alternative products, thus contributing to reducing the shortage of the scarce building materials. Similarly, if the prices of

5

o-storey houses rise more briskly than condo prices, this should induce
.lders to construct more houses and fewer condos, thus contributing to
.n of the relative scarcity of individual houses.

, for every one of the questions put above, any answer involves a trade-off. We
do everything. We are facing time and financial constraints. What is our best
.ice? You have decided to go to university. As a result, most of you are forgoing the
.arnings that some of your friends might now be making by working full-time. You
have given up these early earnings, you pay tuition fees, and you may also encounter
additional lodging costs to acquire a university degree. These are your **opportunity
costs** of going to university. In general, the opportunity cost is the value of what one
must give up in order to acquire something else. The trade-off in this case is that you
will learn quite a lot in university, and that, most likely, you will increase your future
income. Economists have devised a computation method that allows them to conclude
that, on average, even abstracting from the acquired knowledge, this is a good decision.

Everyone faces trade-offs and opportunity costs. Take the general manager of a
National Hockey League (NHL) team. This person has a budget constraint. The
team can spend only so many million dollars on the players' payroll. Indeed, with the
new collective agreement that was signed in 2005 between the NHL players and owners, there is a payroll cap—a maximum amount that no general manager is allowed to
surpass to pay players on the team roster; this amount was set at US$39 million for
the 2005–2006 season and at US$50 million for the 2007–2008 season.

Even general managers who have the good fortune of having a team loaded with talented players must make hard choices. Should they hold on to their star defencemen,
their star forwards, or their top goalie? To which ones of their best forwards should
they make the best salary offer? After the Tampa Bay Lightning beat the Calgary
Flames in the final of the 2004 Stanley Cup, the team's management made substantial
salary offers (US$6 million per season) to their Canadian-born star forwards Vincent
Lecavalier and Martin St-Louis, deciding in the process to let go their starting goalie,
Nicolai Khabibulin, without whose heroics they could not have won the Stanley Cup.
Obviously, the Lightning would have liked to retain the services of Khabibulin (who
also ended up getting over US$6 million per year) but the Tampa Bay Lightning man-
agement faced a payroll constraint. The opportunity cost of keeping Lecavalier and
St-Louis, the trade-off of that decision, was losing the services of Khabibulin. The
Lightning management staff figured that losing Lecavalier or St-Louis would have
been more detrimental to the team (performance-wise or revenue-wise). The Calgary
Flames, the Edmonton Oilers, and the Ottawa Senators faced similar trade-offs after
their nearly successful run at the Stanley Cup in 2004, 2006, and 2007.

Most of microeconomics, and even some macroeconomics, is based on a search for
efficiency. Economists call this *constrained optimization*. Given the time and financial or
resources constraints, what is the best that can be done? What is the optimal decision
if the agent wishes to maximize some criterion (profits, growth, happiness, etc.)?

Macroeconomics   The definitions of economics provided by Adam Smith and Karl
Marx are perhaps more relevant to macroeconomics. Macroeconomists ask questions
such as: Why are some nations rich and others poor? How do the standards of living
of an entire population rise? How can we avoid wasting the productive capabilities of
unemployed labour? While such questions can also be given some answers at the
microeconomic level, macroeconomists deal with aggregates: the production of an
entire economy, such as that of Canada; the level of employment, or unemployment,
in all of Canada or in a province or territory of Canada; the overall level of exports to
foreign markets and imports from abroad; the average price level or the rate of growth
of aggregate prices—that is, the rate of inflation. Macroeconomics also deals with
government policies that affect the entire economy: monetary policy, as reflected in
interest rates or the stock of money and possibly in the exchange rate of the Canadian dollar; and fiscal policy, as reflected in the overall level of government expenditures and the various tax rates.

The field of macroeconomics is said to have been created by John Maynard Keynes when he tried to explain the deep recession of the 1930s through arguments that were not connected to the malfunctioning of individual markets but rather to **paradoxical** effects that were arising when the intended behaviour of individuals led to exactly opposite aggregate results when all of these individuals acted in a similar way. Macro-economics as a field separate from microeconomics owes its existence from the possi-ble occurrence of what is called the **fallacy of composition.** One cannot assume that what is true of the parts will still be true of the whole. There might be a contradiction between what can be ascertained at the level of the individual and what can be said at the aggregate level. For instance, while each of us can get to work downtown more quickly if we drive our cars there instead of taking a bus or riding a bicycle, it will not be true anymore if all of us drive our cars to work, as streets will become overrun with traffic, resulting in traffic jams.

The paradox that Keynes himself underlined is called the *paradox of saving* or the *paradox of thrift.* While it is in the interest of every individual to save as much as pos-sible instead of consuming, saving one's income instead of spending it will have detri-mental consequences on the overall economy, at least when the economy is not fully employed. As individuals try to save more, less will be spent on consumer goods; therefore, firms will lose sales and make less profit and will be induced to hire fewer personnel. In the end, employees and owners will wind up with less income, and hence will not be able to save as much as intended. The intended increase in saving does not materialize and instead creates unemployment.

Macroeconomists are interested in the economic system as a whole, while microeconomists are mainly concerned with the study of individual markets or agents in isolation.

While the principle of scarcity does not apply to all of macroeconomics—for instance, when the rate of unemployment is high, labour resources or at least some labour resources are idle and hence are not scarce—there still exist trade-offs that entail difficult choices. One of these is the trade-off between inflation and unemploy-ment—meaning that low unemployment normally makes inflation rise and high unemployment normally makes inflation fall. Things need not always be that way; for instance, the Canadian economy has benefited from low rates of unemployment since the end of the 1990s without any increase in the inflation rate. In general, however, the trade-off between inflation and unemployment poses one of the fundamental dilemmas of national economic policy. The mechanisms underlying this trade-off are a key topic in macroeconomics.

Other such macroeconomic dilemmas may also exist. Should the government change the income distribution arising from the market even if such transfers weaken economic growth (this may also be considered a microeconomic question—the issue of equity versus efficiency)? Or should the size of the government sector be reduced, even though a larger public sector may be conducive to a more stable economy with fewer fluctuations? These are difficult questions that may go beyond the pure techni-cal advice that economists can offer.

■ INSIDE THE ECONOMIST'S TOOL KIT

Let us now look at some important analytical devices employed by economists to explain social phenomena.

■ Economics as a Discipline

Although economics is clearly the most rigorous of the social sciences, it nevertheless looks decidedly more "social" than "scientific" when compared with, say, physics. An economist must be a jack of several trades, borrowing modes of analysis from numer-ous fields. Mathematical reasoning is often used in economics, but so is historical

A **paradox** is a contradic-tion between two principles that operate at different levels; it often involves an outcome that is contrary to intuition.

The **fallacy of composi-tion** is the error of believ-ing that what is true of each part of a system will also be true of the system as a whole.

study. And neither looks quite the same as when practised by a mathematician or a historian. Statistics play a major role in modern economic inquiry, although economists had to modify standard statistical procedures to fit their kinds of data.

■ The Need for Abstraction

Some students find economics unduly abstract and "unrealistic." The stylized world envisioned by economic theory seems only a distant cousin to the world they know. There is an old joke about three people—a chemist, a physicist, and an economist—stranded on a desert island with an ample supply of canned food but no tools to open the cans. The chemist thinks that lighting a fire under the cans would burst the cans. The physicist advocates building a catapult with which to smash the cans against some boulders. The economist's suggestion? "Assume we have a can opener."

Economic theory *does* make some unrealistic assumptions; you will encounter some of them in this book. But some abstraction from reality is necessary because of the incredible complexity of the economic world, not because economists like to sound absurd.

Compare the chemist's simple task of explaining the interactions of compounds in a chemical reaction with the economist's complex task of explaining the interactions of people in an economy. Are molecules motivated by greed or altruism, by envy or ambition? Do they ever imitate other molecules? Do forecasts about them influence their behaviour? People, of course, do all these things and many, many more. It is therefore vastly more difficult to predict human behaviour than to predict chemical reactions. If economists tried to keep track of every feature of human behaviour, they would never get anywhere. Thus:

> Abstraction from unimportant details is necessary to understand the functioning of anything as complex as the economy.

Abstraction means ignoring many details so as to focus on the most important elements of a problem.

An analogy will make clear why economists **abstract** from details. Suppose you have just arrived for the first time in Toronto. You are now at Pearson Airport—the point marked *A* in Maps 1 and 2, which are alternative maps of part of Toronto. You want to

MAP 1	Detailed Road Map of Toronto

SOURCE: Map © by Rand McNally

Note: *A* indicates Pearson Airport and *B* indicates the Rogers Centre.

drive to the Rogers Centre, point *B* on each map. Which map would be more useful?

Map 1 has complete details of the Toronto road system. This makes it hard to read and hard to use as a way to find the Rogers Centre. For this purpose, Map 1 is far too detailed, although for some other purposes (for example, locating some small street downtown) it may be far better than Map 2.

In contrast, Map 2 omits many minor roads—you might say they are *assumed away*—so that the highways and major arteries stand out more clearly. As a result of this simplification, one route from Pearson Airport to the Rogers Centre clearly emerges. We can take Highway 427 heading south, then take the Gardiner Expressway. Although we *might* find a route by poring over the details in Map 1, most strangers to the city would be better off with Map 2. Similarly, economists try to *abstract* from a lot of confusing details while retaining the essentials.

Map 3, however, illustrates that simplification can go too far. It shows little more than the major highways that pass through the Oshawa–Toronto–Hamilton part of Ontario, and therefore will not help a visitor find the Rogers Centre. Of course, this map was never intended to be used as a detailed tourist guide, which brings us to an important point:

> There is no such thing as one "right" degree of abstraction and simplification for all analytic purposes. The proper degree of abstraction depends on the objective of the analysis. A model that is a gross oversimplification for one purpose may be needlessly complicated for another.

Economists are constantly seeking analogies to Map 2 rather than Map 3, treading the thin line between useful generalizations about complex issues and gross distortions of the pertinent facts. For example, suppose you want to learn why some people are fabulously

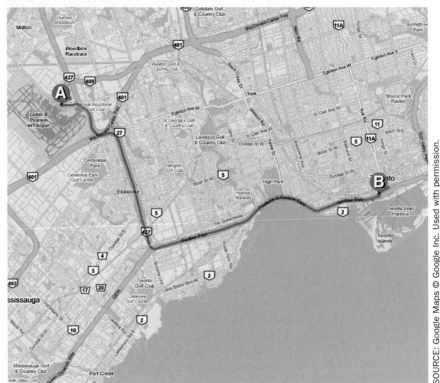

MAP 2   Major Toronto Arteries and Highways

MAP 3   Oshawa–Toronto–Hamilton Area

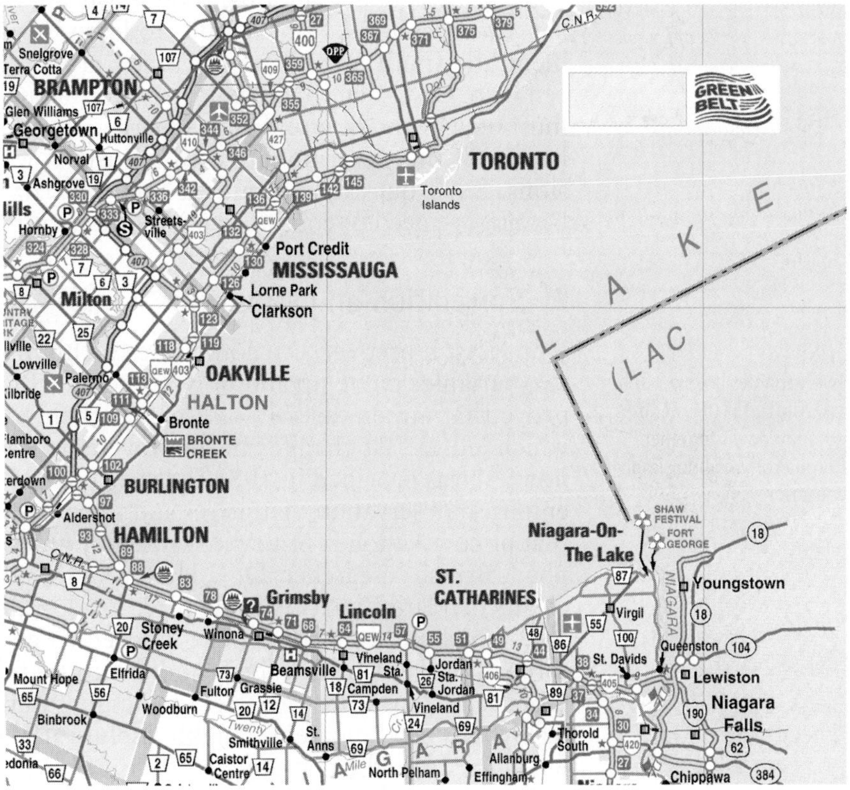

SOURCE: Google Maps © Google Inc. Used with permission.

SOURCE: © Queen's Printer for Ontario, 2006. Reproduced with permission.

rich while others are abjectly poor. People differ in many ways, too many to enumerate, much less to study. The economist must ignore most of these details to focus on the important ones. The colour of a person's hair or eyes is probably not important for the problem but, unfortunately, the colour of his or her skin probably is because racial discrimination can depress a person's income. Height and weight may not matter, but education probably does. Proceeding in this way, we can pare Map 1 down to the manageable dimensions of Map 2. But there is a danger of going too far, stripping away some of the crucial factors, so that we wind up with Map 3.

The Role of Economic Theory

Some students find economics "too theoretical." To see why we can't avoid it, let's consider what we mean by a **theory.**

To an economist or natural scientist, the word *theory* means something different from what it means in common speech. In science, a theory is *not* an untested assertion of alleged fact. The statement that aspirin provides protection against heart attacks is not a theory; it is a *hypothesis*, which will prove to be true or false once the right sorts of experiments have been completed. Instead, a theory is a deliberate simplification (abstraction) of reality that attempts to explain how some relationships work. It is an *explanation* of the mechanism behind observed phenomena. Thus, gravity forms the basis of theories that describe and explain the paths of the planets. Similarly, price theory (discussed in Parts II and III) seeks to describe and explain how buyers and sellers interact in markets to determine prices.

People who have never studied economics often draw a false distinction between *theory* and *practical policy*. Politicians and businesspeople, in particular, often reject abstract economic theory as something that is best ignored by "practical" people. The irony of these statements is that:

It is precisely the concern for policy that makes economic theory so necessary and important.

To analyze policy options, economists are forced to deal with *possibilities that have not actually occurred*. For example, to learn how to shorten periods of high unemployment, they must investigate whether a proposed new policy that has never been tried can help. Or to determine which environmental programs will be most effective, they must understand how and why a market economy produces pollution and what might happen if the government taxed industrial waste discharges and automobile emissions. Such questions require some *theorizing*, not just examination of the facts, because we need to consider possibilities that have never occurred.

Correlation and Causation

The facts, moreover, can sometimes be highly misleading. Data often indicate that two variables move up and down together. But this statistical **correlation** does not prove that either variable *causes* the other. A most famous example in economics, which led to vast changes in the way statistical research is conducted in macroeconomics, was provided in 1980 in the heyday of *monetarism*—the theory, based on the empirical observation that prices and the money supply grow in tandem, which claims that price inflation is primarily caused by an excessive growth rate of the money supply. A British researcher, D. F. Hendry, showed that he could find a nearly perfect fit (high correlation) between the price level in the United Kingdom and another variable, which until then had been ignored by economists but which was closely monitored by a government agency and the entire population. He further showed that this other variable was very good at predicting future values of the inflation rate. Unfortunately, this new, apparently highly useful variable was the amount of cumulative rainfall in the United Kingdom!

Further in relation to rainy days, we can offer another illuminating example of possible spurious correlation. When it rains, people drive their cars more slowly and there are also more traffic accidents. But no one thinks that it is the slower driving

A **theory** is a deliberate simplification of relationships used to explain how those relationships work.

Two variables are said to be **correlated** if they tend to go up or down together. Correlation need not imply causation.

that causes more accidents when it's raining. Rather, we understand that both phenomena are caused by a common underlying factor—more rain. How do we know this? Not just by looking at the correlation between data on accidents and driving speeds. Data alone tell us little about cause and effect. We must use some simple *theory* as part of our analysis. In this case, the theory might explain that drivers are more apt to have accidents on rain-slicked roads.

Similarly, we must use theoretical analysis, and not just data alone, to understand *how*, if at all, different government policies will lead to lower unemployment or *how* a tax on emissions will reduce pollution.

> Statistical correlation need not imply causation. Some theory is usually needed to interpret data.

Even if we are persuaded that statistical correlation in a given instance implies correlation, causality may go one way or another. One of the best-known relationships in economics is the positive relationship between the stock of money and the price level. Although all economists would agree that such a relationship does exist, two different causal stories, based on two different theories, have been put forward for more than 200 years. In one story, based on monetarism (the modern incarnation of the old *quantity theory of money*), the amount of money in the economy explains, or causes, the price level. In the alternative story, nearly just as old—the *Banking school of economics* view—it is the price level that explains, or causes, the amount of money. Two hundred years of studies have not allowed economists to know for sure which theory is the correct one. Indeed, the dominance of one or the other theory has moved in cycles. At times, as in the 1970s and 1980s, the quantity theory of money looked like the only serious contender, whereas in the 1950s and over the last few years, the Banking school view has been incorporated into several macroeconomic theories.

There are now statistical methods to assess causality but, unfortunately, even these sophisticated methods are usually unable to cut through the controversy and provide definite answers. In addition, taking into account the timing of events won't do. This is called, from Latin, the **post hoc, ergo propter hoc fallacy** (translation: *before this, therefore because of this*). For instance, consumers who are planning to purchase last-minute Christmas gifts or who wish to take advantage of Boxing Day sales and New Year's sales may decide to take out cash from the automatic teller machines a few days in advance (because they don't have, or don't want to use, credit cards). But can we say that sales around Christmas time went up because the amount of cash in the economy started to rise in the previous week (as shown in Table 1)? Or should we say instead that the amount of cash has risen because of the planned Christmas shopping spree? If the latter is more correct, then an event of the past (the increase in cash) is being caused by an event in the future (the Christmas sales), and hence the knowledge of timing will not be helpful in this case.

The *post hoc, ergo propter hoc* fallacy is the error of assuming that if some event occurred before another, then the first one must have caused the second.

> Despite all of the difficulties involved, assessing causality is crucially important in economics. Theories based on the same facts will yield different predictions, because they rely on different causation mechanisms.

Having a causal story also allows the economist to know which policy should be put into place. For instance, if causality runs from the price level to the amount of money in the economy, then those who work in central banks and are responsible for keeping prices stable should not worry so much about the level of the money stock or the growth rate of the money stock. Instead, they should be concerned about other factors that might have an impact on the price level or on the growth rate of aggregate prices—particularly the inflation rate. But in order to assess these other factors, they need to *theorize*; they need an economic model.

TABLE 1	
More Cash Circulating around Christmas	
	Paper Cash in Circulation (millions of dollars)
December 5, 2007	$48,104
December 12, 2007	48,269
December 19, 2007	49,330
December 26, 2007	50,724
January 2, 2008	50,157
January 9, 2008	48,156

SOURCE: Bank of Canada, *Weekly Financial Statistics*, BFS Table B2, February 1, 2008.

What Is an Economic Model?

An **economic model** is a simplified, small-scale version of some aspect of the economy. Economic models are often expressed in equations, by graphs, or in words.

An **economic model** is a representation of a theory or a part of a theory, often used to gain insight into cause and effect. The notion of a "model" is familiar enough to children, and economists—like other scientists—use the term in much the same way that children do.

A child's model airplane looks and operates much like the real thing, but it is much smaller and simpler, so it is easier to manipulate and understand. Engineers for Bombardier also build models of planes. Although their models are far larger and much more elaborate than a child's toy, they use them for much the same purposes: to observe the workings of these aircraft "up close" and to experiment with them to see how the models behave under different circumstances. ("What happens if I do this?") From these experiments, they make educated guesses as to how the real-life version will perform.

Economists use models for similar purposes. The late A. W. Phillips, the famous engineer-turned-economist who discovered what is now called the *Phillips curve* was talented enough to construct a working model of the determination of national income in a simple economy by using coloured water flowing through pipes. For years, this contraption has graced the basement of the London School of Economics. Although we will explain the models with words and diagrams, Phillips's engineering background enabled him to depict the theory with tubes, valves, and pumps.

Because many of the models used in this book are depicted in diagrams, for those of you who need review, we explain the construction and use of various types of graphs in the appendix to this chapter. Don't be put off by seemingly abstract models. Think of them as useful road maps. And remember how hard it would be to find your way around Toronto without one.

SOURCE: Science Museum/Science & Society Picture Library

A. W. Phillips built this model in the early 1950s to illustrate Keynesian theory.

WHY ECONOMISTS (SOMETIMES) DISAGREE

"If all the earth's economists were laid end to end, they could not reach an agreement," the saying goes. Politicians and reporters are fond of pointing out that economists can be found on both sides of many public policy issues. If economics is a science, why do economists so often disagree? After all, astronomers do not debate whether the earth revolves around the sun or vice versa.

This question reflects a misunderstanding of the nature of science. Disputes are normal at the frontier of any science. For example, astronomers once did argue vociferously over whether the earth revolves around the sun. Nowadays, they argue about gamma-ray bursts, dark matter, the Big Bang, and other esoterica. These arguments go mostly unnoticed by the public because few of us understand what they are talking about. But economics is a *social* science, so its disputes are aired in public and all sorts of people feel competent to join economic debates.

Is There Consensus among Canadian Economists?

Economists actually agree on much more than popular opinion would have it. Surveys about the opinions of economists were first published in the United States in 1979 and such surveys were repeated in 1992 and 2003. Similar surveys were also conducted in European countries, and in Canada, a survey of members of the Canadian Economics Association was done in 1986 by Walter Block and Michael Walker, two researchers at the Fraser Institute, a think-tank located in Vancouver. Their results were published in 1988 in the journal *Canadian Public Policy*. The propositions that brought the highest degree of consensus are listed below. (*Note:* Responses such as

"No answer" and "Agree with provisions" were discarded, so the totals do not add up to 100 percent; clearly when a large percentage of economists "agree" with a proposition, this implies that the proposition receives even wider support, since there are also economists who approve of the proposition "with provisions.")

- A ceiling on rents reduces the quantity and quality of housing available. (80 percent agree, 4.7 percent disagree)
- Tariffs and import quotas reduce general economic welfare. (70 percent agree, 4 percent disagree)
- Flexible exchange rates offer an effective international monetary arrangement. (58 percent agree, 6 percent disagree)
- The redistribution of income in the developed industrial nations is a legitimate task for the government. (56 percent agree, 15 percent disagree)
- A minimum wage increases unemployment among young and unskilled workers. (68 percent agree, 15 percent disagree)
- Fiscal policy has a significant stimulative impact on a less than fully employed economy. (47 percent agree, 14 percent disagree)
- Taxes represent a better approach to pollution control than imposition of pollution ceilings. (49 percent agree, 17 percent disagree)
- Wage–price controls should be used to control inflation. (4 percent agree, 73 percent disagree)
- The fundamental cause of the rise in oil prices in the 1970s was the monopoly power of the large oil companies. (14 percent agree, 66 percent disagree)
- The government should be an employer of last resort and initiate a guaranteed job program. (14 percent agree, 61 percent disagree)

The above survey results are comforting: They disprove the saying that when asked about a given problem, ten different economists will give eleven different answers! There are issues, however, that clearly divide Canadian economists. Some of the most divisive issues, at least in 1988, but most probably still today, are the following:

- The distribution of income in the developed industrial nations should be more equal. (35 percent agree, 30 percent disagree)
- The economic power of labour unions should be significantly curtailed. (26 percent agree, 38 percent disagree)
- Antitrust laws should be used vigorously to reduce monopoly power from its current level. (33 percent agree, 27 percent disagree)
- The money supply is a more important target than interest rates for monetary policy. (32 percent agree, 40 percent disagree)
- Inflation is primarily a monetary phenomenon. (42 percent agree, 24 percent disagree)
- In the short run, unemployment can be reduced by increasing the rate of inflation. (30 percent agree, 26 percent disagree)
- The corporate state as depicted by John Kenneth Galbraith (see "A Canadian-Born Economist Who Wrote a String of Bestsellers" on the next page) accurately describes the context and structure of advanced economies (13 percent agree, 44 percent disagree).

Once again, all of these propositions give some indication of the sort of issues with which economists become intertwined. Note that nearly all of these nonconsensual propositions have clear and substantial policy implications. Yet, they are far from being settled. In that sense, economics is an evolutionary science. Amusingly, it should be pointed out that while American and Canadian economists do have closely resembling opinions on the above propositions, European economists have sometimes given a yes answer where a majority of Canadian economists would answer no, and vice versa, thus demonstrating that economics is indeed a social science that incorporates cultural traits, despite being based on mathematical reasoning and empirical analysis.

A Canadian-Born Economist Who Wrote a String of Bestsellers

John Kenneth Galbraith (1908–2006) is perhaps North America's most famous economist, but also a highly controversial one among his peers, as many of his ideas were thought to be either subversive to existing theory or just plain wrong. Born in Canada, Galbraith first studied at the Ontario Agricultural College (now the University of Guelph) and the University of Toronto. He then moved to California, where he completed a Ph.D. in agricultural economics. He was immediately hired by Harvard University, where he eventually became a professor. He was in charge of the administration of price controls during World War II, an experience that led to his peculiar description of the behaviour of large firms, in particular in his bestseller *The New Industrial State* (1967), where he claims that corporate planning supersedes market mechanisms. A prolific and witty writer, Galbraith was a left-leaning liberal economist who argued that the private sector has overextended, to the detriment of the public sector and the environment.

SOURCE: Hulton Archive/Getty Images

The Role of Assumptions

An important cause of disagreements among economists is that theorizing is based on assumptions. As we saw in the previous section, abstraction and theorizing require simplifying assumptions. In making such assumptions, economists may exclude variables that they judge to be irrelevant but they may also assume things that they know to be false in themselves. Fruitful assumptions are those that lead to a long string of deductions and to predictions that were not intuitively obvious from the start.

Assumptions play a key role in economic analysis. Changing the assumptions will lead to different results and most likely to different policy recommendations. Whatever the quality of the analysis, if the assumptions are wrong—if they do not adequately reflect stylized facts or the behaviour of people—the conclusions reached are most likely to be wrong as well. Keynes once said that it was preferable to be approximately right than precisely wrong. Economists who are using a different set of assumptions will most likely disagree on the implications of their theories or models.

Take the case of the National Hockey League (NHL). The collective agreement signed in 2005 contains a clause forcing the richest teams—high-revenue teams like the Toronto Maple Leafs and the Montreal Canadiens—to make equalization payments to the poorest teams—the teams with the lowest revenues. Will such an income redistribution toward low-revenue teams improve their performance on the ice? The answer depends on the motivations that drive the behaviour of the NHL owners. If the owners are assumed to maximize profits, as is usually alleged by economists, the prediction is that such equalization payments will have no impact whatsoever, as owners of low-revenue teams will simply pocket the additional money. However, if the owners are assumed to maximize winning, being constrained only by the fact that they want to avoid financial losses, they will use the additional funds to obtain or retain good players in an effort to improve the on-ice performance of their teams.

As another example of the importance of assumptions, think of the fiscal predictions of the Government of Canada. For many years now, the Department of Finance has been underpredicting the size of the federal budget surplus, while other economists, working for trade unions, banks, and forecasting agencies have been much closer to reality. Does that mean that the economists in the Department of Finance are just plain incompetent and are unable to assess and model the expenditures and revenues of the federal government? No. It simply means that the economists at the Department of Finance are using much more cautious and conservative assumptions when making their forecasts; for instance, assuming slightly too low future rates of economic growth, which decrease forecasted government revenues, or slightly too high interest rates, which increase forecasted government payments on debt servicing.

> Different assumptions in economics will often lead to different conclusions, different predictions, and different policy recommendations. For this reason, it is important to clearly spell out our assumptions.

Why don't economists all accept the same assumptions? Besides the reasons that will be offered in the next section, it should be pointed out that an assumption may be quite appropriate in some circumstances and invalid in others. A problem that all economists face is ascertaining the domain of validity of an assumption. Does it apply to all agents, all industries, or all countries, or only to a subset of them? For instance, in the case of NHL hockey, could it be that some owners try to maximize profits (like the owners of the Toronto Maple Leafs?), while others try to maximize on-ice performance?

The Role of Value Judgments

Many disputes among economists are not scientific disputes at all. Sometimes the pertinent facts are simply unknown. For example, the appropriate financial penalty to levy on a polluter depends on quantitative estimates of the harm done by the pollutant. But good estimates of this damage may not be available. Similarly, although there is wide scientific agreement that the earth is slowly warming, there are disagreements over how costly global warming may be. Such disputes make it difficult to agree on a concrete policy proposal.

Another important source of disagreements is that economists, like other people, come in all political stripes: conservative, middle-of-the-road, liberal, radical. Each may have different values, and so each may hold a different view of the "right" solution to a public policy problem—even if they agree on the underlying analysis. Here are two examples:

1. We suggested earlier in this chapter that policies that lower inflation are likely to raise unemployment. Many economists believe they can measure the amount of unemployment that must be endured to reduce inflation by a given amount. But they disagree about whether it is worth having, say, 300,000 more people out of work for a year to cut the inflation rate by 1 percent.

2. In designing an income tax, society must decide how much of the burden to put on upper-income taxpayers. Some people believe the rich should pay a disproportionate share of the taxes. Others disagree, believing it is fairer to levy the same income tax rate on everyone.

While one would think that economists cannot answer questions like these any more than nuclear physicists could have determined whether dropping the atomic bomb on Hiroshima was a good idea, economists do engage in discussions on these issues on the basis of economic arguments. For instance, about the design of tax policies, some economists reason that the rich should not pay too much in taxes because economic growth and prosperity depend on how much the rich can afford to save. But then how much is too much? Ultimately, such decisions rest on moral judgments that can be made only by the citizens of a province or territory, or of the country, through their elected representatives.

> Although economic science can contribute theoretical and factual knowledge on a particular issue, the final decision on policy questions often rests either on information that is not currently available or on social values and ethical opinions about which people differ, or on both.

■ Two Views of Scientific Research

Value judgments permeate not just policy decisions, but the whole scientific process. There are two views of scientific research: the naive and the modern views, as illustrated in Figure 1. In the naive view, economists first collect objective statistical facts and observe agent behaviour; then, from this, they formulate grand theories and build models that represent a subset of these theories; third, they test the models, make predictions, and collect new facts. The models can thus either be rejected because statistical techniques or new facts falsify the theory and its model, or the model is found to be compatible with statistical analysis and new events, in which case, we can say that it is well corroborated. In the latter case, further work can be done to improve the model and its theory, and economic policies can be proposed in line with the lessons drawn from the model. Under this view, economics is a science where models get better and better, and where bad theories are progressively weeded out, to be forever abandoned. The naive view of science makes disagreements in economics nearly impossible to understand. Why wouldn't all economists finally agree on the improved, correct model?

The main two reasons for continuing disagreement among economists have already been spelled out: The facts may be uncertain and economists, like everyone in society, have opinions. Some economic "laws" may be verified in some countries or industries but not in others. In addition, statistical techniques rarely yield clear-cut results. Quite a lot of data massaging must be done to obtain statistics that correspond to the specification of the model or to obtain meaningful results. As the saying goes, the data must be tortured until they confess! The second reason is that economists have political opinions, feelings, cultural experiences, pecuniary interests, and vested interests from past research that will interfere at every stage of scientific enquiry. For instance, who would believe that economists working for tobacco producers, or whose research is being subsidized by tobacco associations, would not arrive at biased conclusions regarding the social costs of smoking? The way economic facts are collected, summarized, classified, organized, and interpreted depends to a large extent on the *a priori* opinions of the researcher. The stylized facts and the conclusions that arise from this exercise depend on ideology; they are not just the outcome of a detached quest for knowledge.

In addition, whether a given model will seem to be confirmed or disparaged by the test results will, to a large extent or at least to some extent, depend on the *a priori* opinions of the researcher. Researchers in social sciences tend to hold on tenaciously to ideas that took years of effort to develop, and will tend to find unconvincing any evidence that conflicts with their pet theories. In social sciences, the observer (the economist) has an influence on reality or at least on the perception of what reality is.

FIGURE 1

Research in Economics:
Two Views

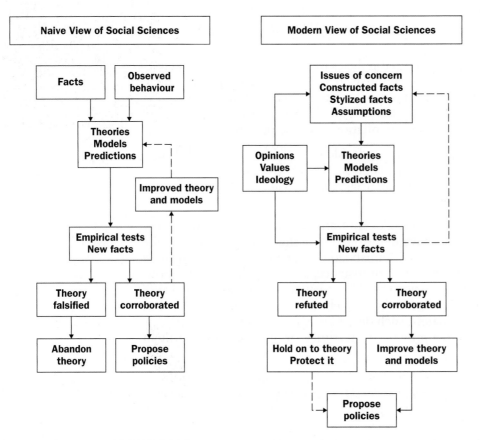

In other academic fields, this is called the *postmodern view*. Although we do not fully espouse this view of knowledge, the limits to objective research in economics must be recognized. Indeed, acknowledging these limits helps us to understand why well-trained economists can hold diverging views on a given economic topic, whatever the facts, and why highly intelligent researchers often cannot agree on a single model and a single policy proposition.

In the naive view of research in the social sciences, researchers are impervious to ideological or pecuniary influences. In the modern view, prior opinions and values have an impact at every stage of research.

Still, this does not mean that *anything goes*. When arguing a position, an economist puts forward assumptions, abstractions, models, a string of coherent implications, and historical or empirical evidence. Every stage of the argument needs to be justified.

The Influence of Political Winds

Figure 1 presented the modern view of scientific research. Philosophers who examine how research in the social sciences is being conducted claim that opinions and ideology do have an impact on the facts that are uncovered, the models and the theories that are put forward, and the policies that are recommended or advocated by researchers. This modern view of scientific research corresponds quite well with a comment made recently by Paul Samuelson, which appears at the bottom of this boxed feature. Samuelson (1915–) was the 1970 recipient of the Bank of Sweden Prize in Economic Sciences in Memory of Alfred Nobel. Samuelson received this prize—the equivalent of a Nobel Prize in Economics—the second year that it was awarded. Besides being an obviously bright and creative researcher, Samuelson is the author of the very first modern principles of economics textbook, *Economics*, first published in 1948. This textbook has been an inspiration for all first-year economics textbooks, including the one you are now reading. As you will see, Samuelson is rather sarcastic, but the main point is that research and theorizing are not done in a vacuum; these activities are influenced by society, our own beliefs, and even self-interest (money). This should help to explain why economists disagree on certain issues—even the most important ones. The difficulty of pursuing conclusive experiments, and hence the absence of absolute knowledge, makes it more likely that values and ideology will have some impact on the theories and the models that will be produced.

Political winds do have an influence on economists, just like important events, such as a deep recession or periods of high inflation, will have an impact on the agenda being pursued by economists.

In the foreword to his 2006 book with co-editor William A. Barnett, *Inside the Economist's Mind: Conversations with Eminent Economists*, Samuelson wrote:

I conclude with an unworthy hypothesis regarding past and present directions of economic research. Sherlock Holmes said, 'Cherchez la femme.' . . . We economists do primarily work for our peers' esteem, which figures in our own self-esteem.

When post-Depression Roosevelt's New Deal provided exciting job opportunities, first the junior academic faculties moved leftward. To get back ahead of their followers, subsequently the senior academic faculties shoved ahead of them. As post-Reagan, post-Thatcher electorates turned rightward, follow the money pointed, alas, in only one direction. So to speak, we eat our own cooking.

SOURCE: Time & Life Pictures/Getty Images

We economists love to quote Keynes's final lines in his 1936 *General Theory* ["Practical men, who believe themselves to be quite exempt from any intellectual influences, are usually the slaves of some defunct economist. Madmen in authority, who hear voices in the air, are distilling their frenzy from some academic scribbler of a few years back."]—for the reason that they cater so well to our vanity and self-importance. But to admit the truth, madmen in authority can *self-generate* their own frenzies without needing help from either defunct or *avant-garde* economists. What establishment economists brew up is as often what the Prince and the Public are already wanting to imbibe. We guys don't stay in the best club by proffering the views of some past *academic* crank or academic sage.

SOURCES: Paul A. Samuelson, "Reflections on How Biographies of Individual Scholars Can Relate to a Science's Biography," in Paul A. Samuelson and William A. Barnett (eds.), *Inside the Economist's Mind: Conversations with Eminent Economists* (Boston: Blackwell Publishing, 2007), pp. ix–x; John Maynard Keynes, *The General Theory of Employment, Interest and Money* (London: Macmillan, 1936), p. 383.

SUMMARY

1. There are many possible definitions of economics. In the past, economics has been defined as being concerned with:

   a. The causes of the wealth of nations

   b. The laws that regulate income distribution

   c. The laws of motion of capitalism

2. Two further definitions could be offered today:

   a. Economics is a method of analyzing individual and social behaviour, especially as it relates to market phenomena.

   b. Economics is the study of behaviour conditioned by scarcity.

3. Microeconomics deals with consumers, firms, industries, or markets taken in isolation. Macroeconomics deals with economic systems taken as a whole, and thus confronts fallacies of composition.

4. Because of the great complexity of human behaviour, economists are forced to *abstract* from many details, to make generalizations that they know are not quite true, and to organize what knowledge they have in terms of some theoretical structure called a *model*.

5. Correlation need not imply causation, and the timing of events may not properly reflect what is the cause and what is the effect.

6. Economists use simplified models to understand the real world and predict its behaviour, much as a child uses a model railroad to learn how trains work.

7. Although these models, if skillfully constructed, can illuminate important economic problems, they rarely can answer the questions that confront policy makers. Value judgments are needed for this purpose, and the economist is no better equipped than anyone else to make them.

8. Economists agree among themselves on several fundamental issues, but as the reading of any newspaper will demonstrate, they disagree on some issues of doctrine and on many policy issues. There are several reasons that can explain such a situation.

   a. The facts are uncertain or statistics hard to come by.

   b. Different economists may start with different assumptions.

   c. Models or theories are hard to disprove, so different economic theories will be held and promoted concurrently by various schools of thought.

   d. Economists come in all political stripes.

9. There are two views of science, the naive and the modern view. In the naive view, all economists should end up accepting the same model. By contrast, the modern view says that value judgments, political opinions, and vested interests influence every step of scientific research, which helps to explain why there are disagreements among economists. Still, economists share the method of justifying every step of their arguments.

KEY TERMS

Economics 4	Fallacy of compostion 7	Correlation 10
Opportunity cost 6	Abstraction 8	*Post hoc, ergo propter hoc* fallacy 11
Paradox 7	Theory 10	Economic model 12

DISCUSSION QUESTIONS

1. Think about how you would construct a model of how your college or university is governed. Which officers and administrators would you include and exclude from your model if the objective was one of the following:

   a. To explain how decisions on financial aid are made

   b. To explain the quality of the faculty

   Relate this to the map example in the chapter.

2. Relate the process of abstraction to the way you take notes in a lecture. Why do you not try to transcribe every word uttered by the lecturer? Why don't you write down just the title of the lecture and stop there? How do you decide, roughly speaking, on the correct amount of detail?

3. Explain why a government policy maker cannot afford to ignore economic theory.

4. Provide another possible example of the *post hoc, ergo propter hoc* fallacy.

5. Provide an example where correlation may not entail causation, besides the examples mentioned in the chapter.

6. Provide different kinds of reasons as to why economists would disagree on whether the power of labour unions ought to be curtailed.

7. Describe in your own words the differences that you see between the old and the new views of social sciences.

APPENDIX *Using Graphs: A Review*

As noted in the chapter, economists often explain and analyze models with the help of graphs. Indeed, this book is full of them. But that is not the only reason for studying how graphs work. Most people will deal with graphs in the future, perhaps frequently. You will see them in newspapers. If you become a doctor, you will use graphs to keep track of your patients' progress. If you join a business firm, you will use them to check profit or performance at a glance. This appendix introduces some of the techniques of graphic analysis—tools you will use throughout the book and, more important, very likely throughout your working career. Students who have some acquaintance with geometry and feel quite comfortable with graphs can safely skip this appendix.

■ GRAPHS USED IN ECONOMIC ANALYSIS

Economic graphs are invaluable because they can display a large quantity of data quickly and because they facilitate data interpretation and analysis. They enable the eye to take in at a glance important statistical relationships that would be far less apparent from written descriptions or long lists of numbers.

■ TWO-VARIABLE DIAGRAMS

Much of the economic analysis found in this and other books requires that we keep track of two **variables** simultaneously.

> A **variable** is something measured by a number; it is used to analyze what happens to other things when the size of that number changes (varies).

For example, in studying how markets operate, we will want to keep one eye on the *price* of a commodity and the other on the *quantity* of that commodity that is bought and sold.

For this reason, economists frequently find it useful to display real or imaginary figures in a two-variable diagram, which simultaneously represents the behaviour of two economic variables. The numerical value of one variable is measured along the horizontal line at the bottom of the graph (called the *horizontal axis*), starting from the **origin** (the point labelled "0"), and the numerical value of the other variable is mea-

sured up the vertical line on the left side of the graph (called the *vertical axis*), also starting from the origin.

> The "0" point in the lower-left corner of a graph where the axes meet is called the origin. Both variables are equal to zero at the **origin**.

Figures 2(a) and 2(b) are typical graphs of economic analysis. They depict an imaginary *demand curve*, represented by the blue dots in Figure 2(a) and the heavy blue line in Figure 2(b). The graphs show the price of natural gas on their vertical axes and the quantity of gas people want to buy at each price on the horizontal axes. The dots in Figure 2(a) are connected by the continuous blue curve labelled *DD* in Figure 2(b).

Economic diagrams are generally read just as one would read latitudes and longitudes on a map. On the demand curve in Figure 2, the point marked *a* represents a hypothetical combination of price and quantity of natural gas demanded by customers in Calgary. By drawing a horizontal line leftward from that point to the vertical axis, we learn that at this point the average price for gas in Calgary is 30¢ per cubic metre. By dropping a line straight down to the horizontal axis, we find that consumers want 8 billion cubic metres per year at this price, just as the statistics in Table 2 show. The other points on the graph give similar information. For example, point *b* indicates that if natural gas in Calgary costs only 20¢ per cubic metre, quantity demanded would be higher—it would reach 12 billion cubic metres per year.

Notice that information about price and quantity is *all* we can learn from the diagram. The demand curve will not tell us what kinds of people live in Calgary, the sizes of their homes, or the condition of their furnaces. It tells us about the quantity demanded at each possible price—no more, no less.

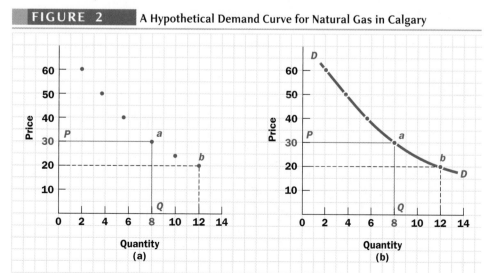

| FIGURE 2 | A Hypothetical Demand Curve for Natural Gas in Calgary |

Note: Price is in cents per cubic metres; quantity is in billions of cubic metres per year.

TABLE 2					
Quantities of Natural Gas Demanded at Various Prices					
Price (per cubic metre)	20¢	30¢	40¢	50¢	60¢
Quantity demanded (billions of cubic metres per year)	12	8	5.6	3.8	2

A diagram abstracts from many details, some of which may be quite interesting, so as to focus on the two variables of primary interest—in this case, the price of natural gas and the amount of gas that is demanded at each price. All of the diagrams used in this book share this basic feature. They cannot tell the reader the "whole story," any more than a map's latitude and longitude figures for a particular city can make someone an authority on that city.

■ THE DEFINITION AND MEASUREMENT OF SLOPE

One of the most important features of economic diagrams is the rate at which the line or curve being sketched runs uphill or downhill as we move to the right. The demand curve in Figure 2 clearly slopes downhill (the price falls) as we follow it to the right (that is, as consumers demand more gas). In such instances, we say that *the curve has a negative slope, or is negatively sloped, because one variable falls as the other one rises.*

The **slope of a straight line** is the ratio of the vertical change to the corresponding horizontal change as we move to the right along the line or, as it is often said, the ratio of the "rise" over the "run."

The four panels of Figure 3 show all possible types of slope for a straight-line relationship between two unnamed variables called Y (measured along the vertical axis) and X (measured along the horizontal axis). Figure 3(a) shows a *negative slope*, much like our demand curve in the previous graph. Figure 3(b) shows a *positive slope*, because variable Y rises (we go uphill) as variable X rises

(as we move to the right). Figure 3(c) shows a *zero slope*, where the value of Y is the same irrespective of the value of X. Figure 3(d) shows an *infinite slope*, meaning that the value of X is the same irrespective of the value of Y.

Slope is a numerical concept, not just a qualitative one. The two panels of Figure 4 show two positively sloped straight lines with different slopes. The line in Figure 4(b) is clearly steeper. But by how much? The labels should help you compute the answer. In Figure 4(a) a horizontal movement, AB, of 10 units ($13 - 3$) corresponds to a vertical movement, BC, of 1 unit ($9 - 8$). So the slope is $BC/AB = 1/10$. In Figure 4(b), the same horizontal movement of 10 units corresponds to a vertical movement of 3 units ($11 - 8$). So the slope is $3/10$, which is larger— the rise divided by the run is greater in Figure 4(b).

By definition, the slope of any particular straight line remains the same, no matter where on that line we choose to measure it. That is why we can pick any horizontal distance, AB, and the corresponding slope triangle, ABC, to measure slope. But this is not true for curved lines.

Curved lines also have slopes, but the numerical value of the slope differs at every point along the curve as we move from left to right.

The four panels of Figure 5 provide some examples of *slopes of curved lines.* The curve in Figure 5(a) has a negative slope everywhere, and the curve in Figure 5(b) has a positive slope everywhere. But these are not the only possibilities. In Figure 5(c) we encounter a curve that has a positive slope at first but a negative slope later on. Figure 5(d) shows the opposite case: a negative slope followed by a positive slope.

We can measure the slope of a smooth curved line numerically *at any particular point* by drawing a *straight* line that *touches*, but does not *cut*, the curve at the point in question. Such a line is called a **tangent** to the curve.

The **slope of a curved line** at a particular point is defined as the slope of the straight line that is tangent to the curve at that point.

Figure 6 shows tangents to the blue curve at two points. Line tt is tangent at point T, and line rr is tangent

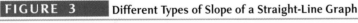

FIGURE 3   Different Types of Slope of a Straight-Line Graph

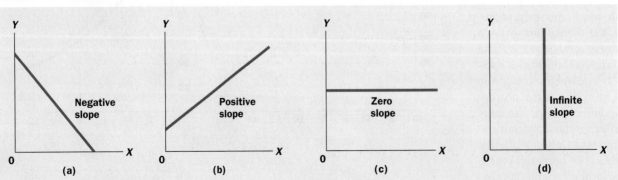

FIGURE 4   How to Measure Slope

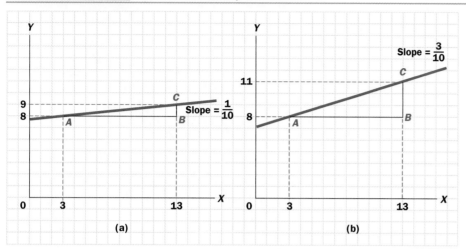

(a)   (b)

FIGURE 5   Behaviour of Slopes in Curved Graphs

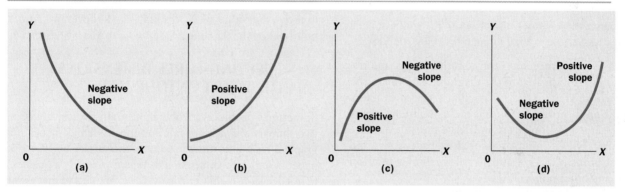

(a)   (b)   (c)   (d)

at point R. We can measure the slope of the curve at these two points by applying the definition. The calculation for point T, then, is the following:

Slope at point T = Slope of line tt

$$= \frac{\text{Distance BC}}{\text{Distance BA}}$$

$$= \frac{(1 - 5)}{(3 - 1)} = \frac{-4}{2} = -2$$

A similar calculation yields the slope of the curve at point R, which, as we can see from Figure 6, must be smaller numerically. That is, the tangent line rr is less steep than line tt:

Slope at point R = Slope of line rr

$$= \frac{(5 - 7)}{(8 - 6)} = \frac{-2}{2} = -1$$

EXERCISE Show that the slope of the curve at point G is about 1.

What would happen if we tried to apply this graphical technique to the high point in Figure 5(c) or to the low point in Figure 5(d)? Take a ruler and try it. The tangents that you construct should be horizontal, meaning that they should have a slope exactly equal to zero. It is always true that where the slope of a *smooth* curve

FIGURE 6   How to Measure Slope at a Point on a Curved Graph

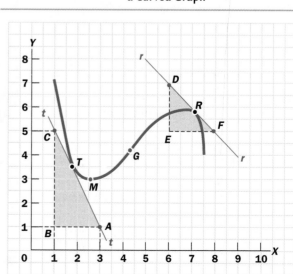

changes from positive to negative, or vice versa, there will be at least one point whose slope is zero.

Curves shaped like smooth hills, as in Figure 5(c), have a zero slope at their *highest* point. Curves shaped like valleys, as in Figure 5(d), have a zero slope at their *lowest* point.

RAYS THROUGH THE ORIGIN AND 45° LINES

The point at which a straight line cuts the vertical (Y) axis is called the **Y-intercept.**

The **Y-intercept** of a line or a curve is the point at which it touches the vertical axis (the Y-axis). The X-intercept is defined similarly.

For example, the Y-intercept of the line in Figure 4(a) is a bit less than 8.

Lines whose Y-intercept is zero have so many special uses in economics and other disciplines that they have been given a special name: a **ray through the origin,** or a **ray.**

Figure 7 shows three rays through the origin, and the slope of each is indicated in the diagram. The ray in the centre (whose slope is 1) is particularly useful in many economic applications because it marks points where X and Y are equal (as long as X and Y are measured in the same units). For example, at point A we have $X = 3$ and $Y = 3$; at point B, $X = 4$ and $Y = 4$. A similar relation holds at any other point on that ray.

How do we know that this is always true for a ray whose slope is 1? If we start from the origin (where both X and Y are zero) and the slope of the ray is 1, we know from the definition of slope that

$$\text{Slope} = \frac{\text{Vertical change}}{\text{Horizontal change}} = 1$$

This implies that the vertical change and the horizontal change are always equal, so the two variables must always remain equal. Any point along that ray (for example, point A) is exactly equal in distance from the horizontal and vertical axes (length DA = length CA)—the number on the X-axis (the abscissa) will be the same as the number on the Y-axis (the ordinate).

Rays through the origin with a slope of 1 are called 45° lines because they form an angle of 45° with the horizontal axis. A **45° line** marks off points where the variables measured on each axis have equal values.[1]

If a point representing some data is above the 45° line, we know that the value of Y

---

[1]The definition assumes that both variables are measured in the same units.

FIGURE 7   Rays Through the Origin

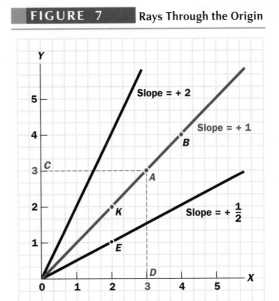

exceeds the value of X. Similarly, whenever we find a point below the 45° line, we know that X is larger than Y.

SQUEEZING THREE DIMENSIONS INTO TWO: CONTOUR MAPS

Sometimes problems involve more than two variables, so two dimensions just are not enough to depict them on a graph. This is unfortunate, because the surface of a sheet of paper is only two-dimensional. When we study a business firm's decision-making process, for example, we may want to keep track simultaneously of three variables: how much labour it employs, how much raw material it imports from foreign countries, and how much output it creates.

Luckily, economists can use a well-known device for collapsing three dimensions into two—a *contour map.* Figure 8 is a contour map of the summit of the highest mountain in the world, Mt. Everest, on the border of Nepal and Tibet. On some of the irregularly shaped "rings" on

FIGURE 8   A Geographic Contour Map

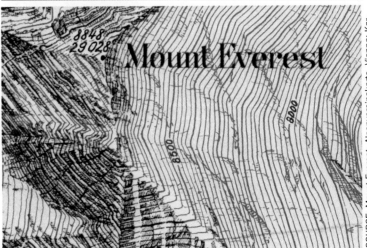

SOURCE: Mount Everest. Alpenvereinskarte. Vienna: Kartographisce Anstalt Freytag-Berndt und Artaria, 1957,1988.

this map, we find numbers (like 8500) indicating the height (in metres) above sea level at that particular spot on the mountain. Thus, unlike the more usual sort of map, which gives only latitudes and longitudes, this contour map (also called a topographical map) exhibits *three* pieces of information about each point: latitude, longitude, and altitude.

Figure 9 looks more like the contour maps encountered in economics. It shows how some third variable, called Z (think of it as a firm's output, for example), varies as we change either variable X (think of it as a firm's employment of labour) or variable Y (think of it as the use of imported raw material). Just like the map of Mt. Everest, any point on the diagram conveys three pieces of data. At point A, we can read off the values of X and Y in the conventional way (X is 30 and Y is 40), and we can also note the value of Z by finding out on which contour line point A falls. (It is on the $Z = 20$ contour.) So point A is able to tell us that 30 hours of labour and 40 metres of cloth produce 20 units of output per day. The contour line that indicates 20 units of output shows the various combinations of labour and cloth a manufacturer can use to produce 20 units of output. Economists call such maps **production indifference maps.**

A **production indifference map** is a graph whose axes show the quantities of two inputs that are used to produce some output. A curve in the graph corresponds to some given quantity of that output, and the different points on that curve show the different quantities of the two inputs that are just enough to produce the given output.

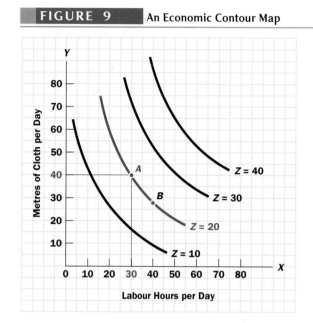

FIGURE 9   An Economic Contour Map

Although most of the analyses presented in this book rely on the simpler two-variable diagrams, contour maps will find their applications, especially in the appendixes to Chapters 5 and 7.

SUMMARY

1. Because graphs are used so often to portray economic models, it is important for students to acquire some understanding of their construction and use. Fortunately, the graphics used in economics are usually not very complex.

2. Most economic models are depicted in two-**variable** diagrams. We read data from these diagrams just as we read the latitude and longitude on a map: each point represents the values of two variables at the same time.

3. In some instances, three variables must be shown at once. In these cases, economists use contour maps, which, as the name suggests, show "latitude," "longitude," and "altitude" all at the same time.

4. Often, the most important property of a line or curve drawn on a diagram will be its **slope**, which is defined as the ratio of the "rise" over the "run," or the vertical change divided by the horizontal change. Curves that go uphill as we move to the right have positive slopes; curves that go downhill have negative slopes.

5. By definition, a straight line has the same slope wherever we choose to measure it. The slope of a curved line changes, but the slope at any point on the curve can be calculated by measuring the slope of a straight line tangent to the curve at that point.

KEY TERMS

Variable   19

Origin (of a graph)   19

Slope of a straight (or curved) line   20

Tangent to a curve   20

Y-intercept   22

Ray through the origin, or ray   22

45° line   22

Production indifference map   23

TEST YOURSELF

1. Portray the following hypothetical data on a two-variable diagram:

Academic Year	Total Enrollment	Enrollment in Economics Courses
2002–2003	3,000	300
2003–2004	3,100	325
2004–2005	3,200	350
2005–2006	3,300	375
2006–2007	3,400	400

Measure the slope of the resulting line, and explain what this number means.

2. From Figure 6, calculate the slope of the curve at point M.

3. Colin believes that the number of job offers he will get depends on the number of courses in which his grade is B+ or better. He concludes from observation that the following figures are typical:

Number of grades of B+ or better	0	1	2	3	4
Number of job offers	1	3	4	5	6

Put these numbers into a graph like Figure 2(a). Measure and interpret the slopes between adjacent dots.

4. In Figure 7, determine the values of X and Y at point K and at point E. What do you conclude about the slopes of the lines on which K and E are located?

5. In Figure 9, interpret the economic meaning of points A and B. What do the two points have in common? What is the difference in their economic interpretation?

2

THE ECONOMY: MYTH AND REALITY

When you cannot measure, your knowledge is meagre and unsatisfactory.

MAXIM ATTRIBUTED TO LORD KELVIN

I've come loaded with statistics, for I've noticed that a man can't prove anything without statistics.

MARK TWAIN

This chapter introduces you to the Canadian economy and its role in the world. It may seem that no such introduction is necessary, for you have probably lived your entire life in Canada. Every time you work at a summer or part-time job, pay your college or university bills, or buy a slice of pizza, you not only participate in the Canadian economy—you also observe something about it.

But the casual impressions we acquire in our everyday lives, though sometimes correct, are often misleading. We can see the trees but not necessarily the forest. We often harbour misconceptions about some very basic economic facts about the Canadian economy. There are many popular myths held by Canadians about the nature of the economy, such as the belief that we are inundated with imported goods, mostly from China, and that we produce very little in Canada today. The object of this chapter is to offer some important useful facts about the nature and evolution of the Canadian economy so as to dispel such misconceptions, and in the chapters that follow, to offer a framework for analyzing theories of how the economy works.

CONTENTS

THE CANADIAN ECONOMY: A THUMBNAIL SKETCH

Canada is a country that scores high on the United Nations *Human Development Index* (HDI)—an index that focuses on three measurable aspects of human welfare: life expectancy, literacy/school enrollment, and income level. While Canadian society performs very well in all three dimensions of human development, one cannot overlook Canada's relative success and maturity as an industrial economy. Yet, when analyzed from the perspective of the Group of Seven (G7) industrialized countries (Canada, France, Germany, Italy, Japan, the United Kingdom, and the United States), its population and, to a lesser extent, its economy appear comparatively small. With over 33 million inhabitants, Canada's population is slightly over one-tenth of that of the United States and one-third of that of Mexico, its two closest neighbours and trading partners on the North American continent. However, despite its relatively small demographic base, the Canadian economy produces a monetary value of its total output that exceeds that of, say, Mexico, when measured on the basis of a common currency unit. With a wide capacity in terms of human, physical, and natural resources, Canada places itself securely within the top tier of high-income countries internationally.

Inputs or **factors of production** are the labour, machinery, buildings, and natural resources used to make outputs.

Outputs are the goods and services that consumers and others want to acquire.

Why are some countries rich and others poor? As mentioned previously, that is one of the central questions facing economists. To try to answer this question, it is useful to think of the economic system as a machine that takes **inputs,** such as labour and other things we call **factors of production,** and transforms them into **outputs,** the things that people want to consume. On the basis of this relationship between inputs and outputs, the Canadian economic machine performs this task reasonably well. Of course, there are some countries, especially within the G7, that seem to accomplish this task even better, but there are many more that do not perform this function as well. Hence, a country like the United States holds the top rank when compared with other countries on the basis of such measures as output per person. Other less fortunate countries, such as Sierra Leone and Niger, are found at the bottom of the scale, with output per capita at less than one-fiftieth of that of Canada.

The 6.5 billion people in the world produced about US$45 trillion worth of goods and services in 2006. However, as Figure 1 shows, the G7 industrial economies, which accounted for just less than 12 percent of the earth's population, generated approximately 67 percent of world output. Given its low relative weight and the large gap between the United States and the other G7 countries, Canada's gross domestic product (GDP) per capita stood slightly below the G7 average in U.S. dollars, when adjusting for cost of living differences (at purchasing power parities) across the seven major industrialized countries.

Although Canada is a rich country and remains an important destination internationally for economic migrants seeking to improve their level of economic well-being, the ten provinces and three territories constituting Canada were not created equal. Population densities vary greatly among the regions of Canada, with enor-

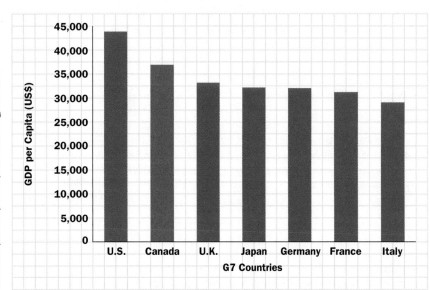

FIGURE 1   **2006 Gross Domestic Product (GDP) per Capita in 7 Industrial Countries**

SOURCE: Organisation for Economic Co-operation and Development (OECD), *OECD Statistics v. 4.4*, Dataset 1 (Gross Domestic Product), Dataset 3 (Total Population). www.oecd.org/statistics

Gross domestic product (GDP) per capita was obtained using current PPPs in U.S. dollars.

mous clustering in the south-central regions of the country. For example, while there are close to 12 inhabitants per square kilometre in the province of Ontario, there are only 0.01 people per square kilometre in the territory of Nunavut. Although much less pronounced, output per person also varies regionally. For instance, income per capita is now highest in Alberta, partly as a result of its vast oil wealth, while provinces such as Newfoundland and Labrador find themselves closer to the other extremity of the income scale, with their average provincial incomes being less than two-thirds of the Alberta average.

An Advanced Market Economy

Many economists would argue that part of the reason for the success of the Canadian economy in achieving a relatively high level of economic well-being relates to the fact that we have developed a sophisticated market economy with an appropriate balance of private and public ownership of property. While being a "land of opportunity" in creating incentives for private initiative, Canada has created a sophisticated social safety net that provides support, both financially and in kind, when the market fails for some of its citizens.

An economy with a mixture of private and public goods is sometimes referred to as a *mixed economy*, and all economies internationally could be said to be mixed. However, one can imagine on one end of the spectrum a pure market economy in which all goods are produced by private enterprises and sold in privately organized markets to individual consumers. In such a *free enterprise system*, all goods would be rationed on the basis of the prices that they fetch for their owners, and the decision to produce and sell one's products in the marketplace would be guided exclusively by the profit motive. Hence, in a pure *capitalist economy*, where individuals could hold and acquire ownership of capital goods so as to derive an income in excess of what they could get solely from their labour services, production and distribution would be purely in private hands. For example, the United States has one of the most "marketized" and "privatized" economies on earth, with even many of the public utilities being run by private companies.

At the other end of the spectrum, we have *command economies*, where decisions regarding the level and the composition of total output is set by a central authority, as in the former Soviet Union and, to a lesser extent, in such countries as China and Cuba today. While the actual ownership of the physical productive resources may or may not be in the hands of a central authority, the decision regarding what to produce is made by a central agency that normally sets specific objectives or plans for the respective public enterprises. This is why such economies have often been termed *planned economies*. This is not to suggest that no economic planning is actually undertaken in a market economy. Private enterprises, as much as public enterprises, must plan the combination of various inputs so as to fulfill orders and meet their commitments. However, in a *private enterprise economy*, it is the reaction to price signals arising from the marketplace that determines the amount of goods produced as well as who will get to consume these goods, based on an individual's ability to pay. Instead, in a command economy, the objective is set by a central authority, which decides what goods to be produced and who will get to consume them, sometimes regardless of an individual's income.

With the breakup of the Soviet Union in the late 1980s, many economies of Eastern Europe and Asia that constituted the former Soviet bloc moved away from the planned system and began to restructure their economies to fit more closely the market model prevailing in Western Europe and North America. Over the last two decades, these former socialist economies found themselves in a transitional phase as they moved from a planned to a market system and, for this reason, they are frequently referred to as *transition economies*. Although the terms *transition* and *emerging economies* are sometimes used broadly to describe any economy that is in the process of restructuring from a more regulated economy to a less regulated market economy (say, in the developing world), it is primarily the constellation of former socialist countries of Eastern Europe and parts of Asia that are most appropriately described as *transition economies*.

One should not, however, confuse a transition economy with a mixed economy. As was previously stated, all economies in the world today are mixed economies, regardless of whether they are market, socialist, or transition economies. All have a specific mixture of private/public production and consumption of goods and services. For instance, if you take the example of health care and compare the Canadian and American systems of delivery of medical services, you can easily distinguish how the two countries differ in terms of the private/public mix. In the American case, the market for health care services is dominated by private providers who ration these services largely on the basis of an individual's ability to pay (whether this is related to one's wealth or to how well endowed one is with private health insurance). In the Canadian case, as well as in many Western European countries, health care systems have features that are closer to the command economy model. In Canada, health care services are provided by provincial governments on the basis of the Canada Health Act to whoever needs medical services, without the intervention of the market and the price mechanism in allocating such services. A similar difference can be found in the area of higher education, where delivery is done largely through quasi-public institutions. The price mechanism (that is, tuition fees) plays a less important role in Canada and in many European countries than in the United States because of the varying degrees of direct government subsidies that are provided to Canada's and other countries' educational institutions.

The private/public composition of goods and services reflects policy preferences of governments that have been fashioned by the history of each country. Over time, the structure of output in an economy changes primarily because of political forces at work in reshaping those preferences. Hence, during the early post-World War II period, political forces internationally had moved in the direction that favoured more public sector involvement in the economy. During the 1970s and 1980s under the influence of Thatcherism in the United Kingdom and Reaganomics in the United States, the pendulum swung in the opposite direction, as governments sold off public assets and retreated somewhat from direct involvement in the provision of goods and services. Although the public sector share of production has declined somewhat from the earlier post-World War II period, Canada's uniqueness is its continued large public sector with close to one-quarter of total production flowing from public sector activities, thereby making it a mixed economy *par excellence*.

Gross domestic product (GDP) is a measure of the size of the economy—the total amount it produces in a year. *Real GDP* adjusts this measure for changes in the purchasing power of money, that is, it corrects for inflation.

The standard measure of the total output of an economy is called **gross domestic product** (or **GDP**), a term that appears frequently in the news media. In an advanced market economy such as ours, the share of GDP that passes through markets is enormous. Although government purchases of goods and services in Canada amount to about 22 percent of GDP, much of this is purchased from private businesses. Direct government production of commodities is rare, but the public sector supply of services is quite significant in Canada, with health care delivery and education subsidies being prime examples.

■ A Relatively "Open" Economy

All nations trade with one another and, as one of Canada's most distinguished economists, Harold A. Innis, pointed out long ago, the economic history of Canada has been shaped very much by foreign trade. From the time of its first European contact, Canada was integrated into the world economy by establishing itself solidly as a producer of primary products and an importer of manufactured goods. While its share of primary commodities has declined significantly over time in this era of globalized product markets, exports now constitute a large and growing share of Canada's GDP. In 2007, our annual exports were about $535 billion and our imports about $503 billion. That's quite a significant amount of money transiting through the foreign sector. But, while very important, some may argue that Canada's international trade often gets a lot more attention than it deserves. The fact is that we still produce a large portion of what we consume and consume a great deal of what we produce, as Figure 2 shows. In 1959, the average of exports and imports was less than 20 percent of GDP. By 2000, this share had peaked at over 40 percent and then bottomed out at slightly less than 34 percent of

GDP by 2007. This was a hefty jump and turnaround in less than half a century, and the effect was to render the Canadian economy generally more dependent on foreign trade. However, these figures suggest that close to two-thirds of what Canadians buy annually is still made in Canada today.

Among the most serious misconceptions about the Canadian economy is the myth that this country no longer manufactures anything but, rather, imports everything from, say, low-wage countries such as China. Indeed, about 33 percent of Canada's GDP was imported in 2007. However, out of the total merchandise imports from the rest of the world, less than 10 percent came from China, thereby reflecting about 2.5 percent of GDP. It is true that Chinese goods constitute a growing share of our imports, but the fact still remains that two-thirds of all of our imports of goods and services originate from a relatively high-wage country and our principal trading partner—the United States.

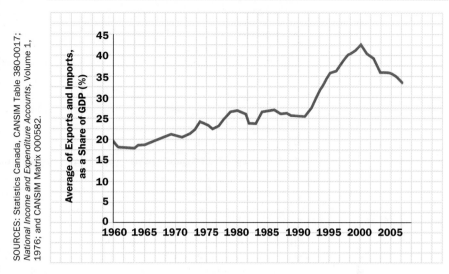

FIGURE 2 Share of Canada's Gross Domestic Product (GDP), Exported and Imported, 1959–2007

SOURCES: Statistics Canada, CANSIM Table 380-0017; *National Income and Expenditure Accounts*, Volume 1, 1976; and CANSIM Matrix 000582.

An economy is called relatively **open** if its exports and imports constitute a large share of its GDP.

An economy is considered relatively **closed** if they constitute a small share.

Economists use the terms **open economy** and **closed economy** to indicate how important international trade is to a nation. A common measure of "openness" is the average of exports and imports, expressed as a share of GDP. Table 1, which lists the average of the exports and imports of commodities (excluding services) for nine countries, shows that Canada, together with such disparate countries as Germany and Mexico, could be classified as moderately open economies in 2006, but clearly not as open as the Netherlands, with over 50 percent of its GDP being dependent on foreign trade. On the other hand, the United States, together with countries such as Japan, are relatively closed economies with shares of GDP a bit less than 15 percent level. Despite its growing importance in world trade, China remains a highly closed economy.

TABLE 1	
Openness of Various National Economies, 2006	
Country	Openness Ratio (%)
Netherlands	67
Germany	35
Mexico	31
Canada	30
Russian Federation	24
United Kingdom	22
Japan	14
United States	11
China	3

SOURCE: World Trade Organization (WTO), *Statistics Database;* and OECD, *OECD in Figures,* 2007 edition; China Statistical Yearbook 2007, The People's Bank of China. China's GDP was converted from Yuan to U.S. dollars at the exchange rate of December 2006 (1:7.8238).

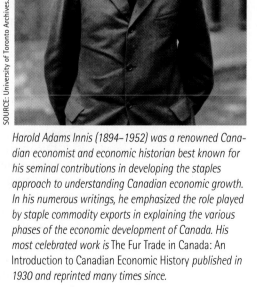

SOURCE: University of Toronto Archives.

Harold Adams Innis (1894–1952) was a renowned Canadian economist and economic historian best known for his seminal contributions in developing the staples approach to understanding Canadian economic growth. In his numerous writings, he emphasized the role played by staple commodity exports in explaining the various phases of the economic development of Canada. His most celebrated work is The Fur Trade in Canada: An Introduction to Canadian Economic History *published in 1930 and reprinted many times since.*

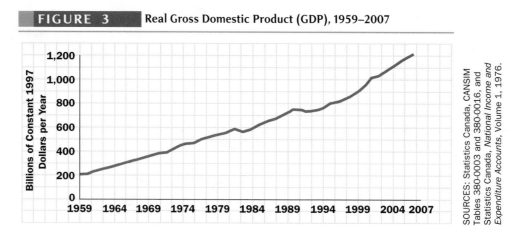

FIGURE 3   Real Gross Domestic Product (GDP), 1959–2007

SOURCES: Statistics Canada, CANSIM Tables 380-0003 and 380-0016, and Statistics Canada, *National Income and Expenditure Accounts*, Volume 1, 1976.

◾ A Growing Economy . . .

The next salient fact about the Canadian economy is its growth—it gets bigger almost every year (see Figure 3). Gross domestic product in 2007 was around $1.5 trillion, which is about $45,000 per Canadian. Once adjusted for inflation, Canada's *real* GDP was about 5.5 times as large in 2007 as it was in 1959. Of course, there were many more people in Canada in 2007 than there were 48 years earlier, but even correcting for population growth, Canada's real GDP *per capita* was about three times higher in 2007 than in 1959. That's still not a bad performance: Living standards have tripled in less than half a century.

◾ But with Bumps along the Growth Path

Although the cumulative growth performance depicted in Figure 3 is impressive, Canada's economic growth has been quite irregular. We have experienced alternating periods of good and bad times, which are called *economic fluctuations* or sometimes just *business cycles.* In some years—two major ones since 1980—GDP actually declined. Such periods of *declining* economic activity are called **recessions.**

A **recession** is a period of time during which the total output of the economy falls.

The bumps along the Canadian economy's historic growth path are barely visible in Figure 3, but they stand out more clearly in Figure 4, which displays the same data in a different way and extends them back further, to before the Great Depression. Instead of plotting the *level* of real GDP each year, Figure 4 plots its *growth rate*—the percentage change from one year to the next. Now the booms and busts that delight or distress people—and even swing elections—stand out clearly. For example, following periods of stunning decline during the Great Depression and then spectacular growth during the World War II era, we had fairly sustained growth from the mid-1950s to the mid-1970s. On the other hand, over the last quarter of a century, Canada went through two severe recessions—in both cases severe enough to have contributed to the defeat of the governments in power. In the early 1980s, Canada went through what some then dubbed as a "great recession"—an economic slump important enough to have helped in the defeat of John Turner's Liberals in 1984 by the Progressive Conservative Party led by Brian Mulroney. In much the same way, after a serious dip in GDP in the early 1990s, Canada's very weak performance at the time possibly contributed to the election of Jean Chrétien's Liberals in 1993.

One important consequence of these ups and downs in economic growth is that unemployment varies considerably from one year to the next (see Figure 5). During the Great Depression of the 1930s, unemployment peaked at about 20 percent of the labour force, but it fell to a mere 1 percent during World War II. Since the 1970s, Canada's unemployment rate showed a significant upward trend. Only during the last decade has the unemployment rate fallen to a low point of 6.0 percent by 2007—its lowest rate in 30 years. In human terms, the sustained high level of unemployment

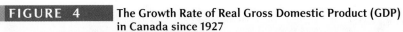

FIGURE 4   **The Growth Rate of Real Gross Domestic Product (GDP) in Canada since 1927**

SOURCES: Statistics Canada, CANSIM Tables 380-0016 and 380-0003, and *National Income and Expenditure Accounts*, Vol. 1, 1976.

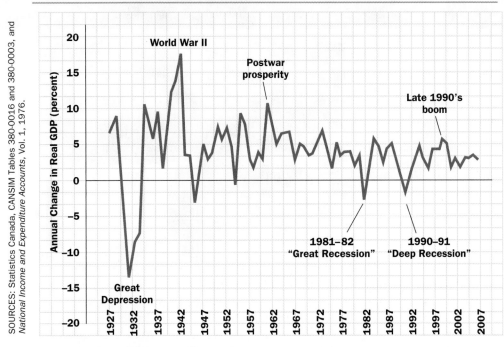

FIGURE 5   **The Unemployment Rate in Canada, 1921–2007**

SOURCES: Statistics Canada: CANSIM Table 282-0002; *Historical Labour Force Statistics, 1976–1977*; and *Historical Statistics of Canada*, 1983, Series D127, D132, and D143.

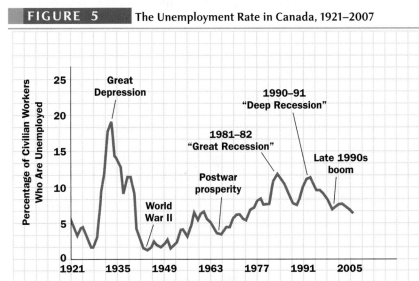

Note: Prior to 1976, Statistics Canada's definition of the working-age population included persons 14 years of age and over, rather than the present 15 years of age and over. This threshold age that defines who is included statistically in the potential labour force should not be confused with the legal working age, which varies between 12 and 17 among provinces.

since the 1970s has meant a "lost generation" of jobless workers, especially young ones, many of whom were excluded from standard labour market activity during the 1980s and the 1990s. Understanding why joblessness varies so dramatically and what can we do about it are major reasons for studying economics.

THE INPUTS: LABOUR AND CAPITAL

Let's now return to the analogy of an economy as a machine turning inputs into outputs. The most important input is human labour: the men and women who run the machines, work behind the desks, and serve you in stores.

Unemployment Rates in Europe

For roughly the first quarter-century after World War II, unemployment rates in the industrialized countries of Europe were significantly lower than those in North America. During the late 1970s, the situation reversed itself, as countries that had been used to full employment with unemployment rates in the range of 1–2 percent were often faced with double-digit unemployment rates. It is noteworthy that one important exception was the United Kingdom; unlike France, Germany, Italy, and Sweden, the United Kingdom did not join the euro zone in 1999. Put on a comparable basis by the U.S. Bureau of Labor Statistics, unemployment rates in the nine countries in 2007 were as shown in the accompanying table.

Country	Unemployment Rate
Canada	5.3%
United States	4.6
Australia	4.4
Japan	3.9
France	8.6
Germany	8.7
Italy	6.1
Sweden	6.1
United Kingdom	5.4

SOURCE: © Joel Stettenheim/Corbis

■ The Canadian Workforce: Who Is in It?

Out of slightly over 33 million Canadians, about 17 million (or about half of the population) held jobs in 2007. Fifty-three percent of these workers were men; 47 percent were women. This ratio represents a drastic change from two generations ago, when most women worked only at home (see Figure 6). Indeed, the massive entrance of women into the paid labour force was one of the major social transformations of Canadian life during the second half of the twentieth century. In 1950, just 22 percent of women worked in the marketplace; now, about 63 percent do.

As Figure 7 shows, the percentage of women in the labour forces of other industrial countries has also been growing. The expanding role of women in the labour

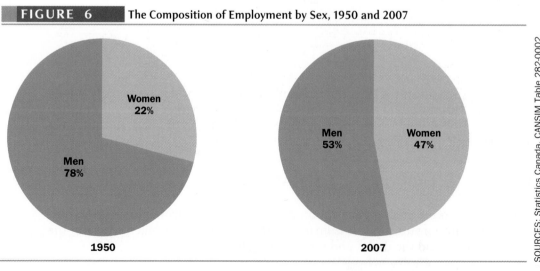

FIGURE 6   The Composition of Employment by Sex, 1950 and 2007

1950

2007

SOURCES: Statistics Canada, CANSIM Table 282-0002 and Statistics Canada publication *Historical Statistics of Canada*, 1983.

market has raised many controversial questions about how government should deal with gender discrimination in the workplace, who should bear the cost of maternity leave, and so on.

In contrast to women, the percentage of teenagers in the workforce has dropped significantly since its peak in the mid-1970s (see Figure 8). Young men and women aged 15 to 19 accounted for 10.9 percent of employment in 1974 but only 5.8 percent in 2006. As the baby boom gave way to the baby bust, people under 20 became scarce resources! Still, close to 900,000 teenagers hold jobs in the Canadian economy today—a number that has been pretty stable in the past few years. Most teenagers fill low-wage jobs at fast-food restaurants, retail outlets, and the like. Relatively few can be found holding full-time positions in the nation's factories and offices.

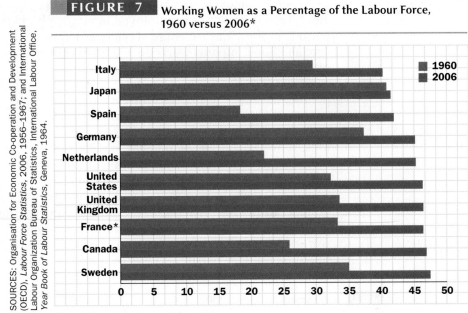

FIGURE 7 Working Women as a Percentage of the Labour Force, 1960 versus 2006*

SOURCES: Organisation for Economic Co-operation and Development (OECD), *Labour Force Statistics, 2006, 1956–1967*; and International Labour Organization Bureau of Statistics, International Labour Office, *Year Book of Labour Statistics*, Geneva, 1964.

* Data for France is for the years 1962 and 2006.

The Canadian Workforce: What Does It Do?

What do these 17 million working Canadians do? The only real answer is: almost anything you can imagine. At the end of 2006, there were 703,900 teachers and

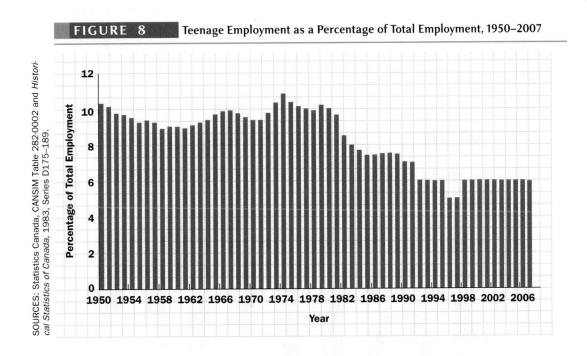

FIGURE 8 Teenage Employment as a Percentage of Total Employment, 1950–2007

SOURCES: Statistics Canada, CANSIM Table 282-0002 and *Historical Statistics of Canada*, 1983, Series D175–189.

professors employed; 480,500 nurses; 467,100 employed in art, culture, recreation, and sports; over a million employed in retail; 540,600 chefs, cooks, and related occupations in food and beverage service; 231,600 in protective services; 195,900 child care and home support workers; 372,800 in the construction trades; 810,000 machine operators and assemblers in manufacturing; and so on.

Figure 9 shows the breakdown by major sector. It holds some surprises for most people, because the majority of Canadian workers—like workers in all developed countries—produce services, not goods. In 2007, about 76 percent of all workers in Canada were employed in the service sector, with the vast majority in private service jobs. The remaining 24 percent were employed in the goods-producing sector, including agriculture. The once popular image of the typical worker as a blue-collar worker, often depicted on prime time television in both Canada and the United States—Homer Simpson, if you will—is really quite misleading.

Federal, provincial/territorial, and local governments employed over 3 million people in 2006 but, contrary to a popular misconception, few of these civil servants worked for the *federal* government. Federal employment (including reservists and full-time military personnel) was only about 393,000 or about 12.5 percent of total public sector employment in Canada, a number that declined significantly during the early and mid-1990s as successive federal governments sought to cut expenditures to combat their ballooning budget deficits. Finally, approximately 350,000 Canadians worked in agriculture and about 2.5 million were self-employed in 2006.

As Figure 10 shows, *all* industrialized countries have become "service economies." This shift toward the service sector can be attributed to at least two fundamental causes. As household real income has risen over time, a growing proportion of household spending has shifted toward consumer services and away especially from the primary sector's output that fulfills some of our most basic needs. Indeed, unlike even a half century ago when, for instance, relatively few ate at restaurants or travelled much, nowadays consumers rely on a vast variety of commercial services, such as

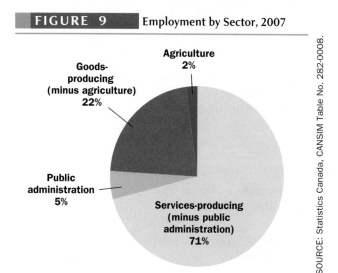

FIGURE 9   Employment by Sector, 2007

SOURCE: Statistics Canada, CANSIM Table No. 282-0008.

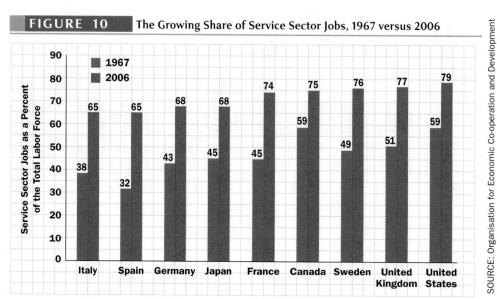

FIGURE 10   The Growing Share of Service Sector Jobs, 1967 versus 2006

SOURCE: Organisation for Economic Co-operation and Development (OECD), *Labour Force Statistics*, 2007, and 1956–1967. www.oecd.org/statistics

mobile phone and Internet services, day care services and the like, that fulfill needs often associated with a society that has attained a much higher level of affluence.

To a considerable degree, this historical shift to services has also been made possible by the growing efficiency of production resulting from the large-scale introduction of labour-saving technology in the goods-producing sector of the economy. With the production of more and more manufacturing products using fewer and fewer workers, it has been possible to free up labour from the primary and secondary sectors to meet this growing demand for services. If you look at the historical series on the sector shares of employment in Table 2, already by the late nineteenth century, these forces were at work in Canada as we moved from an agricultural-based society to a services economy. However, in more recent

TABLE 2			
Percentage Distribution of Employment by Major Sectors, Canada 1881–2006			
Year	Primary	Secondary	Tertiary
1881	51%	29%	20%
1891	50	26	24
1901	44	28	28
1911	40	27	33
1921	37	26	37
1931	33	16	51
1951	23	33	44
1961	14	30	56
1971	9	28	63
1981	7	25	68
1991	5	22	73
2001	5	20	75
2006	4	20	76

Note: The primary sector includes agriculture, fishing, logging, and mining and oil wells; the secondary sector includes manufacturing and construction; and the tertiary or services sector includes transportation, communications and other utilities, trade, finance, insurance and real estate, community, business and personal services, and public administration.

SOURCES: Statistics Canada, CANSIM Table 282-0008; Statistics Canada, *Historical Statistics of Canada,* 1983; Statistics Canada, *Historical Labour Force Statistics;* and various references; and W. L. Marr and D. G. Patterson, *Canada: An Economic History* (Toronto: Macmillan of Canada, 1980), Table 7:3.

decades, it may be argued that this "services revolution" has also occurred with the arrival of the "Information Age." Activities related to computers, to research, to the transmission of information by teaching and publication, and other information-related activities are providing many of the new jobs, notably in the public services. This means that, in the rich industrial countries, workers who moved out of both agriculture and manufacturing jobs into the services sectors have not gone predominantly into low-skill jobs such as dishwashing or housecleaning. Many have found employment in high-skill producers' service jobs in which education and experience provide a great advantage. However, there are also many who have found employment in relatively low-skill and low-wage consumers' service jobs, such as at McDonald's and Tim Hortons.

■ The Canadian Workforce: What It Earns

When taken together, these workers' wages account for over 60 percent of the total income that the production process generates in Canada. That adds up to an average hourly wage of over $20—plus fringe benefits like vacation, worker's disability, dental insurance, pensions and so on, which can contribute to as much as an additional 30 to 40 percent for some workers. With an average workweek of about 35 hours, a typical weekly paycheque in Canada is about $750 before taxes (but excluding the value of benefits). That is hardly a princely sum, and most university graduates can expect to earn substantially more. Indeed, according to the 2001 census of Canada, workers holding a university degree earned 91 percent more (on average) than those holding a high school certificate. Similarly wide differences in earnings according to the degree of schooling are also quite characteristic of the labour market in other industrial countries. It would thus appear that forgoing a few extra years of labour-market earnings would not be such a high price to pay for practically doubling your stream of earnings over your lifetime!

However, average wages throughout Northern Europe tend to exceed Canadian rates. Workers in a number of other industrial countries now receive higher compensation than either Canadian or American workers do—a big change from the situation a few decades ago. As illustrated in Figure 11, after converting into U.S. dollars, workers in Canadian manufacturing industries in 2006 made substantially less than those in Germany, Belgium, the Netherlands, Sweden, France, and the United

SOURCE: U.S. Department of Labor, Bureau of Labor Statistics, *International Comparisons of Hourly Compensation Costs for Production Workers in Manufacturing, 2006*, Table 2. USDL: 06-2020, November 2008. Retrieved from http://www.bls.gov/news.release/pdf/ichcc.pdf

FIGURE 11

Average Hourly Compensation Rates in Manufacturing, 2006

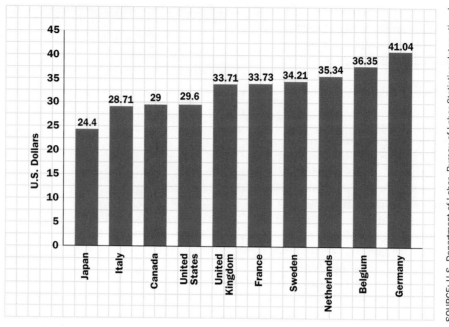

Kingdom, and almost the same hourly compensation as workers in the United States. Canadian compensation levels did, however, exceed those of Japan and Italy. While this has rendered Canadian industry more competitive internationally, in our low inflation environment since the early 1990s, Canadian workers did not keep abreast of wage developments in a number of other industrial countries.

■ Capital and Its Earnings

The rest of national income (after deducting for the sliver of income that goes to the owners of land and natural resources) mainly accrues to the owners of *capital*—the machines and buildings that make up the nation's industrial plant.

The total market value of these business assets—a tough number to estimate—is believed to be in the neighbourhood of $3.5 trillion. With a rate of return to the ownership of capital of, say, about 7 percent before taxes, total capital earnings come to around $250 billion in Canada. Of this, corporate profits constitute approximately two-thirds of total earnings, while the rest is mainly interest income.

Public opinion polls routinely show that people are quite confused about the level of profits in our society. For instance, in polls conducted in the United States, it was found that the man and the woman on the street believe that profits account for about 30 percent of the price of a typical product. While the actual figure varies significantly across industries in Canada, corporate profits before taxes accounted for about 14 percent of the dollar value of total output in 2007. This figure (the share of profits in the value of a typical product) should not

FIGURE 12   Rate of Return on Capital (All-Industries Average), Canada, 1980–2006

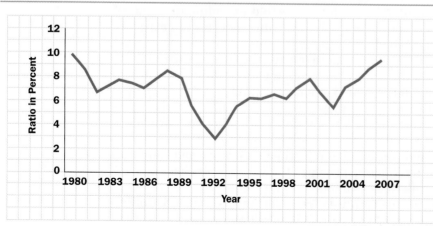

SOURCE: Statistics Canada, CANSIM II, Series V219184 and V3871947.

be confused, however, with the *rate* of profit, which is a ratio of the dollar value of profits in a given period to the value of the capital advanced. While we have assumed this rate to be about 7 percent on average, over the last quarter-century, this ratio has gone from as low as 3 percent annually for the all-industries average in some recession years (such as in 1992) to as high as 10 percent as the economy was approaching a business cycle peak in Canada (in 1980) (see Figure 12).

■ THE OUTPUTS: WHAT DOES CANADA PRODUCE?

What does all this labour and capital produce? Consumer spending accounts for about 60 percent of GDP. And what an amazing variety of goods and services it buys. Canadian households spend roughly 60 percent of their budgets on services, with housing commanding the largest share. For instance, in 2005, an average household with children spent $2,070 annually on health care, $2,420 on education, and, among many other services, $1,510 on personal care. The other 30 percent of Canadian budgets was spent on goods—ranging from food purchased from stores at $9,630 to clothing at $3,760 per household in 2005.

This leaves about 40 percent of GDP for all nonconsumption uses. That includes government services (hospital care, schooling for young people, and spending on national defence), business purchases of machinery and industrial structures, and consumer purchases of new houses.

■ THE CENTRAL ROLE OF BUSINESS FIRMS

When we peer inside the economic machine that turns inputs into outputs, we see primarily private companies whose principal objective is pecuniary gain. Astonishingly, we have about 2.5 million active business establishments in Canada—about one for every 13 people!

The owners and managers of these businesses hire people, acquire or rent capital goods, and arrange to produce things consumers want to buy. Sound simple? It isn't. Over 7,000 businesses fail every year. A few succeed spectacularly. Some do both. Indeed, it has been estimated that, on average, only one out of every five firms survives after only ten years of existence in Canada. Fortunately for the Canadian economy, the lure of riches induces thousands of people to start new businesses every year. Indeed, this high turnover of business enterprises in a market economy was long ago described as a process of "creative destruction" by a famous economist, Joseph A. Schumpeter (1883–1950).

A number of our larger firms do business all over the world, especially in the continental context of the North American Free Trade Agreement (NAFTA). However, there are perhaps still many more foreign-based *multinational corporations* doing business in this country. Historically, Canada has been primarily on the receiving end of *foreign direct investment*, with a high number of foreign-owned subsidiaries established here. The role played by multinationals has been a controversial one in Canada. However, some people would claim that, in this era of global markets, it has now become practically impossible to determine the true "nationality" of global corporations—which may have factories in ten or more countries, sell their wares all over the world, and have stockholders in dozens of nations. (See the boxed feature "What's the Nationality of a Global Corporation?" on the next page.) Most profits of large Canadian-based companies like Nortel are generated abroad, for example, and the Honda you drive was probably assembled in Alliston, Ontario.

Firms compete with other companies in their *industry*. Most economists believe that this *competition* is the key to industrial efficiency. A sole supplier of a commodity will find it easy to make money, and may therefore fail to innovate or control costs. Its management is liable to become relaxed and sloppy. But a company besieged by dozens of competitors eager to take its business away must constantly seek ways to innovate, to cut costs, and to build a better mousetrap. The rewards for business success can be magnificent. But the punishment for failure is severe.

What's the Nationality of a Global Corporation?

Have we entered a new era, with the inexorable convergence on a form of business organization that we now call the "global corporation"—an institution that is footloose, borderless, and capable of rendering national economic policies irrelevant? Or do multinational corporations continue to be shaped by the culture, institutions, and policies of their "home" countries? This remains a highly debated question of great concern to policy makers. For instance, Robert E. Reich, who was U.S. Secretary of Labour in the Clinton administration during the 1990s, was extremely concerned and, just before joining the government, argued that it was nearly impossible to define the nationality of a multinational corporation. In his 1991 book *The Work of Nations,* he wrote:

> What's the difference between an "American" corporation that makes or buys abroad much of what it sells around the world and a "foreign" corporation that makes or buys in the United States much of what it sells? . . . The mind struggles to keep the players straight. In 1990, Canada's Northern Telecom was selling to its American customers telecommunications equipment made by Japan's NTT at NTT's factory in North Carolina.
>
> If you found that one too easy, try this: Beginning in 1991, Japan's Mazda would be producing Ford Probes at Mazda's plant in Flat Rock, Michigan. Some of these cars would be exported to Japan and sold there under Ford's trademark.
>
> A Mazda-designed compact utility vehicle would be built at a Ford plant in Louisville, Kentucky, and then sold at Mazda dealerships in the United States. Nissan, meanwhile, was designing a new light truck at its San Diego, California, design center. The trucks would be assembled at Ford's Ohio truck plant, using panel parts fabricated by Nissan at its Tennessee factory, and then marketed by both Ford and Nissan in the United States and in Japan. Who is Ford? Nissan? Mazda?

The same can be said nowadays of a notable number of large "Canadian" corporations, such as Nortel and Bombardier, whose foreign activities often rival their operations here in Canada. However, although terms such as "global," "multinational," and "transnational" corporations are used quite loosely in the media, even economists

SOURCE: © AP / Wide World Photos

are not in general agreement about how to define a multinational corporation. Which dimensions of a corporation do we choose? Do we define it on the basis of its geographic structure of ownership, its management, the international distribution of its sales, or the geographical distribution of its production? Partly to shed light on this difficult issue, at about the same time that Robert Reich had raised his question in the early 1990s, the United Nations Conference on Trade and Development (UNCTAD) developed a *Transnationality Index* (TNI) to which the UN refers regularly in its annual *UN Investment Report.* The TNI is calculated as a weighted average of three key indicators of "transnationality" of corporations: the proportion of foreign sales to total sales, the proportion of foreign assets to total assets, and the proportion of foreign employment to total employment. When ranked on the basis of the TNI, some major Canadian-based companies, such as the Thomson Corporation, have tended to be placed very high on the UN list of highly globalized corporations.

SOURCE: Robert B. Reich, *The Work of Nations* (New York: Knopf, 1991), pp. 124, 131.

■ WHAT'S MISSING FROM THE PICTURE? GOVERNMENT

Thus far, we have the following capsule summary of how the Canadian economy works: About 2.5 million private businesses, energized by the profit motive, employ about 17 million workers and about $3.5 trillion of capital. These firms bring their enormously diverse wares to market, where they try to sell them to over 33 million consumers.

Households and businesses are linked in a tight circle, depicted in Figure 13, a circular flow model that is discussed in greater detail in macroeconomics. For the time being, it will suffice to say that firms use their receipts from sales to pay wages to employees and interest and profits to the people who provide capital. These income flows, in turn, enable consumers to purchase the goods and services that companies produce. This circular flow of money and goods lies at the centre of the analysis of how the national economy works. All these activities are linked by a series of interconnected markets, some of which are highly competitive and others of which are less so.

FIGURE 13	The Circular Flow of Goods and Money

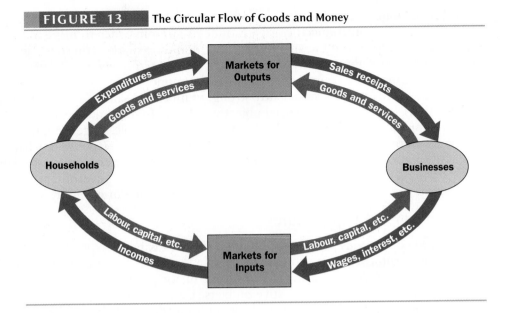

All very well and good. But the story leaves out something important: the role of *government*, which is pervasive even in our decidedly free-market economy. Just what does government do in the Canadian economy—and why?

Although an increasing number of tasks seem to get assigned to the state each year, the traditional role of government in a market economy revolves around five jobs:

- Making and enforcing the laws
- Regulating business
- Providing certain goods and services such as national defence
- Levying taxes to pay for these goods and services
- Redistributing income

Every one of these tasks is steeped in controversy and surrounded by intense political debate. We conclude this chapter with a brief look at each.

The Government as Referee

For the most part, power is diffused in our economy, and people "play by the rules." But, in the scramble for competitive advantage, disputes are bound to arise. Did Company A live up to its contract? Who owns that disputed piece of property? In addition, some unscrupulous businesses are liable to step over the line now and then. We saw some spectacular examples over the last decade with Bre-X, Nortel, and Hollinger, among others, that have rocked the corporate world in Canada and have necessitated government involvement, often as a regulatory referee. Also, we see major industrial strife, which can have significant consequences on the Canadian economy and which usually involves government mediation.

The government enters, therefore, as rule maker, referee, and arbitrator. The federal Parliament and provincial and local governments pass the laws that define the rules of the economic game. The executive branches of all three governmental levels share the responsibility for enforcing them. And the courts interpret the laws and adjudicate disputes.

The Government as Business Regulator

In market economies, governments must interfere with the workings of the marketplace in many ways and for myriad reasons—such as regulating the use of hazardous products and protecting the consumer against misleading advertising in the marketplace. Since market economies are vulnerable to abusive and detrimental market practices, governments have often introduced competition legislation in order to make markets work more efficiently. Given the small size of our domestic market, there is a greater tendency for industrial concentration. Canada's federal *anti-combines legislation* is there to protect competition against encroachment by monopoly, even though some critics would argue that it is not sufficiently strong. In much the same way, some government regulations seek to promote social objectives that unfettered markets do not foster—environmental regulations are a particularly obvious example. In general, it may be said that government regulations in the marketplace represent a response to what could be described generally as a problem of *market failure*. But there are some, especially from the business community, who would probably argue that "government failures" are sometimes a more serious problem than market failures in our economy.

Government Expenditures

The most contentious political issues often involve taxing and spending because those are the government's most prominent roles. In the federal House of Commons as well as in the various provincial legislatures, our major political parties have frequently battled fiercely over their respective budgets. Under the Chrétien and Martin Liberals, the federal government managed a significant turnaround in the state of the public finances, from huge deficits in 1993 to large surpluses at the end of their terms of office. But this turnaround had serious consequences, leading to, among other things, what nowadays are termed *fiscal imbalances* between the federal government and the provinces, which the Harper government sought to redress somewhat in 2007. During 2007, the federal government spent about $230 billion—an amount that is literally beyond comprehension for many of us, unless measured as a proportion of Canada's GDP. The first pie chart in Figure 14 shows where this money went. Over one-third went to social services and programs including *pensions and income security* programs funded by the federal government; 10 percent went largely in the form of *transfers for health care* administered by the provinces; and 11 percent went to *protection*, including national defence. Adding in *interest on the public debt*, these four functions alone accounted for about 70 percent of federal spending. The rest went for miscellaneous other purposes including education, transportation and communication, housing, environment, and foreign aid.

The consolidated government spending at the provincial, territorial and local levels was about $370 billion in 2007. As shown in the second pie chart in Figure 14, health care claimed the largest share of provincial budgets (28 percent), with education a close second (23 percent). Despite this vast outpouring of public funds, many observers

FIGURE 14   The Allocation of Government Expenditures, 2007

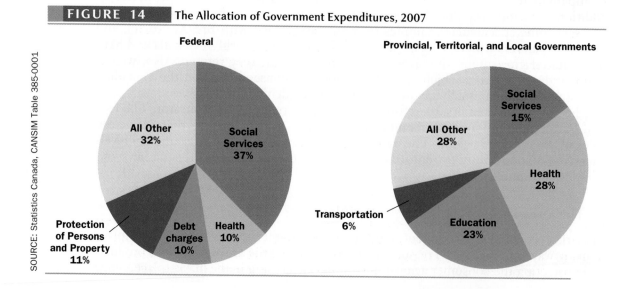

SOURCE: Statistics Canada, CANSIM Table 385-0001

believe that serious social needs still remain unmet. Critics argue that our health care system is poorly funded, our educational system is lacking, and our public infra-structures (such as bridges and roads) are inadequate, while there are others who feel that not enough is spent on the military or foreign aid.

Although the scale and scope of government activity in Canada is substantial, it remains on the low end when we compare it to other leading economies. Figure 15 is a bar graph showing government expenditure as a percentage of GDP for ten industrialized countries. We see that the share of government in the Canadian economy is the third-lowest in this group of countries.

■ Taxes in Canada

The government spends, thereby injecting money into the market system, but it also withdraws money from the economy when it collects taxes. The state of govern-ment finances is usually mea-sured by its net spending—the difference between what the government spends and what it receives in tax revenues.

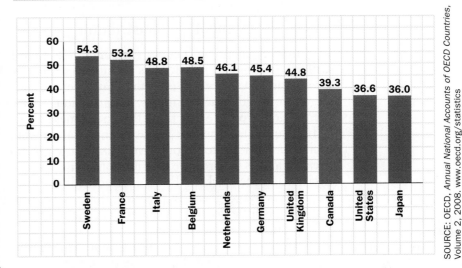

FIGURE 15 Government Spending as a Percentage of GDP in Selected Countries, 2006

SOURCE: OECD, *Annual National Accounts of OECD Countries,* Volume 2, 2008. www.oecd.org/statistics

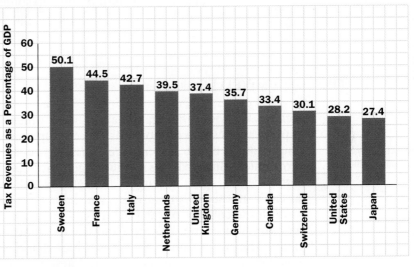

FIGURE 16 The Tax Burden in Selected Countries, 2006

SOURCE: OECD, *Annual National Accounts of OECD Countries,* Volume 2, 2008. www.oecd.org/statistics

When we consider taxes, the first thing that comes to mind is that there seems to be a tax on everything. Income and payroll taxes are withheld from our paycheques, the fed-eral Goods and Services Tax and provincial sales taxes are added to our purchases, prop-erty taxes are levied on our homes—and then there are gasoline taxes, liquor and tobacco taxes, and even taxes on our telephone services.

When asked, not surprisingly, most Canadians would like to pay fewer taxes. How-ever, while anti-tax sentiments have frequently been expressed by certain interest groups in Canada and sometimes also by certain politicians, we have not had the same kind of anti-tax movement that gripped the U.S. political scene during the 1980s and 1990s. For one thing, most Canadians tend to accept the fact that taxes are a neces-sary cost to ensure a greater role for a viable public sector in a mixed economy. More-over, by international standards, one can hardly say that Canadians are overly taxed. Figure 16 compares the fraction of income paid in taxes in Canada with those paid by residents of other industrial countries. In fact, in terms of tax burden, we are just above the Swiss, who are the perhaps the least taxed in Western Europe. This is not to suggest that Canadians have not shown a growing preference for lower taxes. With rising budget surpluses since the late 1990s, the federal government, together with a number of provincial governments, has implemented policies in recent years to reduce taxes in Canada.

The Government as Redistributor

In a market economy, people earn incomes according to what they have to sell. Unfortunately, many people have nothing to sell but unskilled labour, which commands a paltry price. Others lack even that. Such people fare poorly in unfettered markets. In extreme cases, they are homeless, hungry, and ill. Robin Hood transferred money from the rich to the poor. Some think the government should do the same; others disagree.

If poverty amid riches offends your moral sensibilities—a personal judgment that each of us must make for ourselves—two basic remedial approaches are possible. The socialist idea is to force the distribution of income to be more equal by overriding the decisions of the market. "From each according to his ability, to each according to his needs" was Marx's ideal. In practice, things were not quite so noble under socialism. But there is little doubt that incomes in the old Soviet Union were more equally distributed than those in Canada.

For many economists, the idea is to let free markets determine the distribution of *before-tax* incomes, but then to use the tax system and **transfer payments** to reduce inequality—just as Robin Hood did. This is the rationale for, among other things, **progressive taxation** and the antipoverty programs colloquially known as *welfare*. Canadians who support redistribution line up solidly behind this approach. But which ways are the best, and how much is enough? No simple answers have emerged from debate on these highly contentious questions.

Transfer payments are sums of money that certain individuals receive as outright grants from the government rather than as payments for services rendered.

A tax is **progressive** if the ratio of taxes to income rises as income rises.

CONCLUSION: IT'S A MIXED ECONOMY

Ideology notwithstanding, all nations at all times blend public and private ownership of property in some proportions. All rely on markets for some purposes, but all also assign some role to government. Hence, people speak of the ubiquity of **mixed economies.** But mixing is not homogenization; different countries can and do blend the state and market sectors in different ways. Even today, the Russian economy is a far cry from the Italian economy, which is vastly different from that of Hong Kong.

A **mixed economy** is one with some public influence over the workings of free markets. There may also be some public ownership mixed in with private property.

With the collapse of the Berlin Wall in November of 1989, the formerly socialist economies of Eastern Europe and Russia went through and continue to undergo a painful transition from a system in which markets played a subsidiary role to one in which they have become dominant. These nations have changed the mix—dramatically—from a command economy to a system based on private property and the dominance of the marketplace. A central concern of this book is to help you to understand the essential workings of contemporary market economies and to answer the question: *What does the market do well, and what does it do poorly?* This task begins in the next chapter.

SUMMARY

1. The Canadian economy scores high when measured by international standards and as a member of the G7 industrial nations. Although being an advanced market economy, it is also a **mixed** and **open** economy.

2. The Canadian economy has grown dramatically over the years. But this growth has been interrupted by periodic **recessions,** during which unemployment rises.

3. Canada has a diverse workforce whose composition by age and sex has been changing substantially. Relatively few workers these days work in factories or on farms; most work in service industries.

4. Employees take home most of the nation's income. Most of the rest goes, in the forms of interest and profits, to those who provide the capital.

5. Governments at the federal, provincial/territorial, and local levels employ about 18 percent of the Canadian workforce (including the Armed Forces). Collectively, these governments both spend and take in taxes at the rate of about one-third of GDP. This percentage is higher than in the United States at about 27 percent but lower than most Western European countries, including the United Kingdom.

6. In addition to raising taxes and making expenditures, the government in a market economy serves as referee and enforcer of the rules, regulates business in a variety of ways, and redistributes income through taxes and **transfer payments.** For all these reasons, we say that we have a **mixed economy,** which blends private and public elements.

KEY TERMS

Inputs 26

Outputs 26

Factors of production, or Inputs 26

Gross domestic product (GDP) 28

Open economy 29

Closed economy 29

Recession 31

Transfer payments 42

Progressive tax 42

Mixed economy 42

DISCUSSION QUESTIONS

1. Which are the two biggest national economies on earth? Why are they so much bigger than the others?

2. What is meant by a *factor of production?* Have you ever sold any on a market?

3. Why do you think that per-capita income in Newfoundland is about two-thirds of that in Alberta?

4. Roughly speaking, what fraction of Canadian labour works in factories? In service businesses? In government?

5. Most Canadian businesses are small, but most of the output is produced by large businesses. That sounds paradoxical. How can it be true?

6. What is the role of government in a mixed economy?

3

A FUNDAMENTAL ECONOMIC PROBLEM: SCARCITY AND CHOICE

Our necessities are few but our wants are endless.

INSCRIPTION ON A FORTUNE COOKIE

Understanding what the market system does well and what it does badly is this book's central task. But to address this complex question, we must first answer a simpler one: What do economists expect the market to accomplish?

The most common answer is that the market mechanism resolves what is often called *the* fundamental economic problem: how best to manage the resources of society, doing as well as possible with them, despite their scarcity. All decisions are constrained by the scarcity of available resources, whether they are physical or financial. Since resources are scarce, all economic decisions involve *trade-offs*. Should you use that $10 bill to buy pizza or a new notebook for Econ class? Should General Motors Canada invest more money in assembly lines or in research? A well-functioning market system facilitates and guides such decisions, assigning each hour of labour and each kilowatt-hour of electricity to the task where, it is hoped, the input will best serve the public.

This chapter shows how economists analyze choices like these. The same basic principles, based on the concept of *opportunity cost*, apply to the decisions made by business firms, governments, and society as a whole. Many of the most basic ideas of economics, such as *efficiency, division of labour, comparative advantage, exchange,* and *the role of markets* appear here for the first time.

CONTENTS

ISSUE: *What to Do about the Federal Budget Balance?*

After the long era of deficit fighting in the 1980s and early 1990s and for over a decade since the late 1990s, Canada's federal governments (whether Liberal or Conservative) have targeted significant budget surpluses, which have regularly been vaunted at budget time as one of their most significant achievements, especially when compared to the performance of governments of other Western countries, such as the United States. Indeed, according to the *Public Accounts of Canada*, in the years between fiscal year 1997–1998 and fiscal year 2006–2007, the federal government achieved accumulated surpluses of about $85 billion.

This has meant that, over those ten years, the federal government reduced the federal public debt by roughly an equivalent amount. Yet, without failure, each year before budget time, federal government officials and politicians have agonized and debated over what to do with each annual forecasted budget *surplus*. Having revealed their strong political preference against budget deficits during the previous era, and given the predicted budget surplus, what should they do? Three choices face the federal fiscal authorities: (1) let the financial surplus materialize, thereby saving these funds and reducing the public debt by an equivalent amount; (2) spend the surplus by allocating the predicted funds to public expenditures, therefore choosing to run a balanced budget; or (3) spend the surplus through a cut in taxes, in which case the federal authorities would also be choosing a balanced budget scenario for the fiscal year. Over the last decade, successive federal governments have chosen a mixture of lower corporate and income taxes, greater spending in certain areas (such as on security), and targeted debt reduction.

On the basis of their spending *priorities*, choices were made by the successive federal ministers of Finance. However, everyone must make choices in an economy, particularly since the physical and financial resources that you face are never unlimited. An *optimal decision* is one that is the most desirable alternative *among the possibilities permitted by the available resources*, which are always scarce in this sense.

■ SCARCITY, CHOICE, AND OPPORTUNITY COST

Resources are the instruments provided by nature or by people that are used to create goods and services. Natural resources include minerals, soil, water, and air. Labour is a scarce resource because of time limitations and because skilled workers are rare. Factories and machines are man-made resources. These resources are often referred to as *land*, *labour*, and *capital*. They are also called *inputs* or *factors of production*.

One of the basic themes of economics is scarcity: the fact that **resources** are always limited. Ever since mercantilist times in the sixteenth and seventeenth centuries, when humans began generally to recognize that the earth was round and that the precious metal deposits it contained were finite, writers speculated on the limits of financial resources as measured by the limited stock of gold and silver. By the beginning of the nineteenth century, this concern was extended by classical economists to encompass a more important physical resource: good arable land. Nowadays, economists generally accept that this scarcity principle must be extended to all resources in our physical environment.

Indeed, the scarcity of *physical resources* is more fundamental than the scarcity of funds. Fuel supplies, for example, are not limitless, and some environmentalists claim that we should now be making some hard choices—such as keeping our homes cooler in winter and warmer in summer and living closer to our jobs. Although energy may be the most widely discussed scarcity, the general principle applies to all of the earth's resources—iron, copper, uranium, and so on. Even goods produced by human effort are in limited supply because they require fuel, labour, and other scarce resources as inputs. We can manufacture more cars, but the increased use of labour, steel, and fuel in auto production will mean that we must cut back on something else, perhaps the production of refrigerators. This all adds up to the following fundamental principle of economics, which we will encounter again and again in this text:

> Virtually all resources are *scarce*, meaning that humans have less of them than we would like. Therefore, choices must be made among a *limited* set of possibilities, in full recognition of the inescapable fact that a decision to have more of one thing means that we will have less of something else.

In fact, one popular definition of economics is the study of how best to use *limited* means to pursue *unlimited* ends. Although this definition, like any short statement, cannot possibly cover the sweep of the entire discipline, it does convey the flavour of a significant portion of the economist's stock in trade.

To illustrate the true cost of an item given limited resources, consider the decision to produce additional cars, and therefore to produce fewer refrigerators. Although the production of a car may cost $15,000 per vehicle, or some other money amount, *its real cost to society is the refrigerators that society must forgo to get an additional car.* If the labour, steel, and energy needed to manufacture a car are sufficient to make 30 refrigerators, the **opportunity cost** of a car is 30 refrigerators. The principle of opportunity cost is so important that we will spend most of this chapter elaborating on it in various ways.

The **opportunity cost** of any decision is the value of the next best alternative that the decision forces the decision maker to forgo.

Opportunity Cost and Money Cost

Because we live in a market economy where (almost) everything has its price, students often wonder about the connection or difference between an item's *opportunity cost* and its *market price*. What we just said seems to divorce the two concepts: The true opportunity cost of a car is not its market price but the value of the other things (like refrigerators) that could have been made or purchased instead.

But isn't the opportunity cost of a car related to its money cost? The normal answer is yes. The two costs are usually closely tied because of the way in which a market economy sets prices. Steel, for example, is used to manufacture both automobiles and refrigerators. If consumers value items that can be made with steel (such as refrigerators) highly, then economists would say that the *opportunity cost* of making a car is high. But, under these circumstances, strong demand for this highly valued resource will bid up its market price. In this way, a well-functioning price system will assign a high price to steel, which will therefore make the *money cost* of manufacturing a car high as well. In summary:

> If the market functions well, goods that have high opportunity costs will also have high money costs. In turn, goods that have low opportunity costs will also have low money costs.

Yet it would be a mistake to treat opportunity costs and explicit monetary costs as identical. For one thing, the market does not always function well, and hence assigns prices that do not accurately reflect opportunity costs.

Moreover, some valuable items may not bear explicit price tags at all. We encountered one such example in Chapter 1, where we noted that the opportunity cost of a college or university education may differ sharply from its explicit money cost. Why? Because one important item is typically omitted from the money–cost calculation: the *market value of your time,* that is, the wages you could earn by working instead of attending school. Because you give up these potential wages, which can amount to $20,000 per year or more, so as to acquire an education, they must be counted as a major part of the opportunity cost of going to university.

Other common examples where money costs and opportunity costs diverge are goods and services that are given away "free." For example, some early settlers during colonial times destroyed natural amenities such as forests, beaver, and buffalo herds, which had no or very low market price, leaving later generations to pay the opportunity costs in terms of lost resources. Similarly, you incur no explicit monetary cost to acquire an item that is given away for free. But if you must wait in line to get the "free" commodity, you incur an opportunity cost equal to the value of the next best use of your time.

◼ *Optimal* Choice: Not Just *Any* Choice

How do people and firms make decisions? There are many ways, some of them based on hunches with little forethought; some are even based on superstition or the advice of a fortune teller. Often, when the required information is scarce and the necessary research and calculations are costly and difficult, the decision maker will settle on the first possibility that he can "live with"—a choice that promises to yield results that are not too bad, and that seem fairly safe. The decision maker may be willing to choose this course even though he recognizes that there might be other options that are better, but are unknown to him. This way of deciding is called *satisficing*.

In this book, like most books on traditional economic theory, we will assume that decision makers seek to do better than mere satisficing. Although sacrificing a certain degree of realism, we will assume that they seek to reach decisions that are optimal, in other words, decisions that do better in achieving the decision maker's goals than any other possible choice. We will assume that the required information is available to the decision maker and study the procedures that enable her to determine which of the possible choices is optimal to her.

An **optimal decision** is one that best serves the objectives of the decision maker, whatever those objectives may be. It is selected by explicit or implicit comparison with the possible alternative choices. The term *optimal* connotes neither approval nor disapproval of the objective itself.

> An **optimal decision** is one that is selected after implicit or explicit comparison of the consequences of each of the possible choices and that is shown by analysis to be the one that most effectively promotes her goals.

We will study optimal decision making by various parties: by consumers, by producers, and by sellers, in a variety of situations. The methods of analysis for determining what choice is optimal in each case will be remarkably similar. So, if you understand one of them, you will already be well on your way to understanding them all. A technique called *marginal analysis* will be used for this purpose. But one fundamental idea underlies any method used for optimal decision making: To determine whether a possible decision is or is not optimal, its consequences must be compared with those of each of the other possible choices.

◼ SCARCITY AND CHOICE FOR A SINGLE FIRM

The **outputs** of a firm or an economy are the goods and services it produces.

The **inputs** used by a firm or an economy are the labour, raw materials, electricity and other resources it uses to produce its outputs.

The nature of opportunity cost is perhaps clearest in the case of a single business firm that produces two **outputs** from a fixed supply of **inputs**. Given current technology and the limited resources at its disposal, the more of one good the firm produces, the less of the other it will be able to make. Unless managers explicitly weigh the desirability of each product against the other, they are unlikely to make rational production decisions.

Consider the example of Jones, a farmer whose available supplies of land, machinery, labour, and fertilizer are capable of producing the various combinations of soybeans and wheat listed in Table 1. Obviously, devoting more resources to soybean production means that Jones can produce less wheat.

Table 1 indicates, for example, that if Jones grows only soybeans, the harvest will be 40,000 bushels. But if he reduces his soybean production to 30,000 bushels, he can also grow 38,000 bushels of wheat. Thus, *the opportunity cost of obtaining 38,000 bushels of wheat is 10,000 fewer bushels of soybeans.* Put another way, the opportunity cost of 10,000 more bushels of soybeans is 38,000 bushels of wheat. The other numbers in Table 1 have similar interpretations.

TABLE 1		
Production Possibilities Open to a Farmer		
Bushels of Soybeans	Bushels of Wheat	Label in Figure 1
40,000	0	A
30,000	38,000	B
20,000	52,000	C
10,000	60,000	D
0	65,000	E

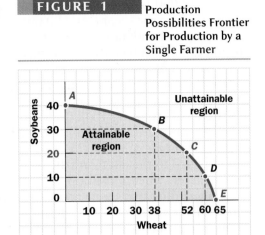

FIGURE 1   Production Possibilities Frontier for Production by a Single Farmer

Note: Quantities are in thousands of bushels per year.

The Production Possibilities Frontier

Figure 1 presents this same information graphically. Point *A* indicates that one of the options available to the farmer is to produce 40,000 bushels of soybeans and zero wheat. Thus, point *A* corresponds to the first line of Table 1, point *B* to the second line, and so on. Curves similar to *AE* appear frequently in this book; they are called **production possibilities frontiers.** Any point *on or inside* the production possibilities frontier is attainable. Points *outside* the frontier cannot be achieved with the available resources and technology.

Because resources are limited, the production possibilities frontier always slopes downward to the right. The farmer can *increase* wheat production (move to the right in Figure 1) only by devoting more land and labour to growing wheat. But this choice simultaneously *reduces* soybean production (the curve must move downward) because less land and labour remain available for growing soybeans.

Notice that, in addition to having a negative slope, our production possibilities frontier *AE* has another characteristic; it is "bowed outward." What does this curvature mean? In short, as larger and larger quantities of resources are transferred from the production of one output to the production of another, the additions to the second product decline.

Suppose farmer Jones initially produces only soybeans, using even land that is comparatively most productive in wheat cultivation (point *A*). Now he decides to switch some land from soybean production into wheat production. Which part of the land will he switch? If Jones is sensible, he will use the part relatively most productive in growing wheat. As he shifts to point *B*, soybean production falls from 40,000 bushels to 30,000 bushels as wheat production rises from zero to 38,000 bushels. A sacrifice of only 10,000 bushels of soybeans "buys" 38,000 bushels of wheat.

Imagine now that this farmer wants to produce still more wheat. Figure 1 tells us that the sacrifice of an additional 10,000 bushels of soybeans (from 30,000 bushels to 20,000 bushels) will yield only 14,000 more bushels of wheat (see point *C*). Why? The main reason is that *inputs tend to be specialized.* As we noted at point *A*, the farmer was using resources for soybean production that were relatively more productive in growing wheat. Consequently, their relative productivity in soybean production was low. When these resources are switched to wheat production, the yield is high.

But this trend cannot continue forever, of course. As more wheat is produced, the farmer must utilize land and machinery with a greater productivity advantage in growing soybeans and a smaller productivity advantage in growing wheat. This is why

A **production possibilities frontier** shows the different combinations of various goods that a producer can turn out, given the available resources and existing technology.

the first 10,000 bushels of soybeans forgone "buys" the farmer 38,000 bushels of wheat, whereas the second 10,000 bushels of soybeans "buys" only 14,000 bushels of wheat. Figure 1 and Table 1 show that these returns continue to decline as wheat production expands: The next 10,000-bushel reduction in soybean production yields only 8,000 bushels of additional wheat, and so on.

As we can see, the *slope* of the production possibilities frontier graphically represents the concept of *opportunity cost*. Between points *C* and *B*, for example, the opportunity cost of acquiring 10,000 additional bushels of soybeans is shown on the graph to be 14,000 bushels of forgone wheat; between points *B* and *A*, the opportunity cost of 10,000 bushels of soybeans is 38,000 bushels of forgone wheat. In general, as we move upward to the left along the production possibilities frontier (toward more soybeans and less wheat), the opportunity cost of soybeans in terms of wheat increases. Looking at the same thing the other way, as we move downward to the right, the opportunity cost of acquiring wheat by giving up soybeans increases—more and more soybeans must be forgone per added bushel of wheat and successive addition to wheat output occur.

■ The Principle of Increasing Costs

We have just described a very general phenomenon with applications well beyond farming. The **principle of increasing costs** states that as the production of one good expands, the opportunity cost of producing another unit of this good generally increases.

This principle is not a universal fact—exceptions arise frequently. But it does seem to be a technological regularity that applies to a wide range of economic activities. As our farming example suggests, the principle of increasing costs is based on the fact that resources tend to be at least somewhat specialized. So we lose some of their productivity when those resources are transferred from doing what they are relatively *good* at to what they are relatively *bad* at. In terms of diagrams such as Figure 1, the principle simply asserts that the production possibilities frontier is bowed outward.

Perhaps the best way to understand this idea is to contrast it with a case in which no resources are specialized so costs do not increase as output proportion changes. Figure 2 depicts a production possibilities frontier for producing black shoes and brown shoes. Because the labour and machinery used to produce black shoes are just as good at producing brown shoes, the frontier is a straight line. If the firm cuts back its production of black shoes by 10,000 pairs, it can get 10,000 additional pairs of brown shoes, no matter how big the shift is between these two outputs. It loses no productivity in the switch because resources are not specialized.

More typically, however, as a firm concentrates more of its productive capacity on one commodity, it is forced to employ inputs that are better suited to making another commodity. The firm is forced to vary the proportions in which it uses inputs because of the limited quantities of some of those inputs. This fact also explains the typical curvature of the firm's production possibilities frontier.

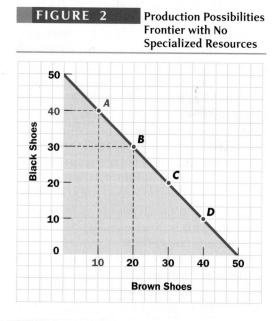

FIGURE 2   Production Possibilities Frontier with No Specialized Resources

Note: Quantities are in thousands of pairs per week.

■ SCARCITY AND CHOICE FOR THE ENTIRE SOCIETY

Like an individual firm, the entire economy is also constrained by its limited resources and technology. If the public wants more planes and helicopters, it will have to give up some boats and automobiles. If it wants to build more factories and stores, it will have to build fewer homes and sports arenas. In general:

> The position and shape of the production possibilities frontier that constrains society's choices are determined by the economy's physical resources, its skills and technology, its willingness to work, and how much it has devoted in the past to the construction of factories, research, and innovation.

Let us illustrate the nature of society's choice by an example where we must decide between national defence and civilian consumption. There has long been public pressure on successive federal governments to protect our sovereignty in Canada's Arctic. Given the enormous cost of equipping the Canadian Navy with more icebreakers, we would have to forfeit a certain amount of civilian consumption, such as fewer automobiles. Indeed, just like a single firm, the economy as a whole in this example faces a production possibilities frontier for icebreakers and autos, determined by its technology and the available resources of land, labour, capital, and raw materials. This production possibilities frontier may look like curve *BC* in Figure 3. If most workers are employed in auto plants, car production will be large, but the output of icebreakers will be small (as at point *D*). If the economy transfers resources out of auto manufacturing when consumer demand declines, with the budget approval of the House of Commons, the government can alter the output mix toward the production of more icebreakers (the move from *D* to *E*). However, something is likely to be lost in the process because some physical resources may be specialized and not be easily transferable from one industry to another, thereby encountering some increasing costs as this transfer of resources is made. For instance, the rubber tires used in car manufacturing would not be of much use in the production of icebreakers nor would the existing car manufacturing plants. The principle of increasing costs strongly suggests that the production possibilities frontier curves downward toward the horizontal axis and explains its curvature.

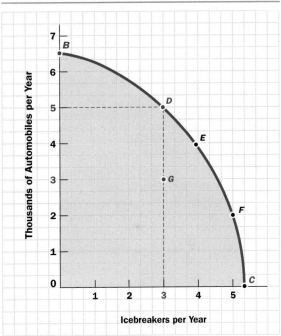

FIGURE 3 Production Possibilities Frontier for the Entire Economy

We may even reach a point where the only resources left are not very useful outside of auto manufacturing. In that case, even a large sacrifice of automobiles will get the economy few additional icebreakers. That is the meaning of the steep segment, *FC*, on the frontier. At point *C*, there is little additional output of icebreakers as compared to point *F*, even though at *C* automobile production has been given up entirely.

> The downward slope of society's production possibilities frontier implies that hard choices must be made. Unless resources are not fully utilized, civilian consumption (automobiles) can be increased only by decreasing defence spending, not by rhetoric or wishing. The curvature of the production possibilities frontier implies that, as public spending increases, it becomes progressively more expensive to "buy" additional "defence" (icebreakers) in terms of the resulting sacrifice of civilian consumption.

■ Scarcity and Choice Elsewhere in the Economy

We have emphasized that limited resources force hard choices on business managers and society as a whole. But the same type of choices arises elsewhere—in households, universities, and other nonprofit organizations, as well as the government.

HARD CHOICES IN THE REAL WORLD

Commenting on the choices made by consumers over the last decade in Canada, which witnessed a growth in disposable income of high-income groups while that of low-income households stagnated, the 2006 report from Industry Canada's Office of Consumer Affairs clearly shows the link between changing household budgets (scarcity) and choice:

> The changes in disposable income . . . have had repercussions on the marketplace. In the area of housing, for example, there is a general trend among high-income earners to acquire large homes with considerable amenities, such as improved storage areas, double garages and two or more bathrooms. . . .
>
> At the other end of the income scale, the situation is markedly different. Approximately 6 percent of Canadian households faced overcrowded housing conditions in 2000, that is, the number of bedrooms in the home was insufficient for the size and make-up of the household.
>
> Food is another area affected by substantial changes in consumers financial situations. . . . Statistics Canada reports that Canadian consumers' spent a higher proportion of their food dollars on meals outside the home (primarily in restaurants) in the 1990s than they did in the 1980s. . . . Not surprisingly, high-income earners led the growth in restaurant spending.
>
> Low-income earners are in a different position: Statistics Canada's 1998–1999 *National Population Health Survey* reported that more than 10 percent of Canadians (an estimated 3 million people) were living in food-insecure households. In addition, the

SOURCE: Ronnie Comeau/iStockPhoto

Institute for Research on Public Policy reports that food banks opened between 1997 and 2002. . . . These developments suggest that, far from boosting restaurant and grocery store business, many low-income Canadians rely on charity for part of their food budget, or sometimes do without, as they are unable to fully participate in the market-based food retail sector.

SOURCE: Industry Canada, Office of Consumer Affairs, *Consumer Trends Report*, May 18, 2006. Retrieved from http://strategis.ic.gc.ca/epic/internet/inoca-bc.nsf/en/ca02093e.html

---

The nature of opportunity cost is perhaps most obvious for a household that must decide how to divide its income among the goods and services that compete for the family's attention. If a family buys an expensive new car, it may be forced to cut back sharply on some other purchases. This fact does not make it unwise to buy the car. But it does make it unwise to buy the car until the family considers the full implications for its overall budget. If the family members are to utilize their limited resources most effectively, they must recognize the opportunity costs of the car—the things they will forgo as a result—perhaps a vacation and an expensive new TV set.

? ISSUE REVISITED: *Coping with the Budget Balance*

As already noted, even a relatively wealthy country like Canada must cope with the limitations dictated by scarce resources. The necessity for choice imposed on the various levels of government by the limited amount they feel they can afford to spend is, in some ways, similar in character to the problem faced by business firms and households. For the goods and services that it buys from others, a government must prepare a budget similar to that of a very large household. For the items it produces itself (education, police protection, public transport, and so on) it faces a production possibilities frontier much like a business firm does. Even though all levels of government in Canada spent about $550 billion in 2007, some of the most acrimonious debates between the government in power and its critics over the last decade have been about how to allocate the federal budget surplus among competing ends. Even if unstated, the concept of opportunity cost is central to these debates.

◼ THE CONCEPT OF EFFICIENCY

So far, our discussion of scarcity and choice has assumed that either the firm or the economy always operates on its production possibilities frontier rather than *below* it. In other words, we have tacitly assumed that, whatever the firm or economy decides to do, it does so **efficiently**.

> Economists define efficiency as the absence of waste. An efficient economy wastes none of its available resources and produces the maximum amount of output that its technology permits.

To see why any point on the economy's production possibilities frontier in Figure 3 represents an efficient decision, suppose for a moment that society has decided to produce three icebreakers. The production possibilities frontier tells us that if three icebreakers are to be produced, then the maximum number of automobiles that can be made is 5,000 (point *D* in Figure 3). The economy is therefore operating efficiently only if it produces 5,000 automobiles rather than some smaller amount such as 3,000 (as at point *G*).

Point *D* is efficient, but point *G* is not, because the economy is capable of moving from *G* to *D*, thereby producing 2,000 more automobiles without giving up any icebreakers (or anything else). Clearly, failure to take advantage of the option of choosing point *D* rather than point *G* constitutes a wasted opportunity—an inefficiency.

Note that the concept of efficiency does not tell us which point on the production possibilities frontier is *best*. Rather, it tells us only that any point *below* the frontier cannot be best, because any such point represents wasted resources. For example, should society ever find itself at a point such as *G*, the necessity of making hard choices would (temporarily) disappear. It would be possible to increase production of *both* icebreakers *and* automobiles by moving to a point such as *E*.

Why, then, would a society ever find itself at a point below its production possibilities frontier? Why are resources wasted in real life? The most important reason in today's economy is *unemployment*. When many workers are unemployed, the economy must be at a point such as *G*, below the frontier, because by putting the unemployed to work, some in each industry, the economy could produce both more icebreakers *and* more automobiles. The economy would then move from point *G* to the right (more icebreakers) and upward (more automobiles) toward a point such as *E* on the production possibilities frontier. Only when no resources are wasted is the economy operating on the frontier.

Inefficiency occurs in other ways, too. A prime example is assigning inputs to the wrong task—as when wheat is grown on land best suited to soybean cultivation. Another important type of inefficiency occurs when large firms produce goods that smaller enterprises could make better because they can pay closer attention to detail, or when small firms produce outputs best suited to large-scale production. Some other examples are the outright waste that occurs because of favouritism (for example, promotion of an incompetent brother-in-law to a job he cannot do very well) or restrictive labour practices (for example, requiring a railroad to keep a firefighter on a diesel-electric locomotive where there is no longer a fire to tend).

A particularly deplorable form of waste is caused by discrimination in the workplace against women, visible minorities, immigrants, or aboriginal people. When a job is given, for example, to a white male in preference to an immigrant woman who is more qualified, society sacrifices potential output and the entire community is apt to be affected adversely. Every one of these inefficiencies means that the community obtains less output than it could have, given the available inputs.

> A set of outputs is said to be produced **efficiently** if, given current technological knowledge, there is no way one can produce larger amounts of any output without using larger input amounts or giving up some quantity of another output.

◼ THE THREE COORDINATION TASKS OF ANY ECONOMY

In deciding how to **allocate its scarce resources**, every society must somehow make three sorts of decisions:

Allocation of resources refers to the society's decisions on how to divide up its scarce input resources among the different outputs produced in the economy and among the different firms or other organizations that produce those outputs.

- First, as we have emphasized, it must figure out *how to utilize its resources efficiently*; that is, it must find a way to reach its production possibilities frontier.
- Second, it must decide *which of the possible combinations of goods to produce*—how many icebreakers, automobiles, and so on; that is, it must select one specific point on the production possibilities frontier.
- Third, it must decide *how much of the total output of each good to distribute to each person*, doing so in a sensible way that does not assign meat to vegetarians and wine to teetotalers.

There are many ways in which societies can and do make each of these decisions—to which economists often refer as *how*, *what*, and *to whom?* For example, a central planner may tell people how to produce, what to produce, and what to consume, as the authorities used to do, at least to some extent, in the former Soviet Union. But in a market economy, no one group or individual makes all such resource allocation decisions explicitly. Rather, consumer demands and production costs allocate resources *automatically* and *anonymously* through a system of prices and markets. For our introduction to the ways in which markets do all this, let's consider each task in turn.

SPECIALIZATION FOSTERS EFFICIENT RESOURCE ALLOCATION

Production efficiency is one of the economy's three basic tasks, and societies pursue it in many ways. But one source of efficiency is so fundamental that we must single it out for special attention: the tremendous productivity gains that stem from *specialization*.

The Importance of the Division of Labour

Division of labour means breaking up a task into a number of smaller, more *specialized* tasks so that each worker can become more adept at a particular job.

Adam Smith (1723–1790), the founder of modern economics, first marvelled at how **division of labour** raises efficiency and productivity when he visited a pin factory. In a famous passage near the beginning of his monumental book, *The Wealth of Nations* (1776), he described what he saw:

> One man draws out the wire, another straightens it, a third cuts it, a fourth points it, a fifth grinds it at the top for receiving the head. To make the head requires two or three distinct operations; to put it on is a peculiar business, to whiten the pins is another; it is even a trade by itself to put them into the paper.[1]

Smith observed that by dividing the work to be done in this way, each worker became quite skilled in a particular specialty, and the productivity of the group of workers as a whole was greatly enhanced. As Smith related it:

> I have seen a small manufactory of this kind where ten men only were employed. . . . Those ten persons . . . could make among them upwards of forty-eight thousand pins in a day. . . . But if they had all wrought separately and independently . . . they certainly could not each of them have made twenty, *perhaps not one pin in a day.*[2]

In other words, through the process of the division of labour and specialization, ten workers accomplished what might otherwise have required thousands. This was one of the secrets of the Industrial

SOURCE: ©Bettmann/Corbis

---

[1] Adam Smith, *The Wealth of Nations* (New York: Random House, 1937), p. 4.
[2] Ibid., p. 5.

Revolution, which helped lift humanity out of the abject poverty that had been its lot for centuries.

The Principle of Comparative Advantage

But specialization in production fosters efficiency in an even more profound sense. Adam Smith noticed that *how* goods are produced can make a huge difference to productivity. But so can *which* goods are produced. The reason is that people (and businesses, and nations) have different abilities. Some can repair automobiles, whereas others are wizards with numbers. Some are handy with computers, and others can cook. An economy will be most efficient if people specialize in doing what they do best and then trade with one another, so that the accountant gets her car repaired and the computer programmer gets to eat tasty and nutritious meals.

This much is obvious. What is less obvious—and is one of the great ideas of economics—is that two people (or two businesses, or two countries) can generally gain from trade *even if one of them is more efficient than the other in producing everything*. A simple example will help explain why.

Some lawyers can type better than their administrative assistants. Should such a lawyer fire her assistant and do her own typing? Not likely. Even though the lawyer may type better than the assistant, good judgment tells her to concentrate on practising law and leave the typing to a lower-paid assistant. Why? Because the *opportunity cost* of an hour devoted to typing is an hour less time spent with clients, which is a far more lucrative activity.

This example illustrates the principle of **comparative advantage** at work. The lawyer specializes in arguing cases despite her advantage as a typist because she has a *still greater* advantage as an attorney. She suffers some direct loss by leaving the typing to a less efficient employee, but she more than makes up for that loss by the income she earns selling her legal services to clients.

> One country is said to have a **comparative advantage** over another in the production of a particular good *relative to other goods* if it produces that good less inefficiently than it **produces** other goods, as compared with the other country.

Precisely the same principle applies to nations. The theory of comparative advantage is often used to analyze international trade patterns. A country that is particularly well endowed with a natural resource, because of the availability of a particular quality of land or other natural circumstance, or is simply better adept at producing certain items—such as wheat in Canada, coffee in Brazil, and cameras in Japan—should specialize in those items, producing more than it wants for its own use. The country can then take the money it earns from its exports and purchase from other nations the items that it does not make for itself. And this is still true if one of trading nations is the most efficient producer of almost everything.

The underlying logic is precisely the same as in our lawyer–typist example. Canada might, for example, be better than Mexico at manufacturing cars and textile fabrics. But if Canada is vastly more efficient at producing cars and only slightly more efficient at making fabrics, it pays for Canada to specialize in car manufacture, for Mexico to specialize in fabrics, and for the two countries to trade. This principle, sometimes also called the *law of comparative advantage*, was discovered by David Ricardo (1772–1823), one of the giants in the history of economic analysis, almost 200 years ago.

Even if one country (or one worker) is worse than another country (or another worker) in the production of *every* good, it is said to have a *comparative advantage* in making the good at which it is *least inefficient*—compared to the other country. Ricardo discovered that two countries can gain by trading even if one country is more efficient than another in the production of *every* commodity. Precisely the same logic applies to individual workers or to businesses.

In determining the most efficient patterns of production and trade, it is comparative advantage that matters. Thus, a country can gain by importing a good from abroad even if that good can be produced more efficiently at home. Such imports make sense if they enable the country to specialize in producing those goods at which it is *even more efficient*.

From an Isolated Island Economy to the International Economy

Let us consider a simple, although somewhat unrealistic, example of two individuals independently shipwrecked on a remote tropical island, named Robinson Crusoe and Friday, somewhat as in Daniel Defoe's classic 1719 English novel. To survive, each individual requires a daily intake of proteins (say, found in fish in the sea) and of vitamins (to be found in fruit growing on the island). Let us assume that Friday, having come originally from a far-off island, is highly skilled at fishing, while Robinson Crusoe does not know how to fish and is therefore less productive at acquiring fish. Let us suppose further that, if Friday dedicates half of his day to gathering fruit and the other half to fishing along the shoreline, at best he can gather two fruit and trap four fish daily. On the other hand, if Robinson Crusoe similarly dedicates half of his day to each of the two activities, he can harvest only two of each. This information is found in the table below, showing that Friday is a bit more productive than Robinson Crusoe with a total daily output of six and four food items, respectively—a daily joint output of ten food items.

Output per Day of Labour before Specialization

	Quantity of Fruit	Quantity of Fish	Daily Output of Food Items
Friday	2	4	6
Robinson Crusoe	2	2	4
Total joint output	4	6	10

The principle of comparative advantage states that, if instead of each going their separate ways and producing both goods in isola-

tion for a daily maximum of ten items for the island economy, the two should cooperate by specializing in what they are relatively best at producing, which in the case of Friday is fishing (a more skilled activity) while for Robinson Crusoe it is gathering fruit (a less skilled activity). Indeed, Friday must give up twice as many fish as Robinson Crusoe in order to gather one additional fruit. Clearly, with specialization and the division of labour, both could *potentially* be better off. As shown in the following table, if each would specialize, the total daily number of items of output would rise by 20 percent—from ten to twelve food items daily.

Output per Day of Labour after Specialization

	Quantity of Fruit	Quantity of Fish	Daily Output of Food Items
Friday	0	8	8
Robinson Crusoe	4	0	4
Total joint output	4	8	12

This same principle also forms the basis of the theory of comparative advantage as applied to international trade, whereby our analogy of the tropical island is extended to our planet as a whole. If instead of Robinson Crusoe and Friday, we replace them with, say, Costa Rica, producing bananas, and Canada, producing fish, both countries could potentially enhance their welfare if, owing to different natural endowments, they specialize in what they are comparatively good at producing and then trade with each other.

■ SPECIALIZATION LEADS TO EXCHANGE

The gains from specialization are welcome, but they create a problem: With specialization, people no longer produce only what they want to consume themselves. The workers in Adam Smith's pin factory had no use for the thousands of pins they produced each day; they wanted to trade them for things like food, clothing, and shelter. Similarly, the administrative assistant has no personal use for the legal briefs she types. Thus, specialization requires some mechanism by which workers producing pins can *exchange* their wares with workers producing such things as cloth and potatoes, and office workers can turn their typing skills into things they want to consume.

Without a system of exchange, the enhanced productivity achieved by comparative advantage and the division of labour would do society little good. With it, standards of living have risen enormously. As we observed in Chapter 1, such exchange could benefit *all* participants.

Unless someone is deceived or misunderstands the facts, a *voluntary* exchange between two parties must make both parties better off—or else why would each party agree? Trading increases production by permitting specialization, as we have just seen. But even if no additional goods are produced as a result of the act of trading, the welfare of society is increased because each individual acquires goods that are more suited to his or her needs and tastes.

Although people can and do trade goods for other goods, a system of exchange works better when everyone agrees to use some common item (such as pieces of paper with unique markings printed on them) for buying and selling things. Enter *money*.

Then workers in pin factories, for example, can be paid in money rather than in pins, and they can use this money to purchase cloth and potatoes. Textile workers and farmers can do the same.

These two phenomena—specialization and exchange (assisted by money)—working in tandem led to vast improvements in humanity's well-being. But what forces induce workers to join together so that society can enjoy the fruits of the division of labour? And what forces establish a smoothly functioning system of exchange so that people can first exploit their comparative advantages and then acquire what they want to consume? One alternative is to have a central authority telling people what to do. Adam Smith explained and extolled yet another way of organizing and coordinating economic activity—markets and prices can coordinate those activities.

■ MARKETS, PRICES, AND THE THREE COORDINATION TASKS

Smith noted that people are adept at pursuing their own self-interests, and that a **market system** harnesses this self-interest remarkably well. As he put it—with clear religious overtones—in doing what is best for themselves, people are "led by an invisible hand" to promote the economic well-being of society as a whole.

Those of us who live in a well-functioning advanced market economy like that found in Canada tend to take the achievements of the market for granted, much like the daily rising and setting of the sun. Few bother to think about, say, what makes Costa Rican pineapples show up daily in Ontario supermarkets. Although the process by which the market guides the economy in such an orderly fashion is subtle and complex, the general principles are well known.

The market deals with efficiency in production through the profit motive, which discourages firms from using inputs wastefully. Valuable resources (such as energy) command high prices, giving producers strong incentives to use them efficiently. The market mechanism also guides firms' output decisions, matching quantities produced to consumer preferences. A rise in the price of wheat because of increased demand for bread, for example, will persuade farmers to produce more wheat and devote less of their land to soybeans.

Finally, a price system distributes goods among consumers in accord with their tastes and preferences, using voluntary exchange to determine who gets what. Consumers spend their incomes on the things they like best (among those they can afford). But the ability to buy goods is hardly divided equally. Workers with valuable skills and owners of scarce resources can sell what they have at attractive prices. With the incomes they earn, they can purchase generous amounts of goods and services. Those who are less successful in selling what they own receive lower incomes and so can afford to buy less. In extreme cases, they may suffer severe deprivation.

This, in broad terms, is how a market economy solves the three basic problems facing any society: how to produce any given combination of goods efficiently, how to select an appropriate combination of goods to produce, and how to distribute these goods sensibly among people. As we proceed through the following chapters, you will learn much more about these issues. You will see that they constitute the central theme that

A **market system** is a form of economic organization in which resource allocation decisions are left to individual producers and consumers acting in their own best interests without central direction.

SOURCE: ©Robert W. Ginn/PhotoEdit

permeates not only this text, but the work of economists in general. As you progress through this book, keep in mind two questions:

* What does the market do well?
* What does it do poorly?

There are numerous answers to both questions, as you will learn in subsequent chapters.

> Society has many important goals. Some of them, such as producing goods and services with maximum efficiency (minimum waste), can be achieved extraordinarily well by letting markets operate more or less freely.

Free unregulated markets will not, however, achieve all of society's goals. For example, they often have trouble keeping unemployment low. In fact, the unfettered operations of markets may even run counter to some goals, such as protection of the environment. Many observers also believe that markets do not necessarily distribute income in accord with ethical or moral norms.

But even in cases in which markets do not perform well, there may be ways of harnessing the power of the market mechanism to remedy some of its deficiencies, as you will learn in later chapters.

■ LAST WORD: DON'T CONFUSE ENDS WITH MEANS

Economic debates often have political and ideological overtones. However, the central theme of this chapter should be construed as neither a *defence of* nor an *attack on* the capitalist system. Most of the formerly socialist countries of Europe and even countries such as the People's Republic of China and Cuba have recognized that the market mechanism can be a very helpful instrument in the pursuit of economic goals and, to varying degrees, have succeeded in marketizing their economies.

The point is not to confuse ends with means in deciding how much to rely on market forces. Those on the left and the right of the political spectrum surely have different goals. But the means chosen to pursue these goals should, for the most part, be chosen on the basis of how effective the selected means are, not on some ideological prejudgments.

Even Karl Marx emphasized that the market is remarkably efficient at producing an abundance of goods and services that had never been seen in precapitalist history. Such wealth can be used to promote conservative goals, such as reducing tax rates and increasing military spending, or to facilitate goals favoured by the left, such as providing more generous public aid for the poor through increased public spending.

Certainly, the market cannot deal with every economic problem. Indeed, we have just noted that the market is the *source* of a number of significant problems that are not handled well by market techniques. The analysis in this book is intended to help you identify both the objectives that the market mechanism can reliably achieve and those that it will fail to promote or, at least, not promote very effectively.

SUMMARY

1. Supplies of all **resources** are limited. Because resources are **scarce**, an **optimal decision** is one that chooses the best alternative among the options that are possible with the available resources.

2. With limited resources, a decision to obtain more of one item is also a decision to give up some of another. What we give up is called the **opportunity cost** of what we get. The opportunity cost is the true cost of any decision.

3. When markets function effectively, firms are led to use resources efficiently and to produce the things that consumers want most. In such cases, opportunity costs and money costs (prices) correspond closely. When the market performs poorly, or when important, socially costly items are provided without charging an appropriate price, or are given away free, opportunity costs and money costs can diverge.

4. A firm's **production possibilities frontier** shows the combinations of goods it can produce, given the current technology and the resources at its disposal. The frontier is usually bowed outward because resources tend to be specialized.

5. The **principle of increasing costs** states that as the production of one good expands, the opportunity cost of producing another unit of that good generally increases.

6. Like a firm, the economy as a whole has a production possibilities frontier whose position is determined by its technology and by the available resources of land, labour, capital, and raw materials.

7. A firm or an economy that ends up at a point below its production possibilities frontier is using its resources inefficiently or wastefully. This is what happens, for example, when there is unemployment.

8. Economists define **efficiency** as the absence of waste. It is achieved primarily by the gains in productivity brought about through **specialization** that exploits **division of labour** and **comparative advantage** and by a system of exchange.

9. Two countries (or two people) can gain by specializing in the activity in which each has a *comparative* advantage and then trading with one another. These gains from trade remain available even if one country is inferior at producing everything.

10. If an exchange is voluntary, both parties must benefit, even if no additional goods are produced.

11. Every economic system must find a way to answer three basic questions: How can goods be produced most efficiently? How much of each good should be produced? How should goods be distributed among users?

12. The **market system** works very well in solving some of society's basic problems, but it fails to remedy others and may, indeed, create some of its own. Where and how it succeeds and fails constitute the central theme of this book and characterize the work of economists in general.

KEY TERMS

Resources   46

Opportunity cost   47

Optimal decision   48

Outputs   48

Inputs   48

Production possibilities frontier   49

Principle of increasing costs   50

Efficiency   53

Allocation of resources   53

Division of labour   54

Comparative advantage   55

Market system   57

TEST YOURSELF

1. A person rents a house for which she pays the landlord $12,000 per year. The house can be purchased for $100,000, and the tenant has this much money in a bank account that pays 4 percent interest per year. Is buying the house a good deal for the tenant? Where does opportunity cost enter the picture?

2. Graphically show the production possibilities frontier for the nation of Stromboli, using the data given in the following table. Does the principle of increasing cost hold in Stromboli?

3. Consider two alternatives for Stromboli in 2007. In case (a), its inhabitants eat 60 million pizzas and build 6,000 pizza ovens. In case (b), the population eats 15 million pizzas but builds 18,000 ovens. Which case will lead to a more generous production possibilities frontier for Stromboli in 2008?

4. Jasmine's Snack Shop sells two brands of potato chips. Brand X costs Jasmine 60 cents per bag, and Brand Y costs her $1. Draw Jasmine's production possibilities frontier if she has $60 budgeted to spend on potato chips. Why is it not "bowed out"?

Stromboli's 2007 Production Possibilities	
Pizzas per Year	Pizza Ovens per Year
75,000,000	0
60,000,000	6,000
45,000,000	11,000
30,000,000	15,000
15,000,000	18,000
0	20,000

DISCUSSION QUESTIONS

1. Discuss the resource limitations that affect:

   a. the poorest person on earth

   b. Bill Gates, one of the richest people on earth

   c. a farmer in Saskatchewan

   d. the government of Indonesia

2. If you were president of your college or university, what would you change if your budget was cut by 10 percent? By 25 percent? By 50 percent?

3. If you were to leave college or university, what things would change in your life? What, then, is the opportunity cost of your education?

4. Raising chickens requires several types of feed, such as corn and soy meal. Consider a farm in the former Soviet Union. Try to describe how decisions on the number of chickens to be raised, and the amount of each type of feed to use in raising them, were made under the old communist regime. If the farm is now privately owned, how does the market guide the decisions that used to be made by the central planning agency?

5. Canada is a relatively wealthy country. Think of a recent case in which the decisions of the Canadian government were severely constrained by scarcity. Describe the trade-offs that were involved. What were the opportunity costs of the decisions that were actually made?

SUPPLY AND DEMAND: AN INITIAL LOOK

The funny thing is that the sophisticated economist sometimes errs by assuming that every transaction marks the intersection of a demand curve and a supply curve, while the economically unsophisticated noneconomist forgets that most observed transactions are at the intersection of a demand curve and a supply curve.

ROBERT M. SOLOW (1924–), 1987 RECIPIENT OF THE SVERIGES RIKSBANK PRIZE IN ECONOMIC SCIENCES IN MEMORY OF ALFRED NOBEL, 1997

In this chapter, we study the economist's most basic investigative tool: the mechanism of supply and demand. Whether your Econ course concentrates on macroeconomics or microeconomics, you will find that the so-called law of supply and demand is a fundamental tool of economic analysis. Economists use supply and demand analysis to study issues as diverse as inflation and unemployment, the effects of taxes on prices, government regulation of business, and environmental protection. Supply and demand curves—graphs that relate price to quantity supplied and quantity demanded, respectively—show how prices and quantities are determined in a competitive market.[1]

A major theme of the chapter is that governments around the world and throughout recorded history have tampered with the price mechanism. As we will see, these bouts with Adam Smith's "invisible hand" have produced undesirable side effects that often surprised and dismayed the authorities. The invisible hand fights back!

CONTENTS

---

[1] This chapter, like much of the rest of this book, uses many graphs like those described in the appendix to Chapter 1. If you have difficulties with these graphs, we suggest that you review that material before proceeding.

PUZZLE: *What Happened to Oil Prices?*

Since 1949, the dollars of purchasing power that a buyer had to pay to buy a barrel of oil has remained remarkably steady, and gasoline has continued to be a bargain. But there were two exceptional time periods—one from about 1975 through 1985, and one beginning in August 2005—when oil prices exploded, and filling up the automobile gas tank became painful to consumers. Clearly, supply and demand changes must have been behind these developments. But what led them to change so much and so suddenly? Later in the chapter, we will provide excerpts from a newspaper story about the a recent oil crisis that describes some dramatic events behind suddenly shifting supply, and will help to bring the analysis of this chapter to life.

SOURCE: Image courtesy of Cdnauto.org

THE INVISIBLE HAND

The invisible hand is a phrase used by Adam Smith to describe how, by pursuing their own self-interests, people in a market system are "led by an invisible hand" to promote the well-being of the community.

Adam Smith, the father of modern economic analysis, greatly admired the price system. He marvelled at its accomplishments—both as an efficient producer of goods and as a guarantor that consumers' preferences are obeyed. Although many people since Smith's time have shared his enthusiasm for the concept of the **invisible hand,** many have not. In countless instances, the public was outraged by the prices charged on the open market, particularly in the case of housing rents, interest rates, and insurance rates and thought they could do better by legislative decree.

Attempts to control interest rates (which are the price of borrowing money) go back hundreds of years before the birth of Christ, at least to the code of laws compiled under the Babylonian king Hammurabi in about 1800 B.C. Our historical legacy also includes a rather long list of price ceilings on foods and other products imposed in the reign of Diocletian, emperor of the declining Roman Empire. More recently, Canadians have been offered the "protection" of a variety of price controls. Laws have placed ceilings on some prices (such as rents) to protect buyers, whereas legislation has placed floors under other prices (such as farm products) to protect sellers. Yet, somehow, everything such regulation touches seems to end up in even greater disarray than it was before. Despite rent controls, rents in Toronto have soared. Despite laws against "scalping," tickets for popular shows and sports events sell at tremendous premiums—tickets to the Stanley Cup, for example, often fetch hundreds or even thousands of dollars on the "grey" market. To understand what goes wrong when we tamper with markets, we must first learn how they operate unfettered. This chapter takes a first step in that direction by studying the machinery of supply and demand. Then, at the end of the chapter, we return to the issue of price controls.

Every market has both buyers and sellers. We begin our analysis on the consumers' side of the market.

DEMAND AND QUANTITY DEMANDED

People commonly think of consumer demands as fixed amounts. For example, when product designers propose a new computer model, management asks: "What is its market potential?" That is, just how many are likely to be sold? Similarly, government bureaus conduct studies to determine how many engineers or doctors the Canadian economy will require (demand) in subsequent years.

Economists respond that such questions are not well posed—that there is no single answer to such a question. Rather, they say, the "market potential" for computers or the number of engineers that will be "required" depends on a great number of influences, including the price charged for each.

The **quantity demanded** of any product normally depends on its price. Quantity demanded also depends on a number of other determinants, including population size, consumer incomes, tastes, and the prices of other products.

The **quantity demanded** is the number of units of a good that consumers are willing and can afford to buy over a specified period of time.

Because prices play a central role in a market economy, we begin our study of demand by focusing on how quantity demanded depends on price. A little later, we will bring the other determinants of quantity demanded back into the picture. For now, we will consider all influences other than price to be fixed. This assumption, often expressed as "other things being equal," is used in much of economic analysis. As an example of the relationship between price and demand, let's think about the quantity of milk demanded. If the price of milk is very high, its "market potential" may be very small. People will find ways to get along with less milk, perhaps by switching to fruit juice or soda. If the price of milk declines, people will tend to drink more milk. They may give their children larger portions or switch away from juices and sodas. Thus:

There is no one demand figure for milk, or for computers, or for engineers. Rather, there is a different quantity demanded at each possible price, all other influences being held constant.

A **demand schedule** is a table showing how the quantity demanded of some product during a specified period of time changes as the price of that product changes, holding constant all other determinants of quantity demanded.

The Demand Schedule

Table 1 shows how such information for milk can be recorded in a **demand schedule.** It indicates how much milk consumers in a particular area are willing and able to buy at different possible prices during a specified period of time, other things held equal. Specifically, the table shows the quantity of milk that will be demanded in a year at each possible price ranging from $1.50 to $0.90 per litre. At a relatively low price, such as $1 per litre, customers wish to purchase 7 billion litres per year. But if the price was to rise to, say, $1.40 per litre, quantity demanded would fall to 5 billion litres.

Common sense tells us why this happens. First, as prices rise, some customers will reduce the quantity of milk they consume. Second, higher prices will induce some customers to drop out of the market entirely—for example, by switching to soda or juice. On both counts, quantity demanded will decline as the price rises.

As the price of an item rises, the quantity demanded normally falls. As the price falls, the quantity demanded normally rises, all other things held constant.

TABLE 1		
Demand Schedule for Milk		
Price per Litre	Quantity Demanded	Label in Figure 1
$1.50	4.5	A
1.40	5.0	B
1.30	5.5	C
1.20	6.0	E
1.10	6.5	F
1.00	7.0	G
0.90	7.5	H

Note: Quantity is in billions of litres per year.

The Demand Curve

The information contained in Table 1 can be summarized in a graph like Figure 1, which is called a **demand curve.** Each point in the graph corresponds to a line in the table. This curve shows the relationship between price and quantity demanded. For example, it tells us that to sell 7 billion litres per year, the price must be $1.00. This relationship is shown at point *G* in Figure 1. If the price was $1.40, however, consumers would demand only 5 billion litres (point *B*). Because the quantity demanded declines as the price increases, the demand curve has a negative slope.[2]

A **demand curve** is a graphical depiction of a demand schedule. It shows how the quantity demanded of some product will change as the price of that product changes during a specified period of time, holding constant all other determinants of quantity demanded.

[2] If you need to review the concept of slope, refer back to the appendix to Chapter 1.

Demand Curve for Milk

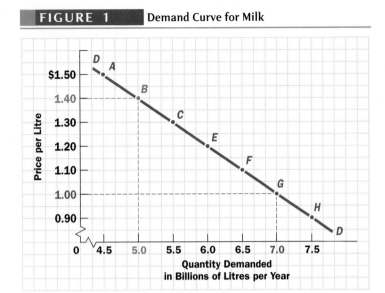

Quantity Demanded
in Billions of Litres per Year

Notice the last phrase in the definitions of the demand schedule and the demand curve: "holding constant all other determinants of quantity demanded constant." What are some of these "other things," and how do they affect the demand curve?

Shifts of the Demand Curve

The quantity of milk demanded is subject to a variety of influences other than the price of milk. Changes in population size and characteristics, consumer incomes and tastes, and the prices of alternative beverages such as soda and orange juice presumably change the quantity of milk demanded, even if the price of milk does not change.

Because the demand curve for milk depicts only the relationship between the quantity of milk demanded and the price of milk, holding constant all other factors, a change in milk price moves the market for milk from one point on the demand curve to another point on the same curve. However, a change in any of these other influences on demand causes a **shift of the entire demand curve.** More generally:

A **shift in a demand curve** occurs when any relevant variable other than price changes. If consumers want to buy *more* at any and all given prices than they wanted previously, the demand curve shifts to the right (or outward). If they desire *less* at any given price, the demand curve shifts to the left (or inward).

A change in the price of a good produces a movement *along* a fixed demand curve. By contrast, a change in any other variable that influences quantity demanded produces a shift of the *entire* demand curve.

If consumers want to buy more milk at every given price than they wanted previously, the demand curve shifts to the right (or outward). If they desire less at every given price, the demand curve shifts to the left (or inward toward the origin).

Figure 2 shows this distinction graphically. If the price of milk falls from \$1.30 to \$1.10 per litre, and quantity demanded rises accordingly, we move along demand curve D_0D_0 from point C to point F, as shown by the red arrow. If, on the other hand, consumers suddenly decide that they like milk better than they did formerly, or if more children are born who need more milk, the entire demand curve shifts outward from D_0D_0 to D_1D_1, as indicated by the blue arrows, meaning that at *any* given price consumers are now willing to buy more milk than before. To make this general idea more concrete, and to show some of its many applications, let us consider some specific examples of those "other things" that can shift demand curves.

Movements along versus Shifts of a Demand Curve

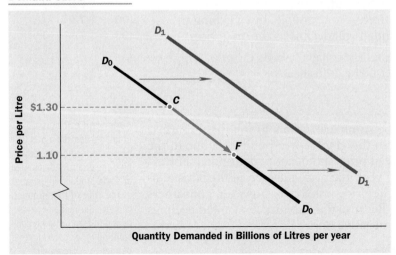

Quantity Demanded in Billions of Litres per year

Consumer Incomes   If average incomes rise, consumers will purchase more of most goods, including milk, even if the prices of those goods remain the same. That is, increases in income normally shift demand curves outward to the right, as depicted in Figure 3(a), where the demand curve shifts outward from D_0D_0 to D_1D_1, establishing a new price and output quantity.

Population   Population growth affects quantity demanded in more or less the same way as increases in average incomes. For instance, a larger population

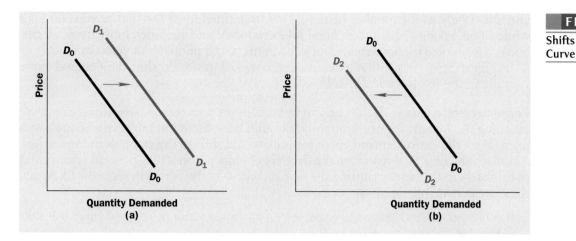

FIGURE 3

Shifts of the Demand Curve

will presumably want to consume more milk, even if the price of milk and average incomes do not change, thus shifting the entire demand curve to the right, as in Figure 3(a). Increases in particular population segments can also elicit shifts in demand—for example, Canada experienced a miniature population boom between the late 1970s

The Ups and Downs of Milk Consumption

The accompanying graph shows the evolution of per-capita milk consumption in Canada between 1986 and 2006. What is striking in the appearance of this graph is that the consumption of the various grades of milk does not change in sync. In fact, quite the contrary can be observed. While the per-capita consumption of whole milk (3.25%) and 2% milk has been cut approximately in half over the last 20 years, the consumption of 1% milk and skim milk has soared. This obviously is related to growing concerns among Canadians about the dangers of cholesterol, saturated fat, and calorie intake (and not much to changes in relative prices). But these concerns have not stopped the annual consumption of cream from rising by

more than 60 percent over the last 20 years, from 5.0 to 8.6 litres per Canadian—thus creating doubt about this explanation. The overall per-capita consumption of fluid milk, including chocolate milk, decreased from 100 litres per year in 1986 to 83 litres per year in 2006—a 17 percent reduction. This decrease may be attributed to an aging and changing population, whose diet does not necessarily include dairy products, but also to competition from highly publicized beverages such as sodas and bottled water. In addition, although not shown in the graph, figures indicate that the consumption of ice cream has diminished over the last 20 years, being replaced by more yogurt consumption.

Canadians Consuming More Low-Fat Milk—*and* Cream (annual per-capita consumption in litres, 1986–2006)

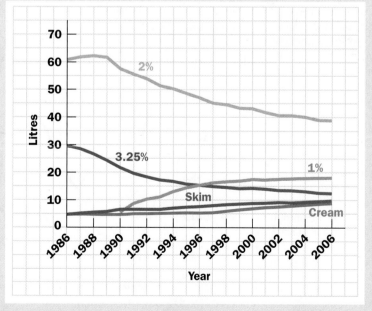

SOURCE: Data is based on Statistics Canada CANSIM database http://cansim2.statcan.ca. Tables 003-0012 and 051-000. (Calculations done by AAFC-AID, Dairy Section)

and mid-1990s, as the number of annual births jumped from 350,000 to 400,000 for a while. This group (which is dubbed Generation Y and includes most users of this book) has sparked higher demand for such items as cell phones and video games.

In Figure 3(b), we see that a decrease in population should shift the demand curve for milk to the left from D_0D_0 to D_2D_2.

Consumer Preferences   If the dairy industry mounts a successful advertising campaign extolling the benefits of drinking milk, families may decide to buy more at any given price. If so, the entire demand curve for milk would shift to the right, as in Figure 3(a). Alternatively, a medical report on the dangers of kidney stones may persuade consumers to drink less milk, thereby shifting the demand curve to the left, as in Figure 3(b). Again, these are general phenomena:

> If consumer preferences shift in favour of a particular item, its demand curve will shift outward to the right, as in Figure 3(a).

An example is the ever-shifting "rage" in children's toys—especially video game consoles such as PlayStation 3, Xbox 360, and PSP. These items become the object of desperate hunts as parents snap them up for their offspring, and stores are unable to keep up with the demand.

Prices and Availability of Related Goods   Because soda, orange juice, and coffee are popular drinks that compete with milk, a change in the price of any of these other beverages can be expected to shift the demand curve for milk. If any of these alternative drinks becomes cheaper, some consumers will switch away from milk. Thus, the demand curve for milk will shift to the left, as in Figure 3(b). Other price changes may shift the demand curve for milk in the opposite direction. For example, suppose that cookies, which are often consumed with milk, become less expensive. This may

Volatility in Gasoline Prices

The accompanying graph shows the volatility of gasoline prices in the Ottawa–Gatineau area. The upper curve shows the highest price observed during one day of each month from September 2005 to June 2007, the lower curve indicates the lowest price observed during the same day, and the middle line is an average of the two measures. The volatility from one day of one month to one day of another, as can be seen from all three curves, is remarkable, as is the volatility of gas prices between one retailer and another, as shown by the distance between the upper and the lower lines. Sometimes all gas stations offered nearly the same price, but on other days there was a large discrepancy. Gas prices also seemed to peak in the spring and summer, when presumably there is an increase in gas demand due to increased vehicular travel.

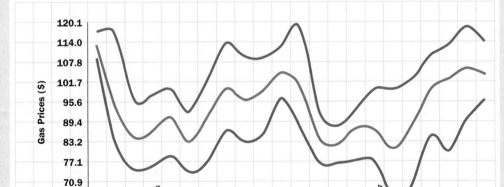

Ottawa–Gatineau Gas Prices on One Day in Each Month, 2005–2007

SOURCE: GasPricesInOttawa.com © 2007, Gas Prices in Ottawa. Retrieved from http://www.gaspricesinot-tawa.com/GasPriceStatistics.aspx

TABLE 2	
The Demand for Milk in a Nutshell	
There is a movement *along* the demand curve, and hence the quantity of milk demanded . . .	
. . . increases if . . .	. . . decreases if . . .
The price of milk falls	The price of milk rises
The *entire* demand curve for milk *shifts* . . .	
. . . up if	. . . down if
Consumers' incomes rise (in general). Population rises.	Consumers' incomes fall (in general). Population falls.
A milk advertising campaign is successful (preferences change favourably).	Medical reports emphasize health dangers related to milk (preferences change unfavourably).
The prices of alternative drinks rise.	The prices of alternative drinks fall.
The prices of goods normally consumed with milk decrease.	The prices of goods normally consumed with milk increase.

induce some consumers to drink more milk and thus shift the demand curve for milk to the right, as in Figure 3(a). In general:

> Increases in the prices of goods that are substitutes for the good in question (as soda is for milk) move the demand curve to the right. Increases in the prices of goods that are normally used together with the good in question (called *complements*, such as cookies and milk) shift the demand curve to the left.

This is just what happened when a frost wiped out almost half of Brazil's coffee bean harvest in 1995. The largest coffee producers raised their prices by 45 percent, and, as a result, the demand curve for alternative beverages such as tea shifted to the right. Then in 1998, coffee prices dropped about 34 percent, which in turn caused the demand curve for tea to shift toward the left (or toward the origin).

Although the preceding list does not exhaust the possible influences on quantity demanded, we have said enough to suggest the principles followed by demand and shifts of demand. These are summarized in Table 2, where, once again, the fundamental distinction between, on the one hand, a movement along the demand curve (and hence a change in the quantity demanded) and on the other hand, a move of the entire demand curve, is very noticeable. Let's turn now to the supply side of the market.

SUPPLY AND QUANTITY SUPPLIED

Like quantity demanded, the quantity of milk that is supplied by business firms such as dairy farms is not a fixed number; it also depends on many things. Obviously, we expect more milk to be supplied if there are more dairy farms or more cows per farm. Cows may give less milk if bad weather deprives them of their feed. As before, however, let's turn our attention first to the relationship between the price and quantity of milk supplied.

Economists generally suppose that a higher price calls forth a greater **quantity supplied.** Why? Remember our analysis of the principle of increasing cost in Chapter 3 (page 50). According to that principle, as more of any farmer's (or the nation's) resources are devoted to milk production, the opportunity cost of obtaining another litre of milk increases. Farmers will therefore find it profitable to increase milk production only if they can sell the milk at a higher price—high enough to cover the additional costs incurred to expand production.

The **quantity supplied** is the number of units that sellers want to sell over a specified period of time.

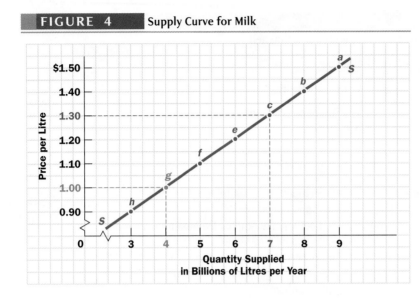

FIGURE 4   Supply Curve for Milk

TABLE 3		
Supply Schedule for Milk		
Price per Litre	Quantity Supplied	Label in Figure 4
$1.50	9	a
1.40	8	b
1.30	**7**	**c**
1.20	6	e
1.10	5	f
1.00	**4**	**g**
0.90	3	h

Note: Quantity is in billions of litres per year.

In other words, it normally will take higher prices to persuade farmers to raise milk production. This idea is quite general and applies to the supply of most goods and services.[3] As long as suppliers want to make profits and the principle of increasing costs holds:

> As the price of any commodity rises, the quantity supplied normally rises. As the price falls, the quantity supplied normally falls.

■ The Supply Schedule and the Supply Curve

Table 3 shows the relationship between the price of milk and its quantity supplied (if the market for milk was a free competitive market, which it isn't in Canada, as we will see later on in this chapter). Tables such as this one are called **supply schedules;** they show how much sellers are willing to provide during a specified period at alternative possible prices. This particular supply schedule tells us that a low price like $1.00 per litre will induce suppliers to provide only 4 billion litres, whereas a higher price like $1.30 will induce them to provide much more—7 billion litres.

As you might have guessed, when such information is plotted on a graph, it is called a **supply curve.** Figure 4 is the supply curve corresponding to the supply schedule in Table 3, showing the relationship between the price of milk and the quantity supplied. It slopes upward—it has a positive slope—because quantity supplied is higher when price is higher. Notice again the same phrase in the definition: "holding constant all other determinants of quantity supplied." What are these "other determinants"?

■ Shifts of the Supply Curve

Like quantity demanded, the quantity supplied in a market typically responds to many influences other than price. The weather, the cost of feed, the number and size of dairy farms, and a variety of other factors all influence how much milk will be brought to market. Because the supply curve depicts only the relationship between the price of milk and the quantity of milk supplied, holding constant all other influences, a change in any of these other determinants of quantity supplied will cause the entire supply curve to shift. That is:

> A change in the price of the good causes a movement *along* a fixed supply curve. Price is not the only influence on quantity supplied, however. If any of these other influences change, the *entire* supply curve shifts.

A **supply schedule** is a table showing how the quantity supplied of some product changes as the price of that product changes during a specified period of time, holding constant all other determinants of quantity supplied.

A **supply curve** is a graphical depiction of a supply schedule. It shows how the quantity supplied of some product will change as the price of that product changes during a specified period of time, holding constant all other determinants of quantity supplied.

---

[3] This analysis is carried out in much greater detail in later chapters.

Figure 5 depicts this distinction graphically. A rise in price from $1.10 to $1.30 will raise quantity supplied by moving along supply curve $S_0 S_0$ from point f to point c. Any rise in quantity supplied attributable to an influence other than price, however, will shift the *entire* supply curve outward to the right from $S_0 S_0$ to $S_1 S_1$, as shown by the blue arrows. Let us consider what some of these other influences are and how they shift the supply curve.

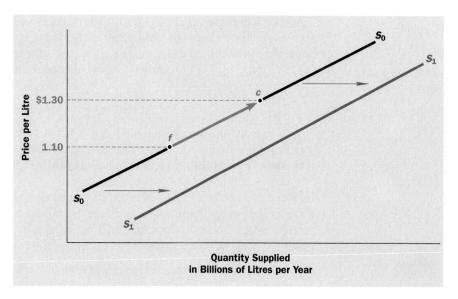

FIGURE 5

Movements along versus Shifts of a Supply Curve

Size of the Industry We begin with the most obvious influence. If more farmers enter the milk industry, the quantity supplied at any given price will increase. For example, if each farm provides 600,000 litres of milk per year at a price of $1.10 per litre, then 10,000 farmers would provide 6 billion litres, but 13,000 farmers would provide 7.8 billion. Thus, when more farms are in the industry, the quantity of milk supplied will be greater at any given price—and hence the supply curve will move farther to the right.

Figure 6(a) illustrates the effect of an expansion of the industry from 10,000 farms to 13,000 farms—a rightward shift of the supply curve from $S_0 S_0$ to $S_1 S_1$. Figure 6(b) illustrates the opposite case: a contraction of the industry from 10,000 farms to 6,250 farms. The supply curve shifts inward to the left from $S_0 S_0$ to $S_2 S_2$. Even if no farmers enter or leave the industry, results like those depicted in Figure 6 can be produced by expansion or contraction of the *existing* farms.

Technological Progress Agriculture, just like most industries, benefits from innovation and technological progress. As funny as it may sound, cows are now much more productive than they used to be. Farmers have discovered all sorts of ways to improve their milk production. For instance, some farmers have found that classical music helps cows to relax while being milked, thus increasing their milk production. Other farmers are using automatic milking machines with electronic devices that allow cows to be

FIGURE 6   Shifts of the Supply Curve

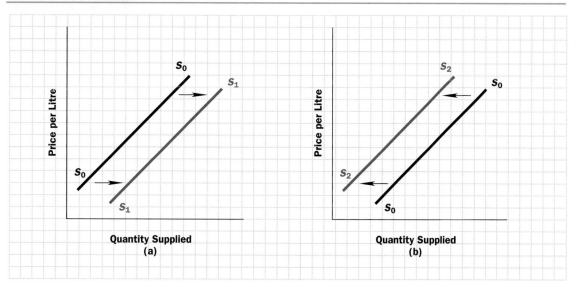

milked when they *want* to be milked, thus also raising milk production. These innovations reduce the cost of producing each litre of milk. Thus, for any given price, farmers are able to produce more milk; that is, the supply curve will shift outward to the right, as in Figure 6(a). This example, again, illustrates a general influence that applies to most industries:

> Technological progress that reduces costs will shift the supply curve outward to the right.

Similarly, automakers have been able to reduce production costs since industrial technology invented robots that can be programmed to work on several different car models. This technological advance has shifted the supply curve outward.

Prices of Inputs   Changes in input prices also shift supply curves. Suppose a drought raises the price of animal feed. Farmers will have to pay more to keep their cows alive and healthy and consequently will no longer be able to provide the same quantity of milk at each possible price. This example illustrates that:

> Increases in the prices of inputs that suppliers must buy will shift the supply curve inward to the left.

Prices of Related Outputs   Dairy farms sell products other than milk. If cheese prices rise sharply, farmers may decide to use some raw milk to make cheese, thereby reducing the quantity of milk supplied. On a supply–demand diagram, the supply curve would then shift inward, as in Figure 6(b).

Similar phenomena occur in other industries, and sometimes the effect goes the other way. For example, suppose that the price of beef goes up, which increases the quantity of meat supplied. That, in turn, will raise the number of cowhides supplied even if the price of leather does not change. Cowhides and meat are *joint* products. Thus, a rise in the price of beef will lead to a rightward shift in the supply curve of leather. In general:

> A change in the price of one good produced by a multiproduct industry may be expected to shift the supply curves of other goods produced by that industry.

The factors that cause a movement along the supply curve on the one hand (and hence in the quantity supplied) and that cause a move of the entire supply curve on the other hand, are summarized in Table 4.

TABLE 4	
The Supply of Milk in a Nutshell	
There is a movement *along* the supply curve, and hence . . .	
. . . the quantity of milk *supplied* . . .	
. . . increases if . . .	. . . decreases if . . .
The price of milk rises.	The price of milk falls.
The *entire* supply curve for milk *shifts* . . .	
. . . to the right (there is an increase in supply) if . . .	. . . to the left (there is a decrease in supply) if . . .
The number of milk producers rise.	The number of milk producers fall.
Technical progress occurs.	Technical regress occurs.
The prices of inputs fall.	The prices of inputs rise.
The price of cheese (alternative product outlets) falls.	The price of cheese (alternative product outlets) rises.

SUPPLY AND DEMAND EQUILIBRIUM

To analyze how an unfettered market determines price, we must compare the desires of consumers (demand) with the desires of producers (supply) to see whether the two plans are consistent. Table 5 and Figure 7 help us do this.

Table 5 brings together the demand schedule from Table 1 and the supply schedule from Table 3. Similarly, Figure 7 puts the demand curve from Figure 1 and the supply curve from Figure 4 on a single graph. Such graphs are called **supply–demand diagrams,** and you will encounter many of them in this book. Notice that, for reasons already discussed, the demand curve has a negative slope and the supply curve has a positive slope. That is generally true of supply–demand diagrams.

In a competitive market, price and quantity are determined by the intersection of the supply and demand curves. At only one point in Figure 7, point *E*, do the supply curve and the demand curve intersect. At the price corresponding to point *E*, which is $1.20 per litre, the quantity supplied and the quantity demanded are both 6 billion litres per year. This means that at a price of $1.20 per litre, consumers are willing to buy exactly what producers are willing to sell.

At a lower price, such as $1.00 per litre, only 4 billion litres of milk will be supplied (point *g*) whereas 7 billion litres will be demanded (point *G*). Thus, quantity demanded will exceed quantity supplied. There will be a **shortage** equal to 7 minus 4, or 3 billion litres. Price will thus be driven up by unsatisfied demand. Alternatively, at a higher price, such as $1.50 per litre, quantity supplied will be 9 billion litres (point *a*) and quantity demanded will be only 4.5 billion (point *A*). Quantity supplied will exceed quantity demanded—creating a **surplus** equal to 9 minus 4.5, or 4.5 billion litres.

Because $1.20 is the price at which quantity supplied and quantity demanded are equal, we say that $1.20 per litre is the equilibrium price (or the "market clearing" price) in this market. Similarly, 6 billion litres per year is the equilibrium quantity of milk. The term **equilibrium** merits a little explanation, because it arises so frequently in economic analysis.

An equilibrium is a situation in which there are no inherent forces that produce change. Think, for example, of a pendulum resting at its centre point. If no outside force (such as a person's hand) pushes it, the pendulum will remain exactly where it is; it is therefore in equilibrium.

If you give the pendulum a shove, however, its equilibrium will be disturbed and it will start to move. When it reaches the top of its arc, the pendulum will, for an

A **supply–demand diagram** graphs the supply and demand curves together. It also determines the equilibrium price and quantity.

A **shortage** is an excess of quantity demanded over quantity supplied. When there is a shortage, buyers cannot purchase the quantities they desire at the current price.

A **surplus** is an excess of quantity supplied over quantity demanded. When there is a surplus, sellers cannot sell the quantities they desire to supply at the current price.

An **equilibrium** is a situation in which there are no inherent forces that produce change. Changes away from an equilibrium position will occur only as a result of "outside events" that disturb the status quo.

FIGURE 7   Supply–Demand Equilibrium

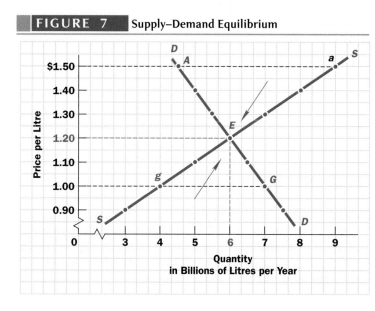

TABLE 5				
Determination of the Equilibrium Price and Quantity of Milk				
Price per Litre	Quantity Demanded	Quantity Supplied	Surplus or Shortage?	Price Direction
$1.50	4.5	9	Surplus	Fall
1.40	5	8	Surplus	Fall
1.30	5.5	7	Surplus	Fall
1.20	6	6	Neither	Unchanged
1.10	6.5	5	Shortage	Rise
1.00	7	4	Shortage	Rise
0.90	7.5	3	Shortage	Rise

instant, be at rest again. This point is not an equilibrium position, for the force of gravity will pull the pendulum downward. Thereafter, gravity and friction will govern its motion from side to side. Eventually, the pendulum will return to its original position. The fact that the pendulum tends to return to its original position is described by saying that this position is a *stable* equilibrium. That position is also the only equilibrium position of the pendulum. At any other point, inherent forces will cause the pendulum to move.

The concept of equilibrium in economics is similar and can be illustrated by our supply-and-demand example. Why is no price other than $1.20 an equilibrium price in Table 5 or Figure 7? What forces will change any other price?

Consider first a low price such as $1.00, at which quantity demanded (7 billion litres) exceeds quantity supplied (4 billion litres). If the price was this low, many frustrated customers would be unable to purchase the quantities they desired. In their scramble for the available supply of milk, some would offer to pay more. As customers sought to outbid one another, the market price would be forced up. Thus, a price below the equilibrium price cannot persist in a free market because a shortage sets in motion powerful economic forces that push the price upward.

Similar forces operate if the market price exceeds the equilibrium price. If, for example, the price should somehow reach $1.50, Table 5 tells us that quantity supplied (9 billion litres) would far exceed the quantity demanded (4.5 billion litres). Producers would be unable to sell their desired quantities of milk at the prevailing price, and some would undercut their competitors by reducing the price. Such competitive price cutting would continue as long as the surplus remained—that is, as long as quantity supplied exceeded quantity demanded. Thus, a price above the equilibrium price cannot persist indefinitely.

We are left with a clear conclusion. The price of $1.20 per litre and the quantity of 6 billion litres per year constitute the only price–quantity combination that does not sow the seeds of its own destruction. It is thus the only equilibrium for this market. Any lower price must rise, and any higher price must fall. It is as if natural economic forces place a magnet at point E that attracts the market, just as gravity attracts a pendulum.

The pendulum analogy is worth pursuing further. Most pendulums are more frequently in motion than at rest. However, unless they are repeatedly buffeted by outside forces (which, of course, is exactly what happens to economic equilibria in reality), pendulums gradually return to their resting points. The same is true of price and quantity in a free market. They are moved about by shifts in the supply and demand curves that we have already described. As a consequence, markets are not always in equilibrium. But, if nothing interferes with them, experience shows that they normally move toward equilibrium.

The **law of supply and demand** states that in a free market the forces of supply and demand generally push the price toward the level at which quantity supplied and quantity demanded are equal.

■ The Law of Supply and Demand

In a free market, the forces of supply and demand generally push the price toward its equilibrium level, the price at which quantity supplied and quantity demanded are equal. Like most economic "laws," some markets will occasionally disobey the **law of supply and demand**. Markets sometimes display shortages or surpluses for long periods of time. Prices sometimes fail to move toward equilibrium. But the "law" is a fair generalization that is right far more often than it is wrong.

■ EFFECTS OF DEMAND SHIFTS ON SUPPLY–DEMAND EQUILIBRIUM

Figure 3 showed how developments other than changes in price—such as increases in consumer income—can shift the demand curve. We saw that a rise in income, for example, will shift the demand curve to the right, meaning that at any given price, consumers—with their increased purchasing power—will buy more of the good than before. This, in turn, will move the equilibrium point, changing both market price and quantity sold.

The Ups and Downs of Burqa Prices

Céline Galipeau is a Radio-Canada (French CBC) reporter who travelled through Afghanistan in March 2006 and then again in November 2006 disguised as an Afghan. In this interview about her latest trip, Galipeau coincidentally gives an illuminating example of the laws of supply and demand tied to the prices of burqas—an Afghan or Pakistani garment that covers the entire female body, with a net or grille over the eyes to allow the wearer to see.

I noticed that the situation of women has experienced a setback. In March 2006 I could see many women in the streets of Kabul without a headscarf, or with just a hidjab. Not so now. Women are scared. The price of burqas is increasing because the demand for them is becoming extremely strong. Women fear the comeback of the Talibans, they fear the conservatives, who are more and more influential in the government and in the rest of the country. The barometer of all this is the price of burqas. Whenever it goes up, it implies that there is insecurity in the country, as all women want to purchase burqas again to protect themselves.

SOURCE: Translated from a transcript of the radio interview conducted by Christiane Charette, Radio-Canada, November 9, 2006. The transcript is available in French at http://www.radio-canada.ca/radio/christiane/modele-document.asp?docnumero=28107&numero=1880

This market adjustment is shown in Figure 8(a). It adds a supply curve to Figure 3(a) so that we can see what happens to the supply–demand equilibrium. In the example in the graph, the quantity demanded at the old equilibrium price of $1.20 increases from 6 billion litres per year (point E on the demand curve D_0D_0) to 7.5 billion litres per year (point R on the demand curve, D_1D_1). We know that $1.20 is no longer the equilibrium price, because at this price quantity demanded (7.5 billion litres) exceeds quantity supplied (6 billion litres). To restore equilibrium, the price must rise. The new equilibrium occurs at point T, where the price is $1.30 per litre and both quantities demanded and supplied are 7 billion litres per year. This example illustrates a general result, which is true when the supply curve slopes upward:

Any influence that makes the demand curve shift outward to the right, and does not affect the supply curve, will raise the equilibrium price and the equilibrium quantity.[4]

Everything works in reverse if consumer incomes fall. Figure 8(b) depicts a leftward (inward) shift of the demand curve that results from a decline in consumer

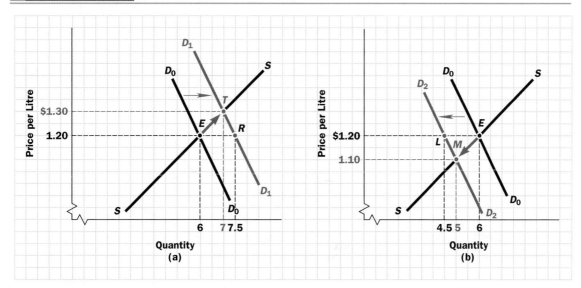

FIGURE 8   The Effects of Shifts of the Demand Curve

Note: Quantity is in billions of litres per year.

---

[4] For example, when incomes rise rapidly, in many developing countries the demand curves for a variety of consumer goods shift rapidly outward to the right. In Japan, for example, the demand for used Levi's jeans and Nike running shoes from the United States skyrocketed in the early 1990s as status-conscious Japanese consumers searched for outlets for their then-rising incomes.

incomes. For example, the quantity demanded at the previous equilibrium price ($1.20) falls from 6 billion litres (point E) to 4.5 billion litres (point L on the demand curve D_2D_2). The initial price is now too high and must fall. The new equilibrium will eventually be established at point M, where the price is $1.10 and both quantity demanded and quantity supplied are 5 billion litres. In general:

> Any influence that shifts the demand curve inward to the left, and that does not affect the supply curve, will lower both the equilibrium price and the equilibrium quantity.

SUPPLY SHIFTS AND SUPPLY–DEMAND EQUILIBRIUM

A story precisely analogous to that of the effects of a demand shift on equilibrium price and quantity applies to supply shifts. Figure 6 described the effects on the supply curve of milk if the number of farms increases. Figure 9(a) now adds a demand curve to the supply curves of Figure 6 so that we can see the supply–demand equilibrium. Notice that at the initial price of $1.20, the quantity supplied after the shift is 7.8 billion litres (point I on the supply curve S_1S_1), which is 30 percent more than the original quantity demanded of 6 billion litres (point E on the supply curve S_0S_0). We can see from the graph that the price of $1.20 is too high to be the equilibrium price; the price must fall. The new equilibrium point is J, where the price is $1.10 per litre and the quantity is 6.5 billion litres per year. In general:

> Any change that shifts the supply curve outward to the right, and does not affect the demand curve, will lower the equilibrium price and raise the equilibrium quantity.

This must always be true if the industry's demand curve has a negative slope, because the greater quantity supplied can be sold only if the price is decreased so as to induce customers to buy more.[5] The cellular phone industry is a case in point. As more providers have entered the industry, the cost of cellular service has plummeted. Some cellular carriers have even given away telephones as sign-up bonuses.

Figure 9(b) illustrates the opposite case: a contraction of the industry. The supply curve shifts inward to the left and equilibrium moves from point E to point V, where the price is $1.40 and quantity is 5 billion litres per year. In general:

> Any influence that shifts the supply curve to the left, and does not affect the demand curve, will raise the equilibrium price and reduce the equilibrium quantity.

FIGURE 9   Effects of Shifts of the Supply Curve

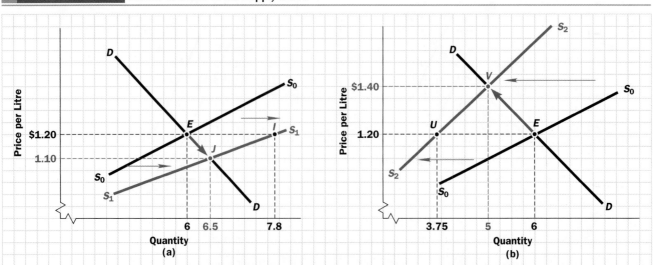

Quantity
(a)

Quantity
(b)

---

[5] Graphically, whenever a positively sloped curve shifts to the right, its intersection point with a negatively sloping curve must always move lower. Just try drawing it yourself.

Many outside forces can disturb equilibrium in a market by shifting the demand curve or the supply curve, either temporarily or permanently. In 1998, for example, gasoline prices dropped because recession in Asia reduced demand, and a reduction in use of petroleum resulted from a mild winter. Often these outside influences

PUZZLE RESOLVED: *Those Leaping Oil Prices*

The disturbing recent behaviour of the price of gasoline, and of the oil from which it is made, is attributable to large shifts in both demand and supply conditions. North Americans are, for example, driving more and are buying gas-guzzling vehicles, and the resulting upward shift in the demand curve raises price. The rapid development of China over the last decade is also said to have led to rising demand pressures on oil and gasoline.

On the supply side, instability in the Middle East and in Russia has undermined the production and distribution of oil. For instance, in 2004, the price of crude oil rose briskly when Iraqi oil lines were blasted and when it was announced that the largest Russian oil producer was on the brink of bankruptcy. Also the price of crude oil doubled, reaching $78 a barrel in the summer of 2006 when market participants started to fear that the war between Lebanon and Israel might lead to oil supply cuts, only to fall later when the war ended. But it all looks like small change now with the price of crude oil reaching $145 in July 2008.

High oil prices have become the norm since August 2005 as a consequence of the devastation brought about by Hurricane Katrina. The following newspaper story describes the impact of this natural disaster on Canadian gasoline prices.

Canadian Gasoline Prices Soar

Motorists in Canada's biggest cities were jolted awake Wednesday by a stunning jump in gas prices—in some centres costs rose as much as 20 cents a litre—in the wake of the devastating impact of Hurricane Katrina on the U.S. energy sector. In Toronto, prices were running around the $1.19 a litre mark at some stations. Overnight in Vancouver, gas prices jumped 12 cents to about $1.13 a litre. In Fredericton, prices at some stations went up to $1.19, an increase of about eight cents a litre. Lineups were reported at places still offering regular unleaded for $1.11. According to Torontogasprices.com, the highest per-litre price reported over the past 24 hours was in Newmarket, Ont., where costs hit $1.29.

The price hikes come on the heels of reports of extensive damage to oil platforms in the Gulf of Mexico that sent crude oil prices surging above $70 (U.S.) overseas for a second consecutive day on Wednesday in what some analysts described as an "evolving energy crisis" as a result of the hurricane. Hurricane Katrina touched land just east of New Orleans on Monday, leaving as much as 80 per cent of that historic city underwater. "Besides the human tragedy unfolding in Louisiana, Mississippi and Alabama—replete with looting, shootings and dramatic rescues—there is an evolving crisis in the Gulf of Mexico's oil and gas industry," BMO Nesbitt Burns chief economist Sherry Cooper said. "Oil futures hit a record settlement of $70 per barrel as traders awaited damage reports from U.S. oil and gas refineries in the Gulf."

The U.S. Coast Guard said at least seven rigs were adrift, while eight refineries have shut down because of the damage caused by the hurricane. According to some estimates, about 95 per cent of the daily oil output from the Gulf of Mexico is out of commission, resulting in soaring commodity prices and surging gasoline costs across much of North America.

"Given that the United States produces 7.75 million barrels of oil per day including natural gas liquids, Hurricane Katrina has knocked out roughly one-fifth of all domestic production," Ms. Cooper said. "To put this in perspective, the U.S. would need to find either a new Canada, Venezuela, Mexico, or Saudi Arabia to replace this loss based on what these countries sell to the United States."

Source: Terry Weber, "Canadian Gasoline Prices Soar," *The Globe and Mail*, August 31, 2005. Reprinted with permission of *The Globe and Mail*.

change the equilibrium price and quantity by shifting either the supply curve or the demand curve. If you look again at Figures 8 and 9, you can see clearly that any event that causes either the demand curve or the supply curve to shift will also change the equilibrium price and quantity.

■ Application: Who Really Pays That Tax?

Supply and demand analysis offers insights that may not be readily apparent. Here is an example. Suppose your provincial government raises the gasoline tax by 10 cents per litre. Service station operators will then have to collect 10 additional cents in taxes on every litre they pump. They will consider this higher tax as an addition to their costs and will shift it to you and other consumers by raising the price of gas by 10 cents per litre. Right? No, wrong—or rather, partly wrong.

The gas station owners would certainly *like* to shift the entire tax to buyers, but the market mechanism will allow them to shift only *part* of it—perhaps 6 cents per litre. They will then be stuck with the remainder—4 cents in our example. Figure 10, which is just another supply–demand graph, shows why.

The demand curve is the red curve DD. The supply curve before the tax is the black curve S_0S_0. Before the new tax, the equilibrium point is E_0 and the price is $1.00. We can interpret the supply curve as telling us at what price sellers are willing to provide any given quantity. For example, they are willing to supply quantity $Q_1 =$ 50 million litres per year if the price is $1.00 per litre.

So what happens as a result of the new tax? Because they must now turn 10 cents per litre over to the government, gas station owners will be willing to supply any given quantity only if they get 10 cents more per litre than they did before. Therefore, to get them to supply quantity $Q_1 = 50$ million litres, a price of $1.00 per litre will no longer suffice. Only a price of $1.10 per litre will now induce them to supply 5 million litres. Thus, at quantity $Q_1 = 50$, the point on the supply curve will move up by 10 cents, from point E_0 to point M. Because firms will insist on the same 10-cent price increase for any other quantity they supply, the *entire* supply curve will shift up by the 10-cent tax—from the black curve S_0S_0 to the new blue supply curve S_1S_1. And, as a result, the supply–demand equilibrium point will move from E_0 to E_1 and the price will increase from $1.00 to $1.06.

The supply curve shift may give the impression that gas station owners have succeeded in passing the entire 10-cent increase on to consumers—the distance from E_0 to M—but look again. The *equilibrium* price has only gone up from $1.00 to $1.06. That is, the price has risen by only 6 cents, not by the full 10-cent amount of the tax.

FIGURE 10

Who Pays for a New Tax on Products?

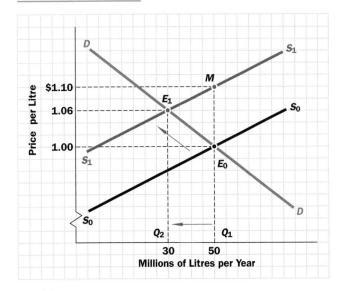

The gas station will have to absorb the remaining 4 cents of the tax.

Now this really *looks* as though we have pulled a fast one on you—a magician's sleight of hand. After all, the supply curve has shifted upward by the full amount of the tax, and yet the resulting price increase has covered only part of the tax rise. However, a second look reveals that, like most apparent acts of magic, this one has a simple explanation. The explanation arises from the *demand* side of the supply–demand mechanism. The negative slope of the demand curve means that when prices rise, at least some consumers will reduce the quantity of gasoline they demand by reducing their car usage. Others will replace gas-guzzling older cars with ones that provide reduced fuel consumption. That will force sellers to give up part of the price increase. In other words, firms must absorb the part of the tax—4 cents—that consumers are unwilling to pay.

Economic Aspects of the War on Drugs

For years now, governments have engaged in a highly publicized "war on drugs." Billions of dollars have been spent on trying to stop illegal drugs at countries, borders. In some sense, interdiction has succeeded: Police officers have seized literally tons of cocaine and other drugs. Yet these efforts have made barely a dent in the flow of drugs to European and North American city streets. Simple economic reasoning explains why.

When drug interdiction works, it shifts the supply curve of drugs to the left, thereby driving up street prices. But that, in turn, raises the rewards for potential smugglers and attracts more criminals into the "industry," which shifts the supply curve back to the right. The net result is that increased shipments of drugs to Montreal or Vancouver docks replace much of what the authorities confiscate. This is why many economists believe that any successful antidrug program must concentrate on reducing demand, which would lower the street price of drugs, not on reducing supply, which can only raise it.

Some people suggest that the government should go even further and legalize many drugs. Although this idea remains a highly controversial position that few are ready to endorse, the reasoning behind it is straightforward.

How would things differ if drugs were legal? Because South American farmers earn pennies for drugs that sell for hundreds of dollars on the streets of Vancouver and Toronto, we may safely assume that legalized drugs would be vastly cheaper. In fact, according to one estimate, a dose of cocaine would cost less than 50 cents. That, proponents point out, would reduce drug-related crimes dramatically. When, for example, was the last time you heard of a gang killing connected with the distribution of cigarettes or alcoholic beverages?

Some specialists, such as University of Ottawa criminologist Line Beauchesne, argue that legalization should be accompanied by reg-

ulation. Drugs would be freely accessed in standardized form from Crown corporations, as is now the case for alcohol and the Liquor Control Board of Ontario, for instance. This would improve the quality of these currently illegal drugs, just as adulterated alcohol was eliminated when alcohol was once more legalized, thus reducing health risks for consumers.

The argument against legalization of drugs is largely moral: Should the state sanction potentially lethal substances? But there is an economic aspect to this position as well: The vastly lower street prices of drugs that would surely follow legalization would increase drug use. Thus, while legalization would almost certainly reduce crime, it may also produce more addicts. If you think the increase in quantity demanded would be large, you are unlikely to find legalization an attractive option.

SOURCE: Nick Procaylo/Canadian Press.

But note that the equilibrium quantity Q_1 has fallen from 50 million litres to $Q_2 = 30$ million litres—so both consumers and suppliers lose out in some sense.

This example is not an oddball case. Indeed, the result is almost always true. The cost of any increase in a tax on any commodity will usually be paid partly by the consumer and partly by the seller. This is so no matter whether the government says that it is imposing the tax on the sellers or on the buyers. Whichever way it is phrased, the economics are the same: The supply–demand mechanism ensures that the tax will be shared by both of the parties.

◼ BATTLING THE INVISIBLE HAND: THE MARKET FIGHTS BACK

Lawmakers and rulers have often been dissatisfied with the outcomes of free markets. From biblical times to the space age, they have battled the invisible hand. Sometimes, rather than trying to adjust the workings of the market, governments have tried to raise or lower the prices of specific commodities by decree. In many such cases, the authorities felt that market prices were, in some sense, immorally low or immorally high. Penalties were therefore imposed on anyone offering the commodities in question at prices above or below those established by the authorities. Such legally imposed constraints on prices are called *price ceilings* and *price floors*. To see their result, we will focus on the use of price ceilings.

Restraining the Market Mechanism: Price Ceilings

A **price ceiling** is a maximum that the price charged for a commodity cannot legally exceed.

The market has proven itself a formidable foe that strongly resists attempts to get around its decisions. In case after case where legal **price ceilings** are imposed, virtually the same series of consequences ensues:

1. *A persistent shortage develops because quantity demanded exceeds quantity supplied.* Queuing (people waiting in lines), direct rationing (with everyone getting a fixed allotment), or any of a variety of other devices, usually inefficient and unpleasant, must substitute for the distribution process provided by the price mechanism. Example: Rampant shortages in Eastern Europe and the former Soviet Union helped precipitate the revolts that ended communism.

2. *An illegal, or "black," market often arises to supply the commodity.* Usually some individuals are willing to take the risks involved in meeting unsatisfied demands illegally. Example: Although most states ban the practice, ticket "scalping" (the sale of tickets at higher than regular prices) occurs at most popular sporting events and rock concerts.

3. *The prices charged on illegal markets are almost certainly higher than those that would prevail in free markets.* After all, lawbreakers expect some compensation for the risk of being caught and punished. Example: Illegal drugs are normally quite expensive. (See the accompanying Policy Debate box, "Economic Aspects of the War on Drugs" on page 77.)

4. A substantial portion of the price falls into the hands of the illicit supplier instead of going to those who produce the good or perform the service. Example: With the introduction of official ticket resellers such as TicketExchange, hockey fans can buy secondhand tickets to watch the Toronto Maple Leafs. The NHL team gets a share of the resale, and it is believed that prices will be cheaper than if scalping laws prohibited such resale.

5. *Investment in the industry generally dries up.* Because price ceilings reduce the monetary returns that investors can legally earn, less capital will be invested in industries that are subject to price controls. Even fear of impending price controls can have this effect. Example: Price controls on farm products in Zambia have prompted peasant farmers and large agricultural conglomerates alike to cut back production rather than grow crops at a loss. The result has been thousands of lost jobs and widespread food shortages.

Case Study: Rent Controls in New York City

FIGURE 11

Supply–Demand Diagram for Rental Housing

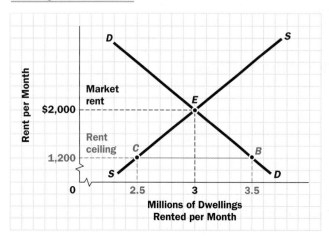

These points and others are best illustrated by considering a concrete example involving price ceilings. New York is the only major city in North America that has continuously legislated rent controls in much of its rental housing since World War II. Rent controls, of course, are intended to protect the consumer from high rents. But most economists believe that rent control does not help the cities or their residents and that, in the long run, it leaves almost everyone worse off. As we saw in Chapter 1, 80 percent of economists agreed without restriction that a ceiling on rents reduces the quantity and quality of housing available. Elementary supply–demand analysis shows us why.

Figure 11 is a supply–demand diagram for rental units in New York. Curve *DD* is the demand curve and curve *SS* is the supply curve. Without controls, equilibrium would be at point *E*, where rents average $2,000 per month and 3 million housing units are occupied. If rent controls are effective, the ceiling price must be below the equilibrium price of $2,000. But with a low rent ceiling, such as $1,200, the quantity of housing demanded will be 3.5 million units (point *B*) whereas the quantity supplied will be only 2.5 million units (point *C*).

The diagram shows a shortage of 1 million apartments. This theoretical concept of a "shortage" manifests itself in New York City as an abnormally low vacancy rate—typically about half the national urban average. Naturally, rent controls have spawned a lively black market in New York. The black market raises the effective price of rent-controlled apartments in many ways, including bribes, so-called key money paid to move up on a waiting list, or the requirement that prospective tenants purchase worthless furniture at inflated prices.

According to Figure 11, rent controls reduce the quantity supplied from 3 million to 2.5 million apartments. How does this reduction show up in New York and in other cities that have rent control? First, some property owners, discouraged by the low rents, have converted apartment buildings into office space or other uses. Second, some apartments have been inadequately maintained. After all, rent controls create a shortage, which makes even dilapidated apartments easy to rent. Third, some landlords have actually abandoned their buildings rather than pay rising tax and fuel bills. These abandoned buildings rapidly become eyesores and eventually pose threats to public health and safety.

With all of these problems, why does rent control persist in New York City? And why do other cities, in Canada and elsewhere, sometimes move in the same direction?

Part of the explanation is that most people simply do not understand the problems that rent controls create. Another part is that landlords are unpopular politically. But a third, and very important, part of the explanation is that not everyone is hurt by rent controls—and those who benefit from controls fight hard to preserve them. In New York and in other cities such as Paris, many tenants still pay rents that are only a fraction of what their apartments would fetch on the open market. They are, naturally enough, quite happy with this situation. This last point illustrates another very general phenomenon:

Virtually every price ceiling or floor creates a class of people that benefits from the regulations. These people use their political influence to protect their gains by preserving the status quo, which is one reason why it is so difficult to eliminate price ceilings or floors.

■ Case Study: Rent Controls in Canada

While most economists agree that rent freezes or strict rent controls, as exist in New York and in some European cities such as Paris, have devastating effects on the quality and quantity of rental housing, some economists argue that second-generation rent controls, like those that have been put into place in many Canadian cities since the mid-1970s (although some were discontinued in the 1990s), have achieved their purposes without generating disastrous effects. These second-generation rent regulations provide annual rent guideline increases, allowing, for instance, 2.1 and 2.6 percent increases in Ontario in 2006 and 2007, respectively. Rental unit owners can apply for further increases when they undertake major repairs and upgrading of their properties and when they face above-normal increases in property taxes and heating or electricity costs. This allows owners to earn a *fair* or *reasonable* rate of return on their residential investment (much as regulated monopolies are allowed to earn a fair rate of return).

Research done for the Canada Mortgage and Housing Corporation seems to demonstrate that there is "no convincing evidence that rent regulations, as they existed in various provinces in Canada . . . had significant effects on rents, on the construction of rental units, or on vacancy rates." In addition, rent controls had no reported effect on the proportion of occupied rental units that were in need of major repairs.

In addition to protecting tenants from unreasonable rent increases and ensuring rental unit owners a fair or reasonable rate of return on their investment, proponents of second-generation rent controls claim that these controls take away some of the monopolistic power of rental unit owners, thus somewhat reducing the overall average rental cost. In addition, they claim, rent controls tend to stabilize rent prices, preventing major rent increases when the market is tight (when vacancy rates are low) and also preventing rents from falling when the market is slack (when vacancy rates are high and owners of rental units would normally take a beating). Whether or not these claims are correct, rent control still remains an issue in several Canadian provinces, in particular in cities where few downtown rental apartments are affordable.

Restraining the Market Mechanism: Price Floors

Interferences with the market mechanism are not always designed to keep prices low. Agricultural price supports and minimum wage laws are two notable examples in which the law keeps prices *above* free-market levels. Such **price floors** are typically accompanied by a standard series of symptoms:

> A **price floor** is a legal minimum below which the price charged for a commodity is not permitted to fall.

1. *A surplus develops as sellers cannot find enough buyers.* Example: Surpluses of various agricultural products have been a persistent—and costly—problem for the U.S. government. The problem is even worse in the European Union (EU), where the common agricultural policy holds prices even higher. This policy accounts for about half of all EU spending.
2. *Where goods, rather than services, are involved, the surplus creates a problem of disposal.* Something must be done about the excess of quantity supplied over quantity demanded. For instance, both the U.S. government and the European Union have often been forced to purchase, store, and then dispose of large amounts of surplus agricultural commodities.
3. *To get around the regulations, sellers may offer discounts in disguised—and often unwanted—forms.* Back when airline fares were regulated by the government, airlines offered more and better food and more stylishly uniformed flight attendants instead of lowering fares. Today, the food is worse, but tickets cost much less.
4. *Regulations that keep prices artificially high encourage overinvestment in the industry.* Even inefficient businesses whose high operating costs would doom them in an unrestricted market can survive beneath the shelter of a generous price floor. This is why airline industries throughout the world went through painful "shakeouts" of the weaker companies since the 1980s, after they were deregulated and allowed to charge market-determined prices.

Once again, a specific example is useful for understanding how price floors work.

Case Study: Farm Price Supports

One of the ironies of world capitalism is that those countries that most strongly argue in favour of free competitive markets and trade liberalization are precisely those countries that have the most extensive agricultural price support programs. Both the United States and the European Union heavily subsidize their agricultural sectors, including sugar beet, cotton, and wheat growers and dairy farmers. Indeed, these agricultural subsidies were an important component of the Doha round of trade negotiations, set up by the World Trade Organization, and the negotiations faltered in 2006 precisely on this issue.

American farm price supports began during the Great Depression when unemployed people could not afford to buy food and farmers were going broke in droves in the midst of excess supplies of agricultural products. Farm price supports in Europe got started a few years after World War II, as the founding members of the European Union were slowly emerging from more than a decade of food shortages.

One of the consequences of these price supports has been the creation of unsellable surpluses—more output of crops such as grains than consumers were willing to buy at the inflated prices yielded by the supports. Warehouses were filled to overflowing. New storage facilities had to be built, and the government was forced to set up programs in which grain from the unmanageable surpluses was shipped to poor foreign countries to combat malnutrition and starvation in those nations. Realistically, if price supports are to be effective in keeping prices above the equilibrium level, then *someone* must be prepared to purchase the surpluses that invariably result. Otherwise, those surpluses will somehow find their way into the market and drive down prices, undermining the price support program. The buyer of the surpluses has usually turned out to be the government, which makes its purchases at the expense of taxpayers who are forced to pay twice—once through taxes to finance the government purchases, and a second time in the form of higher prices for the farm products bought by the public.

Figure 12 illustrates the likely consequences of price support programs. Curve *DD* is the demand curve for a farm product, say wheat, and S_0S_0 is the supply curve. If there was no subsidization program, market forces would bring the price of wheat to $140 per tonne and 150 million tonnes would be produced and sold. If the government was to impose by decree a price of $220 per tonne, only 100 million tonnes would be demanded and 190 million tonnes would be produced. There would thus be a surplus of 90 million tonnes, produced in excess of the quantities being demanded at the $220 price. The government would have to purchase the surplus and store it away, waiting for an increase in demand. This additional demand could come from Third World markets, where the overproduction is now being dumped (at any price), potentially putting Third World farmers out of business.

An alternative is for government to pay a subsidy to wheat producers, thus shifting the supply curve to S_1S_1 (in perfect symmetry to the shift in the supply curve that was induced by an increase in the gasoline tax, as shown in Figure 10). This downward shift in the supply curve occurs because the net cost of production for the wheat grower will be reduced by the amount of the subsidy per tonne. In the case illustrated in Figure 12, to sustain a support price of $220 per tonne of wheat, which would induce a production of 190 millions of tonnes, the price being demanded on the market would have to fall to $108 and the government would be forced to grant a subsidy of $112 per tonne. It is estimated by the Organisation for Economic Co-operation and Development (OECD) that the government subsidy per tonne of wheat has been $150 per tonne in the European Union, $112 in the United States, $28 in Canada, and $7 in Australia over the 1999–2003 period.

Another possibility is to impose **quotas.** Farmers would be allowed to produce only a certain amount of wheat or to farm only a given amount of land. In the former case, the supply curve would become vertical at the production level of 100 tonnes of wheat. In the latter case, the supply curve would shift backward until it became S_2S_2. Through these restricting mechanisms, the quantities being supplied would be exactly equal to the quantities being demanded at the $220 price. In this case, there would no

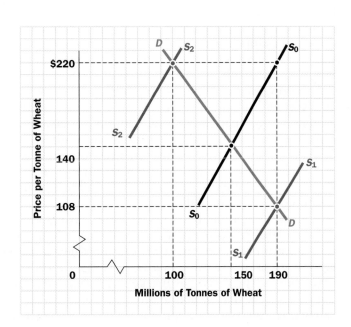

FIGURE 12

Price Support Programs

A **producer's quota** is the maximum amount that a producer is allowed to produce or the maximum area that a farmer is allowed to farm.

longer be a government subsidy, but output (and consumption) would be reduced relative to the free competitive market solution, and prices paid by consumers would be higher: $220 dollars.

■ Case Study: Farm Products Supply Management in Canada

In Canada, several farm products are produced under a form of quota system, where supply is managed by a central agency and products are marketed at set prices. There are many such agencies, such as the Canadian Dairy Commission, which covers milk, cream, cheese, and butter; the Canadian Egg Marketing Agency; the Canadian Turkey Marketing Agency, and the Chicken Farmers of Canada, which obviously cover eggs and poultry.

Although the details are different, all of these organizations operate under similar principles. The national agency first makes an estimate of future demand by both domestic consumers and processors of farm products; an estimate of possible exports and imports is also made. These estimates indicate the required level of national production. Production quotas are then assigned to each provincial board, in proportion to shares previously agreed upon. The provincial boards in turn allot quotas to registered local producers. The farmers then sell their products at prices that have been set by the national or the provincial agencies, taking into consideration a cost-of-production formula designed to provide a fair rate of return on the operations of an efficient farmer. Revenues are often pooled, as they are in the case of the Canadian Wheat Board, which markets the wheat, durum, and barley produced by western Canada farmers, although no quotas are imposed in this case.

Supply management of Canadian farm products as it now exists was mainly put in place in the 1970s. Before that, farm products faced unstable markets and highly variable producer revenues, with unpredictable production cycles and situations in which producers undercut each other when demand relative to supply was weak. Since consumers cannot drastically change their eating habits, a small excess supply of farm products can lead to a large decrease in farm product prices, thus leading to substantial decreases in farm revenues, as it did at the time of the Great Depression. Price support and supply management have been introduced to avoid this drawback of free competitive markets. There were some hitches in the initial stages of supply management, when quotas were not properly enforced or when overly high quotas, in particular in the dairy industry in 1975, were mistakenly granted, thus leading to huge surpluses. This is not the case today. Through quotas, national agencies attempt to strike the best balance between the supply of and the demand for agricultural products, thus ensuring stable prices for the consumers and stable revenues for the producers. A system with properly set quotas thus avoids the excess production associated with pure price support programs, with their storage and disposal costs.

The downside of the quota system is that milk and other dairy products, eggs, chickens, and bread are perhaps more expensive than they would otherwise be on average in a competitive market without quotas, as is obvious from Figure 12. Consumers are not alone in possibly paying higher prices: Milk quotas now sell for $30,000 per cow, which means that anybody who wants to start a dairy farm needs at least $1.2 million, since an efficient farm requires at least 40 head of cattle. But this may be the price that must be paid for a stable agricultural sector.

Another advantage of the farm product marketing boards is that these boards act as a countervailing force to the power of processors of farm products. These processors are often large firms that can take advantage of farmers, so it is argued that without the marketing boards, farm product producers would be at a disadvantage when negotiating prices. In other words, the forces of supply and demand were already distorted before the arrival of marketing boards. Indeed, the Canadian Wheat Board claims explicitly that by acting on behalf of all wheat and barley producers in western Canada, it exercises monopoly power that allows it to extract higher revenues for

POLICY DEBATE

Should the Canadian Wheat Board Be Dismantled?

Conservatives are popular in western Canada, but free-market policies are not welcomed by all Westerners. In the fall of 2006, the Harper federal government initiated steps to dismantle the Canadian Wheat Board. As of mid 2008, the government and the Wheat Board are still battling in court. The following newspaper story illustrates well the ideological conflict between those who believe in the laws of supply and demand and those who believe that markets are not as perfect as economists would like them to be.

Mr. Chorney, a 41-year-old grain farmer, believes the federal government is about to make an enormous mistake by dismantling the monopoly power of the Canadian Wheat Board. "They're really floundering on this issue," he says.

The debate over the future of the Wheat Board runs to the heart of Western Canadian history and politics, pitting traditional Prairie collectivism against the ideology of the free market. It's an issue that has waxed and waned over the years. Now, the federal government is on the brink of creating what it calls "marketing choice," a world in which farmers could choose either to sell their product on their own, or to whatever version of the Wheat Board survived the end of the monopoly. . . .

Ken Ritter is the elected chairman of the Canadian Wheat Board. Mr. Ritter was first elected as an opponent of the Wheat Board monopoly, but after nine months of handling the board's rail-transport negotiations, he had a change of mind. "I saw how the other players had . . . almost scorn for farmers. They felt they should run their railroad exactly the way they want, and farmers' economic interests were minimized," he says. "I'm a believer in a market economy. But in a market economy, the players all have to have reasonable weight to be effective. That's what

the Wheat Board helps farmers do. The main grain traders are huge corporations who hold some 83 per cent of the market. If you're not big, you're not in the game." . . .

Cherilyn Jolly-Nagel, the president of the Western Canadian Wheat Growers Association, is one of those who can't wait to see the market opened up to competition. She's a 27-year-old graduate of an agriculture college who runs a 6,500-acre operation with her husband in western Saskatchewan, and she sees herself as part of farming's new wave, a savvy group of young farmers able to find more money in international markets. "The current system doesn't allow me to capitalize on what I see as marketing opportunities," Ms. Jolly-Nagel says. . . .

Mr. Chorney, whose family has farmed an area 40 kilometres north of Winnipeg for the past 77 years, scoffs at the assertions of the Western Canadian Wheat Growers. He doesn't want to get into a debate about ideology; he's interested in the bottom line. The Canadian Wheat Board is the largest seller of wheat and barley in the world, with sales in the range of $3-billion to $4-billion a year. It was granted a monopoly over wheat exports by the government in 1943 and has been a constant target for U.S. trade challenges. One of the most well-known studies of the Wheat Board, hotly contested by economists on both sides of the debate, argued that over a 14-year period the board averaged sales of $265-million more per year than would have been realized by multiple sellers.

SOURCE: Joe Friesen, "Farmers fretting over Wheat Board's future." Posted October 10, 2006, on *GlobeandMail.com* at http://www.theglobeandmail.com. Reprinted with permission of *The Globe and Mail*.

western grain growers. This also explains why other farmers (for instance, potato growers in Prince Edward Island and in some northeastern U.S. states) organize themselves into cooperatives.

◼ A Can of Worms

Our case studies—rent controls and farm price support programs—illustrate some of the possible side effects of price floors and ceilings, but barely hint at others. Problems that we have not yet mentioned may arise, such as favouritism and corruption. For instance, with price ceilings, there are shortages and someone must decide who gets the limited quantity that is available. In the former Soviet Union, queuing for certain goods was quite common. Even so, Communist Party officials and other favoured groups were somehow able to purchase the scarce commodities that others could not buy. Misallocation of resources is also likely to occur. For example, Russian farmers used to feed their farm animals bread instead of unprocessed grains because price ceilings kept the price of bread ludicrously low. Praiseworthy intentions—here the government's desire to provide all Russian citizens with low-cost food—may cause serious damage elsewhere in the economy.

■ A SIMPLE BUT POWERFUL LESSON

The law of supply and demand in unfettered markets looks simple enough. Tampering with the price mechanism by imposing ceilings or floors can generate all kinds of major negative side effects. Despite this, modern governments still interfere and impose regulations. Why is this so? There are essentially two reasons. The first explanation is that many people in authority still do not understand the law of supply and demand. But there is sometimes a deeper reason. The law of supply and demand assumes that market mechanisms are unhampered to start with, and that none of the market participants have any control over supply or demand. But this is clearly not the case in many, perhaps in most, markets. Even in agricultural markets, which are usually considered excellent illustrations of supply and demand laws, farmers are squeezed by input suppliers and large purchasers such as supermarket chains, which flex their market power muscles. As the quote at the beginning of the chapter reminds us, the free competitive market mechanisms of supply and demand are powerful indeed, but we must not forget that most markets are neither free nor fully competitive, but rather are dominated by a few large participants on either the supply or the demand side.

SUMMARY

1. The quantity of a product that is demanded is not a fixed number. Rather, **quantity demanded** depends on such factors as the price of the product, consumer incomes, and the prices of other products.

2. The relationship between quantity demanded and price, holding constant all other things, can be displayed graphically on a **demand curve.**

3. For most products, the higher the price, the lower the quantity demanded. As a result, the demand curve usually has a negative slope.

4. The quantity of a product that is supplied depends on its price and many other influences. A **supply curve** is a graphical representation of the relationship between **quantity supplied** and price, holding constant all other influences.

5. For most products, supply curves have positive slopes, meaning that higher prices lead to supply of greater quantities.

6. A change in quantity demanded that is caused by a change in the price of the good is represented by a movement *along* a fixed demand curve. A change in quantity demanded that is caused by a change in any other determinant of quantity demanded is represented by a **shift of the demand curve.**

7. This same distinction applies to the supply curve: Changes in price lead to movements along a fixed supply curve; changes in other determinants of quantity supplied lead to shifts of the entire supply curve.

8. A market is said to be in **equilibrium** when quantity supplied is equal to quantity demanded. The equilibrium price and quantity are shown by the point on the supply–demand graph where the supply and demand curves intersect. The **law of supply and demand** states that price and quantity tend to gravitate to this point in a free market.

9. Changes in consumer incomes, tastes, technology, prices of competing products, and many other influences lead to shifts in either the demand curve or the supply curve and produce changes in price and quantity that can be determined from **supply-demand diagrams.**

10. A tax on a good generally leads to a rise in the price at which the taxed product is sold. The rise in price is generally less than the tax, so consumers usually pay less than the entire tax.

11. Consumers generally pay only part of a tax because the resulting rise in price leads them to buy less and the cut in the quantity they demand helps to force price down.

12. An attempt to use government regulations to force prices above or below their equilibrium levels is likely to lead to **shortages** or **surpluses,** to black markets in which goods are sold at illegal prices, and to a variety of other problems. The market always strikes back at attempts to repeal the law of supply and demand.

13. A **ceiling** imposed on the price of a good will generally lead to a **shortage** of this good. A **floor** imposed on prices will generally lead to a **surplus.** The only way to avoid these surpluses is to impose **quotas** on the amounts that can be produced.

KEY TERMS

Invisible hand 62	Supply schedule 68	Law of supply and demand 72
Quantity demanded 63	Supply curve 68	Price ceiling 78
Demand schedule 63	Supply–demand diagram 71	Price floor 80
Demand curve 63	Shortage 71	Producer's Quota 81
Shift in a demand curve 64	Surplus 71	
Quantity supplied 67	Equilibrium 71	

TEST YOURSELF

1. What shapes would you expect for demand curves for the following:

   a. A medicine that means life or death for a patient

   b. French fries in a food court with kiosks offering many types of food

2. The following are the assumed supply and demand schedules for hamburgers in Unitown:

Demand Schedule		Supply Schedule	
Price	Quantity Demanded per Year (thousands)	Price	Quantity Supplied per Year (thousands)
$2.25	12	$2.25	30
2.00	16	2.00	28
1.75	20	1.75	26
1.50	24	1.50	24
1.25	28	1.25	22
1.00	32	1.00	20

   a. Plot the supply and demand curves and indicate the equilibrium price and quantity.

   b. What effect would a decrease in the price of beef (a hamburger input) have on the equilibrium price and quantity of hamburgers, assuming all other things remained constant? Explain your answer with the help of a diagram.

   c. What effect would an increase in the price of pizza (a substitute commodity) have on the equilibrium price and quantity of hamburgers, assuming again that all other things remain constant? Use a diagram in your answer.

3. Suppose the supply and demand schedules for bicycles are as they appear below.

   a. Graph these curves and show the equilibrium price and quantity.

Price	Quantity Demanded per Year (millions)	Quantity Supplied per Year (millions)
$160	40	24
200	36	28
240	32	32
280	28	36
320	24	40
360	20	44

   b. Now suppose that it becomes unfashionable to ride a bicycle, so that the quantity demanded at each price falls by 8 million bikes per year. What is the new equilibrium price and quantity? Show this solution graphically. Explain why the quantity falls by less than 8 million bikes per year.

   c. Suppose instead that several major bicycle producers go out of business, thereby reducing the quantity supplied by 8 million bikes at every price. Find the new equilibrium price and quantity, and show it graphically. Explain again why quantity falls by less than 8 million.

   d. What are the equilibrium price and quantity if the shifts described in Test Yourself Questions 3(b) and 3(c) happen at the same time?

4. The following table summarizes information about the market for principles of economics textbooks:

Price	Quantity Demanded per Year	Quantity Supplied per Year
$40	4,200	200
50	2,200	600
60	1,200	1,200
70	700	2,000
80	550	3,000

   a. What is the market equilibrium price and quantity of textbooks?

   b. To quell outrage over tuition increases, the president of the university places a $50 limit on the price of textbooks. How many textbooks will be sold now?

   c. While the price limit is still in effect, automated publishing increases the efficiency of textbook production. Show graphically the likely effect of this innovation on the market price and quantity.

5. How are the following demand curves likely to shift in response to the indicated changes?

   a. The effect of a drought on the demand curve for umbrellas

   b. The effect of higher popcorn prices on the demand curve for movie tickets

   c. The effect on the demand curve for coffee of a decline in the price of Coca-Cola

6. The two accompanying diagrams show supply and demand curves for two substitute commodities: tapes and compact discs (CDs).

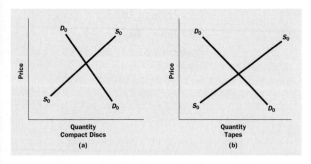

(a) Quantity Compact Discs
(b) Quantity Tapes

a. On the right-hand diagram, show what happens when rising raw material prices make it costlier to produce tapes.

b. On the left-hand diagram, show what happens to the market for CDs.

7. Consider the market for milk discussed in this chapter (Tables 1, 3, and 5 and Figures 1, 4, and 7). Suppose that the government decides to fight kidney stones by levying a tax of 40 cents per litre on sales of milk. Follow these steps to analyze the effects of the tax:

a. Construct the new supply schedule (to replace Table 3) that relates quantity supplied to the price that consumers pay.

b. Graph the new supply curve constructed in Test Yourself Question 7(a) on the supply–demand diagram depicted in Figure 7. What are the new equilibrium price and quantity?

c. Does the tax succeed in its goal of reducing the consumption of milk?

d. How much does the equilibrium price increase? Is the price rise greater than, equal to, or less than the 40-cent tax?

e. Who actually pays the tax, consumers or producers? (This may be a good question to discuss in class.)

8. (More difficult) The demand and supply curves for T-shirts in Touristtown are given by the following equations:

$$Q = 24{,}000 - 500P \qquad Q = 6{,}000 + 1{,}000P$$

where P is measured in dollars and Q is the number of T-shirts sold per year.

a. Find the equilibrium price and quantity algebraically.

b. If tourists decide they do not really like T-shirts that much, which of the following might be the new demand curve?

$$Q = 21{,}000 - 500P \qquad Q = 27{,}000 - 500P$$

Find the equilibrium price and quantity after the shift of the demand curve.

c. If, instead, two new stores that sell T-shirts open up in town, which of the following might be the new supply curve?

$$Q = 4{,}000 + 1{,}000P \qquad Q = 9{,}000 + 1{,}000P$$

Find the equilibrium price and quantity after the shift of the supply curve.

(Hint: See the appendix to this chapter.)

DISCUSSION QUESTIONS

1. How often do you rent videos? Would you do so more often if a rental cost half as much? Distinguish between your demand curve for home videos and your "quantity demanded" at the current price.

2. Discuss the likely effects of the following:

a. Rent ceilings on the market for apartments

b. Floors under wheat prices on the market for wheat

Use supply–demand diagrams to show what may happen in each case.

3. Suppose that Canadian quotas on milk have been miscalculated, not taking sufficient account of the reduction in births in Canada in the twenty-first century, and that huge milk and butter surpluses have accumulated. In an effort to reduce surpluses, the government offers to pay dairy farmers to slaughter cows. Use two diagrams, one for the milk market and one for the meat market, to illustrate how this policy should affect the price of meat. (Assume that meat is sold in an unregulated market.)

4. It is claimed in this chapter that either price floors or price ceilings reduce the actual quantity exchanged in a market. Use a diagram or diagrams to test this conclusion, and explain the common sense behind it.

5. The same rightward shift of the demand curve may produce a very small or a very large increase in quantity, depending on the slope of the supply curve. Explain this conclusion with diagrams.

6. Suppose that you expect the price of gasoline to go up in the very near future, say, in a few days. How would that change your demand for gasoline today? If everyone had the same expectations, what would happen to the demand curve for gasoline? Assuming that the supply curve will remain unchanged, what is the likely effect on the current price of gasoline?

7. From 1997 to 2005 in Canada, the number of working men over 25 years old grew by 12 percent; the number of working women in the same age group grew by 20 percent. During this time, average wages for men grew by 17.5 percent, while the average wages for women grew by 25 percent. Which of the following two explanations seems more consistent with the data?

a. Women decided to work more, raising their relative supply (relative to men).

b. Discrimination against women declined, raising the relative (to men) demand for female workers.

APPENDIX: *The Simple Algebra of Market Equilibrium*

Economists often resort to systems of two equations to deal with simple problems of supply and demand. Question 8 in the Test Yourself section provides an example of such a two-equation system. Knowing how to solve such systems will allow you to compute the equilibrium price and the equilibrium output when you are given supply and demand equations. In economics, the two key variables, price and quantity, are often called P and Q. Thus, the demand and supply curves could be given by:

$$Q = a - bP \qquad \text{(the demand equation)}$$

$$Q = c + dP \qquad \text{(the supply equation)}$$

where a, b, c, and d are the parameters being involved, b and d both being positive numbers.

The first equation represents demand because there is a negative relationship between quantities and prices, as there should be with a demand curve, whereas in the second equation, there is a positive relationship between quantities and prices, as is normally the case for a supply curve. For every \$1 increase in price, quantities demanded decrease by b units; similarly, for every \$1 increase in price, quantities supplied increase by d units.

What is the graphical representation of these two equations? Usually, in algebra, the variable on the left-hand side of an equation, such as $y = a + bx$, is to be found on the vertical axis (the y-axis). But economists do the opposite: As you must have noted, prices P are found on the vertical axis, and quantities Q are on the horizontal axis, so that our two equations can be reinterpreted as being:

$$P = a/b - (1/b)Q$$
(the demand curve)

$$P = -c/d + (1/d)Q$$
(the supply curve)

Thus, the slope of the demand curve as it appears on a demand and supply diagram is equal to $-1/b$ while the slope of the supply curve is $+1/d$, as shown in Figure 13. The vertical intercept of the demand curve (when $Q = 0$) is thus a/b. The horizontal intercepts of the demand and supply curves (when $P = 0$), as can be seen by looking at the two equations with which we started, are obviously a and c, respectively.

What are the equilibrium price and quantity, located at the intersection of the demand and supply curves? To find out, we must solve our system of two equations with two unknown variables (P and Q). One way to do so is to get rid of the Q variable by multiplying the second equation by -1 and subtracting it from the first equation:

$$Q = a - bP$$

$$-Q = -c - dP$$

thus getting:

$$0 = (a - c) - (b + d)P$$

Solving for P, we immediately obtain the equilibrium price:

$$P^* = \frac{a - c}{b + d}$$

Having found the value of P we then need only to introduce this value in either of the two equations of the system to find the equilibrium quantity. If there is no mistake, the value of Q should turn out to be the same, regardless of the chosen equation. Let us introduce the value of P^* in the demand equation. We get the equilibrium quantity:

$$Q^* = a - bP^* = a - b\frac{(a - c)}{(b + d)}$$

$$Q^* = \frac{ad + cb}{b + d}$$

You now know how to find the market equilibrium price and quantity when you are given the demand and supply equations. Obviously, any change in the intercepts of the curves or in the slopes of the curves will modify the equilibrium values.

FIGURE 13 The Algebra of Supply and Demand

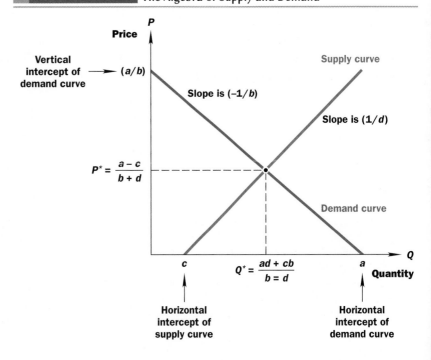

THE BUILDING BLOCKS OF DEMAND AND SUPPLY

T he next four chapters describe and analyze the basic building blocks with which economists analyze markets and their two essential elements: buyers (consumers) and sellers (producers). As in a piece of machinery, all the parts of a market operate simultaneously together, so there is no logical place to begin the story. Furthermore, the heart of the story is not found in the individual components, but in the way they fit together. The four central microeconomics chapters start off with the separate components, but then assemble them into a working model of how firms determine price and output simultaneously. Then Chapter 9 deals with stocks and bonds as tools that help business firms obtain the finances they need to operate and as earnings opportunities for potential investors in firms.

5

CONSUMER CHOICE:
INDIVIDUAL AND MARKET DEMAND

My work may have sometimes assumed too much rationality, but I believe it has been an antidote to the extensive research that does not credit people with enough rationality.

GARY S. BECKER (1930–), 1992 RECIPIENT OF THE SVERIGES RIKSBANK PRIZE IN ECONOMIC SCIENCES IN MEMORY OF ALFRED NOBEL, 1996

Y ou are about to start a new school year, and your favourite clothing store is having a sale. So you decide to stock up on jeans. How do you decide how many pairs to buy? How is your decision affected by the price of the jeans and the amount of money you earned in your summer job? How can you get the most for your money? Economic analysis provides some rational ways to make these decisions. Do you think about your decision as an economist would, either consciously or unconsciously? Should you? By the end of the chapter, you will be able to analyze such purchase decisions using concepts called *utility* and *marginal analysis*.

Chapter 4 introduced you to the idea of supply and demand and the use of supply and demand curves to analyze how markets determine prices and quantities of products sold. This chapter will investigate the underpinnings of the demand curve, which, as we have already seen, shows us half of the market picture.

CONTENTS

PUZZLE: *Why Shouldn't Water Be Worth More Than Diamonds?*

When Adam Smith lectured at the University of Glasgow in the 1760s, he introduced the study of demand by posing a puzzle. Common sense, he said, suggests that the price of a commodity must somehow depend on what that good is worth to consumers—on the amount of *utility* that the commodity offers. Yet, Smith pointed out, some cases suggest that a good's utility may have little influence on its price.

Smith cited diamonds and water as examples. He noted that water has enormous value to most consumers; indeed, its availability can be a matter of life and death. Yet water often sells at a very low price or is even free of charge, whereas diamonds sell for very high prices even though few people would consider them necessities. We will soon be in a position to see how marginal analysis, the powerful method of analysis introduced in this chapter, helps to resolve this paradox.

SOURCE: © din/Shutterstock

SOURCE: © Thinkstock/Getty Images

SCARCITY AND DEMAND

When economists use the term *demand*, they do not mean mere wishes, needs, requirements, or preferences. Rather, *demand* refers to actions of consumers who, so to speak, put their money where their mouths are. *Demand* assumes that consumers *can* pay for the goods in question and that they are also *willing* to pay out the necessary money. Some of us may, for example, dream of owning a racehorse or a Lear jet, but only a few wealthy individuals can turn such fantasies into effective demands.

Any individual consumer's choices are subject to one overriding constraint that is at least partly beyond that consumer's control: The individual has only a limited income available to spend. This scarcity of income is the obvious reason why less affluent consumers demand fewer computers, trips to foreign countries, and expensive restaurant meals than wealthy consumers do. The scarcity of income affects even the richest of all spenders—the government. The Canadian federal government spends billions of dollars on the armed services, postsecondary education, and a variety of other services, but governments rarely, if ever, have the funds to buy everything they want.

Because income is limited (and thus is a scarce resource), any consumer's purchase decisions for different commodities must be *interdependent*. The number of movies that Jane can afford to see depends on the amount she spends on new clothing. If John's parents have just sunk a lot of money into an expensive addition to their home, they may have to give up a vacation trip. Thus, no one can truly understand the demand curves for movies and clothing, or for homes and vacation trips, without considering demand curves for alternative goods.

The quantity of movies demanded, for example, probably depends not only on ticket prices but also on the prices of clothing. Thus, a big sale on shirts might induce Jane to splurge on several, leaving her with little or no cash to spend on movies. So, an analysis of consumer demand that focuses on only one commodity at a time leaves out an essential part of the story. Nevertheless, to make the analysis easier to follow, we begin by considering products in isolation. That is, we employ what is called *partial analysis*, using a standard simplifying assumption. This assumption requires that all other variables remain unchanged. Later in the chapter and in the appendix, we will tell a fuller story.

UTILITY: A TOOL TO ANALYZE PURCHASE DECISIONS

In the Canadian economy, millions of consumers make millions of decisions every day. You decide to buy a movie ticket instead of a paperback novel. Your roommate decides to buy two tubes of toothpaste rather than one tube or three tubes. How do people make these decisions?

Economists have constructed a simple theory of consumer choice based on the hypothesis that each consumer spends her or his income in the way that yields the greatest amount of satisfaction, or *utility*. This seems to be a reasonable starting point, because it says only that people do what they prefer. To make the theory operational, we need a way to measure utility.

A century ago, economists envisioned utility as an indicator of the pleasure a person derives from consuming some set of goods, and they thought that utility could be measured directly in some kind of psychological units (sometimes called *utils*) after somehow reading the consumer's mind. Gradually, they came to realize that this was an unnecessary and, perhaps, impossible task. How many utils did you get from the last movie you saw? You probably cannot answer that question because you have no idea what a util is. Neither does anyone else.

But you may be able to answer a different question like, "How many hamburgers would you give up to get that movie ticket?" If you answer "three," no one can say how many utils you get from seeing a film, but they can say that you get more from the movie than from a single hamburger. When economists approach the issue in this manner, hamburgers, rather than the more vague *utility*, become the unit of measurement. They can say that the utility of a movie (to you) is three hamburgers.

Early in the twentieth century, economists concluded that this indirect way of measuring consumer benefit gave them all they needed to build a theory of consumer choice. One can measure the benefit of a movie ticket by asking how much of some other commodity (like hamburgers) you are willing to give up for it. Any commodity will do for this purpose, but the simplest, most commonly used choice, and the one that we will use in this book, is money.[1]

The Purpose of Utility Analysis: Analyzing How People *Behave*, Not What They *Think*

Here, a very important warning is required: Money (or hamburgers, for that matter) can be a very imperfect measure of utility. The reason is that measuring utility by means of money is like measuring the length of a table with a rubber yardstick. The value of a dollar changes—sometimes a great deal—depending on circumstances. For example, if you win $10 million in the lottery, an additional dollar can confidently be expected to add much less to your well-being than it would have one week earlier. After you hit the jackpot, you may not hesitate to spend $9 on a hamburger, whereas before you would not have spent more than $3. This difference does not mean that you now love hamburgers three times as much as before. Consequently, although we use money as an indicator of utility in this book, it should not be taken as an indicator of the consumer's psychological attitude toward the goods he or she buys.

So why do we use the concept of money utility? There are two good reasons. First, we do know how to approach *measuring* it (see next section), but we do not know how

---

[1] Note to Instructors: You will recognize that, although not using the terms, we are distinguishing here between neo-classical *cardinal utility* and *ordinal utility*. Moreover, throughout the book, *marginal utility in money terms* (or *money marginal utility*) is used as a synonym for the *marginal rate of substitution* between money and the commodity.

to measure what is going on inside the consumer's mind. Second, and much more important, it is extremely useful for analyzing demand behaviour—what consumers will spend to buy some good, even though it is *not* a good indicator of what is going on deep inside their brains.

▪ Total Versus Marginal Utility

The **total utility** of a quantity of a good to a consumer (measured in money terms) is the maximum amount of money that he or she is willing to give up in exchange for it.

Thus, we define the **total monetary utility** of a particular bundle of goods to a particular consumer as *the largest sum of money that person will voluntarily give up in exchange for those goods.* For example, imagine that you love pizza and are planning to buy four pizzas for a party you are hosting. You are, as usual, a bit low on cash. Taking this into account, you decide that you are willing to buy the four pies if they cost up to $52 in total, but you're not willing to pay more than $52. As economists, we then say that the *total utility* of four pizzas to you is $52, the maximum amount you are willing to spend to have them.

Total monetary utility (from which we will drop the word "monetary" from here on) measures your dollar evaluation of the benefit that you derive from your total purchases of some commodity during some selected period of time. *Total* utility is what really matters to you. But to understand which decisions most effectively promote total utility, we must make use of a related concept, **marginal** (monetary) **utility.** The word *marginal* must not be taken as meaning something of little importance. Quite the contrary—in economics, the concepts associated with the word *marginal* are of supreme importance. *Marginal* in economics is understood as *something additional. Marginal utility* is the additional utility derived from an increment of one unit.

The **marginal utility** of a commodity to a consumer (measured in money terms) is the maximum amount of money that she or he is willing to pay for *one more unit* of that commodity.

Your marginal utility of some good, X, is defined as *the addition to total utility that you derive by consuming one more unit of X.* If you consumed two pizzas last month, marginal utility indicates how much additional pleasure you would have received by increasing your consumption to three pizzas. Marginal utility provides *a tool* with which you can analyze how much of a commodity that you must buy to make your total utility as large as possible. Before showing how marginal utility helps to find what quantity of purchases makes total utility as large as possible, we must first discuss how these two figures are calculated and just what they mean.

Table 1 helps to clarify the distinction between marginal and total utility and shows how the two are related. The first two columns show how much *total* utility (measured in money terms) you derive from various quantities of pizza, ranging from zero to eight per month. For example, a single pizza pie is worth (no more than) $15 to you, two are worth $28 in total, and so on. The *marginal* utility is the *difference* between any two successive total utility figures. For example, if you have consumed three pizzas (worth $40.50 to you), an additional pie brings your total utility to $52. Your marginal utility is thus the difference between the two, or $11.50.

Remember: Whenever we use the terms *total utility* and *marginal utility*, we define them in terms of the consumer's willingness to part with *money* for the commodity, not in some unobservable (and imaginary) psychological units.

▪ The Principle of Diminishing Marginal Utility

With these definitions, we can now propose a simple hypothesis about consumer tastes:

The more of a good a consumer has, the less *marginal* utility an additional unit contributes to overall satisfaction, if all other things remain unchanged.

Economists use this plausible proposition widely. The idea is based on the assertion that every person has a *hierarchy* of uses for a particular commodity. All of these uses are valuable, but some are more valuable

TABLE 1
Your Total and Marginal Utility for Pizza This Month

(1) Quantity (Q) Pizzas per Month	(2) Total Utility (TU)	(3) Marginal Utility (MU) = (ΔTU/ΔQ)	(4) Point in Figure 1
0	$0.00		
1	15.00	$15.00	A
2	28.00	13.00	B
3	**40.50**	12.50	C
4	**52.00**	**11.50**	D
5	60.00	8.00	E
6	65.00	5.00	F
7	68.00	3.00	G
8	68.00	0.00	H

Note: Each entry in Column (3) is the difference between successive entries in Column (2). This is what is indicated by the zigzag lines.

than others. Take pizza, for example. Perhaps you consider your *own* appetite for pizza first—you buy enough pizza to satiate your own personal taste for it. But pizza may also provide you with an opportunity to satisfy your social needs. So instead of eating all the pizza you buy, you decide to have a pizza party. First on your guest list may be your boyfriend or girlfriend. Next priority is your roommate, and, if you feel really flush, you may even invite your economics instructor! So, if you buy only one pizza, you eat it yourself. If you buy a second pizza, you share it with your special friend. A third is shared with your roommate, and so on.

The point is: Each pizza contributes something to your satisfaction, but each *additional* pizza contributes less (measured in terms of money) than its predecessor because it satisfies a lower-priority use. This idea, in essence, is the logic behind the **principle of diminishing marginal utility,** which asserts that the more of a commodity you already possess, the smaller the amount of (marginal) utility you derive from acquisition of yet another unit of the commodity.

The third column of Table 1 illustrates this concept. The marginal utility (abbreviated MU) of the first pizza is $15; that is, you are willing to pay *up to* $15 for the first pie. The second is worth no more than $13 to you, the third pizza only $12.50, and so on, until you are willing to pay only $5 for the sixth pizza (the MU of that pizza is $5).

Figure 1, a marginal utility curve, shows a graph of the numbers in the first and third columns of Table 1. For example, point *D* indicates that the MU of a fourth pizza is $11.50. So, at any higher price, you will not buy a fourth pizza.

Note that the curve for marginal utility has a negative slope; it also illustrates how marginal utility diminishes as the quantity of the good rises. Like most laws, however, the principle of diminishing marginal utility has exceptions. Some people want even more of some good that is particularly significant to them as they acquire more, as in the case of addiction. Stamp collectors and alcoholics provide good examples. The stamp collector who has a few stamps may consider the acquisition of one more to be mildly amusing. The person who has a large and valuable collection may be prepared to go to the ends of the earth for another stamp. Similarly, an alcoholic who finds the first beer quite pleasant may find the fourth or fifth to be absolutely irresistible. Economists generally treat such cases of increasing marginal utility as anomalies. For most goods and most people, marginal utility declines as consumption increases.

Table 1 illustrates another noteworthy relationship. Observe that as someone buys more and more units of the commodity—that is, as that person moves further down the table—the *total* utility numbers get larger and larger, while the *marginal* utility numbers get smaller and smaller. The reasons should now be fairly clear. The marginal utility numbers keep declining, as the principle of diminishing marginal utility tells us they will. But *total* utility keeps rising as long as marginal utility remains positive. A person who owns ten compact disks, other things being equal, is better off (has higher total utility) than a person who possesses only nine, as long as the MU of the tenth CD is positive. In summary:

The **principle of diminishing marginal utility** asserts that additional units of a commodity are worth less and less to a consumer in money terms. As the individual's consumption increases, the marginal utility of each additional unit declines.

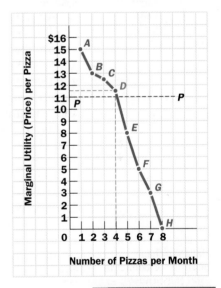

FIGURE 1

A Marginal Utility (or Demand) Curve: Your Demand for Pizza This Month

As a rule, as a person acquires more of a commodity, total utility increases and marginal utility from that good decreases, all other things being equal. In particular, when a commodity is very scarce, economists expect it to have a high marginal utility, even though it may provide little total utility because people have so little of the item.

Using Marginal Utility: The Optimal Purchase Rule

Now let us use the concept of marginal utility to analyze consumer choices. Consumers must always choose among the many commodities that compete for their limited supply of dollars. How can you use the idea of utility to help you understand the purchase choices permitted by those dollars that best serve your preferences?

You can obviously choose among many different quantities of pizza, any of which will add to your total utility. But which of these quantities will yield the greatest net benefits? If pizza was all that you were considering buying, in theory the choice would involve a simple calculation. We would need a statistical table that listed all of the alternative numbers of pizzas that you may conceivably buy. The table should indicate the *net* utility that each possible choice yields. That is, it should include the total utility that you would get from a particular number of pizzas, minus the utility of the other purchases you would forgo by having to pay for them—their opportunity cost. We could then simply read your optimal choice from this imaginary table—the number of pizzas that would give you the highest net utility number.

Even in theory, calculating optimal decisions is, unfortunately, more difficult than that. No real table of net utilities exists; an increase in expenditure on pizzas would mean less money available for clothing or movies, and you must balance the benefits of spending on each of these items against spending on the others. All of this means that we must find a more effective technique to determine optimal pizza purchases (as well as purchases of clothing, entertainment, and other things). That technique is **marginal analysis.**

Marginal analysis is a method for calculating optimal choices—the choices that best promote the decision maker's objective. It works by testing whether, and by how much, a small change in a decision will move things toward or away from the goal.

To see how marginal analysis helps consumers determine their optimal purchase decisions, first recall our assumption that you are trying to maximize the total *net* utility you obtain from your pizza purchases. That is, you are trying to select the number of pies that maximizes the total utility the pizzas provide you *minus the total utility you give up with the money you must pay for them.*

We can compare the analysis of the optimal decision-making process to the process of climbing a hill. First, imagine that you consider the possibility of buying only one pizza. Then suppose you consider buying two pizzas, and so on. If two pizzas give you a higher total net utility than one pizza, you may think of yourself as moving higher up the total net utility hill. Buying more pizzas enables you to ascend that hill higher and higher, until at some quantity you reach the top—*the optimal purchase quantity.* Then, if you buy any more, you will have overshot the peak and begun to descend the hill.

Figure 2 shows such a hill and describes how your total net utility changes when you change the number of pizzas you buy. It shows the upward-sloping part of the hill, where the number of purchases has not yet brought you to the top. Then it shows the point (*M*) at which you have bought enough pizzas to make your net utility as large as possible (the peak occurs at four pizzas). At any point to the right of *M*, you have overshot the optimal purchase. You are on the downward side of the hill because you have bought more than enough pizzas to best serve your interests; you have bought too many to maximize your net utility.

How does marginal analysis help you to find that optimal purchase quantity, and how does it warn you if you are planning to purchase too little (so that you are still on the ascending portion of the hill) or too much (so that you are descending)? The numerical example in Table 1 will help reveal the answers. The marginal utility of, for example, a third pizza is $12.50. This means that the total utility you obtain from three pizzas ($40.50) is exactly $12.50 higher than the total utility you get from two pizzas ($28). As long as marginal utility is a positive number, the more you purchase, the more total utility you will get.

That shows the benefit side of the purchase. But such a transaction also has a debit side—the amount you must pay for the purchase. Suppose that the price is $11 per pizza. Then the marginal *net* utility of the third pizza is marginal utility minus price, $12.50 minus $11, or $1.50. This is the amount that the third pizza adds to your total net utility. (See the third and fourth lines of Table 1.) So you really *are* better off with three pizzas than with two.

We can generalize the logic of the previous paragraph to show how marginal analysis solves the problem of finding the optimal purchase quantity, given the price of the commodity being purchased.

FIGURE 2

Finding Your Optimal Pizza Purchase Quantity: Maximizing Total Net Utility

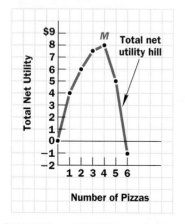

Total Net Utility equals Total Utility minus Total Expenditure (Price × Quantity)

RULE 1:   If marginal net utility is positive, the consumer must be buying too small a quantity to maximize total net utility. Because marginal utility exceeds price, the consumer can increase total net utility further by buying (at least) one more unit of the product. In other words, since marginal net utility (which is marginal utility minus price) tells us how much the purchase of an additional unit raises or lowers total net utility, a positive marginal net utility means that total net utility is still going uphill. The consumer has not yet bought enough to get to the top of the hill.

RULE 2:   No purchase quantity for which marginal net utility is a negative number can ever be optimal. In such a case, a buyer can get a higher total net utility by cutting back the purchase quantity. The purchaser would have climbed too far on the net utility hill, passing the topmost point and beginning to descend.

This leaves only one option. The consumer cannot be at the top of the hill if marginal net utility ($MU - P$) is greater than zero—that is, if MU is greater than P. Similarly, the purchase quantity cannot be optimal if marginal net utility at that quantity ($MU - P$) is less than zero—that is, if MU is less than P. The purchase quantity can be optimal, giving the consumer the highest possible total net utility, only if:

Marginal net utility = MU − P = 0; that is, if MU = P

Consequently, the hypothesis that the consumer chooses purchases to make the largest net contribution to total utility leads to the following *optimal purchase rule:*

It always pays the consumer to buy more of any commodity whose marginal utility (measured in money) exceeds its price, and less of any commodity whose marginal utility is less than its price. When possible, the consumer should buy a quantity of each good at which price (P) and marginal utility (MU) are exactly equal—that is, at which

MU = P

because only these quantities will maximize the *net total utility* that the consumer gains from purchases, given the fact that these decisions must divide available money among all purchases.[2]

Notice that, although the consumer really cares about maximizing total *net* utility (and marginal utility is not the goal), we have used marginal analysis as a *guide* to the optimal purchase quantity. Marginal analysis serves only as an analytic method—as a means to an end. This goal is maximization of total net utility, not marginal utility or marginal net utility. In Chapter 8, after several other applications of marginal analysis, we will generalize the discussion to show how thinking "at the margin" allows us to make optimal decisions in a wide variety of fields besides consumer purchases.

Let's briefly review graphically how the underlying logic of the marginal way of thinking leads to the optimal purchase rule, $MU = P$. Refer back to the graph of marginal utilities of pizzas (Figure 1). Suppose that Paul's Pizza Parlour currently sells pizzas at a price of $11 (the dashed line PP in the graph). At this price, five pizzas (point E) is *not* an optimal purchase because the $8 marginal utility of the fifth pizza is less than its $11 price. You would be better off buying only four pizzas because that choice would save $11 with only an $8 loss in utility—a net gain of $3—from the decision to buy one less pizza.

You should note that, in practice, there may not exist a number of pizzas at which MU is *exactly* equal to P. In our example, the fourth pizza is worth $11.50, whereas the fifth pizza is worth $8—neither of them is *exactly* equal to their $11 price. If you could purchase an appropriate (in-between) quantity (say, 4.38 pizzas), then MU would, indeed, exactly equal P. But Paul's Pizza Parlour will not sell you 4.38 pizzas,

---

[2] Economists can equate a dollar price with marginal utility only because they measure marginal utility in money terms (or, as they more commonly state, because they deal with the marginal rate of substitution of money for the commodity). If marginal utility were measured in some psychological units not directly translatable into money terms, a comparison of P and MU would have no meaning. However, MU could also be measured in terms of any commodity other than money. (Example: How many pizzas are you willing to trade for an additional ticket to a basketball game?)

so you must do the best you can. You buy four pizzas, for which MU comes as close as possible to equality with *P*.

The rule for optimal purchases states that you should not buy a quantity at which MU is higher than price (points like *A*, *B*, and *C* in Figure 1) because a larger purchase would make you even better off. Similarly, you should not end up at points *E*, *F*, *G*, and *H*, at which MU is below price, because you would be better off buying less. Rather, you should buy four pizzas (point *D*), where *P* = MU (approximately). Thus, marginal analysis leads naturally to the rule for optimal purchase quantities.

> The decision to purchase a quantity of a good that leaves marginal utility greater than price cannot maximize total net utility, because buying an additional unit would add more to total utility than it would increase cost. Similarly, it cannot be optimal for the consumer to buy a quantity of a good that leaves marginal utility less than price, because then a reduction in the quantity purchased would save more money than it would sacrifice in utility. Consequently, the consumer can maximize total net utility only if the purchase quantity brings marginal utility as close as possible to equality with price.

Note that price is an objective, observable figure determined by the market, whereas marginal utility is subjective and reflects consumer tastes. Because individual consumers lack the power to influence the price, they must adjust purchase quantities to make their subjective marginal utility of each good equal to the price given by the market.

■ From Diminishing Marginal Utility to Downward-Sloping Demand Curves

We will see next that the marginal utility curve and the demand curve of a consumer who maximizes total net utility are one and the same. The two curves are identical. This observation enables us to use the optimal purchase rule to show that the principle of diminishing marginal utility implies that demand curves typically slope downward to the right; that is, they have negative slopes.[3] To do this, we use the list of marginal utilities in Table 1 to determine how many pizzas you would buy at any particular price. For example, we see that at a price of $8, it pays for you to buy five pizzas, because the MU of the fifth pizza ordered is $8. Table 2 gives several alternative prices and the optimal purchase quantity corresponding to each price derived in just this way. (To make sure you understand the logic behind the optimal purchase rule, verify that the entries in the right-hand column of Table 2 are, in fact, correct.) This *demand schedule* appears graphically as the *demand curve* shown in Figure 1. This demand curve is simply the blue marginal utility curve. This is true, because at any given price, the consumer will find it best to buy the quantity at which marginal utility is equal to the given price. So at any given quantity of the commodity, the price at which it will be bought will equal its marginal utility. That is, at each quantity, the curve tells us the price at which it will be bought, so it is a demand curve. But the curve also tells us the marginal utility at any such quantity, so it is also a marginal utility curve. You can also see its negative slope in the graph, which is a characteristic of demand curves.

Let's examine the logic underlying the negatively sloped demand curve a bit more carefully. If you are purchasing the optimal number of pizzas and then the price falls, you will find that your marginal utility for that product is now *above* the newly reduced price. For example, Table 1 indicates that at a price of $12.50 per pizza, you would optimally buy three pizzas, because the MU of the fourth pizza is only $11.50. If the price falls below $11.50, it then pays to purchase more—it pays to buy the fourth

TABLE 2

List of Optimal Quantities of Pizza for You to Purchase at Alternative Prices

Price	Quantity of Pizzas Purchased per Month
$ 3.00	7
5.00	6
8.00	5
11.50	**4**
12.50	3
13.00	2
15.00	1

Note: For simplicity of explanation, the prices shown have been chosen to equal the marginal utilities in Table 1. In-between prices would make the optimal choices involve fractions of pizzas (say, 2.6 pizzas).

[3] If you need to review the concept of slope, refer to the Chapter 1 Appendix discussion on graphic analysis.

pizza because its MU now exceeds its price. The marginal utility of the next (fifth) pizza is only $8. Thus, if the price falls below $8, it would pay you to buy that fifth pizza. So, the lower the price, the more the consumer will find it advantageous to buy, which is what is meant by saying that the demand curve has a negative slope.

Note the critical role that the principle of diminishing marginal utility plays here. If *P* falls, a consumer who wishes to maximize total utility must buy more, to the point that

Do Consumers Really Behave "Rationally" and Maximize Utility?

It may strike you that this chapter's discussion of the consumer's decision process—equating price and marginal utility—does not resemble the thought processes of any consumer you have ever met. Most consumers make rather complex decisions very quickly, provided they believe that their choice is sufficiently informed. Consumers do not try to handle all possible alternatives. Instead, they make sure that a few self-imposed criteria are being met. They make fast and frugal decisions, often based on simple rules. Buyers make decisions instinctively, without any calculation of marginal utilities or anything like them. That is true—yet it need not undermine the pertinence of the discussion.

When you give a command to your computer, you actually activate some electronic switches and start some operations in what is referred to as *binary code*. Most computer users do not know they are having this effect and do not care. Yet they are activating binary code nevertheless, and the analysis of the computation process does not misrepresent the facts by describing this sequence. In the same way, if a shopper divides her purchasing power among various purchase options in a way that yields the largest possible utility for her money, she *must* be following the rules of marginal analysis, even though she is totally unaware of this choice.

A growing body of experimental evidence, however, has pointed out some persistent deviations between reality and the picture of consumer behaviour provided by marginal analysis. Experimental studies by groups of economists and psychologists have turned up many examples of behaviour that seem to violate the optimal purchase rule. For instance, one study offered two groups of respondents what were really identical options, presumably yielding similar marginal utilities. Despite this equality, depending on differences in some irrelevant information that was also provided to the respondents, the two groups made very different choices.

One group of subjects received the information in parentheses, and the other received the information in brackets. . . .

[*Problem 1*]. Imagine that you are about to purchase . . . a calculator for ($15)[$125]. The calculator salesman informs you that the calculator you wish to buy is on sale for ($10)[$120] at the other branch of the store, located a 20-minute drive away. Would you make the trip to the other store?

The responses to the two versions of this problem were quite different. When the calculator cost $125 only 29 percent of the subjects said they would make the trip, whereas 68 percent said they would go when the calculator cost only $15.

Thus, in this problem *both* groups were really being told they could save $5 on the price of a product if they took a 20-minute trip to another store. Yet, depending on an irrelevant fact, whether the product was a cheap or an expensive model, the number of persons willing to make the same trip to save the same amount of money was very

different. The point is that human purchase decisions are affected by the environment in which the decision is made, and not only by the price and marginal utility of the purchase.

Another example of how environment can affect our decisions has been provided by an experiment conducted by Jack L. Knetsch, a professor at Simon Fraser University, in collaboration with Daniel Kahneman, who shared the Nobel Prize in Economics in 2002 for his research on human judgment and decision making, and Richard H. Thaler, a professor at the University of Chicago.

SOURCE: Courtesy of Texas Instruments Incorporated.

Samples of the residents of Toronto and Vancouver were asked a series of questions over the telephone about whether they thought that a particular economic action was "fair." In some cases, alternative versions of the same question were presented to different groups of respondents. For each question, respondents were asked to judge whether the action was completely fair, acceptable, somewhat unfair, or very unfair. In reporting the results, the first two categories were combined and called "acceptable" and the last two were combined and called "unfair." Perceptions of fairness strongly depended on whether the question was framed as a reduction in gain or an actual loss. For example:

[*Question 1a*]. A shortage has developed for a popular model of automobile, and customers must now wait two months for delivery. A dealer has been selling cars at list price. Now the dealer prices this model at $200 above list price.
Acceptable: 29 percent; Unfair: 71 percent

[*Question 1b*]. A shortage has developed for a popular model of automobile, and customers must now wait two months for delivery. A dealer has been selling these cars at a discount of $200 below list price. Now the dealer sells this model only at list price.
Acceptable: 58 percent; Unfair: 42 percent

The marginal (negative) benefit to the customers is the same in both situations, but still the $200 surcharge (which is perceived as a loss) is considered more unfair than the elimination of a $200 discount (which is perceived as the reduction of a gain). This is called the *loss aversion effect* or the *endowment effect*.

SOURCE: Daniel Kahneman, Jack L. Knetsch, and Richard H. Thaler, "The endowment effect, loss aversion and status quo bias," *Journal of Economic Perspectives*, 5(3), Winter 1991, p. 203. Reprinted with permission.

MU falls correspondingly. According to the principle of diminishing marginal utility, the only way to do this is to increase the quantity purchased.

Although this explanation is a bit abstract, we can easily rephrase it in practical terms. We have noted that individuals put commodities to various uses, each of which has a different priority. For you, buying a pizza for your date has a higher priority than using the pizza to feed your roommate. If the price of pizzas is high, it makes sense for you to buy only enough for the high-priority uses—those that offer high marginal utilities. When price declines, however, it pays to purchase more of the good—enough for some lower-priority uses. The same general assumption about consumer psychology underlies both the principle of diminishing marginal utility and the negative slope of the demand curve. They are really two different ways of describing consumers' assumed attitudes.

CONSUMER CHOICE AS A TRADE-OFF: OPPORTUNITY COST

We have expressed the optimal purchase rule as the principle guiding a decision about how much of one commodity to buy. However, we have already observed that the scarcity of income lurking in the background turns every decision into a trade-off. Given each consumer's limited income, a decision to buy a new car usually means giving up some travel or postponing furniture purchases. The money that the consumer gives up when she makes a purchase—her expenditure on that purchase—is only one measure of the true underlying cost to her.

The real cost is the *opportunity cost* of the purchase—the commodities that she must give up as a result of the purchase decision. This opportunity cost calculation has already been noted in Chapters 1 and 3—we must always consider the real cost of our purchase decisions, which take into account how much of *other* things they force us to forgo. Any decision to buy implies some such trade-off because scarcity constrains all economic decisions. Although their dilemmas may not inspire much pity, even billionaires face very real trade-offs: Invest $200 million in an office building, or go for the $200 million hockey team?

This last example has another important implication. The trade-off from a consumer's purchase decision does not always involve giving up another *consumer good*. This is true, for example, of the choice between consumption and saving. Consider a high school student who is deciding whether to buy a new car or to save the money to pay for college or university. If he saves the money, it can grow by earning interest, so that the original amount plus interest earned will be available to pay for tuition and board three years later. A decision to cut down on consumption now and put the money into the bank means that the student will be wealthier in the future because of the interest he will earn. This, in turn, will enable the student to afford more of his school expenses at the future date when those expenses arise. So the opportunity cost of a new car today is the forgone opportunity to save funds for the future. We conclude:

> From the viewpoint of economic analysis, the true cost of any purchase is the opportunity cost of that purchase, rather than the amount of money that is spent on it.

The opportunity cost of a purchase can be either higher or lower than its price. For example, if your computer cost you $1,800, but the purchase required you to take off two hours from your job that pays $20 per hour, the true cost of the computer—that is, the opportunity cost—is the amount of goods you could have bought with $1,840 (the $1,800 price plus the $40 in earnings that the purchase of the computer required you to give up). In this case, the opportunity cost ($1,840, measured in money terms) is higher than the price of the purchase ($1,800). (For an example in which price is higher than opportunity cost, see Test Yourself Question 4 at the end of the chapter.)

Consumer's Surplus: The Net Gain from a Purchase

The optimal purchase rule, MU (approximately) = P, assumes that the consumer always tries to maximize the money value of the total utility from the purchase *minus* the amount spent to make that purchase.[4] Thus, any difference between the price consumers *actually* pay for a commodity and the price they would be *willing* to pay for that item represents a net utility gain in some sense. Economists give the name **consumer's surplus** to that difference—that is, to the net gain in total utility that a purchase brings to a buyer. The consumer is trying to make the purchase decisions that maximize

Consumer's surplus = Total utility (in money terms) − Total expenditure

Thus, just as economists usually assume that business firms maximize total profit (equal to total revenue minus total cost), they often assume that consumers maximize consumer's surplus, that is, the difference between the total utility of the purchased commodity and the amount that consumers spend on it.

The concept of *consumer's surplus* seems to suggest that the consumer gains some sort of free bonus, or surplus, for every purchase. In many cases, this idea seems absurd. How can it be true, particularly for goods whose prices seem to be outrageous?

The answer relies on the fact that both parties must gain from a voluntary exchange or else one of them will refuse to participate. The same must be true when a consumer makes a *voluntary* purchase from a supermarket or an appliance store. If the consumer did not expect a net gain from the transaction, he or she would simply not bother to buy the good. Even if the seller was to "overcharge" by some standard, that would merely reduce the size of the consumer's net gain, not eliminate it entirely. If the seller is so greedy as to charge a price that wipes out the net gain altogether, the punishment will fit the crime: The consumer will refuse to buy, and the greedy seller's would-be gains will never materialize. The basic principle states that every purchase that is not on the borderline—that is, every purchase except those about which the consumer is indifferent—must yield *some* consumer's surplus.

But how large is that surplus? At least in theory, it can be measured with the aid of a table or graph of marginal utilities (Table 1 and Figure 1). Suppose that, as in our earlier example, the price of a large pizza is $11 and you purchase four pizzas. Table 3 reproduces the marginal utility numbers from Table 1. It shows that the first pizza is worth $15 to you, so at the $11 price, you reap a net gain (surplus) of $15 minus $11, or $4, by buying that pizza. The second pizza also brings you some surplus, but less than the first one does, because the marginal utility diminishes. Specifically, the second pizza provides a surplus of $13 minus $11, or $2. Reasoning in the same way, the third pizza gives you a surplus of $12.50 minus $11, or $1.50. It is only the fourth pizza—the last one that you purchase—that offers little or no surplus because, by the optimal purchase rule, the marginal utility of the last unit is approximately equal to its price.

We can now easily determine the total consumer's surplus that you obtain by buying four pizzas. It is simply the sum of the surpluses received from each pizza. Table 3 shows that this consumer's total surplus is

$4 + $2 + $1.50 + $0.50 = $8

This way of looking at the optimal purchase rule shows why a buyer must always gain some consumer's surplus if she buys more than one unit of a good. Note that the price of each unit remains the same, but the marginal utility diminishes as more units are purchased. The last unit bought yields only a tiny consumer's surplus because MU (approximately) = P. But all prior units must have had marginal utilities greater than the MU of the last unit because of diminishing marginal utility.

We can be more precise about the calculation of the consumer's surplus with the help of a graph showing marginal utility as a set of bars. The bars labelled *A, B, C,* and *D* in Figure 3 come from the corresponding points on the marginal utility curve (demand curve) in Figure 1. The consumer's surplus from each pizza equals the marginal utility of that pizza minus the price you pay for it. By representing

> **Consumer's surplus** is difference between the value to the consumer of the quantity of Commodity *X* purchased and the amount that the market requires the consumer to pay for that quantity of *X*.

TABLE 3

Calculating Marginal Net Utility (Consumer's Surplus) from Your Pizza Purchases

Quantity	Marginal Utility	Price	Marginal Net Utility (Surplus)
0			
1	$15.00	$11.00	$4.00
2	13.00	11.00	2.00
3	12.50	11.00	1.50
4	11.50	11.00	0.50
Total			$8.00

---

[4] Again, in practice, the consumer can often only approximately equate MU and *P*.

consumer's surplus graphically, we can determine just how much surplus you obtain from your entire purchase by measuring the area between the marginal utility curve and the horizontal line representing the price of pizzas—in this case, the horizontal line *PP* represents the (fixed) $11 price.

In Figure 3, the bar whose upper-right corner is labelled *A* represents the $15 marginal utility you derive from the first pizza; the same interpretation applies to the bars *B*, *C*, and *D*. Clearly, the first pizza that you purchase yields a consumer's surplus of $4, indicated by the shaded part of bar *A*. The height of that part of the bar is equal to the $15 marginal utility minus the $11 price. In the same way, the next two shaded areas represent the surpluses offered by the second and third pizzas. The fourth pizza has the smallest shaded area because the height representing marginal utility is (as close as you can get to being) equal to the height representing price. Sum up the shaded areas in the graph to obtain, once again, the total consumer's surplus ($4 + $2 + $1.50 + $0.50 = $8) from a four-pizza purchase.

The consumer's surplus derived from buying a certain number of units of a good is obtained graphically by drawing the person's demand curve as a set of bars whose heights represent the marginal utilities of the corresponding quantities of the good,

FIGURE 3

Graphic Calculation of Consumer's Surplus

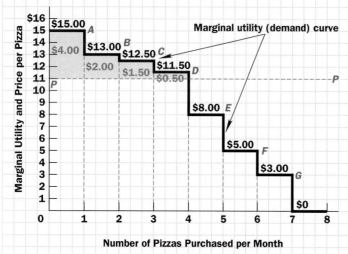

Resolving the Diamond–Water Puzzle

We can now use marginal utility analysis to analyze Adam Smith's paradox (which he was never able to explain) that diamonds are very expensive, whereas water is generally very cheap, even though water seems to offer far more utility. The resolution of the diamond–water puzzle is based on the distinction between marginal and total utility.

The *total* utility of water—its role as a necessity of life—is indeed much higher than that of diamonds. But price, as we have seen, is not related directly to *total* utility. Rather, the optimal purchase rule tells us that price tends to equal *marginal* utility. We have every reason to expect the marginal utility of water to be very low, whereas the marginal utility of a diamond is very high.

Given normal conditions, water is comparatively cheap to provide, so its price is generally quite low. Consumers thus use correspondingly large quantities of water. The principle of diminishing marginal utility, therefore, pushes down the marginal utility of water for a typical household to a low level. As the consumer's surplus diagram (Figure 3) suggests, this also means that its *total* utility is likely to be high.

In contrast, high-quality diamonds are scarce (partly because a monopoly keeps them so). As a result, the quantity of diamonds consumed is not large enough to drive down the MU of diamonds very far, so buyers of such luxuries must pay high prices for them. As a commodity becomes more scarce, its *marginal* utility and its market price rise, regardless of the size of its *total* utility. Also, as we have seen, because so little of the commodity is consumed, its *total* utility is likely to be comparatively low, despite its large *marginal* utility.

Thus, like many paradoxes, the diamond–water puzzle has a straightforward explanation. In this case, all one has to remember is that:

Scarcity raises price and *marginal* utility, but it generally reduces *total* utility. And although total utility measures the benefits consumers get from their consumption, it is marginal utility that is equal (approximately) to price.

and then drawing a horizontal line whose height is the price of the good. The sum of the heights of the bars above the horizontal line—that is, the area of the demand (marginal utility) bars above that horizontal line(the shaded areas)—measures the *total* consumer's surplus that the purchase yields.

Income and Quantity Demanded

Our application of marginal analysis has enabled us to examine the relationship between the *price* of a commodity and the quantity that will be purchased. But things other than price also influence the amount of a good that a consumer will purchase. As an example, we'll look at how quantity demanded responds to changes in *income*.

To be concrete, consider what happens to the number of ballpoint pens a consumer will buy when his real income rises. It may seem almost certain that he will buy more ballpoint pens than before, but that is not necessarily so. A rise in real income can either increase or decrease the quantity of any particular good purchased.

Why might an increase in income lead a consumer to buy fewer ballpoint pens? People buy some goods and services only because they cannot afford anything better. They may purchase used cars instead of new ones. They may use inexpensive ballpoint pens instead of finely crafted fountain pens or buy clothing secondhand instead of new. If their real incomes rise, they may then drop out of the used-car market and buy brand-new automobiles or buy more fountain pens and fewer ballpoint pens. Thus, a rise in real income will reduce the quantities of cheap pens and used cars demanded. Economists have given the rather descriptive name **inferior goods** to the class of commodities for which quantity demanded falls when income rises.

The upshot of this discussion is that economists cannot draw definite conclusions about the effects of a rise in consumer incomes on quantity demanded. But for most commodities, if incomes rise and prices do not change, quantity demanded will increase. Such an item is often called a *normal good*.

> An **inferior good** is a commodity whose quantity demanded falls when the purchaser's real income rises, all other things remaining equal.

FROM INDIVIDUAL DEMAND CURVES TO MARKET DEMAND CURVES

So far in this chapter, we have studied how *individual demand curves* are obtained from the logic of consumer choice. But to understand how the market system works, we must derive the relationship between price and quantity demanded *in the market as a whole*—the **market demand curve.** It is this market demand curve that plays a key role in the supply–demand analysis of price and output determination that we studied in Chapter 4.

> A **market demand curve** shows how the total quantity of some product demanded by *all* consumers in the market during a specified period of time changes as the price of that product changes, holding constant all other things.

Market Demand as a Horizontal Sum

If each individual pays no attention to other people's purchase decisions when making his or her own, we can easily derive the market demand curve from consumers' individual demand curves: As we will see next, we simply *add* the individual consumers' demand curves, as shown in Figure 4. The figure gives the individual demand curves *DD* and *ZZ* for two people, Alex and Naomi, and the total (market) demand curve, *MM.* Alex and Naomi are both consumers of the product.

We can derive this market demand curve in the following straightforward way:

Step 1: Pick any relevant price, say, $10.

Step 2: At that price, determine Alex's quantity demanded (9 units) from his demand curve in Figure 4(a) and Naomi's quantity demanded (6 units) from her demand curve in Figure 4(b). Note that these quantities are indicated by the line segment labelled *AA* for Alex and that labelled *NN* for Naomi.

Step 3: Add Naomi's and Alex's quantities demanded at the $10 price (segment *AA* + segment *NN* = 9 + 6 = 15) to yield the total quantity demanded by the market at that price. This gives segment *CC*, with total quantity demanded equal to

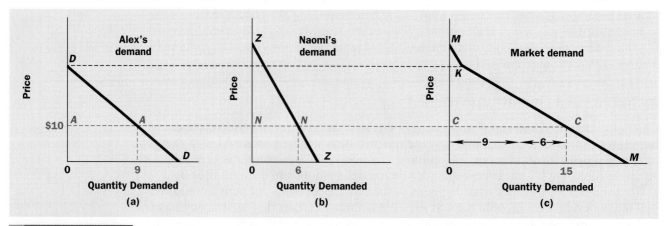

FIGURE 4

The Relationship Between Total Market Demand and the Demand of Individual Consumers Within That Market

The "law" of demand states that a lower price generally increases the amount of a commodity that people in a market are willing to buy. Therefore, for most goods, market demand curves have negative slopes.

15 units, in Figure 4(c). Notice that the addition constitutes a *horizontal* movement in the graph because we are adding quantities purchased and those quantities are measured by horizontal distances from the zero point of the graph.

Now repeat the process for each alternative price to obtain other points on the market demand curve until the shape of the entire curve *MM* appears. (The sharp angle at point *K* on the market curve occurs because that point corresponds to the price at which Alex, whose demand pattern is different from Naomi's, first enters the market. At any higher price, only Naomi is willing to buy anything.) That is all there is to the adding-up process. (Question: What would happen to the market demand curve if, say, another consumer entered the market?)

The "Law" of Demand

Just as for the case of an individual's demand curve, we expect the total quantity demanded by the market to move in the opposite direction from price. Economists call this relationship the **"law" of demand.**

Notice that we have put the word *law* in quotation marks. By now you will have observed that economic laws are not always obeyed, and we will see in a moment that the "law" of demand is not without exceptions. But first let us see why the "law" usually holds.

Earlier in this chapter, we explained that individual demand curves usually slope downward because of the principle of diminishing marginal utility. If individual demand curves slope downward, then the preceding discussion of the adding-up process implies that market demand curves must also slope downward. This is just common sense; if every consumer in the market buys fewer pizzas when the price of pizza rises, then the total quantity demanded in the market must surely fall.

But market demand curves may slope downward even if individual demand curves do not, because not all consumers are alike. Consider two examples where the individual's demand curve does not slope downward. If a bookstore reduces the price of a popular novel, it may draw many new customers, but few of the customers who already own a copy will buy a second one, despite the reduced price. Similarly, true devotees of pizza may maintain their pizza purchases unchanged even if prices rise to exorbitant levels, whereas others would not eat pizza even if you gave it to them free of charge. But the market prices of books and pizzas can still have a negative slope. As the price of pizza rises, less enthusiastic pizza eaters may drop out of the market entirely, leaving the expensive pie to the more devoted consumers. Thus, the quantity demanded declines as price rises, simply because higher prices induce more people to give up pizza completely. And for many commodities, lower prices encourage new customers to come into the *market* (for example, new book buyers), and it is these "fair weather" customers (rather than the negative slope of *individual* demand curves) that can be most important for the "law" of demand.

This is also illustrated in Figure 4, in which only Naomi will buy the product at a price higher than D. At a price lower than D, Alex will also purchase the product. Hence, below point K, the market demand curve lies farther to the right than it would have if Alex had not entered the market. Put another way, a rise in price from a level below D to a level above D would cut quantity demanded for two reasons: (1) because Naomi's demand curve has a negative slope and (2) because it would drive Alex out of the market.

We conclude, therefore, that the "law" of demand stands on fairly solid ground. If individual demand curves slope downward, then the market demand curve surely will, too. Furthermore, the market demand curve may slope downward, even when individual demand curves do not.

■ Exceptions to the "Law" of Demand

Some exceptions to the "law" of demand have been noted. One common exception occurs when people judge quality on the basis of price—they perceive a more expensive commodity as offering better quality. For example, many people buy name-brand aspirin, even if right next to it on the drugstore shelf they see an unbranded, generic aspirin with an identical chemical formula selling at half the price. The consumers who do buy the name-brand aspirin may well use comparative price to judge the relative qualities of different brands. They may prefer Brand X to Brand Y *because* X is slightly more expensive. If Brand X were to reduce its price below that of Brand Y, consumers might assume that it was no longer superior and actually reduce their purchases of X.

Another possible cause of an upward-sloping demand curve is snob appeal. If part of the reason for purchasing a $300,000 Rolls-Royce is to advertise one's wealth, a decrease in the car's price may actually reduce sales, even if the quality of the car remains unchanged. This is sometimes called the *Veblen effect*, named after the analysis of conspicuous consumption pursued by Thorstein Veblen (1857–1929), a well-known economist and sociologist in the early 1900s. Veblen thought that a substantial part of consumption is designed to signal one's status in society. Thus, teenagers in poor neighbourhoods will wear expensive sneakers or jewelry as a way to signal their relative wealth. Other types of exceptions have also been noted by economists. But, for most commodities, it seems reasonable to assume that demand curves have negative slopes.

This chapter has begun to take us behind the demand curve, to discuss how it is determined by the preferences of individual consumers. Chapter 6 will explore the demand curve further by examining other things that determine its shape and the implications of that shape for consumer behaviour.

SUMMARY

1. Economists distinguish between **total and marginal utility**. Total utility, or the benefit a consumer derives from a purchase, is measured by the maximum amount of money he or she would give up to obtain the good. Rational consumers seek to maximize (net) total utility, or **consumer's surplus**: the total utility derived from a commodity minus the value of the money spent in buying it.

2. Marginal utility is the maximum amount of money that a consumer is willing to pay for an *additional* unit of a particular commodity. *Marginal* utility is useful in calculating the set of purchases that maximizes net *total* utility.

3. The **principle of diminishing marginal utility** is a psychological hypothesis stating that as a consumer acquires more and more of a commodity, the marginal utility of additional units of the commodity decreases.

4. To maximize the total utility obtained by spending money on Commodity X, given the fact that other goods can be purchased only with the money that remains after buying X, the consumer must purchase a quantity of X such that the price equals (or approximately equals) the commodity's marginal utility (in monetary terms).

5. If the consumer acts to maximize utility, and if her marginal utility of some good declines when she purchases larger quantities, then her demand curve for the good will have a negative slope. A reduction in price will induce her to purchase more units, leading to a lower marginal utility.

6. Abundant goods tend to have low prices and low marginal utilities regardless of whether their total utilities are high or low. That is why water can have a lower price than diamonds despite water's higher total utility.

7. An **inferior good**, such as secondhand clothing, is a commodity of which consumers buy less when they get richer, all other things held equal.

8. Consumers usually earn a surplus when they purchase a commodity voluntarily. This means that the quantity of the good that they buy is worth more to them than the money they give up in exchange for it. Otherwise they would not buy it. That is why consumer's surplus is normally positive.

9. The true economic cost of the purchase of a commodity, X, is its opportunity cost—that is, the value of the alternative purchases that the acquisition of X requires the consumer to forgo. The money value of the opportunity cost of a unit of good X can be higher or lower than the price of X.

10. A rise in a consumer's income can push quantity demanded either up or down. For normal goods, the effect of a rise in income raises the quantity demanded; for inferior goods, which are generally purchased in an effort to save money, a higher income reduces the quantity demanded.

11. The demand curve for an entire market is obtained by taking a horizontal sum of the demand curves of all individuals who buy or consider buying in that market. This sum is obtained by adding up, for each price, the quantity of the commodity in question that every such consumer is willing to purchase at that price.

KEY TERMS

Total utility   94

Marginal utility   94

The principle of diminishing marginal utility   95

Marginal analysis   96

Consumer's surplus   101

Inferior good   103

Market demand curve   103

The "law" of demand   104

TEST YOURSELF

1. Which gives you greater *total* utility, 12 litres of water per day or 20 litres per day? Why?

2. At which level do you get greater *marginal* utility: 12 litres per day or 20 litres per day? Why?

3. Which of the following items are likely to be normal goods for a typical consumer? Which are likely to be inferior goods?
   a. Expensive perfume
   b. Paper plates
   c. Secondhand clothing
   d. Overseas trips

4. Emily buys an air conditioner that costs $600. Because the air in her home is cleaner, its use saves her $150 in curtain cleaning costs over the lifetime of the air conditioner. In money terms, what is the opportunity cost of the air conditioner?

5. Suppose that strawberries sell for $2 per basket. Jim is considering whether to buy zero, one, two, three, or four baskets. On your own, create a plausible set of total and marginal utility numbers for the different quantities of strawberries (as we did for pizza in Table 1) and arrange them in a table. From your table, calculate how many baskets Jim would buy.

6. Draw a graph showing the consumer's surplus Jim would get from his strawberry purchase in Test Yourself Question 5 and check your answer with the help of your marginal utility table.

7. Consider a market with two consumers, Jasmine and Jim. Draw a demand curve for each of the two consumers and use those curves to construct the demand curve for the entire market.

DISCUSSION QUESTIONS

1. Describe some of the different ways you use water. Which would you give up if the price of water was to rise a little or if you were to be taxed a little more on the amount of residential water that you use? If it were to rise by a fairly large amount? If it were to rise by a very large amount?

2. Suppose that you wanted to measure the marginal utility of a commodity to a consumer by directly determining the consumer's psychological attitude or strength of feeling toward the commodity rather than by seeing how much money the consumer would give up for the commodity. Why would you find it difficult to make such a psychological measurement?

3. Some people who do not understand the optimal purchase rule argue that if a consumer buys so much of a good that its price equals its marginal utility, she could not possibly be behaving optimally. Rather, they say, she would be better off quitting while she was ahead, or buying a quantity such that marginal utility is much greater than price. What is wrong with this argument? (*Hint:* What opportunity would the consumer then miss? Is it maximization of marginal or total utility that serves the consumer's interests?)

4. What inferior goods do you purchase? Why do you buy them? Do you think you will continue to buy them when your income is higher?

APPENDIX *Analyzing Consumer Choice Graphically*

The consumer demand analysis presented in this chapter, although correct as far as it goes, has one shortcoming: By treating the consumer's decision about the purchase of each commodity as an isolated event, it conceals the fact that consumers must *choose* among commodities because of their limited budgets. The analysis so far does not explicitly indicate the hard choice behind every purchase decision—the sacrifice of some goods to obtain others.

The idea is included implicitly, of course, because the purchase of any commodity involves a trade-off between that good and money. If you spend more money on rent, you have less to spend on entertainment. If you buy more clothing, you have less money for food. But to represent the consumer's *choice* problem explicitly, economists have invented two geometric devices, the *budget line* and the *indifference curve*, which are described in this appendix.

■ GEOMETRY OF AVAILABLE CHOICES: THE BUDGET LINE

Suppose, for simplicity, that only two commodities are produced in the world: cheese and rubber bands. The decision problem of any household is then to allocate its income between these two goods. Clearly, the more it spends on one, the less it can have of the other. But just what is the trade-off? A numerical example will answer this question and introduce the graphical device that economists use to portray the trade-off.

Suppose that cheese costs $2 per kilogram, boxes of rubber bands sell at $3 each, and a consumer has $12 at his disposal. He obviously has a variety of choices, as displayed in Table 4. For example, if he buys no rubber bands, the consumer can go home with six kilograms of cheese, and so on. Each of the combinations of cheese and rubber bands that the consumer can afford can be shown in a diagram in which the axes measure the quantities purchased of each commodity. In Figure 5, kilograms of cheese are measured along the vertical axis, the number of boxes of rubber bands is measured along the horizontal axis, and a labelled point represents each of the combinations enumerated in Table 4. This budget line *AE* shows the possible combinations of cheese and rubber bands that the consumer can buy with $12 if cheese costs $2 per kilogram and a box of rubber bands costs $3. For example, point *A* corresponds to spending everything on cheese; point *E* corresponds to spending everything on rubber bands. At intermediate points on the budget line (such as *C*), the consumer buys some of both goods (at *C*, two boxes of rubber bands and three kilograms of cheese), which together use up the $12 available.

If a straight line connects points *A* through *E*, the blue line in the diagram, it traces all possible ways to divide the $12 between the two goods. For example, at point *D*, if the consumer buys three boxes of rubber bands, he will have enough money left to purchase only 1½ kilograms of cheese. This is readily seen to be correct from Table 4. Line *AE* is therefore called the **budget line.**

> The **budget line** for a household graphically represents all possible combinations of two commodities that it can purchase, given the prices of the commodities and some fixed amount of money at its disposal.

TABLE 4				
Alternative Purchase Combinations for a $12 Budget				
Boxes of Rubber Bands (at $3 each)	Expenditure on Rubber Bands	Remaining Funds	Kg of Cheese (at $2 each)	Label in Figure 5
0	$0	$12	6	A
1	3	9	4.5	B
2	6	6	3	C
3	9	3	1.5	D
4	12	0	0	E

FIGURE 5	A Budget Line

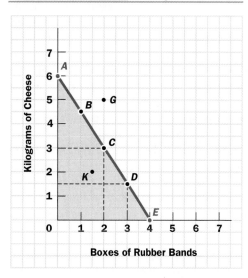

■ Properties of the Budget Line

Let us now use *r* to represent the number of boxes of rubber bands purchased by the consumer and *c* to indicate the amount of cheese that he acquires. Thus, at $2 per kilogram, he spends on cheese a total of $2 times the number of kilograms of cheese bought, or $2c. Similarly, the consumer spends $3r on rubber bands, making a total of $2c$ plus $3r$, which must equal $12 if he spends the entire $12 on the two commodities. Thus, $2c + 3r = 12$ is the equation of the budget line. It is also the equation of the straight line drawn in the diagram.[5]

Note also that the budget line represents the *maximum* amounts of the commodities that the consumer can afford. Thus, for any given purchase of rubber bands, it indicates the greatest amount of cheese that his money can buy. If the consumer wants to be thrifty, he can choose to end up at a point *below* the budget line, such as *K*. Clearly, then, the choices he has available include not only those points on the budget line, *AE*, but also any point in the shaded triangle formed by that line and the two axes. By contrast, points above the budget line, such as *G*, are not available to the consumer, given his limited budget. A bundle of five kilograms of cheese and two boxes of rubber bands would cost $16, which is more than he has to spend.

Changes in the Budget Line

The position of the budget line is determined by two types of data: the prices of the commodities purchased and the income at the buyer's disposal. We can complete our discussion of the graphics of the budget line by examining briefly how a change in either prices or income affects the location of that line.

Obviously, any increase in the income of the household increases the range of options available to it. Specifically, *increases in income produce parallel shifts in the budget line*, as shown in Figure 6. The reason is simple: An increase in available income of, say, 50 percent, if spent entirely on these two goods, would permit the consumer's family to purchase exactly 50 percent more of *either* commodity. Point *A* in Figure 5 would shift upward by 50 percent of its distance from the origin, whereas point *E* would move to the right by 50 percent.[6] Figure 6 shows three such budget lines corresponding to incomes of $9, $12, and $18, respectively.

Finally, we can ask what happens to the budget line when the price of some commodity changes. In Figure 7, when the price of the rubber bands *decreases*, the budget line moves outward, but the move is no longer parallel because the point on the cheese axis remains fixed. Once

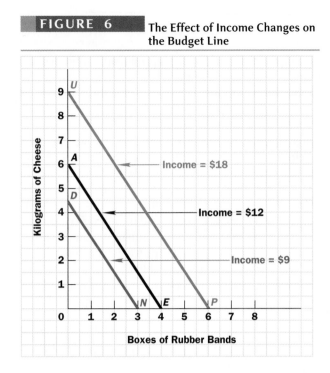

FIGURE 6   The Effect of Income Changes on the Budget Line

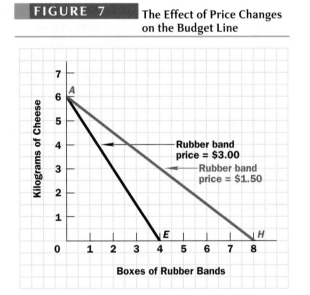

FIGURE 7   The Effect of Price Changes on the Budget Line

again, the reason is fairly straightforward. A 50 percent reduction in the price of rubber bands (from $3.00 to $1.50) permits the consumer to buy twice as many boxes of rubber bands with his $12 as before: Point *E* moves rightward to point *H*, where the buyer can obtain eight boxes of rubber bands. However, since the price of cheese has not changed from point *A*, the amount of cheese that can be bought for $12 is unaffected. This gives the general result that *a reduction in the price of one of the two commodities swings the budget line outward along the axis representing the quantity of that item while leaving the location of the other end of the line unchanged.* Thus a fall in the price of rubber bands from $3.00 to $1.50 swings the price line from *AE*

---

[5] You may have noticed one problem that arises in this formulation. If every point on the budget line, *AE*, is a possible way for the consumer to spend his money, he must be able to buy *fractional* boxes of rubber bands. Perhaps the purchase of 1½ boxes can be interpreted to include a down payment of $1.50 on a box of rubber bands to be purchased on the next shopping trip!

[6] An algebraic proof is simple. Let *M* (which is initially $12) be the amount of money available to the consumer's household. The equation of the budget line can be solved for *c*, obtaining $c = -(3/2)r + M/2$. This equation corresponds to a straight line with a slope of $-3/2$ and a vertical intercept of $M/2$. A change in *M*, the quantity of money available, will not change the *slope* of the budget line; rather, it will lead to parallel shifts in that line.

to blue line *AH*. This happens because at the higher price, $12 buys only four boxes of rubber bands, but at the lower price, it can buy eight boxes.

■ WHAT THE CONSUMER PREFERS: PROPERTIES OF THE INDIFFERENCE CURVE

The budget line indicates what choices are *available* to the consumer, given the size of his income and the commodity prices fixed by the market. Next, we must examine the consumer's *preferences* to determine which of these available possibilities he will choose.

After much investigation, economists have determined what they believe to be the minimum amount of information they need about a purchaser in order to analyze his choices. Economists need know only how a consumer *ranks* alternative bundles of available commodities, deciding which bundle she likes better, but making no effort to find out *how much* more she likes the preferred bundle. Suppose, for instance, that the consumer can choose between two bundles of goods, Bundle *W*, which contains three boxes of rubber bands and one kilogram of cheese, and Bundle *T*, which contains two boxes of rubber bands and three kilograms of cheese. The economist wants to know for this purpose only whether the consumer prefers *W* to *T* or *T* to *W*, or whether he is *indifferent* about which one he gets. Note that the analysis requires no information about the *degree* of preference—whether the consumer is wildly more enthusiastic about one of the bundles or just prefers it slightly.

Graphically, the preference information is provided by a group of curves called **indifference curves** (Figure 8).

An **indifference curve** is a line connecting all combinations of the commodities that are equally desirable to the consumer.

Any point on the diagram represents a combination of cheese and rubber bands. (For example, point *T* on indifference curve *I*_b represents two boxes of rubber bands and three kilograms of cheese.) Any two points on the same indifference curve (for example, *S* and *W*, on indifference curve *I*_a) represent two combinations of the goods that the consumer likes equally well. If two points, such as *T* and *W*, lie on different indifference curves, the consumer prefers the one on the higher indifference curve.

But before we examine these curves, let us see how to interpret one. A single point on an indifference curve says nothing about preferences. For example, point *R* on curve *I*_a simply represents the bundle of goods composed of four boxes of rubber bands and 1/2 kilogram of cheese. It does *not* suggest that the consumer is indifferent between 1/2 kilograms of cheese and four boxes of rubber bands. For the curve to indicate anything, one must consider at least two of its points—for example, points *S* and *W*. An indif-

ference curve, by definition, represents all such combinations that provide equal utility to the consumer.

We do not know yet which bundle, among all of the bundles he can afford, the consumer will choose to buy; this analysis indicates only that a choice between certain bundles will lead to indifference. Before using indifference curves to analyze the consumer's choice, one must examine a few of its properties. Most important is the fact that:

As long as the consumer desires *more* of each of the goods in question, *every* point on a higher indifference curve (that is, a curve farther from the origin in the graph) will be preferred to *any* point on a lower indifference curve.

In other words, among indifference curves, *higher is better*. The reason is obvious. Given two indifference curves, say, *I*_b and *I*_c in Figure 8, the higher curve will contain points lying above and to the right of some points on the lower curve. Thus, point *U* on curve *I*_c lies above and to the right of point *T* on curve *I*_b. This means that the consumer gets more rubber bands *and* more cheese at *U* than at *T*. Assuming that he desires both commodities, the consumer must prefer *U* to *T*.

Because every point on curve *I*_c is, by definition, equal in desirability to point *U*, and the same relationship holds for point *T* and all other points along curve *I*_b, the consumer will prefer *every* point on curve *I*_c to *any* point on curve *I*_b.

This at once implies a second property of indifference curves: *They never intersect*. This is so because if an indifference curve, say, *I*_b, is anywhere above another indifference curve, say, *I*_a, then *I*_b must be above *I*_a everywhere, because every point on *I*_b is preferred to every point on *I*_a.

Another property that characterizes the indifference curve is its *negative slope*. Again, this holds only if the consumer wants more of both commodities. Consider two points, such as *S* and *R*, on the same indifference curve. If

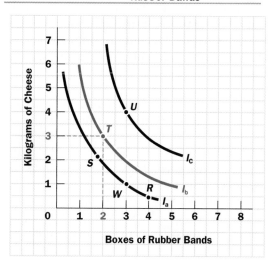

FIGURE 8   Three Indifference Curves for Cheese and Rubber Bands

the consumer is indifferent between them, one point cannot represent more of *both* commodities than the other point. Given that point *S* represents more cheese than point *R* does, *R* must offer more rubber bands than *S* does, or the consumer would not be indifferent about which he gets. As a result, any movement toward the point with the larger number of rubber bands implies a decrease in the quantity of cheese. The curve will always slope downhill toward the right, giving a negative slope.

A final property of indifference curves is the nature of their curvature—the way *they round toward the axes.* They are drawn "bowed in"—they flatten out (they become less and less steep) as they extend from left to right. To understand why this is so, we must first examine the economic interpretation of the slope of an indifference curve.

■ THE SLOPES OF INDIFFERENCE CURVES AND BUDGET LINES

In Figure 9, the average slope of the indifference curve between points *M* and *N* is represented by *RM/RN*.

> The **slope of an indifference curve**, referred to as the *marginal rate of substitution* (MRS) between the commodities, represents the maximum amount of one commodity that the consumer is willing to give up in exchange for one more unit of another commodity.

RM is the quantity of cheese that the consumer gives up in moving from *M* to *N*. Similarly, *RN* is the increased number of boxes of rubber bands acquired in this move. Because the consumer is indifferent between bundles *M* and *N*, the gain of *RN* rubber bands must just suffice to compensate him for the loss of *RM* kilograms of cheese. Thus, the ratio *RM/RN* represents the terms on which the consumer is just willing—*according to his own preference*—to trade one good for the other. If *RM/RN* equals 2, the consumer is willing to give up (no more than) two kilograms of cheese for one additional box of rubber bands. Since the marginal utility of a good was previously defined as the amount of (any commodity) that one is willing to give up to acquire one extra unit of this good, the marginal rate of substitution is simply the ratio of the marginal utility of each good. This implies that if the *RM/RN* ratio in Figure 9 is equal to 2, the marginal utility of one box of rubber bands in terms of kilograms of cheese is 2 and, of course, the marginal utility of one kilogram of cheese in terms of itself is 1. Thus, the marginal rate of substitution implied by a move from bundle *M* to bundle *N* is MRS = MU_r/MU_c where MU_r is the marginal utility of rubber bands and MU_c is the marginal utility of cheese.

The **slope of the budget line,** *BB*, in Figure 9 is also a rate of exchange between cheese and rubber bands, but it no longer reflects the consumer's subjective willingness to trade. Rather, the slope represents the rate of exchange that *the market* offers to the consumer when he gives up money in exchange for cheese and rubber bands. Recall that the budget line represents all commodity combinations that a consumer can get by spending a fixed amount of money. The budget line is, therefore, a curve of constant expenditure. At current prices, if the consumer reduces his purchase of cheese by amount *DE* in Figure 9, he will save just enough money to buy an additional amount, *EF*, of rubber bands, because at points *D* and *F* he is spending the same total number of dollars.

> The **slope of a budget line** is the amount of one commodity that the market requires an individual to give up to obtain one additional unit of another commodity without any change in the amount of money spent.

The slopes of the two types of curves, then, are perfectly analogous in their meaning. The slope of the indifference curve indicates the terms on which the *consumer* is willing to trade one commodity for another, whereas the slope of the budget line reports the *market* terms on which the consumer can trade one good for another.

It is useful to carry our interpretation of the slope of the budget line one step further. Common sense suggests that the market's rate of exchange between cheese and rubber bands should be related to their prices, P_c and P_r, and it is easy to show that this is so. Specifically, the slope of the budget line is equal to the ratio of the prices of the two commodities. To see why, note that if the consumer gives up one box of rubber bands, he has P_r more dollars to spend on cheese. But the quantity of cheese this money

FIGURE 9   Slopes of a Budget Line and an Indifference Curve

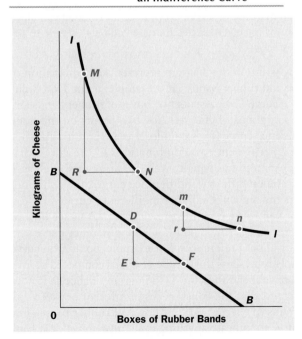

will enable him to buy is *inversely* related to its price; that is, the lower the price of cheese, the more cheese that money can buy—each dollar permits him to buy $1/P_c$ kilogram of cheese. So the additional P_r dollars the consumer has available when he forgoes the purchase of one box of rubber bands permit him to buy P_r times $1/P_c = P_r/P_c$ more kilograms of cheese. Thus, the slope of the budget line, which indicates how much additional cheese the consumer can buy when he gives up one box of rubber bands, is P_r/P_c.

Before returning to our main subject, the study of consumer choice, we pause briefly and use our interpretation of the slope of the indifference curve to discuss the third of the properties of the indifference curve—its characteristic curvature—which we left unexplained earlier. The shape of indifference curves means that the slope decreases with movement from left to right. In Figure 9, at point *m*, toward the right of the diagram, the consumer is willing to give up far less cheese for one more box of rubber bands (quantity *rm*) than he is willing to trade at point *M*, toward the left. This situation occurs because at *M* the consumer initially has a large quantity of cheese and few rubber bands, whereas at *m* his initial stock of cheese is low and he has many rubber bands. In general terms, the curvature premise on which indifference curves are usually drawn asserts that consumers are relatively eager to trade away some part of what they own of a commodity of which they have a large amount but are more reluctant to trade away part of the goods of which they hold small quantities. This psychological premise underlies the curvature of the indifference curve.

We can now use our indifference curve apparatus to analyze how the consumer chooses among the combinations that he can afford to buy—that is, the combinations of rubber bands and cheese shown by the budget line. Figure 10 brings together in the same diagram the budget line from Figure 5 and the indifference curves from Figure 8.

Tangency Conditions

Because, according to the first of the properties of indifference curves, the consumer prefers higher curves to lower ones, he will go to the point on the budget line that lies on the highest indifference curve attainable. This will be point *T* on indifference curve I_b. He can afford no other point that he likes as well. For example, neither point *K* below the budget line nor point *W* on the budget line puts the consumer on such a high indifference curve. Further, any point on an indifference curve above I_b, such as point *U*, is out of the question because it lies beyond his financial means. We end up with a simple rule of consumer choice:

Consumers will select the most desired combination of goods obtainable for their money. The choice will be that point on the budget line at which the budget line is tangent to an indifference curve.

We can see why only the point of tangency, *T* (two boxes of rubber bands and three kilograms of cheese), will give the consumer the largest utility that his money can buy. Suppose that the consumer was instead to consider buying 3½ boxes of rubber bands and one kilogram of cheese. This would put him at point *W* on the budget line and on the indifference curve I_a. But then, by buying fewer rubber bands and more cheese (a move upward and to the left on the budget line), he could get to another indifference curve, I_b, that would be higher and therefore more desirable without spending any more money. It clearly does not pay to end up at *W*. Only the point of tangency, *T*, leaves no room for further improvement.

At a point of tangency, where the consumer's benefits from purchasing cheese and rubber bands are maximized, the slope of the budget line equals the slope of the indifference curve. This is true by the definition of a point of tangency. We have just seen that the slope of the indifference curve is the marginal rate of substitution between cheese and rubber bands, and that the slope of the budget line is the ratio of the prices of rubber bands and cheese. We can therefore restate the requirement for the optimal division of the consumer's money between the two commodities in slightly more technical language:

Consumers will get the most benefit from their money when they choose combinations of commodities whose marginal rates of substitution equal the ratios of their prices. The optimal decision will be such that:

$$MU_r/MU_c = P_r/P_c$$

It is worth reviewing the logic behind this conclusion. Why is it not advisable for the consumer to stop at a point such as *W*, where the marginal rate of substitution

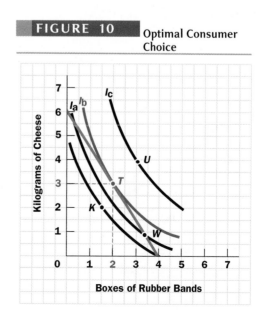

FIGURE 10 Optimal Consumer Choice

(slope of the indifference curve) is less than the price ratio (slope of the budget line)? By moving upward and to the left from W along his budget line, he can instead take advantage of market opportunities to obtain a commodity bundle that he likes better. This will always be true, for example, if the amount of cheese the consumer is *personally* willing to exchange for a box of rubber bands (the slope of the indifference curve) is greater than the amount of cheese for which the box of rubber bands trades *on the market* (the slope of the budget line).

■ Consequences of Income Changes: Inferior Goods

Now consider what happens to the consumer's purchases after a rise in income. We know that a rise in income produces a parallel outward shift in the budget line, such as the shift from BB to CC in Figure 11. The quantity of rubber bands demanded rises from three to four boxes, and the quantity demanded of cheese increases as well. This change moves the consumer's equilibrium from tangency point T to tangency point E on a higher indifference curve.

A rise in income may or may not increase the demand for a commodity. In Figure 11, the rise in income does lead the consumer to buy more cheese *and* more rubber bands, but indifference curves need not always be positioned in a way that yields this sort of result. In Figure 12, as the consumer's budget line rises from BB to CC, the tangency point moves leftward from H to G. As a result, when his income rises, the consumer actually buys *fewer* rubber bands. This implies that for this consumer rubber bands are an *inferior good.*

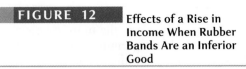

FIGURE 12   Effects of a Rise in Income When Rubber Bands Are an Inferior Good

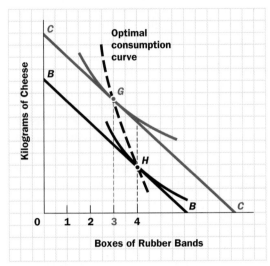

■ Consequences of Price Changes: Deriving the Demand Curve

Finally, we come to the main question underlying demand curves: How does a consumer's choice change if the price of one good changes? We explained earlier that a reduction in the price of a box of rubber bands causes the budget line to swing outward along the horizontal axis while leaving its vertical intercept unchanged. In Figure 13, we depict the effect of a decline in the price of rubber bands on the quantity of rubber bands demanded. As the price of rubber bands falls, the budget line swings from BC to BD. The tangency points, T and E, also move in a corresponding direction, causing the quantity demanded to rise from

FIGURE 11   Effects of a Rise in Income When Neither Good Is Inferior

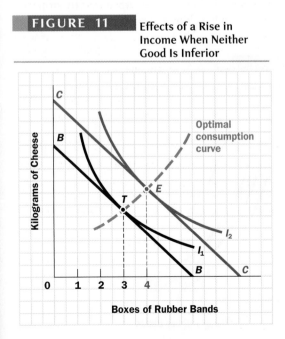

FIGURE 13   Consequences of Price Changes

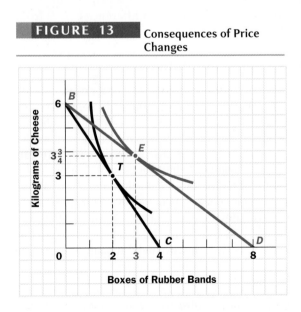

two to three boxes. The price of rubber bands has fallen and the quantity demanded has risen, so the demand curve for rubber bands has a negative slope. The desired purchase of rubber bands increases from two to three boxes, and the desired purchase of cheese also increases, from 3 kilograms to 3¾ kilograms.

The demand curve for rubber bands can be constructed directly from Figure 13. Point *T* shows that the consumer will buy two boxes of rubber bands when the price of a box is $3.00. Point *E* indicates that when the price falls to $1.50, quantity demanded rises to three boxes of rubber bands.[7] These two pieces of information are shown in Figure 14 as points *t* and *e* on the demand curve for rubber bands. By examining the effects of other possible prices for rubber bands (other budget lines emanating from point *B* in Figure 13), we can find all the other points on the demand curve in exactly the same way. The demand curve is derived from the indifference curve by varying the price of the commodity to see the effects of all other possible prices.

The indifference curve diagram also brings out an important idea that the demand curve does not show. A change in the *price of rubber bands* also has consequences for the *quantity of cheese demanded* because it affects the amount of money left over for cheese purchases. In the example illustrated in Figure 13, the decrease in the price of rubber bands increases the demand for cheese from 3 to 3¾ kilograms.

CHOICES WITHOUT SUBSTITUTION

Not all economists agree with the properties of indifference curve analysis as this analysis has been described in this appendix. More precisely, some economists, as well as psychologists, believe that this description incorrectly presents the choices that some consumers take. For instance, while it has been asserted that indifference curves should never cross each other, many researchers have conducted studies that concluded that the subjects under study behaved in such a way that their indifference curves *did* cross each other.

A German researcher, Richard Sippel, has shown that a substantial proportion of consumers do not behave in a way that is consistent with utility maximization. Experiments were conducted in which consumers were given a budget constraint and asked to choose different baskets of goods (video clips, computer games, magazines, Coca-Cola, orange juice, candies, snacks). In each of several experiments, however, the price of these goods was changed. The purpose was to verify that the consumer preferences revealed during these experiments were consistent with generally accepted utility maximization the-

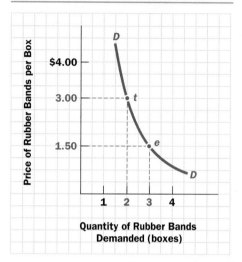

Deriving the Demand Curve for Rubber Bands

ory. However, the behaviour of about 70 percent of the subjects did not correspond to what was to be expected from a consumer maximizing utility subject to a given budget constraint. While some consumers exhibited behaviour that was "nearly" consistent with the theory—meaning that if some of their choices were slightly revised, their behaviour did fit the theory, thus implying that they had made small "errors" in their choices—45 percent of the consumers seemed to be guided by principles different from standard theory.[8]

One possible explanation is that these consumers very clearly separated decisions tied to food (Coca-Cola, orange juice, candies, snacks) from decisions tied to leisure (video clips, computer games, magazines), with trade-offs occurring only within each category of goods. In addition, it may be that the "inconsistent" consumers in the experiment acted in line with the assertion of some economists that consumers have priorities and have a *hierarchy* of needs. Such preferences are called *preferences of a lexicographic nature* and they were first modelled in the 1950s by Rumanian economist Nicholas Georgescu-Roegen (1926–1994). Choices of a lexicographic nature are related to *noncompensatory* choices. For instance, for some people who like red cars, any reduction in the price of an otherwise identical car that was not red would be insufficient to induce them to give up the purchase of a red car.

Figures 15 and 16 describe an example of such a set of preferences. The figures assume that there are two types of goods—necessities and luxury goods, as the classical economists in the days of Adam Smith and David Ricardo theorized. Up to the threshold level shown by the horizontal line at *T*, consumers care only about necessities.

---

[7] How do we know that the price of rubber bands corresponding to the budget line *BD* is $1.50? Because the $12.00 total budget will purchase at most eight boxes (point *D*), the price per box must be $12.00/8 = $1.50.

[8] Reinhard Sippel, "An experiment on the pure theory of consumer's behaviour," *Economic Journal*, September 1997.

Once the threshold is reached and the necessities of life are met, consumers care only about luxuries. In Figure 15, with a low level of income, as illustrated by the budget line B_1B_1, a consumer could purchase only a quantity of necessities, N_1, buying no luxury goods. However, with a higher income level, given by budget line B_2B_2, the consumer would purchase T units of necessities and L_2 units of luxury goods.

FIGURE 15   Choice of a Lexicographic Nature: Effect of a Decrease in the Price of Luxury Goods

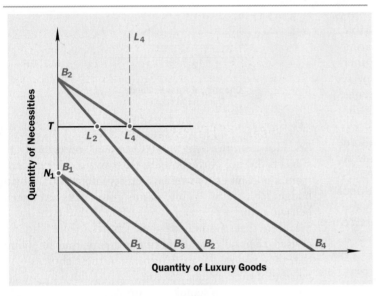

FIGURE 16   Choice of a Lexicographic Nature: Effect of a Decrease in the Price of Necessities

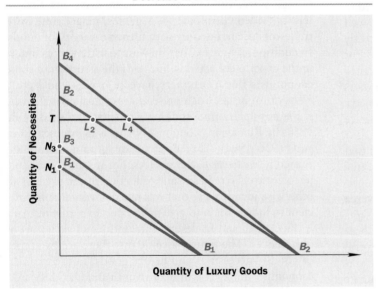

What if the prices of luxury goods were to be cut? This would change nothing to the behaviour of low-income consumers. While their budget constraint would rotate from B_1B_1 to B_1B_3, consumption would remain at N_1 units of necessities. By contrast, high-income consumers, with a new budget constraint given by B_2B_4, would increase their consumption of luxury goods to L_4 units, while still purchasing T necessities.

Now, what if the prices of necessities were cut, as shown in Figure 16? This time, the decrease in price would have an impact on both low-income and high-income consumers. Low-income consumers, moving from a B_1B_1 to B_1B_3 budget constraint, would increase their consumption of necessities from N_1 to N_3, while high-income consumers would see their budget constraint rotate from B_2B_2 to B_2B_4, increasing their purchases of luxury goods to L_4 while still consuming T units of necessities. There is thus an asymmetry here, as the price of luxury goods has no effect on the behaviour of low-income earners, while the price of necessities does have an impact on both low- and high-income consumers, although a different type of impact.

It should also be noted that with preferences of a lexicographic nature, there are no indifference curves. For instance, the consumer choice shown at point L_4 in Figure 15 is preferred to any other combination of luxury and necessary goods that can be found on the left side of the L_4L_4 vertical dashed line.

With choices of a lexicographic nature, there is no substitution effect—there is no trade-off. One kind of good cannot be substituted for another. This gives rise to *vertical* demand curves, as will be discussed on page 122. Some economists (ecological economists in particular) believe that this applies particularly well to some consumption items that carry strong ethical features, such as environmental goods. For instance, some environmentalists want to preserve endangered species, forests, or swamps "at all costs"—provided that their private consumption does not fall below a certain threshold, say, T in Figures 15 and 16 (substituting "Private Consumption" for the label now on the vertical axis and "Quality of the Environment" on the horizontal axis.)

SUMMARY

1. Indifference curve analysis permits economists to study the interrelationships of the demands for two (or more) commodities.

2. The basic tools of indifference curve analysis are the consumer's **budget line** and **indifference curves.**

3. A budget line shows all combinations of two commodities that the consumer can afford, given the prices of the commodities and the amount of money the consumer has available to spend.

4. The budget line is a straight line whose slope equals the ratio of the prices of the commodities. A change in price changes the **slope of the budget line.** A change in the consumer's income causes a parallel shift in the budget line.

5. Two points on an indifference curve represent two combinations of commodities such that the consumer does not prefer one combination over the other.

6. Indifference curves normally have negative slopes and are "bowed in" toward the origin. The **slope of an indifference curve** indicates how much of one commodity the consumer is willing to give up to get an additional unit of the other commodity.

7. The consumer will choose the point on her budget line that gets her to the highest attainable indifference curve. Normally this will occur at the point of tangency between the two curves. This point indicates the combination of commodities that gives the consumer the greatest benefits for the amount of money she has available to spend.

8. The consumer's demand curve can be derived from her indifference curve.

9. Sometimes there is no substitution between goods belonging to different categories (food, leisure, etc.). Also, under some circumstances, for instance when environmental issues are involved, a consumer's choice may reflect a hierarchy of needs, called *preferences of a lexicographic nature*, so that no indifference curve exists.

KEY TERMS

Budget line   107

Indifference curve   109

Slope of an indifference curve
(marginal rate of substitution)   110

Slope of a budget line   110

TEST YOURSELF

1. John Q. Public spends all of his income on gasoline and hot dogs. Draw his budget line under several conditions:

   a. His income is $80, and one litre of gasoline and one hot dog each cost $1.60.

   b. His income is $120, and the two prices remain the same.

   c. His income is $80, hot dogs cost $1.60 each, and gasoline costs $2.00 per litre.

2. Draw some hypothetical indifference curves for John Q. Public on a diagram identical to the one you constructed for Test Yourself Question 1.

   a. Approximately how much gasoline and how many hot dogs will Mr. Public buy?

   b. How will these choices change if his income increases to $120? Is either good an inferior good?

   c. How will these choices change if the gasoline price rises to $2.00 per litre?

3. Explain the information that the *slope* of an indifference curve conveys about a consumer's preferences. Use this relationship to explain the typical curvature of indifference curves.

DEMAND AND ELASTICITY

A high cross elasticity of demand [between two goods indicates that they] compete in the same market. [This can prevent a supplier of one of the products] from possessing monopoly power over price.

U.S. SUPREME COURT, DUPONT CELLOPHANE DECISION, 1956

The particular dispute . . . concerns the definition of the relevant product market. . . . Undeniably, the determination of cross elasticity of demand, which is in theory the truest indicium of the dimensions of a product market, requires some economic or statistical skill. . . . [S]o what is required in the end is an assessment of the economic significance of the evidence; and to this task an economist is almost by definition better suited than is a judge.

SUPREME COURT OF CANADA, CANADA (DIRECTOR OF INVESTIGATION AND RESEARCH) v. SOUTHAM INC. [1997] I S.C.R. 748

I n this chapter, we continue our study of demand and demand curves, which we began in the previous chapter. Here we explain the way economists *measure* how much quantity demanded responds to price changes, and what such responsiveness implies about the revenue that producers will receive if they change prices. In particular, we introduce and explain an important concept called *elasticity* that economists use to examine the relationship between quantity demanded and price.

CONTENTS

ISSUE: *Will Taxing Cigarettes Make Teenagers Stop Smoking?*

Public health experts believe that increased taxes on cigarettes can be a major weapon in the battle to cut teenage smoking. Imagine yourself on a panel of consultants helping a federal parliamentary committee draft new legislation to deal with this issue. As the youngest member of the group, you are asked for your opinion about how effective a big tax increase on cigarettes would be in persuading young people to stop smoking. How would you respond? What sorts of statistical data, if any, would you use to help find your answer? And how might you go about analyzing the relevant numbers?

This chapter will help you answer such questions. As often happens in economics, we will see that careful investigation brings some surprises. This is true in the case of taxes to discourage teenage smoking. A tax on cigarettes may actually benefit teenagers'—and other citizens'—health. And it will, of course, benefit government finances by bringing in more tax money. Nothing surprising so far. Instead, the surprise is this: The more effective the tax is in curbing teenage smoking, the less beneficial it will be to the government's finances, and vice versa; the more the tax benefits the government, the less it will contribute to health. The concept of elasticity of demand will make this point clearer.

ELASTICITY: THE MEASURE OF RESPONSIVENESS

Governments, business firms, supermarkets, consumers, and law courts need a way to measure how responsive demand is to price changes—for example, will a 10 percent cut in the price of commodity X increase quantity of X demanded a little or a lot? Economists measure the responsiveness of quantity demanded to price changes via a concept called *elasticity*. Marketers sometimes use estimates of elasticity to decide how to price their products or whether to add new product models. A relatively flat demand curve like Figure 1(a) indicates that consumers respond sharply to a change

SOURCE: © Royalty-Free/Corbis

FIGURE 1

Hypothetical Demand Curves for Film

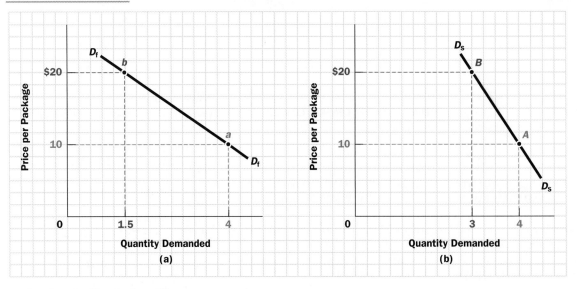

Note: Quantities are in millions of packages of film per year.

in price—the quantity they demand falls by 2.5 units (from 4 units to 1.5 units) when price rises $10. That is, they demand or buy much less of the product when price rises even a little bit. Such a "touchy" curve is called *elastic* or *highly elastic*. A relatively steep demand curve like Figure 1(b), which indicates that consumers respond hardly at all to a price change, is called *inelastic*. In this graph, a $10 price rise cuts quantity demanded by only 1 unit.

The precise measure used for this purpose is called the **price elasticity of demand,** or simply the **elasticity of demand.** We define elasticity of demand as the ratio of the *percentage* change in quantity demanded to the associated *percentage* change in price.

Demand is called *elastic* if, say, a 10 percent rise in price reduces quantity demanded by *more* than 10 percent. Demand is called *inelastic* if such a rise in price reduces quantity demanded by *less* than 10 percent.

Why do we need these definitions to analyze the responsiveness to price shown by a particular demand curve? At first, it may seem that the *slope* of the demand curve conveys the needed information: Curve D_sD_s is much steeper than curve D_fD_f in Figure 1, so any given change in price appears to correspond to a much smaller change in quantity demanded in Figure 1(b) than in Figure 1(a). For this reason, it is tempting to call demand in Panel (a) "more elastic." But slope will not do the job, because the slope of any curve depends on the particular units of measurement, and economists use no standardized units of measurement. For example, cloth output may be measured in yards or in metres, milk in quarts or litres, and coal in tonnes or hundred-weights. Figure 2(a) brings out this point explicitly. In this graph, we return to the pizza example from Chapter 5, measuring quantity demanded in terms of pizzas and price in dollars per pizza. A fall in price from $15 to $11 per pizza (points *A* and *B*) raises quantity demanded at Paul's Pizza Parlour from 280 pizzas to 360 per week—that is, by 80 pizzas.

Now look at Figure 2(b), which provides *exactly* the same information, but measures quantity demanded in *slices* of pizza rather than whole pizzas (with one pizza yielding eight slices). Here, the same price change as before increases quantity demanded, from 8 × 280 = 2,240 slices to 8 × 360 = 2,880 slices—that is, by 640 slices, rather than by 80 pizzas.

Visually, the increase in quantity demanded looks eight times as great in Panel (b) as in Panel (a), but all that has changed is the unit of measurement. The 640-unit increase

The **(price) elasticity of demand** is the ratio of the *percentage* change in quantity demanded to the *percentage* change in price that brings about the change in quantity demanded.

The Sensitivity of Slope to Units of Measurement at Paul's Pizza Parlour

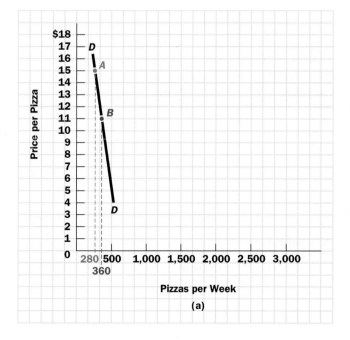
(a)

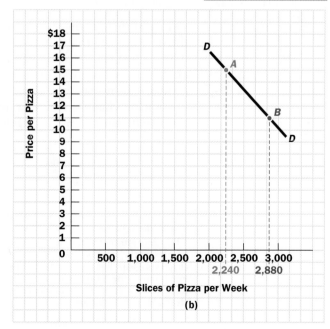
(b)

in Figure 2(b) represents the same increase in quantity demanded as the 80-unit increase in Figure 2(a). Just as you get different numbers for a given rise in temperature, depending on whether you measure it in Celsius or Fahrenheit, so the slopes of demand curves differ, depending on whether you measure quantity in pizzas or in pizza slices. Clearly, then, slope does not really measure responsiveness of quantity demanded to price, because the measure changes whenever the units of measurement change.

Economists created the elasticity concept precisely in response to this problem. Elasticity measures responsiveness on the basis of *percentage* changes in price and quantity rather than on *absolute* changes. The elasticity formula solves the units problem because percentages are unaffected by units of measurement. If the government defence budget doubles, it goes up by 100 percent, whether measured in millions or billions of dollars. If demand for pizza trebles, it rises by 200 percent, whether we measure the quantity demanded in number of pies or slices. The elasticity formula given earlier therefore expresses both the change in quantity demanded and the change in price as *percentages*.[1]

Furthermore, elasticity calculates the change in quantity demanded *as a percentage of the average of the two quantities:* the quantity demanded *before* the change in price has occurred (Q_0) and the quantity demanded *after* the price change (Q_1). In our example, the "before" pizza purchase is 280 (Q_0), the quantity sold after the price fall is 360 (Q_1), and the average of these two numbers is 320. The increase in number of pizzas bought is 80 pizzas, which is 25 percent of the 320 average of the sales before and after the price change. So 25 percent is the number we use as the purchase increase measure in our elasticity calculation. This procedure is a useful compromise between viewing the change in quantity demanded (80 pizzas) as a percentage of the initial quantity (280) or as a percentage of the final quantity (360).

Similarly, the change in price is expressed as a percentage of the average of the "before" and "after" prices, so that, in effect, it represents elasticity at the price halfway between those two prices. That is, the price falls by $4 (from $15 to $11). Because $4 is (approximately) 31 percent of the average of $15 ($P_0$) and $11 ($P_1$) (that is, $13), we say that in this case a 31 percent fall in price led to a 25 percent rise in quantity of pizza demanded.

To summarize, the elasticity formula has two basic attributes:

- Each of the changes with which it deals is measured as a *percentage* change.

- Each of the percentage changes is calculated in terms of the average values of the before and after quantities and prices.

In addition, economists often adjust the price elasticity of demand formula in a third way. Note that when the price *increases*, the quantity demanded usually *declines*. Thus, when the price change is a positive number, the quantity change will normally be a negative number; when the price change is a negative number, the quantity change will normally be a positive number. As a consequence, the ratio of the two percentage changes will be a negative number. We customarily express elasticity as a positive number, however. Hence:

- Each percentage change is taken as an "absolute value," meaning that the calculation drops all minus signs.[2]

---

[1] The remainder of this section involves fairly technical computational issues. On a first reading, you may prefer to go directly to the new section that begins on the next page.

[2] This third attribute of the elasticity formula—the removal of all minus signs—applies only when the formula is used to measure the responsiveness of *quantity demanded* of product X to a change in the *price* of product X. Later in the chapter, we will show that similar formulas are used to measure the responsiveness between other pairs of variables. For example, the elasticity of supply uses a similar formula to measure the responsiveness of quantity supplied to price. In such cases, it is not customary to drop minus signs when calculating elasticity. The reasons will become clearer later in the chapter.

We can now state the formula for price elasticity of demand, keeping all three features of the formula in mind:

Price elasticity of demand = **Change in quantity demanded, expressed as a percentage of the average of the before and after quantities *divided by* the corresponding percentage change in price.**

In our example:

Elasticity of demand for pizzas =

$$\frac{(Q_1 - Q_0)/\text{average of } Q_0 \text{ and } Q_1}{(P_1 - P_0)/\text{average of } P_0 \text{ and } P_1} = \frac{80/320}{4/13} = \frac{25\%}{31\%} = 0.8 \text{ (approximately)}$$

Price Elasticity of Demand and the Shapes of Demand Curves

We noted earlier that looks can be deceiving in some demand curves because their units of measurement are arbitrary. Economists have provided the elasticity formula to overcome that problem. Nonetheless, the shape of a demand curve does convey some information about its elasticity. Let's see what information some demand curve shapes give, with the aid of Figure 3.

1. Perfectly Elastic Demand Curves   Panel (a) of Figure 3 depicts a horizontal demand curve. Such a curve is called *perfectly elastic* (or *infinitely elastic*). At any price higher than $0.75, quantity demanded will drop to zero; that is, the comparative change in quantity demanded will be infinitely large. Perfect elasticity typically occurs when many producers sell a product and consumers can switch easily from one seller to another if any particular producer raises his price. For example, suppose you and the other students in your economics class are required to buy a newspaper every day to keep up with economic events. If news dealer X, from whom you have been buying the newspaper, raises the price from 75 cents to 80 cents, but the competitor, Y, across the street keeps the old price, then X may lose all her newspaper customers to Y. This situation is likely to prevail whenever an acceptable rival product is available at the going price (75 cents in the diagram). In cases in which no one will pay more than the going price, the seller will lose all of her customers if she raises her price by even a penny.

FIGURE 3

Demand Curves with Different Elasticities

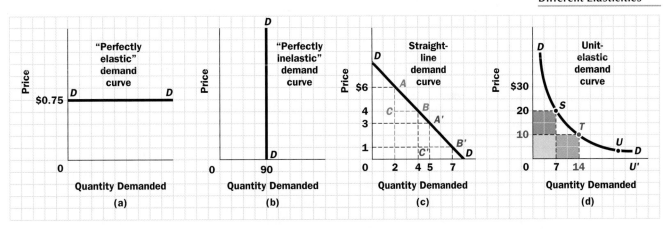

2. Perfectly Inelastic Demand Curves   Panel (b) of Figure 3 shows the opposite extreme: a completely vertical demand curve. Such a curve is called *perfectly inelastic* throughout because its elasticity is zero at every point on the curve. Because quantity demanded remains at 90 units no matter what the price, the percentage change in quantity is always zero, and hence the elasticity (which equals percentage change in quantity divided by percentage change in price) is always zero. In this case, consumer purchases do not respond at all to any change in price.

Vertical demand curves such as the one shown in Panel (b) of Figure 3 occur when a commodity is very inexpensive. For example, you probably will not buy more rubber bands if their prices fall. The demand curve may also be vertical when consumers consider the item in question to be an absolute necessity. For example, if your roommate's grandfather has a heart attack, the family will buy whatever medicine the doctor prescribes, regardless of the price, and will not purchase any more even if the price falls.

3. (Seemingly Simple) Straight-Line Demand Curves   Panel (c) of Figure 3 depicts a case between these two extremes: a *straight-line* demand curve that runs neither vertically nor horizontally. Note that, although the *slope* of a straight-line demand curve remains constant throughout its length, its *elasticity* does not. For example, the elasticity of demand between points A and B in Figure 3(c) is:

$$\frac{\text{Change in } \textbf{\textit{Q}} \text{ as a percentage of average } \textbf{\textit{Q}}}{\text{Change in } \textbf{\textit{P}} \text{ as a percentage of average } \textbf{\textit{P}}} = \frac{2/3}{2/5} = \frac{66.67\%}{40\%} = 1.67$$

The elasticity of demand between points A' and B' is:

$$\frac{\textbf{2 as a percentage of 6}}{\textbf{2 as a percentage of 2}} = \frac{\textbf{33.33 percent}}{\textbf{100 percent}} = 0.33$$

The general point is that:

> Along a straight-line demand curve, the price elasticity of demand grows steadily smaller as you move from left to right. That is so because the quantity keeps getting larger, so that a given *numerical* change in quantity becomes an ever-smaller *percentage* change. But, simultaneously, the price keeps going lower, so that a given numerical change in price becomes an ever-larger percentage change. So, as one moves from left to right along the demand curve, the numerator of the elasticity fraction keeps falling and the denominator keeps growing larger; thus the fraction that is the elasticity formula keeps declining. (For further analysis, see Appendix 1: "The Analytics of Point Elasticity.")

4. Unit-Elastic Demand Curves   If the elasticity of a straight-line demand curve varies from one part of the curve to another, what does a demand curve with the same elasticity throughout its length look like? For reasons explained in the next section, it has the general shape indicated in Figure 3(d). That panel shows a curve with elasticity equal to 1 throughout (a *unit-elastic* demand curve). A unit-elastic demand curve bends in the middle toward the origin of the graph—at either end, it moves closer and closer to the axes but never touches or crosses them.

As we have noted, a curve with an elasticity greater than 1 is called an **elastic demand curve** (one for which the percentage change in quantity demanded will be greater than the percentage change in price); a curve whose elasticity is less than 1 is known as an **inelastic curve.** When elasticity is exactly 1, economists say that the curve is **unit-elastic.**

Real-world price elasticities of demand seem to vary considerably from product to product. Because people can get along without them, moderately luxurious goods, such as expensive vacations, are generally more price elastic—people give them up more readily when their prices rise—than goods such as milk and shirts, which are considered necessities. Products with close substitutes, such as Coke and Pepsi, tend to

A **demand curve** is **elastic** when a given percentage price change leads to a larger percentage change in quantity demanded.

A **demand curve** is **inelastic** when a given percentage price change leads to a smaller percentage change in quantity demanded.

A demand curve is **unit-elastic** when a given percentage price change leads to the same percentage change in quantity demanded.

have relatively high elasticities because if one soft drink becomes expensive, consumers will switch to the other. Also, the elasticities of demand for goods that business firms buy, such as raw materials and machinery, tend to be higher on the whole than those for consumers' goods. This is because competition forces firms to buy their supplies wherever they can get them most cheaply. The exception occurs when a firm requires a particular input for which no reasonable substitutes exist or the available substitutes are substantially inferior. Since aggregate industry estimates are not readily available for Canada, Table 1 gives some well-established estimates of elasticity for some major industries in the U.S. economy.

TABLE 1

Estimates of Price Elasticities

Product	Price Elasticity
Industrial chemicals	0.4
Shoe repairs and cleaning	0.4
Food, tobacco, and beverages	0.5
Newspapers and magazines	0.5
Data processing, precision and optical instruments	0.7
Medical care and hospitalization insurance	0.8
Metal products	1.1
Purchased meals (excluding alcoholic beverages)	1.6
Electricity (household utility)	1.9
Boats, pleasure aircraft	2.4
Public transportation	3.5
China, tableware	8.8

SOURCES: H. S. Houthakker and Lester D. Taylor, *Consumer Demand in the United States*, 2nd ed. (Cambridge, Mass.: Harvard University Press, 1970), pp. 153–158; and Joachim Möller, "Income and Price Elasticities in Different Sectors of the Economy—An Analysis of Structural Change for Germany, the U.K., and U.S." (University of Regensburg, December 1998).

■ PRICE ELASTICITY OF DEMAND: ITS EFFECT ON TOTAL REVENUE AND TOTAL EXPENDITURE

Aside from its role as a measure of the responsiveness of demand to a change in price, elasticity serves a second, very important purpose. As a real-world illustration at the end of this chapter will show, a firm often wants to know whether an increase in price will increase or decrease its total revenue—the money it obtains from sales to its customers. The price elasticity of demand provides a simple guide to the answer:

> If demand for the seller's product is elastic, a price *increase* will *actually decrease* total revenue. If demand is exactly unit-elastic, a rise in price will leave total revenue unaffected. If demand is inelastic, a rise in price will raise total revenue. The opposite changes will occur when price falls.

A corresponding story must be true about the expenditures made by the *buyers* of the product. After all, the expenditures of the buyers are exactly the same thing as the revenues of the seller.

These relationships between elasticity and total revenue hold because total revenue (or expenditure) equals price times quantity demanded, $P \times Q$, and because a drop in price has two opposing effects on that arithmetic product. It decreases P, and, if the demand curve is negatively sloped, it increases Q. The first effect *decreases* revenues by cutting the amount of money that consumers spend on each unit of the good. The second effect *increases* revenues by raising the number of units of the good that the firm sells.

The net effect on total revenue (or total expenditure) depends on the elasticity. If price goes down by 10 percent and quantity demanded increases by 10 percent (a case of *unit elasticity*), the two effects just cancel out: $P \times Q$ remains constant. In contrast, if price goes down by 10 percent and quantity demanded rises by 15 percent (a case of *elastic* demand), $P \times Q$ increases. Finally, if a 10 percent price fall leads to only a 5 percent rise in quantity demanded (*inelastic* demand), $P \times Q$ falls.

We can easily see the relationship between elasticity and total revenue in a graph. First, note that:

> The total revenue (or expenditure) represented by any point on a demand curve (any price– quantity combination), such as point *S* in Figure 4, equals the area of the rectangle under that point (the area of rectangle O*RST* in the figure). This is true because the area of

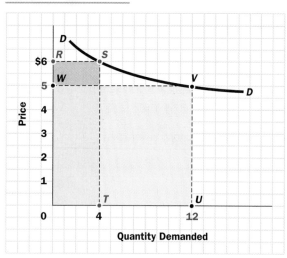

FIGURE 4

An Elastic Demand Curve

a rectangle equals its height times width, or $OR \times RS$ in Figure 4. Clearly, that is price times quantity, which is exactly total revenue.

To illustrate the connection between elasticity and consumer expenditure, Figure 4 shows an elastic portion of a demand curve, *DD*. In this figure, when price falls, quantity demanded rises by a greater percentage, increasing total expenditure. At a price of $6 per unit, the quantity sold is four units, so total expenditure is $4 \times \$6 = \$24$, represented by the vertical rectangle whose upper-right corner is point *S*. When price falls to $5 per unit, 12 units are sold. Consequently, the new expenditure ($60 = \$5 \times 12$), measured by the rectangle $0WVU$, exceeds the old expenditure.

In contrast, Figure 3(d), the unit-elastic demand curve, shows constant expenditures even though price changes. Total spending is $140 whether the price is $20 and 7 units are sold (point *S*) or the price is $10 and 14 units are sold (point *T*).

This discussion also indicates why a unit-elastic demand curve must have the shape depicted in Figure 3(d), hugging the axes closer and closer but never touching or crossing them. When demand is unit-elastic, total expenditure must be the same at every point on the curve. That is, it must equal $140 at point *S* and point *T* and point *U* in Figure 3(d). Suppose that at point *U* (or some other point on the curve), the demand curve were to touch the horizontal axis, meaning that the price would equal zero. Then total expenditure would be zero, not $140. Therefore, if the demand curve remains unit-elastic along its entire length, it can never cross the horizontal axis (where $P = 0$). By the same reasoning, it cannot cross the vertical axis (where $Q = 0$). Because the slope of the demand curve is negative, any unit-elastic curve simply must get closer and closer to the axes as it moves away from its middle points, as illustrated in Figure 3(d). But it will never touch either axis.

We can now see why demand elasticity is so important for business decisions. A firm should not jump to the conclusion that a price increase will automatically add to its profits, or it may find that consumers take their revenge by cutting back on their purchases. For example, when U.S. Heinz's Pet Products Company raised the price of its 9-Lives cat food some years ago, its market share plummeted from 23 percent to 15 percent as customers flocked to other brands. In fact, if its demand curve is elastic, a firm that raises price will end up selling so many fewer units that its total revenue will actually fall, even though it makes more money than before on each unit it sells.

Price *cuts* can also be hazardous—if the elasticity of demand is low. A good example of this is the attitude of the pharmaceuticals industry in the United States, which has fought hard to block imports of lower-priced Canadian generic products. With a very low elasticity of demand for prescription drugs of approximately 0.3, if prices in the United States were to fall to the level of Canadian drug prices, a 10 percent drop in prices would induce only a 3 percent rise in demand. The profits of the American pharmaceuticals industry would undoubtedly take a major hit. Some have estimated a loss of sales revenues for the industry of as much as $50 billion annually if U.S. drug prices were to fall to Canadian levels. Thus, the strategic value to a business firm of a price rise or a price cut depends very much on the elasticity of demand for its product. But elasticity tells us only how a price change affects a firm's revenues; we must also consider the effect of costs on the firm's output decisions, as we will do in Chapter 8.

We said earlier in the chapter that even if a cigarette tax program failed to curb teen smoking, it would benefit the government's tax collectors a great deal. On the other hand, if the program successfully curbed teenage smoking, then government finances would benefit only a little. The logic of this argument should now be clear. If

ISSUE REVISITED: *Will a Cigarette Tax Decrease Teenage Smoking Significantly?*

We're back to the issue with which we began this chapter: Will a tax on cigarettes, which increases their price, effectively reduce teenage smoking? We can express the answer to this question in terms of the price elasticity of demand for cigarettes by teenagers. If that demand elasticity is high, the tax will be effective, because a small increase in cigarette taxes will lead to a sharp cut in purchases by teenagers. The opposite will clearly be true if this demand elasticity is small.

It turns out that young people *are* more sensitive to price increases than adult smokers. The estimates of teenagers' price elasticity of demand for cigarettes range from as low as 0.3 all the way up to 1.65.[3] This means that if, for example, a tax on cigarettes raises their price by 10 percent, the number of teenage smokers will fall by somewhere between 3 and 16.5 percent. As we just noted, adults have been found to have a price elasticity of demand for cigarettes of just 0.2—their response to the 10 percent increase in the price of cigarettes will be a decrease of only 2 percent in the number of adult smokers. So we can expect that a substantial tax on cigarettes that resulted in a significant price increase would cause a higher percentage of teenagers than adults to stop smoking.

teen cigarette demand were inelastic, the tax program would fail to make a dent in teen smoking. That would mean that many teenagers would continue to buy cigarettes and government tax revenue would grow as a result of the rise in tax rate. But when elasticity is high, a price rise *decreases* total revenue (in this case, the amount of tax revenues collected) because quantity demanded falls by a greater percentage than the price rises. That is, with an elastic demand, relatively few teen smokers will remain after the tax increase, so there will be few of them to pay the new taxes. The government will "lose out." Of course, in this case the tax seeks to change behaviour, so the government would no doubt rejoice at its small revenues!

Unfortunately, such a cigarette tax program could easily be derailed because of widespread smuggling and the existence of a black market for cigarettes, as was the case in Canada during the 1980s and early 1990s. If this situation recurred, as the price of cigarette rose, government revenues would plummet due to the unlawful activities, *not* as a result of a decline in teen smoking. The traffic of contraband cigarettes became a serious problem in Canada during the 1980–1990 period because one jurisdiction (Canada) substantially raised excise taxes on cigarettes while another (the United States) did not. Often with the complicity of unscrupulous cigarette producers who have been accused by the Canadian government of engaging in a complex smuggling scheme, "grey" markets also appeared, with Canadian cigarettes being shipped across the Canada–United States border as exports and then reimported at a lower tax rate.

Especially in the area that straddles the borders of the provinces of Quebec and Ontario and New York State, cigarette smuggling ensured that the effective price of cigarettes in Canada did not rise as sharply and teenage smoking did not fall as much, owing to the widespread availability of contraband cigarettes. In an attempt to undermine the unlawful activities and boost government revenues, the federal government sharply lowered the excise tax on a carton of cigarettes in 1994 from $16 to $11. This narrowing of the difference between Canadian and U.S. prices of cigarettes ultimately

---

[3] Sources: David R. Francis, "Demographic Groups Differ in Response to Substance Abuse Policies," *The NBER Digest*, National Bureau of Economic Research, September 1998, www.nber.org; John Tauras, *et al.*, "Effects of Prices and Access Laws on Teenage Smoking Initiation: A National Longitudinal Analysis," *Impac-Teen*, University of Illinois at Chicago Health Research and Policy Centers, April 2001, www.uic.edu/orgs/impacteen; Alexander Ding, "Youth Are More Sensitive to Price Changes in Cigarettes Than Adults," *Yale Journal of Biology and Medicine*, Vol. 76, No. 3, 1 May 2003, pp. 115-124; and Health Canada, *The 2004 Progress Report on Tobacco Control* (Ottawa: Her Majesty the Queen in Right of Canada, 2005).

did check the cross-border smuggling. It also secured more stable government revenues from the excise tax, despite the decline in teen cigarette consumption, which dropped from over 40 percent in the late 1970s to less than 20 percent by the mid-1990s.

■ WHAT DETERMINES DEMAND ELASTICITY?

What kinds of goods have elastic demand curves, meaning that quantity demanded responds strongly to price? What kinds of goods have inelastic demand curves? Several influences affect consumers' sensitivity to price changes.

1. Nature of the Good   *Necessities*, such as basic foodstuffs, normally have relatively inelastic demand curves, meaning that the quantities consumers demand of these products respond very little to price changes. For example, people buy roughly the same quantity of potatoes even when the price of potatoes rises. One study estimated that the price elasticity of demand for potatoes is just 0.3, meaning that when their price rises 10 percent, the quantity of potatoes purchased falls only by 3 percent. In contrast, many *luxury goods*, such as restaurant meals, have rather elastic demand curves. One estimate found that the price elasticity of demand for restaurant meals is 1.6, so that we can expect a 10 percent price rise to cut purchases by 16 percent.

2. Availability of Close Substitutes   If consumers can easily obtain an acceptable substitute for a product whose price increases, they will switch readily. Thus, when the market offers close substitutes for a given product, its demand will be more elastic. Substitutability is often a critical determinant of elasticity. The demand for gasoline is inelastic because we cannot easily run a car without it, but the demand for *any particular brand* of gasoline is extremely elastic, because other brands will work just as well. This example suggests a general principle: The demand for narrowly defined commodities (such as romaine lettuce) is more elastic than the demand for more broadly defined commodities (such as vegetables).

3. Share of Consumer's Budget   The share of the consumer's budget represented by the purchase of a particular item also affects its elasticity. Very inexpensive items that absorb little of a consumer's budget tend to have inelastic demand curves. Who is going to buy fewer paper clips if their price rises 10 percent? Hardly anyone. But many families will be forced to postpone buying a new car, or will buy a used car instead, if auto prices go up by 10 percent.

4. Passage of Time   The time period is relevant because the demand for many products is more elastic in the long run than in the short run. For example, when the price of home heating oil rose in the 1970s, some homeowners switched from oil heat to gas heat. Very few of them switched immediately, however, because they needed to retrofit their furnaces to accommodate the other fuel. So, the short-term demand for oil was quite inelastic. As time passed and more homeowners had the opportunity to purchase and install new furnaces, the demand curve gradually became more elastic.

■ Consequences of the Low Price Elasticity of Food

In Chapter 4, we emphasized the fact that a substantial portion of Canadian agriculture operates under either marketing boards, such as the Canadian Wheat Marketing Board, or under supply management agencies, as is the case for milk and poultry. These impediments to unfettered markets are generally justified by the high potential instability of farm product prices, which can generate substantial changes in farm revenue. The concept of elasticity helps us to understand these features of the agriculture industry. As shown in Table 1, the price elasticity of food, tobacco, and beverages is generally quite inelastic, standing at 0.5. Also, as pointed out earlier, even individual products such as potatoes can be quite price inelastic, at 0.3, while another study done for the Competition Bureau of Canada claims that consumer demand for beef has a price elasticity of 0.55. Thus, increases in supply in the domestic market, due for instance to exports of Canadian products being banned (as was the case in 2003, when an Alberta cow was discovered to have mad cow disease, or in 2000–2001, when Prince Edward Island potatoes were forbidden entry into the United States because of potato wart) can cause prices to fall substantially and to reduce farm incomes sharply.

Figure 5 illustrates what occurs for most agricultural products when there is a sudden increase in domestic supply (the supply curve is shown here as a vertical line, on the assumption that the harvesting season is over and that no more can be brought to market), moving from 9 million units to 10 million units. Prices adjust the quantity being demanded to the quantity being supplied. Because demand is inelastic, while sales in food units need to be larger, total sales revenues are smaller. The figure shows that, with supplied quantities of 9 million units, the price was $10 and total revenues were $90 million. With supply at 9 million units, the price drops to $8 (implying a price elasticity of 10.5%/22.2% = 0.47) and total revenues are now $80 million. In Figure 5, the loss to farmers is the dark green area [(10 − 8) × 9 = 18], while their gain is given by the yellow area [8 × (10 − 9) = 8], with a net loss in revenues of $10 million.

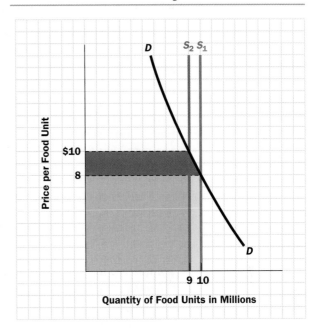

FIGURE 5   Effects of a Supply Shift in an Agricultural Market

ELASTICITY AS A GENERAL CONCEPT

So far we have looked only at how quantity demanded responds to price changes—that is, the price elasticity of demand. But elasticity has a more general use in measuring how any one economic variable responds to changes in another. From our earlier discussion, we know that a firm will be keenly interested in the price elasticity of its demand curve, but its interest in demand does not end there. As we have noted, quantity demanded depends on other things besides price. Business firms will be interested in consumer responsiveness to changes in these variables as well.

Income Elasticity

For example, quantity demanded depends on consumer incomes. A business firm's managers will, therefore, want to know how much a change in consumer income will affect the quantity of its product demanded. Fortunately, an elasticity measure can be helpful here, too. An increase in consumer incomes clearly raises the amounts of most goods that consumers will demand. To measure the response, economists use the **income elasticity of demand,** which is the ratio of the percentage change in quantity demanded to the percentage change in income. Hence, if the average real income of Canadian households went up by, say, 10 percent and purchases of theatre tickets jumped by 20 percent in five years, you could calculate the income elasticity for that period as:

Income elasticity of demand is the ratio of the percentage change in quantity demanded to the percentage change in income.

$$\frac{\textbf{Percentage change in quantity of theatre tickets demanded}}{\textbf{Percentage change in income}} = \frac{20\%}{10\%} = 2$$

Normal goods are goods whose income elasticity is positive.

Inferior goods are goods whose income elasticity is negative.

which suggests a high positive income elasticity that is characteristic of some **normal goods.** Indeed, foreign travel is quite income elastic, with middle-income and higher-income people travelling abroad much more extensively than people with low incomes do. In contrast, jeans, worn by rich and poor alike, show little demand increase as income rises and therefore have low positive income elasticity. On the other hand, the consumption of some goods, such as potatoes, would probably fall as income rises—a relationship perhaps first recognized historically by economic observers examining the post-potato famine consumption behaviour of Irish households in the middle of the nineteenth century. Potatoes are an example of goods that economists refer to as **inferior goods,** whose consumption actually declines as household real income rises. Hence, our measure of the income elasticity of demand could carry a positive or negative sign, depending on whether the good is normal or inferior.

Price Elasticity of Supply

Economists also use elasticity to measure other responses. For example, to measure the response of quantity *supplied* to a change in price, we use the *price elasticity of supply*—defined as the ratio of the percentage change in quantity supplied to the percentage change in price, for example, by what percent the supply of wheat increases when the price (at the time of planting) goes up by, say, 7 percent. The logic and analysis of all such elasticity concepts are, of course, perfectly analogous to those for price elasticity of demand.

Cross Elasticity of Demand

Consumers' demands for many products are substantially affected by the quantities and prices of *other* available products. This brings us to the important concept called *cross elasticity of demand*, which measures how much the demand for product X is affected by a change in the price of another good, Y.

This elasticity number is significantly affected by the fact that some products make other products *more* desirable, but some products *decrease* consumer demand for other products. There are some products that just naturally go together. For example, cream and sugar increase the desirability of coffee, and vice versa. The same is true of mustard or ketchup and hamburgers. In some extreme cases, neither product ordinarily has any use without the other—automobiles and tires, shoes and shoelaces, and so on. Such goods, each of which makes the other more valuable, are called **complements.**

The demand curves of complements are interrelated. That is, a rise in the price of coffee is likely to reduce the quantity of sugar demanded. Why? When coffee prices rise, people drink less coffee and therefore demand less sugar to sweeten it. The opposite will be true of a fall in coffee prices. A similar relationship holds for other complementary goods.

At the other extreme, some goods make other goods *less* valuable. These products are called **substitutes.** Ownership of a motorcycle, for example, may decrease one's desire for a bicycle. If your pantry is stocked with cans of tuna fish, you are less likely to rush out and buy cans of salmon. As you may expect, demand curves for substitutes are also related, but in the opposite direction. When the price of motorcycles falls, people may desire fewer bicycles, so the quantity of bicycles demanded falls. When the price of salmon goes up, people may eat more tuna.

Economists use **cross elasticity of demand** to determine whether two products are substitutes or complements. This measure is defined much like the ordinary price elasticity of demand, except that instead of measuring the responsiveness of the quantity demanded of, say, coffee, to a change in its own price, cross elasticity of demand measures how quantity demanded of one good (coffee) responds to a change in the price of another, say, sugar. For example, if a 20 percent rise in the price of sugar reduces the quantity of coffee demanded by 5 percent (a change of *minus* 5 percent in

Two goods are called **complements** if an increase in the quantity consumed of one increases the quantity demanded of the other, all other things remaining constant.

Two goods are called **substitutes** if an increase in the quantity consumed of one cuts the quantity demanded of the other, all other things remaining constant.

The **cross elasticity of demand** for product X to a change in the price of another product, Y, is the ratio of the percentage change in quantity demanded of X to the percentage change in the price of Y that brings about the change in quantity demanded.

quantity demanded), then the cross elasticity of demand will be:

$$\frac{\textbf{Percentage change in quantity of coffee demanded}}{\textbf{Percentage change in sugar price}} = \frac{-5\%}{20\%} = -0.25$$

Obviously, cross elasticity is important for business firms, especially when rival firms' prices are concerned. Air Canada, for example, knows all too well that it will lose customers if it does not match price cuts by WestJet. Coke and Pepsi provide another clear case in which cross elasticity of demand is crucial. But firms other than direct competitors may well take a substantial interest in cross elasticity. For example, the prices of DVD players and DVD rentals may profoundly affect the quantity of theatre tickets that consumers demand.

The cross elasticity of demand measure underlies the following rule about complements and substitutes:

> If two goods are substitutes, a rise in the price of one of them tends to increase the quantity demanded of the other; so their cross elasticities of demand will normally be positive. If two goods are complements, a rise in the price of one of them tends to decrease the quantity demanded of the other item so their cross elasticities will normally be negative. Notice that, because cross elasticities can be positive or negative, we do *not* customarily drop minus signs as we do in a calculation of the ordinary price elasticity of demand.

This result is really a matter of common sense. If the price of a good rises and buyers can find a substitute, they will tend to switch to the substitute. If the price of Japanese cars goes up and the price of North American cars does not, at least some people will switch to the latter product. Thus, a *rise* in the price of Japanese cars causes a *rise* in the quantity of North American cars demanded. Both percentage changes are positive numbers and so their ratio—the cross elasticity of demand—is also positive.

However, if two goods are complements, a rise in the price of one will discourage both its own use and use of the complementary good. Automobiles and car radios are obviously complements. A large increase in automobile prices will depress car sales, and this in turn will reduce sales of car radios. Thus, a positive percentage change in the price of cars leads to a negative percentage change in the quantity of car radios demanded. The ratio of these numbers—the cross elasticity of demand for cars and radios—is therefore negative.

In practice, courts of law often evaluate cross elasticity of demand to determine whether particular business firms face strong competition that can prevent them from overcharging consumers—hence, the quotations from the U.S. and Canadian Supreme Courts at the beginning of this chapter. The U.S. Supreme Court quotation is one of the earliest examples of the courts using the concept of cross elasticities. It tells us that if two substitute (that is, rival) products exhibit a high cross elasticity of demand (for example, between McDonald's and Burger King), then neither firm can raise its price much without losing customers to the other. In such a case, no one can legitimately claim that either firm has a monopoly. If a rise in Firm X's price causes its consumers to switch in droves to a Firm Y's product, then the cross elasticity of demand for Firm Y's product with respect to the price of Firm X's product will be high. That, in turn, means that competition is really powerful enough to prevent Firm X from raising its price arbitrarily. This relationship explains why cross elasticity is used so often in litigation before courts or government regulatory agencies when the degree of competition is an important issue, because the higher the cross elasticity of demand between two products, the stronger must be the competition between them. So cross elasticity is an effective measure of the strength of such competition.

The cross elasticity issue keeps coming up whenever firms are accused of acting like monopolists. An example that will be discussed later in the "Real-World Application" on page 132, which involved an issue of print media monopoly, was addressed by Canada's Supreme Court in 1997. (Also see "How Large Is a Firm's Market Share? Cross Elasticity as a Test" on page 130 for more on cross elasticity.)

■ CHANGES IN DEMAND: *MOVEMENTS ALONG* THE DEMAND CURVE VERSUS *SHIFTS IN* THE DEMAND CURVE

Demand is a complex phenomenon. We have studied in detail the dependence of quantity demanded on price, and we have noted that quantity demanded depends also on other variables such as consumers' incomes and the prices of complementary and substitute products. Because of changes in these other variables (which we formerly held constant when we studied only the effect of changes in price), demand curves often do not keep the same shape and position as time passes. Instead, they shift about. Chapter 4 showed that shifts in demand curves affect both quantity and price predictably.

Public policy and business discussions often make vague references to "changes in demand." By itself, this expression does not mean anything. Recall from our discussion in Chapter 4 that we must distinguish between a response to a price change—*which shows up as a movement along the demand curve*—and a change in the relationship between price and quantity demanded—*which produces a shift in the demand curve* (in effect, it moves the curve itself).

When price falls, quantity demanded generally rises. This change represents a movement *along* the demand curve. In contrast, an effective advertising campaign may result in people buying more goods at *any given price*. This case involves a rightward *shift* of the demand curve. Such a shift can be caused by a change in the value of any of the variables other than price that affect quantity demanded. Although the distinction between a shift in a demand curve and a movement along it may at first seem trivial, the difference is very significant in practice. Let us pause for a moment to consider how changes in some of these other variables shift the demand curve.

How Large Is a Firm's Market Share? Cross Elasticity as a Test

A firm's "market share" is often a crucial element in anti-merger lawsuits (see Chapter 13) for a simple reason. If the firm supplies no more than, say, 20 percent of the industry's output, courts and regulators presume that the firm is not a monopoly, as its customers can switch their business to competitors if the firm tries to charge too high a price. On the other hand, if the defendant firm in the lawsuit accounts for 90 percent of the industry's output, courts may have good reason to worry about monopoly power (which we cover in Chapter 11).

Such court cases often provide lively debates in which the defendant firms try to prove that they have very small market shares, and the plaintiffs seek to establish the opposite. Each side knows how much the defendant firm actually produces and sells, so what do they find to argue about? The dispute is about *the size of the total relevant market,* which clearly affects the magnitude of the firm's market *share*. Ambiguity arises here because different firms do not produce identical products. For instance, are Rice Krispies in the same market as Cheerios? And how about Quaker Oatmeal, which users eat hot? What about frozen waffles? Are all of these products part of the same market? If they are, then the overall market is large, and each seller therefore has a smaller share. If these products are in different markets, the opposite will be true.

Many observers argue, as Canada's Supreme Court did in the famous Southam case in 1997, that one of the proper criteria for determining the borders of the relevant market is *cross elasticity of demand*. If two products have a high and positive cross elasticity, they must be close enough substitutes to compete closely; that is,

they must be in the same market. But how large must the cross elasticity be before the court decides that two products are in the same market? Although the law has not established a clear elasticity benchmark to determine whether a particular firm is in a relevant market, several courts have determined that a very high cross elasticity number clearly indicates effective competition between two products, meaning that the two items must be in the same market.

SOURCE: © Laura Dwight/Corbis

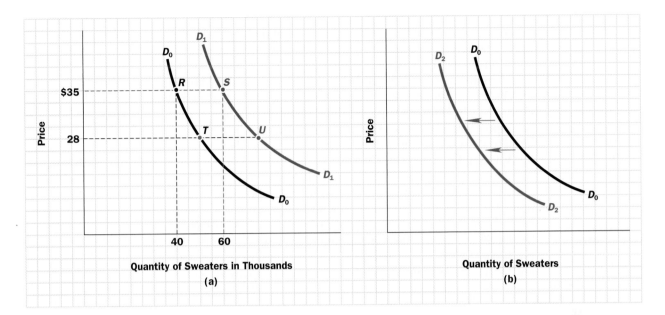

Quantity of Sweaters in Thousands
(a)

Quantity of Sweaters
(b)

Demand Shifters

FIGURE 6

Shifts in a Demand Curve

As an example, consider the effect of a change in consumer income on the demand curve for sweaters. In Figure 6(a), the black curve D_0D_0 is the original demand curve for sweaters. Now suppose that parents start sending more money to their needy sons and daughters at school. If the price of sweaters remains the same, those students are likely to use some of their increased income to buy more sweaters. For example, if the price remains at $35, quantity demanded might rise from 40,000 sweaters (point R) to 60,000 (point S). Similarly, if the price had been $28 and remained at that level, the rise in income might produce a corresponding change from T to U. In other words, we would expect the rise in income to *shift* the entire demand curve to the right from D_0D_0 to D_1D_1. In exactly the same way, a fall in consumer income can be expected to lead to a leftward shift in the demand curve for sweaters, as shown in Figure 6(b).

We can analyze other variables that affect quantity demanded in the same way. For example, increased television advertising for sweaters may lead to a rightward (outward) shift in the demand curve for sweaters, as in Figure 6(a). The same thing might occur if the price of a substitute product, such as jackets, increased, because it would put sweaters at a competitive advantage. If two goods are substitutes, a rise in the price of one of them will tend to shift the demand curve for the other one outward (to the right). Similarly, if a complementary product (perhaps matching pants to go with the sweaters) became more expensive, we would expect the demand curve for sweaters to shift to the left, as in Figure 6(b). In summary:

We expect a demand curve to shift to the right (outward) if consumer incomes rise, if tastes change in favour of the product, if substitute goods become more expensive, or if complementary goods become cheaper. We expect a demand curve to shift to the left (inward) if any of these influences changes in the opposite direction.

THE TIME PERIOD OF THE DEMAND CURVE AND ECONOMIC DECISION MAKING

One more important feature of a demand curve does not show up on a graph. A demand curve indicates, at each possible price, the quantity of the good that is demanded *during a particular time period*. That is, all of the alternative prices considered in a demand curve must refer to the *same* time period. Economists do not compare a price of $10 for commodity X in January with a price of $8 in September.

This feature imparts a peculiar character to the demand curve and complicates statistical calculations. For obvious reasons, actual observed data show different prices and quantities only for different dates. Statistical data may show, for example, the one price that prevailed in January and another that occurred at a later date, when that price had changed. Why, then, do economists adopt the apparently peculiar approach of dealing in a demand curve only with the prices that may conceivably occur (as alternative possibilities) in one and the same time period? The answer is that the demand curve's strictly defined time dimension arises inescapably from the logic of decision making and attempts to reach an **optimal decision**—the decision that moves the decision maker as close to her goal as is possible under the circumstances she faces.

When a business seeks to price one of its products for, say, the following six months, it must consider the range of *alternative* prices available for that six-month period and the consequences of each of these possible prices. For example, if management is reasonably certain that the best price for the six-month period lies somewhere between $3.50 and $5.00, it should perhaps consider each of four possibilities—$3.50, $4.00, $4.50, and $5.00—and estimate how much it can expect to sell at each of these potential prices during that given six-month period. The result of these estimates may appear in a format similar to that of the accompanying table.

> An **optimal decision** is one that best serves the objectives of the decision maker, whatever those objectives may be. It is selected by explicit or implicit comparison with the possible alternative choices. The term *optimal* connotes neither approval nor disapproval of the objective itself.

Potential Six-Month Price	Expected Quantity Demanded
$3.50	75,000
4.00	73,000
4.50	70,000
5.00	60,000

This table supplies managers with the information that they need to make optimal pricing decisions. Because the price that will be selected will be the one at which goods are sold *during the period in question*, all the prices considered in that decision must be alternative possible prices for that same period. The table therefore also contains precisely the information an economist uses to draw a demand curve.

> The demand curve describes a set of hypothetical quantity responses to a set of potential prices, but the firm can actually charge only one of these prices. All of the points on the demand curve refer to alternative possibilities for the *same time period*—the period for which the decision is to be made.

Thus, a demand curve of the sort just described is not just an abstract notion that is useful primarily in academic discussions. Rather, it offers precisely the information that businesses or government agencies need to make rational decisions. However, the fact that all points on the demand curve are hypothetical possibilities for the same period of time causes problems for statistical estimation of demand curves. These problems are discussed in the appendix to this chapter.

REAL-WORLD APPLICATION: CANADA (DIRECTOR OF INVESTIGATION AND RESEARCH) VERSUS SOUTHAM INC.

A notable example highlighting the relevance of the elasticity concept is a case that involved Canada's Competition Tribunal and Southam Inc., a major Canadian print media conglomerate. In the late 1980s, the two daily newspapers serving the Vancouver region (both owned by Southam Inc. through its subsidiary Pacific Press Ltd.)—*The Vancouver Sun* and *The Vancouver Province*—were facing growing competition for advertising revenue from the many smaller newspapers that circulated in the Lower Mainland area of British Columbia. In response, between 1989 and 1991, Southam Inc. acquired a controlling interest in 13 community and specialized newspapers, including a real estate advertising publication and three distribution services. Since this was seen as being in violation of the merger provisions of Canada's Competition Act, the Director of Investigation and Research under the Competition Act applied for an order requiring that Southam divest itself of three of these local newspapers: the *North Shore News*, *The Vancouver Courier*, and the *Real Estate Weekly*.

The Competition Tribunal, however, dismissed the Director's application and ordered that Southam merely divest itself of either the *North Shore News* or the *Real Estate Weekly*. The tribunal's decision was based on a recognition that the two daily

Vancouver newspapers were not in the same market as most of the newly acquired community newspapers and, therefore, that the Competition Act had not been violated. Since the Competition Tribunal's decision did not fully satisfy either of the two parties in the dispute, this decision was subsequently appealed by both the Director of Investigation and Research and Southam Inc. In reexamining the case, the Federal Court of Appeal rejected the earlier Competition Tribunal decision, only to have the latter be once again upheld after a further appeal to the Supreme Court of Canada in 1997.

The issue for the courts with respect to the acquisition of the community newspapers by Southam Inc. had to do with whether the merging of the various print media would lessen competition in Vancouver's retail print advertising market. In turn, this revolved around the issue of whether the two daily Vancouver newspapers and the local community newspapers were in the same product market. If they were found to be in the same market, this would have been deemed to infringe Canada's Competition Act, since it could have led to monopoly abuse in the region.

Based on indirect evidence of substitutability through an assessment of the cross elasticities of demand (see the quotation at the beginning of this chapter), both the original Competition Tribunal and the Supreme Court of Canada concluded that Southam's daily newspapers and the acquired community newspapers were in sufficiently different product markets and therefore did not contravene the Competition Act. In reviewing the evidence based partly on the original tribunal members' perception of the physical characteristics of the products and their demand responsiveness to changes in relative prices, the Supreme Court felt that Southam's acquisition of a large number of community newspapers did not significantly lessen competition in the market for retail print advertising in the Lower Mainland area of British Columbia.

■ IN CONCLUSION

In this chapter, we have continued our study of the demand side of the market. Rather than focusing on what underlies demand formation, as we did in Chapter 5, we applied demand analysis to business decisions. Most notably, we described and analyzed the economist's measure of the responsiveness of consumer demand to changes in price, and we showed how this assessment determines the effect of a firm's price change on the revenues of that enterprise. We illustrated how these concepts throw light not only on business sales and revenues, but also on a number of rather different issues, such as smoking and health and the effectiveness of competition among business firms as studied by courts of law. In the next chapter, we turn to the supply side of the market and move a step closer to completing the framework we need to understand how markets work.

SUMMARY

1. To measure the responsiveness of the quantity demanded to price, economists calculate the **elasticity of demand,** which is defined as the percentage change in quantity demanded divided by the percentage change in price, after elimination of the minus sign.

2. If demand is **elastic** (elasticity is greater than 1), then a rise in price will reduce total expenditures. If demand is **unit-elastic** (elasticity is equal to 1), then a rise in price will not change total expenditures. If demand is **inelastic** (elasticity is less than 1), then a rise in price will increase total expenditure.

3. Demand is not a fixed number. Rather, it is a relationship showing how quantity demanded is affected by price and other pertinent influences. If one or more of these other variables change, the demand curve will shift.

4. Goods that make each other more desirable (hot dogs and mustard, wristwatches and watch straps) are called **complements.** When two goods are such that when consumers get more of one of them, they want less of the other (steaks and hamburgers, Coke and Pepsi), economists call those goods **substitutes.**

5. **Cross elasticity of demand** is defined as the percentage change in the quantity demanded of one good divided by the percentage change in the price of another good. Two substitute products normally have a positive cross elasticity of demand. Two complementary products normally have a negative cross elasticity of demand.

6. A rise in the price of one of two substitute products can be expected to *shift the demand curve* of the other product to the right. A rise in the price of one of two complementary goods tends to shift the other good's demand curve to the left.

7. All points on a demand curve refer to the *same time period—* the time during which the price that is under consideration will be in effect.

KEY TERMS

(Price) elasticity of demand   119

Elastic, inelastic, and unit–elastic demand curves   122

Income elasticity of demand   127

Normal goods   128

Inferior goods   128

Complements   128

Substitutes   128

Cross elasticity of demand   128

Optimal decision   132

TEST YOURSELF

1. What variables other than price and advertising are likely to affect the quantity demanded of a product?

2. Describe the probable shifts in the demand curves for:

   a. Airplane trips when airlines' on-time performance improves

   b. Automobiles when airplane fares increase

   c. Automobiles when gasoline prices increase

   d. Electricity when the average temperature in Canada rises during a particular year (*Note:* The demand curve for electricity in Nunavut and the demand curve for electricity in southern British Columbia should respond in different ways. Why?)

3. Taxes on particular goods discourage their consumption. Economists often say that such taxes "distort consumer demands." In terms of the elasticity of demand for the commodities in question, what sort of goods would you choose to tax to achieve the following objectives?

   a. Collect a large amount of tax revenue

   b. Distort demand as little as possible

   c. Discourage consumption of harmful commodities

   d. Discourage production of polluting commodities

4. Give examples of commodities whose demand you would expect to be elastic and commodities whose demand you would expect to be inelastic.

5. A rise in the price of a certain commodity from $15 to $20 reduces quantity demanded from 20,000 to 5,000 units. Calculate the price elasticity of demand.

6. If the price elasticity of demand for gasoline is 0.3, and the current price is $1.20 per litre, what rise in the price of gasoline will reduce its consumption by 10 percent?

7. Which of the following product pairs would you expect to be substitutes, and which would you expect to be complements?

   a. Shoes and sneakers

   b. Gasoline and sport utility vehicles

   c. Bread and butter

   d. A digital camera and a computer

8. For each of the product pairs given in Test Yourself Question 7, what would you guess about the products' cross elasticity of demand?

   a. Do you expect it to be positive or negative?

   b. Do you expect it to be a large or small number? Why?

DISCUSSION QUESTIONS

1. Explain why elasticity of demand is measured in *percentages.*

2. Explain why the elasticity of demand formula normally eliminates minus signs.

3. Explain why the elasticity of a straight-line demand curve varies from one part of the curve to another.

4. A rise in the price of a product whose demand is elastic will reduce the total revenue of the firm. Explain.

5. Name some events that will cause a demand curve to shift.

6. Explain why the following statement is true: "A firm with a demand curve that is inelastic at its current output level can always increase its revenues by raising its price and selling less." (*Hint:* Refer back to the discussion of elasticity and total expenditure/total revenue on pages 118–123.)

APPENDIX 1 *The Analytics of Point Elasticity*

In this chapter, we have defined price elasticity as the percentage change in quantity demanded over the percentage change in price. While appropriate, this definition is not sufficiently precise mathematically. Economists often refer to the *point elasticity of demand* as being an exact definition of elasticity. Defining P as price, Q as quantity demanded, ΔP as the infinitesimal change in price, and ΔQ as the infinitesimal change in quantity demanded, the point elasticity of demand (η) is simply:

$$\eta = (\Delta Q/Q)/(\Delta P/P)$$

which can be rewritten as:

$$\eta = (\Delta Q/\Delta P)(P/Q)$$

On the right-hand side of the second equation above, we can see that is composed of two elements in parentheses: the reciprocal of the slope of a demand curve, $\Delta Q/\Delta P$ and the ratio of the coordinates of the point on the demand curve, P/Q. From this, you can easily infer that: (1) at any point along a straight-line demand curve, η would *not* be a constant but would be progressing from zero toward infinity as you move from right to left along the curve—that is, from where the demand curve intersects the Q-axis to where it approaches the P-axis, and (2) at the midpoint of a straight-line demand curve, $\eta = 1$.

The proof of a varying point elasticity is quite simple. While the slope, $\Delta Q/\Delta P$, is constant regardless of where it is situated on a straight-line demand curve, the ratio, P/Q, varies a great deal as it moves from one end of the demand curve to the other. In particular, as the curve approaches the Q-axis, the ratio, P/Q, tends to move toward zero, since the numerator, P, is also approaching zero. On the other hand, as the curve approaches the P-axis, the ratio, P/Q, becomes infinitely large as its denominator approaches zero. Furthermore, as shown in Figure 7, at the midpoint of the curve, demand is unit-elastic ($\eta = 1$), while to the left, $\eta > 1$ and to the right, $\eta < 1$. Indeed, moving from left to right on the demand curve, total revenue (PQ) first rises on the elastic portion of the demand curve, reaching a maximum when $\eta = 1$, and then falls as price moves downward along the inelastic portion of the demand curve.

A varying point elasticity of demand has some important implications. For instance, if the objective of a firm is to maximize its total revenue, in addition to other considerations such as costs that might also influence its decision, you would expect the firm to choose an output level at the point where the demand curve facing the firm is unit-elastic. In other words, a revenue-maximizing business enterprise would want to avoid both the inelastic and elastic portions of the demand curve where total revenues would be lower than at the point where $\eta = 1$.

FIGURE 7   **Point Elasticity along a Straight-Line Demand Curve**

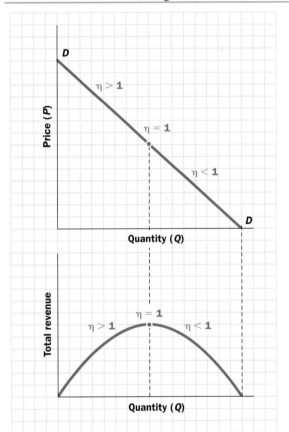

APPENDIX 2 How Can We Find a Legitimate Demand Curve from Historical Statistics?

The peculiar time dimension of the demand curve, in conjunction with the fact that many variables other than price influence quantity demanded, makes it surprisingly difficult to derive a product's demand curve from historical statistical data. Specialists can and often do derive such estimates, but the task is full of booby traps and usually requires advanced statistical methods and interpretation. This appendix seeks to warn you about the booby traps. It implies, for example, that if you become the marketing manager of a business firm after you graduate, and you need demand analysis, you will need experts to do the job. This appendix will also show you some mistakes to look for as you interpret the results, if you have reason to doubt the qualifications of the statisticians you hire to calculate or forecast your demand curve. It also gives an intuitive explanation of the legitimate ways in which demand curves may be determined from the statistics.

The most obvious way to go about estimating a demand curve statistically is to collect a set of figures on prices and quantities sold in different periods, like those given in Table 2. These points can then be plotted on a diagram with price and quantity on the axes, as shown in

Figure 8. We can then draw a line (the dashed line TT) that connects these points (labelled Jan., Feb., and so on) reasonably well, to represent the prices and quantities sold in the months indicated. This line may appear to approximate the demand curve, but unfortunately line TT, which summarizes the data for different points of time, may bear no relationship to the true demand curve. Let us see why, and what can be done about it.

You may notice at once that the prices and quantities represented by the historical points in Figure 8 refer to different periods of time, and that each point on the graph represents an *actual* (not hypothetical) price and quantity sold at a particular period of time (for example, one point gives the data for January, another for February, and so on). The distinction is significant. Over the entire period covered by the historical data (January through May), the true demand curve, which is what an economist really needs to analyze decision problems, may well have shifted because of changes in some of the other variables affecting quantity demanded.

The actual events may appear as shown in Figure 9 In January, the demand curve was given by JJ, but by February the curve had shifted to FF, by March to MM, and so on. This figure shows a separate and distinct demand curve for each of the relevant months, and none of them needs to resemble the plot of historical data, TT.

In fact, the slope of the historical plot curve, TT, can be very different from the slopes of the true underlying demand curves,

TABLE 2					
Historical Data on Price and Quantity					
	January	February	March	April	May
Quantity sold	95,000	91,500	95,000	90,000	91,000
Price	$7.20	$8.00	$7.70	$8.00	$8.20

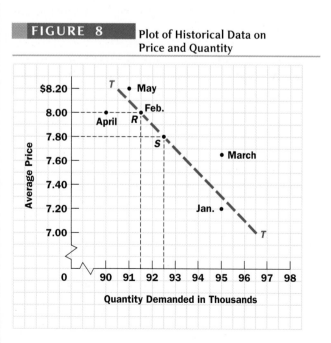

FIGURE 8   Plot of Historical Data on Price and Quantity

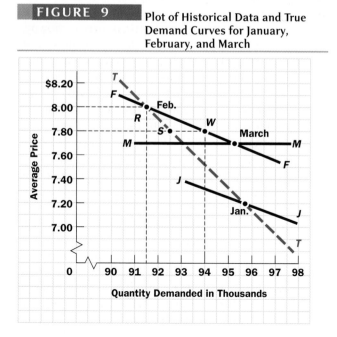

FIGURE 9   Plot of Historical Data and True Demand Curves for January, February, and March

as is the case in Figure 9. As a consequence, the decision maker can be seriously misled if she selects her price on the basis of the historical data. She may, for example, think that demand is quite insensitive to changes in price (as line *TT* seems to indicate), so she may conclude that a price reduction is not advisable. In fact, the true demand curves show that a price reduction would increase quantity demanded substantially, because they are much more elastic than the shape of the estimated curve in Figure 8 would suggest.

For example, if the decision maker was to charge a price of $7.80 rather than $8.00 in February, the historical plot would lead her to expect a rise in quantity demanded of only 1,000 units. (Compare point *R*, with sales of 91,500 units, and point *S*, with sales of 92,500 units, in Figure 8.) The true demand curve for February (line *FF* in Figure 9), however, indicates an increase in sales of 2,500 units (from point *R*, with sales of 91,500 units, to point *W*, with sales of 94,000 units). A manager who based her decision on the historical plot, rather than on the true demand curve, might be led into serious error. Nevertheless, it is astonishing how often people make this mistake in practice, even when using apparently sophisticated techniques.

■ AN ILLUSTRATION: DID THE ADVERTISING PROGRAM WORK?

Some years ago, one of the largest producers of packaged foods in North America conducted a statistical study to judge the effectiveness of its advertising expenditures, which amounted to nearly $100 million per year. A company statistician collected year-by-year figures on company sales and advertising outlays and discovered, to his delight, that they showed a remarkably close relationship to one another: Quantity demanded rose as advertising rose. The trouble was that the relationship seemed just too perfect. In economics, data about demand and any one of the elements that influence it almost never show such a neat pattern. Human tastes and other pertinent influences are just too variable to permit such regularity.

Suspicious company executives asked one of the authors of this book to examine the analysis. A little thought showed that the suspiciously close statistical relationship between sales and advertising expenditures resulted from a disregard for the principles just presented. The investigator had, in fact, constructed a graph of *historical* data on sales and advertising expenditure, analogous to *TT* in Figures 8 and 9 and therefore not necessarily similar to the truly relevant relationship.

It transpired, after study of the situation, that the stability of the relationship actually arose from the fact that, in the past, the company had based its advertising spending on its sales, automatically allocating a fixed percentage of its sales revenues to advertising. The *historical* rela-

tionship between advertising and demand therefore described only the company's budgeting practices, not the effectiveness of its advertising program. If the firm's management had used this curve in planning future advertising campaigns, it might have made some regrettable decisions. *The moral of the story:* Avoid the use of purely historical curves like *TT* in making economic decisions.

■ HOW CAN WE FIND A LEGITIMATE DEMAND CURVE FROM THE STATISTICS?

The trouble with the discussion so far is that it tells you only what you *cannot* legitimately do. But business executives and economists often need information about demand curves—for example, to analyze a pricing decision for next April. How can the true demand curves be found? In practice, statisticians use complex methods that go well beyond what we can cover in an introductory course. Nevertheless, we can (and will) give you a feeling for the advanced methods used by statisticians via a simple illustration in which a straightforward approach helps to locate the demand curve statistically.

The problem described in this appendix occurs because demand curves and supply curves (like other curves in economics) shift from time to time. They do not shift for no reason, however. As we saw in the chapter, they shift because quantity demanded or supplied is influenced by variables other than price, such as advertising, consumer incomes, and so forth. Recognizing this relationship can help us track down the demand curve—if we can determine the "other things" that affect the demand for, say, widgets, and observe when those other things changed and when they did not, we can infer when the demand curve may have been moving and when it probably wasn't.

Consider the demand for umbrellas. Umbrellas are rarely advertised and are relatively inexpensive, so neither advertising nor consumer incomes should have much effect on their sales. In fact, it is reasonable to assume that the quantity of umbrellas demanded in a year depends largely on two influences: their price and the amount of rainfall. As we know, a change in price will lead to a movement *along the demand curve* without shifting it. Heavy rains will *shift the demand curve* outward, because people will need to buy more umbrellas, whereas the curve will shift inward in a drought year. Ideally, we would like to find some dates *when the demand curve stayed in the same position but the supply curve shifted*, so that we can obtain a number of different equilibrium points, all of which lie on or near the same demand curve.

Suppose that rainfall in Winnipeg was as given in Table 3 for the period 1997–2005 and that prices and quantities of umbrellas sold in those years were as indicated by the dots in Figure 10. Notice, first, that in years

TABLE 3								
Hypothetical Annual Rainfall in Winnipeg, 1997–2005								
Year	1997	1998	1999	2000	2001	2002	2003	2004	2005
Centimetres of rain	**65**	45	**70**	**73**	88	54	80	**68**	85

FIGURE 10   Legitimate Demand Curve Estimation from Statistical Data

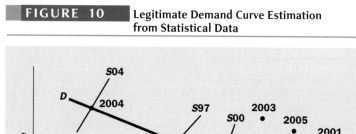

Quantity of Umbrellas Sold

in which rainfall was highest, such as 2001 and 2005, the dots in the graph lie farthest to the right, whereas the dots for low-rain years lie toward the left, meaning that in rainier years more umbrellas were sold, as our hypothesis about the effect of rain on sales suggests. More important for our purposes, for the four years 1997, 1999, 2000, and 2004, rainfall was about the same—nearly 68 centimetres. Thus, the demand curve did *not* shift from one of these years to the next. It is reasonable to conclude that the dots for these four years fell close to the same true demand curve.

But the dots for those four years are quite far apart from one another. This separation means that in those years, with the demand curve in the same position, the supply curve must have been shifting. So, if we wish, we can check this supposition statistically, by observing that the supply curve can be expected to shift when there is a change in the cost of the raw materials that go into the production of umbrellas—cloth, steel for the ribs, and plastic for the handles. Changes in this cost variable can be expected to shift the supply curve but not the demand curve, because consumers do not even know these cost numbers. So, just as the rainfall data indicated in what years the demand curve probably moved and when it did not, the input price data can give us such information about the supply curve.

To see this, imagine that we have a year-by-year table for those input costs similar to the table for rainfall (the cost table is not shown here), and suppose it tells us that in the four years of interest (1997, 1999, 2000, and 2004), those costs were very different from one another. We can infer that the supply curves in those years were quite different even though, as we have just seen, the demand curve was unchanging in the same years. Accordingly, the graph shows line *DD* drawn close to these four dots, with their four supply curves—*SS*97, *SS*99, *SS*00, and *SS*04—also going through the corresponding points, which are the equilibrium points for those four years. We can therefore interpret *DD* as a valid statistical estimate of the true demand curve for those years. We derived it by recognizing as irrelevant the dots for the years with much higher or much lower rainfall amounts, in which the demand curve can be expected to have shifted, and by drawing the statistical demand curve through the relevant dots—those that, according to the data on the variables that shift the curves, were probably generated by different supply curves but a common demand curve.

The actual methods used to derive statistical demand curves are far more complex. The underlying logic, however, is analogous to that of the process used in this example.

PRODUCTION, INPUTS, AND COSTS: BUILDING BLOCKS FOR SUPPLY ANALYSIS

Of course, that's only an estimate. The actual cost will be higher.

AUTO MECHANIC TO CUSTOMER

Suppose you take a summer job working for Al's Building Contractors, a producer of standardized, inexpensive garages. On your first day of work, you find that Al has bought or signed contracts to buy enough lumber, electrical wiring, tools, and other materials to meet his estimated needs for the next two years. The only input choice that has not been made is the number of carpenters that he will hire. So Al is left with only one decision about input purchases: How many carpenters should he sign up for his company? In this chapter, we explore this kind of decision and answer the following question: What input choice constitutes the most profitable way for a business firm to produce its output?

When firms make their supply (output) decisions, they examine the likely demand for the products they create. We have already studied demand in the last two chapters. But to understand the firm's decisions about the supply side of its markets, we must also study its production costs. A firm's costs depend on the quantities of labour, raw materials, machinery, and other inputs that it buys, and on the price it pays for each input. This chapter examines how businesses can select optimal input combinations—that is, the combinations that enable firms to produce whatever output they decide on at the minimum cost for that output. We will discuss the firm's profit-seeking decisions about output and price in Chapter 8.

To make the analysis of optimal input quantities easier to follow, we approach this task in two stages, based on a very important economic distinction: the short run and the long run. We begin the chapter with the simpler, short-run case, in which the firm can vary the quantity of only one input, while all other input quantities are already determined. This assumption vastly simplifies the analysis and enables us to answer two key questions:

- How does the quantity of input affect the quantity of output?
- How can the firm select the optimal quantity of an input?

After that, we deal with the more realistic case where the firm simultaneously selects the quantities of several inputs. We will use the results of that analysis to deduce the firm's cost curves.[1]

CONTENTS

---

[1] Some instructors may prefer to postpone discussion of this topic until later in the course.

PUZZLE: *How Can We Tell If Large Firms Are More Efficient?*

-Modern industrial societies enjoy cost advantages as a result of automation, assembly lines, and sophisticated machinery, all of which often reduce production costs dramatically. But in industries in which equipment with such enormous capacity requires a very large investment, small companies will be unable to reap many of these benefits of modern technology. Only large firms will be able to take advantage of the associated cost savings. When firms can take advantage of such *economies of scale*, as economists call them, production costs per unit will decline as output expands.

But this relationship between large size and low costs does not always fit every industry. Sometimes the courts must decide whether a giant firm should be broken up into smaller units. The most celebrated case of this kind involved American Telephone and Telegraph Company (AT&T), which had a monopoly over most of the phone service in both Canada and the United States for nearly 50 years. AT&T is a descendant of the Bell System, named after the inventor of the telephone, Alexander Graham Bell. The Bell Telephone Company of Canada (which later became Bell Canada, then Bell Canada Enterprises (BCE)—with its affiliates Bell Sympatico, Bell Mobility and Bell ExpressVu—and finally back to Bell Canada Inc.) was part of this North American quasi-monopoly, being one of the regional companies that AT&T owned or controlled. Northern Electric, also owned and controlled by AT&T, was designing and manufacturing telephone equipment for Canada; the company was later known as Northern Telecom and then as the infamous Nortel Networks.

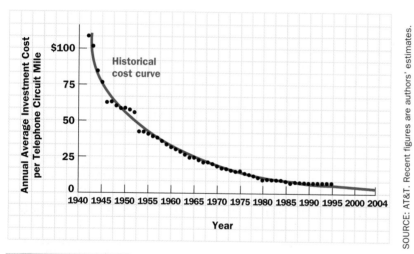

SOURCE: AT&T. Recent figures are authors' estimates.

FIGURE 1

Historical Costs for Long-Distance Telephone Transmissions

Note: Figures are in U..S. dollars per year.

In 1956, as a partial resolution of an antitrust lawsuit filed against AT&T, Bell Canada was let go and survived on its own. The main breakup of the telecommunications monopoly occurred much later, however, in both Canada and the United States, when in 1982, AT&T was dismantled into a series of two dozen regional companies. Starting at about the same time, the Canadian federal government began deregulating the telecommunications industry in a series of decisions in the 1980s and 1990s, allowing competitors into the long-distance phone industry.

Government agencies and analysts who urged a breakup of AT&T argued that such a giant firm had great economic power and deprived consumers of the benefits of competition. Opponents of the breakup, including AT&T itself, pointed out that if AT&T's large size brought significant economies of scale, then smaller firms would be much less efficient producers than the larger one and costs to consumers would have to be correspondingly higher. Who was right? To settle the issue, the courts needed to know whether AT&T had significant economies of scale.

Sometimes data like those shown in Figure 1 are offered to the courts when they consider such cases. The data in the figure, which were provided by AT&T, indicate that as the volume of telephone messages rose after 1942, the capital cost of long-distance communication by telephone dropped enormously and eventually fell below 8 percent of its 1942 level. But economists maintain that this graph does *not* constitute legitimate evidence, one way or another, about the presence of economies of scale. Why do they say this? At the end of this chapter, we will study precisely what is wrong with the evidence presented in Figure 1 and consider what sort of evidence really would legitimately have determined whether AT&T had economies of scale.

■ SHORT-RUN VERSUS LONG-RUN COSTS: WHAT MAKES AN INPUT VARIABLE?

As firms make input and output decisions, their actions are limited by previous commitments to equipment, plant, and other production matters. At any point in time, many input choices are *precommitted* by past decisions. If, for example, a firm purchased machinery a year ago, it has committed itself to that production decision for the remainder of the machine's economic life, unless the company is willing to take the loss involved in replacing that equipment sooner. An economist would say that these temporarily unalterable capital commitments are not variable for the time period in question. Firms that employ unionized labour forces may also incur costs that are temporarily not variable if labour contracts commit the firms to employing a certain number of employees or to using employees for a required number of weeks per year. Costs are not variable for some period if they are set by a longer-term financial commitment, such as a contract to buy a raw material, lease a warehouse, or invest in equipment that cannot be resold or transferred without substantial loss of the investment. Even if the firm has not paid for these commitments ahead of time, legally it must still pay for the contracted goods or services.

■ The Economic Short Run Versus the Economic Long Run

A two-year-old machine with a nine-year economic life can be an inescapable commitment and therefore represent a cost that is not variable for the next seven years. But that investment is not an unchangeable commitment in plans that extend *beyond* those seven years, because by then it may benefit the firm to replace the machine in any case. Economists summarize this notion by speaking of two different "runs" (or periods of time) for decision making: the **short run** and the **long run.**

These terms recur time and again throughout this book. In the short run, firms have relatively little opportunity to change production processes so as to adopt the most efficient way of producing their current outputs, because plant sizes and other input quantities have largely been predetermined by past decisions. Managers may be able to hire more workers to work overtime and buy more supplies, but they can't easily increase factory size, even if sales turn out to be much greater than expected. Over the long run, however, all such inputs, including plant size, become adjustable.

As an example, let's examine Al's Building Contractors and consider the number of carpenters that it hires, the amount of lumber that it purchases, and the amounts of the other inputs that it buys. Suppose the company has signed a five-year rental contract for the warehouse space in which it stores its lumber. Ultimately—that is, in the long run—the firm may be able to reduce the amount of warehouse space to which it is committed, and if warehouse space in the area is scarce in the long run, more can be built. But once he has signed the warehouse contract, Al has relatively little immediate discretion over its capacity. Over a longer planning horizon, however, Al will need to replace the original contract, and he will be free to decide all over again how large a warehouse to rent or construct.

Much the same is true of large industrial firms. Companies have little control over their plant and equipment capacities in the short run. But with some advance planning, they can acquire different types of machines, redesign factories, and make other choices. For instance, General Motors continued producing the Chevrolet Caprice, the Chevrolet Camaro, and other big, rear-wheel-drive cars even though the vehicles were not selling well. That was partly because the company knew that it would need time to convert its plants to manufacture its popular full-size pickup trucks and SUVs, which were in short supply. But after a couple of years, GM engineers were able to convert their plants to truck and SUV production or to close down plants as they did in Boisbriand, Quebec.

Note that the short run and the long run do not refer to the same time periods for all firms; rather, those periods vary in length, depending on the nature of each firm's commitments. If, for example, the firm can change its workforce every week, its machines every two years, and its factory every twenty years, then twenty years will be the long run, and any period less than twenty years will constitute the short run.

The **short run** is a period of time during which some of the firm's cost commitments will *not* have ended.

The **long run** is a period of time long enough for all of the firm's current commitments to come to an end.

Fixed Costs and Variable Costs

A **fixed cost** is the cost of an input whose quantity does not rise when output goes up, one that the firm requires to produce any output at all. The total cost of such indivisible inputs does not change when the output changes. Any other cost of the firm's operation is called a **variable cost**.

This distinction between the short run and the long run also determines which of the firm's costs rise or fall with a change in the amount of output produced by the firm. Some costs cannot be varied, *no matter how long the period in question.* These are called **fixed costs,** and they arise when some types of inputs can be bought only in big batches or when inputs have a large productive capacity. For example, there is no such thing as a "mini" automobile assembly line capable of producing two cars per week, and, except for extreme luxury models, it is impractical to turn out automobiles without an assembly line. For these reasons, the fixed cost of automobile manufacturing includes the cost of the smallest (least expensive) assembly line that the firm can acquire. These costs are called *fixed* because the total amount of money spent in buying the assembly line does not vary, whether it is used to produce 10 cars or 100 cars each day, so long as the output quantity does not exceed the assembly line's capacity.

In the short run, some other costs behave very much as fixed costs do; in other words, they are predetermined by previous decisions and are *temporarily* fixed. But in the longer run, firms can change both their capital and labour commitments. So, in the long run, more costs become **variable.** We will have more to say about fixed and variable costs as we examine other key input and cost relationships.

PRODUCTION, INPUT CHOICE, AND COST WITH ONE VARIABLE INPUT

In reality, all businesses use many different inputs. Nevertheless, we will begin our discussion with the short-run case in which there is *only a single input that is variable*—that is, in which the quantities of all other inputs will not be changed. In doing so, we are trying to replicate in our theoretical analysis what physicists or biologists do in the laboratory when they conduct a *controlled* experiment: changing just one variable at a time to enable us to see the influence of that one variable in isolation. Thus, we will study the effects of variation in the quantity of one input under the assumption that all other things remain unchanged—that is, other things being equal.

TABLE 1

Total Physical Product Schedule for Al's Building Company

(1)	(2)
Number of Carpenters	Total Product (Garages per Year)
0	0
1	4
2	12
3	24
4	32
5	35
6	30

The firm's **total physical product (TPP)** is the amount of output it obtains in total from a given quantity of input.

The **average physical product (APP)** is the total physical product (TPP) divided by the quantity of input. Thus, APP = TPP/X where X = the quantity of input.

Total, Average, and Marginal Physical Products

We begin the analysis with the first of the firm's three main questions: What is the relationship between the quantity of inputs utilized and the quantity of production? Al has studied how many of its inexpensive standardized garages his firm can turn out in a year, depending on the number of carpenters it uses. The relevant data are displayed in Table 1.

The table begins by confirming the common-sense observation that garages cannot be built without labour. Thus, output is zero when Al hires zero labour input (see the first line of the table). After that, the table shows the rising total garage outputs that additional amounts of labour yield, assuming that the firm's employees work on one garage at a time and, after it is finished, move on to the next garage. For instance, with a one-carpenter input, total output is 4 garages per year; with two carpenters helping one another and specializing in different tasks, annual output can be increased to 12 garages. After five carpenters are employed in building a garage, they begin to get in one another's way. As a result, employment of a sixth carpenter actually reduces output from 35 to 30 garages.

Total Physical Product   The data in Table 1 appear graphically in Figure 2, which is called a **total physical product (TPP)** curve. This curve reports how many garages Al can produce with different quantities of carpenters, holding constant the quantities of all other inputs.

Average Physical Product   To understand more about how the number of carpenters contributes to output, Al can use two other physical product relationships given in Table 2. The **average physical product (APP)** measures output per unit of input; it is simply the total physical product divided by the quantity of variable input used. For Al's

TABLE 2

Al's Product Schedules: Total, Average, and Marginal Physical Product and Marginal Revenue Product

(1)	(2)	(3)	(4)	(5)
Number of Carpenters	Total Physical Product (Garages per year)	Marginal Physical Product (Garages per added carpenter)	Marginal Revenue Product (Thousands of $ per year per added carpenter)	Average Physical Product (Garages per carpenter)
0	0			0
		4	$ 60	
1	4			4
		8	120	
2	12			6
		12	180	
3	24			8
		8	120	
4	32			8
		3	45	
5	35			7
		−5	−75	
6	30			5

Note: Each entry in Column (3) is the difference between successive entries in Column (2). This is what is indicated by the zigzag lines.

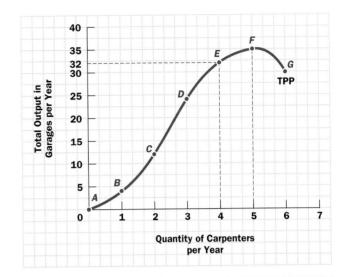

FIGURE 2

Total Physical Product with Different Quantities of Carpenters Used by Al's Firm

firm, it is the total number of garages produced in a year divided by the number of carpenters hired. APP is shown in Column (5) of Table 2. For example, because four carpenters can turn out 32 garages annually, the APP of four carpenters is 32/4, or 8 garages per carpenter.

Marginal Physical Product   To decide how many carpenters to hire, Al should know how many *additional* garages to expect from each *additional* carpenter. This concept is known as **marginal physical product (MPP),** and Al can calculate it from the total physical product data using the same method we introduced to derive marginal utility from total utility in Chapter 5. For example, the marginal physical product of the fourth carpenter is the total output when Al uses four carpenters *minus* the total output when he hires only three carpenters. That is, the MPP of the fourth carpenter = 32 − 24 = 8 garages. We calculate the other MPP entries in the third column of Table 2 in exactly the same way. Figure 3 displays these numbers in a graph called a *marginal physical product curve.*

The **marginal physical product (MPP)** of an input is the increase in total output that results from a one-unit increase in the input quantity, holding constant the amounts of all other inputs.

A Recap

Total physical product: TPP = Total output when quantities of one input change

Average physical product (of an input): APP = TPP/(units of variable input)

Marginal physical product (of an input): MPP = ΔTPP/Δ(one unit of input)

where the Δ symbol represents a *difference*.

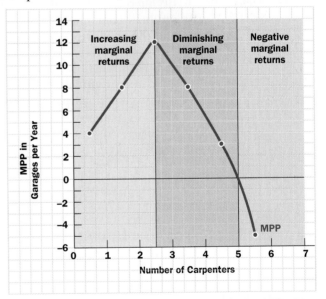

■ Marginal Physical Product and the Principle of Diminishing Marginal Returns

The shape of the marginal physical product curve in Figure 3 has important implications for Al's garage building. Compare the TPP curve in Figure 2 with the MPP curve in Figure 3. The MPP curve can be described as the curve that reports the *rate* at which the TPP curve is changing. MPP is equal to the *slope* of the TPP curve[2] because it tells us

FIGURE 3

Al's Marginal Physical Product (MPP) Curve

---

[2] The same is true of any total and marginal curves: at any output level the marginal is the slope of the total curve. For example, the slope of an individual's total utility curve when he has five apples is the change in his total utility when he acquires a sixth apple. But that, by definition, is the marginal utility of the sixth apple.

how much of an increase in garage output results from each additional carpenter Al hires. Thus, until input reaches three carpenters, the marginal physical product of carpenters *increases* when Al hires more of them. That is, TPP increases at an increasing rate (its slope becomes steeper) between points *A* and *D* in Figure 2. Between three carpenters and five carpenters, the MPP *decreases* but still has *positive* values throughout (that is, it lies above the horizontal axis). Consequently, in this range, TPP is still increasing (its slope, MPP, is greater than zero), but it is increasing more slowly (its slope, MPP, is still positive, but is a declining positive number). That is, in this region, between points *D* and *F* in Figure 2, each additional carpenter contributes garage output, but adds less than the previous carpenter added. Beyond five carpenters, to the right of point *F* in Figure 2, the MPP of carpenters actually becomes *negative:* The total physical product curve starts to decrease as additional carpenters get in one another's way.

Figure 3 is divided into three zones to illustrate these three cases. Note that the marginal returns to additional carpenters increase at first and then diminish. This is the typical pattern, and it parallels what we had to say about the utility of consumption in Chapter 5. Each additional unit adds some production, but at a decreasing rate. In the leftmost zone of Figure 3 (the region of increasing marginal returns), each additional carpenter adds more to TPP than the previous one did.

The **principle of diminishing marginal returns** (also called more simply the principle of diminishing returns), which plays a key role in economics, states that an increase in the amount of any one input, *holding constant the amounts of all others*, ultimately leads to lower marginal returns to the expanding input.

This principle, which some economists call a "law," first arose from the observation, made nearly two centuries ago, that farmers first used the more fertile lands and then less fertile ones, thus achieving lower and lower returns as more land was used. A similar phenomenon occurred in agriculture when more workers were employed on a given tract of land: The use of additional workers yielded smaller and smaller increases to farm production. This led to the principle of variable input proportions, according to which returns to a single input usually diminish. When the quantity of one input increases while all others remain constant, the variable input whose quantity increases gradually becomes more and more abundant relative to the others, and gradually becomes overabundant. (For example, the proportion of labour increases and the proportions of other inputs, such as lumber, decrease.) As Al uses more and more carpenters with fixed quantities of other inputs, the proportion of labour time to other inputs becomes unbalanced. Adding yet more carpenter time then does little good and eventually begins to harm production. At this last point, the marginal physical product of carpenters becomes *negative.*

Many real-world cases seem to follow the law of variable input proportions. In China, for instance, farmers have been using increasingly more fertilizer as they try to produce larger grain harvests to feed the country's burgeoning population. Although its consumption of fertilizer is four times higher than it was 15 years ago, China's grain output has increased by only 50 percent. This relationship certainly suggests that fertilizer use has reached the zone of diminishing returns.

The Optimal Quantity of an Input and Diminishing Returns

We can now address the second question that all firms must ask as they make production decisions: How can the firm select the optimal quantity of an input? To answer this question, look again at the first and third columns of Table 2, which show the firm's marginal physical product schedule. We will assume for now that a carpenter is paid $50,000 per year, and that Al can sell his inexpensive garages for $15,000 each.

Now suppose that Al is considering using just one carpenter. Is this choice optimal? That is, does it maximize his profits? To answer this question we have to consider not only how many garages an additional carpenter provides but also the money value of each garage; that is, we must first translate the marginal *physical* product into its money equivalent. In this case, the monetary evaluation of TPP shows that the answer is no, one

The principle of diminishing marginal returns, often called the **principle of diminishing returns**, asserts that returns to a single input, as all other inputs are held constant, eventually diminish as more of the input is used.

carpenter is not enough to maximize profit, because the marginal physical product of a second carpenter is 8 garages per year, the second entry in marginal physical product Column (3) of Table 2. At a price of $15,000 per garage, this extra output would add $120,000 to total revenue. Because the added revenue exceeds the $50,000 cost of the second carpenter, the firm comes out ahead by $120,000 − $50,000, or $70,000 per year.

Marginal Revenue Product and Input Prices   The additional *money revenue* that a firm receives when it increases the quantity of some input by one unit is called the input's **marginal revenue product (MRP).** If Al's garages sell at a fixed price, say, $15,000, the marginal revenue product of the input equals its marginal physical product multiplied by the output price:[3]

> The **marginal revenue product (MRP)** of an input is the additional revenue that the producer earns from the increased sales when it uses an additional unit of the input.

$$\textbf{MRP} = \textbf{MPP} \times \textbf{Price of output}$$

For example, we have just shown that the marginal revenue product of the second carpenter is $120,000, which we obtained by multiplying the MPP of 8 garages by the price of $15,000 per garage. The other MRP entries in Column (4) of Table 2 are calculated in the same way. The MRP concept enables us to formulate a simple rule for the optimal use of any input. Specifically:

> When the marginal revenue product of an input exceeds its price, it pays the firm to use more of that input. Similarly, when the marginal revenue product of the input is less than its price, it pays the firm to use less of that input.

Let's test this rule in the case of Al's garages. We have observed that two carpenters cannot be the optimal input because the MRP of a second carpenter ($120,000) exceeds his wages ($50,000). What about a third carpenter? Table 2 shows that the MRP of the third carpenter (12 × $15,000 = $180,000) also exceeds his wage; thus, stopping at three carpenters also is not optimal. The same is true for a fourth carpenter, because his MRP of $120,000 still exceeds his $50,000 price. The situation is different with a fifth carpenter, however. Hiring a fifth carpenter is not a good idea because his MRP, which is 3 × $15,000 = $45,000, is less than his $50,000 cost. Thus, the optimal number of carpenters for Al to hire is four, yielding a total output of 32 garages.

Notice the crucial role of diminishing returns in this analysis. When the marginal *physical* product of a carpenter begins to decline, the money value of that product falls as well—that is, the marginal *revenue* product also declines. The producer always profits by expanding input use until diminishing returns set in and reduce the MRP to the price of the input. So Al should stop *increasing* his carpenter hirings when MRP *falls* to the price of a carpenter.

> A common expression suggests that it does not pay to continue doing something "beyond the point of diminishing returns." As we see from this analysis, quite to the contrary, it normally *does* pay to do so! The firm has employed the proper amount of input only when diminishing returns reduce the marginal revenue product of the input to the level of its price, because then the firm will be wasting no opportunity to *add* to its total profit. Thus, the optimal quantity of an input is that at which MRP equals its price (*P*). In symbols:

$$\textbf{MRP} = \textit{P} \textbf{ of input}$$

The logic of this analysis is exactly the same as that used in our discussion of marginal utility and price in Chapter 5. Al is trying to maximize *profits*—the difference between the *total* revenue yielded by his carpenter input and the *total* cost of buying that input. To do so, he must increase his carpenter usage to the point where its price equals its marginal revenue product, just as an optimizing consumer keeps buying until price equals marginal utility.

---

[3] Here it is assumed that the price of the output—the price of each garage—is $15,000, no matter how many garages are produced. But astute readers may wonder what the marginal revenue product would be equal to if Al was forced to gradually reduce the price of his garages when he produced and attempted to sell more garages. We need a new concept— marginal revenue (MR), which will be introduced in Chapter 8. When the price is not constant, MRP = MPP × MR.

Closer to Home: The Diminishing Marginal Returns to Studying

The principle of diminishing marginal returns crops up a lot in ordinary life, not just in the world of business. Consider Jason and his study habits: He has a tendency to procrastinate and then cram for exams the night before he takes them, pulling "all-nighters" regularly. How might an economist describe his payoff from an additional hour of study in the wee hours of the morning, relative to Colin's efforts, who studies for two hours every night?

SOURCE: © Mark Richards/PhotoEdit

■ MULTIPLE INPUT DECISIONS: THE CHOICE OF OPTIMAL INPUT COMBINATIONS[4]

Up to this point we have simplified our analysis by assuming that the firm can change the quantity of only one of its inputs and that the price the product can command does not change, no matter how large a quantity the producer offers for sale (the fixed price is $15,000 for Al's garages). Of course, neither of these assumptions is true in reality. In Chapter 8, we will explore the effect of product quantity decisions on prices by bringing in the demand curve. But first we must deal with the obvious fact that a firm must decide on the quantities of each of the many inputs it uses, not just one input at a time. That is, Al must decide not only how many carpenters to hire, but how much lumber and how many tools to buy. Both of the latter decisions clearly depend on the number of carpenters in his team. So, once again, we must examine the two basic and closely interrelated issues: production levels and optimal input quantities. But this time, we will allow the firm to select the quantities of *many* inputs. By expanding our analysis in this way, we can study a key issue: how a firm, by its choice of production method (also called its production technology), can make up for decreased availability of one input by using more of another input.

■ Substitutability: The Choice of Input Proportions

Just as we found it useful to start the analysis with physical output or product in the one-variable-input case, we will start with physical production in the multiple-variable-input case. Firms can choose among alternative types of technology to produce any given product. Many people mistakenly believe that management really has very little choice when selecting its input proportions. Technological considerations alone, they believe, dictate such choices. For example, a particular type of furniture-cutting machine may require two operators working for an hour on a certain amount of wood to make five desks—no more and no less. But this way of looking at the possibilities is an overly narrow view of the matter. Whoever first said that there are many ways to "skin a cat" saw things more clearly.

In reality, the furniture manufacturer can choose among several alternative production processes for making desks. For example, simpler and cheaper machines might be able to change the same pile of wood into five desks, but only by using more than two hours of labour. Or, the firm might choose to create the desks with simple hand tools, which would require many more workers and no machinery at all. The firm will seek the method of production that is *least costly*.

---

[4] Instructors may want to teach this part of the chapter (up to page 149) now, or they may prefer to wait until they come to Chapters 19 and 20 on the determination of wages, interest rates, profit, and rent.

In advanced industrial societies, where labour is expensive and machinery is cheap, it may pay to use the most automated process. For example, car producers in Canada have curbed their high labour costs by investing in computers that enabled them to manufacture twice as many car engines with the same number of people. But in less developed countries, where machinery is scarce and labour is abundant, making things by hand may be the most economical solution. An interesting example can be found in rural India, where company records are often still handwritten, not computerized, as is widely true in North America.

We conclude that firms can generally substitute one input for another. A firm can produce the same number of desks with less labour, *if* it is prepared to sink more money into machinery. But whether it *pays* to make such a substitution depends on the relative costs of labour and machinery. Several general conclusions follow from this discussion:

- Normally, a firm can choose among different technological options to produce a particular volume of output. Technological considerations rarely fix input proportions immutably.
- Given a target production level, a firm that cuts down on the use of one input (say, labour) will normally have to increase its use of another input (say, machinery). This trade-off is what we mean when we speak of *substituting* one input for another.
- The combination of inputs that represents the *least costly* way to produce the desired level of output depends on the relative prices of the various inputs.

■ The Marginal Rule for Optimal Input Proportions

Choosing the input proportions that minimize the cost of producing a given output is really a matter of common sense. To understand why, let us turn, once again, to marginal analysis of the decision. As before, Al is considering whether to buy more expensive tools that will enable him to produce his garages using fewer carpenters or to do the reverse. The two inputs, tools and carpenters, are substitutes; if the firm spends more on tools, it needs fewer carpenters. *But the tools are not perfect substitutes for labour.* Tools need carpenters to operate them, and tools are not endowed with the judgment and common sense that are needed if something goes wrong. Of course, a carpenter without tools is also not very productive, so Al gains a considerable benefit by acquiring balanced relative quantities of the two inputs. If he uses too much of one and too little of the other, the output of the firm will suffer. In other words, it is reasonable to assume *diminishing returns* to excessive substitution of either input for the other. As he substitutes more and more labour for expensive machinery, the marginal physical product of the added labour will begin to decline.

How should Al decide whether to spend more on tools and less on labour, or vice versa? The obvious—and correct—answer is that he should compare what he gets for his money by spending, say, $100 more on labour or on tools. If he gets more (a greater marginal revenue product) by spending this amount on labour than by spending it on tools, clearly it pays Al to spend that money on labour rather than on tools. As a matter of fact, in that case it pays him to spend somewhat less on tools than he had been planning to do, and to transfer the money he thereby saves to purchasing more carpenter labour. So we have the following three conclusions:

1. If the marginal revenue product of the additional labour that Al gets by spending, say, a dollar more on carpenters is greater than the marginal revenue product he receives from spending the same amount on tools, he should change his plans and devote more of his spending to labour than he had planned and less to tools.
2. If the marginal revenue product of an additional dollar spent on labour is less than the marginal revenue product of an additional dollar spent on tools, Al should increase his spending on tools and cut his planned spending on labour.

3. If the marginal revenue products of an additional dollar spent on either labour or tools are the same, Al should stick to his current purchase plans. There is nothing to be gained by switching the proportions of his spending on the two inputs.[5]

There is only one more step. Suppose, for example, that the MRP per dollar is greater for labour than that for tools. Then, as we have just seen, Al should spend more money on labour than originally planned, and less on tools. But where should this switch in spending stop? Should the transfer of funds continue until Al stops spending on tools altogether, because the MRP per dollar is greater for labour than for tools? Such an answer makes no sense—a worker without tools is not very productive. The correct answer is that, by the "principle" of diminishing returns, when Al buys more and more carpenter time, the initially higher MRP of carpenters will decline. As he spends less and less on tools, tools will become scarcer and more valuable and their initially lower MRP will rise. So, as Al transfers more money from tools to carpenters, the MRPs per dollar for the inputs will get closer and closer to one another, and they will eventually meet. That, then, is when the proportions of Al's spending allocated to the two inputs will have reached the optimal level. At that point, there is no way he can get more for his money by changing the proportions of those inputs that he hires or buys.

■ Changes in Input Prices and Optimal Input Proportions

The common-sense reasoning behind the rule for optimal input proportions leads to an important conclusion. Let's say that Al is producing seven garages at minimum cost. Suppose that the wage of a carpenter falls, but the price of tools remains the same. This means that a dollar will now buy a larger quantity of labour than before, thus increasing the marginal revenue product *per dollar* spent on carpenters—a dollar will now buy more carpenter labour and more of its product than it did before. But because tool prices have not changed, the marginal revenue product obtainable by spending an additional dollar on tools will also be unchanged. So, if Al had previously devoted the right proportions to spending on carpenters and spending on tools, that will no longer be true. If, previously, the marginal revenue product per dollar spent on carpenters equalled the marginal revenue product per dollar spent on tools, now this relationship will have changed so that

Marginal revenue product per dollar spent on carpenters > Marginal revenue product per dollar spent on tools

That is, the proportion between the two inputs will no longer be optimal. Clearly, Al will be better off if he increases his spending on carpenters and reduces his spending on tools.

Looked at another way, to restore optimality, the MRP per dollar spent on carpenters must fall to match the MRP per dollar spent on tools. But, by the principle of diminishing returns, the MRP of carpenters will *fall* when the use of carpenters is increased. Thus, a fall in the price of carpenters prompts Al to use *more* carpenter time. And if the increase is sufficiently large, it will restore equality in the marginal revenue products per dollar spent on the two inputs. In general, we have the common-sense result that:

As any one input becomes more costly relative to competing inputs, the firm is likely to substitute one input for another—that is, to use less of the input that has become more expensive and to use more of competing inputs.

This general principle of input substitution applies in industry just as it does in Al's firm. For a real-world application of the analysis, see the accompanying box, "Input Substitution in the Logging Industry."

---

[5] Calculation of the marginal revenue product per dollar spent on an input is easy if we know the marginal revenue product of the input and the price of the input. For example, we know from Table 2 that the MRP of a third carpenter is $180,000, and his wage is $50,000. Thus, his MRP per dollar spent on his wages is $180,000/$50,000 = $3.60. More generally, the MRP per dollar spent on any input, X, is the MRP of X divided by the price of X.

Input Substitution in the Logging Industry

It is usually believed that the more modern the machines are or the more mechanized an operation is, the better. This is not necessarily so, however. It all depends on the output that can be sold and on the relative cost of the different factors of production. A study done on the efficiency of logging contractors has shown that the most profitable operations were not necessarily those that benefited from the most capital-intensive methods or from the most up-to-date machines. Loggers involved in smaller operations who were the most efficient were those making use of secondhand material. But as the authors of the journal excerpt below argue, this advantage may disappear when the cost of labour rises.

Thirty years ago the entry cost for a pulpwood producer in the South was relatively low: a bob-tail truck, a pair of mules, and a bowsaw. Today, if mechanized felling and skidders are utilized, ownership and operating costs are substantial even for second-hand machines. Among those loggers closest to the entry point, the most efficient were all using depreciated equipment. . . . The aggregate fixed cost, or the minimum capital, required to enter mechanized logging is $144,348. This is approximately the capital value of a used equipment-based logging operation. . . . Within the smaller operations, reducing capital expenses to a minimum was the strategy adopted by the most efficient loggers. Labour efficiency tended to be lower for these operations

as the burden of sustaining production was then transferred from equipment to the workers who were paid for idleness and maintenance work. . . . But it will be increasingly difficult for small contractors to remain competitive if labour costs continue to increase.

SOURCE: L. G. LeBel and W. B. Stuart, "Technical efficiency evaluation of logging contractors using a nonparametric model," *Journal of Forest Engineering*, July 1998, 9(2).

COST AND ITS DEPENDENCE ON OUTPUT

Having analyzed how the firm decides on its input quantities, we now take the next step toward our analysis of the implications for pricing and output quantity of the product it sells to consumers. For this purpose, the firm needs to know, among other things, how much it will cost to produce different output quantities. Clearly, this cost—the amount of money that the firm spends on production—will depend on how much it produces, and what quantities of input it will need to do the job. How do we measure the cost relationships?

Input Quantities and Total, Average, and Marginal Cost Curves

So, we must turn now to the third of the three main questions that a firm must ask: How do we derive the firm's cost relationships from the input decisions that we have just explained? We will use these cost relationships when we analyze the firm's output and pricing decisions in Chapter 8, in which we will study the last of the main components of our analysis of the market mechanism: How much of its product or service should the profit-maximizing firm produce?

The most desirable output quantity for the firm clearly depends on the way in which costs change when output varies. Economists typically display and analyze such information in the form of *cost curves*. Indeed, because we will use marginal analysis again in our discussion, we will need three different cost curves: the *total cost curve*, the *average cost curve*, and the *marginal cost curve*.

NEL

These curves follow directly from the nature of production. The technological production relationships for garage-building dictate the amount of carpenter time, the type and quantity of tools, the amount of lumber, and the quantities of the other inputs that Al uses to produce any given number of garages. This technological relationship for carpenters appeared earlier in Figure 2 (p. 143). From these data on carpenter usage and the price of a carpenter, plus similar information on tools, lumber, and other inputs, and the decision on the optimal proportions among those inputs, Al can determine how much it will cost to produce any given number of garages. Therefore, the relevant cost relationships depend directly on the production relationships we have just discussed. The calculation of the firm's total costs from its physical product schedule that we will use here assumes that the firm cannot influence the market price of carpenters or the prices of other inputs, that these are fixed by union contracts and other such influences. Using this assumption, let us begin with the portion of the cost calculation that applies to carpenters.

The method is simple: For each quantity of output, record from Table 1 or Figure 2 the number of carpenters required to produce it. Then multiply that quantity of carpenters by the assumed annual average wage of $50,000.

Total Variable Costs   In addition to the cost of carpenters, Al must spend money on his other inputs, such as tools and lumber. Furthermore, his costs must include the *opportunity costs* of any inputs that Al himself contributes—such as his own labour, which he could instead have used to earn wages by taking a job in another firm, and his own capital that he has invested in the firm, which he could instead have invested, say, in interest-paying government bonds. The costs of the other inputs are calculated, essentially, in the same manner as the cost of carpenters—by determining the quantity of each input that will optimally be used in producing any given number of garages, and then multiplying that input quantity by its price. To calculate the total cost Al must cover to build, say, four garages per year, we have the following very simple formula:

**The total variable cost of four garages =
(the number of carpenters used ×
the wage per carpenter) +
(the amount of lumber that will be used ×
the price of lumber) +
(the number of pounds of nails that will be
used × the price of nails) + . . .**

Using this calculation and data such as those in Table 1, we obtain directly the total variable costs for different output quantities shown in Table 3. For example, Row (4), Column (2), of Table 3 indicates that if he wants to produce three garages per year, Al needs to purchase quantities of labour time, lumber, and other inputs whose total cost is $54,000. The other numbers in the second column of Table 3 are to be interpreted similarly. To summarize the story:

TABLE 3

Al's (Variable) Cost Schedules

(1)	(2)	(3)	(4)
Total Product (Garages per year)	Total Variable Cost (Thousands of $ per year)	Marginal Variable Cost (Thousands of $ per added garage)	Average Variable Cost (Thousands of $ per garage)
0	$ 0		$ 0
1	28	$28	28
2	44	16	22
3	54	10	18
4	62	8	15.5
5	68	6	13.6
6	75	7	12.5
7	84	9	12
8	100	16	12.5
9	132	32	14.7 (approx.)
10	178	46	17.8

The marginal product relationships enable the firm to determine the input proportions and quantities needed to produce any given output at the lowest total cost. From those input quantities and the prices of the inputs, we can determine the *total variable cost* (TVC) of producing any level of output. Thus, the relationship of total cost to output is determined by the technological production relationships between inputs and outputs and by input prices.

Total, Average, and Marginal Cost Curves   Two other cost curves—the average variable cost (AVC) and marginal variable cost (MVC) curves—provide information crucial for our analysis. We can calculate these curves directly from the total cost curve, just as Table 2 calculated average and marginal physical product from total physical product.

For any given output, *average variable cost* is defined as total variable cost divided by quantity produced. For example, Table 3 shows that the total variable cost of producing seven garages is $84,000, so the average variable cost is $84,000/7 or $12,000 per garage.

Similarly, we define the *marginal variable cost* as the increase in total cost that arises from the production of an additional garage. For example, the marginal variable cost of the fifth garage is the difference between the total cost of producing five garages, $68,000, and the total cost of producing four garages, $62,000. That is, the marginal cost of the fifth garage is $6,000. Figure 4 shows all three curves—the total, average, and marginal variable cost curves. The TVC curve is generally assumed to rise fairly steadily as the firm's output increases. After all, Al cannot expect to produce eight garages at a lower total cost than he can produce five, six, or seven garages. The AVC curve and the MVC curve both look roughly like the letter U—first going downhill, then gradually turning uphill again. We will explore the reason for and implications of this U-shape later in the chapter.

So far, we have taken into account only the *variable* costs of Al's garage-building, or the costs that depend on the number of garages his firm builds. That's why these costs are labelled as "variable" in the table and the graph. But there are other costs, such as the rent Al pays for the company office, that are fixed; that is, they stay the same in total, no matter how many garages he produces, at least within some limits. Of course, Al cannot obtain these fixed-cost inputs for free. Their costs, however, are constants—they are positive numbers and not zero. In Canada, a survey conducted by the Bank of Canada estimates that 37 percent of all business costs are fixed costs.

Total Fixed Cost and Average Fixed Cost Curves
Although variable costs are only part of combined total costs (which include both fixed and variable costs), the *total cost* (TC) curve and the *average cost* (AC) curve that include both types of costs have the same general shape as those shown in Figure 4. In contrast, the curves that record *total fixed costs* (TFC) and *average fixed costs* (AFC) have very special shapes, illustrated in Figure 5 on the next page. By definition, TFC remains the same whether the firm produces a little or a lot—as long as it produces anything at all. As a result, any TFC curve is a horizontal straight line like the one shown in Figure 5(a). It has the same height at every output.

Average fixed cost, however, gets smaller and smaller as output increases, because AFC (which equals TFC/Q) (where Q represents quantity of output) falls as output (the denominator) rises for constant TFC. Businesspeople typically put the point another way: Any increase in output spreads the fixed cost (which they often call "overhead") among more units, meaning that less of it is carried by any one unit. For example, suppose that Al's garage operation's total fixed cost is $12,000 per year.

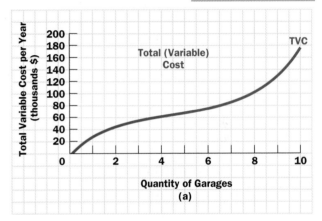

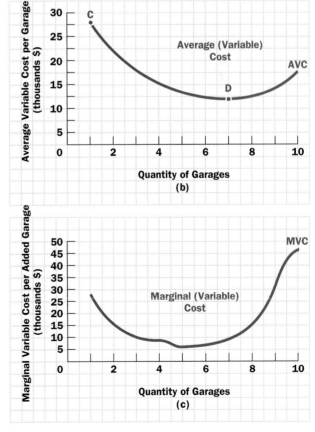

Note: Quantity is in garages per year.

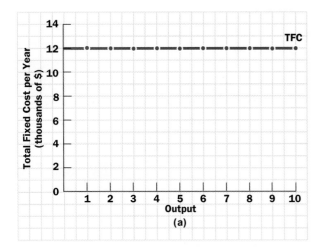

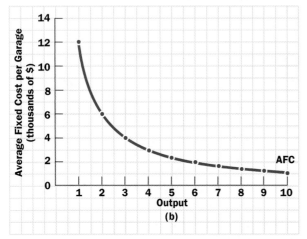

FIGURE 5

Fixed Costs: Total and Average

Note: Output is in garages per year.

TABLE 4			
Al's Fixed Costs			
(1)	(2)	(3)	(4)
Number of Garages	Total Fixed Cost (Thousands of $ per year)	Marginal Fixed Cost	Average Fixed Cost (Thousands of $ per garage)
0	$12		–
1	12	$0	$12
2	12	0	6
3	12	0	4
4	12	0	3
5	12	0	2.4
6	12	0	2
7	12	0	1.7
8	12	0	1.5
9	12	0	1.33
10	12	0	1.2

When he produces only two garages, the entire $12,000 of fixed cost must be borne by those two garages; that is, the average fixed cost is $6,000 per garage. But if Al produces three garages, the fixed cost per garage falls to $4,000 = $12,000/3 (Table 4).

AFC can never reach zero. Even if Al were to produce 1 million garages per year, each garage would have to bear, on the average, one-millionth of the TFC—which is still a positive number (although minuscule). It follows that the AFC curve gets lower and lower as output increases, moving closer and closer to the horizontal axis but never crossing it. This pattern appears in Figure 5(b).

Finally, we may note that marginal fixed costs exhibit a very simple behaviour: *Marginal fixed costs (MFC) are always zero.* Building an additional garage does not add a penny to Al's annual office rent, which is fixed at $12,000 by the lease he and his landlord have signed. Looked at another way, because the total fixed cost stays unchanged at $12,000, no matter how many garages are produced, the marginal fixed cost of, say, a fifth garage is the total fixed cost of five garages minus the total fixed cost of four garages = $12,000 − $12,000 = 0. From now on, we will not refer to the *marginal variable cost* anymore, but will use instead the more simple **marginal cost (MC)** expression.

Marginal cost (MC) is the addition to total cost (TC) resulting from the addition of one unit of output.

A Recap

Total variable costs:	**TVC**
Total fixed costs:	**TFC**
Total costs:	$TC = TVC + TFC$
Average variable costs:	$AVC = TVC/output$
Average fixed costs:	$AFC = TFC/output$
Average (total) costs:	$AC = TC/output = AVC + AFC$
Marginal costs:	$MC = MFC + MVC = 0 + MVC$
	$MC = \Delta TC/\Delta(\text{one unit of output})$

■ The Principle of Diminishing Marginal Productivity and the U-Shaped Average Cost Curve

The preceding discussion of fixed and variable costs enables us to consider the configuration of the **average cost** curve and the production implications of its typical U-shape. The typical curve looks like the one in Figure 4(b) and is roughly U-shaped: The left-hand portion of the curve is downward-sloping and the right-hand portion is upward-sloping. AC declines when output increases in the left-hand portion of the curve for two reasons.

The first reason makes intuitive sense and pertains to the fixed-cost portion of AC and the fact that these fixed costs are divided over more units of product as output increases. As Figure 5(b) shows, the average *fixed* cost curve always falls as output increases, and it falls very sharply at the left-hand end of the AFC curve. Because AC equals AFC plus average variable costs (AVC), the AC curve for virtually any product contains a fixed-cost portion, AFC, which falls steeply at first when output increases. So, as these fixed costs are spread over more units as output increases, the AC curve for any product should have a downward-sloping portion such as *CD* in Figure 4(b), which is characterized by decreasing average cost.

The second reason why AC curves have a downward-sloping section relates to changing input proportions. As the firm increases the quantity of one input while holding other inputs constant, the marginal physical product relationship tells us that MPP will first rise. As a result, average costs will decrease. For example, if Al is using very few carpenters relative to the amounts of other inputs, a rise in the quantity of carpenters will, at first, yield increasing additions to output (in the range of increasing marginal physical product of carpenters illustrated in the left-hand part of Figure 3). As the quantity produced increases, the average cost of output falls.

Now look at any point to the right of point *D* in Figure 4(b). Average cost rises as output increases along this section of the curve. Why does the portion of the curve with decreasing AC end? This is a reflection of the general principle of increasing costs, introduced in Chapter 3. Rising average costs are explained by the principle of diminishing returns, discussed on page 144. Without diminishing returns, average costs would keep falling. But as more carpenters are added to a given number of machines, they run into each other, and thus output rises at a decreasing rate. Also, with more carpenters to supervise, administrators become less efficient at extracting work effort. All of this drives up average costs.

The output at which average costs stop decreasing and begin to rise varies from industry to industry. For instance, fixed costs represent only 21 percent of all costs in the Canadian construction industry; by contrast, in the Canadian information and cultural industries, in transportation and warehousing, and in finance, insurance, and real estate, fixed costs account for 50 percent of all costs. Other things being equal, the greater the relative size of fixed costs, the higher the output at which the switchover occurs. For example, it occurs at a much larger volume of output in automobile production than in farming, which is why no farms are as big as even the smallest auto producer. Automobile producers must be larger than farms because the fixed costs of automobile production are far greater than those in farming, so spreading the fixed cost over an increasing number of units of output keeps AC falling far longer in auto production than in farming. Thus, although firms in both industries may have U-shaped AC curves, the bottom of the U occurs at a far larger output in auto production than in farming.

The **average cost** (AC) is the total cost (TC) divided by the output.

The AC curve for a typical firm is U-shaped. We can attribute its downward-sloping segment to increasing marginal physical products and to the fact that the firm spreads its fixed costs over ever-larger quantities of outputs. Similarly, we can attribute the upward-sloping segment to the principle of diminishing returns, which applies with particular force to the diminishing administrative efficiency of managers that occurs as the firm grows larger.

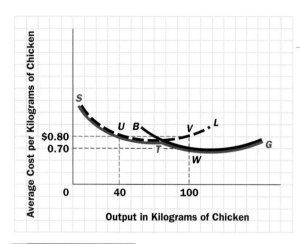

FIGURE 6

Short-Run and
Long-Run Average
Cost Curves

The Average Cost Curve in the Short and Long Run

At the beginning of this chapter, we observed that some inputs are variable and some are precommitted, depending on the pertinent time horizon. It follows that:

The average (and marginal and total) cost curve depends on the firm's planning horizon—how far into the future it tries to look when making its plans. The average (and total) cost curve for the long run differs from that for the short run because, in the long run, input quantities generally become variable.

We can, in fact, be much more specific about the relationships between the short-run and long-run average cost curves. Consider, as an example, the capacity of Naomi's poultry farm. In the short run, she can choose to raise, at most, only the number of chickens that she can crowd into her coops' current capacity. Of course, she can always build more chicken coops. However, if it turns out that the coops are much larger than she needs, Naomi cannot simply undo the excessive space and get back the money that she has spent on it. But, in the long run, after they are sufficiently old to need replacement, she can choose among new coops of different sizes.

If she constructs a smaller coop, Naomi's AC curve looks like curve *SL* in Figure 6. That means that if she is pleasantly surprised as sales grow to 100 kilograms of chicken per week, average cost will be $0.80 per kilogram of chicken (point *V*). She may then wish she had built bigger coops with an AC curve of *BG*, which would have enabled her to cut the cost per kilogram of chicken to $0.70 (point *W*). In the short run, though, Naomi can do nothing about this decision; the AC curve remains *SL*. Similarly, had she built the larger coops, the short-run AC curve would be *BG*, and the farm would be committed to this cost curve even if her sales were to decline sharply.

In the long run, however, Naomi must replace the coops, and she is free to decide all over again how big they should be. If Naomi expects sales of 100 kilograms of chicken per week, she will construct larger coops and have an average cost of $0.70 per kilogram of chicken (point *W*). If she expects sales of only 40 kilograms of chicken per week, she will arrange for smaller buildings with an average cost of $0.80 per kilogram of chicken (point *U*).

In sum, in the long run, a firm will select the plant size (that is, the short-run AC curve) that is most economical for the output level that it expects to produce. The long-run average cost curve therefore consists of all of the *lower* segments of the short-run AC curves. In Figure 6, this composite curve is the blue curve, *STG*. The long-run average cost curve shows the lowest possible short-run average cost corresponding to each output level.

ECONOMIES OF SCALE

We have now put together the basic tools we need to address the question posed at the beginning of this chapter: Does a large firm benefit from substantial economies of scale that allow it to operate more efficiently than smaller firms? To answer this question, we need a precise definition of this concept.

An enterprise's scale of operation arises from the quantities of the various inputs that it uses. Consider what happens when the firm doubles its scale of operations. For example, suppose Al's garage-building firm was to double the number of carpenters, the amount of lumber, the number of tools, and the quantity of every other input that it uses. Suppose as a result that the number of garages built per year increased from 12 to 26; that is, output more than doubled. Because output goes up by a greater percentage than the increase in each of the inputs, Al's production is said to be characterized by **increasing returns to scale** (or **economies of scale**), at least in this range of input and output quantities.

Production is said to involve **economies of scale**, also referred to as **increasing returns to scale**, if, when all input quantities are increased by *X* percent, the quantity of output rises by *more* than *X* percent.

Economies of scale affect operations in many modern industries. Where they exist, they give larger firms cost advantages over smaller ones and thereby foster large firm sizes. Automobile production and telecommunications are two common examples of industries that enjoy significant economies of scale. Predictably, firms in these industries are, indeed, huge.

Technology generally determines whether a specific economic activity is characterized by economies of scale. One particularly clear example of a way in which this can happen is provided by warehouse space. Imagine two warehouses, each shaped like a perfect cube, where the length, width, and height of Warehouse 2 are twice as large as the corresponding measurements for Warehouse 1. Now remember your high-school geometry. The surface area of any side of a cube is equal to the square of its length. Therefore, the amount of material needed to build Warehouse 2 will be 2^2, or four times as great as that needed for Warehouse 1. However, because the volume of a cube is equal to the cube of its length, Warehouse 2 will have 2^3, or eight times, as much storage space as Warehouse 1. Thus, in a cubic building, multiplying the input quantities by four leads to eight times the storage space—an example of strongly increasing returns to scale.

This example is, of course, oversimplified. It omits such complications as the need for stronger supports in taller buildings, the increased difficulty of moving goods in and out of taller buildings, and the like. Still, the basic idea is correct, and the example shows why, up to a point, the very nature of warehousing creates technological relationships that lead to economies of scale.

Our definition of economies of scale, although based on the type of production, relates closely to the shape of the *long-run* average cost curve. Notice that the definition requires that a doubling of *every* input must bring about more than a doubling of output. If all input quantities are doubled, total cost must double. But if output *more* than doubles when input quantities are doubled, then cost per unit (average cost) must decline when output increases. In other words:

> Production relationships with economies of scale lead to long-run average cost curves that decline as output expands.

Figure 7(a) depicts a decreasing average cost curve, but shows only one of three possible shapes that the long-run average cost curve can take. Panel (b) shows the curve for *constant* returns to scale. Here, if all input quantities double, both total cost (TC) and the quantity of output (Q) double, so average cost (AC = TC/Q) remains *constant*. There is a third possibility. Output may also increase, but less than double, when all inputs double. This case of *decreasing* returns to scale leads to a *rising* long-run average cost curve like the one depicted in Panel (c). The figure reveals a close association between the slope of the AC curve and the nature of the firm's returns to scale.

Note that the same production function can display increasing returns to scale in some ranges, constant returns to scale in other ranges, and decreasing returns to scale in yet others. This is true of all the U-shaped average cost curves we have shown, such as that shown in Figure 4(b).

FIGURE 7

Three Possible Shapes for the Long-Run Average Cost Curve

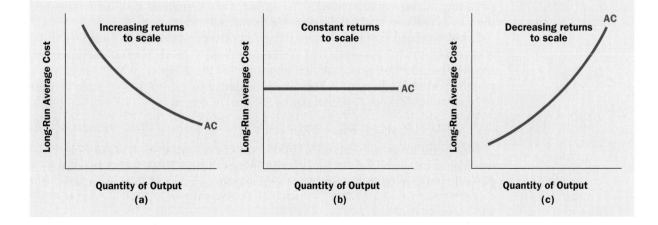

(a)   (b)   (c)

■ The Principle of Diminishing Returns and Returns to Scale

Earlier in this chapter, we discussed the principle of diminishing marginal returns. Is there any relationship between economies of scale and the phenomenon of diminishing returns? At first, the two ideas may seem contradictory. After all, if a producer gets diminishing returns from her inputs as she uses more of each of them, doesn't it follow that by using more of *every* input, she must encounter decreasing returns to scale? In fact, the two principles do not contradict one another, for they deal with fundamentally different issues.

- *Returns to a single input.* This analysis asks the question, How much does output expand if a firm increases the quantity of just *one* input, *holding unchanged all other input quantities?*
- *Returns to scale.* Here the question is, How much does output expand if *all* inputs are increased *simultaneously* by the same percentage?

The principle of diminishing returns pertains to the first question, because it examines the effects of increasing only one input at a time. It is plausible that the firm will encounter diminishing returns as this one input becomes relatively overabundant as compared to the quantities of the firm's other inputs. Thus, for example, the addition of too much carpenter time relative to a given quantity of lumber will contribute relatively little to total garage production, yielding diminishing returns. To get the most benefit out of the hiring of an additional carpenter, the firm needs to acquire more tools and raw materials.

Returns to scale pertain to proportionate increases in *all* inputs and therefore answer the second question. If Al doubles carpenter time and all other inputs as well, the carpenters, clearly, need not become redundant. But increasing the amount of one input without expanding any other inputs clearly threatens redundancy of the expanded item even in a factory where simultaneous expansion of *all* inputs will lead to a very big jump in output. Thus, the principle of diminishing returns (to a single input) is compatible with *any* sort of returns to scale. In summary:

> Returns to scale and returns to a single input (holding all other inputs constant) refer to two distinct aspects of a firm's technology. A production function that displays diminishing returns to *a single input* may show diminishing, constant, or increasing returns when *all input quantities are increased proportionately.*

■ Historical Costs Versus Analytical Cost Curves

In Chapter 5, we noted that all points on a demand curve pertain to the *same* period of time. Decision makers must use this common time period for the analysis of an optimal decision for a given period, because the demand curve describes the alternative choices available *for the period of time to which the decision will apply* . The same is true of a cost curve. All points on a cost curve pertain to exactly the same time period, because the graph examines the cost of each alternative output level that the firm can choose for that period, thus providing the information needed to compare the alternatives and their consequences, and thereby to make an optimal decision for that period.

It follows that a graph of historical data on prices and quantities at *different points in time* is normally *not* the cost curve that the decision maker needs. This observation will help us resolve the problem posed at the beginning of the chapter, which raised the question whether declining historical costs were evidence of economies of scale as information needed to decide on the optimal size of the firm in question.

> All points on any of the cost curves used in economic analysis refer to the same period of time.

One point on an auto manufacturer's cost curve may show, for example, how much it would cost the firm to produce 2.5 million cars during 2009. Another point on the same curve may show what would happen to the firm's costs if, *instead*, it were to produce

3 million cars in that same year. Such a curve is called an *analytical cost curve* or, when there is no possibility of confusion, simply a cost curve. This curve must be distinguished from a diagram of *historical costs*, which shows how costs have changed from year to year.

The different points on an analytical cost curve represent *alternative possibilities*, all for the same time period. In 2009, the car manufacturer will produce either 2.5 million or 3 million cars (or some other amount), but certainly not both. Thus, at most, only one point on this cost curve will ever be observed. The company may, indeed, produce 2.5 million cars in 2005 and 3 million cars in 2009, but the 2009 data are not relevant to the 2008 cost curve which is to be used to analyze the 2008 output decision. By the time 2009 comes around, the cost curve may have shifted, so the 2009 cost figure will not apply to the 2008 cost curve.

Resolving the Economies of Scale Puzzle

Recall the problem that we introduced early in the chapter. We examined the divestiture of AT&T's components and concluded that, to determine whether it made sense to break up such a large company, economists would have to know whether the industry provided economies of scale. Among the data offered as evidence was Figure 1, which showed a precipitous drop in the capital cost of long-distance communications as the volume of calls rose after 1942. But we did not answer a more pertinent question: Why didn't this information constitute legitimate evidence about the presence or absence of economies of scale?

It all boils down to the following: To determine whether a single large firm can provide telephone service more cheaply in, say, 2008 than a number of smaller firms can, we must compare the costs of *both large-scale and small-scale production in 2008*. It does no good to compare the cost of a large supplier in 2008 with its own costs as a smaller firm back in 1942, because that cannot possibly provide the needed information. The cost situation in 1942 is irrelevant for today's decision between large and small suppliers, because no small firm today would use the obsolete techniques employed in 1942.

Since the 1940s, great technical progress has taken the telephone industry from ordinary open-wire circuits to microwave systems, telecommunications satellites, coaxial cables of enormous capacity, and fibre optics. As a result, the *entire* analytical cost curve of telecommunications must have shifted downward quite dramatically from year to year. Innovation must have reduced not only the cost of large-scale operations, *but also the cost of smaller-scale operations*. Until decision makers compare the costs of large and small suppliers *today*, they cannot make a rational choice between single-firm and multifirm production. It is the analytical cost curve, all of whose points refer to the same period, that, by definition, supplies this information.

Figures 8 and 9 show two extreme hypothetical cases, one that entails true economies of scale and one that does not. Both are based on the same historical cost data (in black) with their very sharply declining costs. (This curve is reproduced from Figure 1.) They also show (in blue and red) two possible average cost curves, one for 1942 and one for 2008.

In Figure 8, the analytical AC curve has shifted downward very sharply from 1942 to 2008, as technological change reduced all costs. Moreover, both of the AC curves slope downward to the right, meaning that, in either year, a larger firm has lower average costs. Thus, the situation shown in Figure 8 really does entail scale economies, so that one large firm can serve the market at lower cost than many small ones.

FIGURE 8

Declining Historical Cost Curve with the Analytical Average Cost Curve Also Declining in Each Year

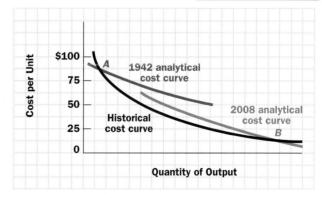

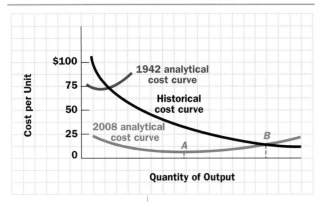

FIGURE 9 Declining Historical Cost Curve with U-Shaped Analytical Cost Curves in Each Year

Now look at Figure 9, which shows exactly the same historical costs as Figure 8. Here, however, both analytical AC curves are U-shaped. In particular, the 2008 AC curve has its minimum point at an output level, *A*, that is less than one-half of the current output, *B*, of the large supplier. Thus, the shape of the analytical cost curves does *not* show economies of scale. This means that, for the situation shown in Figure 9, a smaller company can produce more cheaply than a large one can. In this case, one cannot justify domination of the market by a single large firm on the grounds that its costs are lower—despite the sharp downward trend of historical costs.

In sum, the behaviour of historical costs reveals nothing about the cost advantages or disadvantages of a single large firm. More generally:

Because a diagram of historical costs does not compare the costs of large and small firms *at the same point in time,* it cannot be used to determine whether an industry provides economies of large-scale production. Only the analytical cost curve can supply this information.

Long-distance phone services in both Canada and the United States are still dominated by a few large companies, such as AT&T, Bell Canada, MCI, TELUS, and Sprint. It is perhaps ironic that some of the regional companies that were part of the dismantling of AT&T by the courts in the United States in 1982 have now recombined or are seeking to merge. In Canada, Bell Canada has combined with Aliant, now Bell Aliant Regional Communications, thus regaining some control over the Atlantic provinces and both the urban and regional areas of Quebec and Ontario. There is thus evidence that in this industry, as in cellular and Internet-based long-distance services, there are significant economies of scale and other advantages linked with a larger size.

A different sort of graph can, of course, indicate year by year how costs and outputs vary. Such a graph, which gathers together the statistics for a number of different periods, is not, however, a *cost curve* as that term is used by economists. An example of such a diagram of historical costs appeared in Figure 1 on page 140.

Why do economists rarely use historical cost diagrams and instead deal primarily with analytical cost curves, which are more abstract, more challenging to explain, and more difficult to estimate statistically? The answer is that analysis of real policy problems—such as the desirability of having a single supplier of telephone services for the entire market—leaves no choice in the matter. Rational decisions require analytical cost curves.

■ Cost Minimization in Theory and Practice

Lest you be tempted to run out and open a business, confident that you now understand how to minimize costs, we should point out that business decisions are a good deal more complicated than we have indicated here. Rare is the business executive who knows for sure the exact shapes of his or her marginal physical product schedules, or the precise nature of his or her cost curves. No one can provide an instruction book for instant success in business. What we have presented here is, instead, a set of principles that constitutes a guide to the logic of good decision making.

Business management has been described as the art of making critical decisions on the basis of inadequate information, and our complex and ever-changing world often leaves people no alternative but to make educated guesses. Actual business decisions will at best approximate the cost-minimizing ideal outlined in this chapter. Certainly, practising managers will make mistakes, but when they do their jobs well and the market system functions smoothly, the approximation may prove amazingly good. Although no system is perfect, inducing firms to produce the output they select at the lowest possible cost is undoubtedly one of the jobs the market system does best.

POLICY DEBATE

Should Electricity Be Provided to Northern Ontario Industries at a Discount?

The Government of Ontario, through Ontario's Hydro One, imposes a single provincial rate for all large consumers of energy. However, the cost of producing electricity in the northern part of Ontario is much lower than it is in the rest of Ontario, and is also lower than the cost of importing electricity to Ontario. Industries in northern Ontario are heavy users of electricity, so that electricity costs account for a substantial portion of their total variable costs. The leaders of these industries argue that their future is in jeopardy as a result of the overall increase in the provincial price of electricity. As an alternative, they propose that industries located in northern Ontario take advantage of the lower cost of producing electricity in northern Ontario, thus remaining competitive and keeping their plants and mines open.

But if northern Ontario industries pay a cheaper rate, won't this lead to the adoption or the upkeep of less energy-efficient techniques that will waste electricity resources that would have a higher value in the rest of Ontario or that would force Hydro One to import high-cost electricity? There is a trade-off between preserving jobs and economic activity in northern Ontario and making sure that companies there make more effort to adopt energy-saving measures and technologies that take into account the overall higher cost of electricity.

SOURCE: Tom Grundy/Shutterstock

SUMMARY

1. A firm's total cost curve shows its lowest possible cost of producing any given quantity of output. This curve is derived from the input combination that the firm uses to produce any given output and the prices of the inputs.

2. The **marginal physical product** (MPP) of an input is the increase in total output resulting from a one-unit increase in that input, holding constant the quantities of all other inputs.

3. The **principle of diminishing marginal returns** states that if a firm increases the amount of one input (holding constant all other input quantities), the marginal physical product of the expanding input will eventually begin to decline.

4. To maximize profits, a firm must purchase an input up to the point at which diminishing returns reduce the input's **marginal revenue product** (MRP) to equal its price ($P =$ MRP $=$ MPP $\times$ price).

5. Average and marginal variable cost curves tend to be U-shaped, meaning that these costs decline up to a certain level of output, and then begin to rise again at larger output quantities.

6. The **long run** is a period sufficiently long for the firm's plant to require replacement and for all of its current contractual commitments to expire. The **short run** is any period briefer than the long run.

7. **Fixed costs** are costs whose total amounts do not vary when output increases. All other costs are called **variable costs**. Some costs are variable in the long run but not in the short run.

8. At all levels of output, the total fixed cost (TFC) curve is horizontal and the average fixed cost (AFC) curve declines toward the horizontal axis but never crosses it.

9. TC $=$ TFC $+$ TVC; AC $=$ AFC $+$ AVC; MFC $=$ 0.

10. It is usually possible to produce the same quantity of output in a variety of ways by substituting more of one input for less of another input. Firms normally seek the combination of inputs that is the least costly way to produce any given output.

11. A firm that wants to minimize costs will select input quantities at which the ratios of the marginal revenue product of each input to the input's price—its MRP per dollar—are equal for all inputs.

12. If a doubling of all the firm's inputs just doubles its output, the firm is said to have constant returns to scale. If a doubling of all inputs leads to more than twice as much output, it has **increasing returns to scale** (or **economies of scale**). If a doubling of inputs produces less than a doubling of output, the firm has decreasing returns to scale.

13. With increasing returns to scale, the firm's long-run average costs are decreasing; constant returns to scale are associated with constant long-run average costs; decreasing returns to scale are associated with increasing long-run average costs.

14. Economists cannot tell if an industry offers economies of scale (increasing returns to scale) simply by inspecting a diagram of historical cost data. Only the underlying analytical cost curve can supply this information.

KEY TERMS

Short run   141

Long run   141

Fixed cost   142

Variable cost   142

Total physical product (TPP)   142

Average physical product (APP)   142

Marginal physical product (MPP)   143

Principle of diminishing returns   144

Marginal revenue product (MRP)   145

Average cost (AC)   153

Economies of scale (increasing returns to scale)   154

TEST YOURSELF

1. A firm's total fixed cost is $360,000. Construct a table of its total and average fixed costs for output levels varying from zero to 6 units. Draw the corresponding TFC and AFC curves.

2. With the following data, calculate the firm's AVC and MVC and draw the graphs for TVC, AVC, and MVC. Why is MVC the same as MC?

Quantity	Total Variable Costs
1	$40,000
2	80,000
3	120,000
4	176,000
5	240,000
6	360,000

3. From the data in Test Yourself Questions 1 and 2, calculate TC and AC for each of the output levels from 1 to 6 units and draw the two graphs.

4. If a firm's commitments in 2008 include machinery that will need replacement in 5 years, a factory building rented for 12 years, and a 3-year union contract specifying how many workers it must employ, when, from its point of view in 2008, does the firm's long run begin?

5. If the marginal revenue product of a litre of oil used as input by a firm is $1.20 and the price of oil is $1.07 per litre, what can the firm do to increase its profits?

6. A firm hires two workers and rents 15 hectares of land for a season. It produces 150,000 bushels of crop. If it had doubled its land and labour, production would have been 325,000 bushels. Does it have constant, decreasing, or increasing returns to scale?

7. Suppose that wages are $20,000 per season per person and land rent per hectare is $3,000. Calculate the average cost of 150,000 bushels and the average cost of 325,000 bushels, using the figures in Test Yourself Question 6. (Note that average costs increase when output increases.) What connection do these figures have with the firm's returns to scale?

8. Naomi has stockpiled a great deal of chicken feed. Suppose now that she buys more chicks, but not more chicken feed, and divides the feed she has evenly among the larger number of chickens. What is likely to happen to the marginal physical product of feed? What, therefore, is the role of input proportions in the determination of marginal physical product?

9. Labour costs $10 per hour. Nine workers produce 180 bushels of product per hour, while ten workers produce 196 bushels. Land rents for $1,000 per hectare per year. With ten acres worked by nine workers, the marginal physical product of a hectare of land is 1,400 bushels per year. Does the farmer minimize costs by hiring nine workers and renting ten hectares of land? If not, which input should he use in larger relative quantity?

10. With the help of Tables 3 and 4 in the chapter, compute Al's total cost and average (total) cost.

DISCUSSION QUESTION

1. A firm experiences a sudden increase in the demand for its product. In the short run, it must operate longer hours and pay higher overtime wage rates to satisfy this new demand. In the long run, the firm can install more machines instead of operating fewer machines for longer hours. Which do you think will be lower, the short-run or the long-run average cost of the increased output? How is your answer affected by the fact that the long-run average cost includes the new machines the firm buys, while the short-run average cost includes no machine purchases?

APPENDIX *Production Indifference Curves*

To describe a production function—that is, the relationship between input combinations and the size of a firm's total output—economists use a graphic device called the **production indifference curve**. Each indifference curve indicates *all* combinations of input quantities just capable of producing a *given* quantity of output; thus, a separate indifference curve corresponds to each possible quantity of output. These production indifference curves are perfectly analogous to the consumer indifference curves discussed in the appendix to Chapter 5.

> A production indifference curve (sometimes called an *isoquant*) is a curve showing all the different quantities of two inputs that are just sufficient to produce a given quantity of output.

Figure 10 represents different quantities of labour and land capable of producing given amounts of wheat. The figure shows three indifference curves: one for the production of 220,000 bushels of wheat per year, one for 240,000 bushels, and one for 260,000 bushels. The indifference curve labelled 220,000 bushels indicates that a farm can generate an output of 220,000 bushels of wheat per year using *any one* of the combinations of inputs represented by points on that curve. For example, it can employ ten workers, each over a period of one year, which is ten person-years and 200 hectares of land (point *A*). This is point *A* on the blue curve. Or the farmer can choose the labour–land combination shown by point *B* on the same curve. Because it lies considerably below and to the right of point *B*, point *A* represents a productive process that uses more labour and less land.

Points *A* and *B* can be considered *technologically* indifferent because each represents a bundle of inputs just capable of yielding the same quantity of finished goods. However, the word "indifference" in this sense does not mean that the producer will be unable to decide between input combinations *A* and *B*. Input prices will permit the producer to arrive at a decision.

The production indifference curves in a diagram such as Figure 10 show for each combination of inputs how much output can be produced. Because production indifference curves are drawn in two dimensions, they represent only two inputs at a time. In more realistic situations, firms are likely to need more than two inputs, so, to study the subject, economists must conduct an algebraic analysis. Even so, all the principles we need to analyze such a situation can be derived from the two-variable case.

■ CHARACTERISTICS OF THE PRODUCTION INDIFFERENCE CURVES, OR ISOQUANTS

Before discussing input pricing and quantity decisions, we first examine what is known about the shapes of production indifference curves.

Characteristic 1: *Higher curves correspond to larger outputs.* Points on a higher indifference curve represent larger quantities of *both* inputs than the corresponding points on a lower curve. Thus, a higher curve represents a larger output.

Characteristic 2: *An indifference curve will generally have a negative slope.* It goes downhill as we move toward the right. Thus, if a firm reduces the quantity of one input, and if it does not want to cut production, it must use more of another input.

Characteristic 3: *An indifference curve is typically assumed to curve inward toward the origin near its middle.* This shape reflects the principle of diminishing

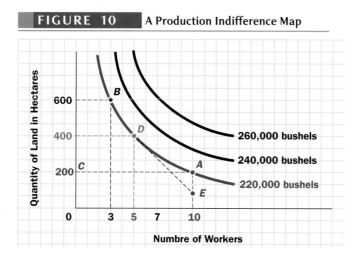

FIGURE 10 A Production Indifference Map

(y-axis: Quantity of Land in Hectares; values 200, 400, 600)
(x-axis: Numbre of Workers; values 3, 5, 7, 10)

260,000 bushels
240,000 bushels
220,000 bushels

returns to a single input. For example, in Figure 10, points B, D, and A represent three different input combinations capable of producing the same quantity of output. At point B, the firm uses a large amount of land and relatively little labour, whereas the opposite is true at point A. Point D is intermediate between the two.

Now consider the choice among these input combinations. When the farmer considers moving from point B to point D, he gives up 200 hectares of land and instead hires two additional workers for a year. Similarly, the move from D to A involves giving up another 200 hectares of land. This time, however, hiring an additional two workers does not make up for the reduced use of land. Diminishing returns to labour as the farmer hires more and more workers to replace more and more land means that the farm now needs a much larger quantity of additional labour—five person-years rather than two—to make up for the reduction in the use of land. Without such diminishing returns, the indifference curve would have been a straight line, DE. The curvature of the indifference curve through points D and A reflects diminishing returns to substitution of inputs.

■ THE CHOICE OF INPUT COMBINATIONS

A production indifference curve describes only the input combinations that *can* produce a given output; it indicates just what is technologically possible. To decide which of the available options suits its purposes best, a business needs the corresponding cost information: the relative prices of the inputs.

The **budget line** in Figure 11 represents all equally costly input combinations for a firm. For example, if farmhands are paid $9,000 per year and land rents for $1,000 per hectare per year, then a farmer who spends $360,000 can hire 40 farmhands but rent no land (point

K), or he can rent 360 hectares but have no money left for farmhands (point J). It is undoubtedly more sensible to pick some intermediate point on his budget line at which he divides the $360,000 between the two inputs. The slope of the budget line represents the amount of land the farmer must give up if he wants to hire one more worker without increasing his budget.

> A budget line is the locus of all points representing every combination of inputs that the producer can afford to buy with a given amount of money and given input prices.

If the prices of the inputs do not change, then the slope of the budget line will not change anywhere in the graph. It will be the same at every point on a given budget line, and it will be the same on the $360,000 budget line as on the $450,000 budget line or on the budget line for any other level of spending. For if the price of hiring a worker for a year is nine times as high as the annual cost of renting a hectare, then the farmer must rent nine fewer hectares to hire an additional farmhand without changing the total amount of money he spends on these inputs. Thus, the slope will be hectares given up per added farmhand = −9/1 = −9.

So, with the input prices given, the slope of any budget line does not change and the slopes of the different budget lines for different amounts of expenditures are all the same. Two results follow: (1) the budget lines are straight lines because their slopes remain the same throughout their length, and (2) because they all have the same slope, the budget lines in the graph will all be parallel, as in Figure 12.

A firm that is seeking to minimize costs does not necessarily have a fixed budget. Instead, it wants to produce a given quantity of output (say, 240,000 bushels) with *the smallest possible budget*.

Figure 12 combines the indifference curve for 240,000 bushels from Figure 10 with a variety of budget lines similar to JK in Figure 11. The firm's task is to find the

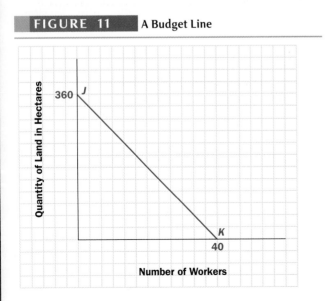

FIGURE 11   **A Budget Line**

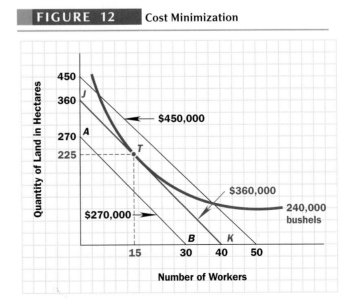

FIGURE 12   **Cost Minimization**

lowest budget line that will allow it to reach the 240,000-bushel indifference curve. Clearly, an expenditure of $270,000 is too little; no point on the budget line, *AB*, permits production of 240,000 bushels. Similarly, an expenditure of $450,000 is too much, because the firm can produce its target level of output more cheaply. The solution is at point *T* where the farmer uses 15 workers and 225 hectares of land to produce the 240,000 bushels of wheat. That budget line, the one that is tangent to the relevant indifference curve, is evidently the lowest budget line that meets the indifference curve anywhere, so it represents the lowest-cost input combination capable of producing the desired output. In general:

> The least costly way to produce any given level of output is indicated by the point of tangency between a budget line and the production indifference curve corresponding to that level of output.

There is thus a tight analogy between consumers who are maximizing their utility and producers who are minimizing their costs. Consumers will choose the combination of goods such that their budget line is tangent to their indifference curve. Producers will choose the combination of inputs such that their budget line is tangent to their production indifference curve. Just as the slope of the consumer indifference curve was called the *marginal rate of substitution*, by analogy, the slope of the producer indifference curve is called the *marginal rate of technical substitution* (MRTS). And, again, analogously, it turns out that this slope (more precisely, its absolute value) is simply equal to the ratio of the marginal physical products of the two inputs. Thus, while utility-maximizing consumers will modify the quantities being purchased to ensure that the ratio of the marginal utilities provided by each good is exactly equal to the ratio of the prices of these two goods, cost-minimizing producers will similarly modify the quantities of inputs in such a way that the ratio of the marginal physical products of

each input is exactly equal to the ratio of the prices of the two inputs.

> The optimal decision of producers will be such that:
>
> $$MPP_w / MPP_l = P_w / P_l$$
>
> where MPP_w and MPP_l are the marginal physical products of workers and land, and where P_w and P_l are the prices of the worker and land inputs.

■ COST MINIMIZATION, EXPANSION PATH, AND COST CURVES

Figure 12 shows how to determine the input combination that minimizes the cost of producing 240,000 bushels of output. The farmer can repeat this procedure exactly for any other output quantity, such as 200,000 bushels or 300,000 bushels. In each case, we draw the corresponding production indifference curve and find the lowest budget line that permits the farm to produce that much. For example, in Figure 13, budget line *BB* is tangent to the indifference curve for 200,000 units of output; similarly, budget line *JK* is tangent to the indifference curve for 240,000 bushels; and budget line *B'B'* is tangent to the indifference curve for 300,000 units of output. This gives us three tangency points: *S*, which gives the input combination that produces a 200,000-bushel output at lowest cost; *T*, which gives the same information for a 240,000-bushel output; and *S'*, which indicates the cost-minimizing input combination for the production of 300,000 bushels.

This process can be repeated for as many other levels of output as we like. For each such output we draw the corresponding production indifference curve and find its point of tangency with a budget line. The blue curve *EE* in Figure 13 connects all of the cost-minimizing points; that is, it is the locus of *S*, *T*, *S'*, and all other points of tangency between a production indifference curve and a budget line. Curve *EE* is called the firm's **expansion path.**

> The expansion path is the locus of the firm's cost-minimizing input combinations for all relevant output levels.

Point *T* in Figure 12 shows the quantity of output (given by the production indifference curve through that point) and the total cost (shown by the tangent budget line). Similarly, we can determine the output and total cost for every other point on the expansion path, *EE*, in Figure 13. For example, at point *S*, output is 200,000 bushels and total cost is $270,000. These data are precisely the sort of information we need to find the firm's total cost curve; that is, they are just the sort of information contained in Table 3, which is the source of the total cost curve and the average and marginal cost curves in Figure 4. Thus:

> The points of tangency between a firm's production indifference curves and its budget lines yield its expansion path, which shows the firm's cost-minimizing input combination

FIGURE 13   The Firm's Expansion Path

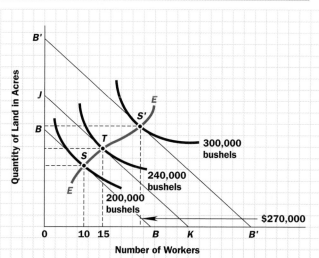

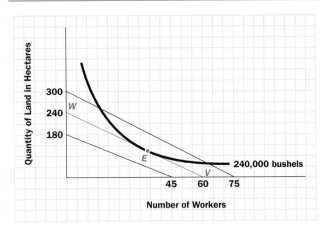

FIGURE 14 Optimal Input Choice at a Different Set of Input Prices

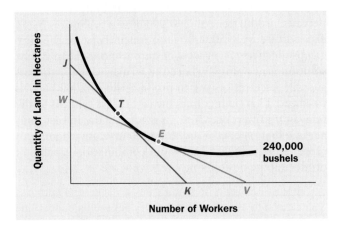

FIGURE 15 How Changes in Input Prices Affect Input Proportions

for each pertinent output level. This information also yields the output and total cost for each point on the expansion path, which is just what we need to draw the firm's cost curves.

Suppose that the cost of renting land increases and the wage rate of labour decreases. These changes mean that the budget lines will differ from those depicted in Figure 12. Specifically, with land becoming more expensive, any given sum of money will rent fewer hectares, so the intercept of each budget line on the vertical (land) axis will shift *downward*. Conversely, with cheaper labour, any given sum of money will buy more labour, so the intercept of the budget line on the horizontal (labour) axis will shift to the *right*. Figure 14 depicts a series of budget lines corresponding to a $1,500 per hectare rental rate for land and a $6,000 annual wage for labour. If input prices change, the combination of inputs that minimizes costs will normally change. In this diagram, the land rent at $1,500 per hectare is more than it was in Figure 12, whereas labour costs $6,000 per year (less than in Figure 12). As a result, these budget lines are less steep than those shown in Figure 12, and point *E* now represents the least costly way to produce 240,000 bushels of wheat.

To assist you in seeing how things change, Figure 15 combines, in a single graph, budget line *JK* and tangency point *T* from Figure 12 with budget line *WV* and tangency point *E* from Figure 14. When land becomes more expensive and labour becomes cheaper, the budget lines (such as *JK*) become less steep than they were previously (see *WV*). As a result, the least costly way to produce 240,000 bushels shifts from point *T* to point *E*, at which the firm uses more labour and less land. As common sense suggests, when the price of one input rises in comparison with that of the other, it will pay the firm to use less of the more expensive input and more of the other input.

In addition to substituting one input for another, a change in the price of an input may induce the firm to alter its level of output. We will cover this subject in the next chapter.

■ FIXED-PROPORTION TECHNOLOGY

Some economists believe that it is more appropriate to describe industrial production as being a series of techniques with fixed coefficients, thus questioning the usual convex shape of production indifference curves. Whereas agricultural production is often described, as we did in this appendix, as a combination of land and labour inputs where substitution is always possible, industrial production usually pertains to labour and machine inputs, the machines being the physical or tangible capital of the firm, for which substitution is not always possible. With capital, fixed coefficients are justified by the claim that once a kind of machine has been chosen, there is only one way to run this machine efficiently. Machines (say, robots in a car-assembling plant) are designed by engineers to be operated by a given number of workers. Such a machine could not function if there were fewer workers to operate it, and there would be no increase in output if more workers were just standing around the machine. In other words, once the technique has been chosen, in the short run there is no (or very little) possible substitution between the two inputs—machines and workers. These two kinds of inputs are strictly complementary. One way to interpret the above is to say that, *before* the choice of technique is made, the production indifference curve must have the convex shape that it has been given in this appendix, indicating that one input can be substituted for another. However, *after* the choice has been made, firms face fixed technical coefficients.

The lack of substitutability between these two inputs is represented by an L-shaped production indifference curve—a production isoquant—as shown in Figure 16. The *ABC* isoquant shows the various input combinations that are possible to produce 10,000 cars per year in a plant. Obviously, to produce 10,000 cars, it is best for the producer to operate at point *B*, with 20 workers and 10 machines. On any other point of the *BC* portion of the isoquant, there would be more workers operating the 10 machines, but still only 10,000 cars would be produced; similarly on any other point of the *AB* portion of the isoquant, 20 workers could be hired to operate more than 10 machines, but output would still remain at 10,000 cars per year since the additional machines would have no one to operate them and therefore would yield no additional output. By contrast, if more machines are put into action and more workers are hired simultaneously, then annual output can increase to 15, 000 cars, as shown by the *DEF* isoquant. Thus, if there is an increase in the demand for the kind of cars produced by this particular plant, say 15,000 cars need to be produced per year, this can be achieved by acquiring additional machines and hiring the required number of workers to operate the additional machines.

Fixed coefficient technologies as shown here are most often used in work that emphasizes the interdependence between industries. It was used in particular in the planned economies of communist countries, where the state had to compute the input amounts required to achieve the target output levels of the plan. The analysis of these interdependencies is called *input–output analysis*, so the L-shaped production isoquants are called *input–output isoquants* or *Leontief isoquants*.

> Production indifference curves arising from fixed coefficient techniques are called *input–output isoquants* or *Leontief isoquants*.

Wassily Leontief (1905–1999), an economist first trained in Russia in the early 1920s who then studied in

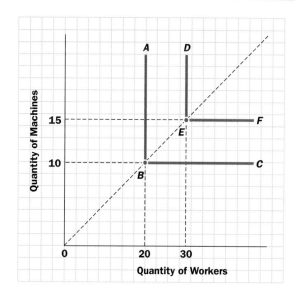

FIGURE 16   Input–Output (Leontief) Production Isoquant

Germany and later taught at Harvard University in the United States, was the main force behind the development of input–output analysis and input–output tables describing entire national economies; hence, the use of his name in this context. Statistics Canada publishes both national and provincial input–output tables on an annual basis. We will discuss further the purpose of input–output analysis in Chapter 14.

SUMMARY

1. A production relationship can be described by a series of **production indifference curves** (also called **isoquants**), each of which shows all input combinations capable of producing a specified amount of output.

2. As long as each input has a positive marginal physical product, production indifference curves will have negative slopes and the higher curves will represent larger amounts of output than the lower curves. Because of diminishing returns, these curves characteristically bend toward the origin near the middle.

3. The optimal input combination for any given level of output is indicated by the point of tangency between a **budget line** and the corresponding production indifference curve.

4. The firm's **expansion path** shows, for each of its possible output levels, the combination of input quantities that minimizes the cost of producing that output.

5. Total cost for each output level can be derived from the production indifference curves and the budget lines tangent to them along the expansion path. These figures can be used to determine the firm's total cost, average cost, and marginal cost curves.

6. When input prices change, firms will normally use more of the input that becomes relatively less expensive and less of the input that becomes relatively more expensive.

7. When substitution between inputs is impossible (that is, when there is strict complementarity of inputs), the production indifference curves are called *input–output isoquants* or *Leontief isoquants*.

KEY TERMS

Production indifference curve (isoquants)   161

Budget line   162

Expansion path   163

TEST YOURSELF

1. Compound Consolidated Corporation (CCC) produces containers using two inputs: labour and glue. If labour costs $10 per hour and glue costs $5 per litre, draw CCC's budget line for a total expenditure of $100,000. In this same diagram, sketch a production indifference curve indicating that CCC can produce no more than 1,000 containers with this expenditure.

2. With respect to Test Yourself Question 1, suppose that wages rise to $20 per hour and glue prices rise to $6 per litre. How are CCC's optimal input proportions likely to change? (Use a diagram to explain your answer.)

3. What happens to the location of the expansion path of the firm in Test Yourself Question 2?

OUTPUT, PRICE, AND PROFIT: THE IMPORTANCE OF MARGINAL ANALYSIS

Business is a good game. . . . You keep score with money.

NOLAN BUSHNELL, FOUNDER OF ATARI (AN EARLY VIDEO GAME MAKER)

Suppose you become president of a firm that makes video games. One of your most critical decisions will be how many video games to produce and at what price to offer them for sale. The owners of the company want to make as much profit as possible. This chapter explores the logic underlying the decisions that lead to achievement of this goal.

With this chapter, we cap off our discussion of the fundamental building blocks of microeconomics. Chapters 5 and 6 dealt with the behaviour of consumers. Then Chapter 7 introduced the other main participant in microeconomics, the firm. The firm's two main roles are, first, to produce its product efficiently and, second, to sell that product at a profit. Chapter 7 described production decisions. Now we turn to the selling decisions. Then, in Chapter 9, we will discuss stocks and bonds as instruments that enable business firms to obtain the money to finance their activities and as an earnings opportunity for individuals who consider investing in firms.

Throughout Part II, we have described how firms and consumers can make *optimal decisions*, meaning that their decisions go as far as possible, given the circumstances, to promote the consumer's and producer's goals. In this chapter, we will continue to assume that business firms seek primarily to maximize total profit, just as we assumed that consumers maximize utility. (See the box, "Do Firms Really Maximize Profits?" on the following page, for a discussion of other objectives of business firms.)

CONTENTS

Do Firms Really Maximize Profits?

Naturally, many people question whether firms really try to maximize profits to the exclusion of all other goals. But businesspeople are like other human beings: Their motives are varied and complex. Given the choice, many executives may prefer to control the *largest* firm rather than the most profitable one. Some may be fascinated by technology and therefore spend so much on research and development that it cuts down on profit. Some may want to "do good" and therefore give away some of the stockholders' money to hospitals and colleges. Different managers within the same firm may not always agree with one another on goals, so that it may not even make sense to speak about "the" goal of the firm. Thus, any attempt to summarize the objectives of management in terms of a single number (profit) is bound to be an oversimplification.

In addition, the exacting requirements for maximizing profits are tough to satisfy. In deciding how much to invest, what price to set for a product, or how much to allocate to the advertising budget, the range of available alternatives is enormous. Also, information about each alternative is often expensive and difficult to acquire. As a result, when a firm's management decides on, say, an $18 million construction budget, it rarely compares the consequences of that decision in any detail with the consequences of all possible alternatives—such as budgets of $17 million or $19 million. But unless all the available possibilities are compared, management cannot be sure that it has chosen the one that brings in the highest possible profit.

Often, management's concern is whether the decision's results are likely to be acceptable—whether its risks will be acceptably low, whether its profits will be acceptably high—so that the company can live satisfactorily with the outcome. Such analysis cannot be expected to bring in the maximum possible profit. The decision may be good, but some unexplored alternative may be even better.

Decision making that seeks only solutions that are acceptable has been called *satisficing*, to contrast it with optimizing (profit maximization). Some analysts, such as the late Nobel Prize winner Herbert Simon of Carnegie-Mellon University, have concluded that decision making in industry and government is often of the satisficing variety. Indeed, several survey studies conclude that satisficing objectives, in contrast to optimizing objectives, rank high among the goals set by managers. In particular, in a survey pursued by both American and Canadian national accountant associations, the leading goal was found to be the achievement of a certain profit level, followed by the achievement of a given return on investment. Maintaining the market share and achieving a certain level of sales were the other two main goals of surveyed firms.

Even if these assertions are true, it does not necessarily make profit maximization a bad assumption. Recall our discussion of abstraction and model building in Chapter 1. A map of Toronto that omits hundreds of roads is no doubt "wrong" if interpreted as a literal description of the city. Nonetheless, by capturing the most important elements of reality, it may help us understand the city better than a map that is cluttered with too much detail. Similarly, we can learn much about the behaviour of business firms by assuming that they try to maximize profits, even though we know that not all of them act this way all of the time.

An **optimal decision** is one that, among all the decisions that are actually possible, best achieves the decision maker's goals. For example, if profit is the sole objective of some firm, the price that makes the firm's profit as large as possible is optimal for that company.

As in the previous three chapters, marginal analysis helps us to determine what constitutes an **optimal decision**. Because that method of analysis is so useful, this chapter summarizes and generalizes what we have learned about the methods of marginal analysis, showing also how this analysis applies in many other situations in which optimality is an issue.

Marginal analysis leads to some surprising conclusions that show how misleading unaided "common sense" can sometimes be. Here's an example. Suppose a firm suffers a sharp increase in its rent or some other fixed cost. How should the firm react? Some would argue that the firm should raise the price of its product to cover the higher rent; others would argue that it should cut its price so as to increase its sales enough to pay the increased rent. We will see in this chapter that both of these answers are incorrect! A profit-maximizing firm faced with a rent increase should neither raise nor lower its price if it does not want to reduce its net earnings.

■ PRICE AND QUANTITY: ONE DECISION, NOT TWO

When your company introduces a new line of video games, the marketing department has to decide what price to charge and how many games to produce. These crucial decisions strongly influence the firm's labour requirements, the consumer response to the product, and, indeed, the company's future success.

PUZZLE 1: *Should You Stick to Your Meal Plan?*

Canuck University is providing students with a dining plan that has the features shown in Table 1. Students must purchase 10 meal tickets at a time. When students purchase their first 10 meals, the total cost is $100, so that the cost per meal is $10; however, once a certain number of meals have been purchased, the cost per meal starts to drop. A new dining hall, providing exactly the same food, is opening right next to the existing one, with 10 meals being offered at an overall cost of $85. An economist surveys the students, asking them whether they will switch to the new dining hall. Students who have already purchased 30 meals should not make the switch. Why is this?

TABLE 1		
Total Cost and Average Cost per Meal: Old Dining Hall		
Cumulative Number of Meals	Total Cost	Average Cost per Meal
10	$100	$10.00
20	200	10.00
30	300	10.00
40	380	9.50
50	460	9.20
60	534	8.90

PUZZLE 2: *Saving the Company by Selling Below Cost!*

A manufacturer of pocket calculators was selling 10 million units per year at a wholesale price of $11 per unit.[1] It found that rising wages and raw material prices had increased its costs to $13 per unit, which was clearly a losing proposition. Yet the availability of competing pocket calculators convinced the firm's managers that they could not get away with a price increase. At this point, a purchasing agent from a foreign country approached the firm and offered to buy an additional 10 million units, but at a price of only $7 per unit. At first, management considered the offer ludicrous, since the $7 price came nowhere near covering the unit cost of $13. But after some analysis, management was able to show that the firm could actually clear up its financial problem by agreeing to the proposed sale, even though it was below cost. At the end of the chapter, we will explain how this was possible.[2]

When the firm selects a *price* and a *quantity* of output that maximize profits, it seems that it must choose two numbers. In fact, however, the firm can pick only one. Once it has selected the *price*, the *quantity* it can sell is up to consumers. Alternatively, the firm may decide how many units it would like to sell, but then the market will determine the *price* at which this quantity can be sold. The firm's dilemma explicitly illustrates the powerful role that consumers play in the market. Management gets two numbers by making only one decision because the firm's demand curve tells it, for any quantity it may decide to market, the highest possible price its product can bring.

To illustrate, we return to Chapter 7's garage-building example. Al's Building Contractors sells garages to individual home owners, and Al is trying to figure out how best to make money on his building operation. To do this, he must estimate his *firm's demand curve*. The firm's demand curve is different from the demand curves we encountered in earlier chapters—the demand curve of an individual consumer and the market demand curve (which is the combined demand of all consumers in the market). Now we are dealing with a single firm (Al's Building Contractors) that is only one among possibly many firms that serve the market. The demand curve of any one supplier depends on the number and activities of the other firms in the market, as each competes for its share of total market demand. The demand curve of a single firm is actually a complicated

---

[1] This example is based on a real case, with the figures doctored to simplify the calculations.

[2] Taken from William J. Baumol, Alan S. Blinder, and William M. Scarth, *Economics: Principles and Policy,* 2nd Canadian ed. (Orlando, FL: Harcourt Brace Jovanovich, 1988), pp. 484, 496–497.

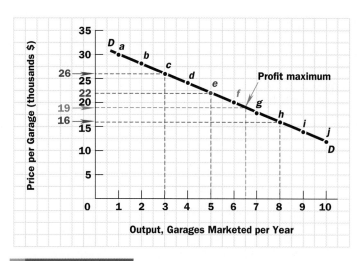

Demand Curve for Al's Garages

matter that we will deal with several times in subsequent chapters.[3] For now, suffice it to say that Al's demand curve will lie closer to the market demand curve (meaning that Al has a greater share of the market), the better his service, the more effective his advertising, the stronger his reputation for quality, and so on.

Suppose Al faces the demand curve for his garages shown as DD in Figure 1. The curve depicts the quantity demanded at each price. For example, the curve shows that at a price of $22,000 per garage (point e), Al's customers will demand five garages. If Al gets greedy and tries to charge the higher price of $26,000 per garage (point c on the curve), he can sell only three garages. If he wants to sell eight garages, he can find the required number of customers only by offering the garages at the lower price of $16,000 each (point h). In summary:

> Each point on the demand curve represents a price–quantity pair. The firm can pick any such pair. It can never pick the price corresponding to one point on the demand curve and the quantity corresponding to another point, however, because such an output cannot be sold at the selected price.

For this reason, we will not discuss price and output decisions separately throughout this chapter, for they are actually two different aspects of the same decision. To analyze this decision, we will make an imperfectly realistic assumption about the behaviour of business firms—the assumption that firms strive for the largest possible total profit to the exclusion of any other goal. We will therefore assume throughout this chapter (and for most of the book) that the firm has only one objective: It wants to make its total profit as large as possible. Our analytic strategy will seek to determine what output level (or price) achieves this goal. But you should keep in mind that many of our results depend on this simplifying assumption, so the conclusions will not apply to every case. Our decision to base the analysis on the profit-maximizing assumption gives us sharper insights, but we pay for it with some loss of realism.

TOTAL PROFIT: KEEP YOUR EYE ON THE GOAL

The **total profit** of a firm is its net earnings during some period of time. It is equal to the total amount of money the firm gets from sales of its products (the firm's total revenue) minus the total amount that it spends to make and market those products (total cost).

Total profit, then, is the firm's assumed goal. By definition, total profit is the difference between what the company earns in the form of sales revenue and what it pays out in the form of costs:

Total profit = Total revenue − Total cost (including opportunity cost)

Total profit defined in this way is called *economic profit* to distinguish it from an accountant's definition of profit. The two concepts of profit differ because an economist's total cost counts the *opportunity cost* of any capital, labour, or other inputs supplied by the firm's owner. For example, let's say that Naomi, who owns a small business, earns just enough to pay her the money that her labour and capital could have earned if they had been sold to others (say, $60,000 per year). Then, as we saw in Chapter 3, economists say that she is earning zero economic profit. (Naomi is just covering all her costs, including her opportunity costs.) In contrast, most accountants would say her profit is $60,000, referring to the difference between her gross receipts and her gross costs.

---

[3] In one case, the relationship between market demand and firm demand is very easy. That is the case where the firm has no competitors—it is a *monopoly*. Since it has the entire market to itself, its demand curve and the market demand curve are one and the same. We deal with monopoly in Chapter 11. Another fairly straightforward case, called *perfect competition*, will be studied in Chapter 10.

ECONOMIC PROFIT AND OPTIMAL DECISION MAKING

Why do economists use this apparently strange definition of profits, in which they subtract not only the costs that would ordinarily be deducted from total revenue, but also the opportunity costs? The answer is that doing so tells us directly whether the firm has made an *optimal* decision, in other words, whether the firm has chosen the price and quantity that maximizes profits. Specifically:

1. If economic profit is positive, then the firm's decisions are optimal; that is, its price and output yield a profit larger than any alternative prices and outputs.
2. If economic profit is zero, then the firm's choices are still satisfactory, because its price and output yield as much profit as the best available alternative.
3. If economic profit is negative, then the choice is not optimal; there exists at least one alternative price–output combination that is more profitable.

This reasoning explains why we pay so much attention to opportunity cost: because it helps us to determine whether or not a decision is optimal. And it works for all decisions, not only those about prices and quantities. But how does it do so? An example will make it clear. Suppose a firm has $100,000 to spend on either packaging or advertising. Suppose further that if the $100,000 is spent on packaging, it will bring in an accounting profit (that is, a profit as ordinarily defined: total revenue minus total ordinary cost, leaving out opportunity cost) of $20,000. If, instead, the (accounting) profit it could obtain from a $100,000 investment in advertising is $X, then by definition, $X is the opportunity cost of the decision to invest in packaging. In other words, $X is the earnings that could have been obtained from the alternative opportunity that the firm gives up by investing in packaging. So, for that decision:

Economic profit = Accounting profit − Opportunity cost = $20,000 − $X

This immediately illustrates our three conclusions above, because:

1. If $X < $20,000, then economic profit > 0, and packaging is the more profitable investment choice,
2. If $X = $20,000, then economic profit = 0, and the two investment options are equally profitable, and
3. If $X > $20,000, then the economic profit of packaging ($20,000 − $X) is negative, and advertising is a more profitable investment than packaging.

The reason economic profit performs this test is simple:

Economic profit of the decision in question = Its accounting profit − Its opportunity cost = Accounting profit of the decision in question − Accounting profit of the best available alternative. So, the economic profit of the decision in question will be positive only if it is more profitable (in the accountant's measurement) than the alternative, and so on.

> **Economic profit** equals net earnings, in the accountant's sense, minus the *opportunity costs* of capital and of any other inputs supplied by the firm's owners.

Total, Average, and Marginal Revenue

To see how total profit depends on output, we must study how the two components of total profit, total revenue (TR) and total cost (TC), behave when output changes. It should be obvious that both total revenue and total cost depend on the output–price combination the firm selects; we will study these relationships presently.

We can calculate **total revenue** directly from the firm's demand curve because, by definition, it is the product of price times the quantity that consumers will buy at that price:

$$TR = P \times Q$$

> The **total revenue (TR)** of a supplier firm is the total amount of money it receives from the purchasers of its products, without any deduction of costs.

Table 2 shows how we derive the total revenue schedule from the demand schedule for Al's garages. The first two columns simply express Figure 1's demand curve in tabular form. The third column gives, for each quantity, the product of price times quantity. For example, if Al sells seven garages at a price of $18,000 per garage, his annual sales revenue will be 7 garages × $18,000 per garage = $126,000.

TABLE 2

Demand for Al's Garages: His Total Revenue Schedule and His Marginal Revenue Schedule

(1)	(2)	(3)	(4)
Garages per Year	Price = Average Revenue per Garage (in thousands)	Total Revenue per Year (in thousands)	Marginal Revenue per Added Garage (in thousands)
0	—	$ 0	
1	$30	30	$30
2	28	56	26
3	26	78	22
4	24	96	18
5	22	110	14
6	20	120	10
7	18	126	6
8	16	128	2
9	14	126	−2
10	12	120	−6

The **average revenue (AR)** is total revenue (TR) divided by quantity.

Figure 2 displays Al's total revenue schedule in graphic form as the black TR curve. This graph shows precisely the same information as the demand curve in Figure 1, but in a somewhat different form. For example, point f on the demand curve in Figure 1, which shows a price–quantity combination of $P = \$20,000$ per garage and $Q = 6$ garages per year, appears as point F in Figure 2 as a total revenue of $120,000 per year ($20,000 per garage × 6 garages). Similarly, each other point on the TR curve in Figure 2 corresponds to the similarly labelled point in Figure 1.

We can speak of the relationship between the demand curve and the TR curve in a slightly different and more useful way than that shown in Figure 1. Because the product price is the revenue per unit that the firm receives, we can view the demand curve as an **average revenue (AR)** curve. To see why this is so, observe that average revenue and total revenue are, by definition, related to one another by the formula $AR = TR/Q$ and, as we have seen, $TR = P \times Q$. Therefore,[4]

$$AR = TR/Q = P \times Q/Q = P$$

As you can see, average revenue and price are just different names for the same thing. The reason should be clear. If a supermarket sells candy bars *at the same price*—say, $1—to each and every customer who wants one, then the average revenue that the store derives from each sale of these candy bars must also be $1.

Marginal revenue (MR) is the addition to total revenue resulting from the addition of one unit to total output. Geometrically, marginal revenue is the slope of the total revenue curve at the pertinent output quantity. Its formula is $MR_1 = TR_1 − TR_0$, and so on.

Finally, the last column of Table 1 shows the **marginal revenue (MR)** for each level of output. Marginal revenue provides us with an analytic tool that we will explain presently. This concept (analogous to marginal utility and marginal cost) refers to the *addition* to total revenue that results from raising output by one unit. Thus, in Table 2, we see that when output rises from two to three garages, total revenue goes up from $56,000 to $78,000, so marginal revenue is $78,000 minus $56,000, or $22,000.

■ Total, Average, and Marginal Cost

The revenue side is, of course, only half of the firm's profit picture. We must turn to the cost side for the other half. As we saw in Chapter 7, average cost (AC) and marginal cost (MC) are obtained directly from total cost (TC) in exactly the same way

FIGURE 2

Total Revenue Curve for Al's Garages

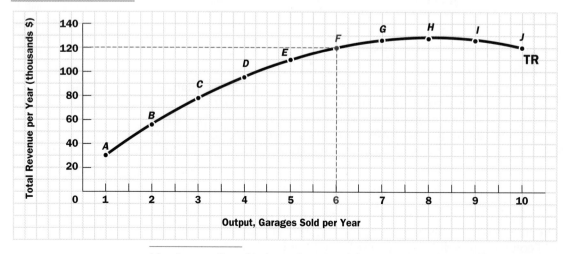

[4] See the appendix to this chapter for a general discussion of the relationship between totals and averages.

TABLE 3			
Al's Total, Average, and Marginal Costs			
(1)	(2)	(3)	(4)
Garages per Year	Total Cost per Year (in thousands)	Marginal Cost per Added Garage (in thousands)	Average Cost per Garage (in thousands)
0	$ 12		—
1	40	$28	$40
2	56	16	28
3	66	10	22
4	74	8	18.5
5	80	6	16
6	87	7	14.5
7	96	9	13.7 (approx.)
8	112	16	14
9	144	32	16
10	190	46	19

that average and marginal revenue are calculated from total revenue.

Figure 3 plots the numbers in Table 3 and thus shows the total, average, and marginal cost curves for Al's garage-building operation. As we learned in Chapter 7, the U-shapes of the average cost and marginal cost curves depicted here are considered typical. The shapes mean that, in any given industry, there is some size of firm that is most efficient in producing the output. Smaller enterprises lose any advantages that derive from a large volume of production, and so their average cost (the cost per unit of output) will be greater than that of a firm operating at the most efficient size of output. Similarly, firms that are too large will suffer from difficulties of supervision and coordination, and perhaps from bureaucratic controls, so that their costs per unit of output will also be higher than those of a firm of the most efficient size.

■ Maximization of Total Profit

We now have all the tools we need to answer our central question: What combination of output and price will yield the largest possible total profit? To study how total profit depends on output, Table 4 brings together the total revenue and total cost schedules from Tables 2 and 3. The fourth column in Table 4—called, appropriately enough, total profit—is just the difference between total revenue and total cost at each level of output.

Because we assume that Al's objective is to maximize profits, it is simple enough to determine the level of production he will choose. The table indicates that by producing and selling six garages per year, Al's garage-building operation earns the highest level of profits it is capable of earning—$33,000 per year (actually, we will see

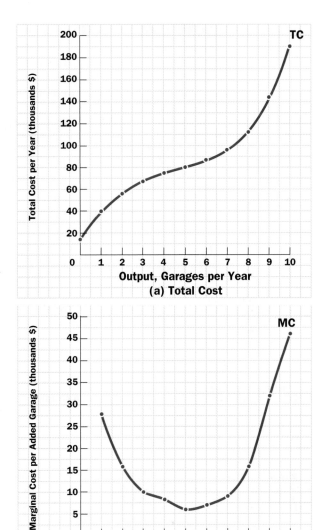

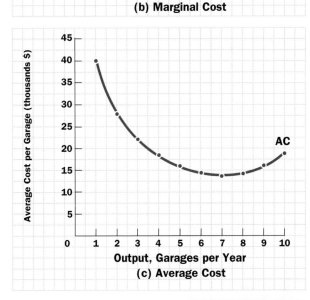

NOTE: Output is in garages per year.

FIGURE 3

Cost Curves for Al's Garages

TABLE 4
Total Revenues, Costs, and Profit for Al's Garages

(1)	(2)	(3)	(4)	(5)
Garages per Year	Total Revenue (TR) (in thousands)	Total Cost (TC) (in thousands)	Total Profit (TR – TC) (in thousands)	Marginal Profit (in thousands)
0	$ 0	$ 12	$–12	$ 2
1	30	40	–10	10
2	56	56	0	12
3	78	66	12	10
4	96	74	22	8
5	110	80	30	3
6	120	87	33	–3
7	126	96	30	–14
8	128	112	16	–34
9	126	144	–18	–52
10	120	190	–70	

in a moment that it pays Al to produce a little more than this amount). Any higher or lower rate of production would lead to lower profits. For example, profits would drop to $30,000 if output were increased to seven garages. If Al were to make the mistake of producing ten garages per season, he would actually suffer a net loss.

Profit Maximization: A Graphical Interpretation

We can present the same information on a graph. In Panel (a) of Figure 4, we bring together into a single diagram the relevant portion of the total revenue curve from Figure 2 and the total cost curve from Figure 3. Total profit, which is the difference between total revenue and total cost, appears in the diagram as the vertical distance between the TR and TC curves. For example, when output is four garages, total revenue is $96,000 (point A), total cost is $74,000 (point B), and total profit is the distance between points A and B, or $22,000.

In this graphical view of the problem, Al wants to maximize total profit, which is the vertical distance between the TR and TC curves. Panel (b) of Figure 4 plots these vertical differences derived from Panel (a) and so it shows the curve of total profit—that is, TR − TC. We see that it reaches its maximum value of about $34,000 (point M) at an output level of six and one-half garages per year—that is, 13 garages every two years. This graph shows that the conclusion we reached by looking at Table 4 was approximately right, but not perfectly accurate. Why? Because the table did not consider the possibility that the labour and material it pays Al to acquire may make it profitable to start on the construction of yet another garage after the first six are completed, with this garage being finished in the next year. We will consider this possibility in more detail in a few paragraphs.

The total profit curve in Figure 4(b) is shaped like a hill. Although such a shape is not inevitable, we expect a hill shape to be typical for the following reason: If a firm produces nothing, it certainly earns no profit. At the other extreme, a firm can produce so much output that it swamps the market, forcing the price down so low that the firm loses money. Only at intermediate levels of output—something between zero and the amount that floods the market—will the company earn a positive profit. Consequently, the total profit curve will rise from zero (or negative) levels at a very small output to positive levels at intermediate outputs; finally, it will fall to negative levels when output gets too large.

FIGURE 4   Profit Maximization: A Graphical Interpretation

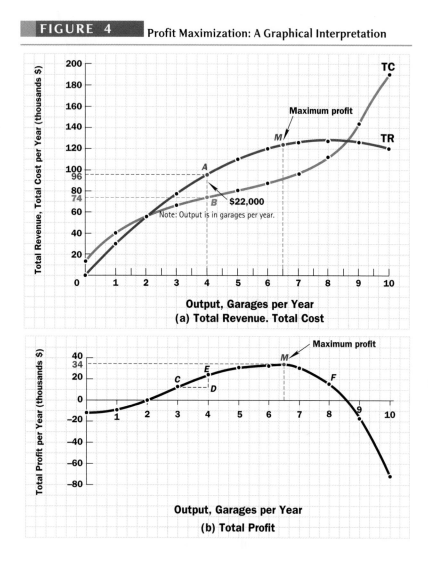

(a) Total Revenue. Total Cost

Note: Output is in garages per year.

(b) Total Profit

Output, Garages per Year

■ MARGINAL ANALYSIS AND MAXIMIZATION OF TOTAL PROFIT

We see from Figure 4 and Table 4 that many levels of output may yield a positive profit, but the firm is not aiming for just any level of profit. Instead, it wants the largest possible profit. If management knew the exact shape of its profit hill, choosing the optimal level of output would be a simple task indeed. It would merely have to locate the point, such as *M* in Figure 4(b), that defined the top of its profit hill. However, management rarely, if ever, has so much information, so a different technique for finding the optimum is required. That technique is marginal analysis—the same set of tools we used to analyze the firm's input purchase decisions in Chapter 7 and the consumer's buying decisions in Chapters 5 and 6.

This time we will use a concept known as **marginal profit** to solve Al's problem. Referring back to Table 4, we see that an increase in Al's output from three to four garages would raise total profit from $12,000 to $22,000; that is, it would generate $10,000 in additional profit, as shown in the last column of Table 4. We call this amount the marginal profit resulting from the addition of the fourth garage. Similarly, marginal profit from the seventh garage would be:

Marginal profit is the addition to total profit resulting from one more unit of output.

Total profit from 7 garages − Total profit from 6 garages =
$30,000 − $33,000 = −$3,000

The marginal rule for finding the optimal level of output is easy to understand:

If the marginal profit from increasing output by one unit is positive, then output should be increased. If the marginal profit from increasing output by one unit is negative, then output should be decreased. Thus, an output level can maximize total profit only if marginal profit is neither positive nor negative—that is, if it equals zero at that output.

For Al's Building Contractors, the marginal profit from the sixth unit of output (a sixth garage) is $3,000. This means that building six garages is not enough. Because marginal profit is still positive at six garages per year, it pays to produce more than six garages per year. However, marginal profit from the seventh garage is $30,000 −$33,000, or −$3,000, so the firm should produce less than seven garages because production of the seventh garage would reduce total profit by $3,000. Only at something between six and seven garages, where marginal profit is neither positive nor negative (as is approximately true for 6.5 garages), can total profit be as big as possible, because neither increasing nor reducing output can add to total profit.

The marginal profit numbers in Table 4 indicate one way in which marginal analysis helps to improve decisions. If we had looked only at the total profit figures in the fourth column of the table, we might have concluded that six garages is the profit-maximizing output for Al. The marginal profit column (column 5) tells us that this is not so. We see that the marginal profit of a seventh garage is −$3,000, so Al should, indeed, produce fewer than seven garages per year. But *the marginal profit of the sixth garage is +$3,000, so it pays Al to produce **more** than six garages.* Thus, a production level somewhere between six and seven garages per year really maximizes profits, as the total profit graph confirms.

The profit hill in Figure 4(b) is a graphical representation of the condition stating that to maximize profit, marginal profit should be zero (or as close to zero

SOURCE: © Royalty-Free/Corbis

as possible). Marginal profit is defined as the additional profit that accrues to the firm when output rises by one unit. For example, when output is increased, say, from three units to four units, or the distance *CD* in Figure 4(b), total profit rises by $10,000 (the distance *DE*) and marginal profit is therefore *DE/CD* (see the triangle *CDE* in the graph). This is precisely the definition of the slope of the total profit curve between points *C* and *E*. In general:

Marginal profit at any output is the slope of the total profit curve at that level of output.

With this geometric interpretation in hand, we can easily understand the logic of the marginal profit rule. At a point such as *C* in Figure 4(b), where the total profit curve is rising, marginal profit (which equals slope) is positive. Profit cannot be maximal at such a point, because we can increase profits by moving farther to the right. A firm that decided to stick to point *C* would be wasting the opportunity to increase profits by increasing output. Similarly, the firm cannot be maximizing profits at a point such as *F*, where the slope of the curve is negative, because there marginal profit (which, again, equals slope) is negative. If it finds itself at a point such as *F*, the firm can raise its profit by decreasing its output.

Only at a point such as *M* in Figure 4(b), where the total profit curve is neither rising nor falling, can the firm possibly be at the top of the profit hill rather than on one of the sides of the hill. Point *M* is precisely where the slope of the curve—and hence the marginal profit—is zero. Thus:

An output decision cannot be optimal unless the corresponding marginal profit is zero.

It is important to recognize that the firm is *not* interested in marginal profit for its own sake, but rather for what it implies about total profit. Marginal profit is like the needle on the temperature gauge of a car: The needle itself is of no concern to anyone, but failure to watch it can have dire consequences.

One common misunderstanding about marginal analysis is the idea that it seems foolish to go to a point where marginal profit is zero. "Isn't it better to earn a positive marginal profit?" This notion springs from a confusion between the quantity one is seeking to maximize (total profit) and the gauge that indicates whether such a maximum has actually been attained (marginal profit). Of course, it is better to have a positive *total* profit than a zero total profit. In contrast, a zero value on the marginal profit gauge merely indicates that all is well—that total profit is at its maximum.

You are likely to have noticed a recurrent theme in this chapter, which is a cornerstone of economic analysis. In any decision about whether to expand an activity, it is always the marginal cost and marginal benefit that are the relevant factors. A calculation based on average data is likely to lead the decision maker to miss all sorts of opportunities, some of them critical.

More generally, if one wants to make optimal decisions, marginal analysis should be used in the planning calculations. This is true whether the decision applies to a business firm seeking to maximize total profit or minimize the cost of the output it has selected, to a consumer trying to maximize utility, or to a less-developed country striving to maximize per-capita output. It applies as much to decisions on input proportions and advertising as to decisions about output levels and prices.

■ Marginal Revenue and Marginal Cost: Guides to Optimization

An alternative version of the marginal analysis of profit maximization can be derived from the cost and revenue components of profit. For this purpose, refer back to Figure 4, where we used total revenue (TR) and total cost (TC) curves to construct the profit hill. There is another way of finding the profit-maximizing solution.

We want to maximize the firm's profit, which is measured by the vertical distance between the TR and TC curves. This distance, we see, is not maximal at an output level such as three units, because there the two curves are growing farther apart. If we move farther to the right, the vertical distance between them (which is total profit) will increase. Similarly, we have not maximized the vertical distance between TR and TC at an output level such as eight units, because there the two curves are coming closer together. We can add to profit by moving farther to the left (reducing output). The conclusion from the graph, then, is that total profit—the vertical distance between TR and TC—is maximized only when the two curves are neither growing farther apart nor coming closer together—that is, when their slopes are equal (in the case of Al's Building Contractors in Figure 4, at 6.5 garages).

Marginal revenue and marginal cost curves, which we learned about earlier in the chapter, will help us understand this concept better. For precisely the same reason that marginal profit is the slope of the total profit curve, marginal revenue is the slope of the total revenue curve—because it represents the increase in total revenue resulting from the sale of one additional unit. Similarly, marginal cost is equal to the slope of the total cost curve. This interpretation of marginal revenue and marginal cost, respectively, as the slopes of the total revenue and total cost curves permits us to restate the geometric conclusion we have just reached in an economically significant way:

Profit can be maximized only at an output level at which marginal revenue is (approximately) equal to marginal cost. In symbols:

MR = MC

The logic of the MR = MC rule for profit maximization is straightforward.[5] When MR is not equal to MC, profits cannot possibly be maximized because the firm can increase its profits by either raising or reducing its output. For example, if MR = $22,000 and MC = $10,000 (Table 5), an additional unit of output adds $22,000 to revenues but only $10,000 to costs. Hence, the firm can increase its net profit by $12,000 by producing and selling one more unit. Similarly, if MC exceeds MR, say, MR = $6,000 and MC = $9,000, then the firm loses $3,000 on its marginal unit, so it can add $3,000 to its profit by reducing output by one unit. Only when MR = MC (or comes as close as possible to equalling MC) is it impossible for the firm to add to its profit by changing its output level.

Table 5 reproduces marginal revenue and marginal cost data for Al's Building Contractors from Tables 2 and 3. The table shows, as must be true, that the MR = MC rule leads us to the same conclusion as Figure 4 and Table 4. If he wants to maximize his profits, Al should produce more than six but fewer than seven garages per year. The marginal revenue of the sixth garage is $10,000 ($120,000 from the sale of six garages less $110,000 from the sale of five garages), whereas the marginal cost is only $7,000 ($87,000 − $80,000). Therefore, MR > MC and the firm should produce more than the sixth unit. The seventh garage, however, brings in only $6,000 in marginal revenue and its marginal cost is $9,000—clearly a losing proposition. Only at about six and one-half units of output does MR equal MC *exactly*.

Because the graphs of marginal analysis will prove so useful in later chapters, Figure 5(a) shows the MR = MC condition for profit maximization graphically. The black curve labelled MR in the figure is the marginal revenue schedule from Table 5. The blue curve labelled MC is the marginal cost schedule. The two curves intersect at point E, which is therefore the point where marginal revenue and marginal

	TABLE 5	
Al's Marginal Revenue and Marginal Cost		
(1)	(2)	(3)
Garages per Year	Marginal Revenue (in thousands)	Marginal Cost (in thousands)
0	—	—
1	$30	$28
2	26	16
3	22	10
4	18	8
5	14	6
6	10	7
7	6	9
8	2	16
9	−2	32
10	−6	46

[5] You may have surmised by now that just as total profit = total revenue − total cost, it must be true that marginal profit = marginal revenue − marginal cost. This is, in fact, correct. It also shows that when marginal profit = 0, we must have MR = MC.

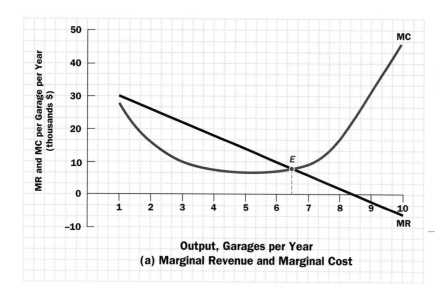

Output, Garages per Year
(a) Marginal Revenue and Marginal Cost

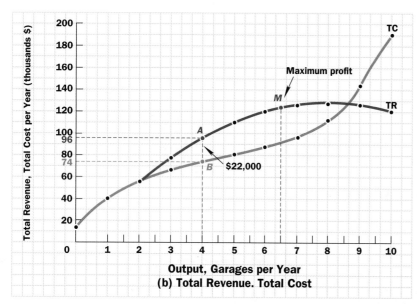

Output, Garages per Year
(b) Total Revenue. Total Cost

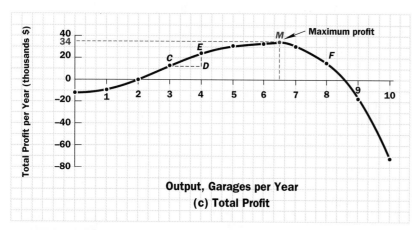

Output, Garages per Year
(c) Total Profit

FIGURE 5

Profit Maximization: Another Graphical Interpretation

Note: Output is in garages per year.

cost are equal. The optimal output for Al is six and one-half units.[6] Panels (b) and (c) in Figure 5, respectively, reproduce the TR and TC curves from Figure 4(a) and the total profit curve from Figure 4(b). Note how MC and MR intersect at the same output at which the distance of TR above TC is greatest, which is also the output at which the profit hill reaches its peak.

■ Finding the Optimal Price from Optimal Output

At the beginning of this chapter, we set two goals: to determine the profit-maximizing output and to find the profit-maximizing price, and emphasized that once we know either of these, it can automatically tell us the other. So far, we have identified the profit-maximizing output, the output level at which MR = MC (6.5 garages per year in our garage-building example). That leaves us with the task of determining the profit-maximizing price.

Fortunately, this task requires only one more easy step. As we said earlier, once the firm has selected the output it wants to produce and sell, the demand curve determines the price it must charge to induce consumers to buy that amount of product. Consequently, if we know that the profit-maximizing output is 6.5 garages, the demand curve in Figure 1 (on page 170) tells us what price Al must charge to sell that profit-maximizing output. To sell an average of 6.5 garages per year (that is, 13 garages every two years), he must price each garage at $19,000 (between points *f* and *g*). The demand curve tells us that this amount is the only price at which this quantity will be demanded by customers.

Once the profit-maximizing output quantity has been determined with the help of the MR = MC rule, it is easy to find the profit-maximizing price with the help of the demand curve. Just use that curve to find out at what price the optimal quantity will be demanded.

---

[6] We must note one important qualification. Sometimes marginal revenue and marginal cost curves do not have the nice shapes depicted in Figure 5(a), and they may intersect more than once. In such cases, although it remains true that MR = MC at the output level that maximizes profits, there may be other output levels at which MR = MC but at which profits are not maximized.

GENERALIZATION: THE LOGIC OF MARGINAL ANALYSIS AND MAXIMIZATION

The logic of marginal analysis of profit maximization that we have just studied can be generalized, because essentially the same argument was already used in Chapters 5 and 7 and will recur in a number of chapters later in this book. To avoid having to master the argument each time all over again, it is useful to see how this concept can be applied in problems other than the determination of the firm's profit-maximizing output.

The general issue is this: Decision makers often are faced with the problem of selecting the magnitude of some variable, such as how much to spend on advertising, or how many bananas to buy, or how many school buildings to construct. Each of these acts brings benefits, so that the larger the number selected by the decision maker, the larger the total benefits that will be derived. Unfortunately, as larger numbers are selected, the associated costs also grow. The problem is to take the trade-off properly into account and to calculate at what point the net gain—the difference between the total benefit and the total cost—will be greatest. Thus, we have the following general principle:

If a decision is to be made about the quantity of some variable, then to maximize

Net benefit = Total benefit − Total cost,

the decision maker must select a value of the variable at which

Marginal benefit = (approximately) Marginal cost

For example, if a community was to determine that the marginal benefit from building an additional school was greater than the cost of an additional school, it would clearly be better off if it built another school. But if the community were planning to build so many schools that the marginal benefit was less than the marginal cost, it would be better off if it switched to a more limited construction program. Only if the marginal benefit and cost are as close as possible to being equal will the community have the optimal number of schools.

We will apply this same concept in later chapters. Again and again, when we analyze a quantitative decision that brings together both benefits and costs, we conclude that the optimal decision occurs at the point where the marginal benefit equals the marginal cost. The logic is the same whether we are considering the net gains to a firm, to a consumer, or to society as a whole.

Application: Fixed Cost and the Profit-Maximizing Price

We can now use our analytic framework to offer an insight that is often unexpected. Suppose there is a rise in the firm's fixed cost; for example, imagine that the property taxes on Al's Building Contractors double. What will happen to the profit-maximizing price and output? Should Al raise his price to cover the increased cost, or should he produce a larger output even if it requires a drop in price? The answer is surprising: Neither!

When a firm's fixed cost increases, its profit-maximizing price and output remain completely unchanged, as long as it pays the firm to stay in business.

In other words, there is nothing that the firm's management can do to offset the effect of the rise in fixed cost. Management must just put up with it. This is surely a case where common sense is not a reliable guide to the right decision.

Why is this so? Recall that, by definition, a fixed cost does not change when output changes. The increase in Al's fixed costs is the same whether business is slow or booming, whether production is 2 garages or 20. This idea is illustrated in Table 6, which also reproduces Al's total profits from Table 4. The third column of the table shows that total fixed cost has risen (from zero) to $10,000 per year. As a result, total profit is $10,000 less than

TABLE 6			
Rise in Fixed Cost: Total Profit Before and After			
(1)	(2)	(3)	(4)
Garages per Year	Total Profit Before (in thousands)	Rise in Fixed Cost (in thousands)	Total Profit After (in thousands)
0	$−12	$10	$−22
1	−10	10	−20
2	0	10	−10
3	12	10	2
4	22	10	12
5	30	10	20
6	33	10	23
7	30	10	20
8	16	10	6
9	−18	10	−28
10	−70	10	−80

180   Chapter 8   OUTPUT, PRICE, AND PROFIT: THE IMPORTANCE OF MARGINAL ANALYSIS

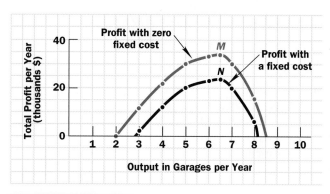

FIGURE 6

Fixed Cost Does Not Affect Profit-Maximizing Output

it would have been otherwise—no matter what the firm's output. For example, when output is four units, we see that total profit falls from $22,000 (second column) to $12,000 (last column).

Because profit is reduced by the same amount at every output level, whatever output was most profitable before the increase in fixed costs must still be most profitable. In Table 6, we see that $23,000 is the largest entry in the last column, which shows profits after the rise in fixed cost. This approximately highest possible profit is attained, as it was before, when output is at six units. The actual profit-maximizing output will remain at 6.5 garages, exactly as before. In other words, the firm's profit-maximizing price and quantity remain unchanged.

This is shown graphically in Figure 6, which displays the firm's total profit hill before and after the rise in fixed cost (reproducing Al's initial profit hill from Figure 4). We see that the cost increase simply moves the profit hill straight downward by $10,000, so the highest point on the hill is lowered just from point M to point N. But the top of the hill is shifted neither toward the left nor toward the right. It remains at the 6.5 garage output level.[7]

PUZZLE 1 RESOLVED: *Marginal Analysis to the Rescue: Why You Should Stick to Your Meal Plan*

We can now put marginal analysis to work and solve Puzzle 1. Although the average cost per meal is still higher in the old dining hall of Canuck University than it is in the new dining hall, what really matters is the marginal cost of a meal. Students who have already purchased 30 meals can now acquire a set of 10 meals by paying an additional $80 (see Table 7). Thus, the marginal price per meal is only $8.00 in the old dining hall, while it is $8.50 in the new hall. Things are even better for those who have already purchased 50 meals, since the marginal cost per meal is now $7.40. So, any student who has already purchased at least 30 meals should stick with the old dining hall.

If you could not resolve the puzzle on your own, do not despair. Even economics students at the prestigious Massachusetts Institute of Technology (MIT) are not immune to error. With a dining plan similar to the one shown in Table 1, they were asked whether they would switch to the new dining hall, and among those for whom the marginal cost of the existing meal plan was lower than that of the new dining hall, 68 percent said that they would switch and gave as their reason that they would "save money"![8] So, 68 percent of MIT economics students misapplied marginal analysis and got the wrong answer in a real-life problem!

TABLE 7

Total Cost and Marginal Cost per Meal: Old Dining Hall

Cumulative Number of Meals	Total Cost	Average Cost per Meal
10	$100	$10.00
20	200	10.00
30	300	10.00
40	380	8.00
50	460	8.00
60	534	7.40

[7] EXERCISE: Does the added fixed cost change the marginal cost? Explain. What does this imply for optimal output?
[8] Richard H. Thaler, "The psychology of choice and the assumptions of economics," in R. H. Thaler (ed.), *Quasi-Rational Economics* (New York: Russell Sage Foundation), 1991, p. 148.

NEL

PUZZLE 2 RESOLVED: *Using Marginal Analysis to Unravel the Case of the "Unprofitable" Calculator*

We can now put the marginal analysis of profit determination to work to solve the second puzzle with which we began this chapter. The example was drawn from reality, and reality never works as neatly as a textbook illustration with a mechanical application of the MR = MC rule. However, we will see that the underlying reasoning does shed useful light on real problems.

In this puzzle, a firm was losing money because the price of its pocket calculator was less than its average cost, and was offered the questionable opportunity to sell more of its product to a foreign buyer at a price that was even lower.

Obviously, this firm was in a bad way financially. As shown in Table 8, its average cost for the product was $13 per unit and yet the price it was charging was only $11 per unit, leading to a $20-million loss on the 10 million units of output that it sold. Management might well have reasoned this way: It would be desirable to expand our volume, but we can't afford to do so. Instead, we must raise our price above our $13 average cost even if it cuts down our sales.

TABLE 8							
Initial Costs and Revenues of the Pocket Calculator							
Units Sold	Total Cost	Average Cost	Marginal Cost	Price	Total Revenue	Total Cost	Profit or Loss
(millions)	(millions of $)	($)		($)	(millions of $)		
10	$130	$13	$3	$11	$110	$130	–$20

While the managers were pondering their dilemma, a foreign purchasing group offered to buy an additional 10 million units of the company's pocket calculators if the company would supply the units at a discount price of $7. On an average cost (AC) calculation, this arrangement seemed disastrous. After all, AC was $13 and the company was already losing money at a price of $11. How could it possibly afford to sell at an even lower price?

But was the proposition so ludicrous? With its marginal costs approximately constant at $3, by accepting the offer from the foreign purchasing group, the company could change its situation from that shown in Table 8 to the one shown in Table 9. We see that the total number of units sold would double, from 10 million to 20 million. Total costs would rise from $130 million to $160 million an increase of $30 million based on the company's marginal cost (MC) of $3 for each of the 10 million additional units. The arithmetic shows that, as a consequence, AC would fall from $130/10 = $13 to $160/20 = $8.

TABLE 9						
Costs and Revenues of the Pocket Calculator Producer after Sales "Below Cost"						
Units Sold	Total Cost	Average Cost	Marginal Cost	Total Revenue	Total Cost	Profit or Loss
(millions)	(millions of $)	($)		(millions of $)		
20	$160	$8	$3	$180	$160	+$20

The last three columns report the resulting "miracle." The apparently ridiculous proposition that 10 million additional pocket calculators be sold at a price below either the old or the new average cost in fact succeeded in eliminating the deficit and actually put the company into the black—to the tune of $20 million in net profit. Just how was this "miracle" accomplished? The answer becomes clear when we apply the rules we have learned in this chapter. In Table 8, it can be seen that AC was indeed

$13, but the corresponding MC figure was only $3. Therefore, every *additional* unit sold to the foreign buyer at a price of $7 brought in a marginal profit of $7 – $3 = $4. In such cases, the more you sell, the better off you are.

This case illustrates a point that frequently arises: Marginal costs are constant instead of rising, while average unit costs decrease, a situation that is not unusual in the manufacturing and service industries. This will be illustrated further in Chapters 11 and 12, when monopolies and oligopolies are discussed.

The same sort of issue faces airlines that offer discounted fares to students (or to senior citizens, or some other group), when those fares are lower than the average cost (including fuel cost, salaries of personnel, and so on) per passenger. If the discounted fares have the effect of filling up seats that would otherwise have flown empty, and if the fares cover more than their *marginal cost* (which consists only of the additional cost of selling the tickets and providing the students with a snack), then those fares clearly are adding to the airline's profits. Nevertheless, such fare discounts sometimes lead to lawsuits by competitors of the airlines that offer such discounted fares.

CONCLUSION: THE FUNDAMENTAL ROLE OF MARGINAL ANALYSIS

We saw in Chapter 7 how marginal analysis helps us to understand the firm's input choices. Similarly, in Chapters 5 and 6, it cast indispensable light on the consumer's purchase decisions. In this chapter, it enabled us to analyze output and pricing decisions. The logic of marginal analysis applies not only to economic decisions by consumers and firms, but also to decisions made by governments, colleges and universities, hospitals, and other organizations. In short, this type of analysis applies to any individual or group that must make optimal choices about the use of scarce resources. Thus, one of the most important conclusions that can be drawn from this chapter, and a conclusion brought out vividly by the examples we have just discussed, is the importance of thinking "at the margin."

Another real-life example not far removed from profit maximization will illustrate how marginal criteria are useful in decision making and in assessing decisions. In 1995, the Ontario government, led by Mike Harris of the Ontario Progressive Conservative Party, announced that it would phase out the Ontario Academic Credit system, thus eliminating the need for Grade 13 in the high school system (presumably to reduce the cost of high school expenditures). A new standardized curriculum was then put into place and in the fall of 1999, the first students under the new system entered Ontario high schools.

In September 2003, four years later, the first Grade 12 graduates from the new Ontario four-year high school curriculum had to compete for admission to colleges and universities with the Grade 13 graduates of the old Ontario five-year high school curriculum. This was called the "Double Cohort." Ontario universities argued that they should be fully compensated, at the going average rate of $6,800 per student (the dollar value of a BIU—the administrative lingo for *basic income unit*—the government subsidy per full-time student) for every additional student that would enter their programs. Was this reasoning correct?

The double-cohort situation caused great concern for both the 2003 Ontario high school graduates and their parents. Many thought that Ontario universities and colleges would accept a smaller proportion of first-year applicants, on the grounds that they had neither the space nor the financial resources to cater to the needs of these new students. And indeed, most Ontario universities did not increase their admission numbers in proportion to the number of new applicants. In limited-enrolment programs, Ontario universities provided only a small number of additional admissions and imposed higher admission requirements for these programs. By contrast, in less popular programs and in programs that required less personal attention, schools maintained the same admission requirements and increased the enrollment numbers. By doing so, universities effectively channelled newly admitted students toward programs that were undersubscribed, filling classes and classrooms that were previously underutilized.

In addition, some Ontario universities imposed on the teaching staff to conduct more courses at night and in some cases, even on Saturdays. The schools thus managed to reduce the marginal cost of admitting a student, while still benefiting in full from the student tuition fee and the government subsidy per student. It therefore can be presumed that the marginal cost of admitting additional students as a result of the double cohort was probably much lower than the average cost of a student. Indeed, the fact that Ontario universities admitted an increased number of unfunded students suggests that the marginal cost of additional students may not be any higher than their tuition fees.

Pressures from the double-cohort parents convinced the Ontario government to grant what the universities were asking for. Ontario universities came out on top of the situation, as they managed to get more than the marginal cost for each additional student who was admitted. This, and a general increase in the dollar value of BIUs, however, helped to correct an unusual situation: The Ontario provincial subsidy per student was the lowest in Canada, while Ontario universities had the highest student–professor ratio at 22:1! In addition, with the arrival of the double-cohort students into graduate programs in September 2007, Ontario universities now receive additional funding for graduate programs.

■ THE THEORY AND REALITY: A WORD OF CAUTION

We have now completed two chapters describing how business managers can make optimal decisions. Can you go to Bay Street and corporate head offices and find executives calculating marginal cost and marginal revenue to decide how much to produce? Not very often—although in some important applications they do. Nor can you find consumers in stores using marginal analysis to decide what to buy. Like consumers, successful businesspeople often rely heavily on intuition and "hunches" that cannot be described by any set of rules. In fact, in a 1993 survey of chief executive

Profit Maximization and Ethical Considerations

We have already questioned whether firms really maximize profits (see the boxed feature near the beginning of this chapter). One of the key notions in economics is that of trade-offs. Maximizing profits may involve tough decisions for managers, decisions that involve ethical considerations. An experiment that illustrates this was conducted by Ariel Rubinstein, a professor at Tel-Aviv University. An electronic questionnaire was conducted with the readers of *Globes,* a newspaper published for Israel's business community. The readers were told that a certain company faced a slowdown in economic activity and that the company executives were considering laying off some of its 196 blue-collar employees. The accompanying table shows the effect on the company's profits when various numbers of workers are retained. The readers were then asked how many employees they would recommend that the company keep. How many would you keep?

If you believe in profit maximization, then the obvious answer is that the company should retain 100 employees (96 workers should be laid off), since this brings the largest expected annual profit: $2 million. Any other decision would lead to lower expected profits. Somewhat surprisingly, less than 30 percent of the 4,600 respondents and only 36 percent of those with an economics degree gave the profit-maximizing answer. The majority recommended that between 144 and 196 employees should be retained.

Employment and Expected Profits	
Number of Workers Who Will Continue to Be Employed	Expected Value of Annual Profit (millions of $)
0 (all workers will be laid off)	Loss of $8
50 (146 workers will be laid off)	Profit of $1
65 (131 workers will be laid off)	Profit of $1.5
100 (96 workers will be laid off)	Profit of $2
144 (52 workers will be laid off)	Profit of $1.6
170 (26 workers will be laid off)	Profit of $1
196 (no layoffs)	Profit of $0.4

A similar questionnaire was administered to graduate students in economics at Harvard and MIT, two universities with prestigious economics departments. Still only 41 percent of these economics students gave the profit-maximizing answer, and half of them thought that a real manager would not choose the profit-maximizing course of action. These students can certainly not be accused of misunderstanding marginal analysis and profit maximization, but when faced with an ethically difficult choice, many of them ignored the profit-maximizing hypothesis.

SOURCE: Ariel Rubinstein, "A sceptic's comment on the study of economics," *Economic Journal,* March 2006, Vol. 116, pp. C1–C9, Blackwell Publishing.

officers (CEOs) conducted by *Inc.* magazine, nearly 20 percent of the respondents admitted to using guesswork to price their products or services.

Note that we have not sought to provide a literal description of business behaviour but rather a model to help us analyze and predict this behaviour. The four chapters that we have just completed constitute the core of microeconomics. We will find ourselves returning again and again to the principles learned in these chapters.

SUMMARY

1. A firm can choose the quantity of its product that it wants to sell or the price that it wants to charge, but it cannot choose both because price affects the quantity demanded.

2. In economic theory, we usually assume that firms seek to maximize **profits**. This assumption should not be taken literally but rather interpreted as a useful simplification of reality.

3. The demand curve of a firm is determined from the market demand curve by the strength of the competitive efforts of the rival firms in the market.

4. **Marginal revenue** is the additional revenue earned by increasing quantity sold by one unit. Marginal cost is the additional cost incurred by increasing production by one unit.

5. Maximum profit requires the firm to choose the level of output at which marginal revenue is equal to (or most closely approximates) marginal cost.

6. Geometrically, the profit-maximizing output level occurs at the highest point on the total profit curve. There the slope of the total profit curve is zero (or as close to zero as possible), meaning that **marginal profit** is zero.

7. A change in fixed cost will not change the profit-maximizing level of output.

8. It will generally pay a firm to expand its output if it is selling at a price greater than marginal cost, even if that price happens to be below average cost.

9. **Optimal decisions** must be made on the basis of marginal cost and marginal revenue figures, not average cost and average revenue figures.

KEY TERMS

Optimal decision   168

Total profit   170

Economic profit   171

Total revenue (TR)   171

Average revenue (AR)   172

Marginal revenue (MR)   172

Marginal profit   175

TEST YOURSELF

1. Suppose that the firm's demand curve indicates that at a price of $12 per unit, customers will demand 2 million units of its product. Suppose that management decides to pick both price and output; the firm produces 3 million units of its product and prices them at $20 each. What will happen?

2. Suppose that a firm's management would be pleased to increase its share of the market, but if it expands its production the price of its product will fall. Will its profits necessarily fall? Why or why not?

3. Why does it make sense for a firm to seek to maximize *total* profit rather than to maximize *marginal* profit?

4. A firm's marginal revenue is $133 and its marginal cost is $90. What amount of profit does the firm fail to pick up by refusing to increase output by one unit?

5. Calculate average revenue (AR) and average cost (AC) in Table 4. How much profit does the firm earn at the output at which AC = AR? Why?

6. A firm's total cost is $800 if it produces one unit, $1,400 if it produces two units, and $1,800 if it produces three units of output. Draw up a table of total, average, and marginal costs for this firm.

7. Draw an average and marginal cost curve for the firm in Question 6 above. Describe the relationship between the two curves.

8. A firm has the demand and total cost schedules given in the following table. If it wants to maximize profits, how much output should it produce?

Quantity	Price	Total Cost
1	$6	$ 1.00
2	5	2.50
3	4	6.00
4	3	7.00
5	2	11.00

DISCUSSION QUESTION

"It may be rational for the management of a firm not to try to maximize profits." Discuss the circumstances under which this statement may be true.

APPENDIX *The Relationships Among Total, Average, and Marginal Data*

You may have surmised that there is a close connection between the average revenue curve and the marginal revenue curve and that there must be a similar relationship between the average cost curve and the marginal cost curve. After all, we derived our average revenue figures from the total revenues and also calculated our marginal revenue figures from the total revenues at the various possible output levels; a similar relationship applied to costs. In fact:

> Marginal, average, and total figures are inextricably bound together. From any one of the three figures, the other two can be calculated. The relationships among total, average, and marginal data are exactly the same for any variable—such as revenue, cost, or profit—to which the concepts apply.

To illustrate and emphasize the wide applicability of marginal analysis, we switch our example from profits, revenues, and costs to a noneconomic variable. As we are about to see, the same concepts can be applied to human body weights. We use this example because calculation of weights is more familiar to most people than calculation of profits, revenues, or costs, and we can use it to illustrate several fundamental relationships between average and marginal figures.

In Table 10, we begin with an empty room. (The total weight of occupants is equal to zero.) A person weighing 55 kilograms enters; total, marginal and average weight are all, then, 55 kilograms. If the person is followed by a person weighing 95 kilograms (marginal weight equals 95 kilograms), the total weight increases to 150 kilograms, average weight rises to 75 kilograms (150/2), and so on.[9]

The rule for converting totals to averages, and vice versa, is:

> Rule 1(a): Average weight equals total weight divided by number of persons.
> Rule 1(b): Total weight equals average weight times number of persons.

This rule naturally applies equally well to cost, revenue, profit, or any other variable.

We calculate marginal weight from total weight by working with the same subtraction process already used to calculate marginal cost and marginal revenue. Specifically:

> Rule 2(a): The marginal weight of, say, the third person equals the total weight of three people minus the total weight of two people.

For example, when the fourth person enters the room, total weight rises from 240 to 320 kilograms, and hence the corresponding marginal weight is $320 - 240$

TABLE 10

Weights of Persons in a Room (in kilograms)

Number of Persons in a Room	Marginal Weight	Total Weight	Average Weight
0		0	—
	55		
1		55	55
	95		
2		150	75
	90		
3		240	80
	80		
4		320	80
	60		
5		380	76
	40		
6		420	70

= 80 kilograms, as is shown in the second column of Table 10. We can also do the reverse—calculate total from marginal weight—through an addition process.

> Rule 2(b): The total weight of, say, three people equals the (marginal) weight of the first person who enters the room plus the (marginal) weight of the second person, plus the (marginal) weight of the third person.

You can verify Rule 2(b) by referring to Table 11, which shows that the total weight of three persons, 240 kilograms, is indeed equal to $55 + 95 + 90$ kilograms, the sum of the preceding marginal weights. A similar relationship holds for any other total weight figure in the table, a fact that you should verify.

In addition to these familiar arithmetic relationships, there are two other useful relationships.

> Rule (3): With an exception (fixed cost) that was discussed in Chapter 7, the marginal, average, and total figures for the first person must all be equal.

That is, when there is only one person in the room whose weight is X kilograms, the average weight will obviously be X, the total weight must be X, and the marginal weight must also be X (because the total must have risen from zero to X kilograms). Put another way, when the marginal person is alone, he or she is obviously the average person and also represents the totality of all relevant persons.

Our final and very important relationship is:

> Rule (4): If marginal weight is lower than average weight, then average weight must decrease when the number of persons increases. If marginal weight exceeds average weight, average weight must increase when the number of persons increases. If the marginal and average weights are equal, the average weight must remain constant when the number of persons increases.

---

[9] In this illustration, "persons in room" is analogous to units of output, "total weight" is analogous to total revenue or cost, and "marginal weight" is analogous to marginal revenue or cost in the discussions of marginal analysis in the body of the chapter.

These three possibilities are all illustrated in Table 10. Notice, for example, that when the third person enters the room, the average weight increases from 75 to 80 kilograms. That increase occurs because this person's (marginal) weight is 90 kilograms, which is above the average and therefore pulls up the average, as Rule 4 requires. Similarly, when the sixth person—who is a 40-kilogram child—enters the room, the average decreases from 76 to 70 kilograms because marginal weight, 40 kilograms, is below average weight and so pulls the average down.

It is essential to avoid a common misunderstanding of this rule. It does *not* state, for example, that if the average figure is rising, the *marginal* figure must be *rising*. When the average rises, the marginal figure may rise, fall, or remain unchanged. The arrival of two persons, both well above the average weight, will push the average up in two successive steps even if the second new arrival is lighter than the first. We see such a case in Table 10, where average weight rises successively from 55 to 75 to 80 kilograms, while the marginal weight falls from 95 to 90 kilograms.

■ GRAPHICAL REPRESENTATION OF MARGINAL AND AVERAGE CURVES

We have shown how, from a curve of total profit (or total cost or total anything else), we can determine the corresponding marginal figure. In the chapter, we noted repeatedly that the marginal value at any particular point is equal to the slope of the corresponding total curve at that point. But for some purposes, it is convenient to use a graph that records marginal and average values directly rather than deriving them from the curve of totals.

We can obtain such a graph by plotting the data in a table of average and marginal figures, such as Table 10. The result looks like the graph shown in Figure 7. In that graph, the number of persons in the room appears on the horizontal axis and the corresponding average and marginal figures appear on the vertical axis. The solid dots represent average weights; the small circles represent marginal weights. For example, point *A* shows that when two persons are in the room, their average weight is 75 kilograms, as recorded on the third line of Table 10. Similarly, point *B*

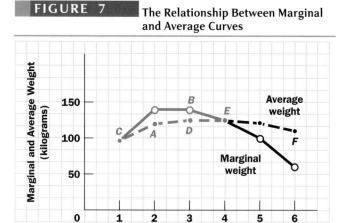

FIGURE 7   **The Relationship Between Marginal and Average Curves**

on the graph represents information provided in the next column of the table—that is, that the marginal weight of the third person who enters the room is 90 kilograms. We have connected these points into a marginal curve and an average curve, represented, respectively, by the solid and the broken curves in the diagram. This is the representation of marginal and average values economists most frequently use.

Figure 7 illustrates two of our rules. Rule 3 says that for the first unit, the marginal and average values will be the same; that is precisely why the two curves start out together at point *C*. The graph also depicts Rule 4 between points *C* and *E*: Where the average curve is rising, the marginal curve lies above the average. (Notice that over part of this range, the marginal curve falls even though the average curve is rising; Rule 4 says nothing about the rise or fall of the *marginal* curve.) We see also that over range *EF*, where the average curve is falling, the marginal curve is below the average curve, again in accord with Rule 4. Finally, at point *E*, where the average curve is neither rising nor falling, the marginal curve meets the average curve; the average and marginal weights are equal at that point, so that the marginal weights to not pull the average weight either upward or downward.

TEST YOURSELF

1. Suppose that the following table is your record of exam grades in your Principles of Economics course:

   Use these data to make up a table of total, average, and marginal grades for the five exams.

Exam Date	Grade		Comment
September 20	65		A slow start
October 10	75		Some improvement
October 31	90		Happy Halloween!
November 20	85		Slipped a little
December 15	95		A fast finish!

2. From the data in your exam-grade table in Test Yourself Question 1, illustrate each of the rules mentioned in this appendix. Be sure to point out an instance where the marginal grade falls but the average grade rises.

9

INVESTING IN BUSINESS: STOCKS AND BONDS

A bargain that is going to become a greater bargain is no bargain.

MARTIN SHUBIK (1926–), CANADIAN-BORN ECONOMIST, YALE UNIVERSITY

A firm does more than select inputs, outputs, and prices—which were the topics of previous chapters. In this chapter, we discuss how real firms finance their activities—notably with stocks and bonds. These days, a very large proportion of the nation's college and university graduates invests money in the stock and bond markets. You probably will as well, if you don't already. For this reason, it is important to understand something about how these markets work. But please do not think that this chapter will turn you into a super speculator who can beat the market consistently. Too many investors have thought that way and ended up losing their life's savings. Indeed, the main lesson of this chapter is that, for good reason, the future behaviour of the stock market is virtually unpredictable. As you look toward the future, the stock market will undoubtedly go up and undoubtedly go down, but the unanswerable question is: When? History repeatedly teaches us that lesson, and as philosopher George Santayana once wrote, "Those who cannot remember the past are condemned to repeat it"—as many stock-market investors have done.[1]

CONTENTS

---

[1] George Santayana, *The Life of Reason, or, The Phases of Human Progress*, Vol. I (New York: C. Scribner's Sons, 1905–06).

PUZZLE 1: *What in the World Happened to the Stock Market?*

Sometimes a picture really is worth a thousand words. Figure 1 shows the remarkable behaviour of share prices between 1986 and 2008 on the Toronto Stock Exchange (TSX), which we will describe later in the chapter. It looks a bit like the Rocky Mountains, rising spectacularly from the fall of 1998 until the end of the summer of 2000, then falling dramatically until the fall of 2002, only to rise again to new summits. The numbers on the scale tell you that the index of the Toronto Stock Exchange—the S&P/TSX composite index—soared from about 5,550 in August 1998 to about 11,250 in August 2000, an astonishing gain of 100% in less than two years! But by September 2002, the index was barely above 6,000, back to where it had been four years before. However, by the end of year 2005, the stock market index regained its record 11,250 level, by 2006 it had gone over the 12,000 mark, and by 2007 it went over 14,000.

Similar index changes rocked other stock market exchanges during this time period, most notably the stock markets of our neighbour: the New York Stock Exchange and the NASDAQ. The latter stock exchange trades the shares of several high-tech companies, including giants such as Intel and Microsoft. In the 1990s, the NASDAQ saw the value of its index treble in less than 18 months, only to lose its entire gain within the next 18 months. As of mid-2007, the NASDAQ was still at only about half the value of its March 2000 peak value.

FIGURE 1   S&P/TSX Stock Market Composite Index, 1986–2008

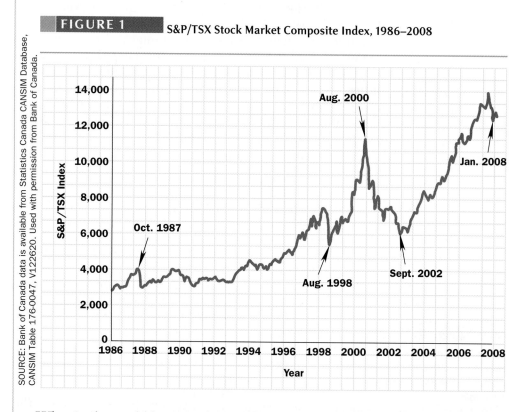

SOURCE: Bank of Canada data is available from Statistics Canada CANSIM Database, CANSIM Table 176-0047, V122620. Used with permission from Bank of Canada.

What in the world happened? In all honesty, most of the world's best economists and leading financial experts were left puzzled by this episode. As we will learn in this chapter, the value of a share of stock is supposed to reflect the current and future profits of the company that issues the stock. But that theory of stock prices will not explain why shares of Nortel (the research and development branch of Bell Canada) sold for $124 per share on the Toronto Stock Exchange in September 2000 and dropped to $0.67 two years later, in August 2002. New Nortel shares , as this book is being completed, are now worth about $10, but it takes ten old Nortel shares to buy a new one!

Alan Greenspan, the chairman of the Federal Reserve (the American central bank), once called the phenomenon that gripped North America in the boom years "irrational exuberance"—and it was certainly that. One of the authors of this book called the upside of the NASDAQ stock market's performance between 1990 and 2004 as the "Wile E. Coyote stock market," after that old nemesis in *Road Runner* cartoons, who would run off cliffs and yet somehow manage to remain in the air— until he looked down.

Apparently, investors in Canadian stocks "looked down" around September 2000. But why then? Why not before? And what made stock prices rise so high in the first place? As we said, the answers to such questions remain shrouded in mystery. Even so, we will be able to throw a little light on the subject by the end of the chapter.

PUZZLE 2: *The Stock Market's Unpredictability*

The stock market is obviously something of an enigma. No other economic activity is reported in such detail in so many newspapers and other media and followed with such concern by so many people. Yet few activities have so successfully eluded prediction of their future. There is no shortage of well-paid "experts" prepared to forecast the future of the market or the price of a particular stock or the earnings of the company to which the stock price is related. But there are real questions about what these experts deliver.

For example, a famous study of leading stock market analysts' predictions of company earnings (on which they based their stock-price forecasts) reports:

[W]e wrote to 19 major Wall Street firms . . . among the most respected names in the investment business.

We requested—and received—past earnings predictions on how these firms felt earnings for specific companies would behave over both a one-year and a five-year period. These estimates . . . were . . . compared with actual results to see how well the analysts forecast short-run and long-run earnings changes. . . .

Bluntly stated, the careful estimates of security analysts (based on industry studies, plant visits, etc.) do very little better than those that would be obtained by simple extrapolation of past trends. . . .

For example . . . the analysts' estimates were compared [with] the assumption that every company in the economy would enjoy a growth in earnings approximating the long-run rate of growth of the national income. It often turned out that . . . this naïve forecasting model . . . would make smaller errors in forecasting long-run earnings growth than . . . [did] the professional forecasts of the analysts. . . .

When confronted with the poor record of their five-year growth estimates, the security analysts honestly, if sheepishly, admitted that five years ahead is really too far in advance to make reliable projections. They protested that, although long-term projections are admittedly important, they really ought to be judged on their ability to project earnings changes one year ahead.

Believe it or not, it turned out that their one-year forecasts were even worse than their five-year projections.[2]

It has been said that an investor may as well pick stocks by throwing darts at the stock market page—it is far cheaper to buy a set of darts than to obtain the apparently useless advice of a professional analyst. Indeed, there have been at least two experiments, one by a U.S. senator and one by *Forbes* magazine, in which stocks picked by dart-throwing actually outperformed the mutual funds, the stocks of which are selected by experts.

Later in this chapter we will suggest an explanation for this poor performance.

---

[2] Burton G. Malkiel, *A Random Walk Down Wall Street* (New York: W. W. Norton, 1990), pp. 140–141.

CORPORATIONS AND THEIR UNIQUE CHARACTERISTICS

Stocks and bonds are created by corporations and are among the primary tools that these companies use to acquire the funds that they need to operate. Corporations play a crucial role in the Canadian economy. Revenues of the top 100 corporations totalled over $1,000 billion in 2007, or the equivalent of nearly 70 percent of Canadian gross domestic product (GDP). The 2007 revenues of the top 50 Canadian corporations—$840 billion—exceeded those of the next largest 450 Canadian corporations. The combined revenues of the three largest Canadian corporations—George Weston Ltd. (food), Manulife Financial Corporation (insurance and financial management), and the Royal Bank of Canada—as can be seen in Table 1, are nearly equal to the entire GDP of countries such as Hungary, the Czech Republic, and New Zealand. The combined revenues of the ten largest Canadian corporations are either equal or larger than the GDP of several other OECD countries: Denmark, Finland, Greece, Ireland, Norway, Poland, and Portugal.[3]

While not all Canadian businesses are corporations—many business owners do not bother to complete the paperwork that would give them this status—all *large* Canadian business firms are corporations. It's a word you've heard used many times, but what, exactly, is a *corporation*?

A **corporation** is a type of firm that is defined by law and to which the law assigns special privileges and special obligations. Three noteworthy features that their legal status entails are the following:

TABLE 1
The Ten Largest Canadian Corporations in 2007

Rank	Corporation/Head Office Location	Revenue (in billions of CDN$)
1	Royal Bank of Canada, Toronto	41.3
2	Manulife Financial Corp., Toronto	35.5
3	George Weston Ltd., Toronto	32.8
4	General Motors of Canada Ltd., Oshawa	31.7
5	Power Corp. of Canada, Montreal	29.4
6	Magna International Inc., Aurora	28.0
7	Alcan Inc., Montreal	26.8
8	The Bank of Nova Scotia, Halifax	26.4
9	The Toronto Dominion Bank, Toronto	25.2
10	Imperial Oil Ltd., Calgary	25.0

SOURCE: *Financial Post 500* 2007 Database. Material reprinted with the express permission of National Post Company, a CanWest Partnership.

A **corporation** is a firm that has the legal status of a fictional individual. This fictional individual is owned by a number of persons, called its *shareholders* or *stockholders,* and is run by a set of elected officers and a board of directors, whose chairman is often also in a powerful position.

- Special limits are placed on the losses that may be suffered by those who invest in these firms.
- These firms are subjected to types of taxation from which other firms are exempt.
- The corporation is considered to be an entity that is distinct from any of its owners or its management, so that the corporation can outlast the association of any and all of the individuals who are currently connected with the firm.

Let us consider the logic behind these three features. To begin with, although it may seem strange, a *corporation* is considered an *individual* in the eyes of the law. Therefore, its earnings, like those of other individuals, are taxed. Thus the legal status leads to what is called "double taxation" of the shareholders. Unlike the earnings of other firms, corporate earnings are taxed twice—once when they are earned by the company and a second time when they go to investors in the form of dividends (and are subject to the personal income tax).

In Canada, all individual shareholders receive a dividend tax credit that removes the effect of double taxation in the case of small corporations. But because the corporate income tax rate on large corporations is higher than that on small corporations, dividends paid out by large corporations are still taxed at a higher rate than any other income. This led to the rising popularity of **income trusts,** which are legal entities that hold income-producing assets. The dividends that these trusts distribute to their unit holders are tax-deductible, so that, in effect, as long as the trust distributes all of its profits, the income trust tax rate on dividends is nil. Prior to decisions by the federal government in 2005 and again in 2006 that somewhat discouraged the creation

Income trusts are legal business entities that pay no tax on distributed dividends.

[3] Organisation for Economic Co-operation and Development, *OECD Figure—2005 edition.* Retrieved from http://www.oecd.org

of income trusts, some corporations, such as Air Canada and Bell Canada, had converted some of their operations into income trusts (Aeroplan and Yellow Pages) to reduce their corporate federal and provincial income taxes and were thinking of further conversions. In addition, large corporations such as the Royal Bank of Canada, CanWest Global Communications, and TELUS, were considering or had announced such conversions, thus avoiding taxation on dividends paid out.

These conversions and announcements of future conversions, which would reduce corporate income taxes collected by federal and provincial governments by more than a billion dollars, induced the federal government to juggle two options: to impose tax rates on income trust profits or to increase the dividend tax credit. The latter option was chosen by the minority Liberal government in 2005, but that was insufficient to stop the avalanche of income trust creation, because foreign investors, pension funds, and registered retirement saving plans still benefited from the existence of income trusts and were pressuring many major Canadian corporations to convert to income trusts. The minority Conservative government was then forced to implement the former option in 2006, taxing income trusts just like any other corporation, thus removing the major benefit of the trusts for corporations.

The move toward income trusts had also been encouraged by changes in provincial legislation (in 1994 in Quebec, but only in 2004–2005 in Ontario and other provinces) that granted **limited liability** to income trusts—a legal advantage previously enjoyed only to corporations. With corporate limited liability, corporate debt is regarded as the obligation of the fictitious legal individual, instead of the liability of each shareholder. In this way, shareholders can lose no more money than they have invested in the firm. In contrast, if you are part or sole owner of a firm that is not a corporation, and it loses money and cannot repay its debts, you can be sued by the people to whom the money is owed, who may be able to force you to pay them out of your own bank account or by selling your vacation home.

> **limited liability** is a legal obligation to a firm's owners to pay back company debt's only with the money they have already invested in the firm.

Limited liability is the main secret of the success of the corporate organizational form, and the reason that some corporations grow so big. Thanks to that provision, individuals throughout the world are willing to invest money in firms whose operations they do not understand and whose management personnel they do not know. Each shareholder receives in return a claim on the firm's profits and, at least in principle, a portion of the company's ownership.

The corporate form is a boon to investors because their liability for loss is limited to their investments. There is also a possible disadvantage to this form of business organization: Corporate income is taxed twice unless a divided tax credit provision applies.

■ FINANCING CORPORATE ACTIVITY: STOCKS AND BONDS

When a corporation needs money to add to its plant or equipment, or to finance other types of investment, it may reinvest its own earnings (rather than paying them out as dividends to shareholders), or print and sell new stock certificates or new bonds, or take out a loan. Stocks and bonds, in the last analysis, are pieces of paper printed by the firm under a variety of legal safeguards. If it can find buyers, the firm can sell these pieces of paper to the investing public when it wants to obtain more money to invest in its operations.

How can a firm obtain money in exchange for such printed paper as a stock or bond certificate? Doesn't the process seem a bit like counterfeiting? If done improperly, there are indeed grounds for the suspicion. But, carried out appropriately, it is a perfectly reasonable economic process. First, let's define our terms.

Common stock represents partial ownership of a corporation. For example, if a company issues 100,000 shares, then a person who owns 1,000 shares owns 1 percent of the company and is entitled to 1 percent of the company's *dividends*, the corporation's annual payments to shareholders. This shareholder's vote also normally counts for 1 percent of the total votes in an election of corporate officers or in a referendum on corporate policy.

> A **common stock** (also called a *share*) of a corporation is a piece of paper that gives the holder of the stock a share of the ownership of the company.

A **bond** is simply an IOU sold by a corporation that promises to pay the holder of the bond a fixed sum of money at the specified *maturity* date and some other fixed amount of money (the *coupon* or *interest payment*) every year up to the date of maturity.

Bonds differ from stocks in several ways. First, the purchaser of a corporation's stock *buys* a share of its ownership and some control over its affairs, whereas a bond purchaser simply *lends* money to the firm and obtains no part of its ownership. Second, whereas shareholders have no idea how much they will receive when they sell their stocks or how much they will receive in dividends each year, bondholders know with a high degree of certainty how much money they will be paid if they hold their bonds to maturity (the date the firm has promised to repay the loan). For instance, a bond with a face value of $1,000 and an $80 *coupon* (the firm's annual interest payment to the bondholder) that matures in 2010 will provide $80 per year every year until 2010, and the firm will repay the bondholder's $1,000 in 2010. Unless the company goes bankrupt, this repayment schedule is guaranteed. Third, bondholders legally have a *prior claim* on company earnings, which means the shareholders receive no money until the firm has paid its bondholders. For all these reasons, bonds are considered less risky investments than stocks.[4]

To return to the question we asked earlier, a new issue of stocks and bonds is generally not like counterfeiting. As long as the funds obtained from the sale of the new securities[5] are used effectively to increase a firm's profit-earning capacity, these funds will automatically yield any required repayment and appropriate interest and dividends to purchasers. Occasionally this payout does not happen. One of the favourite practices of the more notorious nineteenth-century market manipulators was "watering" company stocks—issuing stocks with little or nothing to back them up. The term is originally derived from the practice of some cattle dealers who would force their animals to drink large quantities of water just before bringing them to be weighed for sale.

Similarities Between Stocks and Bonds   In reality, the differences between stocks and bonds are not as clear-cut as just described. Two relevant misconceptions are worth noting. First, the ownership represented by a few shares of a company's stock may be more symbolic than real. A person who holds 0.02 percent of Alcan (aluminum) stock—which, by the way, is a *very large* investment—exercises no real control over Alcan's operations.

In fact, many economists believe that the ownership of large corporations is so diffuse that shareholders or shareholder groups rarely have *any* effective control over management. In this view, a corporation's management is a largely independent decision-making body; as long as it keeps enough cash flowing to shareholders to prevent discontent and *organized* rebellion, management can do anything it wants within the law. Looked at in this way, shareholders, like bondholders, merely provide loans to the company. The only real difference between the two groups, according to this interpretation, is that shareholders' loans are riskier and therefore entitled to higher payments.

Second, bonds actually *can* be a very risky investment. People who try to sell their bonds before maturity may find that the market price happens to be low, so if they need to raise cash in a hurry, they may incur substantial losses. Also, bondholders may be exposed to losses from inflation. Whether the $1,000 promised to the bondholder at the 2010 maturity date represents substantial (or very little) purchasing power depends on what happens to the general price level in the meantime (that is, how much price **inflation** occurs). No one can predict the price level this far in advance with any accuracy. Finally, a firm can issue bonds with little backing; that is, the firm may own little valuable property that it can use as a guarantee of repayment to the lender—the bondholder. This is often true of "junk bonds," and it helps to explain their high risk.

Inflation occurs when prices in an economy rise rapidly. The rate of inflation is calculated by averaging the percentage growth rate of the prices of a selected sample of commodities.

The **interest rate** is the amount that borrowers currently pay to lenders per dollar of the money borrowed—it is the current market price of a loan.

Bond Prices and Interest Rates   What makes bond prices go up and down? A straightforward relationship exists between bond prices and current *interest rates:* Whenever one goes up, the other *must* go down. The term **interest rate** refers to the

[4] An important exception involves so-called junk bonds—very risky bonds that became popular in the 1980s. They were used heavily by people trying to purchase enough of a corporation's stock to acquire control of that firm.
[5] Stocks and bonds are also called *securities*.

amount that borrowers currently pay to lenders per dollar of the money borrowed—it is the current market price of a loan.

For example, suppose that Newfoundland and Labrador Hydro issued some 15-year bonds when interest rates were comparatively low, so the company had to pay only 6 percent to sell the bonds. People who invested $1,000 in those bonds received a contract that promised them $60 per year for 15 years plus the return of their $1,000 at the end of that period. Suppose, however, that interest rates *rise*, so that new 15-year bonds of similar companies now pay 12 percent. An investor with $1,000 can now buy a bond that offers $120 per year. Obviously, no one will now pay $1,000 for a bond that promises only $60 per year. Consequently, the market price of the old Newfoundland and Labrador Hydro bonds must fall.

This example is not entirely hypothetical. Until a few years ago, bonds issued much earlier—at interest rates of 6 percent or lower—were still in circulation. In the 1980s markets, when interest rates were well *above* 6 percent, such bonds sold for prices far below their original values.

> When interest rates *rise*, the prices of previously issued bonds with lower interest earnings must fall. For the same reason, when interest rates *fall*, the prices of previously issued bonds must rise.

It follows that as interest rates change because of changes in government policy or other reasons, bond prices fluctuate. That is one reason why bonds can be a risky investment.

Corporate Choice Between Stocks and Bonds   If a corporation chooses to finance the construction of new factories and equipment through the issue of new stocks or bonds, how does it determine whether bonds or stocks best suit its purposes?

Two considerations are of prime importance. Although issuing bonds generally exposes a firm to more risk than issuing stocks, the corporation usually expects to pay more money to shareholders over the long run. In other words, to the firm that issues them, bonds are cheaper but riskier. The decision about which is better for the firm therefore involves a trade-off between the two considerations of expense and risk.

Why are bonds risky to a corporation? When it issues $20 million in new bonds at 10 percent, a company commits itself to pay out $2 million every year of the bond's life, whether business is booming or the firm is losing money. If the firm is unable to meet its obligation to bondholders in some year, bankruptcy may result.

Stocks do not burden the company with any such risk, because the firm does not promise to pay shareholders *any* fixed amount. Shareholders simply receive whatever is left of the company's net earnings after the firm makes its payments to bondholders. If nothing is left to pay the new shareholders in some years, legally speaking, that is just their bad luck. The higher risk faced by shareholders is the reason they normally obtain higher average payments than bondholders.

> To the firm that issues them, bonds are riskier than stocks because they commit the firm to make a fixed annual payment, even in years when it is losing money. For the same reason, stocks are riskier than bonds to the buyers of securities. Therefore, shareholders expect to be paid more money than bondholders.

■ Plowback, or Retained Earnings

The final major source of funds for corporations, in addition to loans and the issue of stocks and bonds, is **plowback** or **retained earnings.** For example, if a company earns $30 million after taxes and decides to pay only $10 million in dividends to its shareholders and reinvest the remaining $20 million in the firm, that $20 million is called "plowback."

When business is profitable, corporate managers will often prefer plowback to other sources of funding. For one thing, plowback usually involves lower risk. Also, plowback, unlike other sources of funding, does not come under the scrutiny of the

Plowback (or **retained earnings**) is the portion of a corporation's profits that management decides to keep and reinvest in the firm's operations rather than paying out as dividends to shareholders.

provincial and territorial government agencies that regulate stocks. And, of course, plowback does not depend on the availability of eager customers for new company stocks and bonds. An issue of new securities can be a disappointment if there is little public demand when they are offered, but plowback runs no such risk.

Above all, a plowback decision generally does not call attention to the degree of success of management's operations, as a new stock issue does. When stock is issued, the securities regulator (for instance, the Ontario Securities Commission), potential buyers, and their professional advisers may all scrutinize the company carefully. No management has a perfect record, and the process may reveal things management would prefer to be overlooked.

Another reason for plowback's attractiveness is that issuing new stocks and bonds is usually an expensive and lengthy process. In Canada, security commissions require companies to gather masses of data in a *prospectus*—a document that describes a company's financial condition—before any new issue is approved.

Figure 2 shows the relative importance to Canadian nonfinancial corporations (corporations that are not banks or financial intermediaries) of each of the different sources and uses of funds. The left-hand side of Figure 2 indicates that retained earnings were by far the most important source of corporate financing, constituting 63 percent of all of the sources of funds for nonfinancial corporations in 2007. New bond issues and other forms of debt constituted about 30 percent of the total sources of funds, while sales of new stock market shares actually constituted only 6 percent of the sources of funds for nonfinancial corporations.

The right-hand side of Figure 2 shows what these funds were used for. Surprisingly, only 53 percent of the new funds were used for the acquisition of nonfinancial capital—tangible investment (machines, buildings, etc.). The remaining 47 percent was used to acquire financial assets—financial investment. The percentage of retained earnings exceeded the percentage of tangible investment, which implies that the nonfinancial corporate sector lent more to other sectors (notably households) than it borrowed from them. In other words, the retained earnings of the corporations were sufficient to finance all of their investments in tangible capital. Had corporations chosen to acquire smaller amounts of financial assets, they would not have needed to borrow any funds. This situation is relatively new, but it has persisted since 2000.

FIGURE 2   **Sources and Uses of New Funds for Canadian Nonfinancial Corporations, 2007**

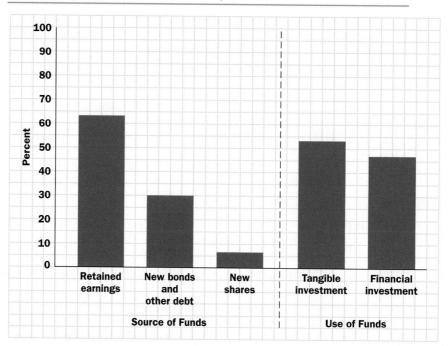

SOURCE: Adapted from Statistics Canada, *National Income and Expenditure Accounts, Quarterly Estimates*, Catalogue 13-001-XIB, Fourth Quarter 2005, Vol. 53, no. 04, March 31, 2006, 50–51.

▪ What Determines Stock Prices?
The Role of Expected Company Earnings

People invest in stocks because they believe (and hope) that the prices of the stocks they have purchased will rise. But will they? To answer that question, one should understand just what determines the price of a stock—but we do not really know the answer. We do know that, as with other things sold in markets, prices are determined by supply and demand. That merely raises the next question: What explains the behaviour of supply and demand? That answer depends on the actions and expectations of the people who have stocks to sell or who wish to buy.

There is one apparently logical answer, although later we will see that there are reasons to question that explanation. This answer is that a stock is simply a share of the ownership of the firm that has issued it. The stock will therefore be valuable if the firm earns a good deal of money in the future, and it will rise in price if the firm earns more than investors had expected. The stock will fall in price if the earnings of the firm are poor or disappointing. That is why professional stock analysts who sell their advice to investors devote most of their efforts to studying individual firms and their markets, hoping to gain some insights into each company's future earnings prospects.

▪ BUYING STOCKS AND BONDS

Although investors can purchase stocks and bonds through any brokerage firm, not all brokers charge the same fees. Bargain brokerage houses advertise in the newspapers' financial pages, offering investors very little service—no advice, no research, no other frills—other than merely buying or selling what the customer wants them to, at lower fees than those charged by higher-service brokerage firms. And during the late 1990s, it became possible to buy and sell shares over the Internet at very low cost.

Many investors are not aware of the various ways in which they can purchase (or sell) stocks. Two noteworthy arrangements are (1) a *market order* purchase, which simply tells the broker to buy a specified quantity of stock at the best price the market currently offers, and (2) a *limit order,* which is an agreement to buy a given amount of stock when its price falls to a specified level. If the investor offers to buy at $18, then the broker will purchase shares if and when the market price falls to $18 per share or less.

Using data taken from 2004 tax returns, Statistics Canada assessed that approximately 3.1 million individual investors receive dividend income from taxable Canadian corporations. This means that *at least* 3.1 million Canadians (14 percent of all tax filers) had invested funds in the stock market, either directly or indirectly through mutual funds.[6] This number however underestimates the total number of Canadian investors in the stock market, as it does not include Canadians who invest only in tax-sheltered vehicles, such as the popular registered retirement savings plans (RRSPs).

▪ Selecting a Portfolio: Diversification

Perhaps the first rule of safe investing is: Always diversify—never put all your eggs in one basket. This was a bitter lesson for employees of Enron, the giant U.S. firm that went bankrupt so spectacularly in 2001. Many of its workers invested much of their savings in high-priced Enron stocks and lost virtually everything when the price of Enron stock later plunged. Similarly, in Canada , when Nortel's stock took a plunge in the early 2000s, tens of thousands of Nortel employees lost both their jobs and their savings, as many of them had invested an overly large proportion of their retirement funds in Nortel shares. A person or an organization's holdings of securities from several different corporations is called a *portfolio* of investments. A portfolio tends to be far less risky than any of the individual securities it contains because of the benefits of **portfolio diversification**. Let's see why.

Portfolio diversification means inclusion of a number and variety of stocks, bonds, and other such items in an individual's portfolio. If the individual owns airline stocks, for example, diversification requires the purchase of a stock or bond in a very different industry, such as breakfast cereal production.

---

[6] Statistics Canada, *The Daily*, October 31, 2005.

If, for example, Alex divides his holdings among Companies A, B, and C, then his portfolio may perform satisfactorily overall even if Company A goes broke. Moreover, suppose that Company A specializes in producing luxury items, which do well in prosperous periods but very badly during recessions, whereas Company B sells cheap clothing, whose cyclical demand pattern differs greatly from that of Company A. If Alex holds stock in both companies, his overall risk is obviously less than if he owned stock in only one. All other things being equal, a portfolio containing many different types of securities tends to be less risky than a portfolio with fewer types of securities.

Increasingly, institutional investors, such as **mutual funds,** have adopted portfolios composed of broad ranges of stocks typifying those offered by the entire stock market. Mutual funds now are among the largest investors in securities. They offer their customers portfolios of various groups of domestic stocks, foreign stocks, and bonds. Small investors can easily put their money into these funds, thereby reducing the risks of owning individual stocks and ensuring that the overall market does not significantly outperform their portfolios. Mutual fund transactions can be carried out by telephone or over the Internet, and investors can also easily check on the past performance of the different funds and obtain other pertinent information. Investors purchasing mutual fund shares should check on the fees charged by different funds, because fees vary surprisingly widely from one fund to another—and the difference can have a large effect on the relative earnings of an investment in a fund.

One kind of mutual fund, called an **index fund,** buys the securities used in one of the standard **stock price indexes** (such as the S&P/TSX Composite Index, a general index computed by Standard and Poor's that represents about 70 percent of the Canadian-based equity listed on the Toronto Stock Exchange; the S&P/TSX 60 that represents 60 large companies listed on the Toronto Stock Exchange; and the Dow Jones Industrial Average (DJIA) index on the New York Stock Exchange, with its listing of 30 "blue chip" companies—companies whose stocks sell at a high price because of public confidence in their long records of steady earnings). A stock price index is an average of the prices of a group of stocks—weighted by the size of each company—that are believed to be representative of the overall stock market (or some specialized segment, such as NASDAQ Canada stocks). When you invest in an index fund, the return on your money will therefore reflect the performance of the entire market, rather than any one or a few securities that you or your broker might have selected instead.

Institutional money managers increasingly use computer programs to decide on their portfolios and to buy or sell huge portfolios of stocks simultaneously and rapidly. Since 1982, some traders have also allowed their computers to decide when to jump in and make massive sales or purchases. This practice is called *program trading*. In 2003, program trading accounted for about 40 percent of the total New York Stock Exchange volume and a considerable amount of the volume in other stock exchanges, in particular the Toronto Stock Exchange, which was the first exchange in the world to computerize. Program trading was heavily criticized for aggravating price fluctuations and contributing to the stock market crash of October 1987. Restrictions are now in place that curb program trading when stock markets decline sharply.

Following a Portfolio's Performance

To enable you to keep track of your investments and how they are performing, newspapers carry daily information on stock and bond prices. Investors also use this information as a basis for decisions on purchase and sale of stocks and bonds, along with minute-by-minute information that can now be found on various websites. Table 2 represents an excerpt from the investing pages of the *Financial Post*, which is an insert in the *National Post*. Similar information can be found in *The Globe and Mail* and also in a simplified format in some other newspapers. The excerpt shows the stock listings of some of the companies included in the S&P/TSX 60, the names of most of which are well known by Canadians. Highlighted in the table is the stock information for TELUS, the western Canada communications giant. In the "Ticker" column, the TELUS stock name abbreviation is given: T.

A **mutual fund,** in which individual investors can buy shares, is a private investment firm that holds a portfolio of securities. Investors can choose among a large variety of mutual funds, such as stock funds, bond funds, and so forth.

An **index fund** is a mutual fund that chooses a particular stock price index and then buys the stocks (or most of the stocks) that are included in the index. The value of an investment in an index fund depends on what happens to the prices of all stocks in that index.

A **stock price index,** such as the S&P/TSX 60, is an average of the prices of a large set of stocks. These stocks are selected to represent the price movements of the entire stock market, or some specified segment of the market, and the chosen set is rarely changed.

TABLE 2
Excerpt from a Stock Market Price Listing for One Day

Stock	Ticker	Close	Netch	%ch	Vol 000s	Day high	Day low	% yield	P/E	52-wk high	52-wk low	Wk %ch	52-wk %ch
Nortel	NT	2.53	+0.02	+0.8	96027	2.57	2.49	n.a.	n.a.	4.02	2.14	+0.4	−32.7
Novelis	NVL	29.95	−0.25	−0.9	3277	28.35	27.74	0.2	n.a.	29.50	18.57	−4.6	+22.9
PennWst	PWT.UN	36.12	−6.09	−14.4	78336	38.49	34.50	11.3	7.2	47.77	31.50	−17.6	+16.7
PetroCan	PCA	47.24	−0.64	−1.3	16926	47.92	46.75	0.8	12.8	59.40	40.25	−1.6	+15.5
Potash	POT	144.40	+3.73	+2.7	4877	146.05	138.58	0.5	23.5	146.05	84.86	+6.5	+51.7
RschMotn	RIM	132.41	+0.51	+0.4	5949	134.10	131.10	n.a.	57.8	134.23	67.95	+1.1	+86.4
RogerCmBNVRCl.B		68.10	+0.91	+1.4	17430	68.64	65.91	0.5	57.7	68.64	41.69	+7.2	+46.7
RoyalBk	RY	50.40	+0.60	+1.2	34279	50.47	49.50	3.2	16.2	51.49	41.305	+1.0	+21.7
ShawComBNVSJR.B		35.52	−1.31	−3.6	32025	37.45	35.22	2.8	16.8	37.45	23.27	+3.1	+48.9
Shoppers	SC	45.12	−0.60	−1.3	3683	45.97	45.03	1.1	24.7	47.20	39.51	−0.4	+13.2
Sun Life Finl	SLF	47.00	−0.22	−0.5	17096	47.73	46.52	2.6	13.5	50.65	41.79	+3.4	+7.3
Suncor	SU	84.34	−1.91	−2.2	23790	85.21	83.25	0.4	11.4	102.18	61.28	−4.6	+33.5
TELUS	T	56.15	−8.78	−13.5	98551	57.40	53.00	2.0	23.5	65.60	42.62	−11.0	+23.0

SOURCE: Chart S&P/TSX 60, *National Post*, 11/02/2006. Material reprinted with the express permission of National Post Company, a CanWest Partnership.

The next column indicates the price of the stock at closing time: $56.15. This is followed by the net change in the closing price from the closing price of the previous day, in this case, −$8.78, indicating that the TELUS stock price on the previous trading day was $64.93 and that the stock took a beating. The TELUS stock value decrease that day (November 2, 2006) was attributed to the fact that the anticipated transformation of TELUS (and of BCE) from corporation to income trust status would either not occur or, if it did occur, would not result in any reduction in corporate taxes. This dollar change is equivalent to the −13.5 percent loss [(−8.78/64.93) × 100] shown in the next column.

The next column indicates the number of shares traded on the previous day (98,551,000), an indication of whether the stock was actively traded (as indeed it was on that day!). The next two numbers indicate the highest ($57.40) and the lowest price ($53.00) attained by the stock during the day, an indication of its volatility. Following that is the yield of the stock, or the dividend per share as a percentage of the closing price (2.0 percent).

The next column reports the price-to-earnings (P/E) ratio (23.5 in the case of TELUS). This figure is the price per share divided by the company's net earnings per share in the previous year, and it is often taken as a basic measure indicating whether the stock's current price overvalues or undervalues the company. However, no simple rule enables us to interpret the P/E figures—for example, a very risky firm or a slowly growing firm with a low P/E ratio may be considered overvalued, whereas a safe, rapidly growing firm with a high P/E ratio may still be a bargain.

Finally, the last four columns give historical data about the TELUS stock prices that allow the investor to put things into perspective: the highest ($65.60) and the lowest ($42.62) price achieved by the listed stock over the last year (the previous 52 weeks); the percentage change in the price of the stock over the last week (−11.0 percent) and over the previous 52 weeks (+23.0 percent).

Table 3 gives similar information about bonds. Corporate bonds are shown here, although on the Canadian bond market, most of the action relates to bond issues by the Government of Canada and its agencies or by provincial governments and hydro corporations, such as Hydro-Québec. Notice that a given company may have several bonds differing in maturity date and coupon rate (the annual interest payment shown in the second column). For example, Loblaw Corporation offers four different bonds. The

TABLE 3

Excerpt from a Bond Price Listing for One Day

Issuer	Coupon [Rate]	Maturity Date	Bid Price	Ask Price	Bid Yld	Ask Yld	Yield Chg
Embridge Inc	6.100	2028-Jul-14		108.36		5.44	−0.022
GMAC Cda	6.250	2007-Aug-22		100.91		5.06	−0.027
GMAC Cda	5.350	2009-Oct-01		99.88		5.39	−0.058
GTAA	5.950	2007-Dec-03	101.60	101.76	4.40	4.25	−0.047
GTAA	6.250	2012-Jan-30	108.61	108.83	4.39	4.34	−0.050
Gaz Met	6.050	2008-Nov-10	103.31	103.62	4.32	4.16	−0.057
Hydro One	7.150	2010-Jun-03	109.77	110.01	4.18	4.11	−0.054
Hydro One	6.400	2011-Dec-01	109.81	110.14	4.23	4.16	−0.054
Loblaw CoLtd	6.000	2008-Jun-02	102.54	102.64	4.31	4.24	−0.056
Loblaw CoLtd	5.750	2009-Jan-22	102.95	103.28	4.33	4.17	−0.059
Loblaw CoLtd	6.500	2011-Jan-19	108.25	108.47	4.33	4.27	−0.050
Loblaw CoLtd	6.450	2028-Feb-09		112.07		5.48	−0.001
ManuF Cap Tr	6.700	2012-Jun-30	111.03	111.34	4.47	4.41	−0.052
Manulife Fin	6.240	2011-Feb-16	107.54	107.85	4.29	4.21	−0.050

highlighted bond pays an annual interest rate of 6.500 percent (the coupon rate) on its face value (assumed to be $100) and its maturity (redemption) date is January 19, 2011. Two prices are provided: the bid price of $108.25 (the highest market price a potential buyer is willing to pay for a bond) and the ask price of $108.47 (the amount a seller has asked for a bond). The bid (ask) yield is simply the coupon divided by the bid (ask) price, in this case 4.33 (4.37) percent. Technically this is called the *current yield*. If the current

"What Is a Share of Google Worth?"

It almost goes without saying that Google is one of the world's leading brands. Its Internet search engine is so ubiquitous that its very name is a verb for looking up information about someone or something.

So when its founders decided to "go public" and offer shares of the company for the public to buy, the announcement set off tremendous speculation about what the company would be worth. Google itself predicted a jaw-dropping price range of US$108 to US$135 for its shares, which would have translated into a company value of US$36 billion. That would put Google right up there with the bluest of the "blue chip" stocks—of the thousands of publicly listed companies in the United States, only about 70 companies have a market value that high.*

On August 19, 2004, Google made its debut on the NASDAQ stock market. Trading under the ticker symbol GOOG (you can "google it," if you like), the stock opened at US$100, which was almost 18 percent higher than its initial offering price of US$85. More than 22 million shares changed hands on that first day of trading, with Google selling a total of 19.6 million shares, thus raising about US$1.2 billion for the company. That price implied a market value of US$27.2 billion. Not bad for an idea conceived by two university grad students!

(As this book went to press, Google had reached as high as US$635 a share.)

SOURCE: © Kim Kulish/Corbis

SOURCES: Paul R. La Monica, "Google Jumps 18% in Debut," CNN Money, August 19, 2004, http://money.cnn.com; Ben Berkowitz, "Is Google Worth $135 a Share?," *MSN Money*, July 26, 2004, http://msn.com; Ben Elgin, "Commentary: Google This: Investor Beware," *Business Week Online*, August 9, 2004, http://www. businessweek.com; "Financial Release: Google Inc. Prices Initial Public Offering of Class A Common Stock," August 18, 2004, http://investor.google.com; and *"2004 Leaders: The Business Week Global 1000," Business Week*, July 26, 2004, http://www.businessweekonline.com.

price of the bond (here around $108) is higher than its face value ($100 by definition), then the current yield will be lower than the coupon rate, as is the case here.

The last column indicates the change in yield since the previous trading day, in this case –0.050, meaning that on the previous day the bid yield (4.28 percent) was lower. A look at this column shows that all bond yields dropped on that day, implying that bond prices rose. This was indeed the case because, as in the case of the stock market listings in Table 2, the bond listings in Table 3 were derived from a November 2, 2006, newspaper (the "Money & Market" pages of *The Globe and Mail*), when financial markets were reacting to the federal government announcement that income trust profits would be taxed. As a result, some investors chose to invest in the bond market instead, pushing up bond prices.

Investors can also find information about the performance of stocks and bonds (and other kinds of investment) on the Internet. For example, an investor who visits the web site, http://www.tsx.com, will find all the information on stocks just described, and a lot more. The difference will be that each individual stock usually has to be viewed separately, whereas the print newspapers allow one to look at large lists of securities and quickly compare them.

■ STOCK EXCHANGES AND THEIR FUNCTIONS

The New York Stock Exchange (NYSE), located on Wall Street in New York, is probably the world's most prestigious stock market. But Canada has a fairly large stock exchange of its own—the Toronto Stock Exchange Group (TSX Group) located in Toronto on Bay Street at the corner of King Street West. The TSX Group, as can be seen in Table 4, is the eighth-largest exchange in the world; it traded the stocks of 3,842 companies in 2006. The Toronto exchange is made up of two stock exchanges, the TSX proper, which deals with "senior" companies (large corporations) and the TSX Venture Exchange, which is devoted to "venture" or "junior" companies that do not yet meet all of the conditions to be listed on the TSX proper. Many Canadian high-tech companies have chosen to be listed in New York on the NASDAQ (the National Association of Securities Dealers Automated Quotations) exchange. The number of Canadian companies that do this is so large that there is a NASDAQ index devoted exclusively to Canadian companies, called the NASDAQ Canada.

TABLE 4	
World's Largest Stock Exchanges, Based on Market Equity Value as of December 2007	
Stock Exchange	Equity value (billions US$)
New York Stock Exchange	15,651
Tokyo Stock Exchange	4,331
Euronext (Amsterdam, Brussels, Lisbon, Paris)	4,223
NASDAQ	4,014
London Stock Exchange	3,852
Shangai Stock Exchange	3,694
Hong Kong Exchanges	2,654
TSX Group	2,187
Deutsche Börse	2,105
Bombay Stock Exchange	1,819

SOURCE: World Federation of Exchanges, WFE Market Highlights, Table 1 Domestic Market Equity Capitalization; http://www.world-exchanges.org/WFE/home.asp

Canada used to have four stock exchanges, located in Toronto, Montreal, Calgary, and Vancouver. But in the late 1990s, stock exchange administrators, faced with the forces of globalization, decided to streamline operations and consolidate all senior stocks in the TSX and eventually all junior stocks into TSX Venture. The Toronto Stock Exchange, which until then was known as the "TSE," then became "TSX." "TSE" is now used by the Tokyo Stock Exchange.

The market for derivatives was first introduced in 1975 in Canada and was assigned to the Montreal Exchange. The TSX purchased the Montreal Exchange in 2008. Derivatives (see the boxed feature "How to Lose Billions: Betting on Derivatives" on page 202) include contracts such as futures options (based for instance on the S&P/TSX 60 index) and interest rate futures that either allow people to speculate or to cover their financial risks. There is also the Winnipeg Commodity Exchange, which deals with futures contracts tied to feed wheat, barley, and canola, thus allowing producers to cover risky positions.

The numbers involved in stock exchange markets are overwhelming. More than 92 million trades were made in 2006 (about 366,000 trades per trading day) on the

SOURCE: RICHARD LAUTENS/Canadian Press

Toronto Stock Exchange (the combined TSX and TSX Venture trades)14 times less, however, than on each of the NYSE and NAS-DAQ. On November 2, 2006, following the federal government announcement that income trust profits would be taxed, a record 614,888 trades were made on the TSX. The average value of a trade within the TSX Group stood at $16,175 per trade. As a result the average daily turnover in 2006 on the Toronto Stock Exchange was $6 billion, about 14 times less than on the NYSE. For all of 2006, more than $1,500-billion worth of stocks were traded in Toronto.[7]

Regulation of the Stock Market

Both the government and the industry itself regulate the Canadian securities markets. At the base of the regulatory pyramid, stock brokerage firms maintain compliance departments to oversee their own operations. At the next level, the Toronto Stock Exchange and Montreal Exchange are responsible for monitoring their member firms' business practices, funding adequacy, compliance, and integrity. The exchanges also use sophisticated computer surveillance techniques to scrutinize trading activity. Finally, there are 13 provincial and territorial securities commissions—one for each of the ten provinces and three territories—that oversee the market's self-regulation.

The lack of a central securities commission similar to the American Securities and Exchange Commission (SEC) has attracted the attention of several politicians, financial institutions, and agencies such as the Bank of Canada, in the wake of the corporate scandals that have rocked financial markets since the early 2000s (see the boxed feature "Corporate Scandals" on the next page). The 13 Canadian securities commissions have representatives on the Canadian Securities Administrators (CSA), an institution designed to help streamline provincial rules into more uniform legislation. The CSA also designates a lead agency in cases where companies must report to more than one jurisdiction. But the CSA does not propose that a national agency take over the role of the 13 agencies. A report called *Canada Steps Up*, produced in October 2006 by a task force set up by the Investment Dealers Association of Canada, essentially recommends (despite the widely held view that proper securities law enforcement is lacking) that Canadians rely more on the market's self-regulation, as this would help to maintain and increase the competitiveness of Canada's capital market. If this report is any indication of things to come, there is little likelihood that the current situation is going to change.

One example of these self-imposed rules involves the steps that markets adopted after the October 1987 stock market crash to cushion future price falls. Starting in 1988, with amendments since then, the NYSE and other stock markets adopted a series of rules called *circuit breakers*, which now halt all trading for one hour, two hours, or the remainder of the trading day when the Dow Jones Industrial Average (a widely followed average price of a sample of stocks) declines below its previous day's closing value by defined percentage amounts (which are adjusted every quarter). These restrictions on trading vary with the severity of the drop in the Dow and with the time of day when the drop occurs. Circuit breakers were designed to head off panics among market participants and forestall crashes like the ones in October 1929 and October 1987. In Canada however, this rule was not introduced until October 1997!

Stock Exchanges and Corporate Capital Needs

Although corporations often raise needed funds by selling stock, they do not normally do so through the stock exchanges. New stock issues are typically handled by a special type of bank, called an *investment bank*. In contrast, the stock markets trade almost exclusively in "secondhand securities"—stocks in the hands of individuals and others

---

[7] World Federation of Exchanges, *WFE Annual Report and Statistics 2006, Equity Tables 1.6 and 1.7*. Retrieved from http://www.world-exchanges.org/WFE/home.asp

CORPORATE SCANDALS

At a time when it was believed that shareholders had finally succeeded in forcing company managers to behave in line with the interest of the owners of the corporations—the shareholders—several scandals erupted in the corporate world in the early 2000s. The names of Enron, WorldCom, Adelphia, and Tyco became known worldwide when their managers were accused (and some of them convicted) of frauds that led to huge bankruptcies. Suddenly, some of the fastest rising stars of the new technology industries were becoming dot-cons instead of dot-coms.

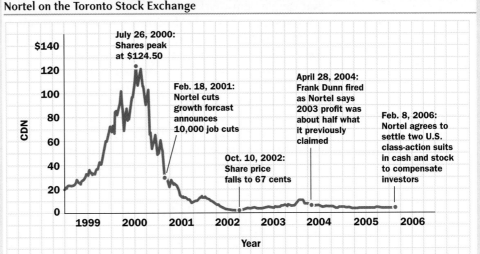

Nortel on the Toronto Stock Exchange

SOURCE: "Nortel on the Toronto Stock Market," Ottawa Sun, February 9, 2006, p. 50.

Canadians have experienced firsthand the consequences of misrepresentation and misinformation. In 2005, Norbourg Asset Management founder Vincent Lacroix was accused of 51 securities violations and of defrauding thousands of individual investors of over $100 million; the trial began in Montreal in May 2007 and Lacroix was convicted and sent to jail. In a highly publicized lawsuit, Toronto-born press tycoon Conrad Black was convicted in July 2007 of three charges of fraud and obstruction of justice and was also sent to prison. Black, who owned over 400 newspapers in North America through his controlling interests in Hollinger Inc., started the *National Post* and also bought Britain's *Daily Telegraph*. The author of two well-documented biographies on Maurice Duplessis (a provincial premier of Quebec until his death in 1959) and Franklin Delano Roosevelt (the American president during the World War II), Black was charged with, among many other things, racketeering, money laundering, and wire fraud for amounts in the hundreds of million dollars. Also since March 2008, U.S. and Canadian regulators have been investigating Eugene Melnyk, the billionaire owner of the NHL's Ottawa Senators, for fraudulent accounting during his time at Biovail, a successful pharmaceutical company.

But the frauds that have generated the greatest interest in Canada are probably those involving Nortel. The accompanying graph might help to explain why. Nortel became a favourite of Canadian investors as its stock market price kept rising to incredible heights in 1999 and the first half of 2000 (up to $124.50 per share). Nortel's main line was the production and the sale of fibre-optic network material, which were doing well in the late 1990s. Many Canadians, as well as most Canadian mutual funds and pension funds, jumped on the bandwagon, purchasing Nortel shares despite the high prices. During that time period, Nortel's CEO John Roth appeared on the cover of every newsmagazine and was named the 2000 "Newsmaker of the Year" by the Canadian edition of *Time* magazine.

When the high-tech bubble began to burst, Roth retired with a $120 million bonus in 2001. About a year later, in the fall of 2002, Nortel's share price had dropped to 67 cents and tens of thousands of its employees had been laid off. The market value of Nortel's shares had dropped from $398 billion, representing about one-third of the entire value of the equity on the Toronto Stock Exchange, to under $5 billion in less than two years. In the meantime, some of Nortel's managers were trying to convince the investors that Nortel was a profitable business, inflating growth forecasts or profit announcements. Profits had been improperly overestimated by billions of dollars, leading to hugely excessive bonuses for the Nortel managers. In February 2006, Nortel agreed to pay out the equivalent of approximately $2.5 billion to settle two class-action suits initiated in the United States (Nortel is also listed on the NYSE) but led by the pension fund of the Ontario Public Sector Employees Union and the Ontario Teachers' Pension Plan Board.

Ironically, although these lawsuits involved Canadians or Canadian firms, most of the action occurred in the United States, since it seems to be nearly impossible to convict anyone in Canada in these types of cases. Even in successful cases, the financial penalties (one or two million dollars) and the prison sentences are very small, compared to the amounts of the swindles (sometimes in the hundreds of millions of dollars). In the United States, however, those found guilty of financial fraud face much more severe penalties; for example, the convicted treasurers and CEOs of Tyco, WorldCom, and Enron received very stiff imprisonment sentences and had to pay huge amounts in compensation and restitution.

Some efforts are being done to change the situation in Canada, including a 2005 amendment to the Canadian Criminal Code that gives increased power to provincial attorneys general to prosecute capital market fraud offences, while offering whistle-blower protection to insiders who expose fraudulent behaviour.

who bought them earlier and now wish to sell them. Thus, the stock market does not provide funds to corporations needing financing to expand their productive activities. The markets provide money only to persons who already hold previously issued stocks.

Nevertheless, stock exchanges perform two critically important functions for corporate financing. First, by providing a secondhand market for stocks, they make individual investment in a company much less risky. Investors know that if they need money, they can always sell their stocks to other investors or to stock market specialists at the current market price. This reduction in risk makes it far easier for corporations to issue new stocks. Second, the stock market determines the current price of the company's stocks. That, in turn, determines whether it will be difficult or easy for a corporation to raise money by selling new stocks.

Some people believe that a company's stock price is closely tied to its operational efficiency, its effectiveness in meeting consumer demands, and its diligence in going after profitable innovation. According to this view, firms that use funds effectively will usually have comparatively high stock prices, and that will enable the firms to raise more money when they issue new stocks through their investment banks and sell them at the high prices determined by the stock market. In this way, the stock market tends to channel the economy's funds to the firms that can make best use of the money. In sum:

> If a firm has a promising future, its stock will tend to command a high price on the stock exchanges. Its high stock price will increase the firm's ability to raise capital by permitting it to amass a large amount of money through the sale of a comparatively small number of new stock shares. Thus, *the stock market helps to allocate the economy's resources to firms that can best use those resources.*

How to Lose Billions: Betting on Derivatives

Derivatives, one of the fastest growing areas of finance, are complex financial instruments so named because they "derive" their value from the price movements of an underlying investment, such as a group of stocks, bonds, or commodities. Businesses buy these contracts in an effort to hedge or insure against sudden changes in interest rates or currency values. But they also can be used to speculate in the markets.

A number of recent spectacular financial failures have been closely tied to the use of derivatives. First was the collapse of a 233-year-old British investment bank, Barings PLC, after one of its employees (a 28-year-old "rogue" futures trader named Nicholas Leeson) "bet the ranch" on the movement of the Japanese stock market and lost $1.46 billion. Then came the meltdown of a private investment fund called Long-Term Capital Management, the management of which happened to include two Nobel Prize–winning economists, Myron Scholes and Robert C. Merton, who shared the prize in 1997. The firm was a so-called hedge fund that used derivatives to place multimillion-dollar bets on movements in such financial instruments as Russian treasury bonds and Danish mortgages. In the fall of 1998, the firm was reported to have lost more than $4 billion (and had to be bailed out by its bankers) when its statistical models failed to predict the movement of global markets.

The most notable episode of all (until a trader produced losses of over $7 billion for French bank Société Générale in January 2008) involved a young Canadian natural gas specialist, Brian Hunter, who was hired in 2004 by Amaranth, a hedge fund created in 2000 by previous Enron employees. When Enron collapsed, Amaranth started to focus its activities on the energy sector, in particular the natural gas market—a highly volatile market. In early 2005, Hunter started to bet on rising natural gas prices, a strategy that became highly successful when Hurricane Katrina hit the north-central Gulf coast

SOURCE: marianad/Shutterstock

of the United States in August 2005, thus halting much of natural gas production in the U.S. south. Natural gas prices were further pushed up when the first month of winter turned out to be unusually cold. The value of Amaranth skyrocketed until the middle of the summer of 2006, and so did the bonuses ($90 million) pocketed by Hunter.

Emboldened by his success, Hunter decided to bet once again on rising prices—but natural gas prices fell instead, with no hurricane in sight and forecasts of a warm 2006–2007 winter. In the fall of 2006, Amaranth could not honour its contracts and went bankrupt, with losses of about $7 billion, which had to be absorbed by the hedge fund industry.

SOURCE: "Wall Street Struggles to Save Big Fund," *Washington Post*, September 24, 1998.; P. Chalmin, "L'histoire édifiante du fonds Amaranth," *Le Monde*, Octobre 24, 2006; Translated by Marc Lavoie (author)

Other people voice skepticism about the claim that the price of a company's stock is closely tied to efficiency. These observers believe that the demand for a stock is disproportionately influenced by short-term developments in the company's profitability and that the market pays little attention to management decisions affecting the firm's long-term earnings growth. These critics sometimes suggest that the stock market is similar to a gambling casino in which hunch, rumour, and superstition have a critical influence on prices. (We will learn more about this view later in the chapter.)

Whether or not stock prices are an accurate measure of a company's efficiency, if a company's stock price is very low in comparison with the value of its plant, equipment, and other assets, or when a company's earnings seem low compared to their potential level, that company becomes a tempting target for a **takeover** attempt. Perhaps the firm's current management is believed not to be very competent and those who seek to take control of the company believe that they can do better. Alternatively, if the demand for a company's stocks is believed to be inordinately influenced by short-term developments, such as temporarily low profits, others may believe that it is a bargain in terms of the low current price of the stock and its more promising future earnings prospects.

A takeover occurs when a group of outside financiers buys a sufficient amount of company stock to gain control of the firm. Often, the new controlling group will simply fire the current management and substitute a new chairman, president, and other top officers.

A **takeover** is the acquisition by an outside group (the raiders) of a controlling proportion of a company's stock. When the old management opposes the takeover attempt, it is called a *hostile takeover attempt.*

■ SPECULATION

Securities dealings are sometimes viewed with suspicion because they are thought to be an instrument of **speculation.** When something goes wrong in the stock market—when, say, prices suddenly fall—observers often blame speculators. Editorial writers, for example, often use the word *speculators* as a term of strong disapproval, implying that those who engage in the activity are parasites who produce no benefits for society and often cause considerable harm. (See "How to Lose Billions: Betting on Derivatives" for a description of a particularly risky speculative instrument, the *derivative.*)

Economists generally disagree with this judgment. They argue that speculators perform two vital economic functions:

Individuals who engage in **speculation** deliberately invest in risky assets, hoping to obtain profits from future changes in the prices of these assets.

- Speculators sell *protection from risk* to other people, much as a fire insurance policy offers protection from risk to a homeowner.
- Speculators help to smooth out price fluctuations by purchasing items when they are abundant (and cheap) and holding them and reselling them when they are scarce (and expensive). In that way, speculators play a vital economic role in helping to alleviate and even prevent shortages.

Some examples from outside the securities markets will help clarify the role of speculators. Imagine that a ticket broker attends a preview of a new musical comedy and suspects it will be a hit. He decides to speculate by buying a large block of tickets for future performances. In that way, he takes over part of the producer's risk, while the play's producer reduces her inventory of risky tickets and receives some hard cash. If the show opens and is a flop, the broker will be stuck with the tickets. If the show is a hit, he can sell them at a premium, if the law allows (and he will be denounced as a speculator or a "scalper").

Similarly, speculators enable farmers (or producers of metals and other commodities whose future price is uncertain) to decrease their risk. Let's say Jasmine and Jim have planted a large crop of wheat but fear its price may fall before harvest time. They can protect themselves by signing a contract with a speculator for future delivery of the crop at an agreed-upon price. If the price then falls, the speculator—not Jasmine and Jim—will suffer the loss. Of course, if the price rises, the speculator will reap the rewards—but that is the nature of risk bearing. The speculator who has agreed to buy the crop at a preset price, regardless of market conditions at the time of the sale, has, in effect, sold an insurance policy to Jasmine and Jim. Surely this is a useful function.

The speculators' second role is perhaps even more important. In effect, they accumulate and store goods in periods of abundance and make goods available in periods of scarcity. Suppose that a speculator has reason to suspect that next year's crop of a storable commodity will not be nearly as abundant as this year's. She will buy some of the crop now, when it is cheap, for resale when it becomes scarce and expensive. In the process, she will smooth out the swing in prices by adding her purchases to the total market demand in the low-price period (which tends to bring the price up at that time), and bringing in her supplies during the high-price period (which tends to push this later-period price down).[8]

Thus, the successful speculator will help to relieve matters during periods of extreme shortage. Speculators have sometimes even helped to relieve famine by releasing supplies they had deliberately hoarded for such an occasion. Of course, speculators are cursed for their high prices when this happens. But those who curse them do not understand that prices would have been even higher if the speculators' foresight and avid pursuit of profit had not provided for the emergency. On the securities market, famine and severe shortages are not an issue, but the fact remains that, nearly by definition, successful speculators tend to reduce price fluctuations by increasing demand for stocks (buying) when prices are low and contributing to supply (selling) when prices are high.

> Far from aggravating instability and fluctuations, to earn a profit speculators iron out fluctuations by buying when prices are low and selling when prices are high.

PUZZLE 1 REDUX: *The Boom and Bust of the Canadian Stock Market*

This last quotation leads to some insights into the remarkable behaviour of the Canadian stock market during the late 1990s and early 2000s—a phenomenon we mentioned at the start of this chapter. (Refer back to Figure 1 on page 188.)

First, many people who buy stocks—both professionals and amateurs—do so for speculative purposes. They may not care (or even know!) what the company does; they care only that its stock price goes up. Second, in a speculative world, where people buy stocks in order to sell them later, a share of stock is basically worth what *someone else* will pay for it. So even if Smart Susan is convinced that Dotcon.com has poor business prospects, it may still be rational for her to buy the stock at $50 per share if she is convinced that she will be able to sell it to Foolish Frank next year for $100 per share. (This idea has been called the "greater fool" theory of investing: It makes sense to buy a stock at a foolishly high price if you can sell it at an even higher price—to an even greater fool!) Third, once something attains the status of a fad, waves of buying can drive prices up to ridiculous levels, as has happened many times in history. Fourth, investors throughout the world undoubtedly fell in love both with information technology (especially the Internet) and the stock market (especially Internet-related stocks) in the late 1990s.

All this set the stage for what is commonly called a financial "bubble." The metaphor is meant to conjure up images of things like balloons and soap bubbles that blow up and up and up . . . until they burst. Indeed, legions of economists were warning about a stock market bubble in 1998, in 1999, and into 2000. The problem is simply stated: No one ever knows when a bubble will burst. And for stock market speculators, timing is everything. Look back at Figure 1 again. Those who claimed at the end of 1999 that stocks were overvalued looked pretty silly when the stock price index gained another 3,000 points in less than one year. (Of course, they subsequently looked pretty smart when prices collapsed!) Indeed, in 1999 and 2000, there were

---

[8] For a diagrammatic analysis of this role of speculation, see Discussion Question 3 at the end of this chapter.

heated discussions in the corridors of many economics departments regarding whether or not the money invested in university pension funds should or should not be removed from the stock market and placed into bonds. Those who wanted to hang on to the stock market (the bulls), even when share prices started to dwindle, argued that similar fears had been voiced around 1998, and that had the pension fund followed the advice of the bears (those who wanted to walk away from the stock market), retirement funds would not have taken advantage of the long and rapid climb in share prices that occurred between 1998 and the summer of 2000. The only thing that is truly predictable about a bubble is that it will burst—*eventually*. But no one ever knows when. As a result, no one could say definitively that *now* was the time to sell stocks and especially technology stocks. As the saying goes, the rest is history.

PUZZLE 2 RESOLVED: *Unpredictable Stock Prices as "Random Walks"*

In one of the puzzles at the beginning of this chapter, we cited evidence indicating that the best professional securities analysts have a forecasting record so miserable that investors may do as well predicting earnings by hunch, superstition, or any purely random process as they would by following professional advice. (See "Sports Moods and Stock Market Prices" to learn about some surprising ways of "predicting" the stock market's performance.)

Does this mean that analysts are incompetent people who do not know what they are doing? Not at all. Rather, there is fairly strong evidence that they have undertaken a task that is basically impossible.

How can this be so? The answer is that to make a good forecast of *any* variable—be it GDP, population, fuel usage, or stock market prices—there must be something in the past whose behaviour is closely related to the future behaviour of the variable whose path we wish to predict. If a 10 percent rise in this year's consumption always produces a 5 percent rise in next year's GDP, this fact can help us predict future GDP

Sports Moods and Stock Market Prices

Some economists have found a way to predict daily changes in the stock market index: Defeats by the home team on the world sports scene bring down domestic stock market prices so, to beat the market, investors need only predict wins and losses of national teams.

An international team of researchers from Norway and the United States has investigated this impact of sports news on stock market prices. They looked in detail at soccer results, those of the final stages of the FIFA World Cup as well as their regional counterparts—the UEFA (Europe) championship, the Copa America (South America), and the Asian Cup. In addition, international results in rugby (from the Six Nations tournament), cricket (One Day Internationals), basketball (Olympics and World Championships), and ice hockey (Olympics, World Championships, World Cup, and Canada Cup) were also examined. While this may seem strange, it is no more bizarre than the many attempts of economists and financial specialists to relate stock market prices to the amount of sunshine, temperature, lunar cycles, or switches from or to Daylight Saving Time.

Many studies have shown that the outcomes of sporting events do have an influence on the well-being of individuals, the perception of their economic situation, and their behaviour. For instance, hospital admissions for heart attacks increased by 25 percent when England lost against Argentina in a shootout during the 1978 Soccer World Cup. In Quebec, it has been shown that the number of suicides is higher in years in which the Montreal Canadiens have been eliminated in the early rounds of the Stanley Cup. So it is perhaps not farfetched to believe that sport outcomes have an impact on the mood of stock market investors and, hence, an impact on stock market prices on the first trading day after a match.

To substantiate this, the researchers found that in soccer, while there is little or no positive effect on stock market prices when a national team wins and continues to the next round, there is a substantial effect when the national team is eliminated from one of the regional cups or when it loses during the World Cup. This impact is particularly strong in countries where soccer is of national interest—Argentina, Brazil, England, France, Germany, Italy, and Spain. As one would expect, the greatest impact occurs during the elimination stage of the World Cup: A loss at that stage causes an average drop of 0.50 percent in the main share index of the losing country. While this may not sound like much, it is substantial from both a statistical and financial point of view. Very similar effects, but of a smaller magnitude, were obtained for basketball, cricket, and rugby. However, ice hockey results appeared to have no effect whatsoever on stock market prices!

SOURCE: A. Edmans, D. Garcia, and Ø. Norli, "Sports sentiments and stock returns," *Journal of Finance*, August 2007, 62(4), pp. 1967–1998.

The time path of a variable such as the price of a stock is said to constitute a **random walk** if its magnitude in one period (say, May 2, 2007) is equal to its value in the preceding period (May 1, 2007) plus a completely random number. That is: Price on May 2, 2007 = Price on May 1, 2007 + Random number, where the random number (positive or negative) can be obtained by a roll of dice or some such procedure.

on the basis of current observations. But if we want to forecast the future of a variable whose behaviour is completely unrelated to the behaviour of *any* current or past variable, there is no objective evidence that can help us make that forecast. Throwing darts or gazing into a crystal ball are no less effective than analysts' calculations.

A mass of statistical evidence indicates that the behaviour of stock prices is largely unpredictable. In other words, the behaviour of stock prices is essentially *random*; the paths they follow approximate what statisticians call **random walks.** A random walk is like the path followed by a sleepwalker. All we know about his position after his next step is that it will be given by his current position plus whatever random direction his next haphazard step will carry him. The relevant feature of randomness, for our purposes, is that it is by nature *unpredictable*, which is just what the word *random* means.

If the evidence that stock prices approximate a random walk stands up to research in the future as it has so far, it is easy enough to understand why stock market predictions are so poor. Analysts are trying to forecast behaviour that is basically random; in effect, they are trying to predict the unpredictable.

Two questions remain. First, does the evidence that stock prices follow a random walk mean that investment in stocks is a pure gamble and never worthwhile? Second, how does one explain the random behaviour of stock prices?

To answer the first question, it is wrong to conclude that investment in stocks is generally not worthwhile. The statistical evidence is that, over the long run, stock prices *as a whole* have followed a fairly marked upward trend, perhaps reflecting the long-term growth of the economy. Thus, the random walk does not proceed in just any direction—rather, it represents a set of erratic movements *around a basic upward trend in stock prices.*

Moreover, it is not in the *overall* level of stock prices that the most pertinent random walk occurs, but in the performance of one company's stock as compared with another firm's stock. For this reason, professional advice may be able to predict that investment in the stock market is likely to be a good thing over the long haul. But, if the random walk evidence is valid, there is no way professionals can tell us *which* of the available stocks is most likely to increase in price—that is, which combination of stocks is best for the investor to buy.

The only appropriate answer to the second question of how to account for the random behaviour of stock prices is that no one is sure of the explanation. There are two widely offered hypotheses—each virtually the opposite of the other. The first asserts that stock prices are random because clever professional speculators are able to foresee almost perfectly every influence that is *not* random. For example, suppose that a change occurs that makes the probable earnings of some company higher than had previously been expected. Then, according to this view, the professionals will instantly become aware of this change and immediately buy enough shares to raise the price of the stock accordingly. Then the only thing for that stock price to do between this year and next is wander randomly, because the professionals cannot predict random movements, and hence they cannot force current stock prices to anticipate them.

The second explanation of the random behaviour of stock prices is at the opposite extreme from the view that all nonrandom movements are wiped out by super-smart professionals. This is the view that people who buy and sell stocks have learned that they cannot predict future stock prices. As a result, they react to *any* signal, however irrational and irrelevant it appears. If the prime minister catches a cold, stock prices fall. If the Canadarm performs well during a space mission, prices go up. According to this view, investors are, in the last analysis, trying to predict not the prospects of the economy or of the company whose shares they buy, but the supply and demand behaviour of other investors, which will ultimately determine the course of stock prices. Because all investors are equally in the dark, their groping around can only result in the randomness that we observe.

The classic statement of this view of stock market behaviour was provided in 1936 by the English economist John Maynard Keynes, a successful professional speculator himself:

> Professional investment may be likened to those newspaper competitions in which the competitors have to pick out the six prettiest faces from a hundred photographs, the prize being awarded to the competitor whose choice most nearly corresponds to the average preferences of the competitors as a whole; so that each competitor has to pick not those faces which he himself finds prettiest, but those which he thinks likeliest to catch the fancy of the other competitors, all of whom are looking at the problem from the same point of view. It is not a case of choosing those which, to the best of one's judgment, are really the prettiest, nor even those which average opinion genuinely thinks the prettiest. We have reached the third degree where we devote our intelligences to anticipating what average opinion expects the average opinion to be. And there are some, I believe, who practice the fourth, fifth and higher degrees.[9]

[9] John Maynard Keynes, *The General Theory of Employment, Interest, and Money* (New York: Harcourt Brace, 1936), p. 156.

SUMMARY

1. Most Canadian manufactured goods are produced by **corporations**.

2. Investors in corporations have greater risk protection than those who put their money into other types of firms because the corporate form gives them **limited liability**— they cannot be asked to pay more of the company's debts than they have invested in the firm.

3. Higher taxation of corporate earnings tends to limit the things in which corporations can invest and may lead to inefficiency in resource allocation.

4. A **common stock** is a share in a company's ownership. A **bond** is an IOU for money lent to a company by the bondholder. Many observers argue that a stock purchase really amounts to a loan to the company—a loan that is riskier than a bond purchase.

5. If **interest rates** rise, bond prices will fall. In other words, if some bond amounts to a contract to pay 8 percent and the market interest rate goes up to 10 percent, people will no longer be willing to pay the old price for that bond.

6. Corporations finance their activities mostly by **plowback** (that is, by retaining part of their earnings and reinvesting the funds in the company). They also obtain funds by selling stocks and bonds and by taking out more traditional loans.

7. If stock prices correctly reflect the future prospects of different companies, it is easier for promising firms to raise money because they are able to sell each stock issue at favourable prices.

8. Bonds are relatively risky for the firms that issue them, but they are fairly safe for their buyers, because they are a commitment by those firms to pay fixed annual amounts to the bondholders whether or not the companies make money that year. Stocks, which do not promise any fixed payment, are relatively safe for the companies but risky for their owners.

9. A portfolio is a collection of stocks, bonds, and other assets of a single owner. The greater the number and variety of securities and other assets a portfolio contains, the less risky it generally is.

10. A **takeover** of a corporation occurs when an outside group buys enough stock to get control of the firm's decisions. Takeovers are a useful way to get rid of incompetent management or to force management to be more efficient. However, the process is costly and leads to wasteful defensive and offensive activities.

11. **Speculation** affects stock market prices, but (contrary to widespread belief) it actually tends to reduce the frequency and size of price fluctuations. Speculators are also useful to the economy because they undertake risks that others wish to avoid, thereby, in effect, providing others with insurance against risk.

12. Statistical evidence indicates that individual stock prices behave randomly (in other words, unpredictably).

KEY TERMS

TEST YOURSELF

1. Suppose that interest rates are 6 percent in the economy and a safe bond promises to pay $3 per year in interest forever. What do you think the price of the bond will be? Why?

2. Suppose that in the economy described in Test Yourself Question 1, interest rates suddenly fall to 3 percent. What will happen to the price of the bond that pays $3 per year?

3. For whom are stocks riskier than bonds? For whom are bonds riskier than stocks?

4. If the price of a company's stock constitutes a random walk, next year its price will equal today's price plus what?

5. Company A sells heaters and Company B sells air conditioners. Which is the safer investment, Company A stock, Company B stock, or a portfolio containing half of each?

6. If you make a lucky prediction about the prices of the stocks of the two companies in question 5 will you earn more or less if you invest in that company rather than the portfolio?

DISCUSSION QUESTIONS

1. If you hold shares in a corporation and management decides to plow back the company's earnings some year instead of paying dividends, what are the advantages and disadvantages to you?

2. If you want to buy a stock, when might it pay you to use a market order? When will it pay to use a limit order?

3. Show in diagrams that if a speculator were to buy when price is high and sell when price is low, he would increase price fluctuations. Why would it be in his best interest *not* to do so? (*Hint:* Draw two supply–demand diagrams, one for the high-price period and one for the low-price period. How would the speculator's activities affect these diagrams?)

4. If stock prices really do take a random walk, can you nevertheless think of good reasons for getting professional advice before investing?

5. Hostile takeovers often end up in court when management attempts to block such a manoeuvure and raiders accuse management of selfishly sacrificing the shareholders' interests. The courts often look askance at "coercive" offers by raiders—an offer to buy, say, 20 percent of the company's stock by a certain date from the first shareholders who offer to sell. By contrast, they take a more favourable attitude toward "noncoercive" offers to buy any and all stock supplied at announced prices. Do you think the courts are right to reject "coercive offers" but prevent management from blocking "noncoercive" offers? Why?

6. In program trading, computers decide when to buy or sell stocks on behalf of large, institutional investors. The computers then carry out those transactions with electronic speed. Critics claim that this practice is a major reason why stock prices rose and fell sharply in the 1980s. Is this idea plausible? Why or why not?

III

MARKETS AND THE PRICE SYSTEM

A **market** comprises a set of sellers and buyers whose activities affect the price at which a particular commodity is sold.

So far, we have talked only about firms in general without worrying about the sorts of markets in which they operate. To understand the different types of competition a firm can face, it is necessary, first, to explain clearly what we mean by the word **market**. Economists do not reserve this term for only an organized exchange, such as the nineteenth-century London stock exchange, operating in a specific location. In its more general and abstract usage, *market* refers to a set of sellers and buyers whose activities affect the price at which a *particular commodity* is sold. For example, two separate sales of Alcan stock in different parts of the country can be considered to take place in the same market, whereas sales of bread in one stall of a market square and sales of compact disks in the next stall may, in our sense, occur in totally different markets.

Economists distinguish among different kinds of markets according to how many firms they include, whether the products of the different firms are identical or different, and how easy it is for new firms to enter the markets. *Perfect competition* is at one extreme (many small firms selling an identical product, with easy entry into the market), and *pure monopoly* (a single firm dominating the market) is at the other extreme. In between are hybrid forms—called *monopolistic competition* (many small firms, each selling slightly different products) and *oligopoly* (a few large rival firms)—that share some of the characteristics of both perfect competition and monopoly.

Perfect competition is far from the typical market form in the Canadian economy. Indeed, it is quite rare. Pure monopoly—literally *one* firm—is also infrequently encountered. Most of the products you buy are no doubt supplied by oligopolies or monopolistic competitors—terms that we will define precisely in Chapter 12.

10

THE FIRM AND THE INDUSTRY
UNDER PERFECT COMPETITION

*Competition . . . brings about the only . . . arrangement of social production which is possible. . . .
[Otherwise] what guarantee [do] we have that the necessary quantity and not more
of each product will be produced, that we shall not go hungry in regard to corn and meat
while we are choked in beet sugar and drowned in potato spirit, that we shall not lack
trousers to cover our nakedness while buttons flood us in millions?*

FRIEDRICH ENGELS (1820–1895) (FRIEND AND COAUTHOR OF KARL MARX), 1847

I ndustries differ dramatically in the number and typical sizes of their firms. Some, such as commercial fishing, encompass a great many very small firms. Others, like automobile manufacturing, are composed of a few industrial giants. This chapter deals with a very special type of market structure—called *perfect competition*—in which firms are numerous and small. We begin by comparing alternative market forms and defining perfect competition precisely. First, as usual, we set out our puzzle.

CONTENTS

PUZZLE: *Pollution Reduction Incentives That Actually Increase Pollution*

Many economists and other citizens concerned about the environment believe that society can obtain cleaner air and water cheaply and effectively by requiring polluters to pay for the damages they cause. (See Chapter 17 for more details.) Yet people often view pollution charges as just another *tax*, and that word can translate into political poison. Some politicians—reasoning that you can move a donkey along just as effectively by offering it a carrot as by poking it with a stick—have proposed *paying* firms to cut down on their polluting emissions. For instance, in 1996, the Chrétien government required oil producers to cut back on the amount of greenhouse gas emissions per barrel of oil in proportion to the increase in the number of extracted barrels, but at the same time, promised to subsidize some of the costs of emission reduction.

At least some theoretical and statistical evidence indicates that such a system of bribes (or, to use a more palatable word, subsidies) does work, *at least up to a point.* Individual polluting firms will, indeed, respond to government payments for decreased emissions by reducing their pollution. But, over the long haul, it turns out that society may well end up with more pollution than before! Subsidy payments to the firms can actually exacerbate pollution problems. How is it possible that subsidies induce each firm to pollute less but in the long run lead to a rise in total pollution? The analysis in this chapter will supplement your own common sense sufficiently to supply the answer.

◼ PERFECT COMPETITION DEFINED

Perfect competition occurs in an industry when that industry is made up of many small firms producing homogeneous products, when there is no impediment to the entry or exit of firms, and when full information is available.

You can appreciate just how special perfect competition is by considering this comprehensive definition. A market is said to operate under **perfect competition** when the following four conditions are satisfied:

1. *Numerous small firms and customers.* Competitive markets contain so many buyers and sellers that each one constitutes a negligible portion of the whole—so small, in fact, that each player's decisions have no effect on price. This requirement rules out trade associations or other collusive arrangements in which firms work together to influence price.

2. *Homogeneity of product.* The product offered by any seller is identical to that supplied by any other seller. (For example, Canada Western Red Winter Wheat is a homogeneous product; different brands of toothpaste are not.) Because products are homogeneous, consumers do not care from which firm they buy, so competition is more powerful.

3. *Freedom of entry and exit.* New firms desiring to enter the market face no impediments that previous entrants can avoid. So new firms can easily come in and compete with older firms. Similarly, if production and sale of the good proves unprofitable, no barriers prevent firms from leaving the market.

4. *Perfect information.* Each firm and each customer is well informed about available products and prices. They know whether one supplier is selling at a lower price than another.

These exacting requirements are rarely, if ever, found in practice. One example that comes close to the perfectly competitive standard is a market for common stocks. On any given day, literally millions of buyers and sellers trade Telus stock; all of the shares are exactly alike; anyone who wishes to sell his or her Telus stock can enter the market easily; and most relevant company and industry information is readily available (and virtually free of charge) in the daily newspapers or on the Internet. Many farming and fishing industries also approximate perfect competition. But it is difficult to find many other examples. Indeed, several sectors of the farming industry, with their marketing boards, do not fulfill the conditions of perfect competition. Our interest in the perfectly competitive model surely does not lie in its ability to describe reality.

Why, then, do we spend time studying perfect competition? The answer takes us back to the central theme of this book. Under perfect competition the market mechanism in many ways performs best. If we want to learn what markets do well, we can put the market's best foot forward by beginning with perfect competition.

As Adam Smith suggested some two centuries ago, perfectly competitive firms use society's scarce resources with maximum efficiency. Also, as Friedrich Engels (Karl Marx's closest friend and coauthor) suggested in the opening quotation of this chapter, only perfect competition can ensure that the economy turns out just those varieties and relative quantities of goods that match consumer preferences. By studying perfect competition, we can learn some of the things an *ideally functioning* market system can accomplish. This is the topic of this chapter and Chapter 14. In Chapters 11 and 12, we will consider other market forms and see how they deviate from the perfectly competitive ideal. Still later chapters (especially Chapter 15 and the chapters in Parts IV and V) will examine many important tasks that the market does *not* perform well, even under perfect competition. All these chapters combined should provide a balanced assessment of the virtues and vices of the market mechanism.

■ THE PERFECTLY COMPETITIVE FIRM

To discover what happens in a perfectly competitive market, we must deal separately with the behaviour of *individual firms* and the behaviour of the *industry* that is constituted by those firms. One basic difference between the firm and the industry under competition relates to *pricing*:

> Under perfect competition, the firm has no choice but to accept the price that has been determined in the market. It is therefore called a **"price taker"** (rather than a "price maker").

The idea that no firm in a perfectly competitive market can exert any control over product price follows from our stringent definition of perfect competition. The presence of a vast number of competitors, each offering identical products, forces each firm to meet but not exceed the price charged by the others, because at any higher price all of the firm's customers would leave it and move their purchases to its rivals.

With two important exceptions, analysis of the behaviour of the firm under perfect competition is exactly as we described in Chapters 7 and 8. The two exceptions relate to the special shape of the perfectly competitive firm's demand curve and the freedom of entry and exit, along with their effects on the firm's profits. We will consider each of these special features of perfect competition in turn, beginning with the demand curve.

Under perfect competition, the firm is a **price taker**. It has no choice but to accept the price that has been determined in the market.

■ The Firm's Demand Curve under Perfect Competition

In Chapter 8, we always assumed that the firm faced a downward-sloping demand curve. That is, if a firm wished to sell more (without increasing its advertising or changing its product specifications), it had to reduce its product price. The perfectly competitive firm is an exception to this general principle.

> A perfectly competitive firm faces a *horizontal* demand curve. This means that it can sell as much as it wants at the prevailing market price. It can double or triple its sales without reducing the price of its product.

How is this possible? The answer is that the perfectly competitive firm is so insignificant relative to the market as a whole that it has absolutely no influence over price. The farmer who sells his barley through a commodities exchange in Winnipeg must accept the current quotation that his broker reports to him. Because there are thousands of farmers, the Winnipeg price per bushel will not budge because farmer Jasmine decides she doesn't like the price and stores a truckload of barley rather than taking it to the grain elevator.

Thus, the demand curve for Jasmine's barley is as shown in Figure 1(a). As we can see, the price she is paid in Winnipeg will be $3 per bushel whether she sells one truck-

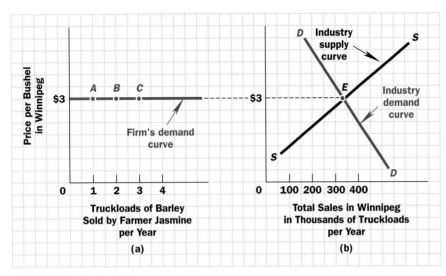

FIGURE 1

Demand Curve for a
Firm under Perfect
Competition

load (point *A*) or two (point *B*) or
three (point *C*). This is because
that $3 price is determined by
the intersection of the *industry's*
supply and demand curves shown
in the right-hand portion of the
graph, Panel (b).

Notice that, in the case of perfect competition, the downward-
sloping industry demand curve in
Figure 1(b) leads to the horizontal demand curve for the individual firm in Figure 1(a). Also
notice that the height of that
horizontal firm demand curve
will be the height of the intersection point, *E*, of the industry sup-
ply and demand curves. So the firm's demand curve will generally not resemble the
demand curve for the industry.

Short-Run Equilibrium for the Perfectly Competitive Firm

We already have sufficient background to study the decisions of a firm operating in a
perfectly competitive market. Recall from Chapter 8 that profit maximization
requires the firm to pick an output level that makes its *marginal cost equal to its marginal revenue:* MC = MR. The only feature that distinguishes the profit-maximizing
equilibrium for the perfectly competitive firm from that of any other type of firm is
its horizontal demand curve. We know from Chapter 8 that the firm's demand curve
is also its average revenue curve because the average revenue a firm gets from selling
a commodity is equal to the price of the commodity. That is, if it sells 100 shirts at a
price of $18 each, then obviously, the average revenue it obtains from the sale of each
shirt will be $18. Because the demand curve tells us the price at which the supplier
can sell a given quantity, this means it also tells us the average revenue it gets per unit
sold when it sells that given quantity. So the firm's demand curve and its average revenue curve are identical. The same curve does two
jobs. But it also does a third job. Because this demand
curve is horizontal, the competitive firm's *marginal*
revenue curve is a horizontal straight line that also
coincides with its demand curve; hence, MR = Price
(*P*). It is easy to see why this is so.

If the price does not depend on how much the firm
sells (which is exactly what a horizontal demand curve
means), then each *additional* unit sold brings in an
amount of additional revenue (the *marginal* revenue)
exactly equal to the market price. So marginal revenue
always equals price under perfect competition because
the firm is a price taker.

Under perfect competition the firm's demand curve, average
revenue curve and marginal revenue curve are all the same.

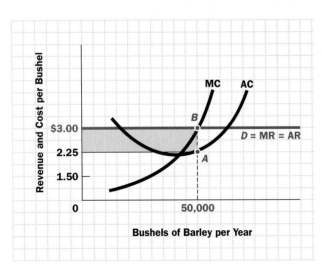

FIGURE 2

Short-Run Equilibrium
of the Perfectly Compet-
itive Firm

As in Chapter 8, once we know the shape and position of a firm's marginal revenue curve, we can use this
information and the marginal cost curve to determine
its optimal output and profit, as shown in Figure 2. As usual, the profit-maximizing
output is that at which MC = MR (point *B*). The demand curve, *D* = MR = AR, is
horizontal because the firm's output is too small to affect market price, as we just saw.

This particular competitive firm produces 50,000 bushels of barley per year—the output level at which MC and MR both equal the market price, $3. Thus:

> Because it is a price taker, the *equilibrium* of a profit-maximizing firm in a perfectly competitive market must occur at an output level at which marginal cost equals price = AR = MR. This is because a horizontal demand curve makes price and MR equal and, therefore, both must equal marginal cost according to the profit-maximizing principle. In symbols:
>
> **MC = MR = P**

This idea is illustrated in Table 1, which gives the firm's total and marginal revenue, total and marginal cost, and total profit for different output quantities. We see from Column (6) that total profit is maximized at an output of about 50,000 bushels where total profit is $37,500. An increase in output from 40,000 to 50,000 bushels incurs a marginal cost ($26,500) that most nearly equals the corresponding marginal revenue ($30,000), confirming that 50,000 bushels is the profit-maximizing output.[1]

The firm could make more revenues if it produced more bushels, as can be seen in Table 1. If it produced 60,000 bushels, its total revenues would rise from $150,000 to $180,000, and it would still make a profit of $11,000. However, as in previous chapters, we assume that firms are maximizing profits. Hence the firm will choose an output of 50,000 bushels—point *B* in Figure 2.

TABLE 1

Revenues, Costs, and Profits of a Perfectly Competitive Firm

(1) Total Quantity	(2) Total Revenue	(3) Marginal Revenue	(4) Total Cost	(5) Marginal Cost	(6) Total Profit
0	$ 0				
		$30			
10	30		$ 32		$ –2
		30		$ 24	
20	60		56		4
		30		11.5	
30	90		67.5		22.5
		30		18.5	
40	120		86		34
		30		26.5	
50	**150**		**112.5**		**37.5**
		30		56.5	
60	180		169		11
		30		93	
70	210		262		–52

Note: Quantity is in thousands of bushels; dollars are in thousands.

Short-Run Profit: Graphic Representation

Our analysis so far tells us how a firm can pick the output that maximizes its profit. It may even be able to earn a substantial profit. But sometimes, even if it succeeds in maximizing profit, the firm may conceivably find itself in trouble because market conditions may make the highest possible profit a *negative* number. If the demand for its product is weak or its costs are high, even the firm's most profitable option may lead to a loss. In the short run, the demand curve can either be high or low relative to costs. To determine whether the firm is making a profit or incurring a loss, we must compare *total* revenue (TR = $P \times Q$) with *total* cost (TC = AC $\times Q$). Because the output (Q) is common to both of these amounts, this equation tells us that the process is equivalent to comparing price (P) with average cost (AC). If $P >$ AC, the firm will earn a profit, and if $P <$ AC, it will suffer a loss.

We can therefore show the firm's profit in Figure 2, which includes the firm's *average cost* curve. By definition, profit per unit of output is revenue per unit *(P)* minus cost per unit (AC). We see in Figure 2 that average cost at 50,000 bushels per year is only $2.25 per bushel (point *A*), whereas *average revenue* (AR) is $3 per bushel (point *B*). The firm makes a profit of AR − AC = $0.75 per bushel, which appears in the graph as the vertical distance between points *A* and *B*.

Notice that, in addition to showing the *profit per unit*, Figure 2 can be used to show the firm's *total profit*. Total profit is the profit per unit ($0.75 in this example) times the number of units (50,000 per year). Therefore, total profit is represented by the *area* of the shaded rectangle whose height is the profit per unit ($0.75) and whose width is the number of units (50,000).[2] In this case, profits are $37,500 per year. In

---

[1] Marginal cost is not precisely equal to marginal revenue, because to calculate marginal costs and marginal revenues with perfect accuracy, we would have to increase output one bushel at a time instead of proceeding in leaps of 10,000 bushels. Of course, that would require too much space! In any event, our failure to make a more careful calculation in terms of individual bushels explains why we are unable to find the output at which MR and MC are *exactly* equal.

[2] Recall that the formula for the area of a rectangle is Area = Height × Width.

general, total profit at any output is the area of the rectangle whose base equals the level of output and whose height equals AR − AC.

> The MC = *P* condition gives us the output that maximizes the perfectly competitive firm's profit. It does not, however, tell us whether the firm is making a profit or incurring a loss. To make this determination, we must compare price (average revenue) with average cost.

■ The Case of Short-Term Losses

The market is obviously treating the farmer in Figure 2 rather nicely. But what if the barley market was not so generous in its rewards? What if, for example, the market price was only $1.50 per bushel instead of $3? Figure 3 shows the equilibrium of the firm under these circumstances. The cost curves are the same in this diagram as they were in Figure 2(a), but the demand curve has shifted down to correspond to the market price of $1.50 per bushel. The firm still maximizes profits by producing the level of output at which marginal cost (MC) is equal to price (*P*) – (MC = P = MR)—point *B* in the diagram. But this time "maximizing profits" really means minimizing losses, as shown by the shaded rectangle.

At the optimal level of output (30,000 bushels per year), average cost is $2.25 per bushel (point *A*), which exceeds the $1.50 per bushel price (point *B*). The firm therefore incurs a loss of $0.75 per bushel times 30,000 bushels, or $22,500 per year. This loss, which is represented by the area of the gold rectangle in Figure 3, is the best the firm can do. If it selected any other output level, its loss would be even greater.

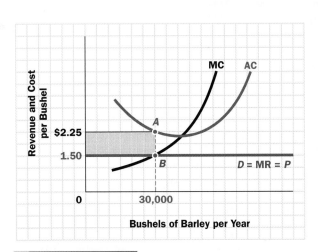

FIGURE 3

Short-Run Equilibrium of the Perfectly Competitive Firm with a Lower Price

A **variable cost** is a cost whose total amount changes when the quantity of output of the supplier changes.

■ Shutdown and Break-Even Analysis

Of course, any firm will accept only a limited amount of loss before it stops production. If losses get too big, the firm can simply go out of business. To understand the logic of the choice between shutting down and remaining in operation, we must return to the distinction between **costs** that are **variable** in the short run and those that are not. Recall from Chapter 7 that costs are not variable (they are said to be *fixed*) if the firm cannot escape them in the short run, either because of a contract (say, with a landlord or a union) or because it has already bought the item whose cost is not variable (for example, a machine).

If the firm stops producing, then its revenue and its short-run variable costs will fall to zero. But its costs that are not variable will remain. If the firm is losing money, sometimes it will be better off continuing to operate until its obligations to pay the fixed costs expire; sometimes it will do better by shutting down immediately and producing nothing. That obviously depends on whether or not by shutting down immediately, the costs it can avoid *immediately* are greater that the revenue it gives up by having nothing to sell any longer. More explicitly, two rules govern the decision:

> Rule 1. The firm will make a loss if total revenue (TR) is less than total cost (TC). In that case, it should plan to shut down, either in the short run or in the long run.

> Rule 2. The firm should continue to operate in the short run if TR exceeds total short-run variable cost (TVC).

The first rule is self-evident. If the firm's revenues do not cover its total costs, then it surely will lose money and, sooner or later, it will have to close. The second rule is a bit more subtle. Suppose that TR is less than TC. If our unfortunate firm continues in operation, it will lose the difference between total cost and total revenue:

Loss if the firm stays in business = TC − TR

However, if the firm stops producing, both its revenues and short-run variable costs become zero, leaving only the *fixed* costs to be paid:

Loss if the firm shuts down = Total fixed costs (TFC) = TC − TVC

Hence, it is best to keep operating as long as its loss if it stays in business is less than its loss if it shuts down:

TC − TR < TC − TVC

or

TVC < TR

That is Rule 2.

We can illustrate Rule 2 with the two cases shown in Table 2. Case A deals with a firm that loses money but is better off staying in business in the short run. If it shuts down, it will lose its entire $60,000 worth of short-run fixed cost. If it continues to operate, its total revenue of $100,000 will exceed its total variable cost (TVC = $80,000) by $20,000. That means continuing operation contributes $20,000 toward meeting fixed costs and reduces losses to $40,000. In Case B, in contrast, it pays the firm to shut down because continued operation merely adds to its losses. If the firm operates, it will lose $90,000 (the last entry in Table 2); if it shuts down, it will lose only the $60,000 in total fixed costs, which it must pay whether it operates or not.

TABLE 2		
The Shutdown Decision		
	Case A	Case B
Total revenue (TR)	$100	$100
Total variable cost (TVC)	80	130
Short-run fixed cost (TFC)	60	60
Total cost (TC)	140	190
Loss if firm shuts down (= Short-run fixed cost)	60	60
Loss if firm does not shut down	40	90

Note: Figures are in thousands of dollars.

FIGURE 4

Shutdown Analysis

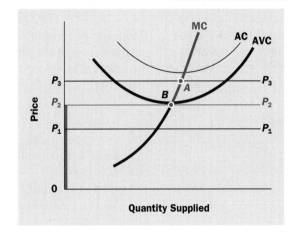

We also can analyze the shutdown decision graphically. In Figure 4, the firm will run a loss whether the price is P_1, P_2, or P_3, because none of these prices is high enough to reach the minimum level of average cost (AC). We can show the *lowest* price that keeps the firm from shutting down by introducing one more short-run cost curve: the average variable cost (AVC) curve. Why is this curve relevant? Because, as we have just seen, it pays the firm to remain in operation if its total revenue (TR) exceeds its total short-run variable cost (TVC). If we divide both TR and TVC by quantity (Q), we get TR/Q = P and TVC/Q = AVC. So, we can state the condition for continued operation equivalently as the requirement that price must exceed AVC. The conclusion is:

The firm will produce nothing unless price lies above the minimum point on the AVC curve.

In Figure 4, price P_1 is below the minimum average variable cost. With this price, the firm cannot even cover its variable costs and is better off shutting down (producing zero output). Price P_3 is higher. Although the firm still runs a loss if it sets MC = P at point A (because AC exceeds P_3), it allows the firm to at least cover its short-run variable costs, so it pays to keep operating in the short run. Price P_2 is the borderline

Hog Prices and Farm Income in a Competitive Market

Because farmers are *price takers*, they simply have to live with the price that is determined by the market's supply and demand. If prices are too low, some of the farms will exit, thus allowing a recovery of prices above average costs. Here is an example.

SOURCE: WizData, inc./Shutterstock

> The hog farm Patrick Ueffing and his two brothers run in Sheffield Mills, Kings County [Nova Scotia], has been in the family name for nearly 44 years. The boys grew up learning the trade under their father, Ted.
>
> The 340-hectare farm is a major stronghold of the faltering hog industry in the province. But Ueffing estimates that if market prices don't dramatically increase and the province refuses to sign off on an industry-wide loan, he may have to consider bankruptcy. . . .
>
> The province's pork industry is facing a crisis that promises to put 60 per cent of hog farmers out of business this winter if the MacDonald Tories don't fork out $6 million to keep them afloat for the next 12 to 18 months, according to Pork Nova Scotia, the hog marketing agency. Hog farmers are losing roughly $40 an animal due to low prices, and high feed and transportation costs. For Ueffing, that loss racks up to $12,000 a week. . . .
>
> The commodity futures price index, a key indicator for economists, forecasts hog prices will jump by roughly $12 over cur-

rent levels, though industry analyst David Robinson cautions that increase will largely be matched by a projected rise in grain price. . . .

> Robinson says the hog market is the hardest hit agricultural sector in the province because it, unlike the dairy and poultry sectors, lacks a supply management board that regulates price.
>
> Pork farmers also need more grain than dairy and poultry farmers to produce a kilogram of market-level product. . . .

SOURCE: "Hog crisis on doorstep of province's largest producer," by Reid Southwick; Jan. 15, 2007, updated Jan. 18, 2007; Nova News Net, Reprinted by permission of the author. Retrieved from http://novanewsnet.ukings.ca/nova_news_3588_9962.html

case. If the price is P_2, the firm is indifferent between shutting down and staying in business and producing at a level where MC = P (point B). P_2 is thus the *lowest* price at which the firm will produce anything. As we see from the graph, P_2 corresponds to the minimum point on the AVC curve.

■ The Perfectly Competitive Firm's Short-Run Supply Curve

The **supply curve of a firm** shows the different quantities of output that the firm would be willing to supply at different possible prices during some given period of time.

Without realizing it, we have now derived the **supply curve of the perfectly competitive firm** in the short run. Why? Recall that a supply curve summarizes in a graph the answers to questions such as, "If the price is so and so, how much output will the firm offer for sale?" We have now discovered two possibilities:

- In the short run, if the price exceeds the minimum AVC, then it pays a competitive firm to produce the level of output at which MC equals P. Thus, for any price above point B in Figure 4, we can read the corresponding quantity supplied from the firm's MC curve, as indicated by the blue portion of the MC curve.
- If the price falls below the minimum AVC, then it pays the firm to produce nothing. Quantity supplied falls to zero, as indicated by vertical red line $0P_2$ in Figure 4.

Putting these two observations together, we conclude that:

The short-run supply curve of the perfectly competitive firm is that portion of its marginal cost curve that lies above the point where it intersects the average (short-run) variable cost curve—that is, above the minimum level of AVC. If price falls below this level, the firm's quantity supplied drops to zero.

■ THE PERFECTLY COMPETITIVE INDUSTRY

Now that we have completed the analysis of the perfectly competitive *firm's* supply decision, we turn our attention next to the perfectly competitive *industry*.

■ The Perfectly Competitive Industry's Short-Run Supply Curve

Once again, we need to distinguish between the short run and the long run, but the distinction is different here. The short run for the *industry* is defined as a period of time too brief for new firms to enter the industry or for old firms to leave, so the number of firms is fixed. By contrast, the long run for the industry is a period of time long enough for any firm to enter or leave as it desires. In addition, in the long run each firm in the industry can adjust its output to its own long-run costs.[3] We begin our analysis of industry equilibrium in the short run.

With the number of firms fixed, it is a simple matter to derive the **supply curve of the perfectly competitive industry** from those of the individual firms. At any given price, we simply *add up* the quantities supplied by each of the firms to arrive at the industry-wide quantity supplied. For example, if each of 1,000 identical firms in the barley industry supplies 45,000 bushels when the price is $2.25 per bushel, then the quantity supplied by the industry at a $2.25 price will be 45,000 bushels per firm × 1,000 firms = 45 million bushels.

> The **supply curve of an industry** shows the different quantities of output that the industry would supply at different possible prices during some given period of time.

This process of deriving the *market* supply curve from the *individual* supply curves of firms is analogous to the way we derived the *market* demand curve from the *individual* consumers' demand curves in Chapter 6. Graphically, what we are doing is *summing the individual supply curves horizontally*, as illustrated in Figure 5. At a price of $2.25, each of the 1,000 identical firms in the industry supplies 45,000 bushels—point *c* in Panel (a)—so the industry supplies 45 million bushels—point *C* in Panel (b). At a price of $3, each firm supplies 50,000 bushels—point *e* in Panel (a)—and so the industry supplies 50 million bushels—point *E* in Panel (b). We can carry out similar calculations for any other price. By adding up the quantities supplied by each firm at each possible price, we arrive at the industry supply curve *SS* in Panel (b).

> The supply curve of the competitive industry in the short run is derived by *summing* the short-run supply curves of all the firms in the industry *horizontally*.

This adding-up process indicates, incidentally, that the supply curve of the industry will shift to the right whenever a new firm enters the industry.

Notice that if the short-run supply curves of individual firms slope upward, then the short-run supply curve of the perfectly competitive industry will slope upward as well. We have seen that the firm's supply curve is its marginal cost curve (above the level of minimum average variable cost), so it follows that rising marginal costs lead to an upward-sloping short-run *industry* supply curve.

FIGURE 5

Derivation of the Industry Supply Curve from the Supply Curves of the Individual Firms

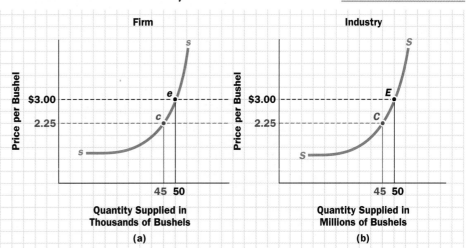

---

[3] The relationship between short-run and long-run cost curves for the firm was discussed in Chapter 7, page 141.

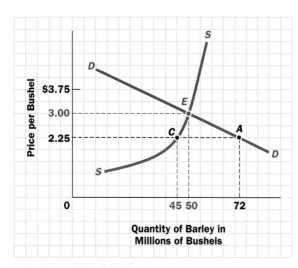

FIGURE 6

Supply–Demand Equilibrium of a Perfectly Competitive Industry

Industry Equilibrium in the Short Run

Now that we have derived the industry supply curve, we need only add a market demand curve to determine the price and quantity that will emerge in equilibrium. We do this for our illustrative barley industry in Figure 6, where the red industry supply curve, carried over from Figure 5(b), is *SS* and the demand curve is *DD*. The only equilibrium combination of price and quantity is a price of $3 and a quantity of 50 million bushels, at which the supply curve, *SS*, and the demand curve, *DD*, intersect (point *E*). At any lower price, such as $2.25, quantity demanded (72 million bushels, as shown by point *A* on the demand curve) will be higher than the 45-million-bushel quantity supplied (point *C*). Thus, the price will be bid up toward the $3 equilibrium. The opposite will happen at a price such as $3.75, which is above equilibrium.

Note that for the perfectly competitive industry, unlike the perfectly competitive firm, the demand curve normally slopes downward. Why? Each firm by itself is so small that if it alone were to double its output, the effect would hardly be noticeable. But if *every* firm in the industry were to expand its output, that would make a substantial difference. Customers can be induced to buy the additional quantities arriving at the market only if the price of the good falls.

Point *E* is the equilibrium point for the perfectly competitive industry, because only at a price of $3 are sellers willing to offer exactly the amount that consumers want to purchase (in this case, 50 million bushels).

Should we expect price actually to reach, or at least to *approximate*, this equilibrium level? The answer is yes. To see why, we must consider what happens when price is not at its equilibrium level. Suppose that the price is lower—say, $2.25. This low price will stimulate customers to buy more; it will also lead firms to produce less than they would at a price of $3. Our diagram confirms that at a price of $2.25, quantity supplied (45 million bushels) is lower than quantity demanded (72 million bushels). Thus, the availability of unsatisfied buyers will probably lead sellers to raise their prices, which will force the price *upward* in the direction of its equilibrium value, $3.

Similarly, if we begin with a price higher than the equilibrium price, we may readily verify that quantity supplied will exceed quantity demanded. Under these circumstances, frustrated sellers are likely to reduce their prices, so price will be forced downward. In the circumstances depicted in Figure 6, in effect a magnet at the equilibrium price of $3 will pull the actual price in its direction, if for some reason the actual price starts out at some other level.

In practice, over a long period of time, prices do move toward equilibrium levels in most perfectly competitive markets. Matters eventually appear to work out as depicted in Figure 6. Of course, numerous transitory influences can jolt any real-world market away from its equilibrium point—a workers' strike that cuts production, a sudden change in consumer tastes, and so on.

Yet, as we have just seen, powerful forces push prices back toward equilibrium—toward the level at which the supply and demand curves intersect. These forces are fundamentally important for economic analysis. If no such forces existed, prices in the real world would bear little resemblance to equilibrium prices, and there would be little reason to study supply–demand analysis. Fortunately, the required equilibrating forces do step in as appropriate to bring markets back toward equilibrium.

Industry and Firm Equilibrium in the Long Run

The equilibrium of a perfectly competitive industry in the long run may differ for two reasons from the short-run equilibrium that we have just studied. First, the number of firms in the industry (1,000 in our example) is not fixed in the long run. Second, as we saw in Chapter 7 (page 141), in the long run, firms can vary their plant size and change other commitments that could not be altered in the short run. Hence, the firm's (and the industry's) long-run cost curves are not the same as the short-run cost curves. These differences can be very important, as we will see.

What will lure new firms into the industry or encourage old ones to leave? The answer is *profits*—economic profits (that is, any part of the firm's earnings that exceeds the average earnings of other firms in the economy and thus exceeds the firm's costs including its opportunity costs). Remember that when a firm selects its optimal level of output by setting MC = P, it may wind up with either a profit, as in Figure 2, or a loss, as in Figure 3. Such profits or losses must be *temporary* for perfectly competitive firms, because new firms are free to enter the industry if profits greater than the average than they can obtain by investing elsewhere are available in our industry. For the same reason, old firms will leave if they cannot cover their costs in the long run. Suppose that firms in the industry earn very high profits, in excess of the normal rates of return currently available. Then new companies will find it attractive to enter the business, and expanded production will force the market price to fall from its initial level. Why? Recall that the industry supply curve is the horizontal sum of the supply curves of individual firms. Under perfect competition, new firms can enter the industry *on the same terms as existing firms.* Thus, new entrants will have the *same* individual supply curves as the old firms. If the market price did not fall, the entry of new firms would lead to an increased number of firms, with no change in output *per firm.* Consequently, the total quantity supplied to the market would be higher, and it would exceed quantity demanded—which, of course, would also drive prices down. Thus, the entry of new firms *must* push the price down.

Figure 7 shows how the entry process works. In this diagram, the demand curve DD and the original (short-run) supply curve S_0S_0 are carried over from Figure 6. The entry of new firms seeking high profits *shifts the industry's short-run supply curve outward to the right*, to S_1S_1. The new market equilibrium at point A (rather than at point E) indicates that price is $2.25 per bushel and that 72 million bushels are produced and consumed. The entry of new firms reduces price and raises total output.

If the price had not fallen, the quantity supplied after the new firms' entry would have been 80 million bushels—point F. Why must the price fall in this case? Because the demand curve for the industry slopes downward: Consumers will purchase the increased output only at a reduced price.

To see the point at which entry stops being attracted by high profits, we must consider how new firm entry affects existing firms' behaviour. At first glance, this notion may seem to contradict the idea of perfect competition; perfectly competitive firms are not supposed to be affected by what competitors do, because no individual firm can influence the industry. Indeed, these barley farmers don't care about the entry of new firms. But they *do* care very much about the market price of barley and, as we have just seen, the entry of new firms into the barley-farming industry lowers the price of barley.

In Figure 8, we juxtapose the diagram of perfectly competitive firm equilibrium (Figure 2) with the perfectly competitive industry equilibrium diagram (Figure 7). Before the new firms' entry, the market price was $3, point E in Figure 8(b), and each of the 1,000 firms produced 50,000 bushels—the point where marginal cost and price were equal, point e in Figure 8(a). Each firm faced the horizontal demand curve D_0 in Figure 8(a). Firms within the industry enjoyed profits because average costs (AC) at 50,000 bushels per firm were less than price.

Now suppose that 600 new firms are attracted by these high profits and enter the industry. Each

FIGURE 7

A Shift in the Industry Supply Curve Caused by the Entry of New Firms

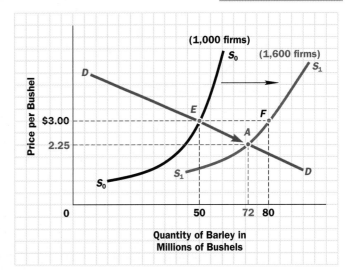

Quantity of Barley in Millions of Bushels

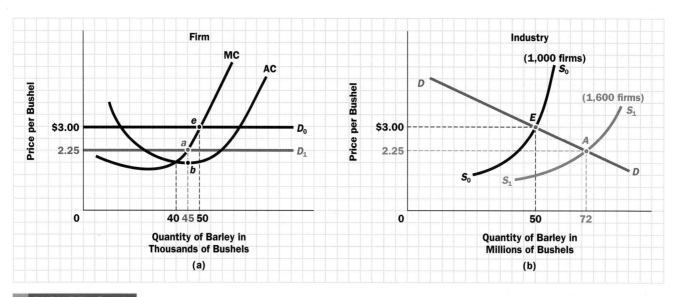

faces the cost structure indicated by the AC and MC curves in Figure 8(a). As a result of the new entrants' production, the industry supply curve in Figure 8(b) shifts to the right, and price falls to $2.25 per bushel. Because the height of the firm's horizontal demand curve is, as we have seen, equal to the industry price, the firm's demand curve must now move down to the blue line D_1 *corresponding to the reduced market price.* Firms in the industry react to this demand shift and its associated lower price. As we see in Figure 8(a), each firm reduces its output to 45,000 bushels (point *a*). But now there are 1,600 firms, so total industry output is 45,000 bushels × 1,600 firms = 72 million bushels, point *A* in Figure 8(b).

At point *a* in Figure 8(a), some profits remain available because the $2.25 price still exceeds average cost (point *b* is below point *a*). Thus, the entry process is not yet complete. New firms will stop appearing only when all profits have been competed away. The two panels of Figure 9 show the perfectly competitive firm and the perfectly competitive industry in long-run equilibrium. Only when entry shifts the industry supply curve so far to the right—S_2S_2 in Figure 9(b)—that each individual firm faces a demand curve that has fallen to the level of minimum average cost—point *m* in Figure 9(a)—will all profits be eradicated and entry cease.[4]

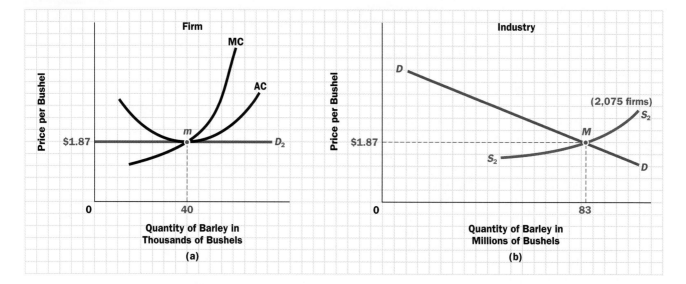

[4] If the original short-run equilibrium had involved losses instead of profits, firms would have exited from the industry, shifting the industry supply curve inward, until all losses were eradicated, and we would end up in a position exactly like Figure 9. *Exercise:* To test your understanding, draw the version of Figure 8 that corresponds to this case.

At the equilibrium point, *m*, in Panel (a), each firm picks its own output level to maximize its profit. As a result, for each firm *P* = MC. But free entry also forces AC to equal *P* in the long run—point *M* in Panel (b) of Figure 9—because if *P* were not equal to AC, firms would either earn profits or suffer losses. That would mean, in turn, that firms would find it profitable to enter or leave the industry, which is not compatible with industry equilibrium. Thus:

> When a perfectly competitive industry is in long-run equilibrium, firms maximize profits so that *P* = MC, and entry forces the price down until it is tangent to the firm's long-run average cost curve (*P* = AC). As a result, in long-run perfectly competitive equilibrium it is always true that for each firm:

$$P = MC = AC$$

Thus, even though every firm earns zero (economic) profit, profits are at the maximum that is sustainable.[5]

Zero Economic Profit: The Opportunity Cost of Capital

Why would there be any firms in the industry *at all* if in the long run they could make no profits? The answer is that the zero profit concept used in economics does not mean the same thing that it does in ordinary, everyday usage. We have already encountered this and discussed its relevance in Chapter 8 (pages 171–174). Here we will explain this important point in a slightly different way.

We have noted repeatedly that when economists measure average cost, they include the cost of *all* of the firm's inputs, *including the opportunity cost of the capital (the funds) or any other inputs, such as labour, provided by the firm's owners.* Because the firm may not make explicit payments to some of the people who provide it with capital, this element of cost may not be picked up by the firm's accountants. So what economists call zero **economic profit** will correspond to a *positive* amount of profit as measured by conventional accounting techniques. For example, if investors can earn 15 percent by lending their funds elsewhere, then the firm must earn a 15 percent rate of return to cover its opportunity cost of capital. The chance for investors to earn 15 percent on their money by putting it into the firm is what attracts them to do so. True, the 15 percent return is no more than the investors can earn by putting their money elsewhere, but that does not make their 15 percent receipt unattractive.

Because economists consider the 15 percent opportunity cost in this example to be the *cost of the firm's capital,* they include it in the AC curve. If the firm cannot earn at least 15 percent on its capital, funds will not be made available to it, because investors can earn greater returns elsewhere. To break even—to earn zero *economic profit*—a firm must earn enough not only to cover the cost of labour, fuel, and raw materials but also the cost of its funds, including the opportunity cost of any funds supplied by the owners of the firm.

An example will illustrate how economic profit and conventional accounting profit differ. Suppose that Canada Savings Bonds pay 8 percent interest, and the owner of a small shop earns 6 percent on her business investment. This shopkeeper might see a 6 percent profit, but an economist would see a 2 percent loss on every dollar she has invested in her business. By keeping her money tied up in her firm, the shop owner gives up the chance to buy government bonds and receive an 8 percent return. With this explanation of economic profit, we can understand the logic behind the zero profit condition for the long-run industry equilibrium.

> Zero profit in the economic sense simply means that firms are earning a return, but that return is just the same as the normal, economy-wide rate of profit in the accounting sense. This result is guaranteed, in the long run, under perfect competition by freedom of entry and exit.

Economic profit equals net earnings, in the accountant's sense, minus the opportunity costs of capital and of any other inputs supplied by the firm's owners.

---

[5] *Exercise:* Show what happens to the equilibrium of the firm and of the industry in Figure 9 if a rise in consumer income leads to an outward shift in the industry demand curve.

■ The Long-Run Industry Supply Curve

We have now seen basically what lies behind the supply-demand analysis that we first introduced in Chapter 4. Only one thing remains to be explained. Figures 5 through 8 depicted short-run industry supply curves and short-run equilibrium. However, because Figure 9 describes long-run perfectly competitive equilibrium, its industry supply curve must also pertain to the long run.

How does the long-run *industry* supply curve relate to the short-run supply curve? The answer is implicit in what we have just discussed. The long-run industry supply curve evolves from the short-run supply curve via two simultaneous processes. First, new firms enter or some existing ones exit, which shifts the short-run industry supply curve toward its long-run position. Second, and concurrently, as in the long run each firm in the industry is freed from its fixed commitments, the cost curves pertinent to its decisions become its long-run cost curves rather than its short-run cost curves. For example, consider a company that was stuck in the short run with a plant designed to serve 20,000 customers, even though it is now fortunate enough to have 25,000 customers. When it is time to replace the old plant, management will want to build a new plant that can serve the larger number of customers more conveniently, efficiently, and cheaply. The reduced cost that results from the larger plant is the pertinent cost to both the firm and the industry in the long run.

Finally, let us note that the long-run supply curve of the perfectly competitive industry (S_2S_2 in Figure 9) must be identical to the industry's long-run *average* cost curve. This is because in the long run, as we have seen, economic profit must be zero. The price the industry charges cannot exceed the long-run average cost (LRAC) of supplying that quantity because any excess of price over LRAC would constitute a profit opportunity that would have attracted new firms and driven price down to average cost. Similarly, price cannot be below LRAC because firms would then have refused to continue to supply that output at this price, output would have fallen, driving price up until it equalled average cost. Therefore, for each possible long-run quantity supplied, the price must equal the industry's long-run average cost. Thus, this long-run industry supply curve is the industry's average cost curve, and that is the cost curve relevant for determination of long-run equilibrium price and quantity in a standard supply–demand diagram.

These ideas are illustrated in Figure 10, in which the short-run industry supply curve, *SS*, lies above and to the left of the long-run average cost curve, LRAC. Consider any industry output—say, 70 million bushels of barley per year. At that output, the long-run average cost is $1.50 per bushel (point *A*). But if the price charged by farmers were given by the short-run supply curve for that output—that is, $2.62 per bushel (point *B*)—then the firms would earn $1.12 in economic profit on each and every bushel they sold.

Such economic profits would induce other firms to enter the industry, which would force prices downward as the industry supply curve shifted outward. As long as this shift did not take *SS* all the way down to LRAC, some economic profits would remain, and so entry would continue. Thus, *SS* must continue to fall until it reaches the position of the long-run average cost curve. Then and only then will entry of new firms cease and long-run equilibrium be attained.

The long-run supply curve of the perfectly competitive industry is also the industry's long-run average cost curve. The industry is driven to that supply curve by the entry or exit of firms and by the adjustment of firms already in the industry.

FIGURE 10

Short-Run Industry Supply and Long-Run Industry Average Cost

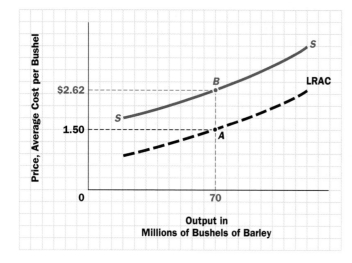

Output in
Millions of Bushels of Barley

POLICY DEBATE

Should Government Regulators Use Perfect Competition as a Guide?

As we have seen here and will discuss further in Chapter 14, perfect competition displays the market mechanism at its best. It prevents firms from earning excess profits, it forces firms to produce the output quantity at which AC is as low as possible, and it has other virtues as well.

As we will see in Chapters 11 and 12, markets where monopoly or oligopoly prevail are very different from perfect competition. In monopolistic or oligopolistic markets, a few large firms may charge high prices that yield large profits, and they may produce output quantities that do not match consumer preferences. Consequently (see Chapter 13), such industries are often *regulated* by government agencies.

But just what should regulation force monopoly or oligopoly firms to do? Should it force them to behave like perfectly competitive firms? Should it force their prices to equal marginal costs? Should it try to break them up into thousands of tiny enterprises?

No one believes that government regulation should go quite that far. Indeed, some

SOURCE: Wendy Kaveney Photography/Shutterstock

economists and others argue that perfect competition is an undesirable and, indeed, impossible goal for such regulated industries.

For example, if those industries are characterized by economies of scale, then breaking them into small firms will raise their costs and consumers will have to pay more, not less. Moreover, as we saw in Chapter 7, where there are economies of scale, the average cost curve must go downhill—the larger the firm's output, the lower its average cost. So marginal cost must be below average cost (see the appendix to Chapter 8 for a review), and a price equal to marginal cost must also be below average cost. Thus, where there are economies of scale, if the firm is forced to charge a price equal to marginal cost it will be forced to go bankrupt!

Even so, many regulators, economists, and others believe that perfect competition is so desirable a state of affairs that regulated firms should be required to come as close to it as possible in their behaviour.

■ PERFECT COMPETITION AND ECONOMIC EFFICIENCY

Economists have long admired perfect competition as a thing of beauty, like one of King Tutankhamen's funerary masks. (And it's just as rare!) Adam Smith's invisible hand produces results that are considered *efficient* in a variety of senses that we will examine carefully in Chapter 14. But one aspect of the great efficiency of perfect competition follows immediately from the analysis we have just completed.

We saw earlier that when the firm is in long-run equilibrium, it must have $P = MC = AC$, as indicated by Figure 9(a). But we know that MC does not equal AC at any point on the AC curve that is moving either downhill or uphill (see the appendix to Chapter 8 if you need to be reminded why this is so). This implies that the long-run competitive equilibrium of the firm will occur at the lowest point (the horizontal point) on its long-run AC curve, which is also where that curve is tangent to the firm's horizontal demand curve.

> In long-run perfectly competitive equilibrium, every firm produces at the minimum point on its average cost curve. Thus, the outputs of perfectly competitive industries are produced at the lowest possible cost to society.

An example will show why it is most efficient if each firm in a perfectly competitive industry produces at the point where AC is as small as possible. Suppose the industry is producing 12 million bushels of barley. This amount can be produced by 120 farms each producing 100,000 bushels, or by 100 farms each producing 120,000 bushels, or by 200 farms each producing 60,000 bushels. Of course, the job can also be done instead by other numbers of farms, but for simplicity let us consider only these three possibilities.

Suppose that the AC figures for the firm are as shown in Table 3. Suppose, moreover, that an output of 100,000 bushels corresponds to the lowest point on the AC curve, with an AC of 70 cents per bushel. Which is the cheapest way for the industry to produce its 12-million-bushel output? In other words, what is the cost-minimizing number of firms for the job? Looking at Column (5) of Table 3, we see that the industry's total cost of producing the 12-million-bushel output is as low as possible if 120 firms each produce the cost-minimizing output of 100,000 bushels.

Why is this so? The answer is not difficult to see. For any *given* industry output, Q, because Q is constant, *total* industry cost (= AC × Q) will be as small as possible if and only if AC (for *each* firm) is as small as possible—that is, if the number of firms doing the job is such that each is producing the output at which AC is as low as possible.

That this kind of cost efficiency characterizes perfect competition in the long run can be seen in Figures 8 and 9. Before full long-run equilibrium is reached (Figure 8), firms may not be producing in the least costly way. For example, the 50 million bushels being produced by 1,000 firms at points *e* and *E* in Figures 8(a) and 8(b) could be produced more cheaply by more firms, each producing a smaller volume, because the point of minimum average cost lies to the left of point *e* in Figure 8(a). This problem is rectified in the long run by the entry of new firms seeking profit. We see in Figure 9 that after the entry process is complete, every firm is producing at its most efficient (lowest AC) level —40,000 bushels.

As Adam Smith might have put it, even though each farmer cares only about his or her own profits, the barley-farming industry as a whole is *guided by an invisible hand* to produce the amount of barley that society wants at the lowest possible cost.

TABLE 3				
Average Cost for the Firm and Total Cost for the Industry				
(1)	(2)	(3)	(4)	(5)
Firm's Output	Firm's Average Cost	Number of Firms	Industry Output	Total Industry Cost
60,000	$0.90	200	12,000,000	$10,800,000
100,000	**0.70**	**120**	**12,000,000**	**8,400,000**
120,000	0.80	100	12,000,000	9,600,000

Note: Output is in bushels.

PUZZLE RESOLVED: *Which Is Better to Cut Pollution— The Carrot or the Stick?*

We end by returning to the puzzle with which the chapter began, because we now have all the tools needed to solve it. Remember that we asked: Should polluters be *taxed* on their emissions, or should they, instead, be offered *subsidies* to cut emissions? A subsidy—that is, a government payment to the firms that comply—would indeed induce firms to cut their emissions. Nevertheless, the paradoxical result is likely to be an *increase* in total pollution. Let us see now why this is so.

First, we must carefully distinguish the effects of the pollution tax and pollution subsidy on the individual firm from the effects on the entire industry. Let us start by examining the effects of a pollution tax on an individual firm. Table 4 shows the total revenues and total costs of a firm, as well as its total profits. Suppose that each unit of output is sold at $4. With no pollution tax or subsidy, the firm will maximize its profits when it produces 50,000 units per year, making a $75,000 total profit. Suppose now that the government imposes a pollution tax of $1.50 per unit of output, as shown in Column (5), assessing that each unit of output generates a given amount of pollution emission. This will increase the firm's total costs and hence reduce total profits, which will now be given by Column (6). The tax will induce the firm to reduce its production to 30,000 units per year, since this is now the output level at which profits are maximized. Despite this, profits are down to $10,000.

But suppose the government chooses the carrot instead of the stick, providing firms with a subsidy of $1.50 for each unit of reduction in their output, with a maximum of $75,000 if they reduce their production by 50,000 units. The subsidy being awarded for each production level is shown in Column (7) of Table 4, and the profits

			TABLE 4				
		Profits with Pollution Tax and with Pollution Subsidy					
(1)	(2)	(3)	(4)	(5)	(6)	(7)	(8)
		No Tax and No Subsidy		With Pollution Tax		With Pollution Subsidy	
Total Quantity	Total Revenue	Total Costs	Total Profits	Tax	Total Profits	Subsidy	Total Profits
0	$ 0	$ 20	$ –20	$ 0	$ –20	$75	$55
10	40	30	10	15	–5	60	70
20	80	45	35	30	5	45	80
30	120	65	55	45	**10**	30	**85**
40	160	92	68	60	8	15	83
50	200	125	**75**	75	0	0	75
60	240	170	70	90	–20	0	70
70	280	220	60	105	–55	0	60

Note: Quantity is in thousands of units; dollars are in thousands.

of the firm, taking into account the subsidies, are shown in Column (8). The subsidy will also induce the firm to reduce its production to 30,000 units per year, since this is now the output level for which profits are maximized (profits can now be as high as $85,000). Thus, whether there is a pollution tax or a pollution subsidy makes no difference to the individual firm: In both cases, output will be reduced and, hence, pollution emissions of the individual firm will be reduced. This surprising result is called the Coase theorem, named after Ronald Coase (1910–), the British economist who taught at the University of Chicago and who first provided this insight.

But the analysis should not stop there. We now must figure out what happens at the industry level. In Figure 11, we have drawn the industry long-run average cost curve (LRAC), *XX*. We now know that this must also be the industry's long-run supply curve, because if the supply curve lies above (to the left of) LRAC, then economic profits will be earned and entry will drive the supply curve to the right. The opposite would occur if the supply was below and to the right of LRAC.

Now, a tax on business firms clearly raises the long-run average costs of the industry. Suppose that it shifts the LRAC, and thus the long-run supply curve, upward from *XX* to *TT* in the graph. This change will move the equilibrium point from *E* to *B* and reduce polluting output from Q_e to Q_b. Similarly, a subsidy reduces average cost, so it shifts the LRAC and the long-run supply curve downward and to the right (from *XX* to *SS*). This change moves the equilibrium point from *E* to *A* and *raises polluting output to* Q_a.

Our paradoxical result follows from the presumption that the more *output* a polluting industry produces, the more *pollution* it will emit. Under the tax on emissions, equilibrium moves from *E* to *B*, so the polluting output falls from Q_e to Q_b. Thus, emissions will fall—just as common sense leads us to expect. But, with the subsidy, industry output will *rise* from Q_e to Q_a. Thus, contrary to intuition and despite the fact that each firm emits less, the industry must pollute more!

What explains this strange result? The answer is the *entry* of new firms. The subsidy will initially bring economic profits to the polluters. As we can see in Table 4, the profits of each individual firm will increase from $75,000 in the no-tax, no-subsidy

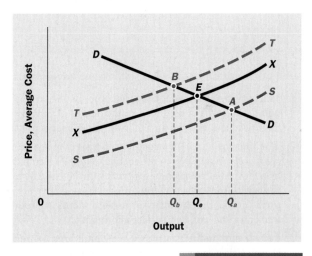

FIGURE 11

Taxes versus Subsidies as Incentives to Cut Pollution

optimal output position to $85,000 in the profit-maximizing situation with a government subsidy. The higher profits thus encourage more polluters to open up for business. Each individual firm produces less and pollutes less than before, but in the long run the entry of new firms, induced by the higher profits arising from the pollution subsidy, drives down the price of the pollution-producing good, and hence leads to higher demanded quantities for this good. Figure 11 tells us that, in a perfectly competitive industry, subsidies *must* lead to increased pollution.

■ A WORD OF WARNING

Now that we have extolled the virtues of the perfect competition market structure, and hence the virtues of free markets, a word of warning is necessary. As pointed out at the beginning of the chapter, there are few markets or industries that meet the stringent requirements of perfect competition. In fact, even in those industries that have plenty of competition—with several small sellers and buyers, a homogenous product, and no barriers to entry—information may not be readily available. In this case, we can speak instead of **pure competition.**

Pure competition is a market structure that has all of the features of perfect competition, except for perfect information.

In the real world, information is often lacking, or asymmetric, and this will induce some market failures. Also, the existence of high transaction costs (between the buyers and the sellers, or the costs of enforcing contracts), which so far have not been taken into consideration, can lead to further market failures. Finally, the Canadian economy, as most foreign economies, is dominated by large firms that purposefully attempt to evade the laws of supply and demand by exercising market power. All of these features imply that the real world may not behave in accordance with the strictures of perfect competition. This is why we need to go beyond this idealized market structure, as we do in the following chapters.

SUMMARY

1. **Markets** are classified into several types depending on the number of firms in the industry, the degree of similarity of their products, and the possibility of impediments to entry.

2. The four main market structures discussed by economists are *monopoly* (single-firm production), *oligopoly* (production by a few firms), *monopolistic competition* (production by many firms with somewhat different products), and *perfect competition* (production by many firms with identical products, free entry and exit, and perfect information).

3. Few, if any, industries satisfy the conditions of **perfect competition** exactly, although some come close. Perfect competition is studied because it is easy to analyze and because it represents a case in which the market mechanism works well, so that it is useful as a yardstick to measure the performance of other market forms.

4. The demand curve of the perfectly competitive firm is horizontal because its output is such a small share of the industry's production that it cannot affect price. With a horizontal demand curve, price, average revenue, and marginal revenue are all equal.

5. The short-run equilibrium of the perfectly competitive firm is at the level of output that maximizes profits—that is, where MR = MC = price. This equilibrium may involve either a profit or a loss.

6. The short-run **supply curve** of the perfectly competitive firm is the portion of its marginal cost curve that lies above its average **variable cost** curve.

7. The industry's short-run supply curve under perfect competition is the horizontal sum of the supply curves of all of its firms.

8. In the long-run equilibrium of the perfectly competitive industry, freedom of entry forces each firm to earn zero **economic profit**, or no more than the firm's capital could earn elsewhere (the opportunity cost of the capital).

9. Industry equilibrium under perfect competition is at the point where the industry supply and demand curves intersect.

10. In long-run equilibrium under perfect competition, the firm chooses output such that average cost, marginal cost, and price are all equal. Output is at the point of minimum average cost. The firm's demand curve is tangent to its average cost curve at its minimum point.

11. The competitive industry's long-run supply curve coincides with its long-run average cost curve.

12. Both a tax on the emission of pollutants and a subsidy payment for reductions in those emissions induce firms to cut emissions. However, under perfect competition, a subsidy

leads to the entry of more polluting firms and the likelihood of a net increase in total emissions by the industry.

13. **Pure competition** entails production of a homogeneous product by several small firms, with free entry and exit, but without perfect information.

KEY TERMS

Market   209

Perfect competition   212

Price taker   213

Variable cost   216

Supply curve of a firm   218

Supply curve of an industry   219

Economic profit   223

Pure competition   228

TEST YOURSELF

1. Under what circumstances might you expect the demand curve of the firm to be:
   a. Vertical?
   b. Horizontal?
   c. Negatively sloping?
   d. Positively sloping?

2. Explain why $P = MC$ in the short-run equilibrium of the perfectly competitive firm, whereas in long-run equilibrium $P = MC = AC$.

3. Explain why it is not sensible to close a business firm if it earns zero economic profits.

4. If the firm's lowest average cost is $48 and the corresponding average variable cost is $24, what does it pay a perfectly competitive firm to do if:
   a. The market price is $49?
   b. The price is $30?
   c. The price is $8?

5. If the market price in a competitive industry were above its equilibrium level, what would you expect to happen?

DISCUSSION QUESTIONS

1. Explain why a perfectly competitive firm does not expand its sales without limit if its horizontal demand curve indicates that it can sell as much as it desires at the current market price.

2. Explain why a demand curve is also a curve of average revenue. Recalling that when an average revenue curve is neither rising nor falling, marginal revenue must equal average revenue, explain why it is always true that $P = MR = AR$ for the perfectly competitive firm.

3. Regarding the four attributes of perfect competition (many small firms, freedom of entry, standardized product, and perfect information):
   a. Which is primarily responsible for the fact that the demand curve of a perfectly competitive firm is horizontal?
   b. Which is primarily responsible for the firm's zero economic profits in long-run equilibrium?

4. We indicated in this chapter that the MC curve cuts the AVC (average variable cost) curve at the *minimum* point of the latter. Explain why this must be so. (*Hint:* Because marginal costs are, by definition, entirely composed of variable costs, the MC curve can be considered the curve of *marginal variable costs*. Apply the general relationships between marginals and averages explained in the appendix to Chapter 8.)

5. **(More difficult)** In this chapter we stated that the firm's MC curve goes through the lowest point of its AC curve and also through the lowest point of its AVC curve. Because the AVC curve lies below the AC curve, how can both of these statements be true? Why are they true? (*Hint:* See Figure 4.)

MONOPOLY

The price of monopoly is upon every occasion the highest which can be got.

ADAM SMITH (1723–1790), 1776[1]

I n Chapter 10, we described an idealized market system in which all industries are perfectly competitive, and in Chapters 14 and 16 we will describe the virtues of that system. In this chapter, we turn to one of the blemishes—the possibility that some industries may be monopolized—and to the consequences of such a flaw in the market system.

We will indeed find that monopolized markets do not match the ideal performance of perfectly competitive markets. Under monopoly, the market mechanism no longer allocates society's resources efficiently. This suggests that government actions to constrain monopoly may sometimes be able to improve the workings of the market—a possibility that we will study in detail in Chapter 13.

But, first, as usual, we start with a real-life puzzle.

CONTENTS

---

[1] But Adam Smith's statement is incorrect! See Discussion Question 4 at the end of the chapter.

PUZZLE: *What Happened to Bell Canada's "Natural Monopoly" in Telephone Service?*

We are all keenly aware of the strong competition in the market for telephone service. How can we miss it? A plethora of firms (old and new) offering telephone service of one kind or another besiege us with television commercials, popup ads on the Internet, and telephone sales pitches. The days of "Ma Bell," the affectionate nickname for Bell Canada—which used to be virtually the only provider of telephone service—are long gone and now seem as quaint and old-fashioned as the horse and buggy. What was it that allowed competition in this industry, which had always been considered by some as a classic example of a "natural monopoly" against which no competitor could be expected to survive (see a fuller definition below)? In this chapter you will learn about the causes and consequences of monopoly and, in the process, obtain insights about the answers to this question.

SOURCE: © H. Armstrong Roberts/Corbis.

MONOPOLY *DEFINED*

A **pure monopoly** is an industry in which there is only one supplier of a product for which there are no close substitutes and in which it is very difficult or impossible for another firm to coexist.

The definition of **pure monopoly** has rather stringent requirements. First, only one firm can be present in the industry—the monopolist must be "the only game in town." Second, no close substitutes for the monopolist's product may exist. Thus, even a city's sole provider of natural gas is not considered a pure monopoly, because other firms offer close substitutes such as heating oil and electricity. Third, there must be some reason why entry and survival of potential competitors is extremely unlikely. Otherwise, monopolistic behaviour and its excessive economic profits could not persist.

These rigid requirements make pure monopoly a rarity in the real world. The telephone company and the post office used to be examples of one-firm industries that faced little or no effective competition, at least in some of their activities. But most firms face at least a degree of competition from substitute products. If only one railroad serves a particular town, it still must compete with bus lines, trucking companies, and airlines. Similarly, the producer of a particular brand of beer may be the only supplier of that specific product, but the firm is not a pure monopolist by our definition. Because many other beers are close substitutes for its product, the firm will lose much of its business if it tries to raise its price far above the prices of other brands.

There is another reason why the unrestrained pure monopoly of economic theory is rarely found in practice. We will learn in this chapter that pure monopoly can have a number of undesirable features. So in markets in which pure monopoly might otherwise prevail, the government has often intervened to prevent monopolization or to limit the discretion of the monopolist to set its price.

If we do not study pure monopoly for its descriptive realism, why *do* we study it? Because, like perfect competition, pure monopoly is a market form that is easier to analyze than the more common market structures that we will consider in the next chapter. Thus, pure monopoly is a stepping stone toward more realistic models. Also, we will understand the possible evils of monopoly most clearly if we examine monopoly in its purest form.

Sources of Monopoly: Barriers to Entry and Cost Advantages

The key requirement for preservation of a monopoly is exclusion of potential rivals from the market. One way to achieve this result is by means of some specific impediment that prevents the establishment of a new firm in the industry. Economists call such impediments **barriers to entry.** Here are some examples.

1. Legal Restrictions   The Canada Post, a Crown corporation, has a monopoly position because the federal government has given it one. Private companies that may want to compete with the postal service directly are prohibited from doing so by law. Local monopolies of various kinds are sometimes established either because the government grants some special privilege to a single firm (for example, the right to operate a food concession in a municipal stadium) or prevents other firms from entering the industry (for instance, by licensing only a single cable television supplier). Monopolies are also sometimes created when a number of firms in a crucial industry are nationalized, as was the case with Hydro-Québec in 1963. As a result, it became one of the largest public electricity utilities in North America.

Barriers to entry are attributes of a market that make it more difficult or expensive for a new firm to open for business than it was for the firms already present in that market.

2. Patents   Some firms benefit from a special, but important, class of legal impediments to entry called **patents.** To encourage inventiveness, the government gives exclusive production rights for a period of time to the inventors of certain products. As long as a patent is in effect, the firm has a protected position and holds a monopoly. For example, Xerox Corporation for many years had (but no longer has) a monopoly in plain-paper copying. Most pharmaceutical companies also obtain monopolies on the medicines they discover. Montreal-based Abbott Laboratories, for instance, has a patent on Humira, a drug that reduces the symptoms of rheumatoid arthritis, generating sales of $1 billion in 2006. This patent expires in 2018, at which point the door will be open for competition from generic makers of the drug. In Canada, there is a huge debate about the length of pharmaceutical patent rights. Canada's research-based pharmaceutical companies argue that Canada's patent protection period is too short, compared with elsewhere, thus impeding drug development. Defenders of the present rules argue against change, on the basis of the merits of competition and low drug prices.

A patent is a privilege granted to an inventor, whether an individual or a firm, that for a specified period of time prohibits anyone else from producing or using that invention without the permission of the holder of the patent.

3. Control of a Scarce Resource or Input   If a certain commodity can be produced only by using a rare input, a company that gains control of the source of that input can establish a monopoly position for itself. Real examples are not easy to find, but the South African diamond syndicate used to come close. The De Beers group, located in Johannesburg, used to control more than 80 percent of the market for diamonds, but now, following diamond discoveries in Canada and Russia, this proportion has fallen to about 60 percent. Future competition might come from laboratory-created diamonds that, according to some sources, are so perfect that many experts are unable to distinguish them from natural diamonds.

4. Deliberately Erected Entry Barriers   A firm may deliberately attempt to make entry into the industry difficult for others. One way is to start costly lawsuits against new rivals, sometimes on trumped-up charges. Another is to spend exorbitant amounts on advertising, as Microsoft did in August 1995 when it launched its Windows 95 operating system thus forcing any potential entrant to match that expenditure.

5. Large Sunk Costs   Entry into an industry will, obviously, be very risky if it requires a large investment, especially if that investment is *sunk*—meaning that it cannot be recouped for a considerable period of time. Thus, the need for a large sunk investment discourages entry into an industry. Many analysts therefore consider sunk costs to be the most important type of "naturally imposed" barrier to entry. For example, the high sunk costs involved in jet airplane production helped Boeing Corporation enjoy a monopoly in the top end of the long-range, wide-body jet airliner market for many years after the launch of the 747 jumbo jet. The rival aircraft manufacturer, Airbus, which with European governments' sponsorship has been able to afford the high investments, has since encroached on Boeing's territory, and hopes to create a monopoly of its own with its new A380 airplane, the "superjumbo" jet, which can seat as many as 550 passengers.

Such barriers can keep rivals out and ensure that an industry is monopolized. But monopoly can also occur in the absence of barriers to entry if a single firm has substantial cost advantages over potential rivals. Two examples of attributes of production that create such advantages are technical superiority and economies of scale.

6. Technical Superiority   A firm whose technological expertise vastly exceeds that of any potential competitor can, for a period of time, maintain a monopoly position. For example, IBM Corporation for many years had little competition in the computer business mainly because of its technological virtuosity. Of course, competitors eventually caught up. More recently, Microsoft Corporation has established a commanding position in the software business, especially for operating systems, through a combination of inventiveness and marketing wizardry.

7. Economies of Scale   If mere size gives a large firm a cost advantage over a smaller rival, it is likely to be impossible for anyone to compete with the largest firm in the industry.

■ Natural Monopoly

A natural monopoly is an industry in which advantages of large-scale production make it possible for a single firm to produce the entire output of the market at lower average cost than a number of firms, each producing a smaller quantity.

This last type of cost advantage is important enough to merit special attention. In some industries, economies of large-scale production or economies of scope (from simultaneous production of a large number of related items, such as car motors and bodies, truck parts, and so on) are so extreme that the industry's output can be produced at far lower cost by a single large firm than by a number of smaller firms. In such cases, we say there is a **natural monopoly**. Once a firm becomes large enough relative to the size of the market for its product, its natural cost advantage may well drive the competition out of business whether or not anyone in the relatively large firm has evil intentions.

A monopoly need not be a large firm if the market is small enough. *What matters is the size of a single firm relative to the total market demand for the product.* Thus, a small bank in a rural town or a gasoline station at a lightly travelled intersection may both be natural monopolies, even though they are very small firms.

Figure 1 shows the sort of average cost (AC) curve that leads to natural monopoly. It has a negative slope throughout, meaning that the more a firm in this industry produces, the lower its average cost will be. Suppose that any firm producing video games has this AC curve and that, initially, there are two firms in the industry. Suppose also that the larger firm is producing 2 million games at an average cost of $25 (point *A*), and the smaller firm is producing 1 million games at an average cost of $30 (point

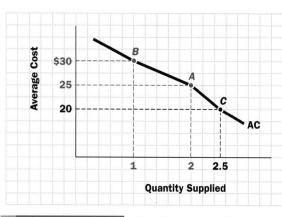

FIGURE 1

Natural Monopoly

Note: Average cost is in dollars per unit; quantity is in millions.

B). Clearly, the larger firm can drive the smaller firm out of business if it offers its output for sale at a price below $30 (so the smaller firm can match the price only by running a loss) but above $25 (so it can still make a profit). Hence, a monopoly may arise "naturally," even in the absence of barriers to entry.

Once the monopoly is established (producing, say, 2.5 million video games—point *C*), the economies of scale act as a very effective deterrent to entry because no new entrant can hope to match the low average cost ($20) of the existing monopoly firm. Of course, the public interest may be well served if the natural monopolist uses its low cost to keep its prices low. The danger, however, is that the firm may raise its price once rivals have left the industry.

Many public utilities operate as *regulated* monopoly suppliers for exactly this reason. It is believed that the technology of producing or distributing their output enables them to achieve substantial cost reductions by producing large quantities. It is therefore often considered preferable to permit these firms to achieve lower costs by having the entire market to themselves, and then to subject them and their prices to regulatory supervision, rather than to break them up into a number of competing firms. We will examine the issues connected with regulation of natural monopolies in detail in Chapter 13. To summarize this discussion:

> There are two basic reasons why a monopoly may exist: barriers to entry, such as legal restrictions and patents, and cost advantages of superior technology or large-scale operation that lead to natural monopoly. It is generally considered undesirable to break up a large firm whose costs are low because of scale economies. But barriers to entry are usually considered to be against the public interest except where they are believed to offer offsetting advantages, as in the case of patents.

The rest of this chapter analyzes how a monopoly can be expected to behave if its freedom of action is not limited by the government.

■ THE MONOPOLIST'S SUPPLY DECISION

A monopoly firm does not have a "supply curve," as we usually define the term. Unlike a firm operating under perfect competition, a monopoly is not at the mercy of the market; the firm does not have to accept the market's price as beyond its control and

Is the Software Industry a Natural Monopoly?

Some leading economists believe the software industry is prone to monopoly. Three influences may incline the industry in this direction, as an article in *InfoWorld* describes:

> One factor is diminishing costs: while the first copy of a software program costs millions to produce, the cost to produce subsequent copies is negligible. The second factor is the network effect in which the value of software increases by the number of people using it and developers creating applications for it. The third factor is the lock-in effect, in which the cost of switching to another system (installation, training, application compatibility) persuades users to stick with current systems. . . . These forces create natural barriers to entry for newcomers, and Microsoft's operating-system dominance is a prime example.

SOURCE: Lynda Radosevich, "Top of the News: How the Software Industry Creates Monopolies," *InfoWorld* 20 (May 25, 1998).

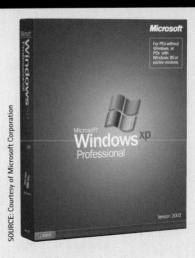

SOURCE: Courtesy of Microsoft Corporation

adjust its output level to that externally fixed price, as the supply curve assumes. Instead, it has the power to set the price, or rather to select the price–quantity combination on the demand curve that suits its interests best.

Put differently, a monopolist is not a *price taker* that must simply adapt to whatever price the forces of supply and demand decree. Rather, a monopolist is a *price maker* that can, if so inclined, raise the product price. Thus, the standard supply–demand analysis described in Chapter 4 does not apply to the determination of price or output in a monopolized industry. But it remains true that, for whatever price the monopolist selects, the demand curve for the product indicates how much consumers will buy.

The demand curve of a monopoly, unlike that of a perfectly competitive firm, is normally downward sloping, not horizontal. This means that a price rise will not cause the monopoly to lose *all* of its customers. But any increase will cost it *some* business. The higher the price, the less the monopolist can expect to sell.

> The market cannot impose a price on a monopolist as it imposes a price on the price-taking perfectly competitive firm. But the monopolist cannot select both price and the quantity it sells. In accord with the demand curve, the higher the price it sets, the less it can sell.

In deciding what price best serves the firm's interests, the monopolist must consider whether profits can be increased by raising or lowering the product's price. Because of the downward-sloping demand curve, the sky is not the limit in pricing by a monopolist. Some price increases are not profitable because they lead to disproportionately large reductions in sales of the products.

In our analysis, we will assume that the monopolist wants to maximize profits. That does not mean that a monopoly is guaranteed a positive profit. If the demand for its product is low, or if the firm is inefficient, even a monopoly may lose money and eventually be forced out of business. However, if a monopoly firm does earn a positive profit, it may be able to keep on doing so in the long run because there will be no entry that competes the profits away.

We can use the methods of Chapter 8 to determine which price the profit-maximizing monopolist will prefer. To maximize profits, the monopolist must compare marginal revenue (the addition to total revenue resulting from a one-unit rise in output) with marginal cost (the addition to total cost resulting from that additional unit). Figure 2 shows a marginal cost (MC) curve and a marginal revenue (MR) curve for a typical monopolist. Recall that the firm's demand curve (DD) is also its average revenue (AR) curve. That is because if a firm sells Q units of output, selling every unit of output at the price P, then the average revenue brought in by a unit of output must be the price, P, because the average of a bunch of equal numbers must be that same number. Because the demand curve gives the price at which any particular quantity can be sold, it also automatically indicates the AR (= price) yielded by that quantity.

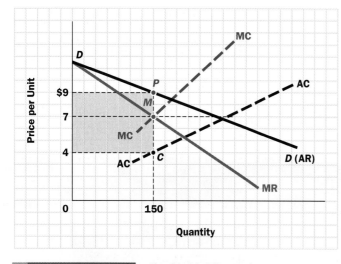

FIGURE 2

Note: Price is in dollars per unit.

Profit-Maximizing Equilibrium for a Monopolist

Notice that the marginal revenue curve is always below the demand curve, meaning that MR is always less than price (P). This important fact is easy to explain. The monopoly firm charges the same price to all of its customers. If the firm wants to increase sales by one unit, it must decrease the price somewhat to all of its customers. When it cuts the price to attract new sales, all previous customers also benefit. Thus, the additional revenue that the monopolist takes in when sales increase by one unit (*marginal revenue*) is the price that the firm collects from the new customer *minus the revenue that it loses by cutting the price paid by all of its old customers*. This means that MR is necessarily less than price; graphically, it implies that the MR curve is below the demand curve, as in Figure 2.

■ Determining the Profit-Maximizing Output

Like any other firm, the monopoly maximizes its profits by setting marginal revenue (MR) equal to marginal cost (MC). It selects point M in Figure 2, where output is 150 units. But point M does not tell us the monopoly price because, as we have just seen, price exceeds MR for a monopolist. To learn what price the monopolist charges, we must use the demand curve to find the price at which consumers are willing to purchase the profit-maximizing output of 150 units. The answer, we see, is given by the height of the demand curve at that output—it is given by point P directly above M. The monopoly price is $9 per unit. Not surprisingly, it exceeds both MR and MC (which are equal at $7).

The monopolist depicted in Figure 2 is earning a tidy profit. This profit is shown in the graph by the shaded rectangle whose height is the difference between price (point P) and average cost (point C) and whose width is the quantity produced (150 units). In the example, profits are $5 per unit, or $750.

To study the decisions of a profit-maximizing monopolist:

1. Find the output at which MR equals MC to select the profit-maximizing output level.

2. Find the height of the demand curve *at that level of output* to determine the corresponding price.

3. Compare the height of the demand curve with the height of the AC curve at that output to see whether the net result is an economic profit or a loss.

We also can show a monopolist's profit-maximization calculation numerically. In Table 1, the first two columns show the quantity and price figures that constitute this monopolist's demand curve. Column (3) shows total revenue (TR) for each output, which is the product of price times quantity. Thus, for 3 units of output, we have TR = $92 × 3 = $276. Column (4) shows marginal revenue (MR). For example, when output rises from 3 to 4 units, TR increases from $276 to $320, so MR is $320 − $276 = $44. Column (5) gives the monopolist's total cost for each level of output. Column (6) derives marginal cost (MC) from total cost (TC) in the usual way. Finally, by subtracting TC from TR for each level of output, we obtain total profit in Column (7).

The table brings out a number of important points. We note first in Columns (2) and (3) that a cut in price may increase or decrease total revenue. When output rises from 1 to 2 units, P falls from $140 to $107 and TR rises from $140 to $214. But when (between 5 and 6 units of output) P falls from $66 to $50, TR falls from $330 to $300. Next we observe, by comparing Columns (2) and (4), that after the first unit, price always exceeds marginal revenue (because the marginal revenue curve *must* lie below the downward-sloping demand [AR] curve). Finally, from Columns (4) and (6) we see that MC = MR = $44 when Q is between 3 and 4 units, indicating that this is the level of output that maximizes the monopolist's total profit. That is confirmed in Column (7) of the table, which shows that at this output profit reaches its highest level, $110, for any of the output quantities considered in the table.

TABLE 1
A Profit-Maximizing Monopolist's Price–Output Decision

		Revenue		Cost		Total Profit
(1) Q	(2) P	(3) TR = P × Q	(4) MR	(5) TC	(6) MC	(7) TR − TC
0	—	$ 0		$ 10		$−10
			$140		$60	
1	$140	140		70		70
			74		50	
2	107	214		120		94
			62		46	
3	92	276		166		**110**
			44		44	
4	80	320		210		**110**
			10		43	
5	66	330		253		77
			−30		45	
6	50	300		298		2

■ Comparing Monopoly and Perfect Competition

This completes our analysis of the monopolist's price–output decision. At this point, it is natural to wonder whether there is anything distinctive about the monopoly equilibrium. To find out, we need a standard of comparison. Perfect competition provides this standard because, as we will learn in Chapter 14, it is a theoretical benchmark of ideal performance against which other market structures can be judged. By comparing the results of monopoly with those of perfect competition, we will see why economists since Adam Smith have condemned monopoly as inefficient.

1. A Monopolist's Profit Persists   The first difference between competition and monopoly is a direct consequence of barriers to entry in monopoly. Profits such as those shown in Figure 2 would be competed away by free entry in a perfectly competitive market, because a positive profit would attract new competitors into the business. A competitive firm must earn *zero economic profit* in the long run; that is, it can earn only enough to cover its costs, including the opportunity cost of the owner's capital and labour. But higher **profit** *can* persist under **monopoly**—if the monopoly is protected from the arrival of new competitors by barriers to entry. This can, then, allow monopolists to grow wealthy at the expense of their consumers. But because people find such accumulations of wealth objectionable, monopoly is widely condemned. As a result, monopolies are generally regulated by government, which often limits the profits they can earn.

> **Monopoly profits** are any excess of the profits earned persistently by a monopoly firm over and above those that would be earned if the industry were perfectly competitive.

2. Monopoly Restricts Output to Raise Short-Run Price   Excess monopoly profit can be a problem. But economists believe that the second difference between competition and monopoly is even more worrisome:

> Compared with the perfectly competitive ideal, the monopolist restricts output and charges a higher price.

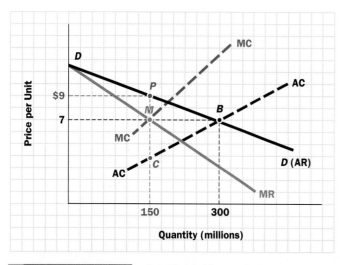

Note: Price is in dollars per unit.

FIGURE 3

Comparison of a Monopoly and a Perfectly Competitive Industry

To see that this is so, let us conduct the following thought experiment. Imagine that a court order breaks up the monopoly firm depicted in Figure 2 (and reproduced as Figure 3) into a large number of perfectly competitive firms. Suppose further that the industry demand curve is unchanged by this event and that the MC curve in Figure 3 is also the (horizontal) sum of the MC curves of all the newly created competitive firms. These may be unrealistic assumptions, as we will soon explain. However, they make it easy to compare the output–price combinations that would emerge in the short run under monopoly and perfect competition.

Before making our comparison, we must note that under monopoly, the firm and the industry are exactly the same entity. But under perfect competition, any one firm is just a small portion of the industry. So when we measure the performance of monopoly against that of perfect competition, we should compare the monopoly with the entire competitive industry, not with an individual competitive firm. In Figure 3, the monopolist's output is point *M* at which MC = MR. The long-run competitive output (point *B*) is greater than the monopoly's because it must be sufficiently large to yield zero economic profit (*P* = AR = AC).

It is self-evident and not very interesting to observe that the output of the monopolist is virtually certain to be larger than that of a tiny competitive *firm*. The interesting issue is how much of the entire industry's product gets into the hands of consumers under the two market forms—that is, how much output is produced by a monopoly as compared with the quantity provided by a similar competitive *industry*.

3. Monopoly Restricts Output to Raise Long-Run Price   As we have seen, monopoly output is determined by the profit-maximization requirement that MC = MR (point *M*). But as we learned in Chapter 10, long-run perfectly competitive equilibrium occurs at point *B* in Figure 3, where price and average cost are equal and economic profit is zero.

By comparing point *B* with the monopolist's equilibrium (point *M*), we see that the monopolist produces fewer units of output than would a competitive industry with the same demand and cost conditions. Because the demand curve slopes downward, producing less output means that the industry gets away with a higher price. The monopolist's price, indicated by point *P* on the demand curve and directly above *M*, exceeds the price that would result from perfect competition at point *B*. This is the essence of the truth behind the popular view that unregulated monopolists "gouge the public." The monopolist deliberately cuts back the amount of output he produces in order to make the product scarcer and thereby force its price upward.

We should note that matters will *always* turn out that way if the average cost curve has a positive slope between the monopoly output level and the competitive output level. That is because we know, in this case, that the MC curve must lie above the AC curve (to review why, see pages 172–173 of Chapter 8). We also have just seen that the MR curve must lie below the demand (AR) curve. It is clear, then, that the point where the MR curve meets the MC curve (the monopoly output) must always lie to the left of the output at which AC and AR meet (the competitive industry output). Consequently, monopoly output will always be the smaller of the two when the curves of the competitive and monopoly industries are identical. With monopoly output lower, its price will always be higher.

4. Monopoly Leads to Inefficient Resource Allocation

We conclude, then, that a monopoly will charge a higher price and produce a smaller output than will a competitive industry with the same demand and cost conditions. Why do economists find this situation so objectionable? Because, as we will learn in Chapter 14, a competitive industry devotes "just the right amount" of society's scarce resources to the production of its particular commodity. Therefore, if a monopolist produces less than a competitive industry, it must be producing too little.

We will see in Chapter 14 that efficiency in resource allocation requires that the marginal utility (MU) of each commodity be equal to its marginal cost. Also, perfect competition guarantees that:

$$MU = P \text{ and } MC = P, \text{ so } MU = MC$$

Under monopoly, consumers continue to maximize their own welfare by setting MU equal to *P*. But the monopoly producer sets MC equal to MR. Because MR is *below* the market price, *P*, we conclude that in a monopolized industry:

$$MU = P \text{ and } MC = MR < P, \text{ so } MC < MU$$

Because MU exceeds MC, too small a share of society's resources is being used to produce the monopolized commodity. Consumers would have a net benefit of MU − MC > 0 if output were increased above the monopoly level by one unit because the added benefit would exceed the added cost. Under monopoly, Adam Smith's invisible hand is sending out the wrong signals. Consumers are willing to pay an amount for an additional unit of the good (its MU) that exceeds what it costs to produce that unit (its MC). But the monopoly refuses to increase production, because if it raises output by one unit, the additional revenue it will collect (MR) will be less than the price the consumer will pay for the additional unit (*P*). The monopolist does not increase production, and resources are allocated inefficiently. To summarize this discussion of the consequences of monopoly:

> Because it is protected from entry, a monopoly firm may earn positive economic profits, that is, profits in excess of the opportunity cost of capital. At the same time, monopoly breeds inefficiency in resource allocation by producing too little output and charging too high a price. For these reasons, some of the virtues of the free market evaporate if an industry becomes monopolized.

■ Monopoly Is Likely to Shift Demand

This analysis need not always apply. For one thing, it has assumed that the market demand curve is the same whether the industry is competitive or monopolized. But is this usually so? The demand curve will be the same if the monopoly firm does nothing to expand its market, but that is hardly plausible.

Under perfect competition, purchasers consider the products of all suppliers in an industry to be identical, so no single supplier has any reason to advertise. But if a monopoly takes over from a perfectly competitive industry, it may very well pay to advertise. If management believes that the creative touch of the advertising agency can make consumers rush to the market to purchase the product whose virtues have been extolled on television, then the firm will allocate a substantial sum of money to accomplish this feat. Take the Eastman Kodak Company, for example. Kodak enjoyed a near monopoly on Canadian film sales from the turn of the century until the 1980s, but that did not stop the company from spending a good deal on advertising. This type of expenditure should shift the demand curve outward. The monopoly's demand curve and that of the competitive industry will then no longer be the same.

The higher demand curve for the monopoly's product may induce it to expand production and therefore reduce the difference between the competitive and the monopolistic output levels indicated in Figure 3. But it may also make it possible for the monopoly to charge even higher prices, so the increased output may not constitute a net gain for consumers.

■ Monopoly Is Likely to Shift Cost Curves

The advent of a monopoly also may shift the average and marginal cost curves. One reason for higher costs is the advertising we have just been discussing. Another reason is the sheer size of the monopolist's organization, which may lead to bureaucratic inefficiencies, coordination problems, and the like.

At the same time, a monopolist may be able to eliminate certain types of duplication that are unavoidable for a number of small, independent firms: One purchasing agent may do the input-buying job where many buyers were needed before; a few large machines may replace many small items of equipment in the hands of the competitive firms. In addition, the large scale of the monopoly firm's input purchases may permit it to take advantage of quantity discounts not available to small competitive firms.

If the consolidation achieved by a monopoly does shift the marginal cost curve downward, monopoly output will tend to move up closer to the competitive level. The monopoly price will then tend to move down closer to the competitive price.

■ CAN ANYTHING GOOD BE SAID ABOUT MONOPOLY?

We conclude that our graphic comparison of monopoly and perfect competition is very artificial. It assumes that all other things will remain the same, even though that is unlikely to happen in reality. For that reason and others, at least in some cases monopoly may not be as damaging to the public interest as the previous discussion suggests. Let us consider some specific ways in which monopoly can offset some of its undesirable consequences.

■ Monopoly May Aid Innovation

Some economists have emphasized that it is misleading to compare the cost curves of a monopoly and a competitive industry *at a single point in time*. Because it is protected from rivals and therefore sure to capture the benefits from any cost-saving methods and new products it can invent, a monopoly has particularly strong motivation to invest in research, these economists argue. If this research bears fruit, the monopolist's costs will be lower than those of a competitive industry in the long run, even if they are higher in the short run. Monopoly, according to this view, may be the hand-maiden of innovation. Although the argument is an old one, it remains controversial. The statistical evidence is decidedly mixed.

Natural Monopoly: Where Single-Firm Production Is Cheapest

Second, we must remember that the monopoly depicted in Figure 2 is not a natural monopoly, because its average costs increase rather than decrease when its output expands. But some of the monopolies you find in the real world are "natural" ones. Where a monopoly is natural, costs of production would, by definition, be higher—possibly much higher—if the single large firm were broken up into many smaller firms. (Refer back to Figure 1.) In such cases, it may serve society's interests to allow the monopoly to continue because consumers benefit from the economies of large-scale production. But then it may be appropriate to regulate the monopoly by placing legal limitations on its ability to set its prices.

CARTELS AS MONOPOLIES

So far we have considered a monopoly to be a single huge firm. But there are times when several firms coordinate their operations—notably their price and output deci-sions—acting as if they were a single giant firm. These firms thus attempt to maxi-mize their joint profits as if they were a single monopoly, instead of each attempting to maximize its profit as an individual firm. Such an organization, when firms collude and coordinate their actions, is called a **cartel**.

A notable cartel is the Organization of Petroleum Exporting Countries (OPEC), which first began making joint decisions on oil production in the 1970s. For a while, OPEC was one of the most spectacularly successful cartels in history. By restricting out-put, its member nations managed to quadruple the price of oil between 1973 and 1974. Unlike most cartels, which come apart because of internal bickering or other reasons, OPEC held together through two worldwide recessions and a variety of unsettling po-litical events. It struck again with huge price increases between 1979 and 1980. In the mid-1980s, its members began to act in ways that did not promote the interest of the entire industry and oil prices tumbled, but prices have since risen and OPEC continues to dominate the world oil market. (See the boxed feature "Oil Prices Fall Further after OPEC Pledge" on page 243 for an example of OPEC decision making.)

OPEC's early success is hardly the norm. Cartels are difficult to organize and even more difficult to enforce. Firms struggle to agree on such things as the amount by which each will reduce its output in order to help push up the price. For a cartel to survive, each member must agree to produce no more output than that assigned to it by the group. Yet once the cartel drives up the price and increases profitability, each member faces the temptation to offer secret discounts that lure some of the very prof-itable business away from other members. When this happens, or even when mem-bers begin to suspect one another of doing so, collusive agreement often begins to come apart. Each member begins suspecting the others and is tempted to cut price first, before the others beat it to the punch.

For this reason, cartels usually adopt elaborate policing arrangements. In effect, they spy on each member firm to ensure that it does not sell more than it is supposed to or shave the price below that chosen by the cartel. This means that cartels are unlikely to succeed or to last very long if the firms sell many, varied products whose prices are difficult to compare and whose outputs are difficult to monitor. In addition, if firms frequently negotiate prices on a customer-by-customer basis and often offer special discounts, a cartel may be almost impossible to arrange.

Many economists consider cartels to be the worst form of market organization, in terms of efficiency and consumer welfare. A successful cartel may end up charging the monopoly price and obtaining monopoly profits. But because the firms do not actu-ally combine operations, cartels offer the public no offsetting benefits in the form of

A **cartel** is a group of sell-ers of a product who have joined together to control its production, sale, and price in the hope of obtain-ing the advantages of monopoly.

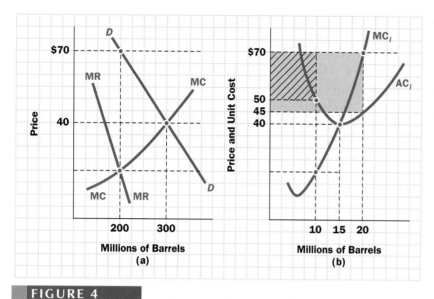

FIGURE 4

Why Cartels Are Unstable

economies of large-scale production. For these and other reasons, open collusion on prices and outputs among firms is illegal in Canada, as we will see in Chapter 13. Outright cartel arrangements rarely occur in Canada, although they are common in some other countries. Only one major exception occurs in Canada: Government regulations have sometimes forced industries such as railroads, gas pipeline transportation, and telecommunications to behave as cartels. Regulations prohibited these firms from undercutting the prices set by the regulatory agencies—an exception that we will discuss in Chapter 13.

FIGURE 4

Why Cartels Are Unstable

Figure 4 illustrates why cartels can easily break down. Figure 4(a) shows the industry market (say, the oil industry). If the cartel firms were acting as competitive firms, output would be 300 million barrels and the price would be $40 per barrel. But with the cartel firms acting together as a monopoly, each firm is assigned quotas of production. The cartel restricts the industry production level at 200 million barrels in such a way that MC = MR, setting a higher price of $70. The situation of each individual member of the cartel is shown Figure 4(b), assuming 20 identical producers. Each producer can produce only 10 million barrels, which it sells at the cartel price of $70 at an individual average cost (AC$_i$) of $50, thus making the profit shown by the striped area—$200 million. At that cartel-fixed price, however, the cartel member could maximize its profits by producing and selling more than the quota that it has been assigned, that is by producing 20 million barrels, where its individual marginal cost (MC$_i$) is $70. In that case, profits would be much larger as shown by the shaded grey area—nearly $500 million, at an AC$_i$ of $45. All that the cheating member would need to do is offer a small price discount that would induce buyers to purchase the additional output, thus reducing the sales of some of the other members of the cartel.

PRICE DISCRIMINATION UNDER MONOPOLY

Price discrimination is
the sale of a given product at different prices to different customers of the firm, when there are no differences in the costs of supplying these customers. Prices are also discriminatory if it costs more to supply one customer than another, but they are charged the same price.

So far we have assumed that a monopoly charges the same price to all of its customers, but that is not always true. In reality, monopoly firms can sell the same product to different customers at different prices, even if that price difference is unrelated to any special costs that affect some customers but not others. Such a practice is called **price discrimination**. Pricing is also said to be discriminatory if it costs more to supply a good to Customer A than to Customer B, but A and B are nonetheless charged the same price.

We are all familiar with cases of price discrimination. For example, suppose that Erik and Emily both mail letters from Toronto, but his goes to Hamilton while hers goes to Vancouver. Both pay the same 52¢ postage even though Vancouver is much farther away from Toronto than Hamilton is. Bargain airline fares are another example. Passenger C, who obtained a student discount, may find herself seated next to Passenger D, who has paid 25 percent more for the same flight and the same taste-free food.

The airline example shows that price discrimination occurs in industries that are not monopolies. Still, it is easier for a monopolist to charge discriminatory prices than it is for a firm that is affected by competition, because price discrimination means that sales to some customers are more profitable than sales to others. Such discrepancies in profitability tempt rivals, including new entrants into the industry, to charge the more profitable consumers somewhat lower prices in order to lure them away from the firm that is "overcharging" them. Price discriminators sneeringly call this type of targeted entry *cream skimming*, meaning that entrants go after the best-paying customers, leaving the low payers (the "skimmed milk") to the discriminator. But, whether desirable or not, such entry certainly makes it more difficult to charge higher prices to the more profitable customers.

Why do firms sometimes engage in price discrimination? You may already suspect the answer: to increase their profits. To see why, let us consider a simple example. Imagine a town with 100 rich families and 1,000 poor ones. The poor families are each willing to buy one video game but cannot afford to pay more than $25. The rich, however, are prepared to buy one per family as long as the price is no higher than $75.

If it cannot price-discriminate, the best the firm can do is to set the price at $25 for everyone, yielding a total revenue of $25 × 1,100 = $27,500. If it charged more, say, $75, it would sell only to the rich and earn just $7,500. If the added cost of producing the 1,000 games for the poorer families is less than the $27,500 − $7,500 = $20,000 in added revenues from the sales to the poor, then the $25 price must be more profitable than the $75 price.

But what if the game maker can charge different prices to the rich and to the poor—and can prevent the poor from reselling their low-priced merchandise to the rich at a markup? Then the revenue obtainable by the firm from the same 1,100 video game output becomes $25 × 1,000 = $25,000 from selling to the poor plus $75 × 100 = $7,500 from selling to the rich, for a total of $32,500. This is clearly a better deal for the firm than the $27,500 revenue obtainable without price discrimination. Profits are $5,000 higher. In general:

> When a firm charges discriminatory prices, profits are normally higher than when the firm charges nondiscriminatory (uniform) prices because the firm then divides customers into separate groups and charges each group the price that maximizes its profits from those customers.

We have constructed our simple example to make the two profit-maximizing prices obvious. In practice, that is not so; the monopolist knows that if it sets a price too high, quantity demanded and hence profits will be too low. The discriminating

Oil Prices Fall Further After OPEC Pledge

Oil prices fell further below the sensitive $40-a-barrel mark today as an OPEC deal to pump more crude outweighed underlying security fears in the Middle East. The price of United States light crude dipped to $38.85 a barrel in morning trade, while Brent crude in London was changing hands at $35.99. Yesterday, OPEC agreed to hike output quotas by two million barrels a day—roughly eight per cent—in a bid to alleviate the escalation in world fuel prices. The move signaled the biggest increase in output in more than six years, although it fell short of what some oil-consuming countries were hoping for. The deal by the 11-member Organization of the Petroleum Exporting Countries also promises to add a further 500,000 barrels a day from the start of August. Faced with renewed terrorism fears and soaring demand from the US and several developing countries, the price of oil has recently leapt to more than $40 a barrel.

SOURCE: Excerpted from "Oil Prices Fall Further After OPEC Pledge," by Scott Reid, *Edinburgh Evening News*, June 4, 2004. Retrieved from http://business.scotsman.com

The National Hockey League as a Cartel

The 30 member clubs of the National Hockey League (NHL) could be considered a cartel, especially since the conclusion of the last round of collective bargaining during the lockout of the 2004–2005 season. The NHL clubs cannot decide individually the salaries for their players. Besides limits to individual salaries, which cannot exceed 20 percent of the team payroll (the total amount paid as salaries to the players), there is now a payroll cap, which was US$39 million, during the first season of the collective agreement, 2005–2006, and $56.7 million during the 2008–2009 season. This is clearly a case of collusion between members of an industry, but it is deemed acceptable because it has been negotiated with the representatives of the NHL Players' Association and incorporated into their collective agreement. Similar limitations exist in the National Football League and the National Basketball Association.

If teams were free to set their own salaries, as was the case in the NHL between 1972 and 2004, the joint profits of the NHL team owners would be much lower. By setting a ceiling on team payrolls, the 30 NHL clubs attempt to achieve higher joint profits, even though some of the individual teams—those with the highest revenues such as the New York Rangers and the Toronto Maple Leafs—could probably afford to pay higher salaries, thus attracting more star free-agent players and potentially generating both higher revenues and higher profits.

What happened before 1972 (before the World Hockey Association was created as a rival league, thus ending the NHL monopoly)? There is substantial evidence that team owners were colluding, offering meagre salaries to star players such as Gordie Howe and Maurice Richard. Today, this would be nearly impossible, with all of the lawyers, agents, and financial advisers surrounding NHL players (thus the need for a salary cap), although Major League Baseball owners were convicted of collusion following the 1985–1987 seasons and had to pay hundreds of million dollars in damages to the players. The owners conspired to keep the salaries low for high-profile players who had become free agents, such as former Montreal Expos player Andre Dawson, offering them ridiculous salary contracts and sharing information on salary offers.

monopolist's problem is determining the different profit-maximizing prices to charge to different customer groups. The solution to this problem is given by another rule of marginal analysis. For simplicity, suppose that the seller proposes charging two different prices to two customer groups, A and B. Profit maximization requires that the price to Group A and the price to Group B are such that they yield the same *marginal* revenue, that is:

The marginal revenue from a sale to a Group A customer must be the same as that from a sale to a Group B customer:

$$MR_a = MR_b$$

The reasoning is straightforward. Suppose that the sale of an additional video game to a Group A customer who lives in Richtown brings in $MR_a = \$28$ in revenue, whereas the corresponding sale to a Group B customer in Poorborough adds only $MR_b = \$12$. Such an arrangement cannot possibly be a profit-maximizing solution. By switching one unit of its shipments from Poorborough, with its B customers, and sending that unit instead to Richtown's A customers, the firm gives up $12 in revenue to gain $28—a net gain of $16 from the same total quantity of sales. Because a similar argument holds for any other pair of marginal revenues that are unequal, profit maximizing clearly requires that the marginal revenue from each group of customers be equal.

The equal-marginal-revenue rule enables us to determine the profit-maximizing prices and sales volumes for two such groups of customers diagrammatically. The two panels of Figure 5 show the demand curves and corresponding marginal revenue curves for customer groups A and B. Suppose that the firm is selling the quantity Q_a to Group A customers at price P_a. How much must the firm then sell to Group B customers, and at what price, to maximize profits? Our rule gives the answer. The marginal revenue from selling to Group A is equal to H—as we see from point J directly above Q_a on the MR curve in Panel (a). The rule tells us that the firm must charge a price to Group B customers that induces them to buy the quantity that yields the same marginal revenue, H. We find this quantity by drawing a horizontal line HH through point J from Panel (a) to Panel (b). The marginal revenues of

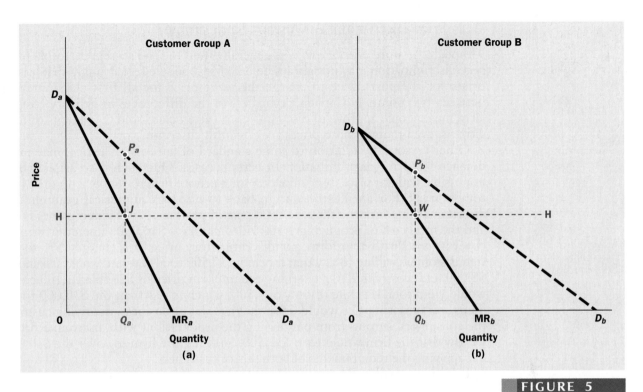

FIGURE 5

Prices and Quantities under Price Discrimination

the two customer groups will clearly be equal where *HH* cuts the Group B marginal revenue curve—at point *W*. The profit-maximizing sales volume to Group B will be Q_b, directly below point *W*. And at sales volume Q_b, the market B price is clearly given by the corresponding point on the market B demand curve, price P_b directly above Q_b.

Given price and output in one of two markets [Figure 5(a)], to determine the profit-maximizing output and price in the other market [Figure 5(b)] under price discrimination, do the following:

1. Draw the demand and marginal revenue curves for the different customer groups (Group A and Group B) side by side.

2. For the first market [Group A, Figure 5(a)], draw a horizontal line through point *J* corresponding to the marginal revenue–quantity combination, which will set the price and quantity for Customer Group A at (P_a, Q_a).

3. Knowing the marginal revenue *H* and output (Q_a), point *J*, for the first market, find the profit-maximizing sales quantity for the second market where the horizontal line cuts the MR curve for the second group of customers, so that the MR levels are the same for both customer groups.

4. Knowing the marginal revenue *H* and point maximizing sales quantity Q_b for the second market, determine the second customer group's profit-maximizing price P_b, point *W*, by locating the point on the demand curve corresponding to the profit-maximizing quantity.

That is not quite the end of the story: We have not yet said anything about costs, and we know that profit maximization must take account of costs as well as revenues. But we can deal with the cost issue quite easily, at least if the marginal cost of a video game is the same whether supplied to an A customer or a B customer. Even under price discrimination, we still have the fundamental MR = MC rule for profit maximization in each market segment (see page 177 in Chapter 8). The extended profit-maximization rule under price discrimination then must be:

$$MR_a = MR_b = MC$$

■ Is Price Discrimination Always Undesirable?

Although the word *discrimination* is generally used to refer to reprehensible practices, *price* discrimination may not always be bad. Most people feel strongly that it is appropriate for the post office to charge the same price for all first-class letters going between two points in Canada, regardless of the differences in delivery costs. Similarly, most people approve of discounts on theatre tickets sold to students or to senior citizens, even though those prices are obviously discriminatory.

Other reasons, in addition to some standard of fairness or justice, may provide a defence for price discrimination in certain cases. One such case arises when it is impossible without price discrimination for a private firm to supply a product that customers want. For an illustration, go back to our first numerical example of price discrimination. Suppose that the total cost of producing 100 video games is $8,000, and the total cost of producing 1,100 video games is $30,000. Then our firm cannot cover its costs with a uniform, nondiscriminatory price. If it charged $75 to the 100 rich customers willing to pay that much, its $7,500 total revenue would fall short of its $8,000 total cost. Similarly, charging the uniform price of $25 to all 1,100 customers would yield total revenue of only $27,500, which is less than the $30,000 total cost. Thus, *any* uniform price would drive the firm out of business, depriving customers of the consumers' surplus from purchasing the product. But with discriminatory prices, we saw that the firm would earn $32,500, enabling the firm to cover the $30,000 cost of supplying the requirements of both sets of customers.

It is even possible that price discrimination can make a product cheaper than it would otherwise be for *all* customers—even those who pay the higher prices. As you may imagine, this can be true only if the production of the commodity involves significant economies of scale. For example, suppose that price discrimination permits the firm to offer lower prices to certain customers, thereby attracting some business that it would not otherwise have. The firm's output will therefore increase. Scale economies will then reduce the firm's marginal costs. If marginal cost falls enough, even the "high-priced" customer group may end up paying less than it would in the absence of price discrimination.

The conclusion from this discussion is not that price discrimination is always a good thing, but rather that it is *sometimes* desirable. In particular, we must recognize that a firm may be unable to cover its costs without price discrimination—a situation that some observers consider to be relatively common.

THE PUZZLE RESOLVED: *Competition in Telephone Service*

We conclude our discussion of monopoly by returning to the puzzle that began this chapter: Why are phone services around the country threatened by competition in an industry that was once considered the very definition of a natural monopoly? The answer has many parts, notably changes in the government's rules and new rulings by the courts. But the main development that made competition in the industry possible is the huge change in telephone service technology.

SOURCE: © AP/Wide World Photos.

Until recently, the market for *local* telephone service was considered a natural monopoly. The primary reason was the need for very expensive transmission facilities, primarily the wires that had to enter every subscriber's home. Canadian governments even disallowed competition in these markets because they believed that it would lead to wasteful duplication of such costly equipment and that this expensive duplication would lead to higher prices. Instead, local utility commissions regulated these monopolies to ensure adequate service and reasonable prices. Because long-distance calls also had to reach the home and office via those costly wires, the firm that owned them would have been in a position to control the industry and perhaps even to turn it into a monopoly once again, if government rules had not prevented it.

Recent changes in communications technology have since made this market riper for competition. Computers and satellite technology have reduced the investment costs of providing phone service. Wherever you live, competition may be on the way with cell phones clearly needing no wires connecting to households. Voice message transmission via the Internet (Voice over Internet Protocol services, or VoIP) is already in existence, far less costly, rapidly improving, and easily supplied by rival providers. Already, the advertisements of cell-phone service suppliers fill many newspaper pages. The local phone companies still have some near-monopoly power in their own geographic territories, but that power seems likely to erode before long.

SUMMARY

1. A **pure monopoly** is a one-firm industry producing a product for which there are no close substitutes.

2. Monopoly can persist only if there are important cost advantages to single-firm operation or **barriers to free entry**. These barriers may consist of legal impediments (**patents**, licensing), the special risks faced by a potential entrant resulting from the need to incur large sunk investments, or the result of "dirty tricks" designed to make things tough for an entrant.

3. One important case of cost advantages is **natural monopoly**—instances in which only one firm can survive because of significant economies of large-scale production.

4. A monopoly has no supply curve. It maximizes its profit by producing an output at which its marginal revenue equals its marginal cost. Its price is given by the point on its demand curve corresponding to that output.

5. In a monopolistic industry, if demand and cost curves are the same as those of a competitive industry, and if the demand curve has a negative slope and the competitive supply curve has a positive slope, then monopoly output will be lower and price will be higher than they will be in the competitive industry.

6. Economists consider the fact that monopoly output tends to be below the competitive level to constitute an (undesirable) inefficiency.

7. Advertising may enable a monopoly to shift its demand curve above that of a comparable competitive industry. Through economies such as large-scale input purchases, a monopoly may be able to shift its cost curves below those of a competitive industry.

8. A group of firms may decide to collude and behave as if it were a monopoly. This is a **cartel**. Because each member of a cartel has a profit incentive to break the rules, cartels are generally unstable organizations.

9. A monopoly may be able to increase its profits by engaging in **price discrimination**—charging higher prices for the same goods to customers who are less resistant to price increases, or failing to charge higher prices to customers whom it costs more to serve.

10. The profit-maximizing discriminatory prices, and corresponding sales volumes, for a firm with several different customer groups can be determined with the help of an extended rule for profit maximization: that the *marginal revenue* from sales to *each* customer group must be equal to one another and to the firm's marginal cost.

11. Price discrimination can sometimes be damaging to the public interest, but at other times it can be beneficial. Some firms cannot survive without it, and price discrimination may even reduce prices to *all* customers if there are substantial economies of scale.

KEY TERMS

Pure monopoly 232	Patents 233	Monopoly profits 238
Barriers to entry 233	Natural monopoly 234	Cartel 241
		Price discrimination 242

TEST YOURSELF

1. Which of the following industries are pure monopolies?
   a. The only supplier of heating fuel in an isolated town
   b. The only supplier of IBM notebook computers in town
   c. The only supplier of digital cameras
   Explain your answers.

2. The following are the demand and total cost schedules for Company Town Water, a local monopoly:

Output in Litres	Price per Litre	Total Cost
50,000	$0.28	$ 6,000
100,000	0.26	15,000
150,000	0.22	22,000
200,000	0.20	32,000
250,000	0.16	46,000
300,000	0.12	64,000

How much output will Company Town Water produce, and what price will it charge? Will it earn a profit? How much? (*Hint:* First compute the firm's MR and MC schedules.)

3. Show from the table in Test Yourself Question 2 that for the water company, marginal revenue (per 50,000-litre unit) is always less than price.

4. A monopoly sells Frisbees to two customer groups. Group A has a downward-sloping straight-line demand curve, whereas the demand curve for Group B is infinitely elastic. Draw the graph determining the profit-maximizing discriminatory prices and sales to the two groups. What will be the price of Frisbees to Group B? Why? How is the price to Group A determined?

DISCUSSION QUESTIONS

1. Suppose that a monopoly industry produces less output than a similar competitive industry. Discuss why this may be considered socially undesirable.

2. If competitive firms earn zero economic profits, explain why anyone would invest money in them. (*Hint:* What is the role of the opportunity cost of capital in economic profit?)

3. Suppose that a tax of $24 is levied on each item sold by a monopolist, and as a result, she decides to raise her price by exactly $24. Why may this decision be against her own best interests?

4. Use Figure 2 to show that Adam Smith was wrong when he claimed that a monopoly would always charge "the highest price which can be got."

5. Cable companies such as Rogers and Videotron have invested vast amounts of money in their fibre-optic networks, which are costly to construct but relatively cheap to operate. They now offer phone services. If both of them were to go bankrupt, why might this *not* result in a decrease in the competition facing Bell Canada? (*Hint:* At what price would the assets of the bankrupt companies be offered for sale?)

6. What does your answer to the previous question tell you about ease or difficulty of entry into telecommunications?

7. A firm cannot break even by charging uniform (nondiscriminatory) prices, but with price discrimination it can earn a small profit. Explain why in this case consumers *must* be better off if the firm is permitted to charge discriminatory prices.

8. It can be proved that, other things being equal, under price discrimination the price charged to some customer group will be higher the less elastic the demand curve of that group is. Why is that result plausible?

BETWEEN COMPETITION AND MONOPOLY

. . . neither fish nor fowl.

JOHN HEYWOOD (C. 1565)

Most productive activity in Canada, as in any advanced industrial society, falls somewhere between the two extreme market forms we have considered so far. So if we want to understand the workings of the market mechanism in a real, modern economy, we must look at hybrid market structures that fall somewhere between perfect competition and pure monopoly. There are two such market forms—*monopolistic competition* and *oligopoly*—that are analyzed extensively by economists and are extremely important in practice.

Monopolistic competition is a market structure characterized by many small firms selling somewhat different products. Here, each firm's output is so small relative to the total output of closely related and, hence, rival products that the firm does not expect its competitors to respond to or even to *notice* any changes in its own behavior.

Monopolistic competition, or something close to it, is widespread in retailing: shoe stores, restaurants, and gasoline stations are good examples. Most firms in our economy can be classified as monopolistic competitors, because even though they are small, such enterprises are abundant. We begin the chapter by using the theory of the firm described in Chapter 8 to analyze a monopolistically competitive firm's price–output decisions, then we consider the role of entry and exit, as we did in Chapter 10.

Finally we turn to oligopoly, a market structure in which a few large firms dominate the market. The steel, automobile, and fibre-optics manufacturing industries are good examples of oligopolies, despite the number of strong foreign competitors. Probably the largest share of Canadian economic output comes from oligopolists. Although they are fewer in number than monopolistic competitors, many oligopoly firms are extremely large, with annual sales exceeding the total outputs of most countries in the world and even of some of the smaller industrial European countries.

CONTENTS

One critical feature distinguishing an oligopolist from either a monopolist or a perfect competitor is that oligopolists care very much about what other individual firms in the industry do. The resulting *interdependence* of decisions, as we will see, makes oligopoly very difficult to analyze and results in a wide range of behaviour patterns. Consequently, economic theory uses not just one but many models of oligopoly (some of which we will review in this chapter), and it is often hard to know which model to apply in any particular situation.

THREE PUZZLING OBSERVATIONS

We need to study the hybrid market structures considered in this chapter because many economic phenomena cannot be explained in terms of perfect competition or pure monopoly. Here are three examples:

Puzzle 1: Why Are There So Many Retailers? You have undoubtedly seen road intersections with gasoline stations on every corner. Often, two or three of them have no customers at the pumps. There seem to be more gas stations than the number of cars warrants, with a corresponding waste of labour, time, equipment, and other resources. Why—and how—do they all stay in business?

Puzzle 2: Why Do Oligopolists Advertise More Than "More Competitive" Firms? Many big companies use advertising as a principal weapon in their battle for customers, and advertising budgets can constitute very large shares of their expenditures. Such firms spend literally billons of dollars per year on advertising, seeking to leap ahead of their rivals. Procter & Gamble, the huge American corporation that manufactures all kinds of consumer goods, is reported to spend $4 billion on advertising (about 10 percent of its revenues in 2004).[1] Yet critics often accuse oligopolistic industries containing only a few giant firms of being "uncompetitive." Farming, in contrast, is considered as close to perfect competition as any industry in our economy, but few, if any, individual farmers spend anything at all on advertising.[2] Why do these allegedly "uncompetitive" oligopolists make such heavy use of combative advertising whereas very competitive farmers do not?

Puzzle 3: Why Do Oligopolists Seem to Change Their Prices So Infrequently? Many prices in the economy change from minute to minute. The very latest prices of commodities such as soybeans, pork bellies, and copper are available online twenty-four hours a day, seven days a week. If you want to buy one of these commodities at 11:45 A.M. today, you cannot use yesterday's price—or even the price from 11:44 A.M. today—because it has probably changed already. Yet prices of products such as cars and refrigerators generally change only a few times a year at most, even during fairly rapid inflation. Firms that sell cars and refrigerators know that product and input market conditions change all the time. Why don't they adjust their prices more often? This chapter will offer answers to each of these questions.

MONOPOLISTIC COMPETITION

For years, economic theory told us little about market forms in between the two extreme cases of pure monopoly and perfect competition. Then, during the 1930s, Edward Chamberlin of Harvard University and Joan Robinson of Cambridge

---

[1] "The Harder Hard Sell," *The Economist* magazine, June 24, 2004. Retrieved from http://www.economist.com and http://www.pg.com.

[2] But farmers' associations, such as dairy groups and hog producers, do spend money on advertising.

University (working separately) partially filled this gap and helped to make economic theory more realistic. The market structure they analyzed is called **monopolistic competition.**

Characteristics of Monopolistic Competition

A market is said to operate under conditions of monopolistic competition if it satisfies four requirements, three of which are the same as those for perfect competition:

- *Numerous participants*—that is, many buyers and sellers, all of whom are small

- *Freedom of exit and entry*

- *Perfect information*—as far as the sellers are concerned

- *Heterogeneous products*—as far as the buyer is concerned, each seller's product differs at least somewhat from every other seller's product

Monopolistic competition refers to a market in which products are heterogeneous but that is otherwise the same as a market that is perfectly competitive.

Notice that monopolistic competition differs from perfect competition in only the last respect. Perfect competition assumes that the products of different firms in an industry are identical, but under monopolistic competition products differ from seller to seller—in terms of quality, packaging, supplementary services offered (such as windshield washing at a gas station), or merely consumers' perceptions. The attributes that differentiate products need not be "real" in any objective or directly measurable sense. For example, differences in packaging or in associated services can and do distinguish otherwise identical products. However, although two products may perform quite differently in quality tests, if consumers know nothing about this difference, it is irrelevant.

In contrast to a perfect competitor, a monopolistic competitor's demand curve is negatively sloped. Because each seller's product is different, each caters to a set of customers who vary in their loyalty to the particular product. If the firm raises its price somewhat, it will drive *some* of its customers to competitors' offerings, but customers who strongly favour the firm's product will not switch. If one monopolistic competitor lowers its price, it may expect to attract some trade from rivals. But, because different products are imperfect substitutes, it will not lure away *all* of the rivals' business.

For example, if Harriet's Hot Dog House reduces its price slightly, it will attract those customers of Sam's Sausage Shop who were nearly indifferent between the two. If Harriet were to cut her prices further, she would gain some customers who have a slightly greater preference for Sam's product. But even a big cut in Harriet's price will not bring her the hard-core sausage lovers who hate hot dogs. Therefore, monopolistic competitors face a demand curve that is negatively sloped, like that of a monopolist, rather than horizontal, like that of a perfect competitor who will lose all of his business if he insists on a higher price than that charged by a rival.

Because consumers see each product as distinct from all others, a monopolistically competitive firm appears to have something akin to a small monopoly. Can we therefore expect it to earn more than zero economic profit? Like perfect competitors, perhaps monopolistic competitors will obtain economic profits in the short run. In the long run, however, high economic profits will attract new entrants into a monopolistically competitive market—not with products *identical* to an existing firm's, but with products sufficiently similar to absorb the excess economic profits.

If McDonald's is thriving at a particular location, it can confidently expect Burger King or some other fast-food outlet to open a franchise nearby shortly. When one seller adopts a new, attractive package, rivals will soon follow suit with slightly different designs and colours of their own. In this way, freedom of entry ensures that the monopolistically competitive firm earns no higher return on its capital in the long run than that capital could earn elsewhere. In other words, the firm earns no excess economic profits. Just as under perfect competition, competition will drive price

Short-Run Equilibrium of the Firm under Monopolistic Competition

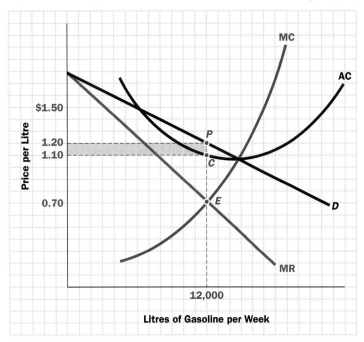

down to equal average cost, including the opportunity cost of capital. In this sense, although its product differs somewhat from everyone else's, the firm under monopolistic competition has no more monopoly *power* than one operating under perfect competition does.

Let us now examine the process that ensures that competition will drive economic profits down to zero in the long run, even under monopolistic competition, and see what prices and outputs that process fosters.

Price and Output Determination under Monopolistic Competition

The *short-run* equilibrium of the firm under monopolistic competition differs little from the equilibrium seen under monopoly. Because the firm faces a downward-sloping demand curve (labelled *D* in Figure 1), its marginal revenue (MR) curve will lie below its demand curve. Like any firm, a monopolistic competitor maximizes profits by producing the output at which marginal revenue equals marginal cost (MC). In Figure 1, the profit-maximizing output for a hypothetical gas station is 12,000 litres per week, and it sells this output at a price of $1.20 per litre (point *P* on the demand curve). The firm makes 10 cents per litre in profits, as depicted by the vertical distance from *C* to *P*.

This analysis, you will note, looks much like Figure 2 in Chapter 11 for a monopoly. The main difference is that monopolistic competitors are likely to face a much flatter demand curve than pure monopolists do, because many products serve as close substitutes for the monopolistic competitor's product. If our gas station raises its price to $1.50 per litre, most of its customers will go across the street. If it lowers its price to $0.70 per litre, it will have long lines at its pumps.

The gas station depicted in Figure 1 is enjoying economic profits. Because average cost at 12,000 litres per week is only $1.10 per litre (point *C*), the station makes a profit of 10 cents per litre on gasoline sales, or $1,200 per week in total, shown by the shaded rectangle. Under monopoly, such profits can persist. Under monopolistic competition, they cannot—because economic profits will entice new firms to enter the market. Although the new gas stations will not offer the identical product, they will offer products that are close enough to take away some business from our firm. (For example, they may sell Petro Canada or Shell gasoline instead of Sunoco gasoline.)

When more firms enter the market, each firm's demand curve will shift downward (to the left). But how far will it shift? The answer is basically the same as it was under perfect competition: Market entry will cease only when the most that the firm can earn is zero economic profit—exactly the same return the firm can earn elsewhere.

Figure 2 depicts the same monopolistically competitive firm as in Figure 1 *after* the adjustment to the long-run equilibrium is complete. The demand curve—and hence also the MR curve—has been pushed down so far by the entry of new rivals that when the firm equates MC and MR in an attempt to maximize profits (point *E*), it simultaneously equates price *(P)* and average cost (AC) so that economic profits are zero (point *P*). As compared to the short-run equilibrium depicted in Figure 1, price in long-run equilibrium is *lower* ($1.15 cents per litre versus $1.20), *more firms* participate in the industry, and each firm produces a *smaller* output (10,000 litres versus

12,000 litres) at a *higher* average cost per litre ($1.15 versus $1.10).[3] In general:

> Long-run equilibrium under monopolistic competition requires that the firm's output be at a level where its demand curve and its average cost curve meet, and there the two curves must be *tangent,* not crossing.

Why? Because if the demand curve was above the average revenue curve or the two curves intersected, firms could produce output quantities at which price would exceed average cost, which means that participants would be earning economic profits, and that would draw an influx of new close-substitute products that would push down the demand curve. Similarly, if the average cost curve were below the demand curve at every point, the firm would incur an economic loss—it would be unable to obtain returns equal to those that its capital can get elsewhere, and firms would leave the industry.

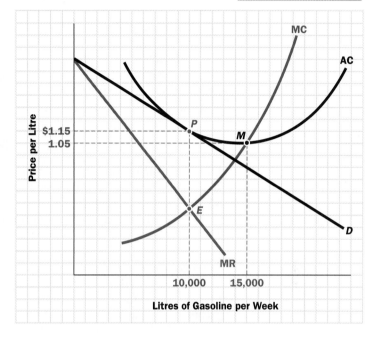

This analysis of entry is quite similar to the perfectly competitive case. Moreover, the notion that firms under monopolistic competition earn exactly zero economic profits seems to correspond fairly well to what we see in the real world. Gas station operators, whose markets fit the characteristics of monopolistic competition, do not earn notably higher profits than do small farmers, who operate under conditions closer to perfect competition.

The Excess Capacity Theorem and Resource Allocation

One economically significant difference arises between perfect and monopolistic competition. Look at Figure 2 again. The tangency point between the average cost and demand curves, point *P,* occurs along the *negatively sloping portion* of the average cost curve, because *P* is the only point where the AC curve has the same (negative) slope as the demand curve. If the AC curve is U-shaped, the tangency point must therefore lie above and to the left of the *minimum point* on the average cost curve, point *M.* In other words, under monopolistic competition, the demand curve hits the average cost curve in a region where average costs are still declining. Average costs have yet to reach their lowest point. By contrast, the perfectly competitive firm's demand curve is horizontal, so tangency must take place at the minimum point on the average cost curve. You can easily confirm this by referring back to Figure 9(a) in Chapter 10. This difference leads to the following important conclusion:

> Under monopolistic competition in the long run, the firm will tend to produce an output lower than that which minimizes its unit costs, and hence unit costs of the monopolistic competitor will be higher than necessary. Because the level of output that corresponds to minimum average cost is naturally considered to be the firm's optimal capacity, this result has been called the *excess capacity theorem of monopolistic competition.* Thus, monopolistic competition tends to lead firms to have unused or wasted capacity.

It follows that if every firm under monopolistic competition were to expand its output, cost per unit of output would be reduced. But we must be careful about jumping

---

[3] *Exercise:* Show that if the demand curve fell still further, the firm would incur a loss. What would then happen in the long run?

to policy conclusions from that observation. It does *not* follow that *every* monopolistically competitive firm *should* produce more. After all, such an overall increase in industry output means that a smaller portion of the economy's resources will be available for other uses; from the information at hand, we have no way of knowing whether that choice leaves us better or worse off in terms of social benefits.

Even so, the situation depicted in Figure 2 probably represents a substantial *inefficiency*. Although it is not clear that society would gain if *every* firm were to achieve lower costs by expanding its production, society *can* save resources if firms combine into *a smaller number of larger companies* that produce the *same total output*. For example, suppose that in the situation shown in Figure 2, 15 monopolistically competitive firms each sell 10,000 litres of gasoline per week. The total cost of this output, according to the figures given in the diagram, would be:

$$\text{Number of firms} \times \text{Output per firm} \times \text{Cost per unit} =$$
$$15 \times 10,000 \times \$1.15 = \$172,500$$

If, instead, the number of stations were cut to 10 and each sold 15,000 litres, total production would be unchanged. But total costs would fall to $10 \times 15,000 \times \$1.05 = \$157,500$, a net saving of \$15,000 *without any cut in total output*.

This result does not depend on the particular numbers that we used in our illustration. It follows directly from the observation that lowering the cost per unit must always reduce the total cost of producing *any* given industry output. That is, producing a *given* output, Q, always must have a lower total cost when average cost is lower: Specifically, if $AC_1 < AC_2$, it must obviously *always* be true that $TC_1 = Q \times AC_1 < Q \times AC_2 = TC_2$. Society must gain in the sense of getting the same total output, Q, as before but at a lower total cost. After all, which do you prefer—a dozen cans of soda for \$0.70 each or the same dozen cans for \$0.55 each?

PUZZLE 1 RESOLVED: *Explaining the Abundance of Retailers*

The excess capacity theorem explains one of the puzzles mentioned at the beginning of this chapter. The highway intersection with four gas stations, where two could serve the available customers with little increase in customer delays and at lower costs, is a real-world example of excess capacity.

The excess capacity theorem seems to imply that too many sellers participate in monopolistically competitive markets and that society would benefit from a reduction in their numbers. However, such a conclusion may be a bit hasty. Even if a smaller number of larger firms can reduce costs, society may not benefit from the change because it will leave consumers with a smaller range of choice. Because all products differ at least slightly under monopolistic competition, a reduction in the number of *firms* means that the number of different *products* falls as well. We achieve greater efficiency at the cost of greater standardization.

In some cases, consumers may agree that this trade-off represents a net gain, particularly if the variety of products available was initially so great that it only confused them. But for some products, most consumers would probably agree that the diversity of choice is worth the extra cost involved. After all, we would probably save money on clothing if every student were required to wear a uniform. But because the uniform is likely to be too hot for some students, too cool for other students, and aesthetically displeasing to almost everyone else, would the cost saving really be a net benefit?

OLIGOPOLY

An **oligopoly** is a market dominated by a few sellers, at least several of which are large enough relative to the total market to be able to influence the market price.

An **oligopoly** is a market dominated by a few sellers, at least several of which are large enough relative to the total market that they may be able to influence the market price.

In highly developed economies, it is not monopoly, but *oligopoly*, that is virtually synonymous with "big business." Any oligopolistic industry includes a group of giant firms, each of which keeps a watchful eye on the actions of the others. Under oligopoly, rivalry among firms takes its most direct and active form. Here one encounters such actions and reactions as frequent new-product introductions, free samples, and aggressive—if not downright nasty—advertising campaigns. A firm's price decision may elicit cries of pain from its rivals, and firms are often engaged in a continuing battle in which they plan strategies day by day and each major decision induces direct responses by rival firms.

Notice that the definition of oligopoly does not mention the degree of product differentiation. Some oligopolies sell products that are essentially identical (such as steel plate from different steel manufacturers), whereas others sell products that are quite different in consumers' eyes (for example, Chevrolets, Fords, and Hondas). Some oligopolistic industries also contain a considerable number of smaller firms (example: soft drink manufacturers), but they are nevertheless considered oligopolies because a few large firms carry out the bulk of the industry's business, and smaller participants must follow their larger rivals' lead to survive at the margins of the industry. Oligopolistic firms often seek to create unique products—unique, at least, in consumers' perceptions. To the extent that an oligopolistic firm can create a unique product in terms of features, location, or appeal, it protects itself from the pressures of competition that will force down its prices and eat into its sales.

Managers of large, oligopolistic firms who have occasion to study economics are somewhat taken aback by the notion of perfect competition, because it is devoid of all harsh competitive activity as they know it. Recall that under perfect competition, firm managers make no price decisions—they simply accept the price dictated by market forces and adjust their output accordingly. As we observed at the beginning of the chapter, a perfectly competitive firm does not advertise; it adopts no sales gimmicks; it does not even know who most of its competitors are. But because oligopolists have some degree of influence on market forces, they do not enjoy the luxury of such anonymity. They worry about prices, spend fortunes on advertising (see "The Mad Scramble to Differentiate the Product" on the next page), and try to understand or even predict their rivals' behaviour patterns.

■ Why Oligopolistic Behaviour Is So Difficult to Analyze

Firms in an oligopolistic industry—in particular, the largest of those firms—have some latitude in choosing their product prices and outputs. Furthermore, to survive and thrive in an oligopolistic environment, firms must take direct account of their rivals' responses. Both of these features complicate the analysis of the oligopolistic

PUZZLE 2 RESOLVED: *Why Oligopolists Advertise but Perfectly Competitive Firms Generally Do Not*

The two reasons for such divergent behaviour should be clear, and they explain the puzzling fact that oligopolists advertise far more than the supposedly far more competitive firms in perfectly competitive markets. First, a perfectly competitive firm can sell all it wants at the current market price, so why should it waste money on advertising? By contrast, General Motors (GM) and Toyota cannot sell all the cars they want at the current price. Because they face negatively sloped (and thus less than perfectly elastic) demand curves, if they want to sell more, they must either reduce prices (to move along the demand curve toward greater quantities) or advertise more (to shift their demand curves outward).

Second, because the public believes that the products supplied by firms in a perfectly competitive industry are identical, if Firm A advertises its product, the advertisement is just as likely to bring customers to Firm B. Under oligopoly, however, consumer products are often *not* identical. Ford advertises to convince consumers that its automobiles are better than GM's or Subaru's. If the advertising campaign succeeds, GM and Subaru will be hurt and probably will respond with more advertising of their own. Thus, the firms in an oligopoly with differentiated products must compete via advertising, whereas perfectly competitive firms gain little or nothing by doing so.

The Mad Scramble to Differentiate the Product

Competition is fierce in the world of business, and companies will go very far indeed to outdo their rivals. In the summer of 2000, Pizza Hut's advertising campaign was literally out of this world: The firm helped to bankroll Russia's space agency by putting a 10-metre-high, $1.25 million ad on a Proton booster rocket.

Not to be outdone, the KFC Corporation constructed an 8,000-square-metre Colonel Saunders logo in the Nevada desert near Rachel (population 98), the so-called "UFO capital of the world," so that extraterrestrials can see it as they approach earth!

SOURCE: "Marketing: Guerrillas in Our Midst," *The Economist*, October 14, 2000, p. 80.

SOURCE: © Courtesy of Pizza Hut

SOURCE: KFC Corp.

firm's behaviour and prevent us from drawing unambiguous conclusions about resource allocation under oligopoly. Oligopoly is much more difficult to analyze than other forms of economic organization, because oligopolistic decisions are, by their very nature, *interdependent*. Oligopolists *recognize* that the outcomes of their decisions depend on their rivals' responses. For example, Ford managers know that their actions will probably lead to reactions by GM, which in turn may require a readjustment of Ford's plans, thereby modifying GM's response, and so on. Where such a sequence of moves and countermoves may lead is difficult enough to ascertain. But the fact that Ford executives recognize this possibility in advance, and may try to second-guess or predict GM's reactions as they initially decide on a marketing tactic, makes even that first step difficult to analyze and almost impossible to predict.

Truly, almost anything can and sometimes does happen under oligopoly. The early railroad kings went so far as to employ gangs of hoodlums who fought pitched battles to try to squelch rival lines' operations. At the other extreme, oligopolistic firms have employed overt or covert forms of collusion to avoid rivalry altogether—to transform an oligopolistic industry, at least temporarily, into a monopolistic one. In other instances, oligopolistic firms seem to have arranged to live and let live, via price leadership (discussed later) or geographic allocations, dividing up customers by agreement among the firms.

■ A Shopping List

Because oligopolies in the real world are so diverse, oligopoly models in the theoretical world should also come in various shapes and sizes. An introductory course cannot hope to explain all of the many oligopoly models. This section offers a quick review of some oligopolistic behaviour models. In the remainder of the chapter, we turn our attention to a particularly interesting set of models that use methods such as game theory to analyze oligopolistic firm behaviour.

1. Ignoring Interdependence   One simple approach to the problem of oligopolistic interdependence is to assume that the oligopolists themselves ignore it—that they behave as if their actions will not elicit reactions from their rivals. Perhaps an oligopolist, finding the "If they think that we think that they think . . . " chain of reasoning too complex, will decide to ignore rivals' behaviour. The firm may then just seek to maximize profits, assuming that its decisions will not affect its rivals' strategies. In this case, economists can analyze oligopoly in the same way they look at monopoly, which we described in Chapter 11. Probably no oligopolist totally ignores all of its major rivals' decisions, but many of them seem to do so as they make their more routine decisions, which are nevertheless often quite important.

2. Strategic Interaction   Although *some* oligopolists may ignore interdependence *some* of the time, models based on such behaviour probably do not offer a general explanation for *most* oligopoly behaviour *most* of the time. The reason is simple: Because they operate in the same market, the price and output decisions of soapsuds makers Brand X and Brand Y *really are* interdependent.

Suppose, for example, that Brand X, Inc. managers decide to cut their soapsuds' price from $1.12 to $1.05, on the assumption that rival Brand Y, Inc. will ignore this move and continue to charge $1.12 per box. Brand X decides to manufacture 5 million boxes per year and to spend $1 million per year on advertising. It may find itself surprised when Brand Y cuts its price to $1.00 per box, raises production to 8 million boxes per year, and sponsors the Grey Cup! In such a case, Brand X's profits will suffer, and the company will wish it had not cut its price in the first place. Most important for our purposes, Brand X managers will learn not to ignore interdependence in the future.

For many oligopolies, then, competition may resemble military operations involving tactics, strategies, moves, and countermoves. Thus, we must consider models that deal explicitly with oligopolistic interdependence.

3. Cartels   The opposite of ignoring interdependence occurs when all firms in an oligopoly try to do something about their interdependence and agree to set price and output, acting as a monopolist would. In a cartel, firms collude directly to coordinate their actions to transform the industry into a giant monopoly. We showed in Chapter 11 why cartels are difficult to organize and even more difficult to enforce.

4. Price Leadership and Tacit Collusion   Overt collusion—in which firms actually meet or communicate directly in some other way to decide on prices and outputs—is quite rare. But some observers think that *tacit collusion*—where firms, without meeting together, try to do unto their competitors as they hope their competitors will do unto them—occurs quite commonly among oligopolists in our economy. Oligopolists who do not want to rock a very profitable boat may seek to find some indirect way of communicating with one another, signalling their intentions and managing the market accordingly. Each tacitly colluding firm hopes that if it does not make things too difficult for its competitors, its rivals will return the favour. For example, three major makers of infant formula—Abbott Laboratories, Bristol-Myers Squibb, and American Home Products—were accused of conspiring against competitors by keeping their wholesale prices only a few cents apart. The formula makers denied any wrongdoing. (See the boxed feature "Acting on Recognized Interdependence versus 'Tacit Collusion'" for another example.)

One common form of tacit collusion is **price leadership,** an arrangement in which one firm in the industry, in effect, makes pricing decisions for the entire group. Indeed, a Bank of Canada survey conducted in 2002–2003 showed that price leadership is a pervasive phenomenon in the Canadian economy.[4] The survey, which is representative of the private unregulated and noncommodity producing segment of the Canadian industry,

Under **price leadership,** one firm sets the price for the industry and the others follow.

[4] See D. Amirault, C. Kwan, and G. Wilkinson, "A Survey of the Price-Setting Behaviour of Canadian Companies," *Bank of Canada Review* (Winter 2004–2005) pp. 29–40; and "Survey of Price-Setting Behaviour of Canadian Companies," Working Paper 2006-35, Bank of Canada.

POLICY DEBATE

Acting on Recognized Interdependence versus "Tacit Collusion"

Competition laws unequivocally prohibit price fixing—collusion among competitors in which they agree on their pricing policies (see Chapter 13). But suppose that the firms in an industry, recognizing their interdependence, simply decide to "go along with" each other's decisions? Is this collusion by long distance? Should it be declared illegal? Should the government require such a firm to "make believe" that it does not know how competitors will respond to its price moves? Must firms act as if they were not interdependent? If such requirements make no sense, what should the government require of oligopolistic firms?

The airline industry constantly illustrates this issue and its complexities. In 1992, American Airlines decided that the vast number of different airline fares and discounts hurt all airlines and that the industry needed a simplified fare structure. American offered a new, simplified pricing plan called "value pricing," in the hope that other airlines would copy that structure widely. But a few weeks later, Northwest Airlines introduced a special vacation travel deal that undercut American's pricing. This led to a price war, and American had to withdraw its plan, losing considerable money in the process. In this case, American's rivals did not go along with a price leader's decision.

In subsequent events, matters worked out differently. The airlines, which have lost money for years, have been seeking ways to cut costs by reducing wages, firing employees, and so on. As part of these cost-cutting efforts, Delta Airlines announced in early 1995 that it was capping payments to travel agents for each ticket sold. As it moved first to make the first such cut in ten years, Delta feared (as we know from its internal memoranda) that if the other airlines did not do the same, travel agents would stop booking passengers on Delta. Everything depended on whether other airlines would support Delta's new policy. They did. Within a week of Delta's

SOURCE: © Peter Christopher/Masterfile

announcement, the seven largest airlines each announced (apparently without consulting one another) that they would adopt Delta's ceiling on payments to travel agents. The travel agents sued, charging tacit collusion. The case was settled out of court with a compromise.

In March 2002, eight of the ten biggest American airlines went all the way and eliminated the ticket commission to travel agents altogether. Air Canada, the dominant airline in Canada, decided to follow their lead in April 2002, thus inducing Canadian travel agents to charge fees to their customers. As a result, a large number of Canadian travellers now book their flights directly on the Internet.

In a price war, each competing firm is determined to sell at a price that is lower than the prices of its rivals, usually regardless of whether that price covers the pertinent cost. Typically, in such a price war, Firm A cuts its price below Firm B's price; B retaliates by undercutting A; and so on and on until some of the competitor firms surrender and let themselves be undersold.

reveals that exactly half of the respondents indicate that there is a price leader in their industry. Other firms are expected to adopt the prices set by the price leader, even though no explicit agreement exists—only tacit consent. Often, the price leader will be the largest firm in the industry. But in some price-leadership arrangements, the leadership role may rotate from one firm to another. For example, analysts suggested that for many years the aluminum industry conformed to the price-leadership model, with Alcoa (Aluminum Company of America) and Alcan (Aluminum Company of Canada) assuming the leadership role at different times.

Price leadership *does* overcome some problems for the firms that result from oligopolistic interdependence, although it does not provide the only possible way of doing so. If Brand X, Inc. acts as price leader for the soapsuds industry, it can predict how Brand Y, Inc. will react to any price increases that it announces: Brand Y will match the increases. Similarly, Brand Z, Inc. executives will be able to predict Brand Y's behaviour as long as the price-leadership arrangement holds up.

One problem besetting price leadership is that, although the oligopolists as an industry may benefit by avoiding a damaging **price war,** the *firms* may not benefit equally. The price-leading firm may be able to enhance its own profits more easily than any of the other firms in the group can. But if the price leader does not consider its rivals' welfare as it makes price decisions, it may find itself dethroned! Like cartels, such arrangements can easily break down.

This is why a price leader may not be the largest firm in the industry nor the firm with the lowest unit costs; instead, it may often be the most representative firm, sometimes called the *barometric leader*, that is, the firm whose average cost represents the average cost in the industry. Price leadership is less likely to break down if the price leader itself is a medium-cost firm. This also explains why there are industrial norms as to how costs ought to be computed, which help the price leader to set prices that will be acceptable to the other oligopolistic firms.

ALTERNATIVE MODELS OF OLIGOPOLY

The study of oligopolies has given rise to a wide variety of models and hypotheses that we partially explore in this section—models that have a long history and have been the subject of intense debate. Because they question some of the principles and main assumptions of standard microeconomic analysis as presented in Chapters 7 and 8 (particularly the principle of diminishing returns and the profit-maximizing assumption), they are seldom found in principles textbooks. We introduce them here because we believe that these alternative models offer significant insights into the real world of oligopolies in which we live.

Sales Maximization

Early in our analysis of the firm we discussed the profit maximization hypothesis, and we noted that firms have other possible objectives. Among these alternative goals, one has attracted much attention: **sales maximization.**

Modern industrial firms often are managed by people who are not the owners of the companies. Paid executives manage the firms, working for the company on a full-time basis. These managers may begin to believe that whatever is good for them as individuals must be good for the company. The owners may be a large and diverse group of shareholders, most of whom own only a tiny fraction of the outstanding stock. They may take little interest in the company's day-to-day operations and may feel no real sense of ownership. In such a situation, managers' goals may influence company decisions more strongly than the owners' goal of profit maximization.

Some statistical evidence, for example, suggests that management's compensation often relates more directly to company *size*, as measured by sales volume, than to *profit*. The president of a large firm generally fetches a much higher salary—and bigger incentive rewards—than the president of a tiny company. Therefore, firm managers may select price–output combinations that maximize *sales* rather than profits. But does sales maximization lead to different outcomes than profit maximization? We shall see shortly that the answer is yes.

The graph in Figure 3 should be familiar by now. It shows the marginal cost (MC) and average cost (AC) curves for a soapsuds firm—in this case Brand X, Inc.—along with its demand and marginal revenue (MR) curves. We have used such diagrams before and thus know that if the company wants to maximize profits, it will select point *A*, where MC = MR. Brand X will produce 2.5 million boxes of soapsuds per year and sell them at $1 each (point *E* on the demand curve above *A*). Because average cost at this level of output is only 80 cents per box, X earns 20 cents economic profit per unit. Total profits are therefore $0.20 × 2,500,000 = $500,000 per year. This is the highest attainable profit level for Brand X.

But what if Brand X chooses to maximize total sales revenue instead? In this case, it will want to keep producing until MR falls to *zero*; that is, it will select point *B*. Why? By definition, MR is the *additional* revenue obtained by raising output by one unit. If the firm wishes to maximize total revenue, then whenever MR is positive, it

A firm's objective is said to be **sales maximization** if it seeks to adopt prices and output quantities that make its total revenue (its "sales"), rather than its profits, as large as possible.

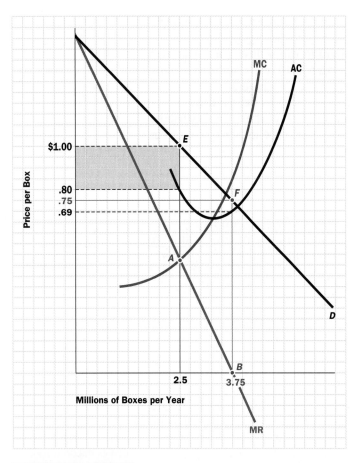

FIGURE 3

Sales-Maximization
Equilibrium

will want to increase output further, and any time that MR becomes negative, X's management will want to decrease output. Only when MR = 0 can management possibly have maximized total sales revenue.[5]

Students should note that point B will also correspond to the point on the demand curve where the price elasticity of demand is unity. This is because, as discussed in Chapter 6 on page 122, when demand is exactly unit-elastic, a small change in price will leave total revenue unaffected. When MR = 0, a small change in quantity leaves total revenue unaffected as well.

Thus the sales-maximizing firm looks to produce a level of output that corresponds to a point on the demand curve where price elasticity = 1.

Thus, if Brand X is a sales maximizer, it will produce 3.75 million boxes of soapsuds per year (point B), and charge 75 cents per box (point F). Because average costs at this level of production are only 69 cents per box, profit per unit is 6 cents and, with 3.75 million units sold, total profit is $225,000. Naturally, this profit is substantially less than what the firm can achieve if it reduces output to the profit-maximizing level. But that is not the goal of Brand X's management. The firm's sales revenue at point B is 75 cents per unit times 3.75 million units, or $2,812,500, whereas at point A it was only $2,500,000 (2.5 million units at $1.00 each). We conclude that:

If a firm is maximizing sales revenue, it will produce more output and charge a lower price than it would if it were maximizing profits.

Figure 3 clearly shows that this result holds for Brand X. But does it always hold? The answer is yes. Look again at Figure 3, but ignore the numbers on the axes. At point A, where MR = MC, marginal revenue must be positive because it equals marginal cost (which, we may assume, is *always* positive—output can normally not be increased at zero additional cost). At point B, MR is equal to zero. Because the marginal revenue curve slopes negatively, the point where it reaches zero (point B) must necessarily correspond to a higher output level than does the point where it cuts the marginal cost curve (point A). Thus, sales-maximizing firms always produce more than profit-maximizing firms and, to sell this greater volume of output, they must charge lower prices.[6]

■ Constant Marginal Costs

We have assumed up to now that all firms face diminishing marginal returns and therefore are confronted with rising marginal costs. The only exception was that of the natural monopoly, as discussed in Chapter 11, page 234. Indeed, in the case of perfect competition, profit maximizing can occur only on the rising portion of the marginal

---

[5] The logic here is exactly the same as the logic that led to the conclusion that a firm maximized profits by setting *marginal profit* equal to zero. If you need to review, consult Chapter 8, especially pages 175–176.

[6] *Exercise:* In the graph, how much below maximum profit is total profit under sales maximization?

cost curve, and hence only this rising portion is truly relevant to economic analysis. There has been, however, a continuous flow of empirical evidence that contradicts these assumptions, going as far back as the mid-1930s, when a vast study program was launched by a team of economists at Oxford University in England—the Oxford Economists' Research Group.

Empirical evidence reveals that most companies in the manufacturing and service industries operate, most of the time, within a range of output where marginal costs (MC) and hence short-run average variable costs (AVC) are constant. This range is associated with engineer-rated capacity—the output capacity of a plant, as defined by the engineers who designed the plant. This implies that average costs are decreasing up to full capacity as defined by the engineers. It is only beyond engineer-rated capacity that marginal costs rise briskly, in a discontinuous way, due to overtime labour costs and breakdowns in machinery. Therefore, as long as the rate of utilization of engineer-rated capacity is below 100 percent, marginal costs are approximately constant and average costs are falling; beyond 100 percent, marginal costs, average variable costs, and average costs are all rising. Indeed it has been argued by the Oxford researchers that firms *normally* operate in the constant marginal cost range. A survey of large American business firms conducted in 1990 by one of the authors of this textbook showed further that 89 percent of the surveyed managers believe that their marginal costs were either constant or decreasing.[7] This empirical view of costs in the manufacturing and service sectors is illustrated in Figure 4.

Students may wonder whether the shapes of the cost curves of Figure 4 contradict the principle of diminishing returns. In one sense they do but in another, they don't. Recall that the principle of diminishing returns is based on all but one factor of production being fixed (see Chapter 7)—a situation that we associated with the short run. What happens in Figure 4 is that while the capacity—the stock of capital—of the corporation or that of its plant is given, as it should be in the short run, the *degree* of utilization of that plant changes depending on the number of workers operating the plant, as well as on the other intermediate inputs, whenever output is increased. Thus, Figure 4 does not formally correspond to the principle of diminishing returns. Rather, it describes a situation where the two inputs, workers and machines in use, are complement inputs, increasing together rather than being substitutes, as was also described in the appendix to Chapter 7, in the "Fixed-Proportion Technology" section on page 164. In the case of many industries, notably manufacturing and services, but not for others (for instance, commodities and farming), this description may be more realistic.

The cost curves represented in Figure 4 help us to better understand the second of the two puzzles presented in Chapter 8. This puzzle examined the situation of a pocket calculator producer who accepted an offer to produce 10 million units at a price ($7) that was apparently below cost. But by doing so, because the marginal cost was constant at $3, the pocket calculator producer managed to reduce the average cost from $13 to $8, as shown in Figure 4. At $8, the average cost was below the average price per unit, which was $9—$11 for the first 10 million units and $7 for the next 10 million units (recall that when price discrimination was discussed in Chapter 11, page 242, constant marginal costs were assumed as well).

Indeed, in the case of manufacturing and services (also called the *secondary* and *tertiary* sectors), it is hard to find

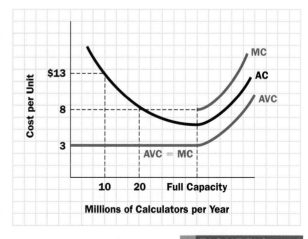

FIGURE 4

The Constant Marginal Costs of a Pocket Calculator Producer

[7]A. Blinder, E. R. D. Canetti, D. E. Lebow, and J. B. Rudd, *Asking About Prices: A New Approach to Understanding Price Stickiness* (New York: Russell Sage Foundation, 1992). Respondents may have somewhat confused marginal costs, which many engineering studies find to be constant, with total average costs, which would then be declining. Indeed, the economists making the survey found that the respondents sometimes had considerable difficulty distinguishing between fixed and variable costs.

real-world examples that do not rely on constant marginal costs. Obviously, the cost of producing one additional copy of a Microsoft Office suite does not increase as more of these copies are produced. As long as there is enough production capacity, additional copies can be produced, packaged, and shipped at a constant cost.

The following story is also instructive. When presenting the usual U-shape of cost curves, one of the authors had to deal with an infuriated student who just would not buy the principle of increasing costs. This student had worked for a publisher and argued very persuasively that average costs always decreased as the number of printed copies increased. The same certainly applies to the textbook you are now using. The more copies of this book that are printed and sold, the lower the average cost is for the publisher. This is because the marginal cost, and hence the average variable cost of a book, remains approximately constant as the number of printed copies increases.

> In oligopolistic industries, marginal costs (and hence average variable costs) are usually constant and total average costs are declining up to full capacity, as defined by the engineers who designed the factory.

Why don't firms operate at full capacity, at a 100 percent rate of capacity utilization, where total average costs (AC) are at their minimal level, as can be seen in Figure 4, instead of keeping reserves of capacity? Why do firms purposefully operate in a zone where there is excess capacity? Several reasons have been advanced. First, there are indivisibilities. A chemical plant may not be efficient unless it is designed to produce a large enough output. Even though expected sales may be lower than this minimal capacity, the managers will go ahead and build the plant, hoping that demand will rise in the future.

Second, firms are producing in an uncertain world and are subjected to fluctuations in sales. The existence of excess capacity allows firms to respond quickly to demand increases, thus keeping or increasing their share of the market. Without this excess capacity, any increase in demand could either not be met or would have to be met at ever-rising costs. The firm would thus either experience losses or it would need to raise prices, thus possibly losing the goodwill of its customers.

Third, the presence of excess capacity allows firms to respond to changes in the structure of demand. For instance, if a firm is producing both two-slice toasters and four-slice toasters, when demand for the latter increases, the firm can quickly retool some of its unutilized plant facilities in order to produce more four-slice toasters, without having to close down temporarily some of its production units to do so. Fourth, the presence of excess capacity acts as a deterrent to entry. Firms that contemplate entry into the industry realize that the existing firms could retaliate by swamping the market with additional products at a lower average cost and at lower prices, thus rendering production less attractive for new entrants.

For all of these reasons, modern firms normally operate below full capacity, in the range where marginal costs are constant. Indeed, several reports indicate that firms consider "normal" or "standard" rates of capacity utilization to be around 80 or 85 percent (see the boxed feature "Surveys of Rates of Capacity Utilization").

Markup Pricing

Besides profit maximizing and sales maximizing, another possible objective of the firm may simply be *satisficing*. Constant marginal costs are often associated with **markup pricing**, which is one variant of a more general pricing method referred to as **cost-plus pricing**. As its name indicates, cost-plus pricing means that prices are set by firms on the basis of their unit costs plus a profit margin. In the specific case of markup pricing, prices are based on the average variable cost, as the following markup formula shows:

$$P = (1 + m)AVC$$

Markup pricing is a specific cost-plus pricing procedure whereby the unit cost measure is the average variable cost, to which a gross costing margin is added.

Cost-plus pricing procedures are an alternative to marginal cost pricing whereby firms set prices by adding an arbitrary costing margin to some measure of unit costs to allow for profit.

Surveys of Rates of Capacity Utilization

Statistics Canada carries out an annual survey called the *Capital and Repair Expenditures Survey*, in which they ask 7,000 companies several questions regarding their capacity utilization rates. One of the survey questions is: "For [2008], this plant has been operating at which percentage of its capacity?"

The survey specifies that "Capacity is defined as maximum production attainable under normal conditions" by taking into account regular holidays. Statistics Canada offers two examples in the survey:

"Plant 'A' normally operates one shift a day, five days a week and, given this operation pattern, capacity production is 150 units

of product for the month. In that month, actual production was 125 units. The capacity use rate for plant 'A' is (125/150) * 100 = 83%.

"Now suppose that plant 'A' had to open for a shift on Saturdays to satisfy an abnormal surge in demand for its product. Given this plant's normal operation schedule, capacity production remains at 150 units. Actual production has grown to 160 units, so capacity use would be (160/150) * 100 = 107%."

On this basis, in the first quarter of 2008, for instance, survey results showed that the rates of capacity utilization in Canadian manufacturing stood at 79.8 percent.

SOURCE: Statistics Canada, *Survey on Capital Expenditures: Preliminary Estimate for 2006 and Intentions 2007-Reporting Guide*, F2, page 3, 2006. Retrieved from http://www.statcan.ca/english/sdds/document/2803_D5_T1_V8_E.pdf

To set prices, firms compute their average variable costs, to which they add a multiple of these average variable costs based on a percentage markup (m), also called the *percentage gross costing margin*. For instance, if the markup is 100 percent, m will be 1 and the price (P) will be twice the size of the average variable cost (AVC). If the markup is 200 percent, m will be 2 and P will be three times the value of AVC, as shown in Figure 5 where AVC is $10 and P equals (1 + 2) 10 = $30. The gross costing margin in percentage terms will be m, while the gross costing margin is m AVC.

Markup pricing is widely used by small firms. When these firms are not simply following their industry's price leader, they set prices in line with the markup formula. Setting prices can be quite an intricate and complex process in a world of interdependent firms, where managers have to make a multitude of decisions. Markup pricing makes use of a fast and frugal rationality: the information and processing requirements are quite simple. A shown in Figure 4, because average variable costs and marginal costs are approximately constant over the range of output that is usually relevant for firms (that is, below full capacity, at rates of capacity utilization below 100 percent), managers and accountants can easily calculate or estimate these unit costs. Managers responsible for setting prices then need only to add the industry standard costing margin to set prices that will simultaneously cover fixed costs and provide for a satisficing profit.

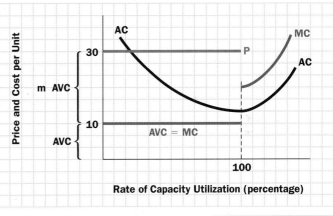

FIGURE 5

Markup Pricing

When one of the authors was visiting the University of Burgundy in Dijon, an economics Ph.D. student there said that his father was in the business of building greenhouses. When asked how his father set the price of his greenhouses, the student blushed and looked very uncomfortable. It turned out that the greenhouse builder asked his accountant to compute the average variable cost, and then simply multiplied this number by two to obtain the selling price of his greenhouses. Obviously the student was embarrassed to admit that his father did not abide by the marginal pricing rule with its profit-maximizing implications, using instead a rule of thumb based on markup pricing.

While some economists believe that markup pricing is a rule that seeks outcomes that are merely acceptable—a satisficing decision rather than an optimal one—others believe that markup pricing is marginal pricing in disguise. These economists point out that as long as output is below full capacity, average variable costs and marginal costs are equal. So, by setting a markup over average variable costs, firms are simply equating marginal revenue with marginal cost, as was shown in the case of monopolies and monopolistic competition. Markup pricing would thus be marginal pricing with imperfect information and a trial-and-error procedure. Low price elasticities would be associated with high markups, whereas cases of high price elasticities would require low markups. In the case of the greenhouse builder, this was probably true to some extent since the Dijon student confirmed that his father sometimes raised the markup when he felt that the purchaser of the greenhouse could afford to pay more (a case of price discrimination)!

There is a problem however with this interpretation. A recent survey of large American businesses has revealed that 84 percent of the respondents thought that they were operating in a range where their price elasticity of demand was below or equal to unity. Indeed, no less than 40 percent claimed that price elasticity was zero, giving a zero answer to the question: "If you cut your prices by, say 10 percent, by what percentage would you expect your unit sales to rise?" But this implies, as pointed out earlier, that marginal revenue is either negative or equal to zero. Since profit maximizing requires that marginal cost be equal to marginal revenue (MC = MR) and since marginal costs cannot be negative, these findings about the demand elasticity faced by firms imply that these firms cannot be maximizing profits.

■ Average Cost Pricing

Average cost pricing is a specific cost-plus pricing procedure whereby a *normal* average cost, which includes fixed costs, is assessed on the basis of *normal* output, to which is added a net costing margin.

While some small firms still use markup pricing, medium- and large-sized firms usually have access to more sophisticated accounting resources, and as a consequence, they tend to use a more sophisticated cost-plus pricing procedure: **average cost pricing**. The formula for average cost pricing (also known as *full cost pricing* or *normal cost pricing*) is just as simple as that of markup pricing, the only difference being that it involves average cost instead of average variable cost. The average cost pricing formula is:

$$P = (1 + n)AC_n$$

In this case, when firms set their prices, they compute their normal average cost (AC_n), that is, the average cost when the firm is operating at its *normal* degree of capacity utilization. Then they add a multiple of this average cost, based on the percentage net costing margin n. The net costing margin is thus $n\,AC_n$. This average cost, in contrast to the discussion in Chapter 8, does not include the opportunity cost of the capital funds that have been invested in the firm (the capital income that could have been obtained if the funds had been invested elsewhere). In other words, AC_n is the average cost as it would be assessed by accountants and not by economists. Thus, $n\,AC_n$ is the accounting profit per unit of output that firms will achieve if sales correspond to normal output.

This is all shown in Figure 6, where it has been assumed that the normal degree of capacity utilization corresponds to 80 percent, whereas full capacity, where marginal costs suddenly rise, corresponds to 100 percent. At a normal average cost of $15 and a percentage net costing margin of 33.33 percent, the price is set at $20. If sales correspond to normal output (here at 80 percent of full capacity), the firm will make a profit of $5 per unit. If firms sell more than normal output, (accounting) profits per unit will exceed $5 (the

FIGURE 6

Average Cost Pricing

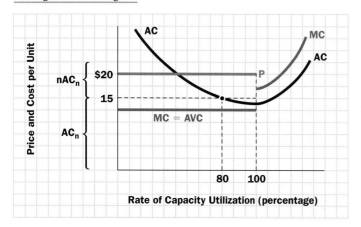

Rate of Capacity Utilization (percentage)

distance between the AC curve and the horizontal price line *PP* will be greater than at the normal 80 percent rate of capacity utilization), and if firms sell less than normal output, (accounting) profits per unit will be less than $5.

Why is average cost pricing based on a normal average cost, rather than on the *actual* average cost corresponding to the actual output level? The reason, once more, has to do with the lack of perfect information. Every different level of output implies a different level of average cost. In many markets, in particular in manufacturing and service industries, prices are set *before* sales and production actually occur. So, firms do not know what the actual output level or the actual level of sales will be, and hence they do not know in advance what the actual average cost will be. To compute average costs and set prices, firms therefore have to rely on a norm—the normal output level, based on the normal rate of utilization of capacity. The normal average cost will thus be assessed by the accountants at this normal output level. Indeed, in many industries, estimates of normal rates of capacity utilization or even estimates of normal average costs are provided by trade associations, so that members of the industry, and in particular the price leader, can set prices that are profitable for all.

Once prices have been set, firms provide catalogues (printed or electronic versions) where they advertise their prices, and for reasons that will be detailed later on, they usually stick to the announced prices. Firms cannot know in advance whether or not their output will be sold within a particular period at those prices, however. Firms can change production levels in reaction to changes in actual sales as opposed to projections, but this adjustment cannot be instantaneous, which explains why firms carry inventories of their goods. When sales exceed production, these inventories decline, and they rise when production exceeds sales. Without these inventories, a firm could miss out on a sale and hence lose part of its market share, as consumers are generally unwilling to wait till a product again becomes available. The number of cars that can be found on car dealers' lots is an obvious example of this. Buyers can purchase a car within an hour by choosing from the cars parked on a dealer's lot, instead of waiting several months for a car to be delivered by the manufacturer.

One issue we have not yet dealt with is that of the determination of the net costing margin *n*. How is that margin fixed? Reports on the pricing procedures followed by large corporations such as General Motors indicate that this margin is often set on the basis of a target rate of return. Firms set the costing margin in such a way that they will realize a certain rate of return on their investments (say, a 15 percent target rate) if sales correspond to the standard or normal rate of capacity utilization. The normal average cost and the costing margin give rise to the *standard* price, which is then the basis for determination of the actual price that will be decided on by the officers of the corporation. The actual price, relative to the standard price, will depend on the pricing strategy, the circumstances, and demand considerations.

Indeed, we will see in Chapter 13 that regulatory agencies that supervise natural monopolies often set prices on the basis of their version of average cost pricing, by allowing regulated monopolies to obtain net costing margins that generate a "fair" rate of return. This fair rate of return is a kind of target rate of return. Thus, these regulators set the prices of regulated monopolies in a way that is not much different from the way that business managers of oligopoly firms set prices when they are free to do so.

A question that is often put to those economists who believe that firms follow one kind or another of cost-plus pricing procedures is: What happens when two firms with different average variable costs or different normal average costs compete in the same market? Will less-efficient firms, which have higher costs, be able to sustain prices that are higher than those of the price leader? When the products of the industry are heterogeneous, as is the case of monopolistic competition, we know that there is some room for price discrepancies. When the products are more homogeneous, all prices have to gravitate around those set by the price leader, so that price followers will have to adjust their costing margins. All other factors being equal, the less efficient firms will thus have to be content with lower costing margins, and as a result, their profit rates (the rate of return on their capital) will be lower than those of the more efficient firms. These lower profit rates will slow down the growth of the less-efficient firms because, as we will see in detail in Chapter 16, these firms will have fewer financial resources to expand their capacity and engage in innovative research and development. Thus, competition reappears through the back door. Even though prices are such that all firms in an oligopolistic industry can earn at least a normal profit rate, the more successful and efficient firms will slowly eliminate the less-efficient ones through faster growth.

> In contrast to markup pricing, average cost pricing cannot be reduced to a case of trial-and-error marginal cost pricing.

The reason for this is that, in normal cost pricing, an increase in fixed costs, such as an increase in overhead (managerial) labour or in the corporate income tax, is shifted onto higher prices through a higher average cost. By contrast, as we saw in Chapter 8, an increase in fixed costs has no effect whatsoever on the profit-maximizing price. Thus, the behaviour of oligopolistic firms following average cost pricing, as is the case of sales-maximizing firms, is definitely different from that of oligopolistic profit-maximizing firms. Indeed, surveys of business managers show that respondents have difficulty distinguishing between fixed and variable costs, so it is dubious that many of them would be able to make use of marginal cost pricing.

■ Sticky Prices

A price is called **sticky** if it does not change often, even when there is a change in either demand or costs.

In a competitive industry with perfect information, you would expect prices to change frequently to reflect changes in costs and in demand. It has long been observed, however, that this is often not the case. This phenomenon is referred to as **sticky prices**. According to the Bank of Canada survey on pricing practices conducted in 2002–2003, while 18 percent of Canadian businesses change prices more than 52 times a year (at least once every week), 35 percent change prices once a year or less and 58 percent change prices four times a year or less. About two-thirds of the firms change prices using a fixed frequency (e.g., weekly, quarterly, annually). On a sector basis, the firms less likely to change prices (once a year on average) are those involved in the community, business, and personal services sectors. Firms in the retail and wholesale sectors are most likely to change prices. As expected, the survey shows that firms with more competitors tend to change prices more often, as do firms that export their products, possibly because they face more foreign competitors. Large firms change prices more often than small firms (five times more frequently), presumably because they have the managerial resources to do so; the managerial staff of smaller firms have too many diversified tasks to set aside time to think about price changes. As surprising as it may sound, firms often claimed that it was easier to change output levels in response to changes in demand than it was to change prices.

Reasons for Changing Prices Firms were asked what motivated their price changes and were given nine choices. Four of the nine were given most often:

1. Price changes by competitors
2. Changes in domestic input costs (non-labour)
3. Changes in the demand for their products or services
4. Changes in wage costs

These reasons certainly cover the two blades of the scissor of supply and demand. Price changes by competitors were by far the most important reason given for changing prices. While this could simply indicate a well-functioning competitive system, 51 percent of the survey respondents identified their industries as being dominated by a price leader. Price changes announced by the price leader would thus be imitated by price followers in an oligopolistic industry, and this would explain why price changes by competitors would be first in the list.

The other apparent demand-side factor, changes in the demand for their products or services, is third in the list, but the survey makers were careless in devising their question: There is nothing there that tells us that firms *raise* prices as demand *increases*.

Since there is a substantial amount of empirical evidence that average costs in manufacturing and service industries decrease as quantities produced increase, it may be that demand *increases* induce some firms to *change* prices by *decreasing* them. Indeed, a U.S. survey similar to the one carried out by the Bank of Canada showed that this counter-intuitive possibility is recognized to be real by a large percentage of respondents.

Supply-side factors do play a key role, with both changes in wage costs and, more important, in non-labour input costs standing out. In a truly competitive industry, changes in the input prices of individual firms should induce no change in prices, since these prices are determined by the market, with the firms being simply price takers. These two reasons for price changes are thus inconsistent with the profit-maximizing model of the competitive firm. On the other hand, the importance of supply-side factors is consistent with monopolistic competition as well as the cost-plus pricing procedures that were presented in this chapter, since prices are set on the basis of unit costs.

Reasons for Sticky Prices We have discussed so far why prices would be modified. But why do firms in some industries hold prices steady even though there may be pressures to change them? Table 1 provides a list of reasons why price changes are infrequent. The column on the right indicates the percentage of Bank of Canada survey respondents who answered that the reason being provided was very important, important, or slightly important. The percentages provided apply only to those firms that had a frequency of no more than four adjustments per year, in order to focus on firms that do have sticky prices.

TABLE 1
Reasons for Infrequent Price Changes

Theories	Description Given in Survey	% of Respondents Who Agreed
1. Cost-based pricing	Prices depend mainly on the costs of labour and raw materials used in producing goods and services. Therefore, prices don't change until costs change.	71.1
2. Customer relations	Prices could not change more often without disturbing customer relations.	69.1
3. Non-price competition	Firms are more likely to amend product characteristics (e.g., warranty, delivery lag) than prices.	46.4
4. Coordination failure—rising prices	Firms delay price increases because they do not want to be the first in the industry to raise prices.	45.4
5. Factor stability	Factors influencing prices do not change often enough to warrant changes.	41.3
6. Explicit contracts	Firms would like to adjust prices more often to reflect market conditions, but fixed-price contracts make it difficult to pass on price increases when a contract is active.	39.4
7. Low inflation	Low inflation rate makes large price changes more noticeable.	39.2
8. Implicit contracts	Firms delay price increases because they have an implied understanding with customers that they will not raise prices in tight markets.	35.1
9. Menu costs	It would be too costly to change prices more often (time, effort, out-of-pocket costs).	30.7
10. Coordination failure—falling prices	Firms delay price cuts because they do not want to be the first in the industry to cut prices.	30.0
11. Sticky information	The information used to review (and ultimately change) prices is available infrequently. Therefore, prices may be slow to adjust to new conditions.	16.5

SOURCES: David Amirault, Carolyn Kwan, and Gordon Anderson, "Survey of Price-Setting Behaviour of Canadian Companies," Working Paper 2006-35, Bank of Canada, p. 21; and "A Survey of the Price-Setting Behaviour of Canadian Companies," *Bank of Canada Review* (Winter 2004–2005), Table 13, p. 30.

The two top reasons presented in Table 1 for sticky prices, according to the senior executives of the surveyed companies, are cost-based pricing and customer relations. Once again, cost-based pricing, or what we have called *cost-plus pricing*, is consistent with the explanations offered by corporate officers. Because prices are based on unit costs (either the average variable cost, with markup pricing, or the normal average cost, with average cost pricing), prices are sticky as long as these unit costs remain unchanged. In the case of the average variable cost, the shape of its curve according to much empirical evidence is flat, so that it does not change whatever the output being produced. The normal average cost is based on a norm (normal output) that remains unaffected, by definition, when actual output levels change. Thus, besides a change in the costing margin, only an increase in unit costs that is external to the firm, **external diseconomies** as they are sometimes called, can cause an increase in prices, a point already made by Italian economist Piero Sraffa (1898–1983) in his famous 1926 critique of the cost curve shapes presented in Chapter 7.

The other major explanation of sticky prices is that of customer relations. Prices are not changed more often because firms do not want to create difficulties for their customers. Indeed, in this survey as in a similar American survey, the fear of antagonizing customers and hence losing future market shares ranked very high. This may be due to the fact that about 85 percent of firms' sales are made to regular customers. Most firms are not in the retail industry, dealing with individual consumers; rather, most firms' main clients are other firms, who purchase intermediate goods as inputs for their own production. Firms therefore must exercise caution in their customer relations and at least give the impression that they are setting fair prices.

A very similar argument seems to support the fourth most popular explanation of sticky prices presented in Table 1: that of coordination failure in the case of potentially rising prices. Firms often prefer to delay price increases because they do not want to be the first company in the industry to raise prices. They feel that if other firms increase prices first, they will avoid antagonizing their own customers. Even firms that described themselves as price leaders recognized this reasoning as an explanation of sticky prices. On the other hand, as can be seen from Table 1, coordination failure in the case of potentially falling prices (ranked tenth) did not appear to play such an important role, as customers will always be happy to benefit from lower prices, although firms could antagonize the other producers in the industry. Indeed,

> **External diseconomies** (and **external economies**) are increases (decreases) in the costs of an individual firm due to changes in the quantities being produced overall in the industry. For example, a rising demand for high-rise apartments can lead to an increase in the price of steel, thus leading to an increase in the production cost of apartments.

PUZZLE 3 RESOLVED: *The Fear of Antagonizing Customers*

The Bank of Canada survey of sticky prices certainly does help us to understand why products supplied by oligopolies or competitive monopolists (such as canned food, cars, televisions, and refrigerators) usually change prices only every few months or even more rarely. Besides the fact that many firms have explicit contracts that specify that prices cannot be changed more often (reason 6 in Table 1), firms fear antagonizing customers (reasons 2 and 4) and also they consider that they have an implicit contract with their customers, that is there is an implied understanding with customers that the firms will not raise prices when markets get tight (reason 8).

In January 1998, southeastern Ontario, southwestern Quebec, and parts of New Brunswick, Nova Scotia, and some U.S. states experienced an incredible ice storm—some 80 hours of freezing rain that wiped out 120,000 kilometres of power lines and telephone cables, 130 transmission towers and 30,000 wooden utility poles, cutting off the power in about a million households.

While for some the blackout lasted less than a day, for others it went on for days, even weeks. The demand for generators and restaurant services rose briskly, as many families were unable to cook food. As demand rose, prices should have shot up, but few businesses dared to take advantage of the tragedy and maximize their profits. Merchants and restaurant owners feared antagonizing their customers and the community by setting what most people would have considered to be unfair prices. They were afraid of losing goodwill and future sales. Those who ventured to raise prices were often the subject of highly negative reports in the press and on television.

price leaders paid little attention to this explanation. An asymmetry of this kind is the source of one of the most famous oligopolistic models—the kinked demand curve.

■ The Kinked Demand Curve Model

The **kinked demand curve** model accounts for the alleged "stickiness" in oligopolistic pricing while retaining the profit-maximizing assumption. For this reason, ever since its inception by members of the Oxford Economists' Research Group, it has always remained quite popular.[8] This model starts from the recognition that when an oligopolist cuts its product's price, it can never predict how rival companies will react. One extreme possibility is that Firm Y will ignore Firm X's price cut; that is, Firm Y's price will not change. Alternatively, Firm Y may reduce its price, precisely matching that of Firm X. Accordingly, the model of oligopolistic behaviour we discuss next uses two different demand curves. One curve represents the quantities a given oligopolistic firm can sell at different prices *if competitors match its price moves,* and the other demand curve represents what will happen if competitors stubbornly *stick to their initial price levels.*

Point *A* in Figure 7 represents our firm's initial price and output: 1,000 units at $8

> A **kinked demand curve** is a demand curve that changes its slope abruptly at some level of output.

each. Two demand curves, *DD* and *dd,* pass through point *A. DD* represents our company's demand if competitors keep their prices fixed, and *dd* indicates what happens when competitors match our firm's price changes.

The *DD* curve is the more elastic (flatter and more responsive) of the two, and a moment's thought indicates why this should be so. If our firm cuts its price from its initial level of $8 to, say, $7, and if competitors do not match this cut, we would expect our firm to get a large number of new customers—perhaps its quantity demanded will jump to 1,400 units. However, if its competitors respond by also reducing their prices, its quantity demanded will rise by less—per-

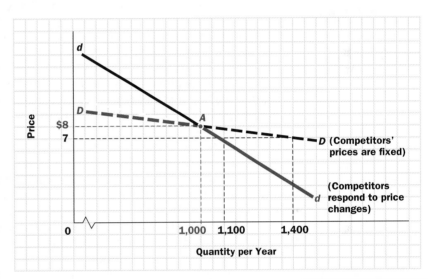

FIGURE 7

The Kinked Demand Curve

haps only to 1,100 units (more inelastic demand curve *dd*). Similarly, when it raises its price, our firm may expect a larger sales flight if its rivals fail to match its increase, as indicated by the relative flatness (elasticity) of the curve *DD* in Figure 7, as compared to *dd,* the firm's demand curve when rivals do match our firm's price changes.

How does this relate to sticky oligopolistic prices? The economists who designed this model hypothesized that a typical oligopolistic firm has good reason to fear the worst. If it lowers its prices and its rivals do not, its sales will seriously cut into its competitors' volume, and so the rivals will *have* to match the price cut to protect themselves. The inelastic demand curve, *dd,* will therefore apply if our firm decides on a price *reduction* (points below and to the right of point *A*).

If, on the contrary, our company chooses to *increase* its price, management expects its rivals to respond differently than they will to a price cut. The price-raising firm will fear that its rivals will continue to sit at their old price levels, calmly collecting customers as they flee from X's higher prices. Thus, this time, for price increases, the relevant demand curve (above *A*) will be *DD.*

---

[8] Variants of this model were constructed by Hall and Hitch in England and by Sweezy in the United States. See R .L. Hall and C. J. Hitch, "Price Theory and Business Behavior," *Oxford Economic Papers* 2 (May 1939), pp.12–45; and P. M. Sweezy, "Demand under Conditions of Oligopoly", *Journal of Political Economy* 47 (August 1939), pp. 568–573.

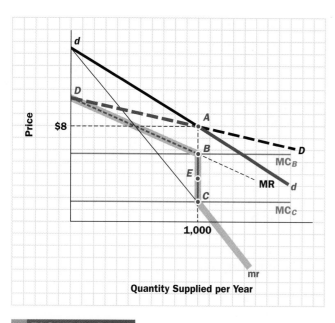

FIGURE 8

The Kinked Demand
Curve and Sticky Prices

In sum, our firm will figure that it will face a segment of the elastic demand curve *DD* if it raises its price and a segment of the inelastic demand curve *dd* if it decreases its price. Its true demand curve will then be given by the heavy blue line, *DAd*. For obvious reasons, it is called a kinked demand curve.

The kinked demand curve represents a "heads you lose, tails you lose" proposition in terms of any potential price changes. If a firm raises its price, it will lose many customers (because in that case its demand is elastic); if it lowers its price, the sales increase will be comparatively small (because then its demand is inelastic). In these circumstances, management will vary its price only under extreme provocation—that is, only if its costs change enormously.

Figure 8 illustrates this conclusion graphically. The two demand curves, *DD* and *dd*, are carried over precisely from Figure 7. The dashed line labelled MR is the marginal revenue curve associated with *DD*, while the solid line labelled *mr* is the marginal revenue curve associated with *dd*. The marginal revenue curve relevant to the firm's decision making is MR for any output level below 1,000 units, but *mr* for any output level above 1,000 units. Therefore, the segmented marginal revenue curve facing the firm is shown by the gold-highlighted line *DBCmr* with two slopes.

The marginal cost curve drawn in the diagram cuts this composite marginal revenue curve at point *E*, which indicates the profit-maximizing combination of output and price for this oligopolist. Specifically, the quantity supplied at point *E* is 1,000 units, and the price is $8, which we read from the blue demand curve *DAd*.

The unique aspect of this diagram is that the kinked demand curve leads to a marginal revenue curve that takes a sharp plunge between points *B* and *C*. Consequently, as long as the marginal cost curve shifts no higher than MC_B and no lower than MC_C, it will intersect the marginal revenue curve on its vertical *BC* segment and thus will *not* lead the firm to change its output decision. Therefore, *the firm's price will remain unchanged.* (Try this for yourself in Figure 8.) Only cost changes large enough to push the MC curve out of the *BC* range will lead to price changes.

If this is, in fact, the way oligopolists view their competitors' behaviour, we can easily see why they may be reluctant to make frequent price changes. We can also understand why price leadership may arise. The price leader firm can raise prices at will, confident that the firm will not be left out on a limb (a kink?) by other firms' unwillingness to follow.

In conclusion, it should be pointed out that while the kinked demand curve model provides a good explanation of why prices are sticky, it does not provide an explanation of why the price is what it is. In Figures 7 and 8, we started by assuming that the price was set at $8. But the model tells us nothing about why it *should* be set at $8. For this, we need some other theory, such as average cost pricing.

THE GAME-THEORY APPROACH

In 1944, the mathematician John von Neumann (1903–1957) and the economist Oskar Morgenstern (1902–1977) contributed a new approach to oligopoly analysis called *game theory*. Game theory is now economists' most widely used analysis of oligopoly behaviour. The theory deals with the issue of interdependence directly, taking for granted that the managers of business firms make decisions on the assumption that rival managers are strategic decision makers. In this model, each oligopolist acts as a competing player in a strategic game.

Game theory uses two fundamental concepts: *strategy* and the **payoff matrix**. A strategy represents a participant's operational plan. In its simplest form, it may refer to just one possible decision, such as "Add a new car to my product line that features a DVD player for backseat passengers," or "Cut the price of my car to $19,500." For simplicity's sake, game-theory analysis often focuses on an oligopoly of two firms—a *duopoly*.

An example will help to explain game theory analysis. Imagine that the market for telecommunications on a low-income Caribbean island is about to be entered by two cell-phone service providers. Say that patent restrictions and other impediments mean that the two companies each have a choice between only one of two cell phones: (1) an expensive, high-tech phone that would have to be sold at a price that gives the seller a low profit margin or, (2) a cheaper, low-tech phone with a high profit margin. Furthermore, under this island government's rules, each firm is required to offer the same phone and price for two years. Table 2 illustrates the resulting payoff matrix for one of the two "players" in this game, Firm A.

This matrix shows how the profits that Firm A can expect to earn depend on the strategy that its sole rival, Firm B, adopts. The choice open to each firm is to select one of the two available strategies—either the "low-tech, high-markup" cell phone or the "high-tech, low-markup" cell phone—without knowing the strategy that the other will choose. The matrix is read like a mileage chart. It shows, for example, that if Firm A chooses the high-tech option (second row of the matrix) and Firm B selects the low-tech option (left-hand column), then A will earn $12 million (lower left-hand square).

> A **payoff matrix**, shows how much each of two competitors (players) can expect to earn, depending on the strategic choices each of them makes.

Firm A's Payoff Matrix in a Game with a Dominant Strategy

		Firm B Strategy	
		Low-tech	High-tech
Firm A Strategy	Low-tech	$10m	$–2m
	High-tech	$12m	$3m

Games with Dominant Strategies

How does game theory analyze Firm A's optimal strategic choice? There are a number of related methods. The most direct way is to search for what is called a **dominant strategy**. Such a strategy is defined as the one that gives the bigger payoff to the firm that selects it, *no matter which of the two strategies the competitor happens to choose.* As a general matter, not all games have such a dominant strategy. But the one illustrated in Table 2 does. Let us see how we know this.

Consider Firm A's decision. Either company can select either the high-tech or the low-tech strategy. Whichever choice B makes, there are two possible profit outcomes for A depending on which strategy it selects. For example, if B selects low-tech, A will either earn $10 million or $12 million, depending its strategy choice (see the left-hand column of Table 2). So the high-tech strategy, with its $12 million payoff, is clearly A's better decision if B selects low-tech. But what if B turns out to pick high-tech, instead? In that case, we see from the right-hand column of the matrix that if A offers the low-tech product, it will lose $2 million while, with that same choice by firm B, A could earn $3 million in profit by choosing high-tech (the lower right-hand entry). So high-tech is again the better choice for A. Clearly, the high-tech option is a *dominant strategy* for firm A, because it will give A a higher profit than the low-tech choice *no matter which option Firm B selects.*

Now let us expand the payoff matrix to show simultaneously the earnings of both firms—not, as before, only those of Firm A. In Table 3, this combined payoff matrix reports the profits that each firm can expect to earn, given its own pricing choice and that of its rival. For example, the upper-left square indicates that if both firms decide to offer the low-tech, high-markup model, both A and B will earn $10 million. We also see that if one firm brings in the high-tech model, whereas the other does not, the high-tech supplier will actually raise its profit to $12 million (presumably by capturing more sales) and drive its rival to a $2 million loss. However, if both firms offer the high-tech model, each will be left with a modest $3 million profit.

> A **dominant strategy** for one of the competitors in a game is a strategy that will yield a higher payoff than any of the other strategies that are possible for the firm, no matter what choice of strategy is made by the firm's competitors.

The Two-Firm Payoff Matrix in a Game with Dominant Strategies

		Firm B Strategy	
		Low-tech	High-tech
Firm A Strategy	Low-tech	A gets $10m / B gets $10m	A gets $–2m / B gets $12m
	High-tech	A gets $12m / B gets $–2m	A gets $3m / B gets $3m

Exercise: Use the same reasoning as above to show that high-tech is also the dominant strategy for Firm B.

Because both firms have a dominant strategy in this example, and it is the same for both, they can both be expected to select it. Each will therefore end up offering the high-tech cell phone, and each will earn $3 million per year.

This example has important implications for policy, because it shows just how competition can force business firms to behave in the way that most benefits consumers, even though it is not the most profitable for the firms. In this example, both firms would have profited most by offering the lower-quality, higher-markup equipment. If they had both chosen the low-tech strategy, they would each have earned $10 million, but at the consumers' expense. However, the presence of a competitor, with its unknown choice, forces each firm to protect itself by offering the better (high-tech) product, even though they end up each earning only $3 million. Of course, if the market had been served by a profit-maximizing monopolist, the lone firm would have selected the more profitable low-tech option, and the public would have been denied the better-quality product.

> The Moral of the Story: A market that is a *duopoly,* that is, a two-firm oligopoly, can serve the public interest better than a monopoly because of the competition between the two duopolists.

Notice that each firm's fear of what its rival will do virtually forces it to offer the high-tech product and to forgo the higher ($10 million) profit that it could earn if it could trust the other to stick to a lower-quality product. This example illustrates why many observers conclude that, particularly where the number of firms is small, companies should not be permitted to confer or exchange information on prices or product quality. If the two rivals were allowed to collude and act like a monopolist, consumers would be damaged in two ways: They would have to pay more in order to provide the resulting additional profits and, besides, as usually is expected to happen under monopoly, consumers would normally get smaller quantities of the products and the products might well be of lower quality.

Games whose payoff matrices have dominant strategies like that in Table 3 have many other interesting applications. They illustrate how people can get trapped into making both themselves and their rivals worse off. For example, a matrix with the same pattern of payoffs applies to people driving polluting cars in the absence of laws requiring emission controls. Each driver runs a polluting auto because she does not trust other drivers to install emission controls voluntarily. So if she alone goes to the expense of equipping her car with pollution controls, most of the pollution—that from all other cars—will remain in the air. She will have paid for the equipment but have gotten little or no cleaner air benefit. So they all end up with a low payoff (breathing polluted air), even though by getting together and all agreeing to do what is needed to cut emissions, they could all end up with a higher payoff in terms of better health, etc.[9]

Still another interpretation explains why the game in Table 3 is known as the "prisoners' dilemma." Instead of a two-firm industry, the prisoners' dilemma involves two burglary suspects who are captured by the police and interrogated in separate rooms. Each suspect has two strategy options: to deny the charge or to confess. If both deny it, both go free, because the police have no other evidence. But if one confesses and the other does not, the silent prisoner can expect the key to his cell to be thrown away while the talker gets off with a light sentence. The dominant solution for each prisoner, then, is to confess and receive the light sentence that results from this choice.

The prisoners' dilemma story confirms the important economic point we made earlier. The reason the two prisoners are both driven to confess, and to bring themselves to justice, is that they are not allowed to communicate. Otherwise, they would collude and promise each other not to confess. The same thing applies to a

---

[9] *Exercise:* Make up a payoff matrix that tells this story.

duopoly. The public interest requires that the duopolists be banned from colluding. If they were permitted to get together and agree on a high price and low-cost, low-quality products, they would earn monopoly profits and the public would suffer the consequences.

The Moral of the Story: It is damaging to the public interest to permit rival firms to collude and to make joint decisions on what prices to charge for their similar products and what quality of product to supply.

Games Without Dominant Strategies

We have already observed that games need not offer dominant strategies. An example is easy to provide. For simplicity, Table 4 again shows only the payoffs for Firm A. But this time the hypothetical payoff numbers are different from those in Table 2.

With these new numbers, neither a low-tech nor a high-tech choice is a dominant strategy for A. Suppose A chooses to go with the low-tech product. Then, if B also happens to select low-tech, A will find itself better off (at a $10 million payoff) than if it had chosen a high-tech product (profit = $3 million). But if B goes the other way and offers the high-tech product, A's payoff will be worse ($7 million) with a low-tech product than with one that is high-tech ($8 million payoff). So which of the two options is better for A depends on B's unforeseeable strategy choice. Neither choice by A offers it foolproof protection, so neither of A's possible strategies is dominant.

The decision for A in Table 4 is now much harder than it was before. How can it go about selecting a strategy? One solution proposed in game theory is called the **maximin criterion.** In this strategy, we may envision the management of Firm A reasoning as follows: "If I choose a low-tech strategy, the worst that can happen to me is that my competitor will select the high-tech counterstrategy, which will make my return $7 million (the blue number in the first row of the payoff matrix). Similarly, if I select a high-tech strategy, the worst possible outcome for me is a $3 million profit" (the blue minimum payoff in the second row of the matrix). How can the managers of Firm A best protect their company from trouble in these circumstances? Game theory suggests that it may be rational to select a strategy based on comparison of the *minimum* payoffs of the different strategies. If the firm's managers want to cut down the risk, they should pick what can be interpreted as an insurance-policy approach. They should select the strategy that will guarantee them the *highest* of these undesirable minimum payoffs. In other words, expecting the worst outcome for any strategy choice it makes, Firm A should pick the strategy that promises the best of those bad outcomes. In this case, the maximin strategy for Firm A is to offer the low tech product, whose worst possible outcome is $7 million, while the worst outcome if it selects the high-tech product is a profit of only $3 million.

Other Strategies: The Nash Equilibrium

We can interpret the maximin strategy as a pessimist's way to deal with uncertainty. A player who adopts this strategy assumes that the worst will always happen: No matter what move she makes, her opponent will adopt the countermove that does her the most damage. The maximin strategy neglects the possibility that opponents will not have enough information to find out the most damaging countermove. It also ignores the possibility of finding common ground, as when two competitors collude to extract monopoly profit from consumers.

Other strategies are less pessimistic, yet still rational. One of the most analytically useful strategies leads to what is called a **Nash equilibrium.** The mathematician John Nash (1928 –) devised this strategy, for which he won the Nobel Prize in economics

TABLE 4

Firm A's Payoff Matrix in a Game Without a Dominant Strategy

	Firm B Strategy	
	Low-tech	High-tech
Low-tech	$10m	$7m
High-tech	$3m	$8m

Firm A Strategy

The **maximin criterion** requires you to select the strategy that yields the maximum payoff on the assumption that your opponent will do as much damage to you as he or she can.

A **Nash equilibrium** results when each player adopts the strategy that gives her the highest possible payoff if her rival sticks to the strategy he has chosen.

in 1994 (after a long period of schizophrenia).[10] The basic idea is simple. In a two-player game, suppose that each firm is trying to decide whether to adopt a red or a blue package for its product. Assume that each firm earns a higher profit if it selects a package colour that differs from the other's. Then, if Firm X happens to select a blue package, it will obviously be most profitable for Y to select a red package. Moreover, it will pay each firm to stick with that choice, because red is Y's most profitable response to X's choice of blue, and vice versa.

In general, a Nash equilibrium describes a situation in which both players adopt moves such that each player's move is the most profitable response to the other player's move. Often, no such mutually accommodating solution is possible. But where it is possible, if both players realize this fact and act accordingly, they may both be able to benefit. For example, note how much worse off both firms would be in the preceding example if Firm Y was determined to damage Firm X, at whatever the cost to itself, and adopted a blue package, just like X's.

■ Zero-Sum Games

There is a special but significant situation involving a simple form of payoff matrix that has even been taken up in popular parlance. It is called a **zero-sum game**. The idea is a simple one and is a useful way to think about many issues. A zero-sum game is one in which whatever one player gains, the other must lose. Thus, when one adds up all the gains and losses, the sum is always zero. If I pick your pocket and find $80 in cash, you are $80 poorer and I am $80 richer, so that the sum of the positive gains and negative losses is clearly zero. But if the money was in a wallet with your driver's licence and credit cards, and I take the money out and then throw the wallet into a river, it is evidently not zero-sum. You have lost not only the money but also the time and cost of replacing the licence and credit cards, whereas I have gained only the money. The payoff matrix of a zero-sum game has a very simple structure. Table 5 provides an example.

The special feature of this matrix is that the payoffs of the two firms add up to $10 million in each and every payoff square. For example, in the lower left-hand square of Table 5, Firm A's payoff is $4 million and Firm B's payoff is $6 million, for a total of $10 million. You can verify that the sum of the two payoffs is $10 million in each of the other three cells, as well.

When game theory was first developed, zero-sum games were all the rage, since game theory was closely associated with parlour games and military operations (notably during the Cold War, when such research was financed by the military), where there are winners and losers. The maximin criterion was then an essential element of game theory, as it was important to avoid disasters. Economists came to realize, however, that zero-sum games were not the most appropriate means of understanding economic behaviour, because economics focuses on voluntary exchange. As already discussed in Chapter 3, if two people trade, it must be because they both believe that they can gain from the exchange (unless one is compelled to do so). The following example should help you understand what we mean.

It was once thought that international trade is a zero-sum game, because it was believed that each trading nation's objective was to get as much gold as possible from other countries in payment for their purchases. If Brazil ships coffee to France, and the French shippers pay 10,000 ounces of gold for the shipment, then on this view of the matter, Brazil has gained and France has lost exactly the same amount—making it a zero-sum transaction. But a little thought tells us that this view is naïve, because it leaves the coffee shipment itself out of the calculation. Trade is not just about money, but also about the goods and services that are traded. If France is too cold to grow good coffee, and Brazil is too hot to produce good wine, and the populations of both countries prefer coffee in the morning and wine in the evening, then it is clear that both will be better off as

A **zero-sum game** is one in which exactly the amount one competitor gains must be lost by other competitors.

TABLE 5

Zero-Sum Payoff Matrix

	Firm B Strategy	
Firm A Strategy	**Strategy 1**	**Strategy 2**
Strategy 1	A gets $10m / B gets 0	A gets $–2m / B gets $12m
Strategy 2	A gets $4m / B gets $6m	A gets $7m / B gets $3m

---

[10] As described in the 2001 movie *A Beautiful Mind*, which was based on the book by Sylvia Nasar.

the result of an exchange of wine for coffee. The game of international trade is far from zero-sum. This is something that must be kept in mind when we consider contentious trade-related issues such as globalization and outsourcing.

Repeated Games

The scenarios described so far involve one-time transactions, as when a tourist passes through a city and makes a purchase at a store that he will never visit again. Most business transactions are different. A firm usually sells its products day after day, often to repeat buyers. It must continuously review its pricing decisions, knowing that its rivals are likely to gain information from any repeated behavioural patterns and adapt their response. The important concept of repeated games also offers significant additional insights about the competitive process under oligopoly.

Repeated games give all of the players the opportunity to learn something about each other's behaviour patterns and, perhaps, to arrive at mutually beneficial arrangements. By adopting a fairly clear pricing behaviour pattern, each firm can attain a reputation that elicits desired responses from competitors.

A **repeated game** is one that is played over again a number of times.

We return to the example of the product introduction war between Firm A and Firm B to show how this approach works. When we studied the payoff matrix for that game, we assumed that in a single play in which neither player knew anything about the other's behaviour pattern, each player was likely to feel forced to adopt its dominant strategy. In other words, each firm offered the low-profit, high-tech product for fear that if it adopted the potentially more profitable low-tech product, its rival would adopt a high-tech product and take customers away. In that way, both firms would end up with low profits.

But when games are repeated, the players may be able to escape such a trap. For example, Firm A can cultivate a reputation for selecting a strategy called *tit for tat*. Each time Firm B chooses a high-tech product, Firm A responds by also introducing a high-tech product, with its limited profit, next time. Firm A also follows a similar repeating strategy if B's product choice is low-tech. After a few repetitions, B will learn that A always matches its decisions. B will then see that it is better off sticking to a more profitable low-tech product. Firm A, too, benefits from its tit-for-tat approach, which will lead both, eventually, to stick permanently to the more profitable low-tech products.

In practice, this amounts to tacit collusion. The two competing firms never actually get together to reach a joint decision on product price and quality, behaviour that is illegal. But they watch one another's behaviour in their repeated game, and each eventually learns to adapt itself and go along with the other's behaviour—which may be anticompetitive and damaging to consumer interests, but offers monopoly profits to the tacit colluders. The courts do not have a clear response to this behaviour, because it is difficult to argue that firms should not consider all publicly and legitimately available information about its rivals, or that firms should not take this observed rival behaviour into consideration when they make their own decisions.

Threats and Credibility   A player can also use *threats* to induce rivals to change their behaviour. The trouble is that, if carried out, the threat may well damage both parties. For example, a retailer can threaten to double its output and drive prices down near zero if a rival imitates its product. However, the rival is unlikely to believe the threat, because such a low price harms the threatener as much as the threatened. Such a threat is simply not *credible*, with one exception.

The possibility can become a **credible threat** if the threatener takes steps that commit it to carry out the action. For example, if Firm A signed an irrevocable contract committing it to double its output if Firm B copied A's product, then the threat would become credible, and B would be forced to believe it. But A can make other commitments that make its threat credible. For example, it can build a large plant with plenty of excess capacity, as we already discussed earlier in this chapter in the section "Constant Marginal Costs." The factory may be very expensive to build, but once built, that cost is irrevocable. If the additional cost of turning out the product, once the plant has been

A **credible threat** is a threat that does not harm the threatener if it is carried out.

built, is very low, then it will pay A to expand its output of the product even at a very low price (if that price exceeds the marginal [variable] cost of the item). So, having built the large factory, the threat to expand output in response to entry becomes credible.

This last possibility leads directly to an important application of game theory: how firms inside an industry ("old firms") can decide strategically on ways to prevent *new* firms from entering into the industry. To create a credible threat to potential entrants, the old firm may well consider building a bigger factory or more plants than it would otherwise want.

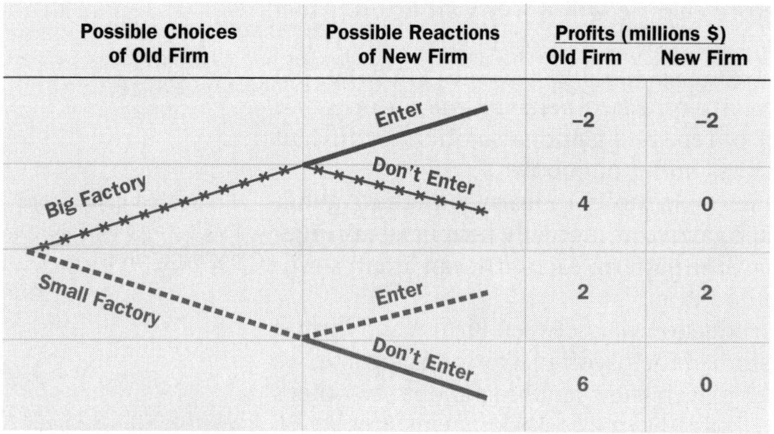

Some hypothetical numbers and a typical game-theory graph will make the story clear. The old firm faces two options: to build a small factory or a big one. Potential entrant firms also face two options: open for business (that is, enter the industry) or do not enter. Figure 9 shows the four resulting possible decision combinations and the corresponding profits or losses that the two firms may expect in each case.

The graph shows that the best outcome for the old firm occurs when it builds a small factory and the new firm decides not to enter. In that case, the old firm will earn $6 million, whereas the new firm will earn nothing, because it never starts up.

Possible Choices of Old Firm	Possible Reactions of New Firm	Profits (millions $) Old Firm	New Firm
Big Factory	Enter	–2	–2
Big Factory	Don't Enter	4	0
Small Factory	Enter	2	2
Small Factory	Don't Enter	6	0

FIGURE 9

Entry and Entry-Blocking Strategy

However, if the old firm *does* decide to build a small factory, it can be fairly sure that the new firm *will* open up for business, because the new firm can then earn $2 million (rather than zero), as shown by the dashed lines. In the process, the old firm's profit will be reduced, also to $2 million.

But if the old firm builds a big factory, its increased output will depress prices and profits. The old firm will now earn only $4 million if the new firm stays out, as shown by the asterisk line, whereas *each* firm will *lose* $2 million if the new firm enters. Obviously, if the old firm builds a big factory, the new firm will be better off staying out of the business rather than subjecting itself to a $2 million loss.

What size factory, then, should the old firm build? When we consider the firms' interactions, the old firm should clearly build the large factory with its excess capacity—because this decision will keep the new firm out of the industry, leaving the old firm with a $4 million profit. The moral of the story: "Wasting" money on excess capacity may not be wasteful to the oligopolist firm if it protects the firm's long-term interest.

Of course, game theory is a much richer topic than we have explained here. For example, game theory also provides tools for economists and business managers to analyze coalitions. It indicates, for cases involving more than two firms, which firms would do well to align themselves together against which others. People other than economists also have used game theory to analyze a variety of complicated problems outside the realm of oligopoly theory. Management training programs employ its principles, as do a number of government agencies (see "Application: Game Theory and the Wireless Communications Industry" on the next page). Political scientists and military strategists use game theory to formulate and analyze strategy.

MONOPOLISTIC COMPETITION, OLIGOPOLY, AND PUBLIC WELFARE

How well or poorly do monopolistically competitive or oligopolistic firms perform, from the viewpoint of the general welfare?

We have seen that their performance *can* leave much to be desired. For example, the excess capacity theorem showed us that monopolistic competition can lead to inefficiently high production costs. Similarly, because market forces may not sufficiently

Application: Game Theory and the Wireless Communications Industry

In 2001, Industry Canada commissioned a study of the Canadian wireless industry to assess the competitiveness and the structure of this industry. As can be seen in the first of the accompanying charts, which gives the subscribers' market shares in 2003, the industry was dominated by three companies—TELUS, Bell Mobility (Bell Canada), and Rogers—with a fourth one, Microcell, being a possible strong competitor. The three remaining market participants were partners of Bell Canada. By the end of 2004, however, Microcell had been taken over by Rogers, at a $1.5 billion cost, providing Rogers with a market share equivalent to that of Bell Canada and its partners. In 2006, Bell assumed responsibility for Aliant Mobility, so that the Canadian wireless communications market is now down to only three competitors; their respective market shares are shown in the second chart.

In our context, what is interesting however is that the 2001 study refers to a previous assessment of the Canadian wireless phone industry that was based on sophisticated developments of game theory, although the authors of the 2001 study show some reservations about their applicability in the case of the wireless industry. Obviously, Industry Canada believes that a field of three competitors is good enough, regardless of what has been "proven" by game theorists!

The analyst goes further, however, to suggest that the number of players in a market place significantly affects the industry's prof-
itability. Nobel Prize game theorist Reinhardt Selten is noted as proving "mathematically" that five is the number of competitors where tacit cooperation between competitors breaks down. In other words, four competitors are too few to ensure a properly functioning competitive market.... [The analyst] speculates that the Canadian market has slightly less than four full competitors (i.e., they suggest the smallest Canadian network operator is only a half a competitor and that tacit cooperation is therefore likely or at least possible.) We have extreme reservations regarding the casual application of theoretical work (such as Selten's) to a real-world situation (such as the Canadian mobile industry). To begin with, Selten's predictions are dependent on specific institutional assumptions regarding commitment possibilities in a quota cartel, which are clearly not satisfied in the mobile wireless market.... In any event, we do know that increasing the number of competitors from two to four has had a significant impact on the competitive status of the Canadian mobile wireless market, resulting in much more price competition as well as service package choice. It should be noted that in some cases, a greater number of wireless providers in a market can lead to poorer customer service.*

*Wall Communications Inc., *A Competitive Assessment of the Canadian Mobile Wireless Industry*, prepared for Industry Canada, November 2001, pp. 61–63.

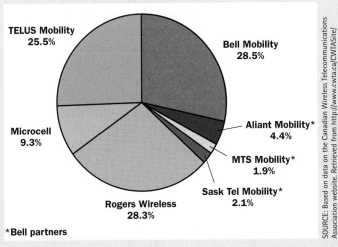

SOURCE: Industry Canada, Wireless Market Share by Company, 2003 of the Telecommunications Service in Canada: An Industry Review, 2004. Reproduced by permission of the Minister of Public Works and Government Services, 2007.

TELUS Mobility 25.5%
Bell Mobility 28.5%
Microcell 9.3%
Aliant Mobility* 4.4%
MTS Mobility* 1.9%
Sask Tel Mobility* 2.1%
Rogers Wireless 28.3%
*Bell partners

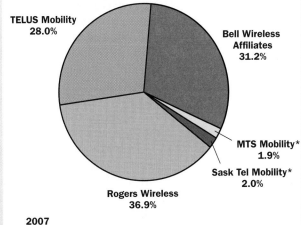

SOURCE: Based on data on the Canadian Wireless Telecommunications Association website. Retrieved from http://www.cwta.ca/CWTASite/english/facts_figures_downloads/SubscribersStats_2005–2006.pdf

TELUS Mobility 28.0%
Bell Wireless Affiliates 31.2%
MTS Mobility* 1.9%
Sask Tel Mobility* 2.0%
Rogers Wireless 36.9%
2007

Wireless Market Share by Company, 2003 and 2007, by Number of Subscribers

restrain their behaviour, oligopolists' prices and outputs may differ substantially from socially optimal levels. In particular, when oligopolists organize themselves into a successful cartel or into a well-disciplined price-leadership structure, prices will be higher and outputs lower than those associated with their perfectly competitive counterparts. Moreover, some people believe that misleading advertising by corporate giants often distorts consumers' judgments, leading them to buy things they do not need and would otherwise not want. Many social critics feel that such corporate giants wield political power, economic power, and power over the minds of consumers—power that undermines the benefits of Adam Smith's invisible hand.

Because oligopoly behaviour varies so widely, the social welfare implications differ from case to case. Some recent economic analysis, however, provides one theoretical

A market is **perfectly contestable** if entry and exit are costless and unimpeded.

case in which oligopolistic behaviour and performance quality can be predicted and judged unambiguously.[11] The analysis also can serve as a model for government agencies that are charged with the task of preventing harmful anticompetitive behaviour by oligopolistic firms. In this theoretical case, called a **perfectly contestable** market, entry into or exit from the market is costless and unimpeded. Here, the constant threat of the possible entry by new firms forces even the largest existing firm to behave well—to produce efficiently and never overcharge. Otherwise, the firm will be threatened with replacement by an entrant that offers to serve customers more cheaply and efficiently.

We define a market as perfectly contestable if firms can enter it and, if they choose, exit it without losing the money they invested. The crucial issue here is not the amount of capital required to enter the industry, but whether an entrant can withdraw the investment if it wishes. For example, if market entry requires investing in highly *mobile* capital (such as airplanes, trucks, or river barges—which can be moved around easily), the entrant may be able to exit quickly and cheaply.[12] For instance, if a car rental company decides to serve the Edmonton area but finds business disappointing, it can easily transfer its cars to, say, the Calgary area.

A profitable market that is also contestable therefore attracts *potential* entrants. Because no barriers to entry or exit exist, firms incur little risk by going into such a market. If their entry turns out to have been a mistake, they can move to another market without loss.

Because perfect competition requires a large number of firms, all of them small relative to the size of the industry, no industry with economies of large-scale production can be perfectly competitive. However, markets that contain a few relatively large firms may be highly contestable, although they are certainly not perfectly competitive. But no real-world industry is *perfectly* contestable, just as no industry is perfectly competitive.

The constant threat of entry forces oligopolists to perform well. Even monopolists must perform well if they do business in a highly contestable market. In particular, perfectly contestable markets have at least two socially desirable characteristics.

First, the freedom of entry eliminates any excess economic profits, so in this respect contestable markets resemble perfectly competitive markets. For example, if the current opportunity cost of capital is 12 percent while the firms in a contestable market are earning a return of 18 percent, then new firms will enter the market, expand the industry's outputs, and drive down the prices of its products to the point at which no firm earns any excess profit. To avoid this outcome, established firms must expand output to a level that precludes excess profit.

Second, inefficient enterprises cannot survive in a perfectly contestable industry because cost inefficiencies invite replacement of the existing firms by entrants that can provide the same outputs at lower cost and lower prices. Only firms operating at the lowest possible cost can survive. In sum, firms in a perfectly contestable market will be forced to operate as efficiently as possible and to charge prices as low as long-run financial survival permits.

The theory of contestable markets has been widely used by courts and government agencies concerned with the performance of business firms and provides workable guidelines for improved or acceptable behaviour in industries in which economies of scale mean that only a small number of firms can or should operate.

A GLANCE BACKWARD: COMPARING THE FOUR MARKET FORMS

We have now completed the set of chapters that has taken us through the four main market forms: perfect competition, monopoly, monopolistic competition, and oligopoly. You have probably absorbed a lot of information about the workings of these

[11] See William J. Baumol, John C. Panzar, and Robert D. Willig, *Contestable Markets and the Theory of Industry Structure*, rev. ed. (San Diego: Harcourt Brace Jovanovich, 1988).
[12] Earlier it was thought that air transportation could be classified as a highly contestable industry, but recent evidence suggests that although this judgment is not entirely incorrect, it requires considerable reservations.

market forms as you read through Chapters 10 through 12, but you may be confused by the details. Table 6 presents an overview of the main attributes of each of the market forms for comparison. It shows that:

- Perfect competition and pure monopoly are concepts useful primarily for *analytical* purposes—we find neither very often in reality. There are many monopolistically competitive firms, and oligopoly firms account for the largest share of the economy's output.
- Profits are zero in long-run equilibrium under perfect competition and monopolistic competition because entry is so easy that high profits attract new rivals into the market.
- Consequently, AC = AR in long-run equilibrium under these two market forms. In equilibrium, MC=MR for the profit-maximizing firm under any market form. However, under oligopoly, firms may adopt the strategies described by game theory or they may pursue goals other than profits; for example, they may seek to maximize sales. Therefore, in the equilibrium of the oligopoly firm, MC may be unequal to MR.
- As we will confirm in Chapter 14, the behaviour of the perfectly competitive firm and industry theoretically leads to an efficient allocation of resources that maximizes the benefits to consumers, given the resources available to the economy. Monopoly, however, can misallocate resources by restricting output in an attempt to raise prices and profits. Under monopolistic competition, excess capacity and inefficiency are apt to result. And under oligopoly, almost anything can happen, so it is impossible to generalize about its vices or virtues.

TABLE 6						
Attributes of the Four Market Forms						
Market Form	Number of Firms in the Market	Frequency in Reality	Entry Barriers	Public Interest Results	Long-Run Profit	Equilibrium Conditions
Perfect competition	Very many	Rare (if any)	None	Good	Zero	MC = MR = AC = AR = P
Pure monopoly	One	Rare	Likely to be high	Outputs not optimal	May be high	MR = MC
Monopolistic competition	Many	Widespread	Minor	Inefficient	Zero	MR = MC AR = AC
Oligopoly	Few	Produces large share of GDP	Varies	Varies	Varies	Varies

SUMMARY

1. Under **monopolistic competition**, there are numerous small buyers and sellers; each firm's product is at least somewhat different from every other firm's product—that is, each firm has a partial "monopoly" over some product characteristics, and thus a downward-sloping demand curve; there is freedom of entry and exit; and there is perfect information.

2. In long-run equilibrium under monopolistic competition, free entry eliminates economic profits by forcing the firm's downward-sloping demand curve into a position of tangency with its average cost curve. Therefore, output will be below the point at which average cost is lowest. As a result, monopolistic competitors are said to have "**excess capacity**."

3. An oligopolistic industry is composed of a few large firms selling similar products in the same market.

4. Under **oligopoly**, each firm carefully watches the major decisions of its rivals and often plans counterstrategies. As a result, rivalry is often vigorous and direct, and the outcome is difficult to predict.

5. One model of oligopoly behaviour assumes that oligopolists ignore interdependence and simply maximize profits or sales. Another model assumes that they join together to form a cartel and thus act like a monopoly. A third possibility is **price leadership**, where one firm sets prices and the others follow suit.

6. A firm that maximizes sales will continue producing up to the point where marginal revenue is driven down to zero. Consequently, a **sales maximizer** will produce more than a profit maximizer and will charge a lower price.

7. Empirical evidence seems to show that many oligopolistic firms operate in the flat range of their marginal cost curve, and hence inside a range where average costs are decreasing, thus also exhibiting excess capacity.

8. There is also substantial evidence that many firms resort to **cost-plus pricing** procedures, assessing a standard price by adding a costing margin to some measure of unit cost. The actual price is set on the basis of the standard price, by taking into account the pricing strategy of the firm, the market circumstances, and the prices set by other firms, in particular those of the price leader when there is one.

9. Smaller firms usually resort to **markup pricing,** setting prices on the basis of average variable costs. Larger firms usually resort to **average cost pricing,** setting prices on the basis of normal average costs, thus taking into account all costs, including fixed costs, in their pricing decision.

10. Large firms often set a net costing margin that allows them to achieve a target rate of return (or fair rate of return) on their investments when sales correspond to the normal rate of capacity utilization.

11. Sticky prices—prices that are adjusted less frequently than would be true under either perfect competition or pure monopoly—seem to arise essentially for two reasons: the prevalence of cost-plus pricing procedures and fears of antagonizing customers and hence losing future market shares.

12. Another explanation of sticky prices—one that still relies on the assumption of profit maximization—is based on the **kinked demand curve** model. If a firm thinks that its rivals will match any price cut but fail to match any price increase, its demand curve becomes "kinked" and its price will be sticky. This model however does not explain why the price is what it is.

13. **Game theory** provides new tools for the analysis of business strategies under conditions of oligopoly.

14. A **payoff matrix,** shows how much each of two competitors (players) can expect to earn, depending on the strategic choices each of them makes. It is used to analyze the reasoning that applies and the possible outcomes when the payoff to any oligopolist depends on what the other oligopolists in the market will do, so that they are all interdependent.

15. A **dominant strategy** for one of the competitors in a game is a strategy that will yield a higher payoff than any of the other strategies that are possible for her, no matter what choice of strategy is made by her competitors. So selection of a dominant strategy, where it is possible, is a good way for a competitor to avoid risk.

16. In a **maximin** strategy, the player takes the strongest possible precautions against the worst possible outcome of any move it selects.

17. In a **Nash equilibrium**, each player adopts the move that yields the highest possible payoff to itself, given the move selected by the other player.

18. A **zero-sum** game is one in which exactly the amount one competitor gains must be lost by other competitors. The zero-sum game is a useful analytic concept, even though it is rare in the real world.

19. In **repeated games**, a firm can seek to acquire a reputation that induces the other player to make decisions that do not damage its interests. It may also promote its goals by means of **credible threats.**

20. Monopolistic competition and oligopoly can be harmful to the general welfare. But because behaviour varies widely, the implications for social welfare also vary from case to case.

KEY TERMS

TEST YOURSELF

1. Using game theory, set up a payoff matrix similar to one that GM's management might employ in analyzing the problem presented in Discussion Question 5.

2. Test Yourself Question 2 at the end of Chapter 11 presented cost and demand data for a monopolist and asked you to find the profit-maximizing solution. Use these same data to find the sales-maximizing solution. In terms of the firm's MR, explain why the answers are different.

3. The producers of Halo 3 spent a lot of money creating the video game, but the cost of producing one additional CD of the game is just a few dollars. Illustrate this situation with a graph, drawing the likely shapes of the average cost and marginal cost curves, showing why marginal cost pricing is unlikely to occur under the circumstances.

4. In the payoff matrix Table 3, which is Firm B's dominant strategy? Show the calculation that leads to that conclusion.

5. You are given a payoff matrix for a *zero-sum* game. You see that, for one pair of strategy choices by the two firms, A's payoff is 9 and B's payoff is 6. For a second set of strategy choices A's payoff is 5. What is B's payoff?

6. CostPlus Enterprise computes its normal average cost to be $40. Its percentage net costing margin is set at 25 percent. The normal cost is computed with an 80 percent rate of capacity utilization. The engineer-rated capacity of the firm is 10,000 units per month. What is the monthly amount of profits that CostPlus Enterprise will make if sales correspond to normal output?

DISCUSSION QUESTIONS

1. How many real industries can you name that are oligopolies? How many that operate under monopolistic competition? Perfect competition? Which of these is most difficult to find in reality? Why do you think this is so?

2. Consider some of the products that are widely advertised on television. By what kind of firm is each produced—a perfectly competitive firm, an oligopolistic firm, or another type of firm? How many major products can you think of that are *not* advertised on TV?

3. In what ways may the small retail sellers of the following products differentiate their goods from those of their rivals to make themselves monopolistic competitors: hamburgers, radios, cosmetics?

4. Pricing of securities on the stock market is said to be carried out under conditions in many respects similar to perfect competition. The auto industry is an oligopoly. How often do you think the price of a share of Ford Motor Company's common stock changes? How about the price of a Ford Taurus? How would you explain the difference?

5. Suppose that General Motors hires a popular singer to advertise its compact automobiles. The campaign is very successful, and the company increases its share of the compact-car market substantially. What is Ford likely to do?

6. A new entrant, Bargain Airways, cuts air fares between Eastwich and Westwich by 20 percent. Biggie Airlines, which has been operating on this route, responds by cutting fares by 35 percent. What does Biggie hope to achieve?

7. If air transportation were perfectly contestable, why would Biggie Airlines (see Discussion Question 8) fail to achieve the ultimate goal of its price cut?

8. Which of the following industries are most likely to be contestable?

   a. Aluminum production

   b. Barge transportation

   c. Automobile manufacturing

   Explain your answers.

9. Since the deregulation of air transportation, a community served by a single airline is no longer protected by a regulatory agency from monopoly pricing. What market forces, if any, restrict the ability of the airline to raise prices as a pure monopolist would? How effective do you think those market forces are in keeping air fares down?

10. Do you feel that, with the current three participants, there is enough competition in the wireless telephone industry? Can you provide anecdotal evidence of why you believe there is enough or not enough competition?

11. What implications do you see for the "laws" of supply and demand if most oligopolistic firms face constant marginal costs and use average cost pricing?

12. Explain, for a repeated game:

   a. Why it may be advantageous to have the reputation of being a tough guy who always takes revenge against anyone who harms your interests.

   b. Why it may be advantageous to have a reputation of irrationality.

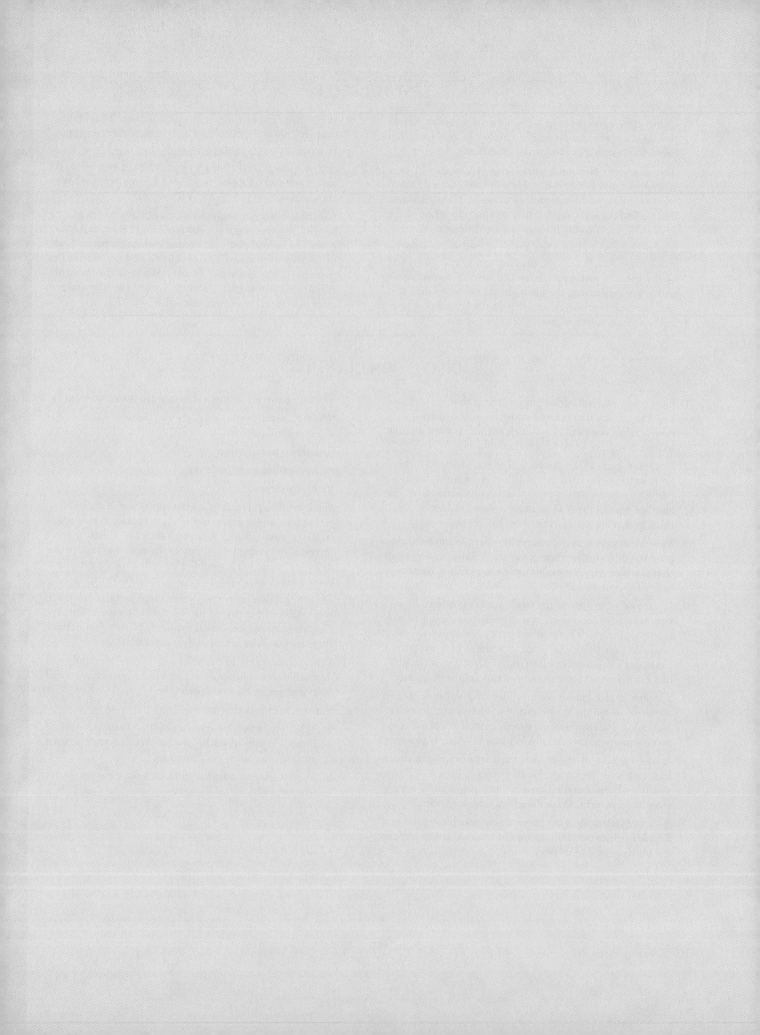

LIMITING MARKET POWER: REGULATION AND COMPETITION POLICY

. . . the one law you can't repeal is supply and demand.

WILLIAM SAFIRE, *THE NEW YORK TIMES,* JULY 13, 1998

To protect the interests of the public when industries are, or threaten to become, monopolistic or oligopolistic, government in Canada uses two basic tools. *Competition policy* seeks to prevent acquisition of *monopoly power* and to ban certain monopolistic practices. All private business firms are subject to the Competition Act. In addition, some industries are *regulated* by rules that constrain firms' pricing and other decisions. Generally, only firms suspected of having the power to act like monopolists are regulated in this way.

CONTENTS

THE PUBLIC INTEREST ISSUE: MONOPOLY POWER VERSUS MERE SIZE

Economies of scale are savings that are obtained through increases in quantities produced. Scale economies occur when an *X* percent increase in input use raises output by *more than X* percent, so that the more the firm produces, the lower its per-unit costs become.

Monopoly power (or market power) is the ability of a business firm to earn high profits by raising the prices of its products above competitive levels and to keep those prices high for a substantial amount of time.

In Chapters 11 and 12, we learned that when an industry is a monopoly or an oligopoly, the result may not be as desirable in terms of the public interest as it would be if the industry was perfectly competitive. Yet for many industries anything like perfect competition is an impossible goal, and perhaps even an undesirable one. This is true, notably, when the industry's technology provides **economies of scale,** meaning, as you will remember, that the more of its product a firm supplies, the lower the cost of supplying a unit of that product. Scale economies therefore mean that in competition between a large firm and a small one, the big one can usually win. As a result, industries with scale economies usually end up having a small number of firms, each of which has a large share of the industry's sales. In other words, such an industry is usually fated to be a monopoly or an oligopoly.

But what is so bad about that? The answer is that sometimes it is not bad at all, because economies of scale allow the larger firms to supply the public at lower cost. In other cases, the public interest will be threatened, because some or all of the firms in the industry will possess **monopoly power.** Monopoly power (or market power) is usually defined as the ability of a firm to earn high profits by raising and keeping the prices of its products substantially above the levels at which those products would be priced in competitive markets. That is, a firm with monopoly power can charge high prices and get away with it—the market will not punish it for doing so. In a competitive industry, in contrast, the market *will* punish a high-price firm by the loss of its customers to rivals with lower prices. Thus, monopoly power is undesirable for several reasons, some of them obvious:

- *High prices reduce the wealth of consumers.* The use of monopoly power is obviously undesirable to consumers because no one likes to pay high prices for purchased commodities. Such high prices may make the firm with monopoly power rich and make the consumers of its products poor. These effects on the distribution of wealth are generally considered undesirable.
- *High prices lead to resource misallocation.* Economists give greater emphasis to a second undesirable effect of prices that exceed the competitive level. Such prices tend to reduce the quantities of the products that consumers demand. In this case, smaller quantities of labour, raw materials, and other inputs will be devoted to production of these high-priced products relative to the quantities that would *best* serve consumer interests. More of those inputs will therefore be transferred to the products of competitive industries. The result will be *underproduction* of the products priced at monopoly levels and *overproduction* of the products of competitive industries. So, as a result of the exercise of monopoly power, the economy does not produce the mix of outputs that best serves the public interest.
- *Monopoly power creates an obstacle to efficiency and innovation.* A firm with monopoly power is a firm that does not face much effective competition—and consequently it does not have as much reason to fear loss of business to others. Where this is so, there is little incentive for management to make the effort to produce efficiently with a minimum of waste or to undertake the expense and risks of innovation. The result is that products may be of poorer quality than they would if the company possessed no monopoly power, and there will be waste in the production process.

The efficiency problems inherent in monopoly power are among the main reasons for governmental intervention controlling business firms' behaviour and other attributes. The critical problem is control of monopoly power and prevention of acts by firms that are designed either to give them (or enhance) monopoly power, or to curb the use of that power to exploit the public.

There is a widespread misconception that all big firms have monopoly power, so that the primary purpose of competition policy or regulatory activity should be to break up as many large firms as possible and to constrain the pricing of all large firms that cannot be broken into smaller ones. But this is not a valid conclusion. It is true that firms that have a very small share of their industry's sales cannot wield market power. For reasons studied in Chapter 10, such small firms are price takers, not price makers. They must simply accept the price determined by supply and demand in a competitive market, or the prices determined by larger firms in their industry if those large firms do have market power. But although firms with small market shares never have market power, the converse is not true: Large firms do not always have market power.

Why? In an oligopoly characterized by fierce rivalry, each firm may be prevented by the actions of its competitors from raising its price above competitive levels. For example, Coca-Cola and Pepsi each have a very large share of the North American soft drink market. It is well known that there is no love between the two companies, so neither dares to raise its prices substantially for fear of driving customers into the arms of its unloved competitor.

Even a monopoly may have little or no monopoly power if entry into its industry is cheap and easy. Such a firm knows that it can retain its monopoly *only if its behaviour is not monopolistic*. If it tries to raise its price to monopoly levels for any substantial period of time, then its rivals will have an opportunity to come in and take some or all of its business away. So in industries where entry is very easy, a large firm will have no monopoly power because the perpetual threat of potential entry will keep it from misbehaving. For this reason, government agencies concerned with monopoly issues explicitly avoid interfering with the actions of firms in industries where entry is cheap and easy.

> The primary threat of monopoly and oligopoly to the public interest is monopoly power. This power can lead to excessive prices that exploit consumers, misallocation of resources, and inefficient and noninnovative firms. But firms that are big do not necessarily have market power.

In Part 1 of this chapter, we will discuss how regulation is used to deal with these issues. In Part 2, we turn to anti-combines policy—a second way of dealing with the problems.

PART 1: REGULATION

We begin with regulation, one of the two traditional instruments used by government to protect consumers from exploitation by firms that are too powerful.

WHAT IS REGULATION?

"**Regulation** of industry" refers to the activities of a number of government agencies that enforce rules about business conduct enacted by Canada's federal Parliament and provincial legislature, or rules that the agencies themselves have adopted. When an industry is suspected of possessing monopoly power and, because of scale economies or for other reasons, it is not considered feasible or desirable to bring effective competition into its markets, the regulatory agency imposes restrictions designed to curb use of the monopoly power. For example, the agency may place ceilings on the prices the regulated firms can charge, or it may require the firm to submit any change it desires in any of its prices to the agency. Such changes, then, are not permitted until they have been approved by the agency, sometimes after extensive (and expensive) hearings (that is, trials) before the agency, in which the opponents and supporters of the proposed changes, as well as their lawyers and their witnesses, have the opportunity to present their opinions.

Regulations designed to limit market power, and economic behaviour more generally, affect industries that together provide perhaps over 10 percent of the gross

Regulation of industry is a process established by law that restricts or controls some specified decisions made by the affected firms; it is designed to protect the public from exploitation by firms with monopoly power. Regulation is usually carried out by a special government agency assigned the task of administering and interpreting the law. That agency also acts as a court in enforcing the regulatory laws.

domestic product (GDP) of Canada. The list includes telecommunications, railroads, electric utilities, oil pipelines, banks, and the stock markets. The federal government and the provinces and territories have regulatory agencies devoted to such tasks.

Despite its good intentions, regulation has been criticized as a cause of inefficiency and excessive costs to the consuming public. The basic fact about regulation and other forms of government intervention that are designed to affect the operations of markets is that *neither* markets *nor* governmental agencies always work perfectly. In an uncontrolled market, for example, monopoly power can damage the public interest, but excessive or poorly conceived regulations or anticompetition decisions also can prove very harmful.

PUZZLE: *Why Do Regulators Often Raise Prices?*

Regulation sometimes forces consumers to pay *higher* prices than they would pay in its absence. For instance, the Canadian Radio-television and Telecommunications Commission (CRTC) is a federal agency that was originally established in 1968 to regulate and supervise the Canadian broadcasting system, including traditional radio and television, as well as cable and pay and specialty services. Recent technological developments permit phone calls to be made over high-speed Internet lines, so it is possible for cable Internet providers to offer Voice over Internet Protocol (VoIP) services to consumers at competitive rates. However, under CRTC rules established in May of 2005, existing telephone carriers such as Bell Canada and TELUS are restricted in their ability to price their own VoIP services and are prevented from using their pricing power to undercut new competitors in the telephone services market.

So why do the CRTC regulators, whose job it is to protect the public interest, deliberately prevent price competition from the incumbent telephone companies? Later in the chapter, you will be able to answer this question.

SOME OBJECTIVES OF REGULATION

Economists recognize a number of reasons that may justify the regulation of an industry.

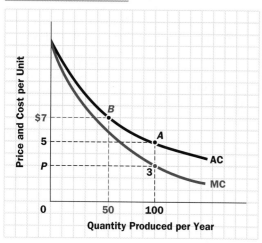

FIGURE 1

Economies of Scale

Control of Market Power Resulting from Economies of Scale and Scope

As we noted at the beginning of this chapter, a major reason for regulation of industry is to prevent the use of or acquisition of market power by regulated firms. In some industries, it is far cheaper to have production carried out by one firm than by many, and the relatively large firms that result may gain market power. One cause is economies of large-scale production. Railroad tracks are a particularly good example of such economies of scale. The total cost of building and maintaining the tracks when 100 trains traverse them every day is not much higher than when only one train uses them. So substantial savings in average cost result when rail traffic increases. As we saw in Chapter 7, scale economies lead to an average cost (AC) curve that goes downhill as output increases (see Figure 1). This means that a firm with a large output can cover its costs at a price lower than a firm whose output is smaller. In the figure, point *A* represents the larger firm whose AC is $5, whereas point *B* is the smaller firm with an AC of $7.

A single, large firm also may have a cost advantage over a group of small firms when it is cheaper to produce a number of different commodities together rather than making each separately in a different firm. Savings made possible by simultaneous production of many different products by one firm are called **economies of scope.** One clear example of economies of scope is the manufacture of both cars and trucks by the same producer. The techniques employed in producing both commodities are similar, which provides a cost advantage to firms that produce both types of vehicles.

In industries characterized by great economies of scale and scope, costs will be much higher if government intervenes to preserve a large number of small, and therefore costly, firms. Moreover, where economies of scale and scope are strong, society will not be able to preserve competition, even if it wants to. The large, multiproduct firm will have so great a cost advantage over its rivals that the small firms simply will be unable to survive.

> Where monopoly production is cheapest, so that competition is not sustainable, the industry is a natural monopoly. When monopoly is cheaper, society may not want to have competition; if competition is not sustainable, it will not even have a choice in the matter.

Even if society reconciles itself to monopoly in such cases, it will generally not want to let the monopoly firm wield its market power without limits. Therefore, it will consider regulating the company's decisions on matters such as pricing. The first and most universal problem facing the regulator is how to prevent the regulated firm from pricing and taking other actions that exploit the public and undermine the efficiency of the market, but to do so in ways that do not destroy the regulated firm or prevent it from serving the public effectively.

■ Universal Service and Rate Averaging

A second type of problem in the analysis of regulation stems from another objective of regulation of the prices and other choices of firms in a regulated industry—the desire for "universal service." By this regulators mean the availability of service to everyone at "reasonable prices," particularly to impoverished consumers and small communities where the limited scale of operations may make costs extremely high. In such cases, regulators may encourage or require a public utility (such as a hydroelectric power supplier) to serve some consumers at a financial loss. This loss on some sales is financially feasible only when the regulated firm is permitted to make up for it by obtaining higher profits on its other sales. Charging higher prices to one set of customers to finance lower prices to another customer group is called **cross-subsidization.**

This sort of cross-subsidization is possible only if the regulated firm is protected from price competition and free entry of new competitors in its other, more profitable markets (in which it charges the higher prices that subsidize the financing of the mandated low prices). If no such protection is provided, potential competitors will sniff out these profit opportunities in the markets where service is supplied at prices well above cost. Many new firms will enter the business and drive prices down in those markets—a practice referred to as *cream skimming.* The entrants choose to enter only the profitable markets and skim away the "cream" of the profits for themselves, leaving the unprofitable markets (the skimmed milk?) to the supplier that had attempted to provide universal service. This phenomenon is one reason why regulatory rules, until recently, made it very difficult or impossible for new firms to enter when and where they saw fit.

Airlines and telecommunications are two industries in which these issues have arisen frequently. In both cases, it was feared that without regulation of entry and rates, or special subsidies, less populous communities would effectively become isolated, losing their airline services and obtaining telephone service only at cripplingly high rates. A number of economists question the validity of this argument for

Economies of scope are savings that are obtained through simultaneous production of many different products. They occur if a firm that produces many commodities can supply each good more cheaply than a firm that produces fewer commodities.

Cross-subsidization means selling one product of the firm at a loss, which is balanced by higher profits on another of the firm's products.

regulation, which, they say, calls for hidden subsidies of rural consumers by everyone else. In fact, with the advent of deregulation of the airline industry, this market has since been taken over to a considerable extent by specialized "commuter" airlines flying much smaller aircraft than the major airlines, which have withdrawn from many such routes.

A similar issue affects Canada Post, which charges the same price to deliver a letter anywhere within Canada, regardless of the distance or the special difficulties and costs of a particular route. To maintain this pricing scheme, some protection of Canada Post from direct competition in many of its activities would be desirable; otherwise, its extreme form of uniform pricing would soon deprive it of its most profitable routes. Thus, the goal of providing universal service leads to the regulation of entry into and exit from the affected industry, and not just price control.

TWO KEY ISSUES THAT FACE REGULATORS

Regulators around the world face at least two critical issues that are of fundamental importance for economic policy. They are at the heart of recent legal battles before regulatory agencies almost everywhere.

Setting Prices to Protect Consumers' Interests and Allow Regulated Firms to Cover Their Costs

When governments regulate prices, they usually want to prevent those prices from being so high that they bring monopoly profits to the firm. At the same time, governments want to set prices at levels that are "compensatory." That is, the prices must be sufficiently high to enable the firms to cover their costs and, consequently, to survive financially. Regulators also are asked to select prices that best serve the public interest. These goals, as we will see next, can often be at odds.

- *Prices intended to promote the public interest may cause financial problems for firms.* The discussion in Chapter 10 implied that the consumer's welfare is most effectively promoted by setting the price of a product equal to that product's marginal cost, and this will be further confirmed in Chapter 14. But as we will show presently, such a rule would condemn many regulated firms to bankruptcy. What should the regulator do in such a case?
- *Preventing firms with monopoly power from earning excessive profits without eliminating all incentives for efficiency and innovation may prove difficult.* The firm's incentive and reward for the effort and expenditure needed to improve efficiency and to innovate is the higher profit that it expects to obtain if it succeeds. But a frequent objective of regulation is to put a ceiling on profit to prevent monopoly earnings. How can monopoly profits be prevented without destroying incentives?

Let's now analyze these issues, which arise frequently in today's crucial regulatory policy debates.

Marginal Versus Average Cost Pricing

Regulatory agencies often have the task of controlling the prices of regulated firms. Acrimonious debate over the proper levels for those prices has filled hundreds of thousands of pages of regulatory-hearing records and has involved literally hundreds of millions of dollars of expenditures in fees for lawyers, expert witnesses, and research. The central question has been: What constitutes the proper formula to set these prices?

Where it is feasible, many economists favour setting price equal to marginal cost because, as we will show in Chapter 14, this pricing policy provides the incentive for firms to produce output quantities that serve consumers' wants most efficiently. However, a serious practical problem often prevents use of marginal cost pricing: In many regulated industries, the firms would go bankrupt if all prices were set equal to marginal costs!

This seems a startling conclusion, but it follows inescapably from three simple facts:

Fact 1. Many regulated industries are characterized by significant economies of large-scale production. As we pointed out earlier, economies of scale are one of the main reasons why certain industries were regulated in the first place.

Fact 2. In an industry with economies of scale, the long-run average cost curve is downward sloping. This means that the long-run average cost falls as the quantity produced rises, as was illustrated by the AC curve in Figure 1. Fact 2 is something we learned back in Chapter 7. The reason, to review briefly, is that where there are economies of scale, if all input quantities are doubled, output will *more than double.* But total costs will double only if input quantities double. Thus, total costs will rise more slowly than output and so average cost must fall. That is, average cost (AC) is simply total cost (TC) divided by quantity (Q), so with economies of scale, $AC = TC/Q$ must decline when Q increases because the denominator, Q, rises more rapidly than the numerator, TC.

Fact 3. If average cost is declining, then marginal cost must be below average cost. This fact follows directly from one of the general rules relating marginal and average data that were explained in the appendix to Chapter 8. Once again, the logic is simple enough to review briefly. If, for example, your average quiz score is 90 percent but the next quiz pulls your average down to 87 percent, then the grade on the most recent test (the marginal grade) must be below both the old and the new average quiz scores. That is, it takes a marginal grade (or cost) that is below the average to pull the average down.

Putting these three facts together, we conclude that in many regulated industries, marginal cost (MC) will be below average cost, as depicted in Figure 1. Now suppose that regulators set the price (or average revenue, AR) at the level of marginal cost. Because P then equals MC, P (= AR) must be below AC and the firm must lose money, so "P equals MC" is simply not an acceptable option. What, then, should be done? One possibility is to set price equal to marginal cost and to use public funds to make up for the deficit. However, government subsidies to large regulated firms are not very popular politically and may also not be sensible.

A second option, which is quite popular among regulators, is to try to set price equal to average cost, where average cost includes a normal return. This is similar to the cost-plus pricing rule discussed on page 266 of Chapter 12, where $P = (1 + n)AC_n$ where n is a percentage net costing margin over normal average cost so as to cover a normal return when the firm is running at a standard rate of capacity utilization. While this is indeed a popular option, it does have certain problems. One problem is that almost every large company produces a number of different varieties and qualities of some product, and many produce thousands of different products, each with its own price. Even GM Canada, a fairly specialized firm that produces many makes and sizes of cars and trucks, also sells home mortgages and quite a few other things. In a multiproduct firm, we cannot even define $AC = TC/Q$, because to calculate Q (total output), we would have to add up all of the apples and oranges (and all of the other different items) that the firm produces. Of course, we know that we cannot add up apples and oranges. Because we cannot calculate AC for a multiproduct firm, it is hardly possible for the regulator to require P to equal AC for each of the firm's products (although regulators sometimes think they can do so).

One way of dealing with the issue is the price-cap approach that was invented by economists but is now widely employed in practice. The procedure and its logic will be described a little later in this chapter.

▪ Preventing Monopoly Profit but Keeping Incentives for Efficiency and Innovation

Opponents of regulation claim that it seriously impairs the efficiency of Canadian industry and reduces the benefits of freely competitive markets. One obvious source of inefficiency is the endless paperwork and complex legal proceedings that prevent the firm from responding quickly to changing market conditions.

In addition, economists believe that regulatory interference in pricing causes economic inefficiency. By forcing prices to differ from those that would prevail in a freely, competitive market, regulations lead consumers to demand a quantity of the regulated product that does not maximize consumer benefits from the quantity of resources available to the economy. (This resource misallocation issue will be discussed in Chapter 15.)

A third source of inefficiency may be even more important. It occurs because regulators often are required to prevent the regulated firm from earning excessive profits, while at the same time offering it financial incentives for maximum efficiency of operation and allowing it enough profit to attract the capital it needs when growing markets justify expansion. It would seem to be ideal if the regulator would permit the firm to earn just the amount of revenue that covers its costs, including the cost of its capital. Thus, if the current rate of profits in competitive markets is 10 percent, the regulated firm should recover its costs plus 10 percent on its investment and not a penny more or less. The trouble with such a rule is that it removes all profit incentive for efficiency, responsiveness to consumer demand, and innovation. In effect, it guarantees just one standard rate of profit to the firm, no more and no less—regardless of whether its management is totally incompetent or extremely talented and hard-working.

Competitive markets do not work this way. Although under perfect competition the average firm will earn just the illustrative 10 percent, a firm with an especially ingenious and efficient management will do better, and a firm with an incompetent management is likely to go broke. It is the possibility of great rewards and harsh punishments that gives the market mechanism its power to cause firms to strive for high efficiency and productivity growth.

When firms are guaranteed fixed returns no matter how well or how poorly they perform, gross inefficiencies often result. For example, many contracts for purchases of military equipment internationally have prices calculated on what is called a cost-plus fixed-fee basis, meaning that the supplier is guaranteed that its costs will be covered and that, in addition, it will receive some prespecified profit. However, such cost-plus fixed-fee arrangements can lead to enormous supplier inefficiencies. A regulatory arrangement that in effect guarantees a regulated firm its cost plus a fair rate of return on its investment obviously has much in common with a cost-plus fixed-fee contract. Fortunately, there are also substantial differences between the two, so regulatory profit ceilings do not always have serious effects on the firm's incentives for efficiency.

How can one prevent regulated firms from earning excessive profits, but also permit them to earn enough to cover their legitimate costs, attract the capital they need and, above all, still allow rewards for superior performance and penalties for poor performance?

Price Caps as Incentives for Efficiency   A regulatory innovation designed to prevent monopoly profits while offering incentives for firms to improve their efficiency is now in use in many countries—for electricity, telephone, and airport services in the United Kingdom, for example, and for telephone rates in Canada, the United States, and many Asian countries.

Under this program, regulators assign ceilings (called **price caps**) for the *prices* (not the profits) of the regulated firms. However, the price caps (which are measured in real, inflation-adjusted terms—in other words, they are adjusted for changes in the purchasing power of money) are reduced each year at a rate based on the rate of cost reduction

A **price cap** is a ceiling above which regulators do not permit prices to rise. The cap is designed to provide an efficiency incentive to the firm by allowing it to keep part of any savings in costs it can achieve.

(productivity growth) previously achieved by the regulated firm. Thus, if the regulated firm subsequently achieves cost savings (by innovation or other means) greater than those it obtained in the past, the firm's real costs will fall more rapidly than its real prices do, and it will be permitted to keep the resulting profits as its reward. Of course, there is a catch. If the regulated firm reduces its costs by only 2 percent per year, whereas in the past its costs fell 3 percent per year, the price cap will also fall at a 3 percent rate. The firm will therefore lose profits, although consumers will continue to benefit from falling real prices. So under this arrangement the firm is automatically punished if its cost-reduction performance does not keep up with what it was able to achieve in the past.

Thus, under price-cap regulation, management is constantly forced to look for ever more economical ways of doing things. This approach clearly gives up any attempt to limit the profit of the regulated firm—leaving the possibility of higher profits as an incentive for efficiency. At the same time, it protects the consumer by controlling the firm's prices. Indeed, it makes those prices lower and lower, in real terms.

■ THE PROS AND CONS OF "BIGNESS"

We have described several goals for regulation, including control of monopoly power and the provision of universal service. Is it desirable, in addition to these regulatory goals, to try to make big firms become smaller? In other words, are the effects of "bigness" always undesirable? We have already seen that only relatively large firms have any likelihood of possessing monopoly power. We also have seen that monopoly power can cause a number of problems, including undesirable effects on income distribution, misallocation of resources, and inhibition of efficiency and innovation.

But we also have seen that big firms, at least sometimes, do not possess monopoly power. More generally, there is another side of the picture. Bigness in industry can also, at least sometimes, benefit the general public. Again, this is true for a number of reasons.

■ Economies of Large Size

Probably the most important advantage of bigness is found in industries in which technology makes small-scale operation inefficient. One can hardly imagine the costs if automobiles were produced in little workshops rather than giant factories. The notion of a small firm operating a long-distance railroad does not even make sense, and a multiplicity of firms replicating the same railroad service would clearly be incredibly wasteful.

On these grounds, most policy makers have never even considered any attempt to eliminate bigness. Of course, it does not follow that every industry in which firms happen to be big is one in which big firms are best. Some observers argue that many firms, in fact, exceed the sizes required for cost minimization.

■ Required Scale for Innovation

Some economists have argued that only large firms have the resources and the motivation for really significant innovation. Many important inventions are still contributed by individuals. But, because it is often an expensive, complex, and large-scale undertaking to put a new invention into commercial production, often only large firms can afford the funds and bear the risks that such an effort demands.

Many studies have examined the relationships among firm size, industry competitiveness, and the level of expenditure on research and development (R&D). Although the evidence is far from conclusive, it does indicate that highly competitive industries composed of very small firms tend not to spend a great deal on research. Up to a point, R&D outlays and innovation seem to increase with size of the firm and the concentration of the industry. One reason for this is that many oligopolistic firms use innovation—new products and new processes—as their primary competitive "weapon," forcing them, as time passes, to maintain and even increase their spending on R&D and other innovative activities.

However, some of the most significant innovations introduced in the twentieth century have been contributed by firms that started very small. Examples include the airplane, alternating current (AC) electricity, the photocopier, and the electronic calculator. Yet, the important successive improvements in those products have characteristically come out of the research facilities of large, oligopolistic enterprises.

The bottom line is that bigness in business firms receives a mixed score. In some cases it can produce undesirable results, but in other cases it is necessary for efficiency and low costs and offers other benefits to the public. A rule requiring regulators to combat bigness per se, wherever it occurs, is likely to have undesirable results and would, in any event, be unworkable.

■ DEREGULATION

Because regulators have sometimes adopted rules and made decisions that were ill-advised and were demonstrably harmful to the public interest, and because the bureaucracy that is needed to enforce regulation is costly and raises business expenses, there have long been demands for reduced regulation. Since the 1980s, successive federal and provincial governments in Canada responded to such arguments by deregulating several industries, such as airlines and natural gas, and eliminating most of the powers of the relevant regulatory agencies. In other industries, such as railways and telecommunications, rule changes now give regulated firms more freedom in decision making. Deregulation is still an ongoing process in some industries in Canada, such as telephone and hydroelectricity.

■ The Effects of Deregulation

One way to deal with the regulation difficulties just discussed is to shut regulation down—that is, simply to leave everything to the market and get rid of the regulators. Many observers think that would be a good idea in a number of cases, but sometimes it would be unacceptable, as in markets that are virtually pure monopolies. Thus, the move toward deregulation has proceeded slowly, by eliminating regulation in some fields and reducing it in others. Deregulation's effects in Canada and elsewhere in North America are still being debated, but several conclusions seem clear.

1. Effect on Prices   There is mixed evidence in both Canada and the United States on the effect of deregulation on prices. An example is the cost of long-distance telephone service for Canadian consumers, which has seen a sharp decline over time (again, in real inflation-adjusted terms), even if deregulation may have led initially to some compensatory upward pressure on local telephone rates. On the other hand, the inflation-adjusted price of airline tickets did fall in the United States but not much in Canada over the last two decades, despite airline deregulation and "open skies" in both countries.

In much the same way, the deregulation of electricity utilities in Ontario has meant significant upward movement in prices since 2002. This is an experience repeated in some U.S. states, such as California, where electricity deregulation was implemented in the late 1990s. On the other hand, prices did show a significant drop, as in Pennsylvania, which is often cited as the state jurisdiction that seemed to have most benefited from electric power deregulation in the United States. Unlike the telephone market, where technology has been the driving force behind lower rates, it would appear that the more competitive environment has not spurred entrepreneurial innovation to the same extent to move prices down in the wholesale and retail markets for electricity.

2. Effects on Local Services   It was widely feared, even by supporters of deregulation in North America, that certain consumers, especially in smaller and more isolated communities, would be deprived of services because smaller numbers of customers would make those services unprofitable. Some predicted that airlines and telephone companies would raise prices sharply or would withdraw altogether from such communities once there was no longer any regulation to force them to stay. While changes did take place as, for instance, with the proliferation of separate user fees for the maintenance and provision of basic telephone services, the outcome was not generally as serious as had been anticipated. Indeed, in the case of North American airline services, larger airlines have left many small communities. Yet, as we have previously mentioned, they have usually been replaced by smaller commuter airlines that have maintained the basic service, although often at a significantly higher price. In addition, the larger airlines inaugurated a new scheduling pattern called the *hub-and-spoke* system (see discussion below), which enabled them to continue to serve less travelled destinations profitably.

3. Effects on Entry   With the elimination of barriers to entry resulting from deregulation, the airline and trucking industries witnessed significant restructuring. In the United States, for instance, older airlines invaded one another's routes, several dozen new airlines sprang up, and about 10,000 new truck operators entered the market. Many of the trucking entrants have since dropped out of the industry, as profits and wages were driven down by competition. Almost all of the new airlines also ran into trouble and were sold to the older airlines. Since 1990, however, many smaller airlines were launched and several remain the most profitable firms in the industry. It is also pertinent to note that although many of the small entrant airlines perished, so did a large number of the very large carriers, including Eastern Airlines, Braniff, Pan Am, and TWA, all of which had once been major enterprises. Many other major companies have been under bankruptcy protection since 2001, such as United Airlines, Delta, Northwest, and US Airways. Indeed, a similar story can be told in Canada, with the disappearance of Canadian Airlines in 2001 and the emergence of new competitors such as WestJet and Jetsgo; the latter collapsed in 2005. In the longer term, it would appear therefore that the pressure has been toward merger and consolidation in the North American airline industry following deregulation.

4. Effects on Unions   Deregulation badly hurts trade unions. In the new competitive environment, firms are under enormous pressure to make sharp cuts in their workforces and to seek concessions from workers through wage rollbacks, cuts in fringe benefits and other aspects of working conditions. Given the strong pressure for retrenchment, it is not surprising that in both Canada and the United States, trade unions have strongly opposed deregulation, from the customer service agents represented by the Canadian Auto Workers in the Canadian airline industry to the Airline Pilots Association in the United States.

5. Effects on Product Quality   The public has been unpleasantly surprised by another effect of deregulation. At least in the case of aviation, increased price competition has been accompanied by sharp reductions in "frills." To cut costs, airlines have made meals less elaborate (to put it mildly) and have limited the number of flights to avoid empty seats—which has increased crowding. To fill planes with more passengers, many airlines turned to "hub and spoke" systems (see Figure 2). Instead of running a flight directly from a low-demand airport, A, to another low-demand airport, B, the airline flies all passengers from Airport A to its "hub" at Airport H, where all passengers, from many points of origin, who are bound for the same destination, Airport B, are brought together and asked to reboard an airplane flying to B. This system clearly saves money and gives passengers more options as the number of flights between hubs and spokes

FIGURE 2

A "Hub and Spoke" Airline Routing Pattern

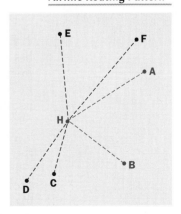

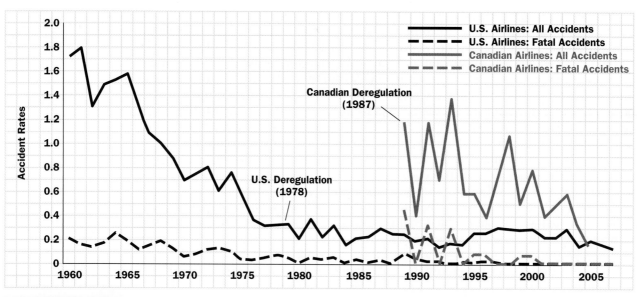

FIGURE 3

U.S. and Canadian
Airline Accident Rates,
1960–2007*

* (1) U.S. airline accident rates: Accidents per 100,000 departures; (2) Canadian airline accident rates: Accidents per 100,000 hours flown.

increases. At the same time, it is less convenient for passengers than a direct flight from origin to destination. Critics of deregulation have placed a good deal of emphasis on the reductions in passenger comfort. Some economists, however, argue that competition would not bring such results unless passengers as a group prefer the reduction in fares to the greater standards of luxury that preceded them.

6. Effects on Safety   In the case of airline deregulation (although the issue can well arise elsewhere), some observers have been concerned that cost cutting after deregulation would lead to skimping on safety measures. As Figure 3 shows, deregulation seems not to have increased the rate of airline accidents in either Canada or the United States. (In Figure 3, the accident rates in each country are not defined in the same way, which accounts for a scale difference in the limited time series for each country.) While there was a significant downward trend prior to deregulation in the United States, the series since deregulation seems to have fluctuated around a relatively stationary trend line in both countries. Since 2001, Canada's federal Parliament and the U.S. Congress have legislated greater security measures pertaining to the airline industry and, therefore, if any airline company may have been cutting corners in terms of safety prior to September 11, 2001, pressure has probably been in the opposite direction since then. At least, the record would suggest that the airline industry has not compromised on passenger safety as a result of deregulation.

7. Effects on Profits and Wages   As the previous discussion suggested, deregulation has generally strengthened competition, and the increased power of competition has, in turn, tended to depress profits and wages. There is evidence that few airlines, including the largest carriers, have been able to earn profits as high as those in other competitive industries, on average, since the deregulation of the airlines more than two decades ago. Recent events such as the threat of terrorism and rising fuel prices have brought several large airlines to the brink of bankruptcy. This, of course, is just the other side of reduced prices to consumers. In some cases, the profit and wage cuts were very substantial and had significant consequences. The recent financial problems for airlines and trucking firms have already been noted, and the pressures for decreases in the very high earnings of airline pilots have prompted frequent confrontations between these workers and the airlines.

THE PUZZLE REVISITED: *Why Regulators Often Push Prices Upward*

We can now return to the puzzle we posed earlier: Why would regulators, who are supposed to protect the interests of the public, raise prices? The answer is that regulators sometimes push for higher prices when they want to prevent the demise of any existing firms or wish to attract more competitors to an industry. Earlier, we saw that strong economies of scale and economies of scope may make it impossible for a number of firms to survive. The largest firm in an industry may have such a big cost advantage over its competitors that it can drive them out of the market while still operating at a profit.

Afraid that unrestrained pricing will reduce the number of firms in an industry, regulatory agencies often attempt to equalize matters by imposing price floors (below which prices cannot be set). Such price floors are designed to permit *all* of the firms in an industry to operate profitably. Hence, in our earlier example of VoIP services in Canada, it is clear that the intention of the CRTC was to attract more firms into the telephone services market, even if consumers might be burdened with higher prices for telephone services.

Some economists maintain that this approach to pricing is a perversion of the idea of competition. The virtue of competition is that, where it occurs, firms force one another to supply consumers with products of high quality at low prices. Any firm that cannot achieve this goal is driven out of business by market forces. A regulatory arrangement may allow efficient and inefficient firms to coexist only by preventing them from competing with one another, but this arrangement merely preserves the appearance of competition while destroying its substance, and it forces consumers to pay the higher prices necessary to keep the inefficient firms alive.

Some economists would argue that deregulation has worked out well, but hardly perfectly, in promoting the welfare of consumers. Indeed, partial deregulation has sometimes proved to be disastrous, as illustrated by what happened in the electricity industry in California in 2001. There, *wholesale* prices were deregulated, but tight ceilings were imposed on *retail* prices. Firms that bought at wholesale and sold at retail incurred great losses when wholesale prices increased, with a brief period of significant power shortages and blackouts being the predictable result. Similar, although less severe, problems have been faced in Ontario since 2002 with the breakup of former Ontario Hydro into successor companies for the generation and distribution of electricity. Since then, the retail price of electricity has remained a political hot potato for successive provincial governments in Ontario.

Despite the somewhat chaotic process that deregulation has created in some regions of North America, there have been exceptions such as the state of Pennsylvania, whose approach to electricity deregulation originally achieved a significant degree of popularity among its residential consumers. Its model of deregulation, with strict retail price caps and state retention of productive assets, allowed for a much smoother transition toward a deregulated environment than, say, in California. Other states, such as New Jersey and Texas, have sought to emulate Pennsylvania's approach.

The battle over deregulation is far from over. Even if those who wish to return to a more regulated environment do not succeed, many areas exist in which regulation of the old-time variety still retains its grip or has been reintroduced in disguised form. In some ways, it may be said that the struggle is not really between supporters of regulation on the one hand and advocates of a completely unregulated market on the other, but between those who desire a market constrained by a high rather than a low regulatory environment. In industries where tremendous overhead costs are present, the inevitable tendency toward monopoly is the norm. Regardless of whether firms are in private or public hands, the dangers of monopoly abuse are ever present.

The Size and Scope of a Competition Case

Alleged violations of the Competition Act are usually dealt with by bringing the accused firm to the Competition Tribunal or by threatening to do so, in the hope that the alleged monopolist will accept a compromise. While a large number of cases have been investigated by the Competition Bureau since the Competition Act was passed in 1986, the vast majority have been settled in the office of Director of Investigation and Research before going to trial. Indeed, even under the old anti-combines legislation, there were very few prosecutions and most of those ended in acquittals.

One of the most famous cases, handled by what was then known as the Combines Investigation Branch, saw criminal charges laid against K.C. Irving Ltd. in 1972 after the company had acquired complete control of all five English-language newspapers in the province of New Brunswick. While the Crown was successful in bringing the lawsuit forward, the Supreme Court's requirement that it be demonstrated "beyond a reasonable doubt" that this was a criminal offence under the old Combines Investigation Act led to the acquittal of K.C. Irving Ltd. in 1978.

The experience in the United States is somewhat different. Antitrust suits are frequent and well-publicized affairs because the accused firms are often the giants of an industry—such famous names as Standard Oil, U.S. Steel, the Aluminum Company of America (Alcoa), General Electric, International Business Machines (IBM), American Telephone and Telegraph (AT&T), and Microsoft have all appeared in such proceedings and have been frequently fined for their offences.

The magnitude of a competition suit is difficult to imagine. After the charges have been filed, it is not unusual for several years to elapse before the case comes to trial. The parties spend this period laboriously preparing their cases. Dozens of lawyers and scores of researchers are likely to participate in this process. The trial itself also can run for years and produce literally volumes of material. As you may imagine, the power of the Crown to haul a company into court on an anti-combines charge is an awesome one. Win, lose, or draw, such a case imposes a very heavy burden on the accused firm, draining its funds, consuming the time and attention of its management, and delaying business decisions until the outcome of the legal proceedings is determined.

Perhaps this is why, in November 2006, the federal government ordered the CRTC to revise its decision on the regulation of telephone services offered through broadband Internet connections. In an unusual move that overturned earlier CRTC decisions, the federal Industry Canada minister at the time argued in favour of reestablishing a level playing field for both incumbent telephone carriers and new Internet providers, which he believed would result in cheaper overall phone services for consumers.

PART 2: ANTI-COMBINES LAWS AND POLICIES

In Part 1 of this chapter, we described the process of regulation, which governments use to oversee monopoly or oligopoly firms that are deemed to have dangerous power to control their markets. In Part 2, we analyze the second of government's instruments for protecting competition: **anti-combines policy.** Anti-combines or competition policy refers to the body of legislation and its enforcement agencies that preclude the deliberate creation of monopoly and prevent powerful firms from engaging in related anticompetitive acts.

Anti-combines policy refers to programs and laws that preclude the deliberate creation of monopoly and prevent powerful firms from engaging in anticompetitive acts.

Dating back to 1889, Canada's anti-combines legislation, as reflected in the original Combines Investigation Act and its provisions in the Criminal Code, has evolved in terms of enforcement and investigative powers accorded to the relevant legal authorities. In its present embodiment, as defined in the Competition Act of 1986, its stated purpose is to maintain and encourage competition in Canada in order to:

- promote the efficiency and adaptability of the Canadian economy
- expand opportunities for Canadian participation in world markets while at the same time recognizing the role of foreign competition in Canada
- ensure that small and medium-sized enterprises have an equitable opportunity to participate in the Canadian economy
- provide consumers with competitive prices and product choices

The Act contains both criminal and civil provisions to prevent abusive practices in the Canadian marketplace and it covers all forms of economic activities, with the exception of industries already regulated by federal and provincial governments.

The application and monitoring of the Act is done through the Competition Bureau (an independent federal government law enforcement agency), while its enforcement is achieved via its Competition Tribunal or other courts, depending on the issue. Normally, at the initiative of the Director of Investigation and Research, the Competition Tribunal proceeds with an inquiry of complaints of alleged violations under the Competition Act. For civil offences, the Director may apply to the Competition Tribunal for an order to forbid the continuation of an abusive trade practice. With criminal offences, the Director provides a statement of evidence to the Department of Justice, which could then choose to prosecute.

Generally, cases are settled at the Competition Tribunal level. However, parties could carry their appeal to the Federal Court (Appeals Division) or ultimately even to the Supreme Court of Canada. Because of the more limited financial resources available to the Director of Investigation and Research or perhaps because of the less litigious nature of Canadian society, only a modest number of cases have reached the Tribunal over the last two decades—a number that is proportionally lower than the number of antitrust cases settled in U.S. courts over a similar period.

While the decision to proceed with a case is made by the Director of Investigation and Research, it is the Competition Tribunal which judges cases and sets the appropriate fines in conspiracy cases. Still, even the threat of being brought in front of the Tribunal is a serious matter to the firm, because of possible punishment if it loses and because fighting the initiative of the Director of Investigation and Research can cost the firm millions of dollars. What justifies investment of so much power in such government agencies as the Competition Tribunal? What exactly do anti-combines laws address? How well has competition policy succeeded? These are some of the issues that we will discuss in the remainder of the chapter.

MEASURING MARKET POWER: CONCENTRATION

Concentration: Definition and Measurement—The Herfindahl Index

It is generally agreed that a firm is not strong enough to violate the Competition Act if it possesses no monopoly power, that is, it does not have the power to prevent entry of competitors or to raise prices substantially above competitive levels. So, in competition lawsuits, one issue that is almost invariably argued about is whether the accused company does or does not have monopoly power. In enforcing anti-combines law, the Crown via the Director of Investigation and Research under the Competition Act, in investigating whether a firm suspected of anti-combines violations is likely to possess monopoly power, must determine the **concentration of the industry** in which the firm carries out its activities.

> **Concentration of industry** measures the share of the total sales or assets of the industry in the hands of the largest firms.

A market or an industry is said to be *highly concentrated* if it contains only a few firms, most or all of which sell a large share of the industry's products. In contrast, an industry with many small firms is said to be *unconcentrated*. Thus, concentration is a useful index of the relative bigness of the firms in the industry. Earlier, we noted that big firms do not always have market power, whereas relatively small firms never (or almost never) do. Still, concentration is one useful piece of evidence in deciding whether market power exists in any case under investigation. In particular, if the accused firm can convince the court that it has no such power, the case is likely to be dismissed by the court.

Concentration is measured in a number of ways. The most straightforward method is to calculate what share of the industry's output is sold by some selected number of the industry's firms. Most often a *four-firm* **concentration ratio** is used for this purpose. Thus, if the four largest firms in an industry account for, say, 58 percent of the industry's sales, we say that the four-firm concentration ratio is 0.58.

> A **concentration ratio** is the percentage of an industry's output produced by its four largest firms. It is intended to measure the degree to which the industry is dominated by large firms.

The **Herfindahl Index (HI)** is an alternative and widely used measure of the degree of concentration of an industry. It is calculated, in essence, by adding together the squares of the market shares of the firms in the industry, although the smallest firms may be left out of the calculation because their small market share numbers have a negligible effect on the result.

Another formula now widely used to measure concentration is the **Herfindahl Index (HI),** also known as the **Herfindahl-Hirschman Index (HHI).** This measure is officially referred to in the 2004 *Merger Enforcement Guidelines* of the Competition Bureau in Canada and is frequently used by the Department of Justice and the Federal Trade Commission in the United States, for example, to decide whether the proposed merger of two firms will lead to excessive concentration in a particular industry. The Herfindahl Index is a broad indicator of competition in a market and it is calculated by determining the market share of each of the firms in the industry, squaring each of these numbers, and then adding them together. Hence, in a market consisting of, say, four firms with market shares of total industry sales (or value added) of 0.1, 0.2, 0.3, and 0.4, respectively (so that the total of these four shares sums to 1), the value of the Herfindahl Index would be: $(0.1)^2 + (0.2)^2 + (0.3)^2 + (0.4)^2 = (0.01) + (0.04) + (0.09) + (0.16) = 0.3$. However, the HI value could range from a high of 1 (in the case of monopoly) to a value approaching zero (when there is a very large number of producers in an industry).

In the United States, the government antitrust authorities consider a market to be unconcentrated if its HI is less than 0.1 and highly concentrated if that number exceeds 0.18. The Herfindahl Index offers at least two advantages over the four-firm concentration ratio. Unlike the latter ratio, HI takes into account data on a much larger percentage of the firms in the market than just the top four. However, the calculation automatically magnifies the weight assigned to the market shares of the larger firms, because the square of a larger number is disproportionately larger than the square of a smaller number. This effect is considered desirable, because these larger firms are the reason the government worries about monopoly power in the market under consideration. It also explains why the HI works as a measure of concentration. The HI number rises when concentration grows because the larger the shares of the market's total sales held by the big firms, the disproportionately larger the squared values of those shares will be.

The usefulness of concentration ratios depends critically on whether a market is properly defined in terms of the appropriate cross elasticities (as discussed in Chapter 6) and its relevant geographic scope. For instance, a recent case involving the U.S. Department of Justice that attempted to prevent the merger in 2006 of two Canadian nickel producers—Inco and Falconbridge Limited—illustrates how the geographic scope of the market is important. Inco's proposed acquisition of Falconbridge would have reduced the number of suppliers of high-purity nickel from three to two, with the merged companies constituting over 80 percent of the world sales of this commodity. For the Antitrust Division of the U.S. Department of Justice, the world was deemed to be the relevant geographic market for this product and the proposed merger of these two Toronto-based companies would have raised the world HI from 0.32 to 0.68, a level that was well in excess of the acceptable HI threshold of 0.18.

Ultimately, policy makers care about concentration ratios if they are a good measure of market power. The question, then, is this: If an industry becomes more concentrated, will the firms necessarily increase their ability to price their products above competitive levels? Many economists have, in fact, concluded that although increased concentration *often* facilitates or increases market power, it does not *always* do so. Specifically, the following three conclusions are now widely accepted:

- If, after an increase in concentration, an industry still has a very low concentration ratio, then its firms are very unlikely to have any market power either before or after the rise in concentration.
- If circumstances in the industry are in other respects favourable for successful price collusion—that is, an agreement among the firms not to undercut one another's prices or not to compete "too much" in other ways—a rise in concentration will facilitate market power. It will do so by reducing the number of firms that need to be consulted in arriving at an agreement and by decreasing

the number of firms that have to be watched to make sure they do not betray the collusive agreement.

• Where entry into and exit from the industry are easy and quite inexpensive, then even when concentration increases, market power will not be enhanced because an excessive price will attract new entrants that will soon force the price down.

■ The Evidence of Concentration in Reality

Concentration data may be the best evidence that we have on the effectiveness of anti-combines programs. Table 1(a) shows 2002 four-firm concentration ratios (based on the value of manufacturing shipment, in percentage terms) and the Herfindahl Indexes calculated on the basis of manufacturing shipment and manufacturing value added for 21 subgroups of the total Canadian manufacturing sector. Concentration varies somewhat from industry to industry: Petroleum and coal products, beverage and tobacco, and primary metal manufacturing are relatively concentrated industries, while clothing, wood products, and plastics and rubber products manufacturing reveal low concentration ratios.

TABLE 1(A)

Concentration Ratios and Herfindahl Indexes for Broad Manufacturing Industry Groups in Canada, 2002

NAICS* 3-Digit	Industry	Four-Firm Ratio (%)	Herfindahl Indexes Manufacturing Shipments	Manufacturing Value Added
311	Food	35.12	0.047	0.056
312	Beverage and tobacco products	66.29	0.128	0.151
313	Textile mills	33.11	0.044	0.047
314	Textile products mills	26.81	0.030	0.034
315	Clothing	12.01	0.009	0.010
316	Leather and allied products	45.90	0.097	0.107
321	Wood products	15.56	0.014	0.013
322	Paper	29.53	0.033	0.036
323	Printing and related support activities	23.80	0.023	0.016
324	Petroleum and coal products	70.00	0.144	0.128
325	Chemical	36.07	0.052	0.047
326	Plastics and rubber products	17.17	0.020	0.021
327	Nonmetallic mineral products	42.40	0.065	0.067
331	Primary metal	51.99	0.109	0.118
332	Fabricated metal products	18.97	0.019	0.015
333	Machinery	19.98	0.029	0.030
334	Computer and electronic products	44.43	0.111	0.064
335	Electrical equipment, appliance and component manufacturing	38.71	0.056	0.052
336	Transportation equipment	44.47	0.100	0.091
337	Furniture and related products	16.75	0.014	0.014
339	Miscellaneous manufacturing	14.38	0.009	0.014

* NAICS = North American Industry Classification System, which was created under the North American Free Trade Agreement to provide common definitions of the industrial structure of Canada, the United States, and Mexico, and a common statistical framework to facilitate analysis of the three economies. The four-firm concentration ratios and Herfindahl Indexes were calculated on the basis of weighted enterprise numbers under the NAICS four-digit classification.

SOURCE: Statistics Canada, *The Daily,* "Annual Survey of Manufactures, 2000, 2001 and 2002." Retrieved from http://www.statcan.ca/Daily/English/040616/d040616d.htm

The concentration ratio in 2002 was highest in the petroleum sector, which has frequently been an object of inquiry by the Director of Investigation and Research under the Combines Investigation Act and, since 1986, the Competition Act.[1] However, these numbers hide major differences within these broad groupings. Let us take, for example, beverage and tobacco products manufacturing. According to Table 1(a), the four-firm concentration ratio was quite high at 66.29 percent in 2002. But when we disaggregate this overall ratio into its two industry components—tobacco manufacturing, with a four-firm ratio of 95.6, as shown in Table 1(b), and beverage manufacturing, with a ratio of 65.3 (not shown in the table)—we immediately notice the wide gap that separates these two subsectors. Hence, if it were not for the large weight of the beverage sector and the low weight of the tobacco industry, the concentration ratio for the combined sector would have been dramatically higher. It is also of interest to note that, despite the industry differences, the cross-sectional HI values for these broad three-digit industrial classifications are all below the threshold of 0.18, thereby indicating less than excessive concentration on average.

TABLE 1(B)

Concentration Ratios and Herfindahl Indexes for Selected Manufacturing Industry Subgroups in Canada, 2002

NAICS* 4-Digit	Industry	Four-Firm Ratio (%)	Herfindahl Indexes Manufacturing Shipments	Manufacturing Value Added
3115	Dairy products	62.4	0.111	0.100
3122	Tobacco	95.6	0.446	0.473
3132	Fabric mills	17.1	0.021	0.025
3141	Textile furnishing mills	45.0	0.066	0.088
3152	Cut-and-sew clothing	10.0	0.005	0.007
3162	Footwear	37.3	0.055	0.050
3212	Veneer, plywood, and engineered wood products	24.7	0.028	0.030
3221	Pulp, paper, and paperboard mills	34.7	0.052	0.060
3231	Printing	23.80	0.023	0.016
3241	Petroleum and coal	70.00	0.144	0.128
3253	Pesticide, fertilizers, and other agricultural chemicals	51.5	0.091	0.072
3261	Plastic products	10.9	0.006	0.006
3274	Lime and gypsum products	73.8	0.192	0.194
3311	Iron and steel mills	73.8	0.176	0.179
3323	Architectural and structural metals	8.6	0.004	0.003
3335	Metalworking machinery	12.7	0.008	0.007
3341	Computer and peripheral equipment	72.4	0.366	0.216
3351	Electrical lighting equipment	36.7	0.050	0.052
3361	Motor vehicle	88.1	0.227	0.293
3371	Household and institutional furniture and kitchen cabinets	12.0	0.007	0.008
3391	Medical equipment and supplies	16.0	0.008	0.008

* NAICS = North American Industry Classification System

SOURCE: Statistics Canada, *The Daily*, "Annual Survey of Manufactures, 2000, 2001 and 2002." Retrieved from http://www.statcan.ca/Daily/English/040616/d040616d.htm

[1] See the six volumes published in the early 1980s (immediately after the two major international oil price shocks) by the Director of Investigation and Research under the Combines Investigation Act describing some of the monopolistic practices in that industry: *The State of Competition in the Canadian Petroleum Industry*, Ottawa: Supply and Services, 1981.

Unlike the historical evolution of these concentration ratios in the United States, which have shown a remarkable stability over the last half-century and gravitated around a lower trend value than in Canadian industry, concentration ratios in Canadian manufacturing delineate a gentle upward trend, both from the evidence provided in Table 2 since 1990 and from evidence going back to 1948.[2] Such a trend may suggest that the competition laws have to some degree been effective in inhibiting whatever underlying trend toward bigness may actually exist, but not completely. However, even this very cautious conclusion has been questioned by some observers. Many point to market forces, particularly the international forces unleashed by the pattern of increasing trade liberalization, and to technological changes that may have produced countervailing forces. These observers argue that anti-combines laws have made little difference in the size and the behaviour of Canadian business.

TABLE 2

The Historical Trend in Concentration in the Canadian Manufacturing Sector, 1990-2002

| Year | Four-Firm Concentration Ratio | | Herfindahl Indexes | | | |
| | | | Based on Shipments | | Based on Valued Added | |
	Simple Average	Weighted Average	Simple Average	Weighted Average	Simple Average	Weighted Average
1990	37.9	22.0	0.079	0.022	0.082	0.020
1992	38.4	22.6	0.088	0.035	0.088	0.032
1994	39.7	24.9	0.091	0.038	0.089	0.035
1996	37.6	24.2	0.086	0.035	0.086	0.033
1998	34.3	27.0	0.084	0.035	0.087	0.035
2000	38.9	24.5	0.089	0.038	0.091	0.038
2002	39.7	25.2	0.087	0.036	0.083	0.034

Note: The weighted averages were calculated on the basis of the four-digit NAICS series, weighted by the respective number of firms in the four-digit subgroups.

Source: Statistics Canada, *Annual Survey of Manufactures*.

■ INDUSTRIAL CONCENTRATION AND FOREIGN OWNERSHIP IN CANADA

There has been much debate historically over the link between foreign ownership of Canadian industry and the degree of industrial concentration. Sir John A. Macdonald's *National Policy of 1879* established a high tariff wall around Canada in support of protectionist manufacturing interests. A number of Canadian economic historians have argued that the *National Policy* laid the foundation for what was to become a highly concentrated branch plant economy dominated by foreign capital. By diverting foreign trade and sheltering domestic manufacturing firms from international competition, Macdonald's high tariff encouraged large American firms to set up shop here. In turn, these foreign corporations were able to take advantage of the lucrative domestic market and benefit from the same protection that the *National Policy*

---

[2] Earlier data can be found in Christopher Green, *Canadian Industrial Organization and Policy*, 3rd ed. (Toronto: McGraw-Hill Ltd., 1990), p. 86, Tables 4–9. Unfortunately, these data are a patchwork of separate time series based on more limited sample sizes and varying weights, thereby making any direct comparison with the post-1990 data difficult. However, broadly speaking, the earlier time series suggest a pattern similar to that found for the post-1990 series displayed in Table 2—a gentle upward movement in the various concentration ratios between the years 1948 and 1985.

accorded to smaller Canadian manufacturers. Since these foreign firms were often subsidiaries of large corporations in the United States, this would have led to a more highly concentrated industrial structure domestically.

At the time of the enactment of the original 1889 anti-combines legislation, there was already some evidence of this increasing concentration of industrial activity in the manufacturing heartland of Canada in part, some would argue, favoured by the growth of foreign direct investment. Since then, it has remained tradition in public parlance to link industrial concentration with the presence of large multinational corporations. This was especially so during the 1960s and early 1970s, when numerous reports pointed to the dominance of foreign capital in Canadian industry. However, over the last few decades, this concern has somewhat abated, particularly since Canada has now become a net exporter of capital.

To what extent is there a link between industrial concentration and foreign ownership of Canadian industry? For instance, according to the *Financial* Post, out of the fifteen largest firms (ranked by sales revenues) operating in Canada, three were majority foreign-owned corporations in 2005—one-fifth of the total. These included an American and a German automobile producer (General Motors and the then DaimlerChrysler) and a major American oil company (Exxon Mobile). While there are undoubtedly big foreign-owned corporations that hold large shares of Canada's domestic market, including the automobile and oil sectors, the link between size (reflecting relative dominance in an industry) and foreign ownership is somewhat tenuous—a conclusion also reached by a number of celebrated studies.[3]

Even when you consider a wider pool of big enterprises, say, the *Financial Post* top 400 largest firms in Canada nowadays, the picture is substantially the same. Indeed, as evidenced in Table 3, this share has actually been declining over the last two decades regardless of industry size classification. For instance, in 1980, 188 of the top 400 firms were 50 percent or more foreign-owned. In 2005, this number had declined to 122 firms—a number that is also slightly over a quarter of the total of the 400 leading firms in terms of sales revenues. This declining share is not particularly surprising and, to some extent, it mirrors the fact that, over the last decade, Canada's international investment position has shifted from being a net importer to a net exporter of capital. This would also explain why Canadian-based corporations, such as Inco Limited, are now more and more under the watchful eye of the American antitrust authorities. (This new phenomenon relating to Canada's international investment position is discussed in greater detail in Chapter 19 of *Macroeconomics: Principles and Policy*.)

TABLE 3								
Evolution of the Number of Foreign-Controlled Firms in Canada, 1980–2005 (number of firms 50% or more foreign-owned)								
Year	Size Classification of Largest Firms							
	Top 50	51–100	101–150	151–200	201–250	251–300	301–350	351–400	Total in Top 400
1980	17	19	25	24	27	24	22	30	188
1987	15	23	18	19	19	27	18	13	152
1998	16	17	20	24	20	20	22	15	154
2005	12	14	18	18	20	8	17	15	122

SOURCES: *Financial Post*, "FP 500," 1981, 1988, 1999, and *National Post Business*, "FP 500," June 2006.

---

[3] National Post Business, "FP 500," June 2006. Indeed, in his famous 1970 study, Gideon Rosenbluth detected no significant relationship during the earlier postwar period between growth of foreign ownership and increasing concentration by industry groups. See Gideon Rosenbluth, "The Relation between Foreign Control and Concentration in Canadian Industry," *Canadian Journal of Economics*, 3(1) (February 1970), pp. 14–38.

A CRUCIAL PROBLEM FOR COMPETITION POLICY: THE RESEMBLANCE OF MONOPOLIZATION AND VIGOROUS COMPETITION

One problem that haunts most anti-combines litigation is that vigorous competition may look very similar to acts that *undermine* competition and support monopoly power. The resulting danger is that the courts will prohibit, or the anti-combines authorities will prosecute, acts that *appear* to be anticompetitive but are really the opposite.

The difficulty occurs because effective competition by a firm is always tough on its rivals. It forces rivals to charge lower prices, to improve product quality, and to spend money on innovations that will cut their costs and improve their products. Competition will legitimately force competitors out of business if they are inefficient and therefore cannot keep their prices low or provide products of acceptable quality. When competition destroys a rival in this way, however, it is difficult to tell whether the firm was, so to speak, murdered or died of natural causes. In both cases, the surviving competitor bears some responsibility for its rival's failure. On the one hand, if the cause of the rival's demise is legitimate competition, consumers will benefit; on the other hand, if the end of the rival was part of a process of monopoly creation, then the public will end up paying. This very real issue constantly recurs in today's anti-combines litigation.

ANTICOMPETITIVE PRACTICES AND ANTI-COMBINES

A central purpose of the anti-combine laws is to prevent "anticompetitive acts," which are actions by a powerful firm that threaten to destroy competitors, or force competitors to compete less vigorously, or prevent the entry of new rivals.

Predatory Pricing

Typical of accusations of anticompetitive behaviour is the claim, made frequently in anticompetition cases, that the defendant has adopted unjustifiably low prices in order to force other firms to lose money, thereby driving competitors out of business. This practice is called **predatory pricing.** Deciding whether pricing is "predatory" is difficult, both for economists and for courts of law, because low prices generally benefit consumers. Therefore, the courts do not want to discourage firms from cutting prices by being too eager to declare that lower prices are intended to destroy a rival.

One principle widely followed by the courts internationally holds that prices are predatory only if they are below either marginal or average variable costs. The logic of this criterion as a test for whether prices are "too low" is that even under perfect competition, prices will not, in the long run, fall below that level, but will equal marginal costs. But even in cases where prices are below marginal or average variable costs, they may be held to be predatory only under two conditions:

- If evidence shows that the low price would have been profitable *only* if it succeeded in destroying a rival or in keeping it out of the market.
- When there is a real probability that the allegedly predatory firm could raise prices to monopoly levels after the rival was driven out, thereby profiting from its venture in crime.

Many major firms—including Air Canada, Bell Canada, and Microsoft—have been accused of predatory pricing. The defendants typically argue that their low prices cover both marginal and average variable costs, that their prices are low because of superior efficiency, and that the lawsuit was brought to prevent the defendants from competing effectively. The courts have generally accepted these arguments. There have been many predatory pricing cases, but few convictions.

Predatory pricing is pricing that threatens to keep a competitor out of the market. It is a price that is so low that it will be profitable for the firm that adopts it only if a rival is driven from the market.

■ The Microsoft Case: Bottlenecks, Bundling, and Network Externalities

The recent litigation involving Microsoft Corporation in the United States and Europe illustrate two other practices that can conceivably be anticompetitive. Microsoft is the enormously successful supplier of computer operating systems that enable you to communicate with and control your personal computer; it also supplies other very popular computer programs. Microsoft's software sales are huge, and the company is clearly a tough and energetic competitor. The difficulty of distinguishing vigorously competitive behaviour from anticompetitive acts is illustrated by the Microsoft antitrust case, in which American and European antitrust authorities accused the firm of various anticompetitive practices.

The Microsoft case raises many issues, two of which are discussed here as illustrations.

Abuse via Bottlenecks   Microsoft's Windows, an operating system that runs on about 90 percent of all personal computers, is a prime example of a problem referred to as a "bottleneck"—a facility or product in the hands of a single firm, without which competitors find it difficult or even impossible to operate. To reach any substantial proportion of personal computer customers, the producer of any word processor, spreadsheet, or graphics program must use Windows, and there seems little likelihood that any alternative to Windows will soon capture a large share of customers.

The bottleneck exists in part because Windows is widely considered a good program, but even more because user compatibility is desirable—computer users need to communicate with one another, and that task is easier if all of them employ the same operating system. That is, there exists a network of users of computer products who want to be able to communicate easily with one another, and who therefore desire compatible software. This preference gives Microsoft a big advantage, because it already has so many users that a new purchaser who values such compatibility will be reluctant to buy a competing product that will make it more difficult to communicate with those many users of the Microsoft products. The bottleneck problem arises because Microsoft itself supplies not only Windows but also many applications (such as Word, a word-processing program; Excel, a spreadsheet program; and Internet Explorer, an Internet browser). There is nothing illegal about simply being the owner of a bottleneck. If company X is a railroad with the only train-bearing bridge over a river because no other rail line had the resources or the initiative to build its own bridge, that is surely not anticompetitive. The worry is that a bottleneck owner, like Microsoft, will use its bottleneck product, Windows, in a way that favours its own programs and handicaps programs supplied by its competitors.

Bundling: Legitimate and Illegitimate   Microsoft has promoted its own products by providing them more cheaply to computer manufacturers if these makers buy a *bundle* of Microsoft programs, rather than just Windows alone. This practice means that rival producers of word processors, spreadsheets, and Internet browsers are handicapped in selling their products to PC owners. The question is whether Microsoft's low bundle price is legitimate or if it constitutes a case of predatory pricing whose only purpose is to destroy competitors. Economists often take the position that a **bundling** discount is legitimate if it is less expensive for the firm to supply several products at once than to supply them one at a time, and if the price cut corresponds to the cost saving. However, they question the legitimacy of the bundle discount if the cost saving is considerably less than the difference between the bundled price and the sum of the prices of the included products (when bought individually). However, even here, it is argued that if the price of the bundle exceeds its marginal cost or its average variable cost, it is not predatory.

Bundling refers to a pricing arrangement under which the supplier offers substantial discounts to customers if they buy several of the firm's products, so that the price of the bundle of products is less than the sum of the prices of the products if they were bought separately.

■ USE OF COMPETITION LAWS TO PREVENT COMPETITION

Finally, let us turn to an issue that some observers consider very serious: the *misuse* of the anti-combines laws to prevent competition. Many firms that have been unable to compete effectively on their own merits have turned to the courts to seek protection from their successful competitors—and some have succeeded.

Firms that try to protect themselves in this way always claim that their rivals have not achieved success through superior ability but rather by means that they call "monopolization." Sometimes the evidence is relatively clear-cut, and the Competition Tribunal can readily discern whether an accused firm has violated the anti-combines laws or whether it has simply been too efficient and innovative for the complaining competitor's tastes. In other cases, the issues are complicated, and only a long and painstaking legal proceeding offers any prospect of resolving them.

In the United States, various steps have been suggested to deal with the misuse of antitrust laws. In one proposal, if the courts decide that a firm has been falsely accused by another of violating the antitrust laws, then (as is done in most countries) the *accuser* will pay the legal costs of the innocent defendant. Another method is to subject such suits to prescreening by a government agency, as is done in Japan. But these issues are hardly open and shut, for there is no such thing as a perfect legal system. Anything that restricts anticompetitive, private anti-combines suits will almost certainly inhibit legitimate attempts by individual firms to defend themselves from genuine acts of monopolization by rival enterprises.

■ CONCLUDING OBSERVATIONS

As we noted at the beginning of this chapter, monopoly and monopoly powers are rightly judged to cause market failure—the "abuse of dominance" in the marketplace entails excessive profits acquired at the expense of consumers desiring greater product choice at competitive prices. The alternative is government intervention, and governments, too, sometimes make imperfect decisions. Thus, before deciding whether to regulate more or deregulate, whether to toughen our competition laws or loosen them, informed citizens should carefully weigh the prospects for market failure against the possibility of government failure in terms of the contemplated change.

Certainly, monopolists have sometimes succeeded in preventing the introduction of useful new products. They have raised prices to consumers and held down product quality. In contrast, large firms have sometimes been innovative and their service to customers has in some cases been considered of high quality.

Government has, at times, made its own missteps. Government authorities can initiate costly lawsuits, sometimes on questionable grounds. It can force regulated firms to adopt pricing rules that may not be beneficial to consumers, and it can even handicap the operations of industries. Yet government does many useful things in beneficially influencing industry behaviour, preventing various monopolistic practices, protecting consumers from impure foods and medications, and so on. A good number of economists and policy makers argue that by the 1970s, government intervention had clearly gone too far in some respects and that deregulation was, consequently, in the public interest. There are others, though, who argue that the deregulation process itself has now gone too far and that a more stringent regulation of industry is desirable. However, the general issue is hardly settled.

SUMMARY

1. Economic **regulation** is adopted to put brakes on the decisions of industries with **monopoly power.**

2. In Canada, regulation of prices and other economic decisions is generally applied only to large firms, including railroads, telecommunications, and gas and electricity supply.

3. In recent years, we have seen a major push toward reduction of regulation. Among the industries that have been deregulated in whole or in part are air, truck, and rail transportation.

4. Among the major reasons given for regulation are (a) **economies of scale** and **economies of scope,** which make industries into natural monopolies; and (b) the universal service goal, which refers to the provision of service to poor people and isolated areas where supply is unprofitable.

5. Regulators often reject proposals by regulated firms to cut their prices, and sometimes the regulators even force firms to *raise* their prices. The purposes of such actions are to prevent "unfair competition" and to protect customers of some of the firm's products from being forced to **cross-subsidize** customers of other products. Many economists disagree with most such actions, arguing that the result is usually to stifle competition and make all customers pay more than they otherwise would.

6. Economists generally agree that a firm should be permitted to cut its price as long as it covers its marginal cost. However, in many regulated industries, firms would go bankrupt if all prices were set equal to marginal costs.

7. By putting ceilings on profits to prevent monopoly earnings, regulation can eliminate the firm's incentive for efficiency and innovation. Price caps, which put (inflation-adjusted) ceilings on prices, rather than profits, are used widely to deal with this problem.

8. *Anti-combines policy* includes those policies and programs designed to control the growth of monopoly and to prevent big business from engaging in "anticompetitive" practices.

9. **Predatory pricing** is pricing that is low relative to the marginal or average variable costs of the firm and so threatens to drive a competitor out of the market. For pricing to be considered predatory, there must also be a likelihood that if the prices do destroy a competitor, the firm will acquire market power enabling it to charge prices well above competitive levels.

10. **Bundling** refers to a price reduction given to customers who purchase several of the firm's products simultaneously. It is considered unobjectionable if it is cheaper for the firm to bundle its products so that the price cut merely passes the savings on to customers. However, bundling can be used to destroy competitors that sell only some of the bundled products.

11. There has been a gentle upward movement in concentration ratios over the last half-century, especially in recent decades. Evidence as to whether anti-combines laws have been effective in preventing monopoly is inconclusive, and observers disagree on the subject.

12. Unregulated monopoly is apt to distribute income unfairly, produce undesirably small quantities of output, and provide inadequate motivation for innovation.

13. Sometimes, however, only large firms may have funds sufficient for effective research, development, and innovation. Where economies of scale are available, large firms may also serve customers more cheaply than can small ones.

KEY TERMS

Economies of scale 286	Cross-subsidization 289	Concentration ratios 299
Monopoly power 286	Price cap 292	Herfindahl Index 300
Regulation 287	Anti-combines policy 298	Predatory pricing 305
Economies of scope 289	Concentration of an industry 299	Bundling 306

DISCUSSION QUESTIONS

1. Why is an electric company in a city often considered to be a natural monopoly? What would happen if two competing electric companies were established? How about telephone companies? How can changes in technology affect your answer?

2. Suppose that a 20 percent cut in the price of coast-to-coast telephone calls brings in so much new business that it permits a long-distance telephone company to cut its charges for service from Toronto to Vancouver, but only by 2 percent. In your opinion, is this practice equitable? Is it a good idea or a bad one?

3. In some regulated industries, regulatory agencies prevented prices from falling, and as a result many firms opened for business in those industries. In your opinion, is

this kind of regulation competitive or anticompetitive? Is it a good idea or a bad one?

4. Regulators are highly concerned about the prevention of predatory pricing. While recognizing that the term does not have a well-defined meaning, Canada's Competition Bureau receives plenty of complaints of predatory pricing. How might you distinguish predatory from non-predatory pricing? If you were the Director of Investigation and Research at the Competition Bureau, what would you do about it?

5. Do you think that it is fair or unfair for rural users of telephone service to be cross-subsidized by other telephone users?

6. To provide incentives for increased efficiency, several regulatory agencies have eliminated ceilings on the profits of

regulated firms but instead put caps on their prices. Suppose that a regulated firm manages to cut its prices in half, but in the process it doubles its profits. Should rational consumers consider this to be a good or a bad development? Why?

7. A shopkeeper sells his store and signs a contract that restrains him from opening another store in competition with the new owner. The courts have decided that this contract is a reasonable restraint of trade. Can you think of any other types of restraint of trade that seem reasonable? Can you think of any that seem unreasonable?

8. Which of the following industries do you expect to have high concentration ratios: motor vehicle production, petroleum, tobacco production, or production of computers? Compare your answers with the data in Tables 1 and 2.

9. Why do you think the specific industries you selected in Discussions Question 8 are highly concentrated?

10. Do you think it is in the public interest to launch an anti-combines suit that costs $1 billion? What leads you to your conclusion?

11. In Japan and a number of European countries, the competition laws were once much less severe than those in Canada and in the United States. Do you think that this difference helped or harmed North American industry in its efforts to compete with overseas producers? Why?

12. Can you think of some legal rules that may discourage the use of competition laws to prevent competition while at the same time not interfering with legitimate anti-combines actions?

13. During the oil crisis in the 1970s, long lines at gas stations disappeared soon after price controls were removed and gas prices were permitted to rise. Should this event be interpreted as evidence that the oil companies have monopoly power? Why or why not?

14. Some economists believe that firms rarely attempt predatory pricing because it would be a very risky act even if it were legal. Why may this be so?

15. Firm X cuts its prices, and competing Firm Y soon goes out of business. How would you judge whether this price cut was an act of legitimate and vigorous competition or an anticompetitive act?

IV

THE VIRTUES AND LIMITATIONS OF MARKETS

L ike most institutions, the market has both shortcomings and benefits, and one of the goals of this book is to describe them both as dispassionately as we can. Chapter 14 describes and analyzes a snapshot picture of the market at its best, showing how remarkably well it can coordinate the vast number of activities and decisions that drive our economy. The next chapter, in contrast, investigates some of the important ways in which the market mechanism, if left entirely to itself, fails to serve the public interest well. In Chapter 15 as well as in Chapter 17, we examine what can be done to remedy these deficiencies—or at least to reduce their undesirable consequences. In Chapter 16, the growth chapter, we depict the economy in motion. There we will see the most incredible accomplishments of the market economy in its ability to bring remarkable increases in standards of living and innovative products that could hardly have been imagined by our ancestors. In short, growth performance of the market has totally outstripped anything our forebears could conceivably have expected. Finally, Chapter 18 introduces you to the tax system and the effects of the government on resource allocation.

THE CASE FOR THE MARKET SYSTEM I: THE PRICE MECHANISM

If there existed the universal mind that . . . would register simultaneously all the processes of nature and of society, that could forecast the results of their inter-reactions, such a mind . . . could . . . draw up a faultless and an exhaustive economic plan. . . . In truth, the bureaucracy often conceives that just such a mind is at its disposal; that is why it so easily frees itself from the control of the market.

LEON TROTSKY, A LEADER OF THE RUSSIAN REVOLUTION

Our study of microeconomics focuses on two crucial questions: What does the market do well, and what does it do poorly? By applying what we learned about demand in Chapters 5 and 6, supply in Chapters 7 and 8, and the functioning of perfectly competitive markets in Chapter 10, we can provide a fairly comprehensive answer to the first part of this question. This chapter describes major tasks that the market carries out well—some, indeed, with spectacular effectiveness.

We begin by recalling two important themes from Chapters 3 and 4. First, because all resources are *scarce*, a society benefits by using them efficiently. Second, to do so, an economy must somehow coordinate the actions of many individual consumers and producers. Specifically, society must somehow choose:

- How much of each good to produce
- What input quantities to use in the production process
- How to distribute the resulting outputs among consumers

CONTENTS

As suggested by the opening quotation (from someone who was certainly in a position to know), these tasks are exceedingly difficult for a centrally planned economy. That overwhelming difficulty was probably a significant factor in contributing to the fall of a number of communist regimes in the late 1980s in Eastern Europe and the former Soviet Union, and the same difficulty shows up today in the few remaining centrally planned economies, such as North Korea. But for the most part those same tasks appear to be rather simple for a market system. This is why observers with philosophies as diverse as those of Adam Smith and the Russian Revolution's Leon Trotsky have admired the market, and why even countries that maintain very strong central governments have now moved toward market economies.

Do not misinterpret this chapter as a piece of salesmanship. Here, we study the market mechanism at its theoretical very best—when every good is produced under the exacting conditions of perfect competition. Some industries in our economy are reasonable approximations of perfect competition, but many others are as different from this idealized world as the physical world is from a frictionless vacuum tube. Just as the physicist uses the vacuum tube to study the laws of gravity, the economist uses the theoretical concept of a perfectly competitive economy to analyze the virtues of the market. We will spend plenty of time in later chapters studying its vices.

PUZZLE: *Toll Bridges and Highways: Is the Price Right?*

SOURCE: JOHN RENNISON/Canadian Press

Toll bridges and highways in Canada are far less prevalent than they are in the United States. The main reason is that, once the relevant Canadian government authorities have paid off the debt that was originally incurred to build these public infrastructures, tolls often disappear. Indeed, once paid for, successive governments have normally chosen to use funds from general tax revenues rather than charge user fees for the upkeep and maintenance of these various infrastructures in Canada.

There are exceptions, however, including the 407 Express Toll Route (ETR) just north of Toronto, which was completed in 1997 and sold to a private consortium in 1999, and the Confederation Bridge, also completed in 1997, which crosses the Northumberland Strait and joins Prince Edward Island to New Brunswick on the Canadian mainland.

Tolls also persist on some international bridges, including the Ambassador Bridge (linking Detroit, Michigan, with Windsor, Ontario), the Blue Water Bridge (joining Port Huron, Michigan, and Sarnia, Ontario), and the Peace Bridge (between Buffalo, New York, and Fort Erie, Ontario). Some cash-strapped provinces and municipalities have also continued to charge tolls; examples are the Angus Macdonald Bridge (linking Halifax and Dartmouth in Nova Scotia) and the Saint John Harbour Bridge in New Brunswick, Given the deteriorating health of some of our bridges and highways, governments have not kept up their bridge and highway maintenance spending in recent years and have often focused on other priorities, such as deficit fighting.

In contrast to the relative scarcity of toll highways and bridges in Canada, Canadians travelling in the United States find that, wherever enough revenues can be efficiently collected, tolls are often charged by the relevant authorities regardless of whether these bridges and highways have been paid for or not. Indeed, anyone travelling by automobile to, say, the New York City area will be struck by the number of toll bridges and highways, despite the fact that many of these, such as the Triborough Bridge (opened in 1936 to connect Manhattan, Queens, and the Bronx), were presumably paid for long ago!

For our puzzle, we have chosen a Canadian example of the relationship between pricing and the efficient use of resources by looking at the appropriate setting of tolls on a privatized highway: the 407 ETR in the Greater Toronto Area (GTA)—described as the world's first all-electronic, barrier-free highway, which stretches 108 kilometres from Burlington to Pickering.

The 407 ETR was originally planned as a freeway that would bypass much of Highway 401 in the GTA to relieve some of the 401 congestion. But, two years after its completion in 1997, the then Conservative provincial government of Premier Mike Harris opted to privatize the 407, clearing the way for user fees to be established.

However, given the high volume of traffic on the 401, most economists would argue that it would have been better to charge a toll for use of the 401, perhaps even a higher one than is now charged on the 407 ETR. But why would anyone want to collect a toll from those unfortunate drivers caught on the 401? Are they not paying a high enough price with their time by being stuck for hours in heavy traffic? Whether you agree or not, before you have finished reading this chapter, you will at least come to understand the logic of this seemingly unfair proposition.

■ EFFICIENT RESOURCE ALLOCATION AND PRICING

The fundamental fact that inputs are scarce means that there are limits to the volume of goods and services that any economic system can produce. In Chapter 3 we illustrated the concept of scarcity with a graphic device called a production possibilities frontier, which we repeat here for convenience as Figure 1. The frontier, curve *BC*, depicts all combinations of bread and butter that a hypothetical society can produce given the limited resources at its disposal. For example, if it decides to produce 300 million kilograms of bread, it will have enough resources left over to produce no more than 500 million kiolgrams of butter (point *D*). Of course, it is possible, then, to produce *fewer* than 500 million kilograms of butter—at a point, such as *G*, below the production possibilities frontier. But if a society makes this choice, it is wasting some of its potential output; that is, it is not operating efficiently.

In Chapter 3 we defined efficiency rather loosely as the absence of waste. Because this chapter discusses primarily how a competitive market economy allocates resources efficiently, we now need a more precise definition. It is easiest to define an **efficient allocation of resources** by saying what it is not. For example, suppose that we could rearrange our resource allocation so that one group of people would get more of the things it wanted, while no one else would have to give up anything. Then, the failure to change the allocation of resources to take advantage of this opportunity would surely be wasteful—that is, inefficient. When society has taken advantage of *every* such opportunity for improvement, so that no such possibilities remain for making some people better off without making others worse off, we say that the allocation of resources is **efficient.**

To see what this implies for our analysis, let us see what an inefficient set of output quantities looks like in our graph. Because point *G* in Figure 1 is below the frontier, there must be points like *E* on the frontier that lie above and to the right of *G*. At point *E*, we get more of *both* outputs without any increase in input, so it is possible to make some people better off without harming anyone. Thus, no point below the frontier can represent an efficient allocation of resources. By contrast, every point on the frontier is efficient because, no matter where on the frontier we start, we cannot get more of one good without giving up some of the other.

An **efficient allocation of resources** is one that takes advantage of every opportunity to make some individuals better off in their own estimation while not worsening the lot of anyone else.

FIGURE 1

Production Possibilities Frontier and Efficiency

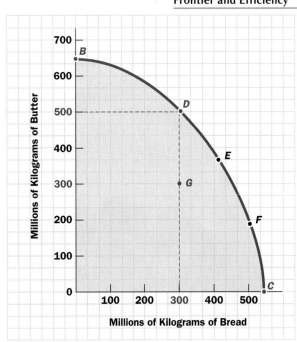

This discussion also shows that, normally, many particular allocations of resources will be efficient; in the example, every combination of outputs that is represented by a point on frontier *BC* can be efficient. As a rule, the concept of efficiency cannot tell us which of these efficient allocations is best for society. Yet, as we shall see in this chapter, we can use the concept of efficiency to formulate surprisingly detailed rules to steer us away from situations in which resources would be wasted.

■ Pricing to Promote Efficiency: An Example

We can use the example in the puzzle about the 407 Express Toll Route in the Greater Toronto Area to illustrate the connection between efficiency and the way that prices can guide efficient choices. Depending on the objective criteria for efficiency, prices can make all the difference between efficiency and inefficiency. This example will show that the price (toll) charged on what are otherwise parallel routes (Highways 401 and 407) to travel from, say, Brampton on the west to Durham on the east (see Figure 2) can make the commuter process more efficient.

To simplify our analysis, we will ignore the fact that, unlike the 401, which is fully publicly owned, the 407 is now essentially a private highway, administered by a private consortium since 1999. This fact is obviously very important, as we will see shortly, but for the moment, we will restrict our analysis to the bare essentials. If both routes were toll-free, given the proximity of the 401 to what are the most densely populated, as well as commercially most active, districts to the south of the highway, the 401 would tend to be the most congested. Since it is desirable to reduce traffic congestion (because traffic jams mean a greater waste of commuter time, greater gasoline consumption, greater damage to the environment, and so on), would a toll on the 401 help in alleviating the traffic and also help the government authority in reducing the debt incurred to build the 407? Most economists would argue that a toll on the most congested route would be appropriate or that, if tolls need to be applied both to raise funds and to service the debt, a higher toll should be imposed for use of the 401.

In reality, of course, we have ignored a very important fact—the 401 is a public highway while the 407 is a private highway, so conflicting objectives are involved. As a private highway saddled with a huge debt and faced with road maintenance costs, the issue becomes one of how to maximize profits to the 407's owners. Hence, we have the reality of a toll on the private route but free use for the public route. While the existence of a toll route does offer choice and does undoubtedly alleviate some of the traffic problems faced by Toronto motorists, a socially more efficient solution would be to have a toll on the most congested highway, not on the least congested.

This example raises another important point with more general implications for economic analysis: Asymmetries in the accessibility of a service or of a resource lead to the systematic overuse of the resource for which there is open access, whether it is the 401 or the fisheries off Newfoundland.[1]

FIGURE 2

Road Map of the Greater Toronto Area

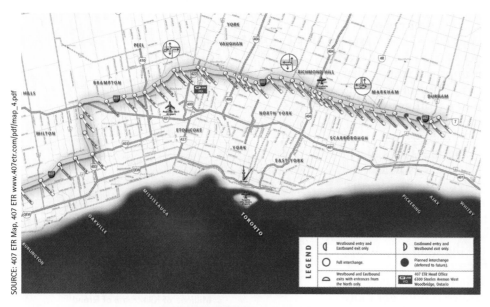

SOURCE: 407 ETR Map, 407 ETR www.407etr.com/pdf/pdf/map_4.pdf

---

[1] Economic historians of the Middle Ages sometimes referred to this outcome as *the tragedy of the commons*.

◼ Can Price Increases Ever Serve the Public Interest?

This discussion raises a point that people untrained in economics always find extremely difficult to accept: Low prices may not always serve the public interest! The reason is pretty clear. If a price, such as a toll charged for crossing a crowded bridge or the price of gasoline, is set "too low," then consumers will receive the "wrong" market signals. Low prices will encourage them to crowd the bridge even more or to consume more gasoline, thereby squandering society's precious resources.

A striking historical illustration brings out the importance of this role of prices. In 1834, a professor of economics at the University of Dublin named Mountifort Longfield lectured about the price system. He offered the following example:

> Suppose the crop of potatoes in Ireland was to fall short in some year [by] one-sixth of the usual consumption. If [there were no] increase of price, the whole . . . supply of the year would be exhausted in ten months, and for the remaining two months a scene of misery and famine beyond description would ensue. . . . But when prices [increase] the sufferers [often believe] that it is not caused by scarcity. . . . They suppose that there are provisions enough, but that the distress is caused by the insatiable rapacity of the possessors . . . [and] they have generally succeeded in obtaining laws against [the price increases] . . . which alone can prevent the provisions from being entirely consumed long before a new supply can be obtained.[2]

You may be intrigued to know that this talk was given some ten years before the great potato famine, which caused unspeakable misery and death by starvation and brought many people from Ireland to North America. The story of the actual potato famine in Ireland is much more complex than Longfield's discussion indicates. Still, the implications of his lecture about the way the price system works are entirely valid.

We can perhaps rephrase Longfield's reasoning more usefully. If the crop fails, potatoes become scarcer. If society is to use its scarce resources efficiently, stretching out the potato supply to last until the next crop arrives, it must cut back on the consumption of potatoes during earlier months—which is just what rising prices will do automatically if free-market mechanisms are allowed to work. However, if the price is held artificially low, consumers will use society's resources inefficiently. In this case, the inefficiency shows up in the form of famine and suffering when people deplete this year's crop months before the next one is harvested.

It is not easy to accept the notion that higher prices can serve the public interest better than lower ones. Politicians who voice this view are in the position of the proverbial parent who, before spanking a child, announces, "This is going to hurt me much more than it hurts you!" Because advocacy of higher prices courts political disaster, the political system often rejects the market solution when resources suddenly become scarcer.

The way that airport officials price landing privileges at crowded airports offers a good example. Airports become particularly congested at "peak hours," just before 9 A.M. and just after 5 P.M. These times are when passengers most often suffer long delays. But many airports continue to charge bargain landing fees throughout the day, even at those crowded hours. That makes it attractive for small corporate jets or other planes carrying only a few passengers to arrive and take off at those hours, worsening the delays. Higher fees for peak-hour landings can discourage such overuse, but they are politically unpopular, and many airports are run by local governments. So we continue to experience late arrivals as a normal feature of air travel. (See the boxed feature "Using Economic Principles to Improve Seat Occupancy Rates on Air Canada Flights" for an example of how the pricing of airline seats deals with the problem of peak-period demand.)

---

[2] Mountifort Longfield, *Lectures on Political Economy Delivered in Trinity and Michaelmas Terms* (Dublin: W. Curry, Jr., and Company; 1834), pp. 53–56.

Using Economic Principles to Improve Seat Occupancy Rates on Air Canada Flights

Ever since the deregulation of the skyways, air carriers have had to make substantial efforts to avoid empty seats and achieve high occupancy rates on their airplanes. The days when airlines could afford to run nearly empty planes across the Atlantic or the North American continent are now long gone (one of the authors once took an Amsterdam–Montreal Canadian Pacific Airlines flight with less than 15 passengers on board a Boeing that could carry about 200 passengers). Airlines now change ticket prices frequently, as they monitor, on a daily or even hourly basis, how scheduled flights are filling up. By moving prices up and down according to demand, air carriers try to induce potential customers to purchase cheap seats on flights that are half-empty, leaving only highly motivated travellers to purchase expensive seats on planes that are already nearly filled or overfilled (called *overbooking*, when an airline sells more tickets than it has seats, this is an endemic phenomenon in the airline industry, as air carriers know, from historical data, that a certain percentage—as high as 15 percent—of the seat holders will cancel their trip at the last minute (the "no-shows"). With this marketing strategy, an airline company improves its load factor—the airline seat occupancy rate—by minimizing the probability of turning down a passenger looking for a specific flight time and hence

losing this passenger to a rival airline. At the same time, the airline company is able to use lower prices to attract flexible passengers from rival carriers.

The accompanying table shows the lowest 2006 Tango fares for a one-way ticket from Toronto to Vancouver on Air Canada flights running during the December holiday period. All of the information was gathered on Halloween: October 31. The most popular flight times and flight days carry high ticket prices, above $400, even though reservations would have been made nearly two months in advance, while flights less in demand have fares as low as $179. Amazingly, leaving one hour earlier or later allows a passenger with some degree of flexibility to save more than $200 ($179 versus $433 on Sunday, December 17).

As one would expect, flights throughout the busy period of December 20–29 are all pretty expensive, except for the late-hour flights on Christmas Day. Also, somewhat surprisingly, there seem to be some benchmark prices. In other words, prices do not change continuously as the seats get filled: Prices change discontinuously along some thresholds. In the table, there are 120 flights, but only 13 different prices.

Note: Prices do not include taxes, fees, and surcharges.

Air Canada Tango Fares, December 2006

Toronto–Vancouver
Flight Departure Time and One-Way Fare

Departure Date	7:00	8:00	8:30	9:00	10:00	11:00	...	20:00	22:45
Fri., 22 Dec.	$179	$179	$416	$328	$179	$179	...	$328	$328
Sat., 16 Dec.	179	428	428	428	328	348	...	348	328
Sun., 17 Dec.	179	433	433	433	179	179	...	328	179
Mon., 18 Dec.	179	411	411	411	179	179	...	179	179
Tue., 19 Dec.	179	179	428	411	318	318	...	318	318
Wed., 20 Dec.	318	348	411	348	348	348	...	348	348
Thu., 21 Dec.	328	433	433	353	388	388	...	328	328
Fri., 22 Dec.	353	433	433	416	388	416	...	433	416
Sat., 23 Dec.	428	428	—	—	—	428	...	383	383
Sun., 24 Dec.	388	388	433	416	353	353	...	353	254
Mon., 25 Dec.	383	411	428	428	328	328	...	219	189
Tue., 26 Dec.	383	383	411	428	411	383	...	348	318
Wed., 27 Dec.	318	383	411	411	383	383	...	348	318
Thu., 28 Dec.	328	388	416	353	353	353	...	328	328
Fri., 29 Dec.	328	353	353	353	353	353	...	353	328

SOURCE: Air Canada. Retrieved on October 31, 2006, from the Air Canada website.

■ Attempts to Repeal the Laws of Supply and Demand: The Market Strikes Back

Keeping prices low when an increase is appropriate can have serious consequences indeed. We have just observed that it can worsen the effects of shortages of food and other vital goods. We know that inappropriately low prices caused chaos in gasoline distribution after the sudden decline in Iranian oil exports in 1979. In times of war, constraints on prices have even contributed to the surrender of cities under military siege, deterring those who would otherwise have risked smuggling food supplies through enemy lines. Low prices also have discouraged housing construction in cities where government-imposed upper limits on rents made building construction a losing proposition.

Of course, in some cases it is appropriate to resist price increases—when unrestrained monopoly would otherwise succeed in gouging the public, when taxes are imposed on products capriciously and inappropriately, and when rising prices fall so heavily on poor people that rationing becomes the more acceptable option. But before tampering with the market mechanism, we must carefully evaluate the potentially serious and even tragic consequences that artificial restrictions on prices can produce.

■ SCARCITY AND THE NEED TO COORDINATE ECONOMIC DECISIONS

Efficiency becomes a particularly critical issue when we concern ourselves with the workings of the economy as a whole, rather than with narrower topics such as choosing among bridge routes or deciding on the output of a single firm. We can think of an economy as a complex machine with literally millions of component parts. If this machine is to function efficiently, we must find some way to make the parts work in harmony.

A consumer in Gimli, Manitoba, may decide to purchase two dozen eggs, and on the same day thousands of shoppers throughout the country make similar decisions. None of these purchasers knows or cares about the decisions of the others. Yet scarcity requires that these demands must somehow be coordinated with the production process so that the total quantity of eggs demanded does not exceed the total quantity supplied. Consumers, supermarkets, wholesalers, shippers, and chicken farmers must somehow arrive at mutually consistent decisions; otherwise, the economic process will deteriorate into chaos, as will millions of other such decisions. A machine cannot run with a few missing parts.

In a planned or centrally directed economy, we can easily imagine how such coordination takes place—although implementation is far more difficult than conception. Central planners set production targets for firms and sometimes tell firms how to meet these targets. In extreme cases, consumers may even be told, rather than asked, what they want to consume.

In contrast, a market system uses prices to coordinate economic activity based on the profit motive. High prices discourage consumption of the scarcest resources and encourage supply, whereas low prices encourage consumption of comparatively abundant resources and discourage supply. In this way, Adam Smith's invisible hand of the market uses prices to organize the economy's production.

The invisible hand has an astonishing capacity to handle enormously complex coordination problems—even those that remain beyond computer capabilities. Like any mechanism, this one has its imperfections, some of them rather serious. But we should not lose sight of the tremendously demanding task that the market constantly does accomplish—unnoticed, undirected, and, in some respects, amazingly well. Let's look at just how the market goes about coordinating economic activity.

■ Three Coordination Tasks in the Economy

We recalled at the beginning of this chapter that any economic system, planned or unplanned, must find answers to three basic questions of resource allocation:

- *Output selection*. How much of each commodity should be produced?
- *Production planning*. What quantity of each of the available inputs should be used to produce each good?
- *Distribution*. How should the resulting products be divided among consumers?

Poland's Transition to a Market Economy

Twenty years have passed since communist regimes collapsed all over Eastern Europe and the former Soviet Union, ending economic central planning and heralding the emergence of a market system in these countries. Nowhere were these changes as dramatic as in Poland, where radical economic reforms constituted no less than "shock therapy."

Poland's transformation into a market economy, although far from complete, has been nearly as drastic as the first postcommunist government hoped. Poland had been saddled with a legendarily incompetent, old-fashioned, and badly managed economy, which in its depths managed to run out of things like matches and salt, its paltry living standards bequeathed by a centrally controlled economy. It reached out to the West for help in creating monetary, budget, trade, and legal regimes, and is now one of the most robust economies in central Europe, and, most recently, one of the newest members of the European Union. Poland is the only transition economy that has experienced substantial growth: Real GDP was over 50 percent higher in 2006 than it was in 1990. Economic liberalization freed entrepreneurs to sell, within loose limits, anything they want at whatever price they can get. Today, there are more than 1.7 million independent firms and 75 percent of the country's GDP is produced in the private sector (up from just 16 percent in 1989).

Despite these positive economic indicators pertaining to the growth rate of the economy, Poland has a long way to go in dealing with crippling unemployment (the highest in the European Union) and low productivity, especially in its agricultural sector. Almost 50 percent of working-age individuals are out of work. Many of its publicly owned industries are still backward, business and personal life remains hampered by bureaucratic red tape and corruption, and Polish farming is antiquated and very inefficient—the agricultural sector produces only 3 percent of GDP but engages 20 percent of the population. Indeed, one observer writes that, from the air, it is easy to identify Poland's national boundary, because the patchwork of tiny fields in Poland is in such contrast to the sprawling expanses of arable land in adjacent countries.

SOURCES: Rudolf Herman, "Rural Poland: Ready for the Chop," *Central European Review*, 1, no. 10 (August 1999); Stanislaw Gomulka, "Macroeconomic Policies and Achievements in Transition Economies, 1989–1999," United Nations' Economic Commission for Europe Annual Seminar, Geneva (May 2, 2000); Michael P. Keane and Eswar S. Prasad, "Poland: Inequality, Transfers, and Growth in Transition," *Finance & Development*, 38, no. 1 (March 2001); and Organisation for Economic Cooperation and Development, *OECD Economic Surveys 2006: Poland* (Paris: OECD, 2006). Retrieved from http://www.sourceoecd.org

SOURCE: © Caro/Alamy

SOURCE: © Raymond Gehman/Corbis

These coordination tasks may at first appear to be tailor-made for a regime of government planning like the one that the former Soviet Union once employed. Yet most economists (even, nowadays, those in the formerly centrally planned economies) believe that it is in exactly these tasks that central direction performs most poorly and, paradoxically, the undisciplined free market performs much better, even though no one directs its overall activities.

Laissez faire refers to a situation in which there is minimal government interference with the workings of the market system. The term implies that people should be left alone in carrying out their economic affairs.

To understand how the unguided market manages the miracle of creating order out of what might otherwise be chaos, let's look at how each of these questions is answered by a system of free and unfettered markets—the method of economic organization that eighteenth-century French economists named **laissez faire**. Under laissez faire, the government acts to prevent crime, enforce contracts, and build roads and other types of public works; it does not set prices, however, and interferes as little as possible with the operation of the market mechanism. How does such an unmanaged economy solve the three coordination problems?

Output Selection   A market system decides what should be produced by individuals who are guided by the profit motive and, in turn, this production is allocated among consumers on the basis of what is called the *"law" of supply and demand*. Where there is a shortage (that is, where quantity demanded exceeds quantity supplied), the market mechanism pushes the price upward, thereby encouraging more production and less consumption of the commodity that is in short supply. Where a surplus arises (that is, where quantity supplied exceeds quantity demanded), the same mechanism works in reverse: The price falls, discouraging production and stimulating consumption.

As an example, suppose that millions of people wake up one morning with a change in taste, and thereafter want more omelettes. As a result, for the moment, the quantity of eggs demanded exceeds the quantity supplied. But, within a few days, the market mechanism swings into action to meet this sudden change in demand, not because of any altruistic tendencies on the part of egg producers but, as Adam Smith noted long ago, by the desire to make a profit. The price of eggs rises, which stimulates egg production. At first, farmers will simply bring more eggs to market by taking them out of storage. Over a somewhat longer time period, chickens that otherwise would have been sold for meat will be kept in the chicken coops laying eggs. Finally, if the high price of eggs persists, farmers will begin to increase their flocks, build more coops, and so on. Thus, a shift in consumer demand leads to a shift in society's resources; more eggs are wanted, so the market mechanism sees to it that more of society's resources are devoted to egg production and marketing.

Similar reactions follow if a technological breakthrough reduces the input quantities needed to produce some item. Electronic calculators are a marvellous example. Calculators used to be so expensive that they could be found only in business firms and scientific laboratories. Then advances in science and engineering reduced their cost dramatically, and the market went to work. With costs sharply reduced, prices fell and the quantity demanded skyrocketed. In their quest for profit, electronic firms flocked into the industry to meet this demand, which is to say that more of society's resources were devoted to producing the calculators that were suddenly in such great demand. These examples lead us to conclude that:

> In a laissez-faire capitalistic economy, the allocation of society's resources among different products depends on where business profits can be maximized, which, in turn, depends on consumer demand (or preferences) and the production costs of the goods demanded.

Notice that no bureaucrat or central planner arranges resource allocation. Instead, an unseen force guides allocation—the lure of profits, which is the invisible hand that guides chicken farmers to increase their flocks when eggs are in greater demand and guides electronics firms to build new factories when the cost of electronic products falls.

Production Planning   Once the market has decided on output composition, the next coordination task is to determine just how those goods will be produced. The production-planning problem includes, among other things, the division of society's scarce inputs among enterprises. Which farm or factory will get how much of which materials? How much of the nation's labour force? Of the produced inputs such as plant and machinery? Such decisions can be crucial. If a factory runs short of an essential input, the entire production process may grind to a halt.

In reality, no economic system can select inputs and outputs separately. The input distribution between the production of cars and the manufacture of washing machines determines the quantities of cars and washing machines that society can obtain. However, it is simpler to think of input and output decisions as if they occur one at a time.

Once again, under laissez faire it is the price system that apportions labour, fuel, and other inputs among different industries in accord with those industries' requirements. The firm that needs a piece of equipment most urgently will be the last to drop out of the market for that product when prices rise. If millers demand more wheat than is currently available, the price will rise and bring quantity demanded back into line with quantity supplied, always giving priority to those users who are willing to pay the most for grain because it is most valuable to them. Thus:

> In an ideal free market, inputs are assigned to the firms that can make the most productive (most profitable) use of them. Firms that cannot make a sufficiently productive use of some input will be priced out of the market for that item.

This task, which sounds so simple, is actually almost unimaginably complex. It is so complex that it has helped to bring down many centrally planned systems. We will return to it shortly, as an illustration of how difficult it is to replace the market by a central planning bureau. But first let us consider the third of our three coordination problems.

Distribution of Products among Consumers   The third task of any economy is to decide which consumer gets each of the goods that has been produced. The objective is to distribute the available supplies to match differing consumer preferences as well as possible. Coffee lovers must not be flooded with tea, for example, while tea drinkers are showered with coffee.

The price mechanism solves this problem by assigning the highest prices to the goods in greatest demand and then letting individual consumers and producers pursue their own self-interests. Consider our example of rising egg prices. As eggs become more expensive, people whose craving for omelettes is not terribly strong will begin to buy fewer eggs. In effect, the price acts as a rationing device that apportions the available eggs among consumers who are willing to pay the most for them.

Thus, the price mechanism has an important advantage over other rationing devices: It can respond to individual consumer preferences. If a centrally planned economy rations eggs by distributing the same amount to everyone (say, two eggs per week to each person), then everyone ends up with two eggs whether he likes eggs or detests them. The price system, on the other hand, permits each consumer to set her own priorities.

There is thus a trade-off between efficiency and equality. The price system carries out the distribution process by rationing goods on the basis of preferences and relative incomes. Notice the last three words of the previous sentence. By rationing products on the basis of those who can best afford them, the price system does favour the rich, and this is a fundamental problem of distribution to which market economies must face up.

However, we may still want to think twice before declaring ourselves opposed to the price system. If equality is our goal, might not a more reasonable solution be to use the tax system to equalize incomes and then let the market mechanism distribute goods in accord with preferences? We take this idea up in Chapter 18, in which we discuss tax policy.

We have just seen, in broad outline, how a laissez-faire economy addresses the three basic issues of resource allocation: what to produce, how to produce it, and how to distribute the resulting products. Because it performs these tasks quietly, without central direction, and with no apparent concern for the public interest, many radical critics have predicted that such an unplanned system must degenerate into chaos. Yet unplanned, market economies are far from chaotic. Quite ironically, it is the centrally planned economies that have often ended up in economic disarray and faced severe shortages of goods, while market economies have shown greater resilience despite the periodic ups and downs of overall market activity. In sharp contrast to the problems of chronic shortages and lack of capacity characteristics of many planned economies, advanced market economies are frequently beset with recurrent problems of excess supply resulting in the chronic underutilization of capacity (a topic that is discussed in *Macroeconomics: Principles and Policy*).

Perhaps the best way to appreciate the accomplishments of market economies is to consider how a centrally planned system must cope with the coordination problem we have just outlined. Let us examine just one of them: production planning.

Input–Output Analysis: The Near Impossibility of Perfect Central Planning

Of the three coordination tasks of any economy, the assignment of input to specific industries and firms has claimed the most attention of central planners. Why? Because the production processes of the various industries are interdependent. Industry X cannot operate without Industry Y's output, but Industry Y, in turn, needs Industry X's product. The output decisions of the two industries cannot escape this (non-vicious) circle. The entire economy can grind to a halt if planners do not solve such production-planning problems satisfactorily. In recent years, failure to adapt to this kind of interdependence has had dire consequences in North Korea, one of the last remaining centrally planned economies. Breakdowns of key economic activities such as the electric supply grid, transportation systems, and other basic industries have each exacerbated the others' failures and created a terrible cycle of economic disaster, contributing to severe famine and cutting the life expectancy of North Koreans by more than six years in the 1990s.[3]

A simple example will further illustrate the point. Unless economic planners allocate enough gasoline to the trucking industry, products will not get to market. And unless planners allocate enough trucks to haul gasoline to gas stations, drivers will have no fuel. Thus, trucking activity depends on gasoline supply, but gasoline supply also depends on trucking activity. We see again that the decision maker is caught in a circle. Planners must decide both truck and gasoline outputs together, not separately.

> Because the output required from any one industry depends on outputs from many other industries, planners can be sure that the production of the various outputs will be sufficient to meet both consumer and industrial demands only by taking explicit account of this interdependence among industries. If they change the output target for one industry, they must also adjust every other industry's output target. But those changes in turn are likely to require readjustment of the first target change that started it all, leading to still more target change requirements, and so on, indefinitely.

For example, if planners decide to provide consumers with more electricity, then more steel must be produced in order to build more electric generators. Of course, an increase in steel output requires more iron ore to be mined. More mining, in turn, means that still more electricity is needed to light the mines, run the elevators, perhaps operate some of the trains that carry the iron ore, and so on and on. Any single change in production triggers a chain of adjustments throughout the economy that require still more adjustments that lead to still more adjustments.

There is a solution to this seemingly intractable problem, at least in theory. To decide how much of each output an economy must produce, the planner must use statistics to form a set of equations, one equation for each product, and then solve those equations simultaneously. The simultaneous solution process prevents interdependence in the analysis—electricity output depends on steel production, but steel output depends on electricity production—from becoming a vicious circle. The technique used to solve these complicated equations, **input–output analysis,** was invented in the late 1920s and early 1930s by the late Russian-born economist Wassily Leontief, who won the 1973 Sveriges Riksbank Nobel Prize in Economic Sciences for his work and whose concerns can be traced as far back as to mid-eighteenth-century French economists interested in explaining the interdependence of the various parts of an economic system.

The equations of input–output analysis illustrated in the box, "Input–Output Equations: An Example," on the next page, take explicit account of the interdependence among industries by describing precisely how each industry's target output

Input–output analysis is a mathematical procedure that takes account of the interdependence among the economy's industries and determines the amount of output each industry must provide as inputs to the other industries in the economy.

---

[3] "Life Expectancy Plummets, North Korea Says," *The New York Times*, May 16, 2001. Retrieved from http://www.nytimes.com

Input–Output Equations: An Example

Imagine an economy with only three outputs: electricity, steel, and coal. Let E, S, and C represent the respective dollar values of these outputs. Suppose that to produce every dollar's worth of steel, $0.20 worth of electricity is used, so that the total electricity demand of steel manufacturers is $0.2S$. Similarly, assume that coal manufacturers use $0.30 of electricity in producing $1 worth of coal, or a total of $0.3C$ units of electricity. Because E dollars of electricity are produced in total, the amount left over for consumers, after subtracting industrial demands for fuel, will be E (available electricity) minus $0.2S$ (used in steel production) minus $0.3C$ (used in coal production). Suppose further that the central planners have decided to supply $15 million worth of electricity to consumers. We end up with the electricity output equation:

$$E - 0.2S - 0.3C = 15$$

The planner will also need such an equation for each of the two other industries, specifying for each of them the net amount intended to be left for consumers after the industrial uses of the product. The full set of equations will then be similar to the following:

$$E - 0.2S - 0.3C = 15$$
$$S - 0.1E - 0.06C = 7$$
$$C - 0.15E - 0.4S = 10$$

These are typical equations in an input-output analysis. In practice, however, such an analysis has dozens and sometimes hundreds of equations with similar numbers of unknowns. This, then, is the logic of input-output analysis.

SOURCE: © Paul Hardy/Corbis

depends on every other industry's target. Only by solving these equations simultaneously for the required outputs of electricity, steel, coal, and so on can planners ensure a consistent solution that produces the required amounts of each product—including the amount of each product needed to produce every other product.

The illustrative input-output analysis that appears in the box is not provided to make you a master at using the technique yourself. Its real purpose is to help you imagine how very complicated the problems facing central planners can become. Their task, although analogous to the one described in the box, is enormously more complex. In any real economy, the number of commodities is far greater than the three outputs in the example! In Canada, some large manufacturing companies deal in hundreds of thousands of items, and probably keep just as many items in inventory.

Planners must ultimately make calculations for each single item. It is not enough to plan the right number of bolts in total; they must make sure that the required number of each size is produced. (Try putting five million large bolts into five million small nuts.) To be sure that their plans will really work, they need a separate equation for every size of bolt and one for every size and type of nut. But then, to replicate the analysis described in the box, they would have to solve several million equations simultaneously! This task would strain even the most powerful computer's capability, but that is not even the main difficulty.

Worse still is the data problem. Each of our three equations requires three pieces of statistical information, making 3×3, or 9, numbers in total. The equation for electricity must indicate how much electricity is needed in steel production, how much in coal production, and how much is demanded by consumers, all on the basis of statistical information that is itself subject to error. Therefore, in a five-industry analysis, 5×5, or 25, pieces of data are needed; a 100-industry analysis requires 100×100, or 10,000, numbers, and a million-item input–output study might need 1 trillion pieces of information. Solving the data-gathering problems is no easy task, to put it mildly. Still other complications arise, but we have seen enough to conclude that:

A full, rigorous central-planning solution to the production problem is a tremendous task, requiring an overwhelming quantity of information and some incredibly difficult calculations. Yet this very complex job is carried out automatically and unobtrusively by the price mechanism in a market economy.

Which Buyers and Which Sellers Get Priority?

Because the supplies of all commodities are limited, some potential customers of a product will end up with none of it. And because demand is not infinite, some potential suppliers of a commodity will find no market available for them. So, which consumers get the scarce commodity, and which firms get to supply the goods? Again, the price mechanism comes to the rescue.

Other things being equal, the price mechanism ensures that those consumers who want a scarce commodity most will receive it, and that those sellers who can supply it most efficiently will get to supply the commodity.

For simplicity, suppose we are dealing here with a commodity such as a painting by a contemporary Canadian artist who can produce similar paintings within a limited time period only by putting increased effort into her work, thereby facing rising opportunity cost represented by the upward-sloping supply curve in Figure 3. Since the artist's paintings have similar characteristics, we will also assume that no one would want to buy more than one painting. The demand curve, *DD*, represents the preferences of six potential customers with widely different tastes. The first customer is willing to pay as much as $700 for a painting, as shown by point *A* on the demand curve (although he would prefer to pay less).

Point *B* represents a second buyer who would purchase a painting at a price of $600, but refuses to spend $700 on it (because he cares less about this artist's paintings than the first consumer does). Similarly, point *C* represents the demand of a third consumer, to whom the artist's paintings are even less important; he is willing to spend only $500 for one. And, points *E*, *F*, and *G* represent consumers with successively lower desires for the artist's work, until the consumer at point *G* is willing to pay only $200 for a painting.

With *SS* as the supply curve, the equilibrium point is *E*, where *SS* and *DD* intersect. Under perfect competition, the market price for a painting will be $400. The buyer at point *A*, to whom a painting is worth $700, will be delighted to buy it for only $400. Similarly, the buyers at points *B*, *C*, and *E* will also each happily buy a painting. But the consumers at points *F* and *G*, to whom a painting is worth less than $400, will not buy paintings. We can see in this example that the paintings will go to the consumers who value them most (in terms of money), and only those who value them least will be deprived of them.

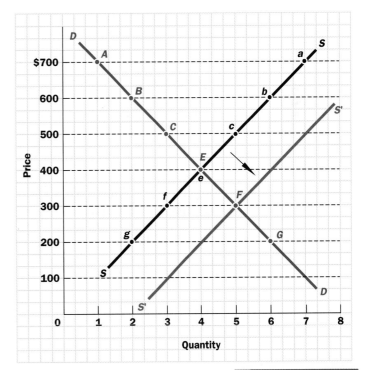

The price mechanism always ranks potential consumers of a good in the order of the intensity of their preference for the good, as indicated by the amount they are willing to spend for it.

FIGURE 3

Supply–Demand Graph Showing That Price Excludes Only Buyers and Sellers Who Care the Least

The price system's priority to consumers who assign most importance to a good goes one step further. Suppose now that the artist gets an apprentice, so that the supply of paintings from this producer increases. In Figure 3, this is represented by the supply curve shifting to the right, from SS to S'S'. Which consumer will get the increased quantity supplied? Answer: Of those consumers who were previously denied the commodity, those who want it most intensely will acquire the product. In the graph, the shift in supply moves the equilibrium point from point E to F, so the point F consumer will now be included in the group of buyers of the artist's paintings (along with points A, B, C, and E consumers), but the point G consumer still does not purchase a painting. The painting is worth more to the point F consumer ($300) than it is to the point G consumer, who values it only at $200.

The price system seems to set the right priorities in deciding which prospective consumers of some specific good do receive some of it and which do not. There is, however, one major problem that arises in this argument, to which we will return in a moment.

First, however, let's look at Figure 3 again, from the producer's point of view. Let us assume that, from the perspective of the painting industry, SS depicts the long-run industry supply curve for paintings. Point g on this curve represents the amount that the industry will supply if the price is $200—that is, the amount that will be supplied by producers whose average cost is no higher than $200, so that the price will cover their cost. Similarly, point f represents the output of all producers whose average cost is no higher than $300, so that the group of suppliers now includes some producing artists that are less efficient (they have higher average cost) than those at point g. At point e, some of the suppliers will have average costs of $400, but none of the suppliers will have an average cost higher than that level. Using the same reasoning, as we move farther along SS to points c, b, and a, increasingly inefficient producers will be included among the suppliers.

Now we examine the supply–demand equilibrium point e, at which price is $400. Which suppliers will be able to market their products at this point? Answer: Those at points g, f, and e, but not producers at points c, b, and a, because no supplier in the last three groups can cover its costs at the equilibrium price. Once again, the price mechanism seems to be doing its job. It ranks producers in order of their efficiency, as measured by long-run average costs, and brings business to the more efficient producers, leaving out the least efficient potential suppliers.

This example illustrates yet another desirable feature of the price mechanism. But there is one obvious fly in the ointment—at least on the demand side of the story—which has often been of serious concern, especially to policy makers interested in the issue of justice in exchange. We saw that consumer G was likely to be denied the scarce commodity we were discussing, because he wanted it less than the other consumers. Consumer G was willing to spend only $200 for the painting, whereas the other consumers were willing to spend more for it. But what if consumer G wanted the commodity very badly, but is also very poor? This is an important moral question—one we will encounter again and again. The price mechanism has sometimes been likened to democracy, but one in which the rule is not "one person, one vote," but rather "one dollar, one vote." In other words, unlike democracy, under the price mechanism, rich consumers' preferences command much more attention than poor consumers' desires do.

HOW AN IDEAL PERFECTLY COMPETITIVE MARKET ACHIEVES EFFICIENCY: A GRAPHIC ANALYSIS

We have indicated how the market mechanism solves the three basic coordination problems of any economy—what to produce, how to produce it, and how to distribute the goods to consumers. Also, we have suggested that these same tasks pose almost insurmountable difficulties for central planners. One critical question remains: Is the allocation of resources that the market mechanism selects *efficient*, according to the precise definition of efficiency presented at the start of this chapter? The answer, under the idealized circumstances of perfect competition, is *yes*. And a simple supply-and-demand diagram can be used to give us an intuitive view of why that is so.

Focusing on the market for a single commodity, let us ask whether either an increase or a decrease in the amount of output produced by the market mechanism can yield a greater total net benefit to consumers and producers. Suppose the current output level of swimming lessons in a swimming pool (number of people being taught) is 20 and the total net benefit to all involved in the activity can somehow be evaluated in money terms at $500 per week. Then, if any other number of students yields a total net benefit less than $500, clearly we have reason to conclude that 20 students is the optimum. We will show that, in equilibrium under perfect competition, the market unerringly and automatically will always drive toward an equilibrium exactly at that optimal output level, without any central direction, or explicit guidance, or planning by anyone. That is one of the major accomplishments of the market mechanism.

To show this, let's begin by defining consumer and producer benefits sufficiently precisely so we can measure them. In Chapter 5 (page 100–101), we already have encountered the concept we need for the consumer benefits: consumer's surplus. And we will introduce a perfectly analogous concept, called *producer's surplus*, for the other side of the market. Suppose Anne would be willing to purchase a full week of swimming lessons at any price up to $140, but when she arrives at the gym she sees that the lessons are available for sale at a price of $90. Because swimming lessons are worth $140 to her, and she has to spend only $90 to obtain them, the purchase provides her with a net benefit of $140 − $90 = $50. If the lessons had been priced at $140, the result of the purchase would have been a wash—she would have given up $140 and received in exchange a service worth exactly $140 to her. But because the market price happens to be $90, she obtains a net gain worth $50 to her—a surplus—from the transaction. So, as we did in Chapter 5, we define:

The **consumer's surplus** from a purchase is equal to the difference between the maximum amount the consumer would be willing, if necessary, to pay for the item bought, and the price that the market actually charges. In a purchase by a rational consumer, the surplus will never be a negative number, because if the price is higher than the maximum amount the potential purchaser is willing to pay, he will simply refuse to buy it.

Producer's surplus is defined exactly analogously. If Ben, a swimming instructor, is willing to provide a week of lessons at any price from $30 up, but the market price happens to be $90, he receives a $60 surplus from the transaction—and is delighted to make such a sale. So we have the definition:

The **producer's surplus** from a sale is the difference between the market price of the item sold and the lowest price at which the supplier would be willing to provide the item.

Now that we know how the two surpluses are defined and how to measure them, our objective is to see how the total surplus to all buyers and sellers in a market is affected by the quantity produced and sold in the market. We will demonstrate a striking result: that at the perfectly competitive market output level—the output level at which the market supply and demand curves intercept—the total surplus for all participants is as large as possible. To do this, we must turn to our familiar supply–demand analysis and use it to show explicitly the roles played by Anne, Ben, and the others involved in the market.

We begin with a table that assumes for simplicity that there are five potential buyers (Anne, Charles, Elaine, etc.) and five potential competing sellers (Ben, Debbie, etc.) in the market for swimming lessons. We see in Table 1 that at the weekly fee of $90 (third column in the table), Anne, to whom a week's lessons are worth $140 (first column) obtains a consumer's surplus of $50 = $140 − $90.

Similarly, at that price, Charles obtains a surplus of just $30. The consumer's surplus for these two customers is shown by the two light blue areas below the blue demand curve DD in Figure 4(a), corresponding to their purchases (two sets of lessons). For example, the left-most blue bar has its bottom at the price of $90 and its top at the $140 that the lessons are worth to Anne, so that the area of Anne's bar is equal to her surplus, $140 − $90 = 50.

> The **consumer's surplus** from a purchase is equal to the difference between the maximum amount the consumer would be willing, if necessary, to pay for the item bought, and the price that the market actually charges.

> The **producer's surplus** from a sale is the difference between the market price of the item sold and the lowest price at which the supplier would be willing to provide the item.

TABLE 1

Consumer's and Producer's Surplus in the Swimming Lesson Market (dollars)

Students	(1) Student's Acceptable Maximum Price	(2) Individual Consumer's Surplus	(3) Actual Price	(4) Cumulative Total Surplus	(5) Individual Producer's Surplus	(6) Instructor's Acceptable Minimum Price	Instructors
Anne	$140	$50	$90	$110 = 50 + 60	$60	$ 30	Ben
Charles	120	30	90	180 = 110 + 30 + 40	40	50	Debbie
Elaine	110	20	90	220	20	70	Frank
George	90	0	90	220	0	90	Harriet
Irene	80	−10	90	180	−30	120	Jack

Similarly, Table 1 shows the producer's surpluses that can be earned by the different potential instructors. For example, it shows that the $90 fee gives Ben a surplus of $60 = $90 − $30, because he would be willing to give the lessons even if the fee was as low as $30. In the same way, we see that Debbie obtains a surplus of $40. These two producers' surpluses are shown in Figure 4(a) by the areas of the first two light pink bars—the areas between the red supply curve SS and the $90 price line for those two sales. We also note that if both Anne and Charles received lessons, and both Ben and Debbie gave lessons, so that two sets of lessons were provided, the total surplus created by the market would be the sum of their four individual surpluses, $50 + 30 + 60 + 40 = $180—which is the second entry in the fourth column in the table. This is also shown by the area DRTUVS in Figure 4(a) that lies between the blue demand curve and the red supply curve when only two sets of lessons are provided.

But comparison of Figure 4(a) and Figure 4(b) shows us clearly that two lessons are not enough to make the total surplus generated by the market as large as possible. Specifically, if Elaine also takes lessons and Frank provides them, this third transaction generates an additional consumer's surplus of $20 and an additional producer's surplus of $20, raising the total to $220. This larger total is shown by summing all the light blue and light pink areas between the demand and supply curves in Figure 4(b). One more set of lessons, the number at which the supply and demand curves intersect at PP, contributes no net gain in surplus, because George and Harriet value the lessons at exactly the prevailing price of $90. In buying and selling the service, these

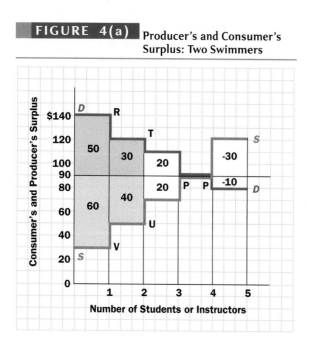

FIGURE 4(a) Producer's and Consumer's Surplus: Two Swimmers

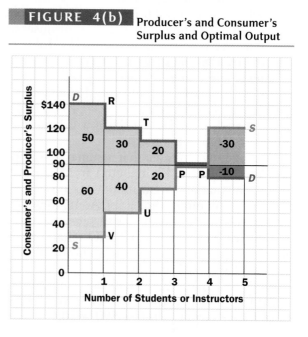

FIGURE 4(b) Producer's and Consumer's Surplus and Optimal Output

two people exchange money and services that are worth exactly the same to them. Increasing output further, by raising it to a fifth set of lessons will actually reduce total surplus, because Irene, the potential student, values the lessons at less than their $90 price while Jack, the potential instructor, considers his work worth $120. If Jack were to provide lessons to Irene, they both would obtain *negative* surpluses, represented by the dark pink and dark blue bars toward the right of the graph. These negative surpluses bring the total surplus down from $220 to $180 (the last two entries in column 4 of the table), clearly a net loss to the economy.

Now we come to the payoff from all this reasoning. Looking at Figure 4(a), we see that if total output stops short of the intersection of the supply and demand curve (interval PP), the light pink and blue areas will not be as large as possible. Similarly, if more than that quantity of swimming lessons is supplied, total surplus is decreased [Figure 4(b)]. Only when the output quantity corresponds to the intersection of the supply and demand curves is the net surplus earned by both buyers and sellers as large as possible. Three conclusions follow:

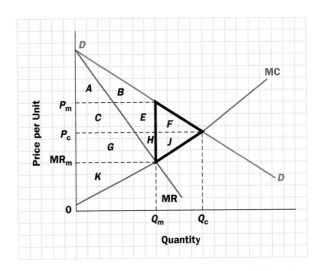

FIGURE 5

Deadweight Loss of a Monopoly

1. Because under perfect competition the equilibrium output will be at the intersection of the supply and demand curves, a regime of perfect competition will select output levels that are optimal in terms of the overall welfare of consumers and producers. They yield as large a sum of consumer's and producer's surpluses as possible.

2. If some influence such as monopoly forces output to be smaller (because price is higher) than that under perfect competition, the public interest will be damaged because the quantity of resources allocated to this market will be less than optimal.

3. If something like a government tax reduction induces suppliers to produce an output larger than the competitive level, that will also be a misallocation of resources damaging to the public welfare.

Applications of Consumer's and Producer's Surpluses: Deadweight Loss

One way to gauge the efficiency of a competitive market is to show how inefficient a monopoly is. Figure 5 provides a comparison of a monopoly and a perfectly competitive industry by highlighting the concepts of consumer's and producer's surpluses that we have just discussed, under the assumption that the horizontal sum of the marginal cost curves of each competitive firm (the supply curve of the competitive industry) would be identical to the marginal cost curve of the monopoly. In the short run, a competitive industry would produce at output Q_c and price P_c, while the monopoly would produce an output Q_m at price P_m (because it chooses the profit-maximizing output that equates marginal cost MC with marginal revenue MR). The area between the marginal curve MC and the demand curve D is filled with triangles and trapezoids that provide geometric measures of the consumer's and producer's surpluses, as summed up in Table 2.

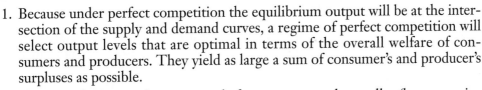

TABLE 2		
Consumer's Surplus and Producer's Surplus Areas in a Perfectly Competitive Industry and in the Case of a Monopoly		
	Perfect Competition	Monopoly
Consumer's surplus	$A + B + C + E + F$	$A + B$
Producer's surplus	$G + H + J + K$	$C + E + G + H + K$
Overall surplus	$A + B + C + E + F + G + H + J + K$	$A + B + C + E + G + H + K$
Deadweight loss		$F + J$

In the case of the competitive industry, with price P_c, the consumer's surplus is the area below the demand curve and above the horizontal line representing the price, the area given by the top five triangles and trapezoids. The producer's surplus is given by the area between the industry supply curve (here the MC curve) and the horizontal line representing the price P_c. The overall surplus available to the entire economy is thus the entire area between the demand curve and the industry supply curve, up to their point of intersection, as indicated in Table 2.

Now take the case of the monopoly, which is producing an output Q_m at price P_m. The consumer's surplus is now reduced to the area given by the top two triangles, below the demand curve and above the horizontal line representing this new price. As to the producer's surplus of the monopoly, it is now given by the area defined by its marginal cost curve and the horizontal line at price P_m up to the vertical line defined by the produced output of the monopoly, Q_m.

Obviously, the monopoly has taken away some of the consumer's surplus. The area given by $C + E$ in Figure 5, which was part of the consumer's surplus, is now part of the monopoly producer's surplus. But this is not the end of the story, since this is not a zero-sum game. The overall surplus of the economy has also decreased by the area given by the two triangles F and J, surrounded by the heavy lines in Figure 5. This area is the **deadweight loss** or the "excess burden" of the monopoly. The existence of the monopoly has led to the appropriation of part of the consumer surplus by the corporate sector but, more importantly from the standpoint of this chapter, because the monopoly does not produce the optimal amount of output, the presence of the monopoly has reduced the overall surplus of the economy.

A deadweight loss can also be shown to exist when taxes are imposed on the economy. Take the case of an excise tax on a retailer, such as the gasoline tax of 10 cents per litre that we analyzed on page 76 of Chapter 4. The impact of such a tax on the economic surplus is illustrated in Figure 6. With no tax, a competitive market would bring supply and demand (represented by the curves S and D) into equilibrium at output Q_0 and price P_0. The areas representing the consumer's surplus and the producer's surplus, and hence the overall economic surplus, are those shown in Table 3.

When a tax is imposed, consumers face a new supply curve, given by S_t, which incorporates the tax being charged to gasoline buyers. The new equilibrium will thus be achieved with Q_t litres of gasoline being sold. The price being charged to buyers of gasoline will be P_d. This price per unit gets subdivided into two parts: the 10 cents per litre

The **deadweight loss** is the loss in economic surplus (consumer's surplus plus producer's surplus) that arises from conditions diverging from those of unhampered perfect competition.

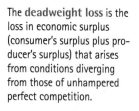

FIGURE 6   Deadweight Loss of an Excise Tax

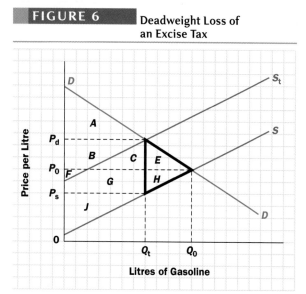

TABLE 3		
Consumer's Surplus and Producer's Surplus before and after the Imposition of a Tax		
	Before Imposition of the Tax	After Imposition of the Tax
Consumer's surplus	$A + B + C + E$	A
Producer's surplus	$F + G + H + J$	J
Private surplus	$A + B + C + E + F + G + H + J$	$A + J$
Government revenue		$B + C + F + G$
Deadweight loss or excess burden of tax		$E + H$

of gasoline tax that is collected by the government, and the price that sellers of gasoline obtain, P_s. What now happens is that the government is able to collect part of the consumer's surplus (the area $B + C$) and part of the producer's surplus (the area $F + G$).

As was the case with the monopoly, however, part of the overall surplus disappears as a consequence of the tax. The deadweight loss in this case is called the *excess burden of the tax*, which will be discussed in Chapter 18. This deadweight loss, as pointed out in Table 3, is the area $E + H$ as defined by the heavy lines in Figure 6. This deadweight loss arises because the tax induces consumers and producers to modify their behaviour, with less gasoline being purchased and sold. We will see in the next chapter, however, that in the case of gasoline, taxes that modify behaviour may have beneficial effects on the economy since gasoline consumption has detrimental effects on our environment.

■ HOW A PERFECTLY COMPETITIVE SETTING WOULD ACHIEVE OPTIMAL OUTPUT: MARGINAL ANALYSIS

There is a second way to look at the optimality of outputs under perfect competition's idealized circumstances, this time relating the discussion directly to the definition of efficiency given at the beginning of this chapter. Because a detailed proof of this assertion for all three coordination tasks is long and time-consuming, we will present the proof only for the task we have just been considering—*output selection*. We will show that, at least in theory, perfect competition does guarantee efficiency in determining the relative quantities of the different commodities that the economy produces.

The proof comes in two steps. First, we derive a criterion for efficient output selection—that is, a test that tells us whether production is being carried out efficiently. Second, we show that the prices that emerge from the market mechanism under perfect competition automatically pass this test.

Step 1: Rule for Efficient Output Selection   We begin by stating the rule for efficient output selection: Efficiency in the choice of output quantities requires that, for each of the economy's outputs, the marginal cost (MC) of the last unit produced be equal to the marginal utility (MU) of the last unit consumed.[4] In symbols:

$$MC = MU$$

This rule is yet another example of the basic principle of marginal analysis that we learned in Chapter 8.

The efficient decision about output quantities is the one that maximizes the total benefit (total utility) to society, minus the cost to society of producing the output quantities that are chosen. In other words, the goal is to maximize the surplus that society gains—total utility minus total cost. But, as we saw in Chapter 8, to maximize the difference between total utility and total cost, we must find the outputs that equalize the corresponding marginal figures (marginal utility and marginal cost), as the preceding efficiency rule tells us.

An example will help us to see explicitly why resource allocation must satisfy this rule to be deemed efficient. Suppose that the marginal utility of an additional kilogram of beef to consumers is $8, but its marginal cost is only $5. Then the value of the resources that would have to be used up to produce one more kilogram of beef (its MC) would be $3 less than the money value that consumers would willingly pay for that additional kilogram (its MU). By expanding the output of beef by one kilogram, society could get more (in MU) out of the economic production process than it was putting in (in MC). We know that the output at which MU exceeds MC cannot be

---

[4] Recall from Chapter 5 that we measure marginal utility in money terms—that is, the amount of money that a consumer is willing to give up for an additional unit of the commodity. Economists usually call this the *marginal rate of substitution* between the commodity and money.

optimal, because society would be better off with an increase in that output level. The opposite is true if the MC of beef exceeds the MU of beef.

Thus, we have shown that, if any product's MU is not equal to MC—whether MU exceeds MC or MC exceeds MU—the economy must be wasting an opportunity to achieve a net improvement in consumers' welfare. This is exactly what we mean by saying society is using resources inefficiently. Just as was true at point G in Figure 1, if MC does not equal MU for some commodity, it is possible to rearrange production to make some people better off while harming no one else. It follows, then, that efficient output choice occurs only when MC equals MU for every good.[5]

Step 2: The Price System's Critical Role   Next, we must show that under perfect competition, the price system automatically leads buyers and sellers to behave in a way that equalizes MU and MC.

To see this, recall from Chapter 10 that under perfect competition it is most profitable for each beef-producing firm to produce the quantity at which the marginal cost equals the price (P) of beef:

$$MC = P$$

This must be so because, if the marginal cost of beef were less than the price, the farmer could add to his profits by increasing the size of the herd (or the amount of grain fed to the animals). The reverse would be true if the marginal cost of beef were greater than its price. Thus, under perfect competition, the lure of profits leads each producer of beef (and of every other product) to supply the quantity that makes $MC = P$.

We also learned, in Chapter 5, that each consumer will purchase the quantity of beef at which the marginal utility of beef in money terms equals the price of beef:

$$MU = P$$

If consumers did not do so, either an increase or a decrease in their beef purchases would leave them better off.

Putting these last two equations together, we see that the invisible hand enforces the following string of equalities:

$$MC = P = MU$$

But if the MC of beef and the MU of beef both equal the same price, P, then they must equal each other. That is, it must be true that the quantity of beef produced and consumed in a perfectly competitive market satisfies the equation:

$$MC = MU$$

This is precisely our rule for efficient output selection. Because the same must be true of every other product supplied by a competitive industry:

> Under perfect competition, producers and consumers will make uncoordinated decisions that we can expect automatically to produce exactly the quantity of each good that satisfies the MC = MU rule for efficiency. That is, under the idealized conditions of perfect competition, the market mechanism, without any government intervention and without anyone else directing it or planning for it, is capable of allocating society's scarce resources efficiently.

■ The Invisible Hand at Work

This is truly an extraordinary result. How can the price mechanism automatically satisfy all of the exacting requirements for efficiency (that marginal utility equals marginal cost for each and every commodity)—requirements that no central planner can hope to handle because of the masses of statistics and the enormous calculations they entail?

---

[5] *Warning:* As described in Chapter 15, markets sometimes perform imperfectly because the decision maker faces a different marginal cost than the marginal cost to society. This situation occurs when the individual who creates the cost can make someone else bear the burden. Consider an example: Firm X's production causes pollution emissions that increase nearby households' laundry bills. In such a case, Firm X will ignore this cost and produce inefficiently large outputs and emissions. We study such problems, called *externalities*, in Chapters 15 and 17.

This seems analogous to a magician suddenly pulling a rabbit out of a hat!

But, as always, rabbits come out of hats only if they were hidden there in the first place. What really is the mechanism by which our act of magic works? The secret is that the price system lets consumers and producers pursue their own best interests—something they are probably very good at doing. Prices are the dollar costs of commodities to consumers, so in pursuing their own best interests, consumers will buy the commodities that give them the most satisfaction per dollar. Under perfect competition, the price the consumer pays is also equal to MC, because the market's incentives lead each supplier to supply that amount at which this is true.

Because $P = MC$ measures the resource cost (in every firm) of producing one more unit of the good, this means that when consumers buy the commodities that give them the most satisfaction for *their money*, they will automatically have chosen the set of purchases that yields the most satisfaction obtainable from the resources used up in producing those purchases. In other words, the market mechanism leads consumers to squeeze the greatest possible benefit out of the social resources used up in making the goods and services they buy. So, if resources are priced appropriately ($P = MC$), when consumers make the best use of their money, they must also be making the best use of society's resources. Ideally, that is the way the market mechanism ensures economic efficiency.

> When all prices are set equal to marginal costs, the price system gives correct cost signals to consumers. It has set prices at levels that induce consumers to use society's resources with the same care they devote to watching their own money, because the money cost of a good to consumers has been set equal to the opportunity cost of the good to society. A perfectly analogous explanation applies to the decisions of producers.

This is the work of the invisible hand. Unlike central planners, consumers need not know how difficult it is to manufacture a certain product or how scarce the inputs required by the production process are. Ideally, everything consumers need to know about supply in making their decisions is embodied in the market price, which, under perfect competition, accurately reflects marginal costs. Similarly, producers do not need to know anything about the psychology and tastes of their individual customers—price movements tell them all they need to know when consumer preferences change.

■ Other Roles of Prices: Income Distribution and Fairness

So far we have stressed the role of prices that economists emphasize most: Prices guide resource allocation. But prices also command the spotlight in another role: Prices influence the distribution of income between buyers and sellers. For example, high rents often make tenants poorer and landlords richer.

This rather obvious role of prices draws the most attention from the public, politicians, and regulators, and we should not lose sight of it.[6] Markets serve only those demands that are backed up by consumers' desire and *ability to pay*. The market system may do well in serving poor families, because it gives them more food and clothing than a less efficient economy would provide. But the market system offers far more to wealthy families. Many people think that such an arrangement represents a great injustice, however efficient it may be.

Often, people oppose economists' recommendations for improving the economy's efficiency on the grounds that these proposals are *unfair*. For example, economists frequently advocate higher prices for transportation facilities at the times of day when the facilities are most crowded. Economists propose a pricing arrangement called *peak, off-peak pricing* under which prices for public transportation are higher during rush hours than during other hours.

The rationale for this proposal should be clear from our discussion of efficiency. A seat on a train is a much scarcer resource during rush hours than it is during other

---

[6] Income distribution is the subject of Part V.

times of the day when the trains run fairly empty. Thus, according to the principles of efficiency outlined in this chapter, seats should be more expensive during rush hours to discourage those consumers with no set schedule from riding the trains during peak periods. The same notion applies to other services. Charges for long-distance telephone calls made at night or on weekends are sometimes lower than those made in the daytime. And in some countries, electricity is cheaper at night, when demand does not strain the supplier's generating capacity.

In fact, between 1987 and 1995, the Ottawa–Carleton Regional Transit Commission (OC Transpo)—the public agency that regulates and provides public transit service in the Ottawa region—used to price its bus fares differentially on the basis of peak-hour usage, with higher fares being charged from 6:00 A.M. to 8:30 A.M. and from 3:00 P.M. to 6:30 P.M. on weekdays. However, OC Transpo discontinued this pricing system due to opposition from critics who pointed out conflicting priorities. For example, if one objective is to reduce traffic congestion, why discourage motorists from using public transportation at the time when it is most necessary to reduce the number of vehicles on the roads, especially if the cross elasticity of demand for automobile use is high and positive? Opponents also pointed to the negative effects on income distribution: Most of the burden of such higher fares would fall on lower-income working people who have no choice about the timing of their trips.

Interestingly, a survey in Great Britain of economists and members of Parliament found that, while high peak-period fares were favored by 88 percent of the economists, only 35 percent of the Conservative Party members of Parliament and just 19 percent of the Labour Party members of Parliament approved of this arrangement (see Table 4). We may surmise that these members of the British Parliament reflected the views of the public more accurately than did the economists. In this case, people simply found the efficient solution unfair, and so they refused to adopt it.

TABLE 4
Replies to a Questionnaire

Question: To make the most efficient use of a city's resources, how should subway and bus fares vary during the day?	Economists	Conservative Party Members of Parliament	Labour Party Members of Parliament
a. They should be relatively low during rush hour to transport as many people as possible at lower costs.	1%	0%	40%
b. They should be the same at all times to avoid making travellers alter their schedules because of price differences.	4	60	39
c. They should be relatively high during rush hour to minimize the amount of equipment needed to transport the daily travellers.	88	35	19
d. Impossible to answer on the data and alternatives given.	7	5	2

SOURCE: Excerpt from Samuel Brittan, *Is There an Economic Consensus?* p. 93. Copyright © 1973. Reproduced by permission of Samuel Brittan.

■ Yet Another Achievement of the Market Mechanism: Growth Versus Efficiency

This chapter has followed the economist's standard approach in evaluating the market mechanism. Economists usually stress efficiency in resource allocation and the role of the market in ensuring such efficiency—the division of resources among alternative uses in a way that misses no opportunity to increase consumer net benefits.

Some other admirers of the market do not place their main emphasis on the free market's efficiency accomplishments. A very diverse group, including businesspeople,

POLICY DEBATE

User Charges for Public Facilities

At a time when budget cutting is the way to popularity for a politician, the notion of charging users for the services that government once gave away for free is under debate. Economists have often advocated such charges for the use of roads, bridges, museums, educational facilities, and the like. Of course, it's true that if the services are provided for "free," the public has to pay for them anyway—just more indirectly through taxes. But if people are asked to pay directly for such services, it can make a big difference.

As an example, let's say a road is financed out of general taxes. In this circumstance, it does not matter how many times Sabrina, the owner of an independent trucking firm, uses the road. She pays the same amount whether she uses it twice a year or every day. But if Sabrina has to pay a toll every time she uses the road, she will have a strong incentive to avoid unnecessary use. That is why advocates of pricing to promote economic efficiency propose more substantial *user charges*, not only for roads and bridges but also for admission to national parks, for the use of publicly owned grazing lands, and for the use of the television and radio spectrums by broadcasters.

Opponents of user charges contend that these fees are unfair to poor people. Besides, it is argued, the use of public facilities such as libraries, museums, and schools should be encouraged rather than impeded by user charges. For instance, in the Montreal area, there is now no charge to cross the many deteriorating bridges that connect Montreal Island to surrounding regions on both the North and South Shores, although tolls were charged on some of the bridges until 1990. But each time user charges are proposed, they are met with the cry, "Should I have to pay an admission fee into my own city?"

With the evolution of technology, however, particularly with the introduction of new electronic toll collection systems that can

SOURCE: Cezar Serbanescu/istockphoto

process vehicles many times faster than the old manual collection system, and with growing pressure from the Canadian public to restore many of these old deteriorating structures and build new ones across the country (while, at the same time, rejecting municipal tax increases), the return of tolls has become a political option once again. Indeed, in June 2007, the Quebec government announced that a new toll bridge is to be built to link Anjou in Montreal with Duvernay in eastern Laval. The new construction—the first privately funded project of this kind in years, with a scheduled 2011 completion date—will be financed by a consortium headed by an Australian multinational firm, the Macquarie Bank Ltd, which also holds a 30 percent share of the Toronto 407 ETR.

politicians, economic historians, leaders in formerly communist economies such as Vladimir Putin, and even Marxists, appreciate the market primarily for a very different reason—the extraordinary growth in output that market economies have achieved and the historically unprecedented abundance that has resulted.

Historians have estimated that before the arrival of the capitalistic market mechanism, output per person grew with glacial slowness. But today, an average Canadian can afford more than *seven* times the quantity of goods and services that an individual's income bought 100 years ago. Undoubtedly, the failure to achieve substantial growth and prosperity (and not just inefficiencies in allocating goods) helped to bring about the fall of communism in Eastern Europe. Even Karl Marx stressed this role of the market mechanism, waxing lyrical in his description of its accomplishments. Chapter 16 will return to this subject, indicating what a market economy can accomplish in terms of economic growth.

■ TOWARD ASSESSMENT OF THE PRICE MECHANISM

In our discussion of the case for the market as an efficient mechanism for allocating goods and services in an economy, we have purposely referred to an ideal state. This is not to suggest that the private enterprise system is an ideal of perfection, without flaw or need for improvement. On the contrary, the market has a number of very serious shortcomings that we will explore in subsequent chapters. But a recognition of these problems should not conceal the price mechanism's enormous accomplishments, especially when measured on the basis of its capacity to generate long-term growth with long spurts of technological progress (to be discussed in Chapter 16) that have been the characteristic feature of modern market economies.

We have shown that, under the proper circumstances, prices are capable of meeting the most exacting requirements of allocative efficiency—requirements that go well beyond any central planning bureau's capacities. Even centrally planned economies use the price mechanism to carry out considerable portions of the task of allocation, most notably in the distribution of consumer goods. No one has invented an instrument for directing the economy that can replace the price mechanism, which no one ever designed or planned for, but which simply grew by itself, a child of the processes of history. Indeed, ever since humans began to recognize the benefits arising from the division of labour, markets and prices appeared to meet the needs of organized exchange of goods and services. Whether at the centre of human activity (as in modern market economies) or at the periphery (as in ancient or modern command economies), the price mechanism has always been present and has played an important allocative function.

Puzzle Revisited: The 407 ETR

Our earlier example of Toronto's 407 Express Toll Route also raises fairness issues. Recall that we had concluded from our analysis that, on purely efficiency grounds, one can argue that a toll is required on the more crowded Highway 401. Instead, there are no user fees on the latter, while on the 407 ETR the user fees on light vehicles, at the time of writing, are 17.6 cents per kilometre during peak hours and 16.8 cents per kilometre during off-peak hours, with additional monthly and/or annual fees. This could add up to a pretty hefty sum for a round trip on the 108-kilometre stretch from Brock Road in Pickering in the east, say, to visit a friend in Burlington living within the proximity of the Highway 403 interchange near Hamilton in the west.

As we discussed earlier, from the social point of view of ensuring an efficient use of the two highways, such a steep price for the use of the less crowded route and no toll whatsoever on the more crowded route seems somewhat irrational. Admittedly, the fact that the 407 ETR is privately owned while the 401 is a public highway does provide an explanation. However, even if both were public, for efficiency reasons, it would be difficult to argue that the 407 should be a toll highway while the 401 should not. The political acceptance of such a toll structure lies in some widely held notions of fairness, because many people would deem it fair to pay for the cost of a recently built highway even if it was in public hands. Some would ask: Why should commuters on the 401 help pay the mortgage on a highway serving primarily those living in closer proximity to the 407? This cross-subsidization would seem unfair. We therefore have a conflict between fairness and efficiency.

An economically questionable pattern of tolls does nothing to ease congestion on Toronto's overcrowded highways and thereby contributes to inefficiency. But one cannot legitimately conclude that the authorities are wrong. Whether this pattern of tolls is or is not desirable must be decided, at least partly, on the basis of the public's sense of what constitutes fairness and justice in pricing. It also depends on the amount that people are willing to pay in terms of delays, inconvenience, and other inefficiencies to avoid apparent injustices.

Economics alone cannot decide the appropriate trade-off between fairness and efficiency. It cannot even pretend to judge which pricing arrangements are fair and which are unfair. But it can and should indicate whether a particular pricing decision, proposed because it is considered fair, will impose heavy inefficiency costs on the community. Economic analysis also can and should indicate how to appraise these costs, so that the issues can be evaluated on a rational, factual basis.

SUMMARY

1. Economists consider an **allocation of resources** to be inefficient if it wastes opportunities to change the use of the economy's resources in any way that makes at least some consumers better off without harming anyone. Resource allocation is considered efficient if there are no such wasted opportunities.

2. Under perfect competition, the market mechanism adjusts prices so that the resulting resource allocation is efficient. It induces firms to buy and use inputs in ways that yield the most valuable outputs per unit of input. It distributes products among consumers in ways that match individual preferences. Finally, it produces commodities whose value to consumers exceeds the cost of producing them and assigns the task of production to the potential suppliers who can produce most efficiently.

3. Resource allocation involves three basic coordination tasks:

   a. How much of each good to produce

   b. What quantities of available inputs to use in producing the different goods

   c. How to distribute the goods among different consumers

4. An optimal allocation of society's resources among the commodities the economy produces and consumes is one that maximizes the sum of the consumers' and producers' surpluses derived by everyone in the community. Perfectly competitive equilibrium achieves this goal, at least in theory.

5. Efficient decisions about what goods to produce require that the marginal cost (MC) of producing each good be equal to its marginal utility (MU) to consumers. If the MC of any good differs from its MU, then society can improve resource allocation by changing the amounts produced.

6. Because the market system induces firms to set MC equal to price, and it induces consumers to set MU equal to price, it automatically guarantees satisfaction of the condition that MC should equal MU.

7. Improvements in efficiency occasionally require some prices to increase so as to stimulate supply or to prevent waste in consumption. This is why price increases can sometimes be beneficial to consumers.

8. In addition to resource allocation, prices influence income distribution between buyers and sellers.

9. The price mechanism can be criticized on the ground that it is unfair because it accords wealthy consumers preferential treatment.

KEY TERMS

Efficient allocation of resources   315

Laissez faire   320

Input–output analysis   323

Consumer's surplus   327

Producer's surplus   327

Deadweight loss   330

TEST YOURSELF

1. What possible social advantages of price increases arise in the following cases?

   a. Charging higher prices for electrical power on very hot days when many people use air conditioners

   b. Raising water prices in drought-stricken areas

2. In the discussion of Figure 3 on page 325, there is a set of numbers indicating how much different buyers would be willing to pay for a painting. Construct a table for these buyers like the first three columns in Table 1, indicating their consumer's surpluses.

3. As in the previous question, use the numbers in Figure 3 to determine the producer's surpluses and complete your table to correspond to the remaining columns of Table 1.

4. Suppose that a given set of resources can be used to make either handbags or wallets. The MC of a handbag is $19 and the MC of a wallet is $10. If the MU of a wallet is $10 and the MU of a handbag is $30, what can be done to improve resource allocation? What can you say about the gain to consumers?

DISCUSSION QUESTIONS

1. Discuss the fairness of the two proposals included in Test Yourself Question 1.

2. Using the concepts of marginal cost (MC) and marginal utility (MU), discuss the nature of the inefficiency in each of the following cases:

   a. An arrangement that offers relatively little coffee and much tea to people who prefer coffee and does the reverse for tea lovers

   b. An arrangement in which skilled mechanics are assigned to ditch digging and unskilled labourers to repairing cars

   c. An arrangement that produces a large quantity of trucks and few cars, assuming that both cost about the same amount to produce and to run, but that most people in the community prefer cars to trucks

3. In reality, which of the following circumstances might give rise to each of the situations described in Discussion Question 2 above?

   a. Regulation of output quantities by a government

   b. Rationing of commodities

   c. Assignment of soldiers to different jobs in an army

4. We have said that the economy's three coordination tasks are output selection, production planning, and product distribution. Which of these is done badly in the cases described in Discussion Questions 2a, 2b, and 2c?

5. In a free market, how will the price mechanism deal with each of the inefficiencies described in Discussion Question 2?

6. In the early months after the end of communism in Eastern Europe, there seems to have been an almost superstitious belief that the market could solve all problems. What sorts of problems do you think the leaders and the citizens of those countries had in mind? Which of those problems is there good reason to believe the market mechanism actually can deal with effectively? What disappointments and sources of disillusionment should have been expected? Which disappointments have resulted?

THE SHORTCOMINGS
OF THE MARKET SYSTEM

*And all economists are therefore schizophrenic: their discipline, derived
from Adam Smith, leads them to favour the market; their self-interest leads them
to favour intervention. . . . We are very clever at finding "special cases"—there are external
effects, there are monopolies, there are imperfections in the market.*

**MILTON FRIEDMAN (1912–2006), 1976 RECIPIENT OF THE SVERIGES RIKSBANK PRIZE IN ECONOMIC
SCIENCES IN MEMORY OF ALFRED NOBEL, *FROM GALBRAITH TO ECONOMIC FREEDOM* (1977), PP. 41–42**

What does the market do well, and what does it do poorly? These questions
are the focus of our microeconomic analysis, and we are well on our way
toward finding their answers. In Chapters 10 and 14, we explained the workings of
Adam Smith's invisible hand, the instrument by which a perfectly competitive economy allocates resources efficiently without any guidance from government. Of
course, that perfectly competitive model is just a theoretical ideal, but our observations of the real world confirm the extraordinary accomplishments of the market
mechanism. Free-market economies have achieved levels of output, productive efficiency, variety in available consumer goods, and general prosperity that are unprecedented in history—and are now the envy of the formerly planned economies. We will
discuss that phenomenal record of production and growth in detail in Chapter 16.

Yet the market mechanism has its weaknesses. In Chapters 11 and 12, we examined one
of these defects—the free market's vulnerability to exploitation by large and powerful
business firms, which can lead to both an inappropriate concentration of wealth and
resource misallocation. Now we take a more comprehensive view of market failures and
study some of the steps that can be taken to remedy them. Clearly, the market does not
do everything we want it to do. Amid the vast outpouring of products in our economy, we
also find appalling poverty, cities choked by traffic and pollution, and hospitals, educational institutions, and artistic organizations in serious financial trouble. Although our
economy produces an overwhelming abundance of material wealth, it seems far less capable of reducing social ills and environmental damage. We will examine the reasons for
these failings and indicate why the price system *by itself* may not be able to deal with them.

Our recognition of the market's limitations does not imply that the public interest
calls for abandoning the market. As we will see, many of the imperfections of this economic system are treatable within the market environment, sometimes even by making use of the market mechanism to cure its own deficiencies.

CONTENTS

PUZZLE: *Why Are Health Care Costs in Canada Rising?*

Canada has a universal health care program (often referred to as "Medicare") under which each province has an insurance plan that reimburses doctors according to a uniform fee schedule; hospitals are put on predetermined overall budgets; and patients pay very low direct, out-of-pocket costs.

SOURCE: © Jens Haas/Corbis

Many observers believe that Canada has created an efficient, user-friendly system, although some critics disagree. But Canadians clearly have *not* succeeded in containing costs. Despite the price controls, Canadian health care costs have been rising persistently faster than the general inflation rate, just as they have in the United States, where there are no such national rules to rein in rising health care prices. Indeed, spending per person rose by 46 percent in Canada between 1996 and 2006, whereas consumer prices rose by only half of that amount—23 percent—during this ten-year period, as can be seen Table 1, which presents the data for 1975–2005. Over the last ten years, health costs have risen much faster than other government expenditures, in all provinces except in Quebec. This has led to rising shares of health spending as a percentage of government expenditures, as shown in Table 2.

TABLE 1

Government Health Spending per Capita, Canada and Provinces/Territories, 1975–2005

Year	Nfld./ Lab.	PEI	NS	NB	QC	ON	MB	SK	AB	BC	Yukon	NWT	Nunavut	Canada
1975–1976	$371.04	$368.40	$336.98	$315.13	$419.18	$391.18	$387.06	$342.79	$403.28	$394.17	$289.59	$369.10	—	$393.15
1985–1986	985.81	974.34	996.11	993.72	1,150.62	1,069.31	1,109.11	1,093.16	1,287.57	1,083.10	1,028.04	1,375.25	—	1,108.38
1995–1996	1,646.57	1,518.14	1,412.21	1,659.62	1,661.73	1,678.73	1,695.61	1,577.45	1,410.68	1,857.97	2,159.10	3,348.86	—	1,663.89
2005–2006	3,097.51	2,669.04	2,818.92	2,789.90	2,500.35	2,792.60	3,152.07	2,997.30	3,183.13	2,854.89	4,762.38	5,303.50	8,026.81	2,806.13

SOURCE: *National Health Expenditure Trends, 1975-2006*, Table F.1.1.2. Reprinted by permission of CIHI.

TABLE 2

Health Spending as a Percentage of Government Expenditures, Canada and Provinces/Territories, 1975–2005

Year	Nfld./ Lab.	PEI	NS	NB	QC	ON	MB	SK	AB	BC	Yukon	NWT	Nunavut	Canada
1975–1976	20.9%	21.2%	25.0%	21.1%	28.1%	27.8%	28.1%	24.0%	24.1%	26.1%	9.5%	10.1%	—	26.6%
1985–1986	23.1%	24.6%	26.1%	24.7%	25.8%	30.0%	25.9%	22.9%	22.9%	28.4%	11.4%	11.35	—	26.7%
1995–1996	24.8%	24.6%	25.3%	25.7%	25.0%	29.6%	27.7%	26.3%	26.3%	29.7%	13.5%	15.4%	—	27.3%
2005–2006	31.9%	30.4%	35.7%	32.7%	27.3%	39.5%	37.5%	33.1%	33.1%	37.1%	19.0%	17.1%	21.6%	34.6%

SOURCE: *National Health Expenditure Trends, 1975-2006*, Table F.1.1.5. Reprinted by permission of CIHI.

Some observers contend that Canadian health services are getting worse, with longer waits for diagnostic tests and surgery and tighter restrictions on treatments available to patients. Does this trend mean that Canadian health services are especially inefficient? There is evidence for such suspicions. So why have Canadians been unable to brake the growth of their health care costs? This chapter will help you to understand the answer to this question, with its important implications for policy.

WHAT DOES THE MARKET DO POORLY?

Although we cannot list all of the market's imperfections, we can list some major areas in which it has been accused of failing:

1. Market economies suffer from severe business fluctuations.
2. The market distributes income unequally.
3. Where power to influence the market exists and is used, the market allocates resources inefficiently. This will generally be the case with monopolies and with monopolistic competition and oligopolies, unless they are part of perfectly contestable markets (as discussed on page 280 of Chapter 12).
4. The market deals poorly with the side effects of many economic activities.
5. The market cannot readily provide public goods, such as national defence.
6. The market may do a poor job of allocating resources between the present and the future.
7. The market mechanism makes public and personal services increasingly expensive, which often induces socially damaging countermeasures by government.

The first item is discussed in *Macroeconomics: Principles and Policy*. The second item will be discussed in the bonus chapter, which can be downloaded from this book's website at http://www.baumolmicro1e.nelson.com. The third item was examined in Chapter 11. This chapter deals with the remaining four. To help us analyze these cases, we will first briefly review the concept of efficient resource allocation, discussed in detail in Chapter 14.

EFFICIENT RESOURCE ALLOCATION: A REVIEW

The basic problem of resource allocation is deciding how much of each commodity the economy should produce. At first glance, the solution may seem simple: the more, the better! But this is not necessarily so.

Outputs are not created out of thin air. We produce them from scarce supplies of fuel, raw materials, machinery, and labour. If we use these resources to produce, say, more jeans, then we must take resources away from some other products, such as backpacks. To decide whether increasing the production of jeans is a good idea, we must compare the utility of that increase with the loss of utility in producing fewer backpacks. This, as you recall, means we must consider the opportunity cost of increased output. It is *efficient* to increase the output of jeans only if society considers the additional jeans more valuable than the forgone backpacks.

To illustrate this idea, we repeat a graph you have seen several times in earlier chapters—a *production possibilities frontier*—but we put it to a somewhat different use here. Curve *ABC* in Figure 1 is a **production possibilities frontier** showing the alternative combinations of jeans and backpacks that the economy can produce by reallocating its resources between production of the two goods. Suppose that point *B*, representing the production of 8 million backpacks and 60 million pairs of jeans, constitutes the *optimal* resource allocation. We assume this combination of outputs is the only one that best satisfies society's wants among all the possibilities that are *attainable* (given the technology and resources as represented by the production frontier). Two questions are pertinent to our discussion of the price system:

1. What prices will get the economy to select point *B*; that is, what prices will yield an *efficient* allocation of resources?
2. How can the wrong set of prices lead to a misallocation of resources?

The **production possibilities frontier** is a curve that shows the maximum quantities of outputs it is possible to produce with the available resource quantities and the current state of technological knowledge.

FIGURE 1

The Economy's Production Possibilities Frontier for the Production of Two Goods

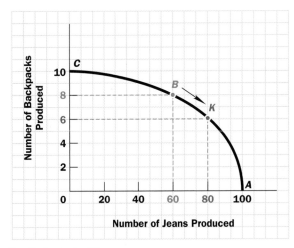

Note: Numbers are in millions per year.

We discussed the first question in detail in Chapter 14, where we saw that:

An efficient allocation of resources requires that each product's price be equal to its marginal cost; that is:

$$P = MC$$

The reasoning, in brief, goes like this: In a free market, the price of any good reflects the money value to consumers of an additional unit—that is, its *marginal utility* (MU). Similarly, if the market mechanism is working well, the *marginal cost* (MC) measures the value (the opportunity cost) of the resources needed to produce an additional unit of the good. That is, MC is the resources cost *caused* by producing another unit of the commodity. Hence, if prices are set equal to marginal costs, then consumers, by using *their own money* in the most effective way to maximize *their own* satisfaction, will automatically be using *society's resources* in the most effective way. In other words, as long as it sets prices equal to marginal costs, the market mechanism automatically satisfies the MC = MU rule for efficient resource allocation that we studied in Chapter 10.[1] In terms of Figure 1, this means that if $P = MC$ for both goods, the economy will automatically gravitate to point *B*, which we assumed to be the optimal point.

This chapter is devoted mainly to the second question: How can the "wrong" prices cause a **misallocation of resources?** The answer to this question is not too difficult, and we can use the case of monopoly as an illustration.

> **Resources are misallocated** if it is possible to change the way they are used or the combination of goods and services they produce and thereby make consumers better off.

The "law" of demand tells us that a rise in a commodity's price normally will reduce the quantity demanded. Suppose, now, that the backpack industry is a monopoly, so the price of backpacks exceeds their marginal cost.[2] This will decrease the quantity of backpacks demanded below the 8 million that we have assumed to be socially optimal (point *B* in Figure 1). The economy will move from point *B* to a point such as *K*, where too few backpacks and too many pairs of jeans are being produced for maximal consumer satisfaction. By setting the "wrong" prices, then, the market induces individual consumers to buy quantities that are inconsistent with maximal welfare of all individuals as a group, and thereby prevents the most efficient use of the economy's resources.

If a commodity's price is higher than its marginal cost, the economy will tend to produce less of that item than would maximize consumer benefits. The opposite will occur if an item's price is lower than its marginal cost.

In the rest of this chapter, we will encounter several other significant instances in which the market mechanism may set the "wrong" prices.

■ EXTERNALITIES: GETTING THE PRICES WRONG

We start with the fourth item on our list of market failures: The market deals poorly with the *incidental* side effects of economic activities. This flaw is one of the least obvious yet most consequential of the price system's imperfections.

> An activity is said to generate a **beneficial** or **detrimental externality** if that activity causes incidental benefits or damages to others not directly involved in the activity and no corresponding compensation is provided to or paid by those who generate the externality.

Many economic activities provide incidental *benefits* to others for whom they are not specifically intended. For example, homeowners who plant beautiful gardens in front of their homes incidentally and unintentionally provide pleasure to neighbours and passersby, even though they receive no payment in return. Economists say that their activity generates a **beneficial externality.** That is, the activity creates benefits that are *external* to, or outside, the intentions and interests of those that are directly involved in the activity. Similarly, some activities incidentally and unintentionally impose *costs* on others. For example, the owners of a motorcycle repair shop create a lot of noise for which they pay no compensation to their neighbours. Economists say these owners produce a **detrimental externality.** Pollution is the classic illustration of a detrimental externality.

---

[1] If you need a review, consult Chapter 14, pages 331–332.
[2] To review why price under monopoly may be expected to exceed marginal cost, you may want to reread Chapter 11, pages 238–239.

To see why externalities cause the price system to misallocate resources, you need only recall that the price system achieves efficiency by rewarding producers who serve consumers well—that is, at the lowest possible cost. This argument breaks down, however, as soon as some of the costs and benefits of economic activities are left out of the profit calculation.

When a firm pollutes a river, it uses up some of society's resources just as surely as when the firm burns coal. However, if the firm pays for coal but not for the use of clean water, we can expect the firm's management to be economical in its use of coal and wasteful in its use of water. By the same token, a firm that provides unpaid benefits to others is unlikely to be generous in allocating resources to the activity, no matter how socially desirable it may be.

In an important sense, the source of the market mechanism's difficulty here lies in society's rules about property rights. Coal mines are *private property;* their owners will not let anyone take coal without paying for it. Thus, coal is costly and so is not used wastefully. But waterways are not private property. Because they belong to everyone in general, they belong to no one in particular. Therefore, anyone can use waterways as free dumping grounds for wastes that spew poisons into the water and use up the water's oxygen that is vital for underwater life. Because no one pays for the use of the socially valuable dissolved oxygen in a public waterway, people will use that oxygen wastefully. The fact that waterways are exempted from the market's normal control procedures is therefore the source of a detrimental externality.

■ Externalities and Inefficiency

Using these concepts, we can see precisely why an externality has undesirable effects on the allocation of resources. In discussing externalities, it is crucial to distinguish between *social* and *private* marginal cost. We define **marginal social cost (MSC)** as the sum of two components: (1) **marginal private cost (MPC),** which is the share of an activity's marginal cost that is paid for by the persons who carry out the activity, plus (2) *incidental cost*, which is the share paid by others.

If an increase in a firm's output also increases the smoke its factory spews into the air, then, in addition to direct private costs (as recorded in the company accounts), the expansion of production imposes incidental costs on others. These costs take the form of increased laundry bills, medical expenditures, outlays for air conditioning and electricity, and the unpleasantness of living in a cloud of noxious fumes. These are all part of the activity's marginal *social* cost.

Where the firm's activities generate detrimental externalities, its marginal social cost will be greater than its marginal private cost, while the business firm will base its pricing only on its private cost because it does not pay the remainder of the social costs of its operation (and generally does not even know how large that remaining cost is). In symbols, MSC > MPC, whereas the price charged by the firm is based on MPC. Therefore, the firm's output must be too big because, in equilibrium, the market will yield an output at which consumers' marginal utility (MU) is equal to the firm's marginal private cost (MU = MPC < MSC). Where there are detrimental externalities, then, the marginal utility is *smaller* than the marginal *social* cost. In such a case, society would necessarily benefit if output of that product was *reduced.* It would lose the marginal utility but save the greater marginal social cost. We conclude that:

> Where a firm's activity causes detrimental externalities, marginal benefits will be less than marginal social costs in a free market. Smaller outputs than those that maximize profits will be socially desirable.

This relationship holds because private enterprise has no motivation to take into account any costs to others for which it does not have to pay. In fact, competition *forces* firms to produce at as low a private cost as possible, because if they don't, rivals will be able to take their customers away. Thus, competition *compels* firms to make extensive use of resources for which they are not required to pay or pay fully. As a

The **marginal social cost (MSC)** of an activity is the sum of its marginal private cost (MPC) plus its incidental costs (positive or negative) that are borne by others who receive no compensation for the resulting damage to their well-being.

The **marginal private cost (MPC)** is the share of an activity's marginal cost that is paid for by the persons who carry out the activity.

The **marginal social benefit (MSB)** of an activity is the sum of its marginal private benefit (MPB) plus its incidental benefits (positive or negative) that are received by others, and for which those others do not pay.

The **marginal private benefit (MPB)** is the share of an activity's marginal benefit that is received by the persons who carry out the activity.

result, goods that cause detrimental externalities will be produced in undesirably large amounts, because they have social costs that are not paid by the supplier firms.

The opposite, of course, holds for the case of external benefits. This situation is one where the **marginal social benefit (MSB)** is greater than the **marginal private benefit (MPB)**. A clear example is an invention produced by Firm A that gives an idea for another new product or process to an engineer from a different firm, B. Firm B clearly benefits from Firm A's research and development (R&D) spending, and B does not pay anything to A for this gain. In that case, the social benefit—the sum of the benefits to the two firms together—will be greater than the private benefit to the inventor Firm A alone. Thus, the marginal private benefit to investment in R&D will be less than the marginal social benefit, and less R&D will be carried out under private enterprise than social optimality requires.

These principles can be illustrated with the aid of Figure 2. This diagram repeats the two basic curves needed for analysis of the firm's equilibrium: a marginal revenue curve and a marginal cost curve (see Chapter 8). These curves represent the *private* costs and revenues of a particular firm (in this case, a paper mill). The mill maximizes profits by providing 50,000 tonnes of output, corresponding to the intersection between the marginal private cost and marginal revenue curves (point *A*).

Now suppose that the factory's wastewater pollutes a nearby estuary, so that its production creates a detrimental externality for which the owners do not pay. Then marginal social cost must be higher than marginal private cost, as shown in the diagram. The output of paper, which is governed by private costs, will be 50,000 tonnes (point *A*)—an excessive amount from the viewpoint of the public interest, given its environmental consequences.

If, instead of being able to impose the external costs on others, the paper mill's owners were forced to pay them, then their private marginal cost curve would correspond to the higher of the two cost curves. Paper output would then fall to 30,000 tonnes, corresponding to point *B*, the intersection between the marginal revenue curve and the marginal *social* cost curve.

Table 3 gives a numerical illustration of detrimental externalities, using the same numerical data that was used for Chapter 10, Table 4, page 227, when we dealt with the puzzle related to pollution taxes and subsidies. When a firm does not take social costs into account, it increases production as long as marginal revenue is above marginal private cost. The profit-maximizing level of production in that case is thus 50,000 tonnes. But the optimum level of production, from society's point of view is only 30,000 tonnes, because at higher producing outputs, the overall marginal social cost is above marginal revenue.

A diagram similar to Figure 2 can show that the opposite relationship will hold when the firm's activity produces beneficial externalities. The firm will produce less

FIGURE 2

Equilibrium of a Firm Whose Output Produces a Detrimental Externality (Pollution)

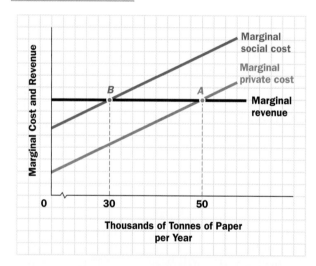

TABLE 3

Profits with Pollution Tax and with Pollution Subsidy

(1)	(2)	(3)	(4)	(5)
Total Quantity	Marginal Revenue	Marginal Private Cost	Incidental Cost	Marginal Social Cost
0	$ 0	$ 0	$ 0	$ 0
10	40	10	15	25
20	40	15	15	30
30	**40**	20	15	**35**
40	40	27	15	42
50	**40**	**33**	15	48
60	40	45	15	60
70	40	50	15	65

Note: Quantity is in thousands of tonnes; dollars are in thousands.

of its beneficial output than it would if it were rewarded fully for its activities' benefits. Thus:

Where the firm's activity generates beneficial externalities, markets will produce too little output. Society would be better off with larger output levels.

We can also see these results with the help of a production possibilities frontier diagram similar to that in Figure 1. In Figure 3, we see the frontier for two industries: electricity generation, which causes air pollution (a detrimental externality), and tulip growing, which makes an area more attractive (a beneficial externality). We have just seen that detrimental externalities make marginal social cost greater than marginal private cost. Hence, if the electric company charges a price equal to its own marginal (private) cost, that price will be less than the true marginal social cost. Similarly, in tulip growing, a price equal to marginal private cost will be above the true marginal cost to society.

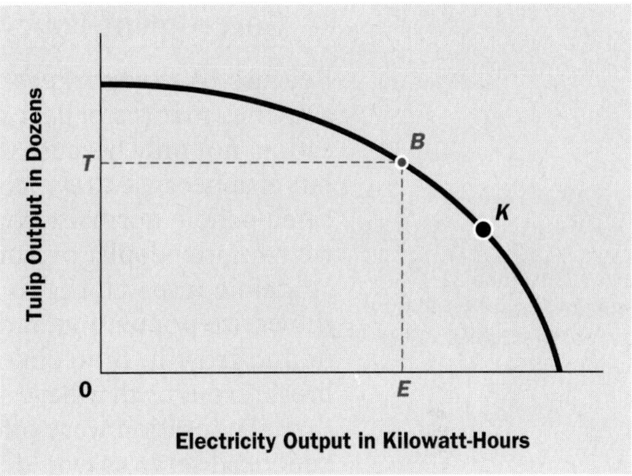

Earlier in the chapter, we saw that an industry that charges a price above marginal social cost will reduce quantity demanded through this high price, and so it will produce an output too small for efficient allocation of resources. The opposite will be true for an industry whose price is below marginal social cost. In terms of Figure 3, suppose that point B again represents the efficient allocation of resources, involving the production of E kilowatt-hours of electricity and T dozen tulips.

Because the polluting electricity-generating company charges a price below marginal social cost, it will sell more than E kilowatt-hours of electricity. Similarly, because tulip growers generate external benefits and so charge a price above marginal social cost, they will produce less than T dozen tulips. The economy will end up with the resource allocation represented by point K rather than that at point B. There will be too much smoky electricity production and too little attractive tulip growing. More generally:

An industry that generates detrimental externalities will have a marginal social cost higher than its marginal private cost. If the price is equal to a firm's own marginal private cost, it will therefore be below the true marginal cost to society. In this way, the market mechanism tends to encourage inefficiently large outputs of products that cause detrimental externalities. The opposite is true of products that cause beneficial externalities; private industry will provide inefficiently small quantities of these products.

Externalities Are Everywhere

Externalities occur throughout the economy. Many are beneficial. A factory that hires unskilled or semiskilled labourers, for example, gives them on-the-job *training* and provides the external benefit of better workers to future employers. Benefits to others are also generated when firms *invent* useful but unpatentable products, or even patentable products that can be imitated by others to some degree. We will discuss the externalities of innovation further in Chapter 16.

Detrimental externalities are also widespread. Pollution by factories, cars, and trucks cause some of our most pressing environmental problems. The abandonment of buildings causes the quality of neighbourhoods to deteriorate and is the source of serious externalities for cities. And these are only two of many significant examples.

Although the market mechanism, acting on its own, does nothing to cure externality problems, there is more to the story. Market economies often have dirty air and rivers and suffer from the effects of improperly disposed toxic wastes, but that does not mean that *non*market economies do any better. The communist countries

FIGURE 3

Externalities, Market Equilibrium, and Efficient Resource Allocation of Eastern Europe and the Soviet Union long were known to have a dismal environmental record. Just one example: the consequences of the 1986 Chernobyl nuclear power plant accident in Ukraine. When communism fell apart in those countries, the horrors of environmental degradation that were revealed were hard to believe. It became abundantly clear that central planning is not a guaranteed cure for environmental difficulties.

Moreover, the market mechanism does offer an effective way of dealing with such difficulties. Although markets hardly can be claimed to protect the environment automatically, they offer us a possibly powerful tool for doing so, as we will see shortly.

Government Policy and Externalities

Because of the market's inability to cope with externalities, governments support activities that are believed to generate external benefits. Governments subsidize education, not only because they know it helps promote equal opportunity for all citizens, but also because they believe it generates beneficial externalities. For example, educated people normally commit fewer crimes than uneducated people do, so the more we educate people, presumably the less we need to spend on crime prevention. Also, academic research that is a by-product of the educational system has often benefited the entire population and has, indeed, been a major contributor to the nation's economic growth. Biotechnology and advanced computing are just two major scientific breakthroughs that have stemmed from university research. We consequently believe that, if education were offered only by profit-making institutions, the outputs of these beneficial services would be provided at less than optimal levels.

Similarly, governments have begun to increase fines on companies that contribute heavily to air and water pollution. This is done, of course, as a disincentive for the creation of socially damaging externalities. In other words, it brings the amounts that business firms pay closer to covering all of the costs that their activities generate.

Externalities are really just failures to price resources so that markets will allocate them efficiently. One effective way to deal with externalities may be to use taxes and subsidies, making polluters pay for the costs they impose on society and paying the generators of beneficial externalities for the incidental benefits of their activities (which can be considered as an offset or deduction from the social cost of the activity). This is called the *Pigovian approach*, because it was first advocated by British economist A. C. Pigou (1877–1956). (For a satirical view of this approach, see the boxed feature "The Politics of Pigovian Taxes.")

For example, firms that generate beneficial externalities should be given *subsidies* per unit of their output equal to the difference between their marginal social costs and their marginal private costs. Similarly, detrimental externalities should be *taxed* so that the firm will have to pay the entire marginal social cost. In terms of Figure 2, after paying the tax, the firm's marginal private cost curve will shift up until it coincides with its marginal social cost curve, so the market price will be set in a manner consistent with efficient resource allocation. In terms of Table 3, by taxing the output of the firm producing the detrimental externality, the government forces private firms to take the social costs into account. If the tax per unit is equal to the marginal social cost (in Table 3, $15,000 per 10,000 tonnes, that is $1.50 per tonne), the firm will be induced to produce the optimal amount from society's point of view (30,000 tonnes).

Although this approach works well in principle, it is often difficult to carry out in reality. Social costs are rarely easy to estimate, partly because they are so widely diffused throughout the community (everyone is affected by pollution) and partly because it is difficult to assess many of the costs and benefits (effects on health, unpleasantness of living in smog) in monetary terms. In Chapter 17, which focuses on environmental problems, we will continue our discussion of the pros and cons of the economist's approach to externalities and will outline alternative policies for their control.

The Politics of Pigovian Taxes

As we pointed out in Chapter 1, most Canadian economists believe that the imposition of taxes that force economic agents to take into account possible social costs represents a good approach to externalities in general and to pollution control in particular. These Pigovian taxes are usually moderately popular among environment-friendly citizens with left-wing tendencies, who tend to favour direct controls and the imposition of pollution ceilings. However, as suggested in the quotation at the beginning of this chapter, there are also some economists who are reluctant to accept the possibility of externalities and the imposition of Pigovian taxes, because they fear that the concept will be used to diminish the role of unfettered markets and to increase government intervention. The following two excerpts, by the same author, illustrate this more conservative point of view—with a good dose of humour.

The first is an excerpt from an article by Terence Corcoran in the *Financial Post*, October 25, 2006:

> Here's a practical question for Pigovians: How many Pigou taxes will it take to achieve specific objectives? Example: Traffic congestion. Specifically, in the case of London, the question is how many taxes, and how high must the taxes be, to effectively achieve the claimed objective of reducing traffic congestion in one of the world's great cities?
>
> Fans of Pigou taxes like to claim London's use of a congestion charge has been a success. London, which already has $4 (all figures US) a gallon gas taxes, also imposes a $16 daily congestion charge on vehicles entering the central core of the city. Pigovians claim—supported by London official propaganda—that the congestion charge, originally set at about $10, had produced a significant response, reducing traffic congestion by 30 per cent.
>
> That's the claim, although a recent visit to London leads me to believe congestion is still an issue. If it was such a success, why did they have to raise the charge, and why is the city now talking about raising it again to about $20? The tax is certainly a cash cow; maybe that's one reason. Another: Maybe it doesn't work all that well.
>
> The latest report from the London authority actually says it's too soon to reach final conclusions. Also, the 30 per cent reduction in congestion is a bit of a statistical game. It compares the amount of time it takes to travel one kilometre within the city before and after the charge was imposed. But it doesn't.

> The total driving time for one kilometre pre-congestion charge was four minutes and 30 seconds. The first two minutes are considered to be normal traffic. The congestion element is listed at two minutes and 30 seconds. The claim is that the congestion portion was reduced by 30 per cent. But that's 30 per cent of the 150 seconds per kilometre that make up the congestion portion, which means that the total congestion reduction is about 45 seconds off the time it takes to travel one kilometre. That's success?
>
> The net effect: Before the congestion charge was imposed, the time to travel one kilometre was 4 mins and 30 secs. Time to travel one kilometre after charge: three minutes, 45 seconds. Actual reduction, or total time saved: equal to about 15 per cent. That's based on the report after the first year of operation. The latest report reduces the numbers a bit. Bottom line analysis: If you were driving, say, 5 kilometres across central London in 2002, pre-charge, it would have taken 22 minutes. To travel the same distance today would take almost 19 minutes. That three minute reduction in travel time today cost $16, soon to rise to $20. At $16, that works out to more than $5 a minute saved.
>
> That's Pigovian tax policy in action—based, one should add, on survey methodology. So Brits now pay two Pigovian taxes: $4 a gallon in gas tax and another $16 in congestion charge. But London is still bogged down in traffic!
>
> So the fundamental question is: How many Pigovian taxes will it take to meet the objective of reducing traffic congestion?

Also by Terence Corcoran, the following is an excerpt from the October 21, 2006, edition of the *Financial Post:*

> Join the Club. Worried about new taxes on gasoline? Welcome to the NoPigou Club. The club's purpose is to counter the ideas of the Pigou Club, an informal assembly of economists and pundits who support the idea of raising gasoline taxes . . . to curb global warming and fight other environmental and economic problems. In the view of the NoPigou Club, the Pigou approach is just another form of central planning dressed up in free-market terminology. To join, comment and add to the discussion visit the NoPigou Club at http://www.nationalpost.com/nopigouclub.

SOURCES: Excerpted from Terence Corcoran, "How many taxes will it take?" Financial Post, 25 October 2006. Reprinted by permission of Terence Corcoran; and "Join the Club," Terence Concoran, *Financial Post*, 10/12/2006. Material reprinted with the express permission of National Post Company, a CanWest Partnership.

POLICY DEBATE
Illegal Drugs Once Again

We mentioned on page 77 of Chapter 4 that some criminologists and economists believe that illegal drugs should be made legal, thus leading to a reduction in their price and the profits made by the underworld. But what about the negative effects that these drugs have on individuals and their communities? Criminologist Line Beauchesne argues that while these drugs should be sold by Crown corporations, each drug should be taxed at a different tax rate. The most dangerous drugs—those that have the worse effects and hence the most detrimental externalities—should be taxed at the highest rates, whereas drugs that are scientifically recognized as less dangerous would be taxed at a lower rate. Beauchesne believes that in this way, consumers would be encouraged to use the less offensive drugs. A counterargument, however, is that if tax rates are too high, it would become profitable once again for organized crime to sell these drugs on the black market—a dilemma that already exists in the case of cigarettes.

SOURCE: Line Beauchesne, "Vers la légalisation réglementée des drogues," *Le Devoir*, November 20, 2006, p. A9.

Externalities Are Everywhere—Even in the National Hockey League!

We earlier defined detrimental externalities as the result of an activity that generates incidental damages to others not directly involved in the activity, with no corresponding compensation. Sports economists argue that the overly high salaries paid to star players or to journeymen by some irresponsible general managers of the National Hockey League (NHL) are a good example of detrimental externalities. When these overly high salaries are being granted, the general managers of the other teams are stuck in a quagmire: Either they also grant ridiculous pay increases to their own players, in which case they jeopardize the financial viability of their team, or they don't, in which case they may lose their best players to rival teams.

In addition, the collective bargaining agreement of the NHL, which deals with labour relations between the owners and the players, contains provisions that allow subsets of players to go to salary arbitration when they are unhappy about the pay offers they get from the team that owns their playing rights. A judge who specializes in labour arbitration then decides whether a player's claim is reasonable or not, by comparing the performance and pay of the player with those of similar players. Thus, when an irresponsible general manager grants absurd pay increases to his players, the players from the 29 other NHL teams can go to arbitration and argue that their salaries are too low! If the judge agreed with the players and their agents, the teams would have to either grant the pay increases

or lose the players at the end of the season. The decisions of a single general manager thus have possible negative financial consequences for all teams—an instance of detrimental externalities. Bad decisions by a few teams lead to salary inflation and weak profits for all teams, as hockey salaries outgrow team revenues.

Two solutions have been advanced to deal with this problem. During the 1994–1995 lockout, the owners proposed a "luxury tax" to penalize teams that grant overly high salaries, with the proceeds being distributed to the poorest teams. Just as in the case of a tax on pollution, the object of the tax is to induce owners to take into account the social cost of their decisions; that is, the potential impact on the financial health of the league. Such a luxury tax was also proposed by the players during the 2004–2005 lockout. But as is now well known, at the time of this second lockout, the NHL owners had lost all faith in this market mechanism and were then looking for a more interventionist solution: the payroll cap. With the payroll cap, the league imposes a maximum payroll on each team. Even if a team owner wishes to spend more on players' salaries and has enough revenues to do so, the league forbids it. The 2004–2005 NHL lockout thus had some ironic features: The players' union was arguing in favour of a market mechanism (the luxury tax), while the team owners were pushing for a "socialist" solution (an identical payroll cap for all teams).

■ PROVISION OF PUBLIC GOODS

A public good is a commodity or service whose benefits are *not depleted* by an additional user and from which it is generally difficult or *impossible to exclude* people, even if the people are unwilling to pay for the benefits.

A private good is a commodity characterized by both depletability and excludability.

A commodity is **depletable** if it is used up when someone consumes it.

A commodity is **excludable** if someone who does not pay for it can be kept from enjoying it.

A second area in which market failure occurs is the provision of what economists call **public goods.** Public goods are socially valuable commodities whose provision, for reasons we will explain, cannot be financed by private enterprise, or at least not at socially desirable prices. Thus, government must pay for public goods if they are to be provided at all. Standard examples of public goods include everything from national defence to coastal lighthouses.

It is easiest to explain the nature of public goods by contrasting them with **private goods,** which are at the opposite end of the spectrum. *Private goods are characterized by two important attributes.* One can be called **depletability.** If you eat an apple or use a litre of gasoline, there is that much less fruit or fuel in the world available for others to use. Your consumption depletes the supply available for other people, either temporarily or permanently.

But a pure public good is like the legendary widow's jar of oil, which always remained full no matter how much oil was poured out. For example, once snow has been removed from a street, improved driving conditions are available to every driver who uses that street, whether 10 or 1,000 cars pass that way. One passing car does not make the road less snow-free for the next driver. The same is true of spraying swamps near a town to kill mosquitoes. The cost of spraying is the same whether the town contains 10,000 or 20,000 persons. A resident of the town who benefits from this service does not deplete its advantages to others.

The other property that characterizes private goods but not all public goods is **excludability,** meaning that anyone who does not pay for the good can be excluded from enjoying its benefits. If you do not buy a ticket, you are excluded from the basketball game. If you do not pay for an electric guitar, the storekeeper will not hand it over to you.

But some goods or services, once provided to anyone, automatically become available to many others whom it is difficult, if not impossible, to exclude from the benefits. When the street is cleared of snow, everyone who uses the street benefits, regardless of who paid for the snowplow. If a country provides a strong military, every citizen receives its protection, even persons who do not want it.

A public good is defined as a good that lacks depletability. Very often, it also lacks excludability. Notice two important implications:

First, because nonpaying users usually cannot be excluded from enjoying a public good, suppliers of such goods will find it *difficult or impossible to collect fees* for the benefits they provide. This is the so-called *free-rider* problem. How many people, for example, would *voluntarily* cough up close to $1,600 a year to support our national defence establishment? Yet this is roughly what it costs per Canadian family. Services such as national defense and public health, which are not depletable and where excludability is simply impossible, *cannot* be provided by private enterprise because people will not pay for what they can get free. Because private firms are not in the business of giving services away, the supply of public goods must be left to government and nonprofit institutions.

The second implication we notice is that, because the supply of a public good is not depleted by an additional user, *the marginal (opportunity) cost of serving an additional user is zero*. With marginal cost equal to zero, the basic principle of optimal resource allocation (price equal to marginal cost) calls for provision of public goods and services to anyone who wants them *at no charge*. In other words, not only is it often *impossible* to charge a market price for a public good, it is often *undesirable* as well. Any nonzero price would discourage some users from enjoying the public good; but this would be inefficient, because one more person's enjoyment of the good costs society nothing. To summarize:

> It is usually *not easily possible* to charge a price for a pure public good because people cannot be excluded from enjoying its benefits. It may also be *undesirable* to charge a price for it because that would discourage some people from benefiting, even though using a public good does not deplete its supply. For both of these reasons, government supplies many public goods. Without government intervention, public goods simply would not be provided.

Referring back to our example in Figure 1, if backpacks were a public good and their production were left to private enterprise, the economy would end up at point *A*, with zero production of backpacks and a far greater output of jeans than is called for by efficient allocation (point *B*). Usually, communities have not let that happen; today they devote a substantial proportion of government expenditure—indeed, the bulk of municipal budgets—to financing of public goods or services believed to generate substantial external benefits. National defence, public health, police and fire protection, and research are among the services governments provide because they offer beneficial externalities or are public goods.

■ ALLOCATION OF RESOURCES BETWEEN PRESENT AND FUTURE

A third area in which market failure occurs is the division of benefits between today and tomorrow. When a society invests, more resources are devoted to expanding its capacity to produce consumer goods in the future. But if we devote inputs to building new factories and equipment that will add to production tomorrow, those resources then become unavailable for consumption now. Fuel used to make steel for a factory cannot be used to heat homes or drive cars. Thus, the allocation of inputs between current consumption and investment—their allocation between present and future—influences how fast the economy grows. Investment in education has a similar role, because people who are educated today are likely to be more effective producers tomorrow, and if education enables them to contribute inventions, that may increase tomorrow's production even more. That is why economists refer to education as "investment in human capital," thereby thinking of more-educated people as analogous to machinery in the factory whose efficiency is increased by modernization.

In principle, the market mechanism should be as efficient in allocating resources between present and future uses as it is in allocating resources among different outputs at any one time. If future demands for a particular commodity, such as personal computers, are expected to be higher than they are today, it pays manufacturers to plan now to build the necessary plant and equipment so they will be ready to turn out the computers when the market expands. More resources are thereby allocated to future consumption.

We can analyze the allocation of resources between present and future with the aid of a production possibilities frontier diagram, such as the one in Figure 1. The question now is how much labour and capital to devote to producing consumers' goods and how much to devote to construction of factories to produce output in the future. Then, instead of jeans and backpacks, the graph will show consumers' goods and number of factories on its axes, but otherwise it will be exactly the same as Figure 1.

The profit motive directs the flow of resources between one time period and another, just as it handles resource allocation among different industries in a given period. The lure of profits directs resources to those products *and those time periods* in which high prices promise to make output most profitable.

■ How Does It Work in Practice?

Some economists have suggested that the market may devote too large a proportion of the economy's resources to immediate consumption. British economist A. C. Pigou argued that people suffer from a "defective telescopic faculty"—that they are too shortsighted to give adequate weight to the future. A "bird in the hand" point of view leads people to spend too much on today's consumption and commit too little to tomorrow's investments.

A second reason why the free market may not invest enough for the future is that investment projects, such as the construction of a new factory, are much greater risks to the individual investor than to the community as a whole. Even if the original investor goes bankrupt and the factory falls into someone else's hands, it can continue turning out goods for the general public. Of course, the profits will not go to the original investor or to his or her heirs. Therefore, the loss to the individual investor will be far greater than the loss to society. For this reason, individual investment for the future may fall short of the socially optimal amounts, even though investments too risky to be worthwhile to any group of private individuals may nevertheless be advantageous to society as a whole.

Third, our economy shortchanges the future when it despoils irreplaceable natural resources, exterminates whole species of plants and animals, floods canyons, "develops" attractive areas into hectares of potential slums, and so on. Worst of all, industry, the military, and individuals bequeath a ticking time bomb to the future when they leave behind lethal and slow-acting toxic residues. For example, nuclear wastes may remain dangerous for hundreds or even thousands of years, but their disposal containers are likely to fall apart long before the contents lose their lethal qualities. Such actions are essentially *irreversible*. If a factory is not built this year, the deficiency in facilities provided for the future can be remedied by building it next year. But a natural canyon, once destroyed, can never be replaced. Global warming is another example of severe environmental damage. It is also an example of *defective telescopic faculty*, which means that inadequate attention is being paid to the future of our planet. More economic resources need to be devoted *now* to safeguard the *future*. For this reason:

> Many economists believe that *irreversible decisions* have a special significance and must *not* be left entirely to the decisions of private firms and individuals—that is, to the market.

Some writers, however, have questioned the general conclusion that the market system will not invest enough for the future. They point out that our economy's prosperity has increased fairly steadily from one decade to the next, and that there is reason to expect future generations to have far higher real average incomes and an abundance of consumer goods. Pressures to increase future investment then may be like taking from the poor to give to the rich—a sort of backward Robin Hood redistribution of income.

Global warming (which will be discussed more in Chapter 17), illustrates quite well all of the difficulties associated with deciding on the optimal allocation of resources between the present and the future. In a 700-page report issued in the fall of 2006, British economist Sir Nicholas Stern described global warming as the greatest and most wide-ranging market failure. He warns that, if no action is taken now in relation to harmful emissions, there is more than a 75 percent chance of global temperatures rising between two and three degrees Celsius over the next 50 years, and that there is a 50 percent chance that average global temperatures could rise by five degrees Celsius.

In this case, Stern and his research team estimate that world per-capita consumption would be lowered by as much as 20 percent compared to what it otherwise might be. To avoid this future loss, Stern recommends that strong measures should be undertaken immediately, such as imposing heavy taxes on carbon-producing industries that are said to cause climate change, in the hope of achieving a smooth transition toward a lower carbon-energy economy. This action would slow down the world economy, but the losses of today would avert bigger losses in the future.

Not surprisingly, the Stern report has generated both high praise and harsh criticism from economists. Besides disagreements on the effects of global warming per se, economists disagree on the measurement of future costs and on how to assess them in terms of current dollars—the problem of *discounting*, which will be discussed in the appendix to Chapter 19.

SOME OTHER SOURCES OF MARKET FAILURE

We have now surveyed some of the most important imperfections of the market mechanism. But our list is not complete, and it can never be. In this imperfect world, nothing ever works out ideally. Indeed, by examining anything with a sufficiently powerful microscope, one can always detect more blemishes. However, some significant items were omitted from our list. We will conclude with a brief description of three of them and discuss a fourth of special current interest in somewhat greater detail.

Imperfect Information: "Caveat Emptor"

In our analysis of the virtues of the market mechanism in Chapter 14, we assumed that consumers and producers have all the information they need to make good decisions. In reality, this is rarely true. When buying a house or secondhand car or when selecting a doctor, consumers are vividly reminded of how little they know about what they are purchasing. The old cliché, "caveat emptor" (let the buyer beware), applies. Obviously, if participants in the market are ill-informed, they will not always make the optimal decisions described in our theoretical models. (For more on this issue, see "Asymmetric Information, Lemons, and Agents," on the next page.)

Yet not all economists agree that imperfect information is really a failure of the market mechanism. They point out that information, too, is a commodity that costs money to produce. Neither firms nor consumers have complete information because it would be irrational for them to spend the enormous amounts needed to get it. As always, compromise is necessary. One should, ideally, stop buying information at the point where the marginal utility of further information is no greater than its marginal cost. With this amount of information, the business executive or the consumer would be able to make what we call *optimally imperfect* decisions.

There is a problem with this viewpoint, however: How do decision makers know that it is worth searching for more information? They must already know the value of what they still have to discover! There is a problem of infinite regress, which is too often ignored by economists and which those involved in real business decisions avoid by following rules of thumb that proved to be successful in the past.

Asymmetric Information, Lemons, and Agents

Have you ever wondered why a six-month-old car sells for so much less than a brand-new one? Economists offer one explanation, having to do with *imperfect information.* The problem is that some small percentage of new automobiles are "lemons" that are plagued by mechanical troubles. The new-car dealer probably knows no more than the buyer about whether a particular car is a lemon. The information known to the two parties, therefore, is said to be *symmetric,* and there is a low probability that a car purchased from a new-car dealer will turn out to be a lemon.

In the used-car market, however, information is *asymmetric.* The person selling the used car knows very well whether the car is a lemon, but the buyer does not. Moreover, a seller who wants to get rid of a relatively new car is likely to be doing so only because it *is* a lemon. Potential buyers realize that. Hence, if a person is forced to sell a good new car because of an unexpected need for cash, he will be stuck with a low price because he cannot *prove* that his car really works well. The moral is that asymmetric information also tends to harm the honest seller.

In addition, asymmetric information leads to the *principal–agent problems,* that are discussed in the text and whose analysis is a major concern of recent economic research. Principal–agent and asymmetric information problems are said to have played a major part in the much-publicized Enron debacle. When that huge energy-trading firm collapsed, stockholders (including Enron employees whose retirement money was invested in the firm) lost their savings. But Enron's management had already deserted the sinking ship with large bonus payments, having sold *their* company stocks while the price was still high.

Asymmetric information is crucial here. The principals know only *imperfectly* whether their agents are serving their interests faithfully and efficiently or are instead neglecting or even acting against the principals' interests to pursue selfish interests of their own. Misuse of the principals' property, embezzlement, and political corruption are extreme examples of such dereliction of duty by agents and, unfortunately, they seem to occur often. Stock options may help to deal with the asymmetric information problem here. If the earnings of corporate management are linked to company profits or based on the market value of company shares, then by promoting the welfare of stockholders, managers will make themselves better off. Shareholders, even though they know only imperfectly what management is doing, can have greater confidence that management will try to serve their interests well.

SOURCE: egd/Shutterstock

■ Transaction Costs

Transaction costs include the costs of obtaining necessary information costs and of the bargaining, implementation, and enforcement related to decision making.

British economist Ronald Coase received the 1991 Sveriges Riksbank Nobel Prize in Economics for his work that emphasized the effects of transaction costs—a feature that is often ignored in economics. When transaction costs are relatively high, the market may be unable to provide an efficient solution to the problem at hand. **Transaction costs** include the costs of obtaining the necessary information for decision making, but they also include the costs associated with bargaining (when the parties involved have to find some arrangement agreeable to all), and the costs associated with reaching a decision. Finally, transaction costs also involve policing and implementation costs once the solution has been reached and a decision has been made.

Take the case of a firm that pollutes a river as part of its production process. People living downstream are negatively affected by this water pollution but the firm does not take into account the social annoyance that it is creating for these people; hence, we have an instance of detrimental externality. If you follow the spirit of Coase's approach, the problem is not so much the existence of the externality but rather a problem of transaction costs. The water pollution problem could be solved by imposing a Pigovian tax on the polluting firm, but there are other possible solutions. The firm could be compelled to adopt a new production process that would greatly reduce pollution, or the people living downstream could get together and construct a plant that would clean up the river water before it reaches their dwellings. The most efficient solution, from society's point of view, depends on the relative costs and benefits of each solution. If there were no transaction costs, the market (that is, the bargaining between the involved parties) would provide the optimal solution. However, with transaction costs, the most efficient solution may never be enforced. For instance, suppose that it is much cheaper to construct a plant that cleans up the water than to install a new production process that reduces pollution. It might turn out to be impossible to get every one of the people living downstream to agree to pay for the water cleaning plant, or the people might never manage to agree to take the polluting firm to court to make it pay for the construction and operation of a water-cleaning plant. Because of these transaction costs, the most efficient solution—constructing a water-cleaning plant—will not be adopted.

In general, with market transaction costs, proper institutions that reduce these transaction costs need to be developed. These may range from large corporations to trade associations that will police its members, and it may involve access to a banking system with proper collateral rules and well-functioning legal recourse. An example of such an institution is the International Joint Commission (IJC), which was created by Canada and the United States in 1909 to manage the lake and river system along the border between the two countries, so as to respect competing interests and in recognition that the actions of each country affect the environment of both countries. This led in 1972 to the first Great Lakes Water Quality Agreement, the purpose of which is to control pollution and remove toxic substances from the Great Lakes–St. Lawrence River system. Other water agreements have since followed, involving in particular the Souris River and the Milk River in western Canada. Another major issue has also been acid rain, which can spread over thousands of kilometres and which led to the IJC 1991 Air Quality Agreement.

Rent Seeking

An army of lawyers, expert witnesses, and business executives crowd our courtrooms and cause enormous costs to pile up through litigation. Business firms seem to sue each other at the slightest provocation, wasting vast resources and delaying business decisions. Why? Because it is possible to make money by such seemingly unproductive activities—through legal battles over profit-making opportunities.

For example, suppose that a municipality awards a contract to produce electricity to Firm A, offering $20 million in profit. It may be worthwhile for Firm B to spend $5 million in a lawsuit against the municipality and Firm A, hoping that the courts will award it the contract (and thus the $20 million profit) instead.

In general, any source of unusual profit, such as a monopoly, tempts firms to waste economic resources in an effort to obtain control of that source of profit. This process, called **rent seeking** (meaning that the firms hope to obtain earnings without contributing to production), is judged by some observers to be a major source of inefficiency in our economy. (For more on rent seeking, see page 456–458 in Chapter 19.)

Rent seeking refers to unproductive activity in the pursuit of economic profit—in other words, profit in excess of competitive earnings.

Moral Hazard

Another widely discussed problem for the market mechanism is associated with insurance. Economists view insurance—which is the provision of protection against risk—as a useful commodity, like shoes or information. But insurance also encourages the very risks against which it provides protection. For example, if an individual has a valuable stamp collection that is fully insured against theft, she has little motivation to protect it against burglars. She may, for example, fail to lock it up in a safe-deposit box. This problem—the tendency of insurance to encourage the source of risk—is called **moral hazard,** and it makes a free market in insurance difficult to operate.

Moral hazard refers to the tendency of insurance to discourage policyholders from protecting themselves from risk.

Principals, Agents, and Recent Stock Option Scandals

Yet another important area of concern about the performance of the unconstrained market is called the "principal-agent problem." The economy contains many activities so large and complex that it is out of the question for them to be organized and operated by those most directly concerned. The most striking example is provided by our representative democracy that is, in theory, run by us. But it is obvious that it would be quite impractical to assemble all of the citizens of the country to discuss and decide on the details of proposed legislation on complex matters such as trade policy or rules for protection of the environment. So, instead, democracy requires us to hire politicians via the election process to run the country on our behalf. In economic terminology, we would say that the citizens are the **principals** in the activity of running the country, and the prime minister and other members of Parliament are the **agents** who are hired by us, the principals, to operate the country on our behalf.

> **Agents** are people hired to run a complex enterprise on behalf of **the principals,** those whose benefit the enterprise is supposed to serve.

A second example, the one on which we will focus here, is the running of a corporation. A giant corporation such as Intel (the largest producer of microprocessors for computers) has thousands of shareholder-owners. And, like citizens of a country, they are also too numerous to run the firm day by day, making the thousands of required decisions. So these principals, too, hire agents—the corporate management—to do the job. The assigned task of the agents is to run the corporation in a way that best promotes the interests of the shareholders.

The main problem that besets this arrangement, like all principal–agent arrangements, is that the agents cannot always be trusted. All too often they put their own interests ahead of those of their principals, in clear dereliction of duty. Indeed, in just this decade so far, there has been what seems like a flood of corporate scandals, with managements having indiscriminately betrayed shareholders and employees while obtaining for themselves hundreds of millions of dollars as their supposedly merited rewards. (For examples, see the feature box in Chapter 9 on "Corporate Scandals.")

Economic analysis suggests a solution to the problem: Arrange for the amount that the agents are paid to depend on the degree to which their actions succeed in benefiting the principals. Pay the agents a lot if they achieve much for the principals, and pay them little if they don't. If such an incentive scheme is established, the agents can do well for themselves only by doing well for the shareholders.

The only trouble with this solution is that it is easier to describe on paper than to carry out in practice. First, it is not easy to measure what the agents have actually accomplished. If the company's sales increased, was that because of something management did, or was it largely an accident? The second problem is that unscrupulous managers can often find ways to get around such rules via legal manoeuvres or by appointing friends and allies to the company's board of directors, rather than evenhanded appointees who can assure the honesty and competence of management.

One seemingly clever device was thought up to do the job of rewarding management for what they achieve: the employee stock option. But corruption within firms and irrational tax laws that undermine their effectiveness, among other impediments, have prevented stock options from doing the job they were intended to do. Let us see why.

> A **stock option** is a contract that permits its owner to buy a specified quantity of stocks of a corporation at a future date, but at the price specified in the contract rather than the stock's market price on the date of purchase.

A **stock option** is, in effect, a contract that allows the person who owns the option to buy a specified quantity of the company's stock at some date in the future that can be chosen, within specified limits, by the owner. But when he pays for the stock, he pays not the price on the day the stock is bought but, rather, the price of the stock on the day the option was obtained. For example, suppose the price of the stock was $40 on February 12, the day the option was acquired. On March 23, the owner considers using the option to buy the stock. If the price has fallen to $30, the option owner will decide not to buy any stock because, if he did, the option contract would require him to spend $40 for a stock worth only $30, clearly a losing proposition. But suppose the stock had gone in the other direction and, on the proposed purchase date, the share's price had risen to $60. Since this means that the option owner could acquire a stock worth $60 for only $40, it would give him an immediate $20 profit—a very good deal.

When the price of the company's stock goes down, stock options are not used. Thus, the owner of the option loses only what she paid for the option, if anything. But if the price of the stock rises, the owner can make a profit by "exercising the option;" that is, by using it to buy the stock and pocketing the difference between the price specified in the option and the value of the stock at the time it is bought.

If stock options are granted to a corporation's management under appropriate rules, they may well be a powerful way to deal with the principal–agent problem in corporations. For if managers who own stock options work harder to make the company successful, their actions can raise the market price of the corporation's stock, thereby benefiting the shareholders as well as themselves. In other words, a gift or sale of stock options to management can help align the interests of shareholders and management: They both want the stock price to rise. Few other instruments can ensure such compatibility between the interest of shareholders and managers.

However, the conditions under which stock options are now granted are far from this ideal. They can, for instance, lead management to focus on short-term gains in stock prices, rather than on the long-run performance of the firm. They reward management even when the firm's performance is worse than that of the industry and that of the stock market as a whole. And subservient boards of directors often provide staggering and probably undeserved managerial compensation in the form of huge gifts of stock options.

Unscrupulous managers have learned ways to manipulate stock options and undermine their benefits to shareholders. For instance, there have been cases in which management sent out misleading information indicating, falsely, that the company was about to make large profits. This raised the price of its stock temporarily, giving the holders of stock options an opportunity to use them quickly to buy the stocks at the low prices specified in the options and quickly sell the shares while their market price was still high, thus making a large profit for themselves. Such problems are best attacked directly by requiring the issue of stock options to management to satisfy provisions such as the following:

1. That exercise of those stock options should not be permitted for some substantial period of time, say five years, after they are initially offered;
2. That the stock options be performance-based, meaning that they are contingent on performance by the firm that exceeds that of comparable firms or of the firm's own past record, with the number of stock options granted to management proportioned to the magnitude of the superiority of the firm's performance;
3. That any such grant of options to management be subject to approval by vote of the firm's shareholders; and
4. That the sale of such shares by top management be made public promptly.

Stock options granted on these terms may well lead to a dramatic change in the incentives facing management—and in the desired direction. If the improved incentives created by options succeed in their purpose of fostering higher earnings, the gift of options to management may involve no cost to shareholders. On the contrary, earnings per share will be higher than they would otherwise have been, and both managers and shareholders will benefit. But unfortunately, the existing rules do not contain such provisions to protect the interests of the shareholders (the principals).

Given the ability of corporate managers to find ways that benefit them rather than the shareholders, and given their ability to control the corporate boards of directors that set their pay conditions, some shareholder organizations such as Mouvement d'éducation et de défense des actionnaires (led by Yves Michaud, a former civil servant and Quebec politician) advocate that the salaries of corporate executives be set as a function of the salary of the average employee in the corporation and as a function of the actual profit of the corporation.

While some believe that these conditions should be voted on and hopefully endorsed at corporate general meetings, others believe that the outrageous pay conditions of top executives are significant examples of market failures and that they have become so disgraceful that governments should regulate these and place limits on them. Previous efforts in that direction, such as the NDP-led Ontario government decision in the 1990s to make public the salaries of all employees beyond $100,000 did not have the expected effect: Instead of slowing down salary inflation among top executives, it triggered an acceleration in executive salary inflation, as executives were able to compare their salaries to those of other executives, using these as bargaining tools to propel their own salaries upward.

MARKET FAILURE AND GOVERNMENT FAILURE

We have pointed out some of the invisible hand's most noteworthy failures. We seem forced to the conclusion that a market economy, if left entirely to itself, is likely to produce results that are, at least in some respects, far from ideal. We have noted in our discussion, either directly or by implication, some of the things that government can do to correct these deficiencies. But the fact that government often *can* intervene in the economy's operation in a constructive way does not always mean that it actually *will* succeed in doing so. Governments cannot be relied on to behave ideally, any more than business firms can be expected to do so.

It is difficult to make this point in a suitably balanced way. Commentators too often stake out one extreme position or the other. Some people think the market mechanism is inherently unfair and biased by the greed of those who run its enterprises and look to the government to cure all economic ills. Others deplore government intervention and consider the public sector to be the home of every sort of inefficiency, graft, and bureaucratic stultification. The truth, as usual, lies somewhere in between.

Governments, like humans, are inherently imperfect. The political process leads to compromises that sometimes bear little resemblance to rational decisions. For example, legislators' versions of the policies suggested by economic analysis are sometimes mere caricatures of the economists' ideas.

Yet often the problems engendered by an unfettered economy are too serious to be left to the free market. The problems of inflation, environmental decay, and the provision of public goods are cases in point. In such instances, government intervention is likely to yield substantial benefits to the general public. However, even when *some* government action is clearly warranted, it may be difficult or impossible to calculate the *optimal* degree of governmental intervention. There is, then, the danger of intervention so excessive that the society might have been better off without it.

In other areas, the market mechanism is likely to work reasonably well, and small imperfections do not constitute adequate justification for government intervention. In any event, *even where government action is appropriate, we must consider market-like instruments as one possible way to correct market mechanism deficiencies.* The tax incentives described earlier in our discussion of externalities are an outstanding example of what we have in mind.

THE COST DISEASE OF SOME VITAL SERVICES IN THE ECONOMY

As our final example, we consider next a problem that is not strictly a *failure* of the market mechanism. Rather, it is a case where the market's behaviour creates that illusion and often leads to ill-advised *government* action that threatens the general welfare. This problem concerns dramatically rising prices, as typified by college and university tuition fees. As a reader of this book, you are well aware that your attendance at school is likely to cost as much as $5,000 per year. Back in the early 1970s, when the two Canadian authors of this book started university, tuition fees were only about $600. In 1988–1989, average undergraduate tuition fees in Canadian universities were $1,185 and they almost quadrupled by 2007–2008, reaching $4,524—an average increase of 7 percent per year during this 19-year period. By contrast, general inflation was at only 2.4 percent per year during the same time period. That is a dramatic rise in cost, and it has not hit only tuition fees. In this section, we will examine the reasons for these rising prices and other disturbing developments in the affected segments of the economy.

Deteriorating Personal Services

Over the years, general standards of living have increased and our material possessions have multiplied. But at the same time, our communities have experienced a decline in the quality of a variety of public and private services. Throughout the world, streets and subways, for example, have grown increasingly dirty. Bus, train, and postal services have all been cut back. Amazingly enough, in the 1800s in suburban London, there were twelve mail deliveries per day on weekdays and one on Sundays! Today, mail service in the United Kingdom is hardly a subject of admiration anymore.

Parallel cutbacks have occurred in the quality of private services. Milk once used to be delivered to homes every day, and it was not necessary to push five buttons successively on the telephone to get to speak to a human being at the bank. Doctors almost never visit patients at home anymore. In many areas a house call, which 50 years ago was a commonplace event, now occurs only rarely. Another example, although undoubtedly a matter for less general concern, is the quality of food served in restaurants. Even some of the most elegant and expensive restaurants serve frozen and reheated meals—charging high prices for what amounts to little more than TV dinners.

Personal Services Are Getting More Expensive

Perhaps most distressing of all, and closely connected with the problems just described, is the persistent and dramatic rise in the *cost* of what we call *personal services*—services that require face-to-face, in-person interaction between the supplier and the consumer, such as health care and education. As a college or universiy student, you know how fast tuition fees have been increasing. But you may not realize that the cost of a hospital stay has been going up even more rapidly. Worse still, the rising cost of health care has endangered adequate and timely universal access to health services. These cost increases have made health care a prime subject of debate in political contests, not only in Canada but in almost every other industrialized country.

Virtually every major industrial nation has tried to prevent health care costs from rising faster than its economy's overall rate of inflation, but none has succeeded, as Figure 4 shows. In this graph, the bar for each country shows its average yearly rate of increase in real (inflation-adjusted) health care spending per person between 1970 and 2005. In some countries, real health care costs have grown even faster than in Canada and the United States.

The cost of education has a similar record—costs per pupil have increased substantially in most countries. Figure 5 shows the average yearly rate of increase in real (inflation-adjusted) education spending per pupil in elementary and secondary schools in a number of countries between 1985 and 2002. The rate of increase in Canada has been below 1 percent in real terms, the lowest of the OECD countries shown. But this is rather unusual, as the other countries, including the United States, have seen the costs of

FIGURE 4

Increased Health Spending per Person between 1970 and 2005

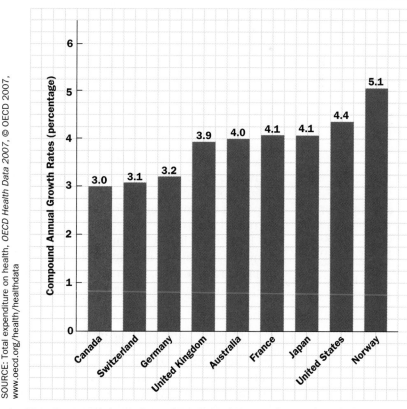

SOURCE: Total expenditure on health, *OECD Health Data 2007*, © OECD 2007, www.oecd.org/health/healthdata

Note: Compounded annual growth rates in real terms (inflation-adjusted); for Japan, the data are for 1970 to 2004; for Australia, the data are for 1969 to 2004.

NEL

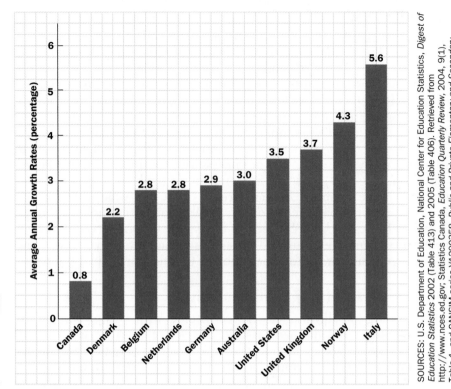

SOURCES: U.S. Department of Education, National Center for Education Statistics, *Digest of Education Statistics* 2002 (Table 413) and 2005 (Table 406). Retrieved from http://www.nces.ed.gov; Statistics Canada, *Education Quarterly Review*, 2004, 9(1), Table 1, and CANSIM series V1200358, *Public and Private Elementary and Secondary Education Expenditures*, and V735319, *Consumer Price Index*.

FIGURE 5

Increased Education Spending per Pupil (Primary and Secondary Schools) Between 1985 and 2002

Note: Average annual growth rates in real terms (inflation-adjusted); the average annual growth rate for Canada is for 1986 to 2001.

their education services rise at a much faster pace than overall inflation. Persistent cost increases have also plagued other services such as postal delivery and libraries. The soaring costs of education, health care, and police and fire protection place a terrible financial burden on provincial/territorial and municipal budgets.

■ Why Are These "In-Person" Services Costing So Much More?

What accounts for the ever-increasing costs? Are they attributable to inefficiencies in government management or to political corruption? Perhaps to some degree to both. But there is also another reason—one that cannot be avoided by any municipal administration no matter how pure its conduct and efficient its bureaucrats and one that affects personal services provided by the private sector of the economy just as severely as it does the public sector. The common influence underlying all of these problems of rising cost and deterioration in service quality, which is *economic* in character and expected to grow even more serious with time, has been called the **cost disease of the personal services.**

The **cost disease of the personal services** is the tendency of the costs and prices of these services to rise persistently faster than those of the average output in the economy.

This "cost disease" stems from the basic nature of personal services: They usually require face-to-face interaction between those who provide the service and those who consume it. Doctors, teachers, and librarians all engage in activities that require direct, in-person interaction. Moreover, the quality of the service deteriorates if less personal time is provided by doctors, teachers, and librarians to each user of their services.

■ Uneven Labour Productivity Growth in the Economy

In other parts of the economy, such as manufacturing, no direct personal contact between the consumer and the producer is required. For instance, the buyer of an automobile usually has no idea who worked on its assembly and could not care less how much labour time went into its production. A labour-saving innovation in auto production need not imply a reduction in product quality. As a result, over the years it has proved far easier for technological change to save labour in manufacturing than to save labour in providing many services. Labour productivity (output per hour worked) in Canadian manufacturing increased by nearly 2 percent per year between 1987 and 2006. In agriculture, labour productivity increased by 3 percent per year over the same period. By contrast, output per hour worked in both education services and health services actually declined by about 0.75 percent per year between 1987 and 2006.[3] Still, the yearly salaries of teachers have grown at approximately the same rate as those of the average worker; that is, salaries barely exceeded the rate of price inflation.[4]

These disparate productivity performances have grave consequences for prices. When manufacturing wages rise 2 percent, the cost of manufactured products need not rise because increased output per worker can make up for the rise in wages. But the nature of many personal services makes it very difficult to introduce labour-saving devices in those parts of the service sector. A 2 percent wage increase for teachers or police officers is not offset by higher productivity and must lead to an equivalent rise in municipal budgets. Similarly, a 2 percent wage increase for hairdressers must lead beauty salons to raise their prices.

In the long run, wages for all workers throughout the economy tend to go up and down together, for otherwise an activity whose wage rate falls seriously behind will tend to lose its labour force. So autoworkers and police officers will see their wages rise at roughly the same rate in the long run. But if productivity on the assembly line advances, while productivity in the police patrol car does not, then police protection grows ever more expensive, relative to manufacturing, as time goes on. Because productivity improvements are very difficult to achieve for most personal services, their costs can be expected to rise more rapidly, year in and year out, than the costs of manufactured products do. Over a period of several decades, this difference in the growth rate of costs of the two sectors adds up, making services enormously more expensive compared with manufactured goods. This imbalance explains why personal services have grown steadily more expensive compared to goods, and they are likely to continue to do so.

A Future of More Goods but Fewer Services: Is It Inevitable?

If some services continue to get ever more expensive in comparison to goods, the implications for life in the future are profound indeed. The cost disease portends a world in which the typical home contains an abundance of goods—luxuries and furnishings that we can hardly imagine. But it is a home surrounded by garbage and perhaps by violence. The cost disease also portends a future in which the services of doctors, teachers, and police officers are increasingly mass-produced and impersonal, and in which arts and crafts are increasingly supplied only by amateurs because the cost of professional work in these fields is too high.

But this future is by no means inevitable. To see why, we must first recognize that the problem's source, paradoxically, is the growth in our economy's productivity—or rather, the *unevenness* of that growth. Trash removal costs go up, not because garbage collectors become *less* efficient but because labour in automobile manufacturing becomes *more* efficient, thus enhancing the sanitation worker's potential value on the automotive assembly line. The sanitation worker's wages must go up to keep him at his garbage removal job.

But increasing productivity in goods manufacturing does *not* make a nation poorer. It does *not* make us unable to afford things that we could afford in the past. Indeed, increasing productivity (that is, more output from each work-hour) means that we can afford more of *all* things—televisions, electric toothbrushes, cell phones, *and* medical care, education, and other services.

---

[3] Centre for the Study of Living Standards, *Capital, Labour and Total Factor Productivity Tables by Province, 1987–2006, NAICS-based*, Table S7. Retrieved from http://www.csls.ca
[4] Statistics Canada. Based on *Teachers' salaries subindex*, CANSIM V102688; *Consumer price index*, CANSIM V735319; *Average weekly earnings*, CANSIM V1597104.

The role of services in the nation's future depends on how we order our priorities. If we value services sufficiently, we can have more and better services—at some sacrifice in the growth rate of manufactured goods. Whether that is a good choice for society is not for economists to say. But society *does* have a choice, and if we fail to exercise it, matters may proceed relentlessly toward a world in which material goods are abundant and many things that most people now consider primary requisites for a high quality of life are scarce.

Government May Make the Problem Worse

How does the cost disease relate to the central topic of this chapter—the market's performance and its implications for the government's economic role? Here the problem is that the market *does* give the appropriate price signals, but government is likely to misunderstand these signals and to make decisions that do not promote the public interest most effectively.

Health care is a good example. The cost disease itself is capable of causing health care costs (say, the price of a hospital stay) to rise more rapidly than the economy's inflation rate because medical care cannot be standardized enough to share in the productivity gains offered by automation and assembly lines. As a result, if we want to maintain standards of care in public hospitals, it is not enough to keep health care budgets growing at the economy's prevailing inflation rate. Those budgets must actually grow *faster* to prevent a decline in quality. For example, when the inflation rate is 2 percent per year, hospitals' budgets may need to increase by 4 percent annually.

In these circumstances, something may seem amiss to a provincial government that increases its hospitals' budgets by only 2 or 3 percent per year. Responsible lawmakers will doubtless be disturbed by the fact that the budget is growing steadily, outpacing the inflation rate, and yet standards of quality at public hospitals continue to slip. If the legislators do not realize that the cost disease is causing the problem, they will look for villains—greedy doctors, corrupt or inefficient hospital administrators, and so on. The net result, all too often, is a set of wasteful rules that hamper the freedom of action of hospitals and doctors inappropriately or that tighten hospital budgets below the levels that demands and costs would require if they were determined by the market mechanism rather than by government.

In many cases, *price restrictions* are proposed for sectors of the economy affected by the cost disease—for medical services, insurance services, and the like. As we know, such price restrictions may merely eliminate the symptoms of the disease, and they can create problems that are sometimes more serious than the disease itself.[5] For instance, it is sometimes said that, to cut down on health costs, governments ought to reduce the salaries of nurses and the fees of physicians. But this cure may lead to the emigration of Canadian nurses and physicians abroad, in particular to the United States, thus worsening the scarcity of health services in Canada. But while the salaries of physicians in Canada are lower than those of physicians in the United States, they are much higher than in Western Europe, for instance, in countries such as France, the United Kingdom, and Finland. Indeed, even within Canada, there are substantial discrepancies between the revenues of a medical doctor located in Alberta or British Columbia and one located in Quebec or Manitoba, whose average gross earnings are nearly $100,000 less per year.

The difficulty, from an economic standpoint, is to assess whether these discrepancies are truly due to market forces or if they arise as a result of acquired social status and more powerful medical associations that manage to get higher fees or salaries for their members from the rest of society. For example, as can be seen from Figure 6, physicians are scarcer in Manitoba than in British Columbia, but that does not stop medical doctors in British Columbia from earning about $100,000 more than their colleagues in Manitoba. Clearly, part of the problem of the Canadian health system arises from the fact that Canadian doctors can so easily be attracted to American high-tech hospitals offering high earnings.

---

[5] See Chapter 4, pages 62 and 77–83.

| FIGURE 6 | Number of Physicians per 100,000 Population by Province/Territory, Canada, 2006 |

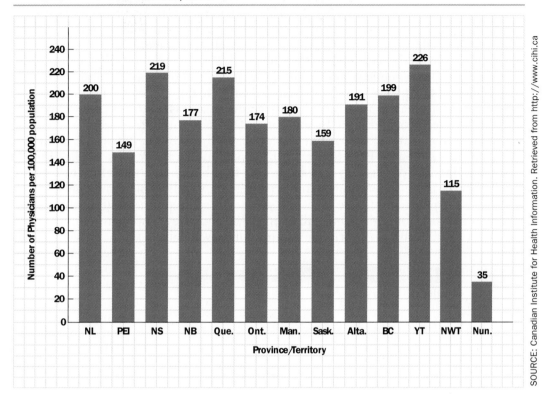

SOURCE: Canadian Institute for Health Information. Retrieved from http://www.cihi.ca

THE PUZZLE RESOLVED: *Explaining the Rising Costs of Canadian Health Care*

This brings us back to the puzzle with which we began the chapter: Why have price controls failed to brake the rise in Canadian health care costs? The answer is that the medical care system in Canada, like the health care system in every other industrial country, is struggling with the effects of the cost disease of the personal services. As we have just seen, legislative fiat cannot abolish the productivity-growth patterns that force health care costs to rise persistently and universally faster than the overall inflation rate. The government-imposed price restrictions on doctors' fees and hospital budgets have, in fact, led to long waiting lists for Canadians who need high-tech medical procedures and have reduced patients' access to high-priced specialists. Some Canadians go to the United States to have surgeries performed more quickly. The provincial governments are also trying to hold down costs by squeezing the list of services covered by public health insurance, dropping such things as vision tests and physical therapy, and forcing Canadians to pay for these things out of their own pockets. The overall quality of service apparently remains high, but the costs have risen persistently more rapidly than the overall inflation rate, just as in the United States, where there is no government-sponsored universal health care program.

With the health services of all countries being afflicted by the cost disease of the personal services, various changes have been suggested. In the United States, where total health expenditures in 2004 represent 15.4 percent of GDP, there have been long-standing suggestions to move toward a universal health care program similar to that in Canada, where the health expenditures-to-GDP ratio is only 9.8 percent.

In Canada, where doctors must either work within the publicly funded system or opt out entirely, treating only patients who pay with their own money, it has been proposed that the health care system be privatized or, rather, that a parallel *insurable* private health care system be created—a kind of mixed system that already exists in most, if not all, countries that have universal health coverage.

Opponents to this change fear that the public system will gradually be dismantled, with users of the public system being condemned to poor services and even longer waiting times. They point out that *health-adjusted* life expectancy is 74.0 and 70.1 years for Canadian females and males, respectively, whereas it is only 71.3 and 67.2 years for their American counterparts. In addition, infant mortality rates in the United States are much higher than they are in Canada or in European countries with universal health care systems.[6] Privatizing health expenditures, besides its implications for income distribution, may do little to provide health services more efficiently. On the other hand, those who favour partial privatization, which would grant Canadians the right to get private insurance on health services already covered by the public system, argue that such a mixed system will help reduce both the cost pressures on the public system and the current overly long waiting lists (see Table 4). To help achieve this, other health experts favour the introduction of limited user fees, as they already exist in many European countries.

If Canadians are unwilling to accept a parallel insurable private system or the introduction of user fees, then they should realize that health services are subjected to the cost disease of the personal services and that, as such, and as the Canadian population gets older, they should be ready to pay more taxes to finance these vital services.

TABLE 4

Health Care Experiences

	Australia	Canada	New Zealand	United Kingdom	United States	Germany
Wait to be seen in emergency room						
Less than 1 hour	47%	**39%**	55%	50%	53%	66%
4 hours or more	17%	**24%**	12%	14%	12%	4%
Wait for an appointment to see a doctor						
Same day	49%	**23%**	58%	45%	30%	56%
Next day	17%	**13%**	23%	16%	17%	13%
6 days or more (or never)	10%	**36%**	3%	15%	23%	13%
Wait for an appointment with a specialist						
Less than 1 week	11%	**10%**	17%	11%	20%	27%
4 months or more	46%	**57%**	40%	60%	23%	22%
Wait for elective surgery						
Less than 1 month	48%	**15%**	32%	25%	53%	59%
4 months or more	19%	**33%**	20%	41%	8%	6%

SOURCE: Nadeem Esmail and Michael Walker, *How Good Is Canadian Health Care? 2006 Report: An International Comparison of Health Care Systems* (Vancouver: Fraser Institute, December 2006). Retrieved from http://www.fraserinstitute.ca/admin/books/files/HowGoodHealthCare2006.pdf. Reprinted by permission of the Fraser Institute.

[6] All of these numbers are taken from the Institute of Health Economics, Alberta, *IHE in Your Pocket: A Handbook of Health Economic Statistics*, 2006.

THE MARKET SYSTEM ON BALANCE

This chapter, like Chapter 14 has deliberately offered a rather unbalanced assessment of the market mechanism. In Chapter 14, we extolled the market's virtues; in this chapter, we catalogued its vices. We come out concluding that the market is either very, very good or it is very, very bad.

There seems to be nothing *moderate* about the quality of performance of a market system. As a means of achieving efficiency in the production of ordinary consumer goods and responding to changes in consumer preferences, it is unparalleled. It is, in fact, difficult to overstate the accomplishments of the price system in these areas. By contrast, the market has proved itself incapable of coping with business fluctuations, income inequality, or the consequences of monopoly and oligopoly. It has proved to be a very poor allocator of resources among outputs that generate external costs and external benefits, and it has shown itself to be incapable of arranging for the provision of public goods. Some of the most urgent problems that plague our society—the deterioration of services in the cities, the despoliation of our atmosphere, the social unrest attributable to poverty—can be ascribed in part to one or another of these market system shortcomings.

Most economists conclude from these observations that although the market mechanism is virtually irreplaceable, the public interest nevertheless requires considerable modifications in the way it works. Proposals designed to deal directly with the problems of poverty, monopoly, and resource allocation over time abound in economic literature. All of them call for the government to intervene in the economy, either by supplying directly those goods and services that, it is believed, private enterprise does not supply in adequate amounts, or by seeking to influence the workings of the economy more indirectly through regulation. We discussed many of these programs in earlier chapters; we will explain others in future chapters.

■ EPILOGUE: THE UNFORGIVING MARKET, ITS GIFT OF ABUNDANCE, AND ITS DANGEROUS FRIENDS

As we said at the end of Chapter 14, economists' analysis of the free market's accomplishments, although valid enough, may fail to emphasize its central contribution. The same can be said of their analysis of the market's shortcomings.

The market's major contribution to the general welfare may well be its stimulation of *productivity*, which has yielded an abundance of consumer goods, contributed to increases in human longevity, created new products, expanded education, and raised standards of living to levels undreamed of in earlier societies. This is an accomplishment that is yet to be discussed (see Chapter 16). The main shortcoming of the market, according to many observers, lies in the arena of justice and injustice, a subject that economists are no more competent to address than anyone else. The perception that markets are cruel and unjust springs from the very heart of the mechanism. The market mechanism has sometimes been described appropriately as the profit system, because it works by richly rewarding those who succeed in introducing attractive new products or in increasing efficiency sufficiently to permit sharp price reductions of other items. At the same time, it is unforgiving to those who fail, subjecting them to bankruptcy and perhaps to poverty.

Both the wealth awarded to those who succeed and the drastic treatment accorded to those who fail are main sources of the markets' productive power. But they also generate disenchantment and opposition. Consider what has happened in the newly "marketized" countries of Eastern Europe. Predictably, as enterprise in these countries was freed from government control, a number of wildly successful entrepreneurs have earned high incomes, leading to widespread resentment among the populace and calls for restrictions on entrepreneurial earnings. These critics do not seem to realize that a market without substantial rewards to successful entrepreneurs is a market whose engine has been weakened, if not altogether removed.

It must be admitted however that the wealth amassed by some of these successful Russian and Eastern European entrepreneurs was acquired not through productive entrepreneurship but through deception and the acquisition of previously state-owned assets at bargain prices, with the help of accomplices within the government. But of course this is not much different from the North American robber barons of the past, who, beyond their great entrepreneurial qualities, used unfair business practices and political protection to acquire vast industrial and financial empires.

Indeed, efficient and effectively competitive markets often elicit support from groups that, at the same time, do their best to undermine that competition. For example, regulators who seek to prevent "excessive competition," and politicians in other countries who arrange for the sale of government enterprises to private owners only to constrain decision making by the new owners at every turn, are, in fact, doing their best to keep markets from working. When the general public demands price controls on gasoline, rents, and health care services, it is expressing its unwillingness to accept the free market's decisions. Businesspeople who tirelessly proclaim their support for the market system, but who seek to acquire the monopoly power that can distort its activities, are doing the same thing. In short, the market has many professed supporters who genuinely believe in its virtues but whose behaviour poses a constant threat to its effectiveness. In other words, a market economy is made up of competing firms that try very hard to eliminate competitors. Competition is good for consumers who will benefit from lower prices, but too much competition, in the form of price wars, for instance, will result in bankruptcies, company closures, and job losses, and will eventually lead to less competition and the appearance of oligopolies.

We cannot take for granted the success of the newly introduced market mechanism in Eastern Europe. The Russian economy, in its transition from communist government control, has come very slowly out of turmoil, as have other economies in Eastern Europe. Even in the older free-enterprise economies, we cannot simply assume that the market will emerge unscathed from the dangerous embrace of its most vocal supporters. The capitalist system does not function in a vacuum. Even in the United States, which is considered to be the most extreme example of free-market capitalism, there are many regulations either imposed by governments or self-imposed by trade associations and professional associations. These regulations help ensure that entrepreneurs pursue fair business practices.

SUMMARY

1. At least seven major imperfections are associated with the market mechanism:

   a. Inequality of income distribution

   b. Fluctuations in economic activity (inflation and unemployment)

   c. Monopolistic output restrictions

   d. Beneficial and detrimental externalities

   e. Inadequate provision of public goods

   f. Misallocation of resources between present and future

   g. Deteriorating quality and rising costs of personal services

2. Efficient resource allocation is a matter of balancing the benefits of producing more of one good against the benefits of devoting the required inputs to some other good's production.

3. A **detrimental externality** occurs when an economic activity incidentally does harm to others who are not directly involved in the activity. A **beneficial externality** occurs when an economic activity incidentally creates benefits for others.

4. When an activity causes a detrimental externality, the activity's **marginal social cost** (including the harm it does to others) must be greater than the **marginal private cost** to those who carry on the activity. The opposite will be true when a beneficial externality occurs.

5. If a product's manufacture causes detrimental externalities, its price will generally not include all of the marginal social

cost it causes, because part of the cost will be borne by others. The opposite is true for beneficial externalities.

6. The market will therefore tend to overallocate resources to the production of goods that cause detrimental externalities and underallocate resources to the production of goods that create beneficial externalities.

7. A **public good** is a commodity (such as the guiding beam of a coastal lighthouse) that is not depleted by additional users. It is often difficult to exclude anyone from the benefits of a public good, even those who refuse to pay for it. A **private good**, in contrast, is characterized by both **excludability** and **depletability**.

8. Free-enterprise firms generally will not produce a public good, even if it is extremely useful to the community, because they cannot charge money for the use of the good.

9. Many observers believe that the market often shortchanges the future, particularly when it makes irreversible decisions that destroy natural resources. Global warming may be such an instance.

10. **Transaction costs,** in particular information costs and bargaining costs when they are overly high, may stop the market from reaching the most efficient solution.

11. Complex and large-scale enterprises such as huge corporations cannot be run day to day or effectively controlled directly by their owners, the **principals.** So they hire **agents** to run the enterprises on their behalf. The danger is that the agents will operate the enterprises so as to favour their own interests rather than those of the principals.

12. Because personal services—such as education, medical care, and police protection—are activities whose inherent value depends on face-to-face, in-person interaction, they are not amenable to labour-saving innovations; they suffer from a **cost disease**. That is, their costs tend to rise persistently and considerably more rapidly than costs in the economy as a whole, where faster productivity increases offset rising input costs. The result can be a distortion in the supply of services by the government; that is, fewer services or services of lesser quality. Examples are public schooling and health services, when the rising cost of such services is attributed to greed and mismanagement or when taxpayers become frustrated by the tax increases that these rising costs generate.

KEY TERMS

Production possibilities frontier   341

Resource misallocation   342

Externalities (detrimental and beneficial)   342

Marginal social cost (MSC)   343

Marginal private cost (MPC)   343

Marginal social benefit (MSB)   344

Marginal private benefit (MPB)   344

Public good   348

Private good   348

Depletability   348

Excludability   348

Transaction costs   352

Rent seeking   353

Moral hazard   353

Principals   354

Agents   354

Stock options   354

Cost disease of the personal services   358

TEST YOURSELF

1. What is the opportunity cost to society of a 100-kilometre trip of a truck? Why may the price of the gasoline used by the truck not adequately represent that opportunity cost?

2. Suppose that, because of a new disease that attacks coffee plants, far more labour and other inputs are required to harvest a kilogram of coffee than before. How may that change affect the efficient allocation of resources between tea and coffee? How would the prices of coffee and tea react in a free market?

3. Give some examples of goods whose production causes detrimental externalities and some examples of goods whose production creates beneficial externalities.

4. Compare cleaning a dormitory room with cleaning the atmosphere of a city. Which is a public good and which is a private good? Why?

5. **(More difficult)** A firm holds a patent that is estimated to be worth $20 million. The patent is repeatedly challenged in the courts by a large number of (rent-seeking) firms, each hoping to grab away the patent. If anyone is free to challenge the patent so that there is free entry into the litigation process, how much will end up being spent in the legal battles? (*Hint:* Under perfect competition, should firms expect to earn any economic profit?)

DISCUSSION QUESTIONS

1. Give some other examples of public goods. In each case, explain why additional users do not deplete the good and why it is difficult to exclude people from using it.

2. Think about the goods and services that your local government provides. Which are "public goods" as economists use the term?

3. Explain why the services of a lighthouse are sometimes used as an example of a public good.

4. Explain why education is not a very satisfactory example of a public good.

5. In recent decades, college and university tuition costs have risen more rapidly than the general price level, even though the wages of the teaching staff have failed to keep pace with the price level. Can you explain why?

6. Discuss the advantages and disadvantages of the current Canadian health system as you understand it. What change, if any, would you recommend? Try to ascertain all of the economic and social implications of your suggested change.

16

THE CASE FOR THE MARKET SYSTEM II: INNOVATION AND GROWTH

Canada's economic competitiveness depends on scientific and technological development and also on the people responsible for this development, especially those engaged in R&D. . . . In 2004, the majority, (64%, or 126,670) of personnel engaged in R&D were employed in business enterprises. . . .

STATISTICS CANADA, *SCIENCE STATISTICS*, JANUARY 2007 EDITION, P. 6.

An activity is said to generate a beneficial or detrimental **externality** if that activity causes incidental benefits or damages to others not directly involved in the activity, and no corresponding compensation is provided to or paid by those who generate the externality.

The past several chapters have tried to provide a balanced evaluation of the market, describing both its shortcomings and its accomplishments. Among its defects we have listed attributes such as vulnerability to monopoly power, **externalities** such as damage to the environment, and a propensity to underproduce public goods. On the virtuous side, we showed how the market can allocate resources more efficiently and more in accord with consumer desires than planning and central direction. But we have saved the best for last—the market's incredible performance in terms of *innovation* and growth, in which it has far exceeded any other type of economy in history, whether ancient or recent.

Although growth is often viewed as a macroeconomic topic, inventions are provided by individuals or individual laboratories, and are brought to market by individual firms. So understanding innovation and its contribution to growth requires microeconomic analysis of the behaviour of individual innovators and firms. This chapter will indicate the magnitude of the market's growth accomplishment and will use our microeconomic tools to analyze how the market has produced that achievement. Part of the discussion may be considered both as a review of some of the analytic tools we have used before and as an additional illustration of the wide variety of subjects they can be used to investigate.

CONTENTS

THE MARKET ECONOMY'S INCREDIBLE GROWTH RECORD

Per-capita income in an economy is the average income of all people in that economy.

The **productivity** of an economy is the value of all goods and services produced there, divided by the total labour time devoted to the economy's productive activities.

The **Industrial Revolution** is the stream of new technology and the resulting growth of output that began in England toward the end of the eighteenth century.

Capitalism is an economic system in which most of the production process is controlled by private firms operating in markets. The investors in these firms (called *capitalists*) own the firms.

In the free-market economies, the growth in **per-capita income** (average income per person) and **productivity** (output per hour of work) has been so enormous that we can hardly comprehend its magnitude. In contrast, average growth rates of per-capita incomes probably approximated *zero* for about 1,500 years before the **Industrial Revolution** (around the time of the conquest of New France by the British in the early 1760s). In 1763, even the wealthiest consumers in England, then the world's richest country, could purchase perhaps only a half-dozen consumer goods that had not been available more than a thousand years earlier in ancient Rome. These new products included (highly inaccurate) hunting guns, (highly inaccurate) watches, paper with printed material on it, window glass, and very little else. No sounds had ever been recorded, so we can never hear the voices of Montcalm and Wolfe on the Plains of Abraham during the Battle of Quebec. No one had travelled on land faster than on horseback. Messages delivered from the Old World to the New required weeks and even months, so that battles were sometimes fought after peace treaties had been signed. And Roman citizens enjoyed a number of amenities, such as hot baths and paved roads, that had practically disappeared long before the French Revolution in 1789.

The economic conditions of the lower economic classes before the Industrial Revolution and for quite a period beyond it are difficult for us to grasp. Regular famines—at least once per decade on average, with starvation widespread and corpses littering the streets—only began to disappear in the eighteenth century. Still, famines continued occasionally well into the nineteenth, and not only in Ireland. For example, in relatively wealthy Belgium, "During the great crisis of 1846, the newspapers would tell daily of cases of death from starvation. . . .[In one town] cases became so frequent that the local policeman was given the job of calling at all houses each day to see if the inhabitants were still alive."[1] Even the living standards of the upper classes were far from enviable.

By comparison, in the past two centuries, per-capita incomes in the typical **capitalist** economy have risen by amounts ranging from several hundred to several thousand percent. Recent decades have yielded an unmatched outpouring of new products and services: colour television, the computer, jet aircraft, the VCR and DVD player, the microwave oven, the hand-held calculator, the BlackBerry, the iPhone, the iPod, and MP3 player, and so on and so on. And the flood of new products continues.[2] Surely part of the reason for the collapse of most of the world's communist regimes was their citizens' desire to participate in the growth miracle of the capitalist economies.

During the twentieth century, the real income of an average Canadian grew by a factor of more than seven.[3] Looked at another way, an average Canadian family living around 1900 could afford only *one-seventh* of the food, clothing, housing, and other amenities that constitute the standard of living today. The change is really incredible. Just try to imagine how your family's life would be changed if it lost more than six out of seven dollars from its consumption expenditure.

We can look at this enormous economic progress from another angle: by examining how much work it takes to acquire the things we purchase. For example, in 1919, the average Canadian worker had to labour nearly an hour to buy a pound of chicken. At today's wages and poultry prices, less than five minutes of labour is required for the purpose! Figure 1 shows how much cheaper a variety of snack foods have become over the past century, as measured in minutes of work.

Food is not the only item that has become much less costly in terms of the labour time needed to pay for it. Figure 2 shows the great cost reductions in terms of minutes

---

[1] Adrien De Meeüs, *History of the Belgians* (New York: Frederick A. Praeger, 1962), p. 305.

[2] "Could the Emperor Tiberius have eaten grapes in January? Could the Emperor Napoleon have crossed the Atlantic in a night? . . . Could Thomas Aquinas have . . . dispatched [a letter] to 1,000 recipients with the touch of a key, and begun to receive replies within the hour?" (J. Bradford DeLong, *The Economic History of the Twentieth Century: Slouching Toward Utopia?*, Chapter 2, p. 3, draft copy. Retrieved from http://www.j-bradford-delong.net).

[3] Real income is not measured in actual dollars but in dollars whose purchasing power is kept unchanged.

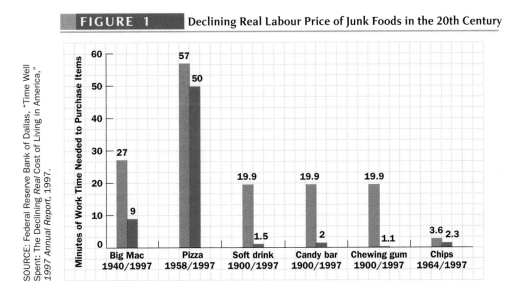

FIGURE 1 Declining Real Labour Price of Junk Foods in the 20th Century

SOURCE: Federal Reserve Bank of Dallas, "Time Well Spent: The Declining *Real* Cost of Living in America," *1997 Annual Report*, 1997.

of work needed to aquire various types of electronic equipment—a cut of 98 percent in the cost of a colour TV between 1954 and 1997, 96 percent in the cost of a VCR between 1972 and 1997, and 99 percent in the cost of a microwave oven between 1947 and 1997. Of course, the most sensational decrease of all has been in the cost of computers. Computer capability is standardized in terms of the number of MIPS (millions of instructions per second) that the computer is capable of handling. In 2008, it cost about 1 minute of labour per 1 MIPS capacity and the number keeps falling. In 1984, it cost the wages of 52 *hours* of labour; in 1970, the cost was 1.24 *lifetimes* of labour; and in 1944, the price was a barely believable 733,000 *lifetimes* of labour.[4] In this chapter, we will investigate the free market's extraordinary record of growth and economic progress, although it should be recognized that the magic of productivity growth has not succeeded in invading every sector of the economy, as discussed at the end of

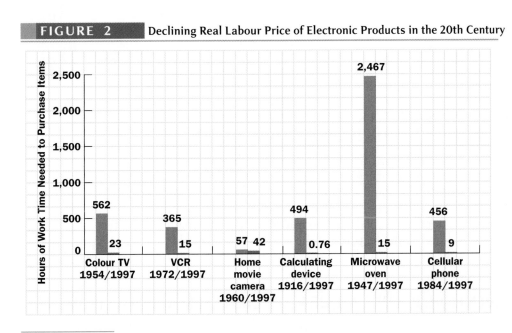

FIGURE 2 Declining Real Labour Price of Electronic Products in the 20th Century

---

[4] All of these figures on changing labour-value prices (except the 2008 figure) are taken from Federal Reserve Bank of Dallas, 1997, "Time Well Spent: The Declining Real Cost of Living in America", *1997 Annual Report*.

FIGURE 3 | Work Time Needed to Buy One Year of University Education in Canada in 2007 versus 1990 and 2001

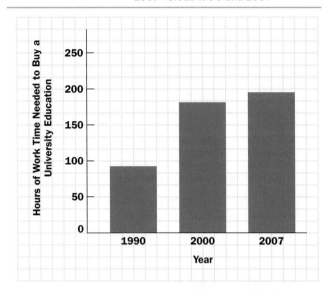

SOURCES: Statistics Canada, "University tuition fees (including compulsory fees)," http://www.statscan.ca/Daily/English/ 060901/d060901a.htm, http://www.statisticscanada.com/ Daily/English/080206/p080206.htm, "Employment, earnings and hours," Catalogue no. 72-002-XIB (table 9); Centre for the Study of Living Standards, "Aggregate Income and Productivity Trends, 1961-2006" (Table 4), http://www.csls.ca

Chapter 15. In particular, the cost of a university education seems to have escaped the cost-reducing effect of productivity growth. Figure 3 shows the evolution of tuition fees for Canadian students. Between 1990 and 2007, the cost of one year of university education, in terms of hours of work, has doubled and risen from 93 to 195 labour hours at the average Canadian wage.

The history of the growth in income per person can be summed up with a graph depicting estimates of the United Kingdom's **GDP** per capita for five centuries (Figure 4). It is clear that the pattern of the graph is characterized by a rising slope that grows dramatically ever steeper.

GDP (gross domestic product) is a measure of the total amount the economy produces domestically in a year.

FIGURE 4 | Real GDP per Capita in the United Kingdom, 1500–2006

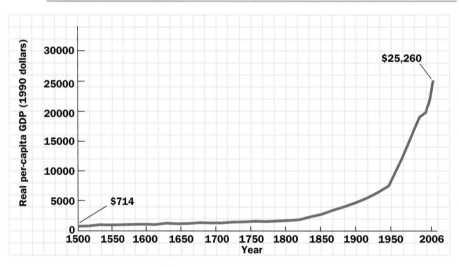

SOURCE: Angus Maddison, *The World Economy: A Millennial Perspective* (Paris: Organisation for Economic Cooperation and Development, 2001), Table B-21, p. 264; EconStats, www.econstats.com/weo/C171.htm.

THE BIG PUZZLE: *What Accounts for the Market System's Incredible Growth Record?*

The conclusion from all this is that the explosion of growth and innovation of the past two centuries is the most sensational economic accomplishment of the market-based economies. Its secret is what the developing countries would most like to learn from the experience of the world's wealthy nations. But that is the basic puzzle: How does one explain this extraordinary performance? The rest of the chapter seeks to describe the features of the market economy that played the primary role in that success story.

INNOVATION, NOT INVENTION, IS THE UNIQUE MARKET SYSTEM ACCOMPLISHMENT

The search for explanations of the capitalist growth miracle must focus on its unprecedented outpouring of innovation, and to that we will soon turn. But first it is important to distinguish the key term *innovation*, from the related word *invention*.

Invention is used by economists to mean what it usually does: the creation of new products or processes or at least the ideas that underlie them. But the term **innovation** means more than that; it refers to the entire extended process of which invention is only the initial step. Innovation includes development of the invention's design to the point at which it is ready for practical use, its introduction to the market, and its subsequent utilization by the economy. The distinction is critical here because it underlies much of the difference between the accomplishments of the capitalist economy and those of any and all of its predecessors, including those earlier economies with remarkable records of invention.

Invention is nothing new. Ancient China, for example, invented paper, the printing press, paper money, playing cards, the spinning wheel, the umbrella, and an elaborate water clock, to name just a few. And at least 800 years before the Industrial Revolution, China had invented piston bellows for making steel, along with gunpowder, suspension bridges, drills for natural gas, the decimal system, and the abacus. Yet China did not conquer the world despite these earlier inventions. Why?

Despite China's talent for the creation of novel technology, its performance in adoption and utilization of these inventions was hardly outstanding. More than once, inventions were diverted to amusement rather than productive use, or, like the wondrous water clock, soon forgotten.[5] Even in the Soviet Union, with its cadre of very capable scientists and engineers, there is evidence of a respectable record of invention, but a remarkably poor record of utilization of these inventions—except in military activity. The reason is that the economic institutions in both ancient China and the Soviet Union not only failed to offer incentives for innovative activity, but actually provided strong motivation for its determined avoidance. In China, inventions often were confiscated by the government, with no reward for the inventors. In the Soviet Union, factory managers resisted the installation of improved equipment or the adoption of improved products because the necessary retooling period could cut down the factory's production, on which the manager's reward was based. In short, although the free market's record of invention is noteworthy, it is its performance in innovation that is unique.

Invention is the creation of new products or processes or the ideas that underlie them.

Innovation is the process that begins with invention and includes improvement to prepare the invention for practical use and marketing of the invention or its products.

◼ SOURCES OF MARKET INNOVATION: THE ROLE OF THE ENTREPRENEUR

There are many obvious sources of innovation. Some innovations are contributed by *universities* and *government research agencies*, which are not inherently market-driven. Then there are the well-known products of *individual inventors*, such as Alexander Graham Bell. Finally, there are the outputs of industrial laboratories in *giant corporations*, for instance, the creation of the Java open-source programming language by Calgary-born James Gosling, in 1994, while part of a development team at the multinational firm Sun Microsystems. These last two sources—the private entrepreneur and the giant corporations—clearly are directly embedded in the workings of the market economy, and it is on them that we will focus.

Here, we use the term **entrepreneur** to refer to an individual who organizes a new business firm. We will deal primarily with the creators of firms that offer new products or new productive technology, that is, with individuals who establish *innovative* firms. Until the end of the nineteenth century, invention was largely the work of independent inventors and their entrepreneur associates who brought the invention to market (though in a number of cases both roles were played by the same individual).

There have always been imaginative, enterprising, and risk-taking individuals who followed the most effective routes to acquisition of wealth, power, and prestige. But the methods they used for the purpose were very different from those that became the norm in the capitalist era. They often sought advancement through military careers supporting the ruling monarch, or as independent robber barons, or organized private

An **entrepreneur** is an individual who organizes a new business firm, particularly a firm that offers new products or new productive technology.

---

[5] This persisted into a much more recent era. Westerners bringing mechanical clocks as gifts to the Chinese emperors found that timekeeping accuracy elicited little appreciation, but marching or dancing figures run by the clockworks were highly valued.

armies as business enterprises and hired them out for money, or they undertook warfare on their own for the wealth they could capture. Sometimes the enterprising individuals sought economic success by way of careers in the government bureaucracy or in the church hierarchy. And such varied activities of enterprising individuals have not disappeared today: Who would deny that a high official in a dictatorial government or a godfather in a Mafioso organization can be enterprising and grow rich? But these forms of entrepreneurial activity rarely lead to increases in productivity of the economy.

In precapitalist societies, the more modern forms of productivity-increasing entrepreneurship were virtually prevented by regimes in which any property accumulated by commercial and productive activity was constantly threatened by government expropriation, and where organizations such as the medieval guilds could punish anyone who attempted to set up in business as a competitor, particularly if that person offered improved productive techniques or innovative products that threatened the guild's monopoly.[6] Until the century after Shakespeare's time, patent monopolies were often awarded by the monarchs, but were given to personal friends of the king and their relatives rather than the inventors. Only with the adoption of laws protecting property from expropriation, enforcing contracts, and providing patents only to inventors could modern entrepreneurship flourish. In what is now Canada, the first patents for inventors were granted in the 1820s. At Confederation, the 1867 British North America Act assigned exclusive legislative authority on patents to the federal government. Initially, Canadian patents could be obtained only by Canadians, but this privilege was extended to foreign inventors by the end of the nineteenth century. Canadian patents are now valid for 20 years.

Breakthrough Invention and the Entrepreneurial Firm

Individual inventors and entrepreneurs continued to be the primary source of innovation in the market economies until the end of the nineteenth century, when large corporations began to play a critical role in the process. But the part played by large corporations is very different from that of the more freewheeling and flexible small enterprises. Research activity in large business organizations is inherently cautious and focuses on small, relatively limited improvements in current technology. The big established firms tend to avoid the great risks that revolutionary breakthroughs involve. The true breakthrough inventions, rather, are often still the domain of small or newly founded enterprises, guided by enterprising owners, although success of an invention can rapidly transform a startup firm into a business giant.

There is no clear boundary between inventions that can be considered revolutionary breakthroughs and those that are "merely" cumulative incremental improvements, but some inventions clearly fall into the former category. For example, electric light, alternating electric current, the internal combustion engine, and the electronic computer must surely be deemed revolutionary. In contrast, successive models of washing machines and refrigerators—with each model more convenient to use and offering more gadgets—clearly constitute a sequence of incremental improvements.

There is a striking degree of asymmetry between small and large firms in their introduction of breakthrough versus incremental invention. A disproportionate number of breakthrough innovations have been carried out by small firms. The list spans the range from A to Z, from air conditioning to the zipper, not to forget the defibrillator, the heart valve, the pacemaker, soft contact lens, and oral contraceptives, and also the airplane, the helicopter, hydraulic brakes, audiotape recorders, FM radio, integrated circuits, microprocessors, personal computers, and portable computers. Some of these have been introduced by Canadians, as shown in Table 1, which gives the 2007 ranking of the 50 greatest Canadian inventions ever, along with the names of their inventors, according to CBC TV viewers. (See also the box "Entrepreneurship and Canadian Inventions").

---

[6] In the Middle Ages, unions of employer craftsmen, called *guilds*, controlled various types of production in a community. An example is the Fishmongers' Guild of London.

TABLE 1
The Greatest Canadian Inventions

1.	Insulin, treatment for diabetes [1921, Frederick Banting, Charles Best]	27.	Pablum [1930, Alan Brown, Theodore Drake, Frederick Tisdall]
2.	Telephone [1876, Alexander Graham Bell]	28.	Lacrosse [First Peoples]
3.	Light bulb [1874, Henry Woodward, Mathew Evans]	29.	Electric oven [1892, Thomas Ahearn]
4.	Five-pin bowling [1908, Thomas F. Ryan]	30.	Steam foghorn [1853, Robert Foulis]
5.	Wonderbra [1964, Louise Poirier]	31.	Walkie-talkie [1942, Donald L. Hings]
6.	Pacemaker [1950, John Hopps, Wilfred Bigelow, John Callaghan]	32.	Alkaline LONG-LASTING Battery [1959, Lewis Urry]
7.	Robertson screw, 1908 [Peter Robertson]	33.	Paint roller [1940, Norman Breakey]
8.	Zipper [1913, Gideon Sundback]	34.	Electronic music synthesizer [1945, Hugh Le Caine]
9.	Electric wheelchair [1952, George Klein]	35.	WeeVac 6 [1990, Wendy Murphy]
10.	Poutine [1957, Fernand Lachance]	36.	Green garbage bag [1950, Harry Wasylyk, Larry Hansen, Frank Plomp]
11.	Cobalt-60 "bomb" cancer treatment [1951, Harold Johns]	37.	Snowblower [1925, Arthur Sicard]
12.	Java programming language [1994, James Arthur Gosling]	38.	Self-propelled combine harvester [1937, Thomas Carroll]
13.	Bloody Caesar [1969, Walter Chell]	39.	Instant mashed potatoes [1962, Edward Asselbergs]
14.	Canadarm [1975, Spar Aerospace/NRC]	40.	Explosives vapour detector [1985, Lorne Elias]
15.	Standard Time [1878, Sir Sandford Fleming]	41.	Marine screw propeller [1833, John Patch]
16.	Electron microscope [1939, James Hillier, Albert Prebus]	42.	Plexiglas [1931, William Chalmers]
17.	Ski-Doo [1922, Joseph-Armand Bombardier]	43.	Key frame animation (filmmaking) [1969, Nestor Burtnyk, Marcelli Wein]
18.	BlackBerry [1999, Mike Lazaridis]	44.	CPR mannequin: "Actar 911" [1989, Dianne Croteau, Richard Brault]
19.	Radio voice transmission [1900, Reginald Fessenden]	45.	G-suit (antigravity, for pilots and astronauts) [1941, Wilbur Rounding Franks]
20.	Birchbark canoe [First Peoples]	46.	Ardox spiral nail [1954, Allan Dove]
21.	Basketball [1892, James Naismith]	47.	Automatic lubricating cup (engines) [1872, Elijah McCoy]
22.	Retractable beer carton handle [1957, Steve Pasjack]	48.	Crash-position indicator [1957, Harry Stevinson]
23.	UV degradable plastics [1971, James Guillet]	49.	Caulking gun [1894, Theodore Witte]
24.	Instant TV replay [1955, CBC's Hockey Night in Canada]	50.	Separable baggage check [1882, John Mitchell Lyons]
25.	Goalie mask [1959, Jacques Plante]		
26.	Marquis wheat [1908, Sir Charles Saunders]		

SOURCE: *The Greatest Canadian Inventions*, from http://cbc.ca/inventions/. Reprinted by permission of CBC Radio-Canada.

So a high proportion of the revolutionary new ideas of the past two centuries have been, and are likely to continue to be, provided by independent innovators who operate small business enterprises. The small entrepreneurial firms have played a leading role in the portion of business **research and development (R&D)** activity that is engaged in the search for the revolutionary breakthroughs that are such a critical part of the growth machine that is provided by the market economy. What drives this activity and what is different about its operation in the market economy? To the extent one can generalize, inventor–entrepreneurs are driven by the prospect that by being first to come up with a better product or better productive technology they can (temporarily) beat out all competitors in the market for their product, and can thereby obtain monopoly profits. In a market economy, however, this source of wealth is available only temporarily, because current and prospective rivals in the market will constantly try to improve on the initial invention and recapture the market. Thus, there is no rest for the innovators. They can never afford to be satisfied with their past achievements if they want their stream of

Research and development (R&D) is the activity of firms, universities, and government agencies that seeks to invent new products and processes and to improve those inventions so that they are ready for the market or other users.

Entrepreneurship and Canadian Inventions

Records suggest that Canadians have patented over a million inventions since Canada's first federal Patent Act came into force in 1869. Some of these inventions have been quite revolutionary and still play major roles in our everyday lives. For instance, two Canadian inventors, Henry Woodward and Matthew Evans, patented the first light bulb in 1875. It was Gideon Sundback who invented the zipper in 1913. Reginald Fessenden, perhaps Canada's most prolific inventor, who held some 500 patents when he died in Bermuda in 1932, is known as the father of radio broadcasting and, among other things, patented a first television system in 1927.

However, not many of the men and women who held these patents had an entrepreneurial mindset and were able to successfully market their products. Fessenden was neither a shrewd businessman nor an accomplished promoter. Woodward and Evans' light bulb would revolutionize the North American lifestyle but, lacking the inner drive and the financial means to promote their invention, they sold their rights to Thomas Edison (the son of Canadian emigrants to the United States), whose name is still synonymous with the development of the electric light bulb even more than a century later because of his entrepreneurial ability.

Other Canadian inventors did become successful entrepreneurs, though. John McLaughlin started a soda pop plant in Toronto in 1890 and patented the modern version of Canada Dry ginger ale in 1907. His bottle with the distinctive label of the map of Canada and the beaver was to become a registered trademark—the "Champagne of Ginger Ales"—which is still a highly recognizable brand today. Its original Canadian logo is still used by its new owners, London-based Cadbury-Schweppes, who bought the brand in 1986.

Another readily recognizable entrepreneurial success story is that of Joseph-Armand Bombardier from Valcourt, Quebec, who designed the first modern snowmobile in 1958 and began commercial production and marketing of the Ski-Doo in 1959. He started in 1922 at the age of 15 to experiment with motorized sleighs and,

four decades later, perfected the Ski-Doo, marking the beginning of a very successful Canadian business firm. Bombardier Inc. is now a major international conglomerate that designs and produces a wide variety of transportation and aerospace equipment, with estimated annual revenues of $18.5 billion in 2007.

More recently, in 1999, Mike Lazaridis and his high-tech company, Research in Motion, located in Waterloo, Ontario, launched the BlackBerry, a wireless hand-held device with a full but miniature QWERTY keyboard. The BlackBerry can accomplish multiple tasks, including e-mail, Web browsing, mobile phone, and fax transmission. By mid 2007, the number of BlackBerry subscribers had reached 9 million.

Many other interesting Canadian inventions, such as the IMax movie system, co-invented in 1968 by Grahame Ferguson, Roman Kroitor, and Robert Kerr, are not found in the list in Table 1.

SOURCE: Photo Courtesy of Research In Motion

monopoly profits to continue. Yesterday's invention soon is ancient history, and unless successor inventions are introduced soon enough by the firm, rivals will succeed in entering the market and will dry up the initial entrepreneur's stream of profits. So the entrepreneurs have no choice. They must seek to generate a stream of innovations, and that is one key part of the market's success story—the market provides a mechanism designed to change innovation from an occasional happening with a large element of accident and chance into a systematic process that ensures, as far as ingenuity and current knowledge permit, the injection of a stream of inventions into the economy.[7]

But what is there about modern market systems that allows this innovation process to flourish? The answer is primarily found in the new institutions that grew up along with the capitalist economy, perhaps partly as a historical accident. We have already mentioned such institutions as sanctity of property (prohibiting arbitrary expropriation by the king and his nobles), enforceability of contracts, and the patent system. These rules were quite new at the time of the Industrial Revolution, and for the first time they assured entrepreneurs and innovators that they could keep the wealth generated by

---

[7] The materials in this paragraph are a brief summary of the analysis of Joseph Schumpeter (1883–1950), who can be judged to have inaugurated the economics of innovation and growth in a book first published in 1911.

their efforts. This assurance not only provided the incentives that attracted individuals into the struggle for innovation, it also served as an irresistible lure for the entry of competitors. The appearance of the early innovating entrepreneurs and their success brought in ever more entrepreneurs, but it also gave rise to ever-fiercer competition using innovation as a weapon. And this provided the driving force for innovation that is present and fully effective only in the market economies.

> The individual inventor and entrepreneur play a critical role in the provision of a constant stream of breakthrough innovations. If they succeed in marketing an innovation, they are rewarded by temporary monopoly profits. But, usually, the profits are soon eroded by competition. So if they want the accumulation of profit to continue, they must provide one innovation after another. This is all possible only in the market economy, with its institutions such as sanctity of property, enforceability of contracts, and the patent system.

This apparently critical and continuing innovative role of the entrepreneur and the small firm may seem to leave little scope for invention by the large enterprise. But that, as we will see next, is a very misleading conclusion.

The Large Enterprises and Their Innovation "Assembly Lines"

As you can see in Figure 5, industrial investment in R&D has risen sharply during the high-tech boom of the late 1990s, reaching its apex in 2001. Increasingly, at least in North America, the financing for innovation has been supplied by large oligopolistic enterprises, rather than by independent inventors or small, newly founded entrepreneurial firms. Today, in Canada, 10 percent of R&D expenditures are made by federal and provincial government agencies, 34 percent by universities, and 56 percent by businesses. However federal and provincial governments fund over 25 percent of the R&D activity in Canada, while the foreign sector (mostly foreign firms) finances nearly 10 percent of this activity. Business enterprises fund a large share of the remainder—nearly 50 percent of total R&D activity—with most of the business outlays being made by larger firms.[8]

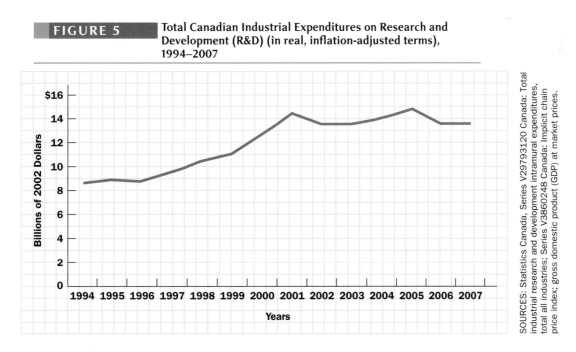

FIGURE 5 Total Canadian Industrial Expenditures on Research and Development (R&D) (in real, inflation-adjusted terms), 1994–2007

SOURCES: Statistics Canada, Series V29793120 Canada: Total industrial research and development intramural expenditures, total all industries; Series V3860248 Canada: Implicit chain price index; gross domestic product (GDP) at market prices.

[8] These figures are taken from a Statistics Canada working paper, Catalogue No. 88F0006XIE, No. 020, Janet Thompson, *Estimates of Canadian Research and Development Expenditures (GERD), Canada, 1994 to 2005, and by Province 1994 to 2003*. In relation to large U.S. firms, in 2001, the 68 largest manufacturing firms (each employing 25,000 or more workers) accounted for 49 percent of R&D in the manufacturing sector of the economy (National Science Board, *Science and Engineering Indicators—2004*, Arlington, VA: National Science Foundation, 2004, http://www.nsf.gov).

Innovation has, in fact, become a prime weapon of choice for competitive battles in substantial sectors of the economy. Of course, prices are still important. But it is improved products and methods of production that really capture the attention of the firm's managers. Product lines as diverse as computers and computer software, automobiles, cameras, and machinery all feature constant improvements, which are instantly and widely advertised. Even seemingly "low-tech" companies, noted for outputs like cleaning and personal care products, employ R&D personnel. These firms are driven to do this by powerful market pressures of competitive innovation.

> The result is a kind of innovation arms race in which no firm in a **high-tech** industry can afford to fall behind its rivals. Indeed, only by staying abreast of the others can the firm hope to preserve its place in the market. In its innovation, it is forced to run as fast as it can just to stand still—because its rivals are doing the same. Any firm that can come up with a better model than its rivals will gain a critical advantage.

Firms in many high-tech industries—such as computers, medical equipment, aeronautics, and even automobiles—struggle for market position in this way. The managers of firms cannot afford to neglect R&D activities. For if a firm fails to adopt the latest technology—even if the technology is created by others—then rival firms can easily take the lead and make disastrous inroads into the slower firm's sales. Often, for the firm, innovation is literally a matter of life and death.

Thus, especially in high-tech sectors, firms dare not leave innovation to chance, or to the haphazard contributions of independent inventors tinkering in their basements and garages. Rather, competitive markets force firms to take over the innovation process themselves and (in the immortal words of the great comedian, W. C. Fields) "to remove all elements of chance" from the undertaking.[9] Many business firms today routinely budget for R&D, hire scientists and engineers to do the job, and systematically decide how to promote and price their innovations.

> This "arms-race" feature of an industry's innovation process probably plays a critical role in the continuing outpouring of innovations that characterize the market economy. The capitalist economy itself has become a giant innovation machine, the predictable output of which is a stream of improved technology. Never in any other type of economy has there existed such an innovation machine—an assembly line that *forces* the economy to bring one invention after another from the drawing board all the way to the market.

We mentioned earlier that that there is a rather sharp differentiation between the contributions to the economy's innovation that are provided by entrepreneurs and those that are offered by established businesses, with their large internal R&D laboratories. In their effort to contain the risks inherent in the innovation process, large business firms have tended to slant their efforts toward incremental improvements rather than revolutionary breakthroughs. User friendliness, increased reliability, marginal additions to application, expansions of capacity, flexibility in design—these and many other types of improvement have come out of the industrial R&D facilities, with impressive consistency, year after year, and often preannounced and preadvertised.

The products of these innovative activities may often be individually modest, making very small improvements in products and productive processes. Nevertheless, taken in the aggregate, they have accomplished a great deal. An example is the airplane. The comfort, speed, and reliability of the modern passenger aircraft and the complexity and power of today's military flying machines clearly have turned the Wright brothers' original revolutionary device into a historical curiosity. Most of the sophistication, speed, and reliability of today's aviation equipment is probably attributable to the combined incremental additions made by routine research activities in corporate facilities.

There are even more startling examples of the magnitude of the innovative contributions of the large companies, whose incremental advances can compound to results

A **high-tech (high-technology)** firm or industry is one whose products, equipment and production methods utilize highly advanced technology that is constantly modified and improved. Examples are the aerospace, scientific instruments, computer, communications, and pharmaceutical industries.

---

[9] This phrase is uttered when Fields, playing a card shark, seeks to lure an unsuspecting novice into a card game, whereupon his intended victim questions the morality of "games of chance." Fields hastens to reassure him: "Young man, when you play with me, all elements of chance have been removed!"

of enormous magnitude. It is reported, for example, that between 1971 and 2008, the "clock speed" of Intel's microprocessor chips—that is, the number of instructions each chip can carry out per second—has increased by some *sixty million percent*, reaching about sixty billion computations per second today. And, between 1968 and 2003, the number of transistors embedded in a single chip has expanded more than *ten million percent*, and the number of transistors that can be purchased for a dollar has grown by *five billion percent*.[10] Added up, these advances surely contributed enormously more computing capacity than was provided by the original revolutionary breakthrough of the invention of the electronic computer. Of course, that initial invention was an indispensable necessity for all of the later improvements. But it is only the combined work of the two together that made possible the powerful and inexpensive apparatus that serves us so effectively today. Other careful observers have extended such examples and have concluded that incremental innovation activities of the large firms have been responsible for a very respectable share of the contribution of innovation to economic growth in the twentieth century and today.

In the growth process, the individual entrepreneurs and the giant firms have played roles that are different, but are essential for one another. The breakthrough ideas have been contributed disproportionately by the entrepreneurs in their pursuit of the temporary monopoly profits that successful innovations promise. The giant firms have specialized in a constant stream of incremental improvements that protect them from destruction by competitors who constantly seek to beat them at the innovation game. Together, the contributions of the two groups have played a critical role in the growth of the market economies.

▨ The Market Economy and the Speedy Dissemination of New Technology

Another attribute of the market economy that is vital for its growth is the fact that new technology now spreads with impressive speed, meaning that obsolete products and processes do not long survive or hold back economic growth. The evidence indicates that dissemination is not only surprisingly rapid, but has also been growing more so with remarkable consistency for more than a century (see "The Speed-Up of Technology Dissemination" box).

What underlies this increase in the rapidity with which inventions spread? It may seem that when a business firm obtains a promising new invention, it will naturally do

The Speed-Up of Technology Dissemination

A recent study of 46 major product innovations found that, in less than a century, the average time between the commercial introduction of a new product and the time of entry of competitors supplying the same or similar products fell precipitously from almost 33 years at the inception of the 20th century to just 3.4 years in the period 1967–1986.* Moreover, as shown in Figure 6, the decline was remarkably steady and persistent.

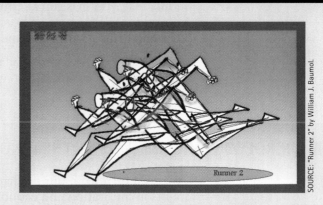

SOURCE: "Runner 2" by William J. Baumol.

* Rajshree Agarwal and Michael Gort, "First Mover Advantage and the Speed of Competitive Entry, 1887–1986," *Journal of Law and Economics*, Vol. XLIV, April 2001, pp. 161–177. The authors report that other studies support their results.

[10] John Markoff, "Technology; Is There Life After Silicon Valley's Fast Lane?," *The New York Times*, Business/Financial Desk, Section C, April 9, 2003, p. 1.

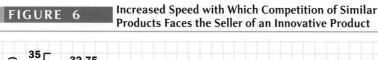

FIGURE 6   Increased Speed with Which Competition of Similar Products Faces the Seller of an Innovative Product

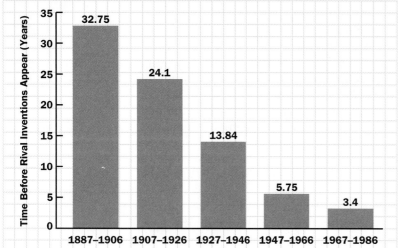

SOURCE: Rajshree Agarwal and Michael Gort, "First Mover Advantage and the Speed of Competitive Entry, 1887–1986," *Journal of Law and Economics*, Vol. XLIV, April 2001, pp. 161–177.

all it can to bar its competitors' access to the new technology so as to retain a competitive advantage over its rivals. In reality, this is often not so. If a firm can get a sufficiently high price by licensing others to use its technology, it may be just as profitable to do that as to reserve the innovations for itself. This is not just a theoretical possibility. Newspaper reports indicate, for example, that more than 20 percent of IBM's profits in 2000 were obtained from its technology licences.

There is another incentive for firms to trade innovations with others, including their competitors. Fearing that their own laboratories may conceivably fail in all R&D undertakings in a particular time period, while competitors may have better luck, firms often enter into agreements with a competitor to *share* all successful future innovations for a specified time period—say, the next five years. Such agreements reduce risk for *both* firms. In photography, for example, one camera manufacturer may introduce an improved automatic-focus device, a second firm may develop an automatic light adjustment, and a third may invent a way to make the camera more compact. Each of these three firms can keep its invention to itself. But if they get together and agree to produce cameras combining all their new features, they will be able to market a product clearly superior to what any could have produced alone. They will also be in a far better position to meet competition from another camera manufacturer.

Cross licensing of patents occurs when each of two firms agrees to let the other use some specified set of its patents, either at a price specified in their agreement or in return for access to the other firm's patents.

For instance, a firm located in Kanata, the high-tech centre in Ottawa, may sign a worldwide patent **cross licensing** agreement with NEC, a firm based in Tokyo, in relation to any of their semiconductor products. IBM cross licenses patents with *each* of its major competitors, and Microsoft now does something very similar. Such agreements are not restricted to high-tech industries. Steel mills, for example, may regularly and routinely exchange information with each other so as to enhance productivity. Firms sometimes train the employees of competing firms or send their own personnel to competing facilities to help set up unfamiliar equipment.[11]

Indeed, business firms provide their technology to others for a profit so commonly that MIT has run a seminar teaching firms how to earn more from their technology rental business. There is even an international association of technology licensing firms—with thousands of members.

Inventions are becoming available more quickly to other firms, including competitors of the firms that own them. Moreover, competitive pressures ensure that these innovations are rapidly put to use.

MICROECONOMIC ANALYSIS OF THE INNOVATIVE FIRM

Next, we turn from our description of the facts related to the market's accomplishments in innovation and economic growth and see what the tools of microeconomic analysis can help us to understand about these achievements.

[11] Eric Von Hippel, *The Sources of Innovation* (New York: Oxford University Press, 1988), p. 79.

Financing the Innovation "Arms Race": Firms with High R&D Costs and Low Marginal Costs

Large-scale innovative activity is expensive. Firms must spend substantial amounts of money, year after year. In some firms, the costs of R&D can account for as much as 40 percent of the company's total costs. If an innovative firm is to stay in business, the products it supplies must be priced so as to enable the firm to recover those expenditures.

This effort requires an approach to pricing that is very different from the one we studied in most of the earlier chapters. There we concluded that, in a competitive market, prices tend to be set approximately equal to marginal costs, assuming this price would bring in enough revenue to keep the firm in business. To see the reason for the difference between this case and that of the innovative firm, consider the case of Jim—an organic wheat farmer—who decides to grow 1,000 more bushels of wheat than he did last year. That level of production will require him to rent x more hectares of land, to buy y more bags of fertilizer and z more bags of seed, to hire h more hours of labour, and to borrow b more dollars from the bank. The prices of these inputs tell Jim how much he must spend to get the added output. If this added cost is divided by the 1,000 added bushels, we have an (approximate) calculation of the marginal cost of a bushel, including the marginal return to capital—Jim's loan payment to the bank. If the price of organic wheat is set by the market so that it covers this amount, evidently price is equal to marginal cost and is also enough to keep the farm in business. It is enough to keep Jim's farm going because *all* of his costs, including the cost of renting more land, are costs of *adding* to his output—in essence, all of his costs take the form of marginal or added costs.

Contrast this case with a software firm that has just spent $20 million to create a valuable new computer program. If the firm supplies one more unit of the program (or even one thousand more units of the program), what is its added cost? The answer is nearly zero: just the cost of making a new CD, packaging it, and shipping it. One of the firm's main costs is that of R&D, but no *added* R&D cost is incurred when another purchaser acquires the already-designed program. So the firm's heavy R&D expenditure contributes nothing to *marginal* cost. A price that covers only the marginal cost of one more copy of the program can hardly amount to more than, say, $5. That price cannot begin to cover the $20 million in R&D cost—a cost the firm will probably have to replicate in the next year to keep the program up to date and up to competitive standards. So, pricing software—or any other products of a firm with high and continuing R&D costs—at marginal cost is a recipe for financial suicide. Prices of the products of innovating firms simply cannot follow the familiar formula: $P = MC$.

> Firms that are forced by competition to spend a great deal on research and development year after year, but that use the results of the R&D to improve a product whose marginal costs are low, cannot expect to recover their R&D costs if they set their prices equal or close to marginal costs, as occurs under perfect competition.

This gives one further justification for the use of cost-plus pricing and, more specifically, average cost pricing, as discussed in the section dealing with alternative views of the oligopolistic firm in Chapter 12. Large oligopolistic firms that engage in costly R&D activities need to earn profits that will allow them both to pay dividends to their shareowners and to fund R&D investment expenditures. For these firms, marginal costs will be constant, and perhaps even decreasing, as we saw in Chapter 12 and, as a result, marginal costs are never above average cost. These firms have no choice but to set prices on the basis of average cost pricing, adding a costing margin that will cover both normal profits and R&D investment expenditures.

This pricing situation is troubling because it can mislead the government agencies charged with preventing firms from acting as monopolists. Many of the people who work in these agencies have been trained using textbooks such as this one, and they have come away from their studies with the valid (but possibly irrelevant) conclusion that under perfect competition, price must equal marginal cost. So, when they encounter prices in innovative firms that are nowhere near marginal costs, their suspicions are sometimes aroused. Is this firm exploiting the public by charging prices higher than marginal costs? Should something be done to make the company price its products as wheat farmer Jim does? We see now that doing so may well bring innovative activity to a virtual standstill. Of course, most of the government authorities who are concerned with monopolistic behaviour know better than that, but their suspicions are nevertheless aroused by finding cases of $P > MC$. In addition, some of them really do misunderstand the issue, and so constitute a threat to innovative activity by business.

The Profits of Innovation

Many discussions of innovation start off with the assumption that innovators can expect to earn very high profits. Indeed, huge rewards do often accrue to those who introduce unusually successful innovations. We have all heard of innovators like Thomas Edison, Alexander Graham Bell, Joseph-Armand Bombardier, and, more recently, Bill Gates, Steven Jobs, and others in the computer industry, who have acquired great riches from their ability to invent, or to bring innovations to market. Of course, for every successful or briefly successful innovator such as Corel's Michael Cowpland, many others have plowed their family savings into new gadgets and lost all they have spent. Quite possibly, inventors on average earn zero economic profits, or even lose money.

This possibility appears even more likely when we consider business investment in R&D. As we saw in Chapter 10, if an industry is perfectly competitive, entry will occur until economic profits are forced down to zero. Put another way, perfect competition permits firms to earn just what they need to pay investors for the funds they provide—no more and no less. This must be so because, if a typical firm in one industry earns more than firms in other industries, investors will put more money into the more profitable industry. Any excess economic profit will lead to an expansion of industry output, which will drive prices down and squeeze profits.

Because there are some barriers to entry into innovation, we cannot be certain that economic profits from invention will tend *exactly* toward zero, but we can expect them to be very low on average. In other words, although inventive activity sometimes pays off handsomely, large R&D investments also can fail spectacularly, so that the average economic profits comes out close to zero. In particular, a large firm with a big R&D division may work simultaneously on many possible innovations. The "law of averages" suggests that some of these efforts will fail and some will succeed. So we should not be surprised to find near-zero economic profit even in industries with a great deal of innovative activity.

Does this conclusion fit the facts? Although we have no systematic study of all inventive activities, high-tech industries provide a useful illustration—especially the computer industry, where many founders have made fortunes and received much publicity. According to corporate management guru Peter F. Drucker, "The computer industry hasn't made a dime . . . Intel and Microsoft make money, but look at all the people who were losing money all the world over. It is doubtful the industry has yet broken even."[12] But is it true? A recent study looked at companies that went public from 1975 to 1992, most of which were high-tech firms, and found their rate of return to be about average (that is, zero economic profit), once the researchers adjusted for risk and company size.[13]

How Much Will a Profit-Maximizing Firm Spend on Innovation?

The legendary "Eureka! I have found it!" scenario, in which the lone inventor working in a basement or garage happens to come up with a brilliant invention, may not

---

[12] As cited in Jane Katz, "To Market, to Market: Strategy in High-Tech Business," *Federal Reserve Bank of Boston Regional Review*, Fall 1996. Retrieved from www.bos.frb.org

[13] Alon Brav and Paul A. Gompers, "Myth or Reality? The Long-Run Underperformance of Initial Public Offerings: Evidence from Venture and Nonventure Capital-Backed Companies," *Journal of Finance* 52, no. 5 (December 1997): 1791–1821.

be amenable to conventional economic analysis. But innovation in a modern corporation is easier to analyze by using the standard tools of the theory of the firm because R&D budgeting looks a lot like other business decisions, such as those about how much to produce or how much to spend on advertising. We can study all of these standard business decisions using the same tools of marginal analysis that we studied in Chapters 5, 7, and 8. The key questions are: How much can we expect firms to spend on R&D? How much can they expect to earn by doing so? And how will competition affect their innovative activity?

We have asked and answered similar questions before, when we studied how basic marginal analysis addresses business decision making. If the firm seeks to maximize its profits, it will expand its spending on R&D up to the point at which the marginal cost of additional R&D equals the marginal revenue.

By now, the logic should be familiar. A level of R&D spending (call it X dollars) at which marginal revenue (MR) is, for example, *greater* than marginal cost (MC) cannot possibly represent the profit-maximizing amount for the company to spend on R&D. For, if MR exceeds MC, the company can increase its profits by spending more than X dollars on R&D. The opposite will be true if MR < MC. In that case, the firm can increase its profits by *decreasing* R&D spending. So X dollars cannot be the optimal level of spending if, at that level of expenditure, either MR > MC or MR < MC. It follows that the profit-maximizing level of spending on R&D can only be an amount—say, Y dollars—at which MR = MC. You will recognize this argument, for we have repeated it many times in earlier chapters when we discussed other business decisions, such as those related to price and quantity of output.

This analysis simultaneously tells us everything, and nothing, about the R&D decision. It tells us everything because its conclusion is correct. If the firm is a profit maximizer, and if we know its MR and its MC curves for R&D investment, then the MR = MC rule does, in theory, tell us exactly how much the profit-seeking firm should invest in R&D. But the discussion so far tells us nothing about the shape of "typical" marginal revenue and marginal cost curves for R&D, nor does it tell us how the competitive pressures that play such an important role in R&D decisions affect those curves. We turn next to these crucial matters.

A Kinked Revenue Curve Model of Spending on Innovation

Our discussion thus far has left a basic question unanswered. If innovation is so expensive and so risky, and if the economic profits expected from innovation approach zero, why do firms do it? Why doesn't every firm refuse to participate in this unattractive game? The answer, at least in part, is that competitive markets leave them no choice. If firms do not keep up with their competitors in terms of product attractiveness and improved process efficiency that lowers costs, they will lose out to their rivals and end up losing money. Clearly, firms prefer *zero* economic profits—profits that yield only normal competitive returns to investors—to *negative* profits and investor flight.

This observation also enables us to investigate how much the firm will spend on R&D, using a microeconomic model very similar to one we encountered in Chapter 12, page 271—the kinked demand curve model that we used to explain why prices tend to be "sticky" in oligopoly markets. The underlying mechanism there was an asymmetry in the firm's expectations about its competitors. The firm hesitates to lower its price for fear that its rivals will match the price cut, causing the firm to end up with only a few new customers but dramatically reduced revenues. But the firm fears that if it *increases* its price, the others will *not* follow suit, so that it will be left all by itself with an overpriced product. A firm with such beliefs will want to set its price at the industry level—no more and no less—and leave it there unless the competitive situation changes drastically.

The innovation story is similar. Imagine an industry with, say, five firms of roughly equal size. Company X sees that each of the other firms in the industry spends approximately $20 million per year on R&D. It will not dare to spend much less than

$20 million on its own R&D because, if it does so, its next model may lack new features as attractive as those of rival products. But Company X sees little point in raising the ante to, say, $30 million because it knows that its competitors will simply follow suit. So we can expect that as time passes, the firms will hesitate to make *any* significant changes in the amount they spend on innovative activity.

But that's not the end of the story. All the firms in the industry will continue to invest the same amount as they have in the past, even if the cost of R&D shifts down moderately or some other minor change occurs, until one of them enjoys a research breakthrough leading to a wonderful new product. That fortunate firm will then expand its investment in the breakthrough product, because doing so will pay off *even if the other firms in the industry match the increase.* Thus the MR curve for the breakthrough firm will move to the right, and so will its profit-maximizing R&D budget level—to an amount larger than $20 million. Other companies in the industry will then be forced to follow. So now the industry norm will no longer be a $20 million annual investment but some larger amount, say, $25 million per firm. No firm will be the first to drop back to the old $20 million level, fearing that its rivals would not follow such a retrenchment move. So the MR = MC equilibrium point will now be $25 million of R&D spending. Again, the common story of armaments races among countries parallels the story of innovation battles among firms.

The process we have just described assumes that competition forces firms in the industry to keep up with one another in their R&D investments. But once they have caught up, the investment level remains fairly constant until one firm breaks ranks and increases its spending. Then, all other firms follow suit, but none dares to drop back. Such an arrangement is described as a **ratchet,** in analogy to the mechanical device that prevents a wound-up spring from suddenly unwinding. This arrangement normally holds technological spending steady, sometimes permits it to move forward, but generally does not allow it to retreat. Thus, we can expect R&D spending to expand from time to time. Once the new level is reached, the ratchet—enforced by the competitive market—prevents firms from retreating to the previous lower level.[14]

Ratcheting acts as a critical part of the mechanism that produces the extraordinary growth records of free enterprise economies and differentiates them from all other known economic systems. Competitive pressures force firms to run as fast as they can in the innovation race just to keep up with the others.

A **ratchet** is an arrangement that permits some economic variable, such as investment or advertising, to increase, but prevents that variable from subsequently decreasing.

▓ Innovation as a Public Good

An innovation, once created, usually does not contribute only to the output of the firm that discovered the breakthrough. At little or no additional cost, the new technology can also add to the outputs produced by other enterprises, often in other industries. This public good property (for review of the concept of *public goods,* see Chapter 15, pages 348–349) of technical knowledge enables those who adopt the innovation (with or without the inventor's permission) to adopt it more cheaply.

In Chapter 15, we used the term *public good* to describe any input or output that is not depleted when used once, but rather can be used over and over by more users with little or no additional cost. Such goods can be costlessly available to the entire public, not just to a single individual. Analogously, R&D expenses need not be duplicated when firms use knowledge repeatedly to produce output. For instance, Thomas Edison and his colleagues worked for many months and used up much material

---

[14] This statement somewhat exaggerates the effectiveness of ratchets in preventing the economy from *ever* sliding backward in its R&D expenditures. In fact, expenditures on R&D did fall back in real terms after the stock market crash of 2000, as shown in Figure 5 on page 375. After all, even in machinery, ratchets sometimes slip. Firms may, for example, be forced to cut back their R&D expenditure if business is extremely bad. They may also make mistakes in planning how much to spend on investment or become discouraged by repeated failures of their research division to come up with salable products. The economy's ratchets are indeed imperfect, but they nevertheless exist. They cannot completely prevent backsliding in R&D expenditure, but they can be a powerful influence that is effective in resisting such retreats.

before they finally found a way to manufacture the first viable light bulb. But they did not have to repeat that outlay to produce their second light bulb. Similarly, if Edison had permitted another firm to use the technology, that firm would not have needed to repeat the expensive research that yielded the first light bulb. Innovation is like the oil lamp in the ancient Hanukkah legend: a lamp that miraculously replenished its fuel and could provide light day after day without any additional oil.

That is one distinguishing feature of any knowledge. Both coal and technical knowledge contribute to output. But when a tonne of coal is used as fuel, it cannot be used again. A second tonne of coal must be mined and burned to run the engine longer. Once technical knowledge is created, however, it can be used over and over again without ever being depleted.

Effects of Process Research on Outputs and Prices

As a last example of how standard analytic tools of microeconomic analysis can help us to deal with innovation, we turn to the effects of innovation on outputs and prices. We will consider a single monopoly firm that makes decisions independently of other enterprises' activities and decisions.

Innovation is often divided into two types: **product innovations**, which consist of the introduction of a new item (such as a photocopying machine or a video camera), and **process innovations**, which entail an improvement in the way in which commodities are produced, making them cheaper to buy. At this point, we will discuss only process innovations, because they are easier to analyze.

A successful process innovation can be expected to expand the output of the product that uses the process, and to reduce the product's price, for a very simple reason: A process innovation normally leads to a downward shift in the firm's marginal and average cost curves but, because it involves no change in the product, it should not cause any change in the demand and marginal revenue curves.

A standard graph familiar from earlier chapters can demonstrate these results. Figure 7 shows MR and DD (demand), the firm's marginal revenue and demand (average revenue) curves, respectively, for the production of widgets. The graph also shows MC_1, the marginal cost curve of widgets *before* the process innovation, and MC_2, the marginal cost curve *after* the innovation is adopted. MC_2 is naturally lower than MC_1 because the innovation has reduced the cost of making widgets. Before the innovation, the quantity produced by our profit-maximizing firm is Q_1, the quantity at which $MR = MC_1$ (at point E_1). The corresponding price is P_1, the point on the demand curve (DD) above quantity Q_1. After the process innovation, the marginal cost curve shifts downward to MC_2. That new marginal cost curve meets the downward-sloping MR curve at point E_2, which lies to the right of E_1. This means that the profit-maximizing output quantity must increase from Q_1 to Q_2, and, because of the downward slope of the demand curve, price must fall from P_1 to P_2. Thus, we have shown, as suggested earlier, that:

A cost-cutting process innovation increases the output and decreases the price of the product that a profit-making firm supplies with the help of the innovation.

A **product innovation** is the introduction of a good or service that is entirely new or involves major modifications of earlier products.

A **process innovation** is an innovation that changes the way in which a commodity is produced.

FIGURE 7

Effect of Process Innovations on Prices and Outputs

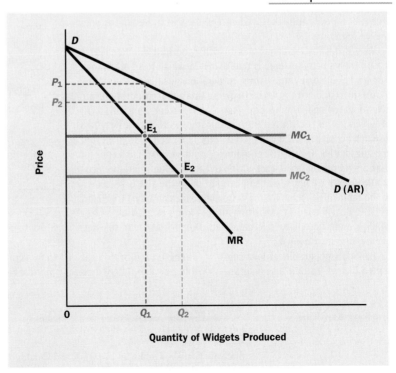

Quantity of Widgets Produced

■ DOES THE MARKET ECONOMY SPEND ENOUGH ON R&D ACTIVITIES?

We have seen that today's market economies turn out innovations at a pace and complexity never seen before in human history. Business firms, governments, universities, and others spend a good deal on research and innovation.

In 2005, more than $26 billion (about 1.9 percent of the Canadian total GDP) was spent on these activities, with business firms, both foreign and domestic, funding about 60 percent of that amount.[15] Yet we may well ask, is this amount too small or too large a share of GDP? That is, would the general public benefit or lose if more resources were devoted to innovation? Some economic analysis suggests that there is a fundamental reason for believing that, despite our impressive successes in this arena, we still do not spend enough.

As usual, there is a trade-off to spending more than we currently do. If we devote more resources to innovation this year, less will be left over to produce clothing, food, or new TV programs—goods and services that contribute primarily to today's consumption rather than tomorrow's. With smaller supplies of these items, their prices will rise. On the other hand, if we devote more resources to innovation, we will probably get better and cheaper products in the future. So, as with any investment, R&D expenditures entail a trade-off between the present and the future. More R&D spending means that consumers get less to consume this year, but they get more and better products in the future. The question is, how much is enough?

Is Canada a Laggard in the Innovation Race?

The fact that half of R&D is conducted by large businesses may help to explain why Canada has a relatively low share of GDP going to R&D compared with many other countries. The accompanying table shows that over the 1981–2004 period, total R&D expenditures in Canada represented only 1.6 percent of GDP (although it has been rising over the last few years). By contrast, the average for all Organisation for Economic Co-operation and Development (OECD) countries is 2.2 percent for the same time period. Some small countries like Finland, Sweden, and Switzerland, well known for being innovative, have ratios that well exceed the OECD average, as does the United States.

Why is this R&D expenditures-to-GDP ratio so low in Canada? A reason that is often offered is that many Canadian firms are branch subsidiaries of some large parent corporations located in the United States. R&D activities in these large multinational corporations are often located near the headquarters of the parent company, most of which are in the United States. This implies that relatively less research activity is being conducted in the large Canadian firms that are subsidiaries of foreign companies. An interesting illustration of that phenomenon is the case of Ireland—the Celtic Tiger—the economic growth of which was so phenomenal in the 1990s. As shown in the table, R&D expenditures in Ireland represent only 1.0 percent of GDP. But this is not surprising since a large proportion of Ireland's economic activity is conducted by foreign-owned businesses, mainly American-owned.

Canada's geographical location next to the United States has some advantages and disadvantages. On the one hand, Canadian

Research and Development Expenditures as a Percentage of GDP, Yearly Average, Selected Countries, 1981–2004

Countries	R&D-to-GDP Ratio
Canada	1.6%
Finland	2.3%
France	2.2%
Ireland	1.0%
Japan	2.7%
Sweden	3.2%
Switzerland	2.5%
United States	2.6%
OECD countries	2.2%
Russian Federation	1.1%

Note: Even these OECD series are not fully comparable, as some countries exclude R&D conducted by regional governments.

SOURCE: "Science and Technology: Gross domestic expenditure on R&D," OECD Factbook 2007—Economic, Environmental and Social Statistics, © OECD 2007, www.oecd.org/bookshop?926402946X

firms have quick access to innovations developed in the United States. On the other hand, Canadian researchers are easily induced to move a few hundred kilometres south to work in American labs and research units.

---

[15] Statistics Canada, Catalogue 13-001-X and Catalogue No. 88F0006XIE, No. 020, Janet Thompson, *Estimates of Canadian Research and Development Expenditures (GERD), Canada, 1994 to 2005, and by Province 1994 to 2003.*

Innovation as a Beneficial Externality

Many economists believe that private enterprise does *not* devote enough resources to innovation, because the acquisition of new technical knowledge generates large *externalities.* Recall from Chapter 15 that an externality is an effect of a business transaction that benefits or hurts persons other than those who directly take part in the transaction.[16] For example, if demand for air travel expands and more planes take off from the local airport, noise pollution affecting nearby residents will increase and they may feel it necessary to spend more money on insulation. Here, the air passengers and the airline are the participants in the transaction, and neighbourhood homes suffer from the damaging externality. A detrimental externality is part of the true social cost of producing a commodity—air transport, in this example. This means that the airline will not pay all of the costs of its flights because, inadvertently or deliberately, it can shift part of the costs to others—which they pay in the form of higher spending on headache medicine or soundproofing. Because lower costs lead firms to produce higher outputs, the ability to escape part of the cost of its operation will lead the airline to overproduce air travel capacity. The result is excessive flight activity and too much noise pollution.

But sometimes externalities *benefit* innocent third parties, rather than harming them, and then those who carry out the transaction reap only part of the benefits. Take the case of the discovery of insulin, which was ranked as the most important Canadian invention in Table 1, on page 373. Daily insulin injections save the lives of millions of diabetic persons throughout the world. The discovery of insulin by Frederick Banting and his assistant Charles Best in a University of Toronto lab run by J. J. R. McLeod earned Banting and McLeod a Nobel Prize in Physiology and Medicine in 1923. (Incidentally, Banting shared with Best the amount of Nobel Prize money that he was awarded.) While this certainly helped the research careers of both Banting and Best, all of the proceeds of insulin treatment went to Connaught Laboratories, which commercialized the production of insulin. Thus, Banting and Best received only a minute portion of the overall benefits that the discovery of insulin brought to the world. This is true of most innovations: They benefit the innovator to some degree, but large parts of the benefits also go to others. Such beneficial externalities mean that a firm that invests in R&D can expect to reap only a fraction of the profits from the innovation.

Consequently, many economists believe that the free market induces private firms to invest less than the socially optimal amount in innovation. They believe that many innovations whose benefits would exceed their costs are never carried out because any firm that spent the money to produce the innovation would get only part of the benefit, and that part would be insufficient to cover the firm's costs. Instead, governments finance a good deal of innovation and research activity, which is carried out in government laboratories and in research institutions such as universities.

The externality problem is probably most severe for what is called **basic research**— that is, research that deals with science and general principles rather than with improvement of a specific product. (Research of the latter sort, which is directly related to commercial or other uses, is called **applied research.**) For example, research on the nature of electricity and magnetism may yield enormous economic benefits in the near or distant future, but for the moment it satisfies only physicists' curiosity. Few business firms will finance such research. Of course, the economy would be much less productive in the long run if no one did it. That is why Canadian governments and a number of other industrialized countries finance basic research, and why economists generally favour such funding.

Why the Shortfall in Innovation Spending May Not Be So Big After All

But the notion that we are spending far too small a share of GDP on innovation is not really very plausible. Looking about us, we see a flood of new products and processes,

Basic research refers to research that seeks to provide scientific knowledge and general principles rather than coming up with any specific marketable inventions.

Applied research is research whose goal is to invent or improve particular products or processes, often for profit. Note, however, that the military and government health-related agencies provide examples of not-for-profit applied research.

[16] For review, see Chapter 15, pages 342–348.

but certainly nothing that suggests a dearth of new technology. And a number of economists are now offering reasons that suggest why there may be no shortfall, or why any shortfall that occurs may be relatively limited.

Here only one of the reasons will be suggested: the existence of profitable markets in *licensing* of innovation to others. As we have seen, many firms permit others, even their closest competitors, to use their private technology—for a fee. That fee becomes the market price for a licence to use the technology. To take this idea to its extreme, imagine that all innovating firms are successful in profitably licensing their technology to every firm and individual that can benefit from it. Then the externality problem would disappear. The reason is straightforward: A beneficial externality, after all, is simply a good deed for which the doer of the deed is not paid, or not paid adequately, for the benefit he or she creates. For this reason, the outputs that yield beneficial externalities can generally be expected to be too low from the general welfare point of view. But if the supplier can somehow arrange to be paid sufficiently, the incentive to supply an adequate amount of the beneficial product will plainly be restored. So a profitable market for technology licences is said to help in "internalizing the externality," by getting the supplier paid for supplying the valuable innovation and by restoring the incentive for further innovation. On the other hand, if there are high transaction costs in arranging such licences, as there could be (see page 352 of Chapter 15), then the licensing benefits will be insufficient and we are back to the argument of insufficient resources devoted to innovation and research.

A related but lesser-known phenomenon occurs when many firms try to reduce their risks by **technology trading**—getting paid for another firm's use of its technology by receiving in exchange the right to use the other firm's technology. This type of deal can be thought of as bartering, rather than selling, technology licences. Either way, the innovator firm receives some compensation for use of its technology by others.

Technology trading is an arrangement in which a firm voluntarily makes its privately owned technology available to other firms either in exchange for access to the technology of the second company or for an agreed-upon fee.

The implication of all this is that, even if innovating firms do not receive full compensation for the benefits that their technology provides to others, those firms seem to have become quite adept at getting some substantial portion of the appropriate payment. The result is that the innovation externalities may not be nearly as serious a handicap to innovation as the theory may have led some observers to suspect.

■ CONCLUSION: THE MARKET ECONOMY AND ITS INNOVATION ASSEMBLY LINE

While most advocates of the market system emphasize its efficiency in allocating resources under given conditions, this may well be a side issue; the greatest strength of capitalism is rather its proven ability to be the most powerful engine of economic growth and innovation ever known. The increased creation, faster dissemination, and accelerated utilization of inventions is surely no accident. There is something about the way the modern economy works that makes it outstrip all of its predecessors in terms of the creation and utilization of new technology—and to do so with little let-up for more than two centuries.

TOWARD SOLUTION OF THE PUZZLE:
How the Market Achieved Its Unprecedented Growth

There can be no single answer to the question we posed earlier in the chapter: Why do all rival economic systems trail so far behind the growth rates of market-based economies? But several key features of the market economy seem clearly to constitute the major elements of the story. A critical difference between the modern market economy and all other types of economies in history, ancient or modern, is that the other economies had no built-in mechanisms that led to widespread *use* of the inventions. By contrast, market economies are built around a number of critical institutions that have made efforts to provide products and processes a very promising route to success. Primary among these from the point of view of growth are the legal institutions that prevent governments from arbitrary expropriation of the wealth acquired through innovation and production; the enforceability of contracts that prevent disorder in the transactions among firms, banks, and between firms and consumers; and the patent system that most directly protects the interests of innovators, entrepreneurs and firms that deal in innovative properties. One consequence has been that vigorous competition now provides a strong incentive for innovative effort and often makes innovative effort a matter of life and death for the business firm. The result has been a kind of innovation arms race, which, in turn, underlies the growing inclusion of innovative activity as a standard part of the internal operations of modern business firms—an assembly line that turns out innovations routinely, much as a meat packing plant turns out sausages.

The market economy *is* different to a substantial degree, and in ways that will make a major difference to economic well-being both now and in the foreseeable future. It is hardly perfection. The market system has brought more effective and fiercer competition, even as it has raised new problems for prevention or control of monopoly. It has led to more rapid resource depletion, but it has also provided ways to use natural resources more efficiently. It has left many other important economic problems unsolved, but it has raised standards of living and accelerated the rate of improvement of these economic standards in the wealthiest countries to a degree that could not have been imagined at the beginning of the Industrial Revolution. The capitalist economy has done this, and continues to do so, not through a series of lucky accidents, but rather through features built solidly into the economy that have turned it into a growth machine that contains and operates its very effective innovation assembly line.

The market system in its perfectly competitive version provides static efficiency in allocating given resources; but the most compelling case for the market economy, despite its frequent oligopolistic features, is its dynamic efficiency—its ability to deliver growth and innovation.

SUMMARY

1. The growth records and **per-capita incomes** achieved by market economies far exceed those attained by any other form of economic organization. **Innovation** is one of the main sources of that economic growth.

2. Small firms created by **entrepreneurs** account for a substantial proportion of the economy's breakthrough inventions, while larger companies specialize in incremental improvements that over time often add up to very major advances.

3. Innovation in free-market economies is stimulated by competition among business firms, which try to outdo one another in terms of the attractiveness of their new and improved products and in the efficiency of their productive processes.

4. Innovative entrepreneurial firms are driven to provide a stream of innovations because otherwise rivals are likely to introduce substitute products that will erode the profits from any one innovation. Among large competing firms

frequent innovation is a matter of life and death because a firm with obsolete products or processes will lose its customers to rivals.

5. The large amounts that competition forces many firms to spend on R&D and the low marginal costs of the consumer goods sometimes produced with the resulting innovations often mean that if the firms set $P = MC$, as is done under perfect competition, the innovating firms will not be able to recover their costs. As a result, firms will set prices on the basis of average cost pricing.

6. As with any other decision, a profit-maximizing firm will invest in R&D up to the point at which the expected MR equals the MC of that expenditure.

7. Competition can force firms to set their R&D spending at levels corresponding to those of their rivals.

8. The typical level of R&D spending in an industry will sometimes increase, but it will rarely decline because no firm dares to be the first to cut back on such spending.

9. Firms often seek to reduce the risks of their R&D activities by entering into agreements with other firms to share one another's technology. They may also sell access to their technology to others.

10. Many economists believe that private investment in innovation will fall short of the socially optimal level, because the externalities from innovation mean that inventors do not obtain all of the benefits of their innovations.

11. **Process innovations** can be shown by MR = MC analysis to increase outputs and decrease prices, even in monopoly firms.

12. The market system in its perfectly competitive version provides static efficiency in allocating resources; but the most compelling case for the market economy, despite its frequent oligopolistic features, is its dynamic efficiency—its ability to deliver growth and innovation.

KEY TERMS

Externality   367

Per-capita income   368

Productivity   368

Industrial Revolution   368

Capitalism   368

GDP (gross domestic product)   370

Invention   370

Innovation   371

Entrepreneur   371

Research and development (R&D)   373

High-tech   376

Cross licensing   378

Ratchet   382

Product innovation   383

Process innovation   383

Basic research   385

Applied research   385

Technology trading   386

DISCUSSION QUESTIONS

1. To understand how much the free-enterprise economy has increased living standards, try to envision the daily life of a middle-class family in a major Canadian city just after Confederation, when the average purchasing power is estimated to have been less than one-ninth of today's. What do you think they ate? How much clothing did they own? What were their living quarters like? What share of their budget was available for vacations and entertainment?

2. Name five common products introduced since you were born.

3. Name some companies that advertise that their products are "new" or "improved."

4. Explain why firms in an industry that spends a large amount of money on advertising may feel locked into their current advertising budgets, with no one firm daring to cut its expenditure. Describe the analogy with competition in innovation.

5. Alexander Graham Bell beat Elisha Grey to the patent office by several hours, so that Bell obtained the patent on the telephone. Imagine how much that patent turned out to be worth. How much do you think Grey got for his effort and expenditure on development of the invention? How does that help explain the possibility that *average* economic profits from innovation are close to zero?

6. If average economic profits from investment in innovation are close to zero, why would many people be anxious to invest in innovation?

7. Explain how firms that share their technology with competitors benefit by improving their ability to compete against new entrants.

8. What are the possible advantages to the general welfare when firms make their technology automatically available to others (while, of course, charging a price for use of the technology)?

9. Why may it be unprofitable for a firm to spend much more on R&D than its competitors do?

10. Define the following terms:

   a. externality

   b. public good

   c. ratchet

   Explain the applicability of these concepts to the innovative economy.

11. From the point of view of the general welfare, do you think spending on R&D in Canada is too low? Too high? Just about right? Why?

17

EXTERNALITIES, THE ENVIRONMENT, AND NATURAL RESOURCES

Markets are simply the mechanisms through which economies work. But markets only work if you factor in all of the costs, and at present they exclude environmental costs. If we can change that, then markets will create an incentive to protect the environment. Carbon is the test case in how you make markets work for the environment on a global scale.

STEWART ELGIE, UNIVERSITY OF OTTAWA, FOUNDER OF ECOJUSTICE CANADA, 2007

E conomics is useful in pointing out both the accomplishments of the market and its shortcomings. But that is only half the battle. Economic analysis would be quite arid if it could not offer us any remedial suggestions for dealing with the market's shortcomings. In Chapter 13, we investigated one of the market's important imperfections: monopoly, or limited competition. In this chapter, we will look at another significant market imperfection studied by microeconomists: *externalities*. In Chapter 15, we learned that externalities—the incidental benefits or damages imposed on people not directly involved in an economic activity—can cause the market mechanism to malfunction. In Part 1 of this chapter, we study a particularly important application of this idea: externalities as a way to explain environmental problems. We will consider the extent to which the price mechanism bears responsibility for these problems and see how that same mechanism can be harnessed to help remedy them. In Part 2 of this chapter, we address a closely related subject: the depletion of natural resources. We will discuss fears that the world is quickly using up many of its vital natural resources and see how the price mechanism can help with this problem as well.

CONTENTS

PUZZLE: *Those Resilient Natural Resource Supplies*

It is a plain fact that the earth is endowed with only finite quantities of such vital resources as oil, copper, tin, and coal. This reality underlies many worried forecasts about the inevitable, and imminent, exhaustion of one resource or another. For instance, on page 409, "The Permanent Fuel Crisis" recalls a number of bleak prophecies about fuel shortages, all of which have so far proved to be off the mark.

In reality, far from running out, available supplies of many key minerals and fuels are *growing*. Known supplies of most minerals have grown at least as fast as production, and in many cases have far outstripped it. For example, in 1950 world reserves of tin were estimated at 6 million metric tonnes (mmt). Between 1950 and 2000, 11 mmt of tin were mined from the earth. Nonetheless, at the end of 2000, world reserves of tin had *increased* to 10 mmt. For iron ore (which is used to make steel), known reserves in 1950 were 19,000 mmt, and production between 1950 and 2000 amounted to about 38,000 mmt, but estimated world reserves at the end of 2000 had risen to 140,000 mmt. A similar odd story is true for zinc, copper, and many more minerals.[1] How is this possible? Aren't the quantities of these resources finite? Economic principles, as we will see later in this chapter, help to clear up these mysteries.

PART 1: THE ECONOMICS OF ENVIRONMENTAL PROTECTION

Environmental problems are not new. For example, in the Middle Ages, English kings repeatedly denounced the massive pollution of the river Thames, which, they reported, had grown so bad that it was impeding navigation of the tiny medieval ships! What *is* new and different is the attention we now give to environmental problems. Much of the increased interest stems from rising incomes, which have reduced our concerns about our most basic needs of food, clothing, and shelter and have allowed us the luxury of concentrating on the *quality* of life.

Economic thought on the subject of environmental degradation preceded the outburst of public concern by nearly half a century. In 1911, the British economist Arthur C. Pigou wrote a remarkable book called *The Economics of Welfare*, which for the first time explained environmental problems in terms of externalities. Pigou also outlined an approach to environmental policy that is still favoured by most economists today and is gradually winning over lawmakers, bureaucrats, and even cautious environmentalists (as the opening quotation suggests). His analysis indicated that a system of monetary *pollution charges* can be an effective means to control pollution. In this way, the price mechanism can remedy one of its own shortcomings!

EXTERNALITIES: A CRITICAL SHORTCOMING OF THE MARKET MECHANISM

An activity is said to generate a beneficial or detrimental **externality** if that activity causes incidental benefits or damages to others not directly involved in the activity, and no corresponding compensation is provided to or paid by those who generate the externality.

In our discussion in Chapter 15, we emphasized that externalities are found throughout the economy. For example, pollution of the air and waterways is to a considerable degree contributed by factories and motor vehicles as an incidental byproduct of their activities that damages other members of society. Similarly, another car's entry onto an overcrowded highway adds to delays that other travellers must endure, thereby causing those drivers and passengers to suffer a *detrimental* **externality.** But externalities can also be *beneficial* to third parties. In Chapter 16, when discussing the microeconomics of innovation and growth, we emphasized that the vital innovative activities, to which society devotes huge quantities of resources, usually provide beneficial externalities to persons who neither invest in innovation nor work in any research and development establishments.

---

[1] U.S. Geological Survey, *Minerals Yearbook*, various years. Retrieved from http://www.minerals.er.usgs.gov

Because those who create harmful externalities do not pay for the damage done to others, they have little incentive to desist. In this way, the market tends to create an undesired abundance of damaging externalities. Similarly, because those who create beneficial externalities are not compensated for doing so, they have little incentive to supply as large a quantity as will best serve the interests of society. Therefore, the market tends to supply an undesirably small amount of such beneficial externalities. In sum, economists conclude that unless something is done about it, the market will provide an overabundance of harmful externalities and an undersupply of desirable ones. Either case is far from ideal.

Externalities have important consequences for the welfare of society and the efficient functioning of the economy. They affect the health of the population and threaten our natural resource heritage. This chapter discusses the character and magnitude of the problem and the methods that can be used to contain its harmful consequences.

In this chapter, we focus on one of the most highly publicized externalities—pollution. Toxic fumes from a chemical plant affect not only the plant's employees and customers, but also other people not directly associated with the plant. Because the firm does not pay for this *incidental* damage, the firm's owners have no financial incentive to limit their emissions of pollution, particularly given that pollution controls cost money. Instead, the polluting firm will find it profitable to continue its toxic emissions as though the fumes caused no external damage to the community.

■ The Facts: Is the World Really Getting Steadily More Polluted?

First, let's see what the facts really are. The popular press often gives the impression that environmental problems have been growing steadily worse and that *all* pollution is attributable to modern industrialization and the profit system. The problems are, indeed, serious and some of them are extremely urgent. But it is nevertheless possible to exaggerate them.

For one thing, pollution is nothing new. Medieval cities were pestholes; streets and rivers were littered with garbage and the air stank of rotting wastes—a level of filth that was accepted as normal. Early in the twentieth century, the automobile was actually hailed for its major *improvement* in the cleanliness of city streets, which until then had fought a losing battle against the proliferation of horse dung.

Since World War II, there has been marked progress in solving a number of pollution problems in North America and Western Europe. Air quality has improved in U.S. cities during the past three decades. Measures of most air pollutants—particulate matter, sulphur dioxide, nitrogen dioxide, carbon monoxide, and lead—are now well below maximum standards set by the U.S. Environmental Protection Agency (EPA), whereas this was not always the case before 1985. Rapid declines in automobile pollution (aided by initiatives such as California's tough Clean Cars Law) have played a large role in this improvement, along with decreases in emissions from power plants. Water quality has also improved. However, despite improvement, many urban areas in the United States and elsewhere still suffer from excessive levels of ground-level ozone, especially during the summer. Ozone (the presence of which high above the earth protects humans from the fiercest part of the sun's ultraviolet radiation) is a primary component of smog—ground-level air pollution.

The Europeans have made progress as well. For example, the infamous killing fogs of London, once the staple backdrop of British mystery fiction, are a thing of the past because of the air quality improvement since 1950. The Thames River has been cleaned up enough to allow large-scale fishing of giant conger eels to resume after a 150-year hiatus. The point is that pollution problems are not a uniquely modern phenomenon, nor is every part of the environment deteriorating relentlessly.

Market economies certainly have no monopoly on pollution. Although it may seem that a centrally planned economy should be able to cope much better with the environmental problems caused by externalities, such economies have in reality been the *biggest* environmental disasters. China, the last large communist society, has some of the world's worst air pollution, mainly from the burning of low-quality, high-sulphur coal and a dearth of pollution control devices. Urban ozone levels in China are far greater than those in Los Angeles, a place that Americans tend to think invented smog.

Grave environmental problems also continue to plague Eastern Europe and the countries of the former Soviet Union. Poland, despite considerable improvement since 1989, continues to battle very serious air pollution problems. Particularly in the cities, high pollution levels contribute to health problems. The collapse of communism in the former Soviet Union revealed a staggering array of environmental horrors, including massive poisoning of air, ground, and water in the vicinity of industrial plants and the devastation of the Aral Sea, once the world's fourth-largest inland sea, but now reduced to less than half its previous size. Many Russians live in environmentally hazardous conditions, and especially severe problems are found in Chechnya, where millions of barrels of oil have seeped into the ground from the region's black-market oil industry. Radioactive pollutants from 50 years of plutonium production, processing, and storage at the Mayak industrial complex have turned nearby Lake Karachay into one of the most polluted places on earth. The result has been widespread illness and countless premature deaths in these areas.[2]

Air pollution in Canada does not seem to have improved recently. Figures 1 and 2 show some Canadian historical data about fine particulate matter and ground-level ozone, which are the two key components of smog that have a negative impact on health, most notably respiratory problems. While no significant trend is discernible in relation to fine particulates—the series is still too short—ground-level ozone measures grew by nearly 1 percent per year over the 1990 to 2005 period. This increase seems to be related mainly to activities in southern Ontario and perhaps in the Quebec and eastern Ontario region, as Figure 2 shows similar regional measures for these two areas. Indeed, the Ontario Ministry of Environment issued 123 smog alerts in Toronto between 2001 and 2006 (about 20 per year), whereas there were only 37 (6 per year) between 1995 and 2000. Such a dramatic increase in pollution is one of the reasons that, in the fall of 2006, the Canadian federal government tabled a Clean

FIGURE 1

Air Quality Trends in Canada

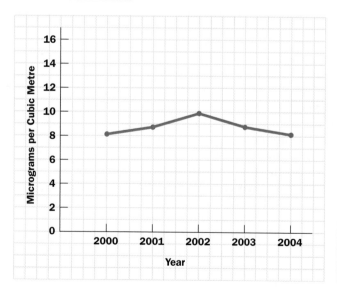

(a) Fine Particulates (PM$_{2.5}$) Indicator, 2000–2005

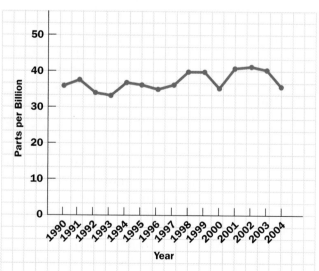

(b) Ground-Level Ozone Indicator, 1990–2005

SOURCE: Statistics Canada, *Canadian Environmental Sustainability Indicators*, Catalogue No. 16-251XIE, 2006 (Figure 3, p. 8, and Figure 1, p. 5).

[2] Central Intelligence Agency, *The World Factbook*. Retrieved from www.cia.gov; "Poland: Areas of Concern," Resource Renewal Institute. Retrieved from http://www.rri.org; and "Russia: Environmental Issues," U.S. Department of Energy, Energy Information Administration. Retrieved from http://www.eia.doe.gov.

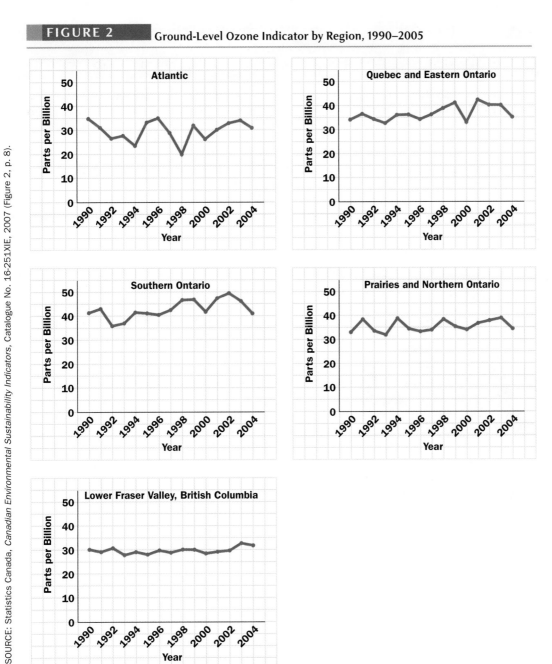

FIGURE 2   Ground-Level Ozone Indicator by Region, 1990–2005

SOURCE: Statistics Canada, *Canadian Environmental Sustainability Indicators*, Catalogue No. 16-251XIE, 2007 (Figure 2, p. 8).

Air Act, the goal of which is to improve air quality both indoors and outdoors and decrease emissions of greenhouse gases. The Act includes short-, medium-, and long-term industrial air pollution targets that will be at least as stringent as those in other countries that are taking lead roles in handling environmental issues.

Smog is not the only problem, however: Freshwater quality is also threatened by industrial activity and bacteria such as blue algae, which thrive on the phosphorus in detergents and fertilizers. As is obvious with water problems, our world is frequently subjected to new pollutants, some far more dangerous than those we have reduced, although less visible and less malodorous. Improperly dumped toxic substances—such as PCBs (polychlorinated biphenyls), chlorinated hydrocarbons, dioxins, heavy metals, and radioactive materials—can cause cancer and threaten life and health in other ways. The danger presented by some of these substances can persist for thousands of years, causing all but irreversible damage.

An Alternative View of Global Warming

The chart that illustrates the evolution of mean global temperatures in the boxed feature on page 395 shows clearly that global temperatures have been rising over the last 125 years. The consensus among environmental specialists—one that is reinforced every year—is that carbon dioxide gases produced by human activity are the main source of global warming, but a small group of scientists disagree. Although the latter are often written off as researchers sponsored by corporations that produce GHG emissions, many ordinary citizens still wonder whether global warming is not just the latest hysterical craze, along the lines of the Y2K computer bug, which many predicted would lead to total chaos on January 1, 2000. Indeed, in 2002, before he became prime minister of Canada, Stephen Harper wrote, "Kyoto is essentially a socialist scheme to suck money out of wealth-producing nations."

Global Warming and the Kyoto Protocol

This photo shows the significant glacial retreat in the Swiss Alps caused by global warming.

But all these problems pale when compared to a global environmental threat—the long-term warming of the earth's atmosphere. Environment Canada measurements show that annual temperatures between 1948 and 2005 have trended upward by 0.1° Celsius in the Atlantic provinces, 0.5° in the Great Lakes/St. Lawrence River area (the corridor between Quebec City and Windsor, Ontario), and 1.3° in the Prairies (Winnipeg, Regina, Calgary, Edmonton) and on the Pacific Coast (Vancouver). Scientists have demonstrated that the documented global warming of the past century, and especially in the past decade, is a consequence of human activities that have increased greenhouse gases (GHG) in the atmosphere (but see the box "An Alternative View of Global Warming").

Most climatologists agree that the carbon dioxide buildup from the burning of fossil fuels such as oil, natural gas, and coal is a prime contributor to this problem. Forecasts of future warming range from 1.8° to 4.0° Celsius by the year 2100, a dramatic change that may shift world rain patterns, disrupt agriculture, threaten coastal cities with inundation, and expand deserts (for more on this topic and for empirical evidence about past and future warming trends, see the box "Global Warming: A Scientific Report").

> Although environmental problems are neither new nor confined to capitalist, industrialized economies, we continue to inflict damage on ourselves and our surroundings.

Most specialists believe that if average temperatures rise more than 2° Celsius, a cataclysmic chain of events could occur and threaten our planet). They argue that the best way to keep global warming under control is to acquiesce to the Kyoto Protocol. This international treaty was signed by Canada and 155 other nations in 1997, but it did not officially come into force until February 2005, when, in a surprise move, Russia decided to ratify it. Canada ratified the Protocol in 2002, committing itself to reducing its GHG emissions to 6 percent below 1990 levels by 2008–2012. But many experts believe that even such reductions will be insufficient to stop global warming and that tougher objectives, such as a 33 percent reduction, are required.

Canada's performance in this regard has been dismal, however. As Figure 3 shows, instead of reducing its greenhouse gas emissions, Canada's emissions in 2005 were 25 percent above the 1990 level—33 percent above the Kyoto target. The federal government plan, as outlined in its 2006–2007 Clean Air Act, is that the Kyoto target be achieved by 2020. Environmentalists such as David Suzuki, however, advocate, that the 1990 emission levels be reduced by 25 percent by 2020 and by 80 percent by 2050 if rises of global temperatures exceeding the possibly catastrophic 2° Celsius are to be avoided. The only good news so far is that Canada reduced GHG emissions *per unit of GDP* by 18 percent between 1990 and 2005 (see Figure 4). This means that lower

Global Warming: A Scientific Report

The World Meteorological Organization and the United Nations Environment Programme established the Intergovernmental Panel on Climate Change (IPCC) in 1988. The IPCC does not carry out research but rather assesses all information relevant to understanding the risk of human-induced (anthropogenic) climate change.

In its third assessment report (TAR), the IPCC concluded that "most of the observed warming over the last 50 years is *likely* to have been due to the increase in greenhouse gas concentrations." In its fourth assessment report, presented in February 2007, the IPCC now believes that this is *very likely*, as shown in its findings below.

The understanding of anthropogenic warming and cooling influences on climate has improved since the Third Assessment Report (TAR), leading to *very high confidence* that the globally averaged net effect of human activities since 1750 has been one of warming. . . .

Warming of the climate system is unequivocal, as is now evident from observations of increases in global average air and ocean temperatures, widespread melting of snow and ice, and rising global average sea level. . . .

At continental, regional, and ocean basin scales, numerous long-term changes in climate have been observed. These include changes in Arctic temperatures and ice, widespread changes in precipitation amounts, ocean salinity, wind patterns and aspects of extreme weather including droughts, heavy precipitation, heat waves and the intensity of tropical cyclones. . . .

Paleoclimate information supports the interpretation that the warmth of the last half-century is unusual in at least the previous 1,300 years. The last time the polar regions were significantly warmer than present for an extended period (about 125,000 years ago), reductions in polar ice volume led to 4 to 6 metres of sea level rise. . . .

Most of the observed increase in globally averaged temperatures since the mid-20th century is *very likely* due to the observed increase in anthropogenic greenhouse gas concentrations. . . . Discernible human influences now extend to other aspects of climate, including ocean warming, continental-average temperatures, temperature extremes and wind patterns. . . .

For the next two decades a warming of about 0.2°C per decade is projected for a range of . . . emission scenarios. Even if the concentrations of all greenhouse gases and aerosols had been kept constant at year 2000 levels, a further warming of about 0.1°C per decade would be expected. . . .

Continued greenhouse gas emissions at or above current rates would cause further warming and induce many changes in the global climate system during the 21st century that would *very likely* be larger than those observed during the 20th century. . . .

Anthropogenic warming and sea level rise would continue for centuries due to the timescales associated with climate processes and feedbacks, even if greenhouse gas concentrations were to be stabilized. . . .

SOURCE: Excerpt from *Contribution of Working Group I to the Fourth Assessment Report of the Intergovernmental Panel on Climate Change*, "Climate Change 2007: The Physical Science Basis—Summary for Policymakers," Geneva, Switzerland, February 2007. Retrieved from http://www.ipcc.ch/SPM2feb07.pdf

MEAN GLOBAL SURFACE AIR TEMPERATURE, 1880–2007

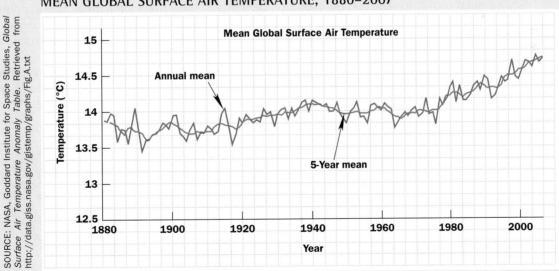

SOURCE: NASA, Goddard Institute for Space Studies, *Global Surface Air Temperature Anomaly Table*. Retrieved from http://data.giss.nasa.gov/gistemp/graphs/Fig.A.txt

amounts of greenhouse gases are being emitted for each good being manufactured and for each commercial activity. Improvements in energy efficiency and the production of energy explain most of this change. But despite this improvement, Canada is still a laggard—Canada, Australia, and the United States have the greatest amounts of GHG emissions per capita and also per unit of GDP among major industrialized countries.

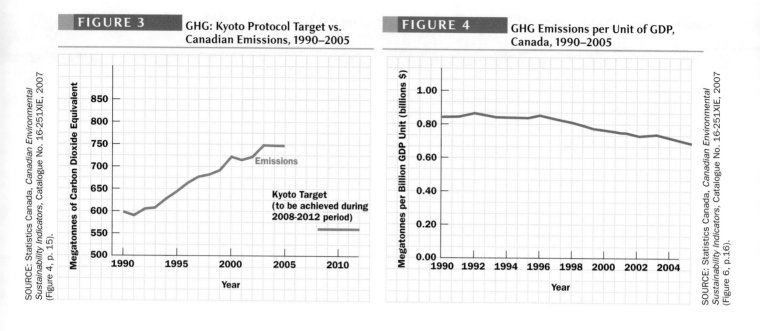

FIGURE 3 GHG: Kyoto Protocol Target vs. Canadian Emissions, 1990–2005

SOURCE: Statistics Canada, *Canadian Environmental Sustainability Indicators*, Catalogue No. 16-251XIE, 2007 (Figure 4, p. 15).

FIGURE 4 GHG Emissions per Unit of GDP, Canada, 1990–2005

SOURCE: Statistics Canada, *Canadian Environmental Sustainability Indicators*, Catalogue No. 16-251XIE, 2007 (Figure 6, p.16).

Trade-Offs in Dealing with Global Warming

Figure 5 helps to explain the difficult conundrum that faces federal politicians. Because GHG emissions are mostly associated with the production and consumption of energy (coal, oil, and natural gas industries, and fossil fuel-fired electricity generation, as well as transportation), this production and consumption accounted for 82 percent of total Canadian emissions in 2005. These energy-related activities also accounted for 90 percent of the growth in emissions from 1990 to 2005. As a consequence, western provinces such as Alberta and Saskatchewan account for a relatively over-large proportion of GHG emissions, with Ontario—a very large car producer—accounting for the largest absolute amounts. These three provinces also account for the biggest emissions increases since 1990. The fact that only three provinces are responsible for a huge amount of Canada's greenhouse gas emissions understandably puts the federal government into a difficult position.

Indeed, it is possible that Canadian government officials who were disinclined to ratify the Kyoto Protocol were hoping that both the United States and Russia would continue to refuse to ratify the agreement, which would have prevented the Protocol

FIGURE 5 GHG Emissions: Provinces and Territories, 1990 and 2005

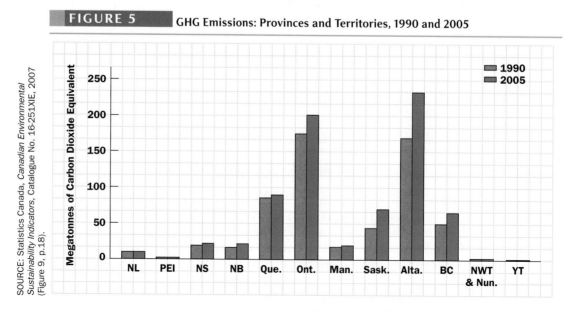

SOURCE: Statistics Canada, *Canadian Environmental Sustainability Indicators*, Catalogue No. 16-251XIE, 2007 (Figure 9, p.18).

from coming into force for lack of sufficient participation. This hope was well founded in the case the United States, but wrong in the case of Russia. Because Russia has greatly reduced its GHG emissions since 1990 as a consequence of the terrible economic debacle that it experienced during its transition to a market economy, it could benefit financially from the Kyoto Protocol since countries that fulfill the Kyoto requirements can sell their rights to produce greenhouse gases to corporations or countries that are unable to meet their emissions reduction obligations.

Also troublesome for the Canadian government are the uncertainties associated with the future economic costs of global warming and the possible trade-off between economic growth and the achievement of the Kyoto targets. As indicated in the 2006 Stern report on global warming mentioned in Chapter 15 on page 351, Canada and Scandinavia may actually derive net benefits from global warming, despite coastal areas being disrupted by rising sea levels, as warmer weather will allow higher agricultural yields, lower heating requirements, and possibly more tourism. Global warming is expected to be the most damaging to southern Europe and most of the developing world. Since Canada's share of worldwide GHG emissions is relatively small, and because world GHG emissions are expected to rise considerably, in particular in India and China, Canadian action needs to be motivated by a desire for world equity and by fears of catastrophic consequences for world peace if the worst-case scenario materializes.

It now seems that a majority of Canadians do want their governments to tackle and reduce GHG emissions. The question is how fast this should be done. In a document released in April 2007, the federal government assessed that meeting its obligations under the Kyoto Protocol would require cutting GHG emissions by one-third in 2008–2012. This would entail a deep economic recession, with GDP falling by about 4 percent relative to the previous year, which is more than 6.5 percentage points relative to the "business as usual" situation. About 275,000 jobs would be lost and natural gas and gasoline prices would need to rise by more than 60 percent.[3] These forecasts have been criticized by environmental specialists, but to some extent they are indicators of what could happen. This is why the federal 2006–2007 Clean Air Act proposes measures designed to meet the Kyoto targets around 2020, not in the 2008–2012 period specified.

Pollution and the Law of Conservation of Matter and Energy

The physical law of conservation of matter and energy tells us that objects cannot disappear—at most they can be changed into something else. Petroleum, for instance, can be transformed into heat (and smoke) or into plastic—but it will never vanish. This means that after a raw material has been used, either it must be used again (recycled) or it becomes a waste product that requires disposal.

If it is not recycled, any input used in production must ultimately become a waste product. It may end up in some municipal dump; it may literally go up in smoke, contributing to atmospheric pollution; or it may be transformed into heat, warming up adjacent waterways and killing aquatic life. But the laws of physics tell us nothing can be done to make used inputs disappear altogether.

We create an extraordinary amount of solid waste. Despite our efforts to reduce waste, each Canadian discards more than 300 kilograms of residential trash every year. If we include nonresidential solid waste, this per-capita number is raised to nearly 800 kilograms per year. This is more than any other OECD country, with the United States, Ireland, and Australia all producing 700 kilograms or more of solid waste per capita every year. Fortunately, in the face of the rising tide of garbage, recycling rates for many commonly used materials (such as aluminum, paper, and glass) are rising in Canada and many other industrial countries.

Still, although recycling has increased over the years, only a small percentage of municipal solid waste in Canada was handled by recycling and resource recovery in

[3] Environment Canada, *The Cost of Bill C-288 to Canadian Families and Business*, April 2007. Retrieved from http://www.ec.gc.ca/doc/media/m_123/report_eng.pdf

2002 (21.6 percent) and 2004 (23.7 percent); this is called the *waste diversion rate*. This is better than in many other industrial countries: The waste diversion rate in Switzerland was 20 percent, and the statistics for Japan, Sweden, the Netherlands, Germany, and Spain are all in the 15 to 20 percent range. By contrast, the United States recycles 28 percent of its municipal solid waste. In Canada, only the province of Nova Scotia does any better, with 33.0 and 35.5 percent waste diversion rates in 2002 and 2004, respectively, thanks to a program that was started in 1996.[4]

Our very existence makes some environmental damage inevitable. To eat and protect ourselves from the elements, people must inevitably use up the earth's resources and generate wastes.

> Environmental damage cannot be reduced to zero. As long as the human race survives, eliminating such damage completely is impossible.

Why do economists believe that, although environmental damage cannot be reduced to zero, the *public interest* requires it to be reduced below its free-market level? Why do economists conclude that the market mechanism, which is so good at providing approximately the right number of hockey sticks and hair dryers, generates too much pollution? Pollution is an externality, which means that it results from a price mechanism malfunction that prevents the market from doing its usual effective job of carrying out consumers' wishes.

Here, the *failure of the pricing system* is caused by a pollution-generating firm's ability to use up some of the community's clean air or water without paying for the privilege. Just as the firm would undoubtedly use oil and electricity wastefully if they were available at no charge, so it will use "free" air wastefully, despoiling it with chemical fumes far beyond the level justified by the public interest. The problem is that *price* has not been permitted to play its usual role here. Instead of having to pay for the pure air that it uses up, a polluting firm gets that valuable resource free of charge.

> Externalities play a crucial role affecting the quality of life. They show why the market mechanism, which is so efficient in supplying consumers' goods, has a much poorer record in terms of environmental effects. The problem of pollution illustrates the importance of externalities for public policy.

SUPPLY–DEMAND ANALYSIS OF ENVIRONMENTAL EXTERNALITIES

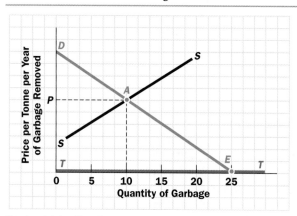

FIGURE 6   Free Dumping of Pollutants as an Inducement to Environmental Damage

Note: Quantity is in millions of tonnes per year.

We can use basic supply–demand analysis to explain both how externalities lead to environmental problems and how these problems can be cured. As an illustration, consider the environmental damage caused by massive garbage generation.

Figure 6 shows a hypothetical demand curve, *DE*, for garbage removal. As usual, this curve has a negative slope, meaning that if garbage removal prices rise, people will demand less removal. They may create less waste, or take more waste to recycling centres, or reuse items rather than throwing them out after one use. (See "Garbage! Economic Incentives to Create Less of It and Recycle More of It" on the next page for an example of financial incentives in action.)

The graph also shows the supply curve, *SS*, of an ideal market for garbage removal. This is the marginal cost for

---

[4] Statistics Canada, *Waste Management Industry Survey: Business and Government Sectors 2004*, February 2007, Catalogue No. 16F0023XIE, Tables A1 and A2, p. 18; Conference Board of Canada, *How Canada Performs: A Report Card on* Canada, 2007, pp. 72–73, retrieved from http://www.conferenceboard.ca; U.S. Environmental Protection Agency, *Municipal Solid Waste Factbook*, retrieved from http://www.epa.gov. Note that recycling is not always as benign as it might seem. The very process of preparing materials for reuse often can produce dangerous emissions. The recycling of waste oil is a good example of this, because used petroleum products are often combined with toxic chemicals that can be released in the recycling process.

Garbage! Economic Incentives to Create Less of It and Recycle More of It

Some communities operate "pay-as-you-throw" programs (PAYT), in which residents are charged for the collection of household garbage based on the amount they throw away. These are user fee systems based on the "polluter pays" principle. This creates a direct economic incentive to generate less garbage and to recycle more of what is generated. Rather than paying a flat fee for waste disposal (or simply receiving waste disposal services without any sense of what the cost is—as is true when a municipality provides trash collection services and pays for them out of general revenues), these programs require residents to pay for municipal waste disposal based on the number of bags or cans of trash placed at the curb or dropped off at a trash disposal facility.

Such a system has been put in place in a number of cities in Canada, including British Columbia's capital, Victoria. Households are limited to one bag of garbage per household per week. Households who have more garbage to dispose of must purchase tags at $3 apiece and attach one to each extra bag. A similar program exists in Orillia, Ontario, where all garbage bags have to be tagged to be picked up. Households get the first 40 tags free and must pay $1.50 for each additional tag.

It is no surprise that this system works! It has been shown that variable rate PAYT programs have substantially reduced the tonnage of waste shipped to disposal facilities. Various studies, mostly done in the United States, estimate that PAYT programs have reduced residential disposal by 14 to 47 percent. About half of this can be attributed to the reduction in generated garbage, while the other half is attributable to increases in recycling. In Orillia, for instance, the amount of material sent to recycling increased by 31 percent over a five-year period once the PAYT program was introduced.

SOURCE: © Bernard Wittich/Visuals Unlimited

SOURCES: Statistics Canada, *Human Activity and the Environment: Annual* Statistics, 2005, Catalogue No. 16-201-XIE, p. 18; Donald N. Dewees, "Pricing Municipal Services: The Economics of User Fees," *Canadian Tax Journal*, 50(2), 2002, pp. 586–599.

garbage removal. In an ideal world, it would include both the private and the social costs, including costs of pollution (such as laundry and doctor's bills, charged to garbage removal suppliers) caused when garbage is burned at the dump. The supply curve shows the prices at which suppliers can be induced to provide any given quantity of output. For the community depicted in the graph, the price of garbage removal is P dollars per tonne, and 10 million tonnes are generated (point A).

But what if the community's government decides to remove garbage "for free"? Of course, the consumer still really pays for garbage removal through taxes, but not in a way that makes each household pay for the quantity of garbage it actually produces. The marginal cost as perceived by consumers is then no longer SS. Rather it becomes the blue line TT, which lies along the horizontal axis, because any household can increase the garbage it throws away at no cost to itself. Now the intersection of the supply and demand curve is no longer point A. Rather it is point E, at which the price is zero, and the quantity of garbage generated is 25 million tonnes—a substantially greater amount.

Similar problems occur in the case of water consumption. Canadians rank as the second-largest per-capita water users in the world, using 1,600 cubic metres of water per person per year. Water use is two to three times that of the average French and average German citizen. This wasteful consumption of water can be attributed to the apparent zero cost of water, since most Canadian cities have no water meters. The impact of people having to pay for their water consumption can be illustrated by the example of the twin cities Ottawa and Gatineau, which are, respectively, on the Ontario and Quebec banks of the Ottawa River. In Ottawa, where there are water meters and where user fees are imposed on water consumption, no restriction on water use is ever needed during the dry months of summer, as additional use of water entails additional costs for consumers, inducing self-restriction (this can be represented once more with the help of Figure 6, where the price of water is P and the horizontal quantities represent quantities consumed: 10 units).

By contrast, in Gatineau, where water seems to be "free," since it is paid for through a lump-sum municipal tax which entails no additional cost when more water is being used, municipal water restrictions have to be imposed every summer, as water in the reservoirs of treatment facilities tend to fall below safe levels. (Reinterpreting Figure 6, the apparent price of water is zero and water quantities consumed without the restrictions would be 25 units.) Local politicians in Canadian cities such as Gatineau usually argue that the costs of installing and monitoring water meters would be too high.

> The magnitude of our pollution problems is largely attributable to the fact that the market lets individuals, firms, and government agencies deplete such resources as clean water and pure air without charging them any money for using up those resources.

It follows that one way of dealing with pollution problems is to charge those who emit pollution, and those who despoil the environment in other ways, a price commensurate with the costs they impose on society.

BASIC APPROACHES TO ENVIRONMENTAL POLICY

In broad terms, there are three ways to control activities that damage the environment:

- *Voluntary efforts*, such as nonmandatory investment in pollution control equipment by firms motivated by social responsibility, or voluntary recycling of solid wastes by consumers.
- *Direct controls*, which either (1) impose legal ceilings on the amount any polluter is permitted to emit or (2) specify how particular activities must be carried out. For example, direct controls may prohibit backyard garbage incinerators or high-sulphur coal burning or require smokestack "scrubbers" to capture the emissions of power plants.
- *Taxes on pollution*, *tradable emissions permits*, or the use of other monetary incentives or penalties to make it unattractive financially for pollution emitters to continue to pollute as usual.

As we will see next, all of these methods have useful roles.

1. Voluntarism   Voluntarism, although admirable, often has proved weak and unreliable. Some well-intentioned business firms, for example, have voluntarily made sincere attempts to adopt environmentally beneficial practices. Yet competition has usually prevented them from spending more than token amounts for this purpose. No business, whatever its virtues, can long afford to spend so much on "good works" that rivals can easily underprice it. As a result, voluntary business programs sometimes have been more helpful to the companies' public relations activities than to the environment.

Yet voluntary measures do have their place. They are appropriate where surveillance and, consequently, enforcement is impractical, as in the prevention of littering by campers in isolated areas, where appeals to people's consciences are the only alternative. And in brief but serious emergencies, which do not allow for time to plan and enact a systematic program, voluntary compliance may be the only workable approach.

Several major cities have, for example, experienced episodes of temporary but dangerous concentrations of pollutants, forcing the authorities to appeal to the public for drastic emissions cuts. Public response to appeals requiring cooperation for short periods often has been enthusiastic and gratifying, particularly when civic pride was a factor. For example, during the 1984 Summer Olympic Games, in which one of the authors participated, Los Angeles city officials asked motorists to car-pool, businesses to stagger work hours, and truckers to restrict themselves to essential deliveries and to avoid rush hours. The result was an extraordinary decrease in traffic and smog, such that the San Gabriel Mountains suddenly became visible behind the city.

Direct controls are government rules that tell organizations or individuals what processes or raw materials they may use or what products they are permitted to supply or purchase.

2. Direct Controls   **Direct controls** have traditionally been the chief instrument of environmental policy in Canada. Under the Constitution, legislative authority for the environment is shared between the provincial and federal governments, and this has sometimes resulted in intergovernmental jurisdictional disputes over recent years. The job of enforcing federal standards often falls to the provinces. A well-known example is that of emissions standards for new vehicles sold in Canada: These standards are set by the federal government but the provincial governments are responsible for the control of pollution after the automobiles or the trucks have been sold.

3. Taxes on Pollution Emissions Most economists agree that relying exclusively on direct controls is a mistake and that, in most cases, *financial penalties*, or **pollution charges,** on polluters can do the same job more dependably, effectively, and economically.

The most common suggestion is that governments permit firms to pollute all they want but be forced to pay a tax for the privilege, in order to make them *want* to pollute less. Under such a plan, the quantity of the polluter's emissions is metered just like the use of electricity. At the end of the month, the government sends the polluter a bill charging a stipulated amount for each litre (or other unit) of emissions. (The amount can also vary with the emissions' quality, with a higher tax rate being imposed on emissions that are more dangerous or unpleasant.) Thus, in such a scheme, the more environmental damage done, the more the polluter pays. Emissions taxes are deliberately designed to *encourage* polluters to take advantage of the tax loophole—by polluting less, the polluter can reduce the amount of tax owed.

In terms of Figure 6, if the tax is used to increase the payment for waste emissions from zero (blue supply line *TT*) and instead forces the polluter to pay its true cost to society (line *SS*), then emissions will be reduced from 25 million to 10 million tonnes.

Businesses *do* respond to such taxes. One well-known example is the Ruhr River basin in Germany, where emissions taxes have been used for many years. Although the Ruhr is a heavily concentrated industrial centre, the rivers that are protected by taxes are clean enough for fishing and other recreational purposes. Firms have also found it profitable to avoid taxes by extracting pollutants from their liquid discharges and recycling them. (See "Making the Polluter Pay" for another example of the response to taxes.)

Emissions Taxes Versus Direct Control

It is important to see why taxes on emissions may prove more effective and reliable than direct controls. Direct controls rely on the criminal justice system for enforcement. But a polluter who violates the rules must first be caught. Then the regulatory agency must decide whether it has enough evidence to prosecute. Next, the agency must win its case in court. Finally, the court must impose a penalty strong enough to matter. If any *one* of these steps does not occur, the polluter gets away with the environmentally damaging activities.

Enforcement Issues Enforcement of direct controls requires vigilance and enthusiasm by the regulatory agency, which must assign the resources and persons needed to carry out enforcement. But in many cases the resources devoted to enforcement are pitifully small. The effectiveness of direct controls also depends on the speed and rigor of the court system. Yet the courts are often slow and lenient. In addition, direct controls work only if the legal system imposes substantial penalties on violators. Whereas U.S. courts sometimes do impose hefty penalties, this is not usually the case in Canada.

For instance, the 2004–2005 report of the enforcement activities carried out under the Canadian Environmental Protection Act of 1999 shows that while there were over 5,000 inspections during that time period, charges were laid in only 23 cases, with 1 conviction and 20 contraventions being assigned. Fines under the Act are usually in the paltry $1,000 to $25,000 range. A more recent case, related to the Fisheries Act, which protects water resources, involved a division of Tembec Inc. that operates in Temiscaming, in northwest Quebec. The firm pleaded guilty to having deposited deleterious substances into the Ottawa River 16 times during 2003 and 2004, despite warnings by an inspector. In May 2006, the firm was ordered to pay a $750,000 penalty.

Pollution charges (taxes on emissions) are taxes that polluters are required to pay. The amount they pay depends on what they emit and in what quantities.

Making the Polluter Pay

In the Netherlands, a set of charges originally intended to cover only the costs of wastewater treatment has produced a classic demonstration of the pollution-preventing power of charges themselves. Since 1970, gradually rising fees for emissions of organic material and heavy metals into canals, rivers, and lakes have spurred companies to cut emissions, but without dictating how. Between 1976 and 1994, emissions of cadmium, copper, lead, mercury, and zinc plummeted 86–97 percent, primarily because of the charges, according to statistical analyses. . . . And demand for pollution control equipment has spurred Dutch manufacturers to develop better models, lowering costs and turning the country into a global leader in the market. The taxes have in effect sought the path of least economic resistance—of least cost—in cleaning up the country's waters.

Industrial Discharges of Selected Heavy Metals into Surface Waters of the Netherlands, 1976–1994

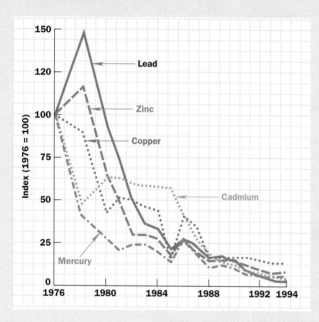

SOURCE: © Lana/Shutterstock

SOURCE: David Malin Roodman, "Getting the Signals Right: Tax Reform to Protect the Environment and the Economy" from Worldwatch Institute, *Worldwatch Paper* 134, 1997 (www.worldwatch.org).

Where more drastic penalties are available, their very magnitude may make the authorities reluctant to impose them. In an extreme case, in which the only legal remedy is to force the closing of an offending plant, the government agency is likely to ignore the offence under local pressure to preserve a community's source of jobs and income. An example of this problem came to light in Saskatchewan in 1984. The Atomic Energy Control Board simply allowed continued violation of federal regulations by the Key Lake Mining Corporation, until an 87-million-litre spill of radioactive water attracted national attention.

In contrast, pollution taxes are automatic and certain. No one need be caught, prosecuted, convicted, and punished. The tax bills are sent out automatically by the untiring tax collector. The only sure way for the polluter to avoid paying pollution charges is to pollute less.

Efficiency in Cleanup   A second important advantage of emissions taxes is that they tend to cost less than direct controls. Statistical estimates for several pollution control programs suggest that the cost of doing the job through direct controls can easily be twice as high as under the tax alternative. Why should there be such a difference?

Under direct controls, emissions cutbacks are usually *not* apportioned among the various firms on the basis of ability to reduce pollution cheaply and efficiently.

Suppose it costs Firm A only 4 cents per litre to reduce emissions, whereas Firm B must spend 20 cents per litre to do the same job. If each firm spews out 2,000 litres of pollution per day, authorities can achieve a 50 percent reduction in pollution by ordering both firms to limit emissions to 1,000 litres per day. This may or may not be fair, but it is certainly not efficient. The social cost will be 1,000 × 4 cents (or $40) to Firm A, and 1,000 × 20 cents (or $200) to Firm B, a total of $240. If the government had instead imposed a tax of 10 cents per litre, Firm A would have done all the cleanup work by itself, at a far lower total cost. Why? Firm A would have eliminated its emissions altogether, paying the 4 cents/litre cost to avoid the 10 cents/litre tax. Firm B would have gone on polluting as before, because the tax would be cheaper than the 20 cents/litre cost of controlling its pollution. In this way, under the tax, *total daily emissions would still be cut by 2,000 litres per day,* but the total daily cost of the program would be $80 (4 cents × 2,000 litres) as opposed to $240 under direct controls.

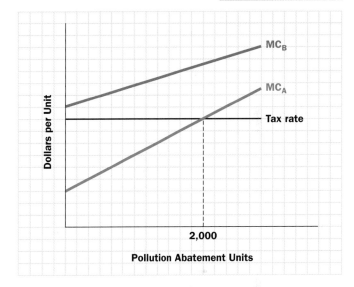

FIGURE 7

The Impact of Emission Taxes on Pollution Abatement

The secret of a pollution tax's efficiency is straightforward. Only polluters that can reduce emissions cheaply and efficiently can afford to take advantage of the built-in loophole—the opportunity to save on taxes by reducing emissions. The tax approach therefore assigns the job to those who can do it most effectively—and rewards them by letting them escape the tax.

In general, if firms face rising marginal costs in pollution abatement, they will reduce pollution until the marginal cost of reducing emissions is lower or equal to the tax per unit of emission. Thus, as shown in Figure 7, firms with low marginal abatement costs (Firm A, given by MC_A) will prefer to reduce emissions by a larger amount than firms with high abatement costs (Firm B, with costs MC_B, which here makes no reduction whatsoever).

Advantages and Disadvantages   Given all these advantages of the tax approach, why would anyone want to use direct controls?

In three important situations, direct controls have a clear advantage:

* *Where an emission is so dangerous that it must be prohibited altogether.*
* *Where a sudden change in circumstances—for example, a dangerous air quality crisis—calls for prompt and substantial changes in conduct, such as temporary reductions in use of cars.* Tax rule changes are difficult and time-consuming, so direct controls will usually do a better job in such a case. The mayor of a city threatened by a dangerous air quality crisis can, for example, forbid use of private passenger cars until the crisis passes.
* *Where effective and dependable pollution metering devices have not been invented or are prohibitively costly to install and operate.* In such cases, authorities cannot operate an effective tax program because they cannot determine the emissions levels of an individual polluter and so cannot calculate the tax bill. This is a good example of transactions costs, as introduced on page 352 of Chapter 15. In this case, the ability of the market mechanism to solve the problem breaks down. An effective option may be to require firms to use "clean" fuel or install emissions-purification equipment. A simple alternative, when metering is impossible or too costly, is to tax the good whose production is associated with pollution instead of attempting to tax the pollution emissions as such. This, as we already saw on page 227 of Chapter 10, will also lead to a reduction of emissions, as less of the polluting good will be sold as a consequence of its higher price.

Another Financial Device to Protect the Environment: Emissions Permits

The basic idea underlying the emissions-tax approach to environmental protection is that financial incentives induce polluters to reduce their environmental damage. But at least one other form of financial inducement can accomplish the same thing: requiring polluters to buy **emissions permits** that authorize the emission of a specified quantity of pollutant. Such permits can be offered for sale in limited quantities fixed by the government authorities at prices set by demand and supply.

Under this arrangement, the environmental agency decides what quantity of emissions per unit of time (say, per year) is tolerable and then issues a batch of permits authorizing (altogether) just that amount of pollution. The permits are sold to the highest bidders, with the price determined by demand and supply. The price is likely to be high if the number of permits offered for sale is small and many firms need permits to carry out their industrial activities because, as more emissions need to be reduced, the marginal cost of reducing emissions is likely to rise. The price of permits is thus influenced by the cost of reducing emissions. If technological progress is such that the cost of emission abatement is reduced, we should expect the price of permits to be reduced as well.

The effect of the marginal cost of emissions reduction on the price of permits is illustrated in Figure 8. Suppose that the government wants to reduce emissions by 2,000 litres per day per polluter on average, as shown by the vertical line *ER*. Once again there are two polluters, one of which, Firm A, has relatively low pollution reduction costs, given by the marginal cost curve MC_A. The price of pollution permits, *P*, will be such that the number of permits that Firm A wishes to sell will be exactly equal to the number of permits that the firm with high pollution reduction costs (Firm B, with marginal cost MC_B) is willing to purchase (in this case, 300 permits will be exchanged). If the government decides to increase the average amount of pollution abatement, the *ER* curve will be shifted to the right, and the price of permits will turn out to be higher. If one firm, say Firm A, introduces more efficient means to reduce emissions and shifts down its emission reduction cost curve (to MC_A'), the price of permits will be lower, at *P'*, and more permits will be exchanged (700, according to the figure).

Emissions permits basically work like a tax—they make it too expensive for firms to continue polluting as much as before. However, the permit approach has some advantages over taxes. For example, it reduces *uncertainty* about the *quantity* of pollution that will be emitted. Under a tax, we cannot be sure about this quantity in advance, because it depends on polluters' response to a given tax rate. In the case of permits, environmental authorities decide on an emissions ceiling in advance, then issue permits authorizing just that amount of emissions.

Take again the case of polluting Firm A and Firm B. They each emit 2,000 litres of pollution per day but each firm has been given the right to produce only 1,000 litres of pollution per day (1,000 units of emission permits). If the price of emission permits turns out to be, say, 12 cents per litre, Firm A can reduce its emissions by 2,000 litres per day, at a cost of 4 cents per litre, for a total cost of $80, and sell 1,000 units of its emission permits, thus getting $120 in the process. Firm A thus makes an accounting profit of $40 ($120 − $80) and an economic profit of $80, since otherwise it would have had to disburse $40 to reduce emissions by 1,000 litres. On the other hand, Firm B, whose pollution control cost is 20 cents per litre (or $200 per 1,000 litres) would rather buy 1,000 units of emission permits from Firm B at 12 cents each, for a total private cost of $120. With this transaction, Firm B also makes an economic profit of $80 since it avoids disbursing $200.

Emissions permits are licences issued by government specifying the maximum amount the licence holder is allowed to emit. The licences are restricted to permit a limited amount of emission in total. Often, they must be purchased from the government or on a special market.

FIGURE 8

Prices of Tradable Pollution Permits as a Function of Emission Reduction Costs

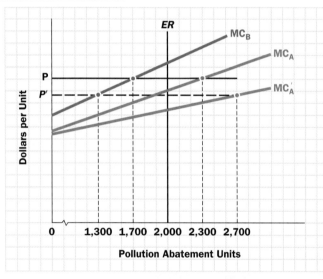

The Kyoto Protocol and Canadian Government GHG Emissions Policies

We have already pointed out that, according to the latest 2005 estimates, Canada is some 33 percentage points above the Kyoto Protocol 2008–2012 GHG emissions targets, with nearly 750 megatonnes of GHG emissions instead of the 560-megatonne target. Without any pollution control policies, it is estimated that GHG emissions would rise to 900 megatonnes by 2020. The federal government has undertaken a series of initiatives to achieve or nearly achieve the Kyoto target around 2020, hoping to curtail GHG emissions to 600 megatonnes—actually the 1990 level (see the accompanying table). The government has also announced that it intends to reduce Canada's GHG emissions by 50 percent by 2050.

But what measures have been taken so far? Many educational campaigns encouraging Canadians to save energy have been and will be pursued. Various subsidies have been granted—the public transit tax credit; insulation grants to homeowners; subsidies for the producers of wind energy; the ecoAuto program, whereby purchasers of fuel-efficient new vehicles such as the Mini Cooper and the Toyota Prius hybrid car could, for a while, get a $1,000 or $2,000 rebate, respectively, whereas purchasers of gas guzzlers are charged an excise tax (Green Levy) of up to $4,000. As valuable as these programs are, they barely make a dent on GHG emissions. The renewable fuel standard, which forces gasoline companies to have a minimum percentage of ethanol in their fuel, also does little to improve the situation, since the transformation of grain into ethanol may actually lead to larger GHG emissions if coal is used in the process.

By contrast, the apparent desire of the federal government to adopt California's strict Clean Cars Law standards with regards to the GHG emissions of new vehicles—which became the American standards in June 2007 when an energy bill was passed requiring that average fuel consumption of new cars be decreased from 8.6 to 6.1 litres per 100 kilometres by 2020—will have a more substantial impact, resulting in an estimated reduction of 15 megatonnes by 2020. The only other measure that, so far, is bound to substantially reduce GHG emissions is the obligation for large industrial emitters (in the oil, gas, mining, and manufacturing industries) to reduce the intensity of their emissions. But this obligation is based on *intensity* reduction (GHG emissions per unit of GDP), not absolute emission reductions, and has too many loopholes; it is estimated that this measure will result in a reduction of only 75 megatonnes of GHG emissions by 2020.

Overall, according to Mark Jaccard, an environmental economist at Simon Fraser University, current government initiatives are likely to reduce Canadian GHG emissions by about 120 megatonnes relative to the "business as usual" scenario. But that scenario yields 900 megatonnes of GHG emissions, so the federal government is unlikely to achieve its own target or that of a delayed Kyoto Protocol target.

According to Jaccard, environmental policies dealing with global warming based on education, subsidies, and other voluntary schemes are inefficient and insufficient. They have been adopted in Canada because they are politically painless policies. As one of the signatories of the Canadian government paper on the negative economic impact of moving quickly toward the Kyoto Protocol target, Jaccard is fully aware of the possible costs of more drastic policies. Nevertheless, to achieve the government target, Jaccard recommends a three-prong approach, based on compulsory policies that have demonstrated their efficiency in achieving targets: an economy-wide Pigovian carbon tax, direct controls with emission caps, and a market for emissions permits.

GHG Emissions: Levels, Targets, and Forecasts, Canada, 1990–2020	
Levels, Targets, and Forecasts	GHG Annual Emissions (in megatonnes)
1990: GHG emissions level	600
2008–2012: Kyoto Protocol target	563
2005: GHG emissions level	747
2020: "Business as usual" scenario	900
2020: Federal government target (2007 Clean Air Act)	600
2020: Jaccard's estimate based on federal initiatives	780

SOURCE: Mark Jaccard and Nic Rivers, *Estimating the Effect of the Canadian Government's 2006–2007 Greenhouse Gas Policies*, C.D. Howe Institute Working Paper, June 2007. Retrieved from http://www.cdhowe.org

As with a tax on emissions, the total daily social cost of the pollution reduction program is $80, as opposed to $240 under direct controls. Emission permits are thus just as efficient as pollution taxes. But this time, the government need not assess the unit cost of emission reduction in order to set the tax rate on emissions that will achieve its target of emission reduction. This task is left to each individual firm, and the forces of market supply and demand will do the rest, inducing the industry to achieve the target imposed by government. Emissions permits thus combine some of the advantages of direct control and emission taxes: The government sets the emissions ceiling or reduction target, and the market provides the incentives. Still, emission permits are no panacea: Proper monitoring is needed; otherwise, firms will shirk by hiding some of their emissions.

When the U.S. Environmental Protection Agency (EPA) first introduced tradable emission permits in 1995, many people were outraged by the notion of such "licences to pollute." Nowadays, one hears of few complaints, because tradable permit programs have turned out to be such a huge success. One of the best examples is the permits market for sulphur dioxide emissions, which cause acid rain, an environmental problem that plagues eastern Canada and arises from industrial activity and electricity-generating utility companies. Half of the acid rain in Canada is due to American activity. In this "cap and trade" program, the EPA sets limitations on total SO_2 emissions and issues the corresponding number of tradable permits. Some of the permits are sold at auctions, so that environmental activists can purchase permits and thus reduce the amount of allowable emissions.

Although the idea of pollution emission permits was first suggested in the 1960s by Canadian economist, the late John H. Dales, formerly from the University of Toronto, no general market for such permits yet exists in Canada (as this book goes to press), although some pilot projects have in operation from 1996 and 2000, while both the Ontario and the Quebec governments have announced in 2008 that they would set up such a permit market. As was pointed out when explaining why Russia finally did endorse the Kyoto Protocol, GHG emission permits constitute one of the market mechanisms designed to facilitate the Protocol targets, and they are most likely to be issued on the eve of the Protocol's 2012 target, by 2008. As a result, Natural Resources Canada has been preparing several plans with the intention of allowing Canada to participate in such a worldwide permit market system. By creating a domestic emissions trading system, Canadian corporations would be able to either buy or sell credits from other countries that also have such a permit system. The 2007 version of the Clean Air Act allows large Canadian GHG emitters to purchase emission permits from abroad. The Canadian government, in its 2007 Throne speech, also promised to establish a domestic carbon emissions trading market.

TWO CHEERS FOR THE MARKET

In Part 1 of this chapter, we have learned that environmental protection cannot be left to the free market. Because of the large externalities involved, the market will systematically allocate insufficient resources to the job. However, this market failure does not imply that we should disregard the price mechanism. On the contrary, we have seen that a legislated market solution based on pollution charges may often be the best way to protect the environment. At least *in this case, the market mechanism's power can be harnessed to correct its own failings.*

We turn now, in the second half of this chapter, to the issue of natural resources, where the market mechanism also plays a crucial role.

PART 2: THE ECONOMICS OF NATURAL RESOURCES

Since Fuel is become so expensive, and will of course grow scarcer and dearer; any new Proposal for saving the [fuel] . . . may at least be thought worth Consideration.

BENJAMIN FRANKLIN, 1744

One of the most significant forms of environmental damage occurs when we waste natural resources. Earlier in this chapter, we saw that externalities can lead to just this sort of waste—as when governments, individuals, or business firms use up clean air and clean water without cost or penalty. There is a close analytic connection between the economics of environmental protection that we have just investigated and the economics of natural resources, to which we now turn.

Nearly 30 years ago, the world was rocked by a sudden "energy crisis." Oil prices shot up and consumers found themselves waiting in long lines to buy gasoline. This event had profound effects throughout the world and ended the widespread assumption that the stock of natural resources was unlimited and simply ours for the taking. Indeed, back in the late 1970s and early 1980s, there was near-panic about the threatened exhaustion of many nat-

SOURCE: © JUPITERIMAGES/Comstock Images/Alamy

ural resources. The front page of a leading magazine even asked, "Are we running out of *everything*?"

Natural resources have always been scarce, and they have often been used wastefully. Nevertheless, we are *not* about to run out of the most vital resources. In many cases, substitutes are available, and will be forthcoming when the price of the natural resources will be high enough for these substitutes to be introduced at a profit.

■ ECONOMIC ANALYSIS: THE FREE MARKET AND PRICING OF DEPLETABLE NATURAL RESOURCES

If statistics on known mineral reserves keep rising as surprisingly as those reported in the puzzle with which this chapter began, we may begin to regard them skeptically and question whether the statistics are wrong or whether we are really not running out of a number of valuable resources, despite their finite supply and their continued use. Is there another indicator of resource depletion that is more reliable? Most economists say there is one—*the price of the resource.*

■ Scarcity and Rising Prices

According to economic analysis, a better indicator of the degree of depletion of a resource is its price. As a resource becomes scarcer, we expect its price to rise for several reasons. One reason is that we do not deplete a resource simply by gradually using up a homogeneous product, every unit of which is equally available. Rather, we generally use up the most accessible and highest-quality deposits first; only then do we turn to less accessible supplies that are more costly to retrieve or deposits of lower purity or quality. Oil is a clear example. First, Canadians relied primarily on their most easily found domestic oil in Alberta. Then they turned to imports, mostly from South America, with their higher transport costs. Today, large shipments come from Algeria, Saudi Arabia, and Venezuela, but half of our oil imports come from Europe, extracted mainly from the North Sea platforms of Norway and the United Kingdom. Now there is crude oil extraction in several other provinces and territories, notably in Saskatchewan and more recently from the ocean floor off Newfoundland, where production seemed too costly until the early 1990s.

For some time now, there has also been slowly growing extraction of the semisolid petroleum imbedded in the Athabasca tar sands in Alberta (also called *synthetic oil* and *crude bitumen*). Because extraction from the oil sands is more costly, increases in the price of crude oil gradually lead to more tar sands extraction becoming a profitable venture (but this causes problems from an environmental point of view: see the box "A Trade-Off between Environmental and Economic Issues"). When the potential of the tar sands is taken into consideration, the estimated Canadian crude oil reserves can be multiplied by a factor of 35, making Canadian reserves the second-largest in the world, behind those of Saudi Arabia, but ahead of those of Iran, Iraq, Kuwait, the United Arab Emirates, and Venezuela, in that order.

> Increasing scarcity of a resource such as oil is not usually a matter of imminent and total disappearance. Rather, it involves exhaustion of the most accessible and cheapest sources so that new supplies become more costly.

■ Supply–Demand Analysis and Consumption

Growing scarcity also raises resource prices for the usual supply–demand reason. As we know, goods in short supply tend to become more expensive. To see just how this process works for natural resources, imagine a mythical mineral, "economite," consistent in quality, which has negligible extraction and transportation costs. How quickly will the reserves of this mineral be used up, and what will happen to its price as time passes?

> The basic law of pricing of a depletable resource tells us that as its stocks are used up, its price in a perfectly competitive market will rise every year by greater and greater dollar amounts.

A Trade-Off between Environmental and Economic Issues

While oil companies are talking about "green" energy, hundreds of miles north of the border between the United States and Canada, they are also making a costly, dirty bet on future supplies that has created a boom in the frontier town of Fort McMurray, Alberta.

Companies like Shell, Chevron, Exxon, and Total are investing billions of dollars to unlock oil from Canada's underground rock formations. These oil sand reserves are huge, potentially rivalling oil reserves found in Saudi Arabia, according to some optimistic estimates. Oil sands production in Canada is expected to triple to 3 million barrels per day by 2015, according to Canada's National Energy Board.

The problem is that Canada's reserves do not flow freely out of the ground. They are packed so tightly that they must first be melted before they can seep out of the rocks. This process is much more costly than extracting conventional oil from the ground. Because the extraction process uses a lot of energy, it also releases many more carbon emissions.

While high oil prices are stimulating interest in alternative energy from clean sources, these prices are also spurring interest in lots of dirtier sources, too. In hopes of countering such developments, BP's most ambitious alternative project is to build a new type of power plant that runs on hydrogen, captures the carbon dioxide, and injects it back into a nearby field to help flush out either oil or natural gas.

"The oil industry has the know-how to do geological storage," said Stephen Bachu, a senior adviser for the Alberta Energy and Utilities Board. "If you ask why it is not done, that is because there is no reason to do it. Either the oil industry will make a profit, and that is why you see carbon dioxide in enhanced oil recovery projects, or the oil companies will do it to avoid paying a penalty."

In the end, experts say, the oil industry may respond only when governments force change. For now, governments are relying mostly on subsidies, but the ultimate answer, they say, probably lies in some form of taxation of carbon dioxide emissions that puts a system of carrots and sticks to work to limit global warming.

SOURCE: Excerpt from Jad Mouawad, "A Refinery Clears the Air to Grow Roses; Oil Industry Moves to Curb Carbon Emissions," *The New York Times*, June 30, 2006. Retrieved from http://nytimes.com. Copyright 2006, The New York Times Company.

Although we can predict the price of economite without knowing anything about its supply or consumer demand for it, we do need to know something about supply and demand to determine what will happen to economite's consumption—the rate at which it will be used up.

Figure 9(a) is a demand curve for economite, *DD*, which shows the amount people want to use up *per year* at various price levels. On the vertical axis, we show how the price must rise from year to year from $100 per tonne in the initial year to $110 in the next year, and so on. Because of the demand curve's negative slope, it follows that consumption of this mineral will fall each year. That is, *if there is no shift in the demand curve, as in Panel (a)*, consumption will fall from 100,000 tonnes initially to 95,000 tonnes the next year, and so on.

In reality, such demand curves rarely stay still. As the economy grows and population and incomes increase, demand curves shift outward—a pattern that has probably been true for most scarce resources. Such shifts in the demand curve will offset at least part

FIGURE 9

Consumption over Time of a Depletable Resource

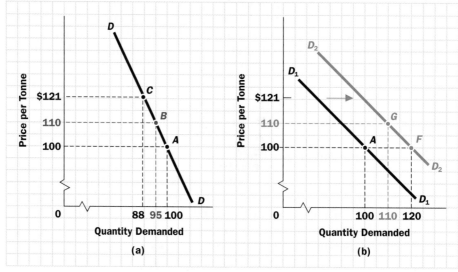

Note: Quantity is in throusands of tonnes per year.

The Permanent Fuel Crisis

Humanity has a long history of panicking about the imminent exhaustion of natural resources. In the thirteenth century, a large part of Europe's forests was cut down, primarily for use in metalworking (much of it for armour). Wood prices rose, and there was a good deal of talk about depletion of fuel stocks.

Economists and other concerned citizens have been making similar sombre predictions ever since. More than 200 years ago, British economist Thomas Robert Malthus (1766–1834) in his famous essay, *An Essay on the Principle of Population* (1798), predicted that food production, which he asserted grew at an arithmetic rate because of limited natural resources, could not keep up with population, which grew exponentially. Countries like China and India (and, earlier, South Korea) are showing that it is possible for poor countries to overcome malnutrition. In Western countries the problem is not the lack of food, as ever-larger population segments suffer from overweight and obesity.

William Stanley Jevons (1835–1882), who is best known as one of the earlier advocates of marginal analysis, was concerned with the possible near-exhaustion of the main fuel of his time—coal. In the book that brought him public recognition, *The Coal Question* (1865), Jevons predicted the end of progress and of the Industrial Revolution because of a lack of coal. Nearly 150 years later, coal is still plentiful, however. In Canada for instance, coal reserves are estimated to last 66 years, and coal still accounts for 69 percent of electricity generated at thermal-electric power stations—17 percent of all electricity generated in Canada. Jevons also predicted that the supplies of petroleum, which had just started to be in use, would soon run out as well. Jevons also feared the attrition of forests: He hoarded such huge quantities of blank writing paper and brown packing paper that his descendants, more than 50 years after his death, still had piles of them.

These predicted episodes of severe shortages, which did not materialize, resemble current announcements about future shortages of oil and other natural resources. One of the most shocking predictions about future problems was in a report to the Club of Rome (an international group of distinguished businessmen, statesmen, and scientists) entitled *The Limits to Growth* (1972), also known as the *Meadows Report* from the names of its two main investigators. Like Malthus, the authors were greatly concerned by the implications of exponential growth, and they concluded that "If the present growth trends in world population, industrialization, pollution, food production, and resource depletion continue unchanged, the limits to growth on this planet will be reached sometime within the next one hundred

years. The most probable result will be a rather sudden and uncontrollable decline in both population and industrial capacity."* This conclusion was mostly attributed to the depletion of nonrenewable natural resources; as resource extraction becomes more and more costly, growth becomes impossible. If this scenario did not materialize, for instance because of newly found natural resources, the authors of the report concluded that fast-rising pollution would lead to rising death rates and decreasing food production rates. To avoid these disastrous scenarios, the authors suggested stopping population growth in 1975 and industrial capital growth in 1985.

SOURCE: © Keith Wood/Stone/Getty Images

The *Meadows Report* created quite a stir because it was quickly followed by the first oil crisis in 1973, with its gasoline shortages and crude oil prices that had doubled. In addition, the report seemed to have solid scientific credentials, as it relied on a computer model based on system dynamics—an approach founded on feedback effects (positive and negative ones) developed at MIT by Jay W. Forrester (1918–) that combines economics and engineering tools.

At a 35-year distance, the *Meadows Report* has some good and bad points. Obviously, at least so far, it missed the mark about depletable resources, as is demonstrated in the puzzle that introduces the current chapter, since depletable natural resources are still plentiful (for instance, the report claimed that the planet would run out of oil in 2022, which at this point does not seem likely). Still, some of the changes that were being advocated—such as the necessary reduction of pollutant emissions, recycling, and the more efficient use of energy and depletable resources—have been either introduced or are in the process of being introduced.

* From an abstract by Eduard Pestel based on *A Report to the Club of Rome* by Donella H. Meadows et al. (New York: Universe Books, 1972).Retrieved from http://www.clubofrome.org/docs/limits.rtf

of the reduction in quantity demanded that results from rising prices. Nevertheless, rising prices do cut consumption growth relative to what it would have been if price had remained unchanged. Figure 9(b) depicts an outward shift in demand from curve D_1D_1 in the initial period to curve D_2D_2 a year later. If price had remained constant at the initial value, $100 per tonne, quantity consumed per year would have risen from 100,000 tonnes to 120,000 tonnes. But because with a given supply curve price must rise, say to $110, quantity demanded will increase only to 110,000 tonnes. Thus, whether or not the demand curve shifts, we conclude:

The ever-rising prices accompanying increasing scarcity of a depletable resource discourage consumption (encourage conservation). Even if quantity demanded grows, it will not grow as much as it would if prices were not rising.

ACTUAL RESOURCE PRICES IN THE MODERN WORLD

How do the facts match up with this theoretical analysis? Not too well, as we will see now. Figure 10 shows the behaviour of the prices of three critical metals—lead, zinc, and copper—since the beginning of the twentieth century. This graph shows the prices of these three resources relative to other prices in the economy (in other words, the *real* prices, after adjustment for any inflation or deflation that affected the purchasing power of the dollar). What we find is that instead of rising steadily, as the theory leads us to expect, zinc prices actually remained amazingly constant, as has the price of lead, even though both minerals are gradually being used up. The price of copper has been all over the map but also has shown no upward trend.

Figure 11 shows the real price of crude oil in Canada since 1947 (again, adjusted for inflation). It gives price at the wellhead—that is, at the point of production, with no transportation cost included. Notice how constant these prices were until the first "energy crisis" in 1973, when oil prices rose precipitously. A second and even more dramatic increase occurred in the late 1970s and early 1980s, but since then real oil prices remained well below their "energy crisis" levels, until 2003, when oil prices increased significantly again.

FIGURE 10   Prices of Lead, Zinc, and Copper, 1900–2003, in Real (Inflation-Adjusted) Terms

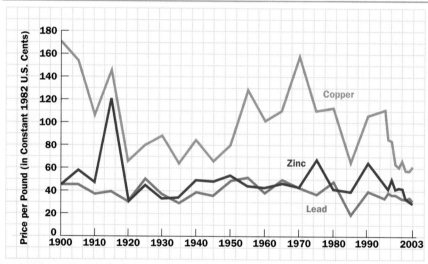

Note: Prices are in constant 1982 U.S. cents, as deflated by the U.S. producer price index for all commodities.

SOURCES: U.S. Bureau of the Census, *Historical Statistics of the United States, Colonial Times to 1970*, Washington, D.C.: 1975; *Statistical Abstract of the United States*, Washington, D.C.: various issues; U.S. Department of Labor, Bureau of Labor Statistics, retrieved from http://www.bls.gov; and U.S. Geological Survey, retrieved from http://www.usgs.gov.

FIGURE 11   Western Canada Crude Oil Wellhead Price, 1947–2006, in Real Terms

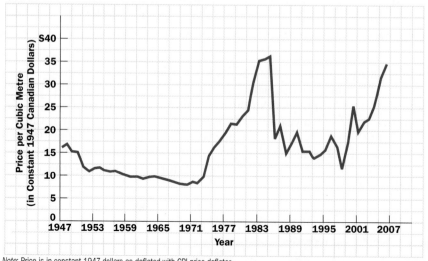

Note: Price is in constant 1947 dollars as deflated with CPI price deflator.

SOURCE: Canadian Association of Petroleum Producers, *CAPP Statistical Handbook*, January 2008, Table 5.1. Retrieved from http://www.capp.ca

Interferences with Price Patterns

How does one explain this strange behaviour in the prices of finite resources, which surely are being used up, even if only gradually? Although many things can interfere with the price patterns that theory leads us to expect, we will mention only four:

1. *Unexpected discoveries of reserves whose existence was previously not suspected.* If we were to stumble upon a huge and easily accessible reserve of economite, which came as a complete surprise to the market, the price of this mineral would obviously fall. This situation is illustrated in Figure 12, where we see that people originally believed that the S_1S_1 curve represented available supply. The discovery of the new economite reserves leads them to recognize that the supply is much larger than previously thought. A rightward shift of the supply curve (curve S_2S_2) results, because the suppliers' cost of any given quantity is reduced by the discovery, so it will pay them to supply a larger quantity at any given price. Like any outward shift in a supply curve, this change can be expected to cause a price decrease (from P_1 to P_2).

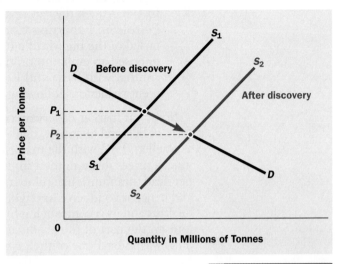

FIGURE 12

Price Effects of a Discovery of Additional Reserves

   A clear historical example was the Spaniards' sixteenth-century discovery of gold and silver in Mexico and South America, which led to substantial drops in European prices of these precious metals. The same effect can result from innovations that use the resources more efficiently. *If a new invention doubles the number of kilometres one can travel on a litre of gasoline, that is tantamount to doubling the supply of petroleum that still remains in the ground.*

2. *The invention of new methods of mining or refining that may significantly reduce extraction costs.* This development can also lead to a rightward shift in the supply curve, as suppliers become able to deliver a larger quantity at any given price. The situation is therefore again represented by a diagram like Figure 12—only now a reduction in cost, not a new discovery of reserves, shifts the supply curve to the right.

3. *Price controls that hold prices down or decrease them.* A legislature can pass a law prohibiting the sale of the resource at a price higher than P^* (see Figure 13). Often this strategy doesn't work; in many cases an illegal black market emerges, where suppliers charge very high prices more or less secretly. But when price controls do work, shortages usually follow. Because the objective is to make the legal ceiling price, P^*, lower than the market equilibrium price, P, then at price P^* quantity demanded (5 million tonnes in the figure) will be higher than the free-market level (4 million tonnes). Similarly, we may expect quantity supplied (2 million tonnes in the figure) to be less than its free-market level (again, 4 million tonnes). Thus, as always happens in these cases, quantity supplied is less than quantity demanded, and a shortage results (measured in Figure 13 by the length of AB, or 3 million tonnes).

4. *Changes in oligopoly power:* As you saw in Figure 11, after a long period of near-constant oil prices, crude oil prices at the wellhead doubled in 1973–1974, in what has been dubbed the *first oil crisis,* and they jumped again between 1979 and 1984—the second oil crisis. In fact, because Canada put in place an energy policy in

FIGURE 13

Controls on the Price of a Resource

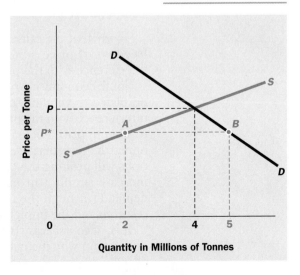

1980, the National Energy Program, that imposed gradual oil price increases among other things, oil prices in Canada did not rise as fast as they did on international markets, so that Figure 11 underestimates oil price increases in the rest of the world during the initial years of the second crisis.

These price changes are not the result of simple supply and demand changes. In 1973–1974, they arose as a result of muscle flexing by the Organization of the Petroleum Exporting Countries (OPEC)—a cartel organization mainly composed of the big Middle East and African oil exporters—when these countries imposed an embargo on the Western countries that had supported Israel in its conflict with Syria and Egypt. The second crisis was the initial result of shipment reductions following the Iranian Revolution and the Iraq–Iran war.

Some oil market observers consider that this market can best be explained as some form of bilateral oligopoly, made up of the OPEC and the big petroleum companies such as Shell and BP, with the major oil-consuming countries having the added potential to impact prices through their import or regulation policies. Mineral extraction (zinc, copper, lead, uranium), like oil extraction, implies large fixed costs and low marginal costs, and hence is conducive to oligopolistic industries. Under that interpretation, the second oil crisis and its accompanying high oil prices were the result of successful collusive behaviour on the part of the producing countries' cartel and the oligopolistic oil companies. This was indeed one of the justifications for setting up the Canadian National Energy Program, which was dismantled between 1984 and 1986. When this book was first being written in 2007, some observers believed that some of the gasoline price increases could be attributed to the overly high profit margins of oil refineries. By 2008, high oil prices were being partly blamed on speculators cornering the commodities market.

We can explain each of our examples of minerals whose price did not rise by one or more of these influences. For example, copper and zinc have benefited from technological changes that lowered their extraction costs. In addition, the development of direct electroplating techniques has made copper production much more efficient. In the case of lead, new mines have held abundant quantities of ore that were much easier to extract and much cheaper to refine than what had been available before. Obviously, real events are more complex than a naïve reading of theoretical models might lead us to believe.

Is Price Interference Justified?

Despite these influences, if a resource does become very scarce and costly to obtain, its price must ultimately rise unless government interferes. Moreover:

In an unfettered market, quantity demanded can never exceed quantity supplied, even if a finite resource is undergoing rapid depletion. The reason is simple: In any free market, price will automatically adjust to eliminate any difference between quantity supplied and quantity demanded.

In theory, any shortage—any excess of quantity demanded over quantity supplied—must be artificial, ascribable to a decision to prevent the price mechanism from doing its job.

To say that the cause is artificial, of course, does not settle the basic issue—whether freedom of price adjustments is desirable when resources are scarce, or whether interference with the pricing process is justified.

Some economists argue that when natural resource prices are jacked up for reasons unrelated to genuine scarcity or rising extraction costs, there is room for government interference with the price mechanism (as was done in Canada during the early 1980s) to smooth price fluctuations and their impact on the rest of the economy. Other economists believe that preventing prices from fully adjusting to new temporary conditions will prolong the period of overly high prices, as this will reduce the incentives to increase supply (through the exploration and discovery of new sites) and reduce demand (through the introduction of energy-saving devices for instance, or through research and the implementation of alternative technologies).

It is, of course, easy to understand why no consumer loves a price rise. It is also easy to understand why many consumers attribute any such price increase to a conspiracy by greedy suppliers that somehow deliberately arrange for shortages to force prices upward. Sometimes, this view is even correct. For example, the members of OPEC have openly and frankly tried to influence the flow of oil in order to increase its price. But it is important to recognize from the principles of supply and demand that when a resource grows scarce, its price will tend to rise automatically, even without any conspiracies or plots.

■ On the Virtues of Rising Prices

Rising prices help to control resource depletion in three basic ways:

1. They discourage consumption and waste and provide an inducement for conservation.
2. They stimulate more efficient resource use by industry, providing incentives for employment of processes that are more sparing in their use of the resource or that use substitute resources.
3. They encourage innovation—the discovery of other, more abundant resources that can serve the same role and of new techniques that permit these other resources to be used economically.

Competition Bureau Concludes Examination into Gasoline Price Spike Following Hurricane Katrina

Various complaints about excessive gasoline prices or price hikes over the past several years have been brought to the attention of Canada's Competition Bureau. On only one occasion, in 2008, did the bureau conclude that there was a breach of the Competition Act. In particular, in the case of Hurricane Katrina, which devastated part of the New Mexico coastline including the city of New Orleans in 2005, the bureau found that:

- The production cost of crude oil did not change during the 45-day period identified.
- The wholesale price of gasoline in Canada rose, tracking the spot price of gasoline in U.S. exchange markets and leading to higher gross refining margins for Canadian and American companies.
- As a result, the retail price of gasoline rose as expected.

- There was no evidence of a conspiracy among North American gasoline refiners.

The Competition Bureau takes the view that "price gouging, or charging high prices at times of actual or anticipated excess demand, is not contrary to the Act." In the case of Hurricane Katrina, 10 percent of American gasoline production was halted. Although reductions in oil or gasoline production can be absorbed by increased imports or by drawing on inventories of crude oil or gasoline, without reducing market supplies, the *uncertainty* over current and future supply conditions is sufficient to push up market prices. Thus, beliefs or expectations, whether right or wrong, have an effect on markets.

SOURCE: Competition Bureau, "Competition Bureau concludes gasoline pricing examinations," *Backgrounder*, March 30, 2006. Retrieved from http://www.competitionbureau.gc.ca

Uranium Prices: Supply and Demand or Oligopolistic Behaviour

The price of oil has been the main focus of this section on natural resources, but the following news report shows that the price of uranium can mainly be explained through supply and demand considerations, and that exploration for new production sites depends on how high the price of the commodity is. The price of uranium U308 traded between US$10 and US$15 for about 15 years, until 2003, when it rose continuously to the current levels. Because exploration takes time, supply cannot respond quickly enough for production to equate demand increases. There is however a second interpretation that can be found in the following article: The price of uranium rises because the prices of alternative energy resources, such as oil, have

been rising. This alternative explanation relies on the presumption that the energy industries are dominated by oligopolies that have the power to raise prices when substitutes become more expensive.

VANCOUVER (CP) — After nearly doubling last year, the price of uranium appears poised to continue its bull run in 2007 as demand for the radioactive fuel continues to outstrip supply, analysts say.

"It is a commodity that has for years been under a lot of pressure from excess supply and now the seeds have been sown and we're beginning to see the flip side of that," said RBC Capital Markets analyst Adam Schatzker, who has forecast the price will average US$100 per pound in 2007.

continued on following page

Uranium Prices: Supply and Demand or Oligopolistic Behaviour (continued)

"There is not a lot of mine production. The inventories that were being sold into the market are disappearing and we're actually in a supply–demand deficit."

Though hedge funds and other speculators are beginning to move into the uranium market, he said the biggest driver to the recent increase in price is a shortfall in supply and growing demand.

New nuclear power plants are being built in China and other parts of the world, while few new major deposits have been developed, leading to demand that is 40% ahead of current supply.

For years the price of uranium removed the incentive to spend the money building any new production or searching for new deposits. With governments selling their inventories the markets were flooded with cheap uranium and there was no need to dig up new deposits.

But those inventories are depleting and uranium users still need the fuel for their reactors.

The price of uranium averaged US$28.15 per pound in 2005 and jumped to an average of $48.10 per pound in 2006. However the spot price for the radioactive metal was a whopping US$72 per pound at the end of the year.

Scotiabank commodity specialist Patricia Mohr has suggested that the current upswing in uranium prices is a "secular" change in global energy markets, due to the price of oil and that nuclear power generation emits virtually no greenhouse gases.

"While exploration activity has surged for uranium—across Canada, Australia, Africa and in Kazakhstan—there has been little improvement in mine production," Mohr wrote in a recent report forecasting an average price of US$80 in 2007, ending the year close to $90. . . .

The shortfall in supply was made worse when Saskatoon-based Cameco, the world's biggest uranium producer, reported flooding at its Cigar Lake mine in northern Saskatchewan, a project it had hoped to bring into production in 2008.

SOURCE: Craig Wong, "Analysts Remain Bullish on Uranium after Nearly Doubling in 2006." © Associated Press, 07 January 2007.

THE PUZZLE REVISITED: *Growing Reserves of Exhaustible Natural Resources*

Earlier we saw, strangely enough, that reserves of many mineral resources have actually been increasing, despite growing world production that uses these resources. This paradox has a straightforward economic explanation: Rising mineral reserves are a tribute to the success of pricing and exploration activity. Minerals are not discovered by accident. Rather, exploration and discovery entail costly work requiring geologists, engineers, and expensive machinery. Industry does not consider this money worth spending when reserves are high and mineral prices are low.

In the twentieth century, every time some mineral's known reserves fell and its price tended to rise, exploration increased until the decline was offset. The law of supply and demand worked. In the 1970s, for example, the rising price of oil led to very substantial increases in oil exploration, which helped to build up reserves. A similar phenomenon occurred following the early 1980s episode of rising oil prices. Demand shifted to other sources of energy, such as natural gas, and, thanks as well to technical progress, the oil fields in the North Sea became profitable enough to produce oil on a large scale, thus unsettling the monopoly power of the OPEC cartel. These episodes also led to the creation and adoption of energy-saving technologies, the use of which were not abandoned when oil prices reversed to their previous low levels.

More recently, the increases in oil prices that have occurred since 2000, and more specifically in 2004 and 2005 (as shown in Figure 11), which are mainly attributed to China's growing demand for oil, have given a boost to both the discovery of conventional oil fields in Canada and the exploitation of the huge fields of Alberta tar sands. Table 1 shows that while conventional crude oil reserves in Canada were declining when crude oil prices were relatively low, as a result of oil being extracted from the oil fields, the situation reversed in 2004 and especially in 2005, when *established* reserves rose, these being defined as the reserves recoverable under current technology and present and anticipated economic conditions, as proved by drilling and testing.

TABLE 1

**Remaining Established Crude Oil Reserves
in Canada, 2002–2006 (millions of cubic metres)**

Year	(1) Remaining at Beginning of Year	(2) Gross Additions	(3) Net Production	(4) = (1 + 2 − 3) Remaining at End of Year	(5) = (4 − 1) Net Change in Reserves during Year
2002	740	59	85	714	−26
2003	714	47	85	676	−38
2004	676	98	82	692	+16
2005	692	215	79	828	+136
2006	828	36	78	785	−42

SOURCE: Canadian Association of Petroleum Producers, *CAPP Statistical Handbook,* November 2006, Table 2.6b; Retrieved from http://www.capp.ca

Very likely, established crude oil reserves in Canada will grow again in 2008–2009, as a consequence of the meteoric climb of oil prices in 2007 and 2008.

SUMMARY

1. Pollution is as old as human history. Contrary to popular notions, some forms of pollution were actually decreasing even before government programs were initiated to protect the environment.

2. Both planned and market economies suffer from substantial environmental problems.

3. The production of commodities *must* cause waste disposal problems unless everything is recycled, but even recycling processes cause pollution (and use up energy).

4. Global warming, tied to greenhouse gas (GHG) emissions, is now considered to be the most pressing environmental problem. How emissions should be reduced and how fast they should be reduced are highly controversial issues in Canada, as they involve economic trade-offs.

5. Pollution is an **externality**—when a factory emits smoke, it dirties the air in nearby neighbourhoods and may damage the health of persons who neither work for the factory nor buy its products. Hence, the public interest in pollution control is not best served by the free market.

6. Pollution can be controlled by voluntary programs, **direct controls**, **pollution charges** (taxes on emissions), and other monetary incentives for emissions reduction.

7. Most economists believe that the monetary incentives approach is the most efficient and effective way to control damaging externalities.

8. The quantity demanded of a scarce resource can exceed the quantity supplied only if something prevents the market mechanism from operating freely.

9. As a resource grows scarce on a competitive market, its price will rise, inducing increased conservation by consumers, increased exploration for new reserves, and increased substitution of other items that can serve the same purpose.

10. In the twentieth century, the relative prices of many resources remained roughly constant, largely because of the discovery of new reserves and cost-saving innovations.

11. In the 1970s, OPEC succeeded in raising petroleum's relative price, but the price increase led to a substantial decline in world demand as well as to an increase in production in countries outside OPEC.

12. *Known reserves* of depletable scarce resources have not tended to fall with time, because as the price of the resource rises with increasing scarcity, increased exploration for new reserves becomes profitable.

KEY TERMS

Externality   390

Direct controls   400

Pollution charges (taxes on emissions)   401

Emissions permits   404

TEST YOURSELF

1. Production of Commodity X creates 10 kilograms of emissions for every unit of X produced. The demand and supply curves for X are described by the following table:

Price	Quantity Demanded	Quantity Supplied
$10	80	100
9	85	95
8	90	90
7	95	85
6	100	80
5	105	75

What is the equilibrium price and quantity, and how much pollution will be emitted?

2. Using the data in Test Yourself Question 1, if the price of X to consumers is $9, and the government imposes a tax of $2 per unit, show that because suppliers get only $7, they will produce only 85 units of output, not the 95 units of output they would produce if they received the full $9 per unit.

3. With the tax described in Test Yourself Question 2, how much pollution will be emitted?

4. Compare your answers to Test Yourself Questions 1 and 3 and show how large a reduction in pollution emissions occurs because of the $2 tax on the polluting output.

DISCUSSION QUESTIONS

1. What sorts of pollution problems would you expect in a small African village? In a city in India? In the People's Republic of China? In Toronto?

2. Suppose you are assigned the task of drafting a law to impose a tax on smoke emissions. What provisions would you put into the law?

   a. How would you decide the size of the tax?

   b. What would you do about smoke emitted by a municipal electricity plant?

   c. Would you use the same tax rate in densely and sparsely settled areas?

   What information will you need to collect before determining what you would do about each of the preceding provisions?

3. Discuss some valid and some invalid objections to letting rising prices eliminate shortages of supplies of scarce resources.

4. Why may an increase in fuel prices lead to more conservation after several years have passed than it does in the months following the price increase? What does your answer imply about the relative sizes of the long-run and short-run elasticity of demand for fuel?

5. Should Canada fully implement the Kyoto Protocol and do everything possible to achieve the target agreed to in 1997? Why, or why not? What kind of economic reasons can you give?

6. Average fuel consumption of new cars will have to be diminished by about 30 percent by 2020. What is the likely effect on the price of cars? What effect should this measure have on the retail price of gasoline? What impact should it have on oil exploration? Explain with the help of supply and demand diagrams.

18

TAXATION AND RESOURCE ALLOCATION

If taxes grow beyond a moderate limit, they cease to be taxes and turn into devices for the destruction of the market economy.

LUDWIG VON MISES (1881–1973), *HUMAN ACTION,*
YALE UNIVERSITY PRESS, NEW HAVEN, 1949, CH. 28.

Taxes are what we pay for civilized society.

OLIVER W. HOLMES, JR. (1841–1935),
U.S. SUPREME COURT ASSOCIATE JUSTICE, 1927

"Nothing is certain but death and taxes," proclaims an old adage. But, in recent decades, politics has turned this aphorism on its head. Nowadays, it seems, the surest route to political death is to raise taxes—and the surest route to winning elections is to cut them.

Larry O'Brien, a successful businessman and a newcomer to politics, stunned all observers by easily beating out his two experienced opponents to become the mayor of Ottawa in 2006 on the basis of a single pledge—not to increase property taxes. Politicians who are not in power can easily convince themselves that they can reduce wasteful expenditures and hence reduce the amount of taxes required to finance public expenditures. Once in power, however, reality strikes back. Newly elected politicians discover the personal services cost disease that we discussed in Chapter 15—the fact that many vital services, such as health care, education, and garbage removal, suffer from low productivity growth and hence entail costs that are likely to rise faster than overall inflation and government revenues (naturally, Ottawa city taxes did increase!).

In Canada, but even more so in the United States, many organizations advocate tax reductions—in Canada, the best-known ones are the C.D. Howe Institute, the Montreal Economic Institute, and the Fraser Institute. The latter even celebrates "Tax Freedom Day" every year. These advocacy groups claim that taxes stifle entrepreneurship, burden citizens, and reduce the efficiency of market processes, as argued by the first of the two quotations at the top of this page. But taxes are also the means through which our society can be more civilized, as argued in the second of these quotations. Taxes pay for public health, public education, child care, clean streets, and security, as well as for transfer programs such as social welfare and Employment Insurance. In addition, the government uses the tax system to promote social goals. For example, we learned in the previous chapter that policy makers can use taxes to correct misallocations of resources caused by externalities.

This chapter discusses the types of taxes that are used to raise revenues for government purposes, the effects of taxes on resource allocation and income distribution, and the principles that may help to distinguish "good" taxes from "bad" ones.

CONTENTS

ISSUE: *Should the Goods and Services Tax Be Abolished?*

In January 2006, Stephen Harper became the prime minister of Canada, bringing in a minority Conservative government after 12 years of Liberal government. In his electoral platform, Harper, who holds a master's degree in economics from the University of Calgary, proposed to reduce the federal Goods and Services Tax (GST) from 7 percent to 5 percent. The plan was implemented in July 2006 and January 2008, when the GST rate was reduced from 7 to 6 percent, and then to 5 percent. During the election campaign, the plan to cut the GST was bluntly called "stupid economics" by the Liberals, and similar statements were made when the tax was actually reduced.

Ironically, the GST was introduced in 1991 by then Conservative Prime Minister Brian Mulroney and Finance Minister Michael Wilson. The GST replaced a tax that was much less comprehensive—the Manufacturer's Sales Tax (MST), which was imposed at the wholesale level on manufacturers' goods. The introduction of the GST created a lot of resentment among Canadians because, whereas the MST was hidden in the price tag of any produced good, the Conservatives decided, for reasons of transparency, to have the tax appear as an explicit addition to the price tag, as is the case with provincial retail sales taxes. During the 1993 election campaign, the Liberals pledged to eliminate the GST altogether, a promise that helped them to almost entirely wipe out the Conservatives in the House of Commons. However, this promise was not kept and nothing was done until the Conservatives got back into power in 2006 and reduced the GST rate.

So, is the GST a good or a bad tax? On what grounds can we assess the GST? In this chapter, you will learn the principles by which tax systems can be judged.

■ THE LEVEL AND TYPES OF TAXATION

Many Canadians believe that taxes have been gobbling up an ever-increasing share of the Canadian economy. Figure 1, however, shows that this belief is not true. By charting the behaviour of federal, provincial/territorial, and local taxes *as a percentage of gross domestic product* (GDP) for selected years since 1926, we see that the share of federal taxes in GDP has been approximately the same since the 1950s. There was a remarkable increase during World War II, when federal government taxes rose from 8.4 percent of GDP in 1939 to 20.6 percent in 1946, only to fall back to 15.3 percent in 1950. Since then, the proportion of federal taxes of Canadian GDP has been around that 15.3 percent number (or a couple of percentage points more) and was back to nearly 15.0 percent in 2007.

The share of GDP taken by provincial and local taxes climbed substantially between 1960 and 1970, when the welfare state was put in place, with this share going from 8.6 percent in 1960 to 13.9 percent in 1970. The proportion of provincial and local taxes of GDP reached its peak in 1996, at 17.6 percent. Since then it has generally decreased, being at 16.1 percent in 2007. Lately, provincial taxes represent about 12.8 percent of GDP, whereas local taxes represent only 3.1 percent. Overall, adding all levels of government, taxes represent less than one-third of Canada's GDP. Including the compulsory contributions to the Canada Pension Plan and the Quebec Pension Plan would add another 2.5 percent, bringing consolidated tax and compulsory contributions to 33.4 percent of GDP.

Whether these shares are too high or too low is a matter of some debate. But in any event:

The shares of GDP taken in taxes by the federal and provincial/local governments in 2007 are not much different from the shares taken in the 1970s or 1980s. However, there was a clear increase in these shares in the early 1990s and a downward reversal that started in the late 1990s and has continued until now.

Yet, as we noted in Chapter 2, when comparing industrialized countries internationally, Canada is in the low-intermediate class of taxation, along with countries as

FIGURE 1   **Taxes as a Percentage of Gross Domestic Product, 1926–2007**

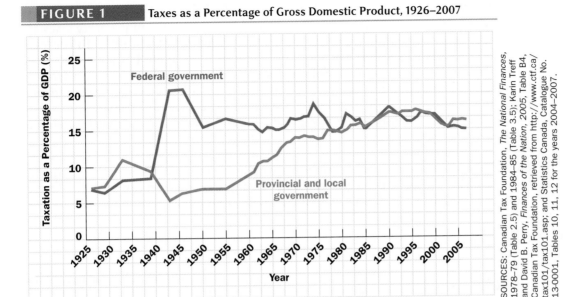

SOURCES: Canadian Tax Foundation, *The National Finances*, 1978–79 (Table 2.5) and 1984–85 (Table 3.5); Karin Treff and David B. Perry, *Finances of the Nation*, 2005, Table B4, Canadian Tax Foundation, retrieved from http://www.ctf.ca/tax101/tax101.asp; and Statistics Canada, Catalogue No. 13-0001, Tables 10, 11, 12 for the years 2004–2007.

Note: 1926–1984 data are based on gross national product (GNP), the total income that Canadian residents earn within a year. Numbers are rounded. The contributions paid to the Canada Pension Plan and the Quebec Pension Plan since 1966 were excluded, while contributions to social insurance were included.

diversified as Spain, Portugal, Greece, the United Kingdom, and New Zealand. Other Anglo-Saxon countries tend to belong in the low-tax category, such as the United States, Australia, and Ireland; also in this category are Japan and Switzerland, where tax shares are at, or below, 30 percent. Other European states belong to the higher tax categories. The Netherlands, Italy, Austria, and Norway are in the high-intermediate class, with taxes raking in about 40 percent of GDP. The other Nordic countries— Denmark, Finland, and Sweden—are in the high-tax group, with a share approaching 50 percent, along with France and Belgium (see Figure 16 in Chapter 2, page 41). Still, despite the economic inefficiencies brought about by taxes, according to most *social indicators*, these high-tax countries seem to be doing better than low-tax countries (see "Are There Any Benefits to High Taxation Rates? An Alternative View" on page 434).

Progressive, Proportional, and Regressive Taxes

Economists classify taxes as *progressive*, *proportional*, or *regressive*. Under a **progressive tax** like the personal income tax, the fraction of income paid in taxes *rises* as a person's income increases. Under a **proportional tax** like the payroll tax, this fraction is constant. Under a **regressive tax** like the notorious *head tax*, which charges every person the same amount, the fraction of income paid to the tax collector *declines* as income rises.[1] Because the fraction of income paid in taxes is called the **average tax rate,** we can reformulate these definitions as they appear in the margin.

Often, however, the average tax rate is less interesting than the **marginal tax rate,** which is the fraction of each *additional* dollar that is paid to the tax collector. The reason, as we will see, is that the *marginal* tax rate, not the *average* tax rate, most directly affects economic incentives.

Direct Versus Indirect Taxes

Another way to classify taxes is to categorize them as either **direct taxes** or **indirect taxes.** This classification is rather unhelpful, but it has been used by lawyers. Direct

A **progressive tax** is one in which the average tax rate paid by an individual rises as income rises.

A **proportional tax** is one in which the average tax rate is the same at all income levels.

A **regressive tax** is one in which the average tax rate falls as income rises.

The **average tax rate** is the ratio of taxes to income.

The **marginal tax rate** is the fraction of each *additional* dollar of income that is paid in taxes.

Direct taxes are taxes being imposed on the individual who is meant to bear the burden of the tax.

Indirect taxes are taxes levied on specific economic activities.

[1] In 1990, Prime Minister Margaret Thatcher caused riots in the United Kingdom by instituting a head tax. Such a head tax, or poll tax, is allowed in municipalities in Newfoundland and Labrador. In Alberta and British Columbia, health insurance premiums are set as fixed amounts per head or per family, with some partial or total relief for low-income residents.

taxes are understood as taxes that are imposed on the individual who is meant to bear the burden of the tax. The primary example is the income tax, but property taxes are also direct taxes, since they are directly imposed on the property owner. In contrast, indirect taxes are levied on the economic activity of some agent but are meant to be ultimately paid by someone else. Sales taxes in their various forms are considered to be typical examples of indirect taxes, because the tax is collected from the vendor but is intended to be paid by the purchaser. We will see later why this classification is not very useful, when we discuss the burden of a tax and how that burden can be shifted to other agents of the economy.

Although both the federal government and provincial governments raise revenues by both direct and indirect taxes, direct taxes are the main source of federal government revenues, while the provincial governments rely more on indirect taxes. North Americans, when compared to Europeans, pay more direct taxes and fewer indirect taxes.

■ THE FEDERAL TAX SYSTEM

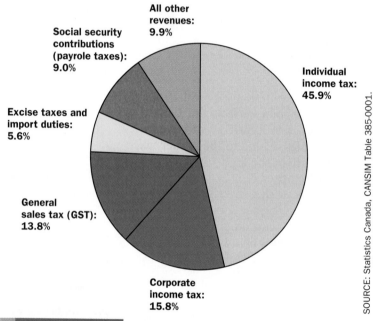

All other revenues: 9.9%

Social security contributions (payrole taxes): 9.0%

Excise taxes and import duties: 5.6%

General sales tax (GST): 13.8%

Corporate income tax: 15.8%

Individual income tax: 45.9%

SOURCE: Statistics Canada, CANSIM Table 385-0001.

FIGURE 2

Sources of Federal Revenue, 2006–2007

The *personal income tax* is by far the federal government's largest source of revenue. The second-largest source is the *Goods and Services Tax*, and the third-largest source of federal government revenue is the *corporate income tax*, a tax on the profits of incorporated businesses. Individual employees and their employers must also make contributions to the social security programs—the fourth-largest source of revenue at the federal level. The federal government also levies *excise taxes*—sales taxes and import duties on goods that are imported into Canada. While import duties used to represent the greatest part of the federal government budgetary revenues between Confederation in 1867 until the end of the 1950s, they now represent barely 1.5 percent of its revenues. The other federal government sources of revenues include taxes on investment income and direct taxes on foreigners or foreign operations. Figure 2 shows the breakdown of federal revenues for the fiscal year 2006–2007. Let us now look at some of these taxes in more detail.

■ The Federal Personal Income Tax

The tax on personal incomes was introduced by the federal government as late as 1917, during World War I. It was then perceived as a temporary measure, one that was costly to administer but that was needed to finance the war. Some 90 years later, the personal income tax has yet to be removed! At the beginning of World War II in 1939, the personal income tax represented only 8 percent of the federal government budgetary revenues, but it now accounts for about 46 percent of all federal government revenues.

April 30 is a key calendar day for all Canadian taxpayers, as they must send in their income tax returns by then, by mail or via the Internet. However, because employers are compelled to *withhold* income taxes from payrolls and then forward those funds to the Canadian Treasury, many individuals do not have to send in any money to pay additional income tax on that day. In fact, many taxpayers pay more than the required amount of income tax during the year and hence receive refund cheques or electronic payments through their banks. Tax withholding ensures that employees pay the required income tax, and as this method is somewhat painless, they might not fully realize that they pay large amounts to the Canadian and provincial treasuries. In many semi-industrialized countries, and even in some industrialized ones such as France until very recently, there is no tax withholding and tax collectors must negotiate the amount to be paid by assessing the earnings of each taxpayer, with taxpayers possibly paying their entire personal income tax on a single day.

The personal income tax is *progressive*. That fact is evident in Table 1, which shows that average tax rates rise as income rises. There are only four marginal rates, each applying to a different income bracket. For instance, in 2007, for a taxable income of between $0 and $37,178, the marginal tax rate was 15 percent. With taxable income between $37,178 and $74,357, any amount beyond $37,178 is taxed at the marginal tax rate of 22 percent. An individual earning $200,000 of taxable income would have to pay taxes equal to $25,854 on her first $120,887, plus 29 percent on the remaining taxable income ($79,113). Thus, her federal income tax is equal to $48,796 (25,854 + 0.29 × 79,113 = 25,854 + 22,942), as shown in the second column of Table 1. The maximum marginal tax rate at the federal level is 29 percent. However, when the provincial personal income tax is taken into account (provincial income taxes are collected by the federal government except in Quebec, which has its own provincial income tax system), the highest marginal rates range from 39 percent, as in Alberta, to 48.64 percent as in Newfoundland and Labrador.

Actually, the income tax is less progressive than it seems because of a variety of **tax shelters** or tax loopholes. Finance Canada keeps track of the amounts forgone by each of them, calling them *personal income tax expenditures*. Let us examine a few major ones.

Tax-Exempt Status for Capital Gains

Public finance specialists define income as the sum of potential consumption expenditures and the increase in wealth. Thus, if you are able to spend $70,000 on consumption goods, while your wealth increases by $30,000, then your income is $100,000. Your wealth may increase either because you have purchased $30,000 worth of new assets or because the assets that you hold are now valued $30,000 more than before, as could be the case if you hold shares on the stock market. In the latter case, you have made a **capital gain** of $30,000. Thus, income is made up of both regular income (wages, salaries, interest and dividend income) and capital gains.

In Canada, as in many other countries, capital gains are taxable only when they are being realized, not when they accrue. In addition, only 50 percent of the realized capital gains are included in taxable income (none of the capital gains arising from the sale of a farm property or shares of a small unincorporated business are taxable as long as these gains do not exceed $500,000). Thus, suppose that you purchased $250,000 worth of mutual funds when you inherited some money from an aunt at the end of 2007. Suppose further that the market value of these funds is $350,000 at the end of 2008. As long as you do not sell your mutual fund shares, your accrued $100,000 capital gain will be **tax-exempt.** By contrast, as shown in Table 2, if you sell all of your shares, the realized capital gain will be taxed and you will have to fork out $14,500 in federal income tax.

Thus, income in the form of capital gains is a tax shelter, since tax can be deferred as long as the capital gain is not realized (or until you die, at which point the Canada

A **tax shelter** is a special provision of the Income Tax Act that reduces or defers taxation if certain conditions are met.

A **capital gain** is the profit made from the sale of an asset at a higher price than was paid for it.

A particular source of income is **tax-exempt** if income from that source is not taxable.

TABLE 1		
Personal Federal Income Tax Rates, 2006			
Taxable Income	Tax	Average Tax Rate	Marginal Tax Rate
$ 0	$ 0	0 %	
			15%
37,178	5,577	15.00	
			22
74,357	13,756	18.50	
			26
120,887	25,854	21.40	
			29
200,000	49,796	24.40	
			29
1,000,000	281,085	28.10	

SOURCE: Authors' calculations and Canada Revenue Agency, T1-2007 tax return form. Retrieved from http://www.cra-arc.gc.ca

TABLE 2	
Federal Taxes Paid on Capital Gains for an Individual Whose Marginal Tax Rate is 29 Percent	
Purchase cost of asset	$250,000
Selling price of asset	350,000
Capital gain	100,000
Taxable income on capital gain	50,000
Tax on capital gain	14,500

Revenue Agency assumes that the assets were sold); in addition, only half of the capital gain is considered as taxable income. The loss in federal tax revenue due to the latter exemption was assessed to be about $2.5 billion in 2007. Still, some economists, most notably former Reform MP Herbert Grubel, argue that capital gains should not be taxed at all because capital gain taxation deters entrepreneurship. Indeed, realized capital gains were not added to taxable income in Canada until 1972.

Registered Retirement and Pension Plans   The most popular tax shelters in Canada are the Registered Retirement Saving Plan (RRSP) and the Registered Pension Plan (RPP). About 40 percent of paid workers are covered by an employer's RPP, while about 30 percent of tax filers in any given year declare contributions to an RRSP. These plans are intended to help and encourage individuals to accumulate funds that will finance their retirement years, hopefully without any further help from government. Furthermore, beyond these effects on individuals' wealth, some economists also believe that these **tax deductions** are good for the community, because they transform an income tax into a form of consumption tax, where saving is exempted from taxation. This, in their view, encourages citizens to save and allows for faster economic growth. Other economists see the RRSP and RPP only as what they are—tax shelters.

> A **tax deduction** is a sum of money that may be subtracted before the taxpayer computes his or her taxable income.

The yearly amounts put aside in an RPP or RRSP are deducted from taxable income. This is another instance of tax deferral, since the sums invested in one of these plans become taxable only when they are taken out of it, usually many years later. In addition, interest income and capital gains within RRSPs and RPPs are also tax-free until pensions are paid or funds are taken out of the registered saving vehicle. The RPP and the RRSP constitute two of the biggest three tax shelters in Canada, with the net loss in federal government tax revenue being forecast as $13 billion and $9 billion, respectively, in 2007.

Tax Benefits for Homeowners   It is often argued that mortgage interest payments and property taxes should be tax-deductible in Canada, as they are in the United States and in some other countries. Homeowners, however, already benefit from a tax shelter. First, there is no tax on the capital gains arising from the sale of the main residence of an individual, which is estimated to result in a loss of $5 billion in tax revenue for the federal government in 2007. Secondly, and this is our main point, homeowners benefit from housing services without paying rent, thus receiving income in kind that is not taxable; this is called *imputed rent*.

To understand why home ownership is a tax shelter, even without a capital gain, it is best to give an example. Take two friends, Jane and Linda, each earning $60,000 a year in taxable income. Suppose that they share a winning lottery ticket, each receiving $200,000 in tax-free cash. Jane purchases a $200,000 home. She has no mortgage or rent payment, but must pay $4,000 in property taxes per year. Linda decides to buy low-risk bonds that yield 5 percent interest, thus getting $10,000 per year in interest payments. She also rents a house that is identical to Jane's and pays $14,000 in rent per year. Most economists would argue that Jane and Linda should pay the same income tax but, under existing rules, they won't. Jane's taxable income remains at $60,000, while Linda's has increased to $70,000. Still, after they have paid their lodging expenditures, both Jane and Linda are left with $56,000 (see Table 3), and both own an asset worth $200,000.

How could this disparity be remedied? One solution would be for both homeowners and renters to be able to deduct their lodging expenditures. In this case, both Jane and Linda would show a taxable income of $56,000. An alternative would be to add imputed rent to Jane's revenue. Jane's net implicit rental income of occupying her own home is $10,000 ($14,000 of rent minus the property tax amount paid, $4,000). Her taxable income would then become $70,000, the same amount as Linda's. The fact

TABLE 3		
Owning versus Renting a Home		
	Jane	Linda
Earnings	$60,000	$60,000
Interest income	0	10,000
Taxable income	60,000	70,000
Expenditures on lodging	4,000	14,000
Amount left over	56,000	56,000

that imputed rent is not included in taxable income represents a major tax shelter that favours homeowners, especially wealthy ones with luxurious houses.

We could list more tax shelters, but enough has been said to illustrate the main point:

Every tax shelter encourages particular patterns of behaviours and favours particular types of people. Furthermore, because most shelters mainly benefit the rich, they erode the progressivity of the income tax.

The Goods and Services Tax (GST)

As pointed out earlier, the Goods and Services Tax (GST) was introduced by the federal government in 1991 and, as its name indicates, it applies to sales of both goods and services. The GST is our Canadian-made version of a value-added tax, a VAT as it is called in Europe and other industrialized countries where this tax generates a high proportion of government revenues.

The GST is intended to be a tax on final consumption, but it is imposed on the sale and import of goods and services at all stages of production. Businesses are granted input tax credits for all GST that they have paid in the course of their activities. Only the final consumer does not benefit from such credits. As a result, the tax yield of the GST is the value of the goods and services sold to consumers times the tax rate, which at the time of writing is 5 percent.

Table 4 provides an example of the GST mechanism. It illustrates the case of food that ends up in a restaurant. A farmer first produces soybeans that are sold to a miller; the miller transforms the soybeans into a bag of soy meal and sells this bag to a factory; the factory transforms the soy meal into a litre of soy sauce, selling it to a restaurant; the restaurant, in the course of providing meals, charges its customers for the use of the soy sauce. At each stage of production, each business adds some value to the product. As Table 4 shows, the farmer initially adds $3; the miller sells his bag for $4, thus providing an added value of $1. A litre of soy sauce sells for $8, so the transformation activity of the factory has an added value of $4; and finally the restaurant generates $2 of added value to the product.

TABLE 4								
The GST Mechanism								
Item	Seller	Buyer	Price without GST	Value Added	GST	Price with GST	Tax Credit	Net Tax
Soybeans	Farmer	Miller	$ 3.00	$ 3.00	$0.15	$ 3.15	$0.00	$0.15
Soy meal	Miller	Factory	4.00	1.00	0.20	4.20	0.15	0.05
Soy sauce	Factory	Restaurant	8.00	4.00	0.40	8.40	0.20	0.20
Seasoning	Restaurant	Consumers	10.00	2.00	0.50	10.50	0.40	0.10
Total				10.00				0.50

At each activity stage, the GST must be paid by the purchaser and collected by the seller for the Canada Revenue Agency (CRA). Initially, the miller paid $0.15 in GST on the purchase of the soybeans. When the miller sells a bag of soy meal to the factory, the factory must pay $0.20 in GST, which is collected by the miller and sent off to the CRA. The miller gets back $0.15 as a GST refund, thus paying a net GST amount of only $0.05. The process continues like this until the final multiple consumers pay $10.50 for the use of a litre of soy sauce, with the restaurant collecting $0.50 of taxes on behalf of the government. This is the end of the process, as consumers cannot get an input tax credit.

Some researchers argue that the GST has led to an increase in the underground economy, with businesses and workers providing services, such as minor house renovations, declining to declare their economic activities and hence evading payment of the GST as well as part of their income tax. Most observers would claim however that the GST has many features that compare favourably with the Manufacturer's Sales Tax that it replaced. The GST taxes consumer goods, but not investment goods, thus helping firms to acquire productivity-enhancing machines. Imported goods are taxed, but exported goods are not, thus helping Canadian producers to be more competitive in world markets. Finally the GST is quite encompassing. Nearly everything being sold is taxed. Basic groceries carry a zero GST rate, while some services benefit from a rate reduction: most health and dental services, financial services, daycare services, and educational services, for instance.

In theory, the GST is a slightly regressive tax, since poorer taxpayers usually spend a larger proportion of their income on goods and services than do high-revenue taxpayers. The exemption on grocery foods, however, tempers this effect. In addition, low-revenue households benefit from a refundable sales **tax credit** when they file their income tax returns. This makes the GST proportional, perhaps even slightly progressive, for people in low-income brackets.

> A **tax credit** is a sum of money that may be subtracted from the amount of tax owed by the taxpayer.

The Corporate Income Tax

The tax on corporate profits is also considered a direct tax, because corporations are fictitious "people" in the eyes of the law. Large corporations currently pay a basic federal marginal tax rate below 20 percent. Smaller businesses pay a lower rate, at 11 percent. When provincial corporate taxes are added, the overall marginal tax rates rise to approximately 30 percent and 16 percent, respectively, depending on the provincial location of the corporation. Because the tax applies only to profits—not to income—all wages, rents, and interest paid by corporations are deducted before the tax is applied.

There is a lot of pressure to reduce corporate tax rates. Think-tanks financed by businesses, such as the C.D. Howe Institute and the Fraser Institute, frequently publish studies providing evidence that high tax rates on capital slow down business activity and reduce foreign direct investment. Despite this, the share of corporate income tax in federal revenues in 2007 was still approximately what it was in the 1970s and 1980s.

Payroll Taxes

Payroll taxes—basically, taxes on wages and salaries—are mainly earmarked to be paid into various trust funds, at least in theory. At the federal level, two main programs are financed by payroll taxes: the Canada Pension Plan (CPP) and the Employment Insurance (EI) program. The costs of both of these social security programs are shared by the employees and the employers. For example, with respect to the Canada Pension Plan, employees must contribute 4.95 percent of their gross wage and the employer must contribute an identical amount. Self-employed workers contribute 9.90 percent, acting as both the employee and the employer. In the case of Employment Insurance, employers pay premiums that are 1.4 times more than those of workers.

On the surface, payroll taxes seem to be *proportional* taxes, but they are actually highly *regressive* for two reasons. First, only wages and salaries are subject to the tax; interest and dividends are not. Second, because there are limits on the benefits that one can draw from the CPP and from the EI program, earnings above a certain level (which changes every year, but between $40,000 and $50,000 depending on the program), are exempted from the tax. Above this limit, the *marginal payroll tax rate* is zero.

Payroll taxes have been subjected to intense debate lately. Worker organizations claim that the dues to the Employment Insurance program, which should be run like an insurance program with contributions approximately covering benefits to unemployed workers, were used by the federal government to finance general expenditures in the late 1990s and early 2000s, thus helping the Liberal government to move the federal budget from a deficit to a surplus position. The program has accumulated huge surpluses, estimated at $46 billion in 2005—more than three times the surplus that is considered safe by accounting standards. Worker organizations, such as the National Union of Public and General Employees, consider that the overlarge contributions constitute a scandal that is much worse than the sponsorship scandal that made the headlines in 2005 and led to the Liberal defeat in the January 2006 federal election. Unions would like the government to pay back employees and their employers. This is unlikely to occur, even though unions have taken the judicial route. Indeed, in 2007, the Supreme Court granted the unions the right to present their case. Future surpluses are unlikely, however, as contribution rates, by law, will be adjusted to balance the EI program.

Public Pension Plans

The Canada Pension Plan (and its equivalent for Quebec workers, the Quebec Pension Plan), financed by payroll taxes, has also been subjected to intense debates. As is the case in most industrialized countries, demographic trends worry economists and politicians alike, as they have important implications for the viability of our social security programs. The Canada Pension Plan relies mostly on a "pay-as-you-go" system, where the payroll tax payments of current workers (and their employees) are paid out to current retirees. The benefit cheques that your grandparents receive each month are not dividends on the contributions that were made on their behalf while they worked. Instead the cheques are paid out of the payroll taxes that your parents (or you) pay each month.

For many years, this pay-as-you-go system managed to give every generation of retirees more in benefits than it had contributed in payroll taxes. Unfortunately, the growth magic stopped working in the 1970s, for several reasons. First, growth in real wages slowed dramatically—indeed it nearly stalled completely—while pension plan benefits continued to grow rapidly. As a result, the burden of financing a public pension plan grew more onerous.

Second, population growth slowed significantly in Canada. Birthrates in this country were high from the close of World War II until about 1960—this was the postwar baby boom—and fell thereafter. The age pyramid is now inverted, except for a bump that corresponds to the children of the baby boomers—the echo boom. The fraction of the Canadian population that is older than age 65 has climbed from only 8.0 percent in 1971 to 10.0 percent in 1984 and 13.2 percent in 2006. It is certain to go much higher in the coming decades as the baby boomers retire. Thus, there are fewer working people available to support each retired person. Indeed Statistics Canada estimates that by 2030, 10 percent of the Canadian population will be *80 years old and over*, while more than 23 percent will be 65 and over!

Third, life expectancy keeps increasing. In 1991, life expectancy for males and females was 72.1 and 79.3 years, respectively; in 2004, these numbers were 77.4 and 82.4 years. In addition, the retirement age kept falling between 1971 and 1995. For instance, in 1971, 78.7 percent of males aged between 55 and 64 were still employed; this fell to 53.7 percent in 1995. As people live longer and retire younger, they spend more and more years in retirement. When the normal Canada Pension Plan retirement age was set at 65, many Canadians did not live that long. Nowadays, most do, and many live 20 years or more beyond retirement.

With the growth magic gone, something had to be done. In 1998, the federal government decided to increase the payroll tax, which gradually moved from 6 percent to 9.9 percent. The government also decided to switch to a partial instead of a full pay-as-you-go program, accumulating funds in advance, taking advantage of investment earnings as would an individual, by investing its reserve funds in bonds and the stock market. While some observers are still worried that future generations will have to carry a heavy burden to support the public pension plans, others believe that the Canada Pension Plan is now on solid ground. (See the boxed feature "Will You Benefit from the Canada Pension Plan When You Retire in 40 Years?")

THE PROVINCIAL/TERRITORIAL AND LOCAL TAX SYSTEM

Personal income taxes and sales taxes are the major sources of revenue for provincial and territorial governments. Municipalities, as well as school boards, rely heavily on

Will You Benefit from the Canada Pension Plan When You Retire in 40 Years?

Many recent surveys have asked Canadians whether they think that the current public pension plans will still exist when they retire. More than half of the members of Generation X—people who are between 25 and 39 years old—doubt that this will be the case. This pessimism, which may be shared by current college and university students, is encouraged by the media, which create some hype by describing doom-and-gloom scenarios, and by private retirement fund companies, which try to attract customers. Still, with the large overhaul of the Canadian Pension Plan in 1998, the Chief Actuary of Canada has certified that the plan is safe for as long as one can reasonably predict.

The confusion over public pension plans is reinforced by the 180-degree turn taken by governments. Not long ago, Canadian governments were providing early retirement incentives, encouraging civil servants, school teachers, nurses, and physicians to stop working and live off their pension benefits. Now the courts are abolishing compulsory retirement, early retirement incentives are being withdrawn, and the Organisation for Economic Co-operation and Development (OECD) is telling governments to raise the age of eligibility for public pensions. "Freedom 55," whereby one could retire as young as 55, is now a dream of the past, especially when stock markets took a beating in the early 2000s, first in Asia and then everywhere else. Trends have been reversed: In nearly all industrialized countries, including Canada, many workers now retire later or start working again after having apparently retired, some because of boredom but many because of financial necessity.

Economists assume that people are rational and are knowledgeable about their options. This is certainly not the case when it comes to pension plans. A Statistics Canada survey showed that many people thought they had pension coverage at work, but they did not. In particular, it was found that among recent immigrants (who are sometimes better educated than their Canadian counterparts) who reported benefiting from a registered pension plan, more than half were in fact working for firms that had no pension plan at all! Also, many individuals could not understand the difference between: a defined benefit pension plan, where future retirement benefits are guaranteed based on earnings and years of experience, and a defined contribution plan, where retirement benefits depend on the rate of return of the invested contributions, and nothing is promised.

SOURCE: Monica Townson, *Growing Older, Working Older: The New Face of Retirement* (Ottawa: Canadian Centre for Policy Alternatives, 2006).

---

property taxes, but their taxing powers are derived from their provincial or territorial legislature. Both levels of government also rely on transfers from higher-level governments. Figures 3 and 4 show the breakdown of provincial/territorial and local government receipts by source. We will now discuss some of these sources, leaving aside income taxes since they have already been discussed extensively.

FIGURE 3

Sources of Provincial and Territorial Governments Revenue, 2006

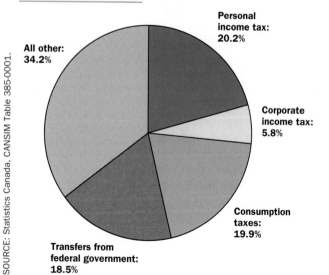

Personal income tax: 20.2%

All other: 34.2%

Corporate income tax: 5.8%

Consumption taxes: 19.9%

Transfers from federal government: 18.5%

SOURCE: Statistics Canada, CANSIM Table 385-0001.

Sales and Excise Taxes

All provincial governments (except for Alberta, where oil royalties fill the gap) impose a retail sales tax, the rate of which stands usually at 7 or 8 percent. In some provinces (such as New Brunswick and Nova Scotia), this tax is harmonized with the GST. In Quebec and Prince Edward Island, the retail sales tax is imposed on top of the GST. In the rest of the provinces, the tax applies to the price before the imposition of the GST— a clear example of Canadian diversity, which rather confuses foreign tourists!

By law, the retail sales tax is imposed on the purchaser for final use. The retailer is viewed as an intermediary, acting on behalf of government. This procedure was adopted because sales taxes are generally considered to be indirect taxes, being levied on the retailer but ultimately being paid by the consumer. When Confederation came about however, the British North America Act gave the provinces the right to collect direct taxes only. The Act was circum-vented when the provinces managed to convince the courts that sales taxes were assessed directly on consumers, with the vendors acting as the collecting agent of the provincial governments, thus showing that the direct–indirect classification is of little help. More will be said later about who really pays the retail sales tax.

The provincial retail sales tax carries many exceptions. Provinces try to exempt production goods, because such a tax puts Canadian producers at a disadvantage relative to foreign ones. All provinces exempt farm machinery and equipment, and most other production machinery is also exempted. There are also widespread exemptions of some consumer goods. All provinces exempt food, prescription drugs, and medical appliances, as well as books and children's clothing. However, some services are also subject to the provincial retail sales tax, such as telecommunications, hotel and motel accommodation, and insurance premiums.

Besides the retail sales tax, there are also some specific sales taxes, called excise taxes, which originally were imposed on luxury goods or activities that were not considered meritorious. Duties and taxes are levied by both the provincial and the federal governments, mainly on tobacco products, all kinds of alcohol, and gasoline and diesel fuel.

| FIGURE 4 | Sources of Local Governments Revenue, 2004–2005 |

SOURCE: Karin Treff and David B. Perry, Finances of the Nation 2005, Canadian Tax Foundation, Table A9. Retrieved from http://www.ctf.ca/tax101/tax101.asp

All other: 4.7%

Property taxes: 40.4%

Transfers from other governments: 39.7%

Sales of goods and services: 15.5%

Property Taxes

Municipalities raise revenue by taxing properties, such as houses and office buildings. Educational and religious institutions are normally exempt from these property tax levies. The usual procedure is to *assess* each taxable property based on its market value and then to place a tax rate on the community's total assessed value that yields enough revenue to cover expenditures on local services. Property taxes generally run between 1 and 3 percent of true market value.

Considerable political controversy has surrounded the property tax for years. Because local property taxes provide the main source of financing for public schools, wealthy communities with expensive real estate are able to afford higher-quality schools than poor communities. A simple arithmetical example will clarify why. Suppose real estate holdings in Richtown average $300,000 per family, whereas real estate holdings in Poortown average only $100,000 per family. If both towns levy a 2 percent property tax to pay for their schools, Richtown will generate $6,000 per family in tax receipts, but Poortown will generate only $2,000.

Glaring inequalities like these have led some provincial and territorial governments to transfer large sums of money to municipalities or to school boards, to ensure that the residents and their children in poorer districts have an equal opportunity to obtain high-quality services and education. This can be seen in Figure 4, where government transfers constitute a large share of local government revenues. The federal government, in part as a result of its recent huge budgetary surpluses, also transfers large sums of money to municipalities.

■ Fiscal Federalism

Figure 3 points out an interesting fact: Grants from the federal government are a major source of revenue to provincial and territorial governments. In addition, grants from the provinces and territories are vital to local governments. This system of transfers from one level of government to the next, which has a long history, is referred to as **fiscal federalism.**

Aid from this source can come either in the form of *conditional grants* or in the form of *unconditional grants.* No strings are attached to unconditional grants, but with conditional grants, money is given from one level of government to the next on the condition that it be spent for a specific purpose. For example, the federal government may grant funds to a province *if* that province promises to use the money to build highways. Or a territorial government may give money to a school board to spend on a specific educational program.

In Canada, *fiscal federalism* mainly refers to the difficult financial relationships that have existed between the federal government and the provinces ever since Confederation. From the very beginning, provinces were strapped for cash, being restricted to direct taxes because they did not dare to impose the highly unpopular personal income tax. The situation became particularly intolerable during the Great Depression, since the Confederation Act assigned social welfare responsibilities to the provinces. The costs of social welfare programs were quickly rising, leading some provinces to levy retail sales taxes through the legal trick that was mentioned earlier. Despite this, the federal government had to step in and provide the provinces with transfers that covered a large share of their expenditures. This fiscal imbalance—the imbalance between the revenues of the provinces and those of the federal government, relative to their constitutional responsibilities—which has been talked about so much since the end of the 1990s, is not a new issue.

At this point, federal transfers to the provinces have evolved into three sets of programs, two conditional programs and an unconditional one. The two conditional programs are the Canada Health Transfer program and the Canada Social Transfer program, both of which are shared-cost programs. The former deals with health care (medical and hospital services). The provinces and territories must respect five principles: Their health services must be universal, accessible, comprehensive, also available to out-of-province residents, and well administered. The other conditional program, the Canada Social Transfer program, deals with social assistance and social services, as well as child care and postsecondary education.

Perhaps the most contentious program is the Equalization Program. Its objective is to provide comparable public services anywhere in Canada, without tax rates being higher in regions with fewer resources and lower incomes. Eligibility to receive equalization funding is determined by a highly complicated formula that measures the revenue-raising capacity of each province and territory against a five-province standard. Currently, only Alberta and Ontario receive no equalization payment, and Saskatchewan receives very little.

The most contentious issue is the composition of the equalization formula. In particular, what should be the components of the formula? Acrimonious debate has arisen about whether revenues derived from depletable natural resources, in particular oil revenues, should be included in, or excluded from, the formula, the point being that the wealth derived from depletable resources could be considered to be temporary. The exact size of the transfers is also a contentious issue, with rich versus poor provinces and natural resource-endowed provinces versus provinces with few natural resources engaged in the debate. There is little chance that the provinces will agree among themselves, so the federal government might have to impose its own view. Unilateral decisions by the federal government may not be the best option, however, as was demonstrated in 1995 when federal Minister of Finance Paul Martin, in his effort to eliminate the federal budget deficit, decided unilaterally to cut into the federal transfers to the provinces and territories. The effects of the damage that the resultant lack of funding did to various provincial and territorial programs, including health care and educational programs, are still being felt more than 12 years later.

■ THE CONCEPT OF EQUITY IN TAXATION

Taxes are judged on two criteria: *equity* (Is the tax fair?) and *efficiency* (Does the tax interfere unduly with the workings of the market economy?). Although economists are mostly concerned with the second criterion, public discussions about tax proposals focus almost exclusively on the first. Let us, therefore, begin our discussion by investigating the concept of equitable taxation.

■ Horizontal Equity

There are three distinct concepts of tax equity. The first, **horizontal equity,** simply asserts that *equally situated individuals should be taxed equally.* Few would quarrel with this principle. But because it is often difficult to apply in practice, violations of horizontal equity can be found throughout Canadian tax laws.

Consider, for example, the personal income tax. Horizontal equity calls for two families with the same income to pay the same tax. But what if one family has eight children and the other has just one? Well, you answer, we must define *equally situated* to include equal family sizes, so only families with the same number of children can be compared on grounds of horizontal equity. But what if one family has unusually high medical expenses, and the other has none? Are they still equally situated? By now, the point should be clear: Determining when two families are equally situated is no simple task. In fact, the Canadian tax provisions contain literally scores of requirements that must be met before two families are construed as equal.

Horizontal equity is the notion that equally situated individuals should be taxed equally.

■ Vertical Equity

The second concept of fair taxation seems to flow naturally from the first. If equals are to be treated equally, it appears that *unequals should be treated unequally.* This precept is known as **vertical equity.**

Just saying this does not get us very far, however, because vertical equity is a slippery concept. Often it is translated into the **ability-to-pay principle,** which states that *those most able to pay should pay the highest taxes.* Unfortunately, this principle still leaves a definitional problem similar to the problem of defining *equally situated*: If two families each earn $80,000, how much less tax should the family with four children pay relative to the family with only one child? In Canada, high-income families pay the same amount of income tax, no matter how many children they have. Still, the ability of the various types of families to pay taxes must be different. Is this fair?

How do we measure the ability to pay?

The nature of each tax often provides a straightforward answer. In income taxation, we measure ability to pay by income; in property taxation, we measure it by property value, and so on.

But an even thornier problem arises when we try to translate this concept into concrete terms. Consider the three alternative income-tax plans listed in Table 5. Families with higher incomes pay higher taxes under all three plans, so all of them can claim to follow the ability-to-pay principle. Yet the three

Vertical equity refers to the notion that differently situated individuals should be taxed differently in a way that society deems to be fair.

*The **ability-to-pay principle** of taxation refers to the idea that people with greater ability to pay taxes should pay higher taxes.*

TABLE 5						
Three Alternative Income Tax Plans						
	Plan 1		Plan 2		Plan 3	
Income	Tax	Average Tax Rate	Tax	Average Tax Rate	Tax	Average Tax Rate
$ 10,000	$ 300	3%	$ 1,000	10%	$1,000	10%
50,000	8,000	16	5,000	10	3,000	6
250,000	70,000	28	25,000	10	7,500	3

plans have radically different distributive consequences. Plan 1 is a progressive tax, like the individual income tax in Canada: The average tax rate is higher for richer families. Plan 2 is a proportional tax: Every family pays 10 percent of its income. This corresponds precisely to the situation in Alberta, where the provincial income tax rate is a flat 10 percent, whatever the income of the individual (beyond a certain threshold). Plan 3 is regressive: Because tax payments rise more slowly than income, the average tax rate for richer families is lower than that for poorer families.

Which plan comes closest to the ideal notion of vertical equity? Many people find that Plan 3, the regressive tax, offends their sense of fairness. But people agree much less over the relative merits of progressive versus proportional taxes. Some people take the notion of vertical equity to be synonymous with progressivity. Other things being equal, progressive taxes are seen as "good" taxes in some ethical sense, whereas regressive taxes are seen as "bad." On these grounds, advocates of greater equality support progressive income taxes and oppose regressive sales taxes. But other people disagree and find proportional taxes to be "fair."

■ The Benefits Principle

Whereas the principles of horizontal and vertical equity, for all their ambiguities and practical problems, at least do not conflict with one another, the final principle of fair taxation often violates commonly accepted notions of vertical equity. According to the **benefits principle of taxation**, those who reap the benefits from government services should pay the taxes.

> The **benefits principle of taxation** holds that people who derive benefits from a service should pay the taxes that finance it.

The benefits principle is often used to justify earmarking the proceeds from certain taxes for specific public services. For example, receipts from gasoline taxes typically go to finance construction and maintenance of roads. Thus, those who use the roads pay the taxes—and roughly in proportion to their usage. Most people seem to find this system fair. But in other contexts—such as public schools and hospitals—the body politic has been loath to apply the benefits principle because it clashes so dramatically with common notions of fairness. (Should sick people pay for public hospitals?) So most public services are financed out of general tax revenues rather than by direct charges for their use.

■ THE CONCEPT OF EFFICIENCY IN TAXATION

Economic efficiency is among the most central concepts of economics. The economy is said to be *efficient* if it has used every available opportunity to make someone better off without making anyone else worse off. In this sense, taxes almost always introduce *inefficiencies*. That is, if the tax were removed, some people could be made better off without anyone being harmed.

However, that is not a terribly pertinent comparison. The government does, after all, need revenue to pay for the services it provides. So, when economists discuss the notion of "efficient" taxation, they are usually seeking taxes that cause the *least amount of inefficiency* for a given amount of tax revenue. Or, in the more colourful words of Jean-Baptiste Colbert, treasurer to King Louis XIV of France, "The art of taxation consists in so plucking the goose to obtain the largest amount of feathers, with the least possible amount of hissing."

> The **burden of a tax** to an individual is the amount one would have to be given to be just as well off with the tax as without it.

To explain the concept of efficient taxation, we need to bring back a concept that was discussed on page 330 of Chapter 14—deadweight loss. Economists define the **burden of a tax** as the amount the taxpayer would have to be given to be just as well off in the presence of the tax as in its absence. An example will clarify this notion and also make clear why:

The burden of a tax normally exceeds the revenue raised by the tax.

Take the case of the new excise tax on fuel-inefficient vehicles that was introduced by the Harper government in its 2007 budget, as briefly mentioned in Chapter 17, page

405. The federal government now collects a "green levy" on gas guzzlers. The excise tax applies to new automobiles (including station wagons, vans and sport utility vehicles) designed primarily to carry passengers. A simple tax schedule is shown in Table 6.

Suppose that Harry, who now drives the full-size Jeep Grand Cherokee SRT8, wants a big SUV. Once the new tax takes effect, he has five different choices, but we will assume that he is considering only the three options shown in the shaded rows in the table. He can buy another Jeep Grand Cherokee and pay $4,000 in tax; he can switch to a Chevrolet Trailblazer with its six-litre motor and avoid half the tax; or he can switch to the slightly smaller Acura MDX and avoid the entire green levy.

If Harry sticks with the Grand Cherokee, we have a case in which the burden of the tax is exactly equal to the tax he pays. Why? Because if someone gave Harry $4,000, he would be in exactly the same position as he was before the tax was enacted. In general:

When a tax induces no change in economic behaviour, the burden of the tax is measured accurately by the revenue collected.

However, this result is not what we normally expect to happen, and it is certainly not what the government intends by levying a tax on gas-guzzling vehicles. Normally, we expect taxes to induce some people to alter their behaviour in ways that reduce or avoid tax payments. So let us look into Harry's other two options.

If Harry decides to purchase a Chevrolet Trailblazer, he pays only $2,000 in tax. But that $2,000 *understates* his burden. Give Harry $2,000 and his tax bill will be covered, but he will still be chagrined by the fact that he no longer drives a Grand Cherokee. How much money would it take to make Harry just as well off as he was before the tax? Only Harry knows for sure. But we do know that it is more than the $2,000 tax that he would pay if he bought the Trailblazer and that it is less than the $4,000 tax that he would have to forfeit to buy another Grand Cherokee; otherwise, he would have chosen the Grand Cherokee. Whatever that (unknown) amount is, the amount by which it exceeds the $2,000 tax bill is called the **excess burden,** or the deadweight loss, of the tax.

Harry's final option makes the importance of understanding excess burden even more clear. If he switches to an Acura MDX, Harry will pay no tax. Are we therefore to say he has suffered no burden? Clearly not, for he longs for the Grand Cherokee that he no longer drives. The general principle is:

The **excess burden** of a tax to an individual is the amount by which the burden of the tax exceeds the tax that is paid.

Whenever a tax induces people to change their behaviour—that is, whenever it "distorts" their choices—the tax has an *excess burden.* In such a case, the revenue collected systematically understates the true burden of the tax.

The excess burdens that arise from tax-induced changes in economic behaviour are precisely the *inefficiencies* we noted at the outset of this section. The basic precept of efficient taxation is to try to devise a tax system that *minimizes* these inefficiencies. In particular:

In comparing two taxes that raise the same total revenue, the one that produces less excess burden is the more efficient.

TABLE 6
"Green Levy" Taxation Schedule

Weighted Fuel Consumption per 100 Kilometres	Green Levy	Vehicle Type
Less than 13 litres	$ 0	Acura MDX
13 litres and more, but less than 14	1,000	Cadillac SRX 4.6
14 litres and more, but less than 15	2,000	Chevrolet Trailblazer 6.0
15 litres and more, but less than 16	3,000	Infiniti QX56
16 litres and more	4,000	Jeep Grand Cherokee SRT8

SOURCE: Canada Revenue Agency. Retrieved from http://www.cra-arc.gc.ca/whatsnew/items/list_veh-e.pdf

Notice the proviso that the two taxes being compared must yield the *same* revenue. We are really interested in the *total* burden of each tax. Because

Total burden = Tax collections + Excess burden

we can unambiguously state that the tax with less *excess* burden is more efficient only when tax collections are equal.

Excess burdens arise when consumers and firms alter their behaviour on account of taxation. So this precept of sound tax policy can be restated the following way:

> In designing a tax system to raise revenue, the government should try to raise any given amount of revenue through taxes that induce the smallest changes in behaviour.

Sometimes, however, a tax is levied not primarily as a revenue raiser, but as a way to induce individuals or firms to alter their behaviour. For example, we mentioned on page 118 of Chapter 6 that higher taxes on cigarettes are one way to reduce teen smoking. Various "green" taxes to combat greenhouse gas emissions (the "carbon" tax), and pollution in general, have also been mentioned in Chapter 17. The possibility of using taxes to change consumer behaviour will be discussed later in this chapter.

Tax Shelters and Excess Burden

We noted earlier that various exemptions make the income tax less progressive than it appears to be on paper. Now that we have learned that tax-induced changes in behaviour lead to excess burdens, we can understand the second reason why tax specialists condemn tax shelters: They make the income tax less *efficient* than it could be. Why? Because most tax shelters involve imposing different tax rates on different types of income. Given a choice between paying, say, a 35 percent marginal tax rate on one type of income and a 15 percent rate on another, most rational taxpayers will favour the latter. Thus:

> When different income-earning activities are taxed at different marginal rates, economic choices are distorted by tax considerations, which in turn impairs economic efficiency.

Our example is hardly hypothetical. Take the case of Ontario and Manitoba, where upper-bracket taxpayers now pay a combined 46.4 percent tax on income that comes in the form of wages or interest but only 23.2 percent on income that comes in the form of capital gains or dividends. It is no wonder, then, that such people shun interest and seek capital gains—often in the stock market.

One major objective shared by tax reformers is to enhance both the equity and efficiency of the personal income tax by closing loopholes and lowering tax rates. As was the motto of the Carter Commission—the Royal Commission on Taxation—that examined the Canadian tax system in 1966 and proposed substantial changes: "A buck is a buck." Politicians regularly promise to simplify Canadian tax law, making it fairer and more streamlined. In particular, there is a lot of talk about a personal income tax with a single tax rate, where nearly all existing deductions and exemptions would be removed. But these promises are difficult to fulfill. Because life is a complicated affair, equitable treatment may require complicated tax rules.

SHIFTING THE TAX BURDEN: TAX INCIDENCE

The incidence of a tax is an allocation of the burden of the tax to specific individuals or groups.

When economists speak of the **incidence of a tax,** they are referring to who actually bears the burden of the tax. In discussing the tax on gas-guzzling autos, we adhered to what has been called the *flypaper theory of tax incidence:* that the burden of any tax sticks where the government puts it. In this case, the burden stays on Harry, our SUV fan. But often things do not work out this way.

Consider, for example, what will happen if the government levies a special $4,000 tax on all SUVs like the Jeep Grand Cherokee. We learned how to deal with such a tax in a supply-and-demand diagram back in Chapter 4, page 76: The supply curve shifts up by the amount of the tax—in this case, $4,000. Figure 5 shows such a shift by the movement from S_0S_0 to S_1S_1. If the demand curve DD does not shift, the market equilibrium moves from point A to point B. The quantity of SUVs declines as Harrys all over Canada react to the higher price by buying fewer SUVs. Notice that the price rises from $50,000 to $53,000, an increase of $3,000. People who continue buying these vehicles therefore bear a burden of only $3,000—less than the tax that they pay!

Does this mean that the tax imposes a *negative* excess burden? Certainly not. What it means is that consumers who refrain from buying the taxed commodity manage to *shift* part of the tax burden away from consumers as a whole, including those who continue to buy SUVs. Automakers now get $49,000 for their SUVs whereas before they got $50,000—a $1,000 loss. Who are the ultimate victims of this **tax shifting?** There are two main candidates. First, obviously, are the automakers themselves or, more precisely, their shareholders. To the extent that the tax reduces auto sales and profits, shareholders bear the burden. The other principal candidates are autoworkers. To the extent that reduced production leads to layoffs or lower wages, these workers bear part of the tax burden.

Notice that it does not matter who, by law, is required to pay the tax. In the example depicted in Figure 5, it is implicitly assumed that the company must pay the $4,000 tax on every vehicle sold, so that its supply curve shifts up as its unit costs (including the tax) go up by the amount of the tax. But assume now, as shown in Figure 6, that consumers have to pay the tax on SUVs, sending $4,000 to the Canada Revenue Agency whenever they purchase a SUV. The 12,000 Canadians who wish to purchase a new SUV at $50,000 are now willing to give only $46,000 to the automaker because they must remit $4,000 to the federal government. From the point of view of the automaker, the demand curve has shifted down as a result of the tax that needs to be paid by consumers, from D_0D_0 to D_1D_1. The final result however is the same as in Figure 5: Only 10,000 consumers will now purchase a SUV at the tax-inclusive price of $53,000, and the SUV maker will get $49,000.

People who have never studied economics almost always believe in the flypaper theory of incidence, which holds that sales taxes are borne by consumers, property taxes are borne by homeowners, and taxes on corporations are borne by shareholders. Perhaps the most important lesson of this chapter is that:

The flypaper theory of incidence is often wrong.

Failure to grasp this point can lead to all sorts of misguided tax legislation, where elected representatives, *thinking* they are placing a tax burden on a group of people, inadvertently place it squarely on another. For instance, effective October 2007, the Quebec government imposed a new "green" gasoline tax on petroleum companies to finance its plan to fight global warming, claiming that consumers would not be saddled with the additional cost because oil companies could afford to absorb the full cost of the

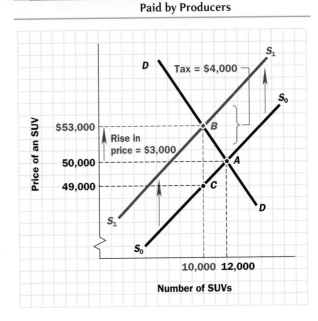

FIGURE 5   The Incidence of an Excise Tax Paid by Producers

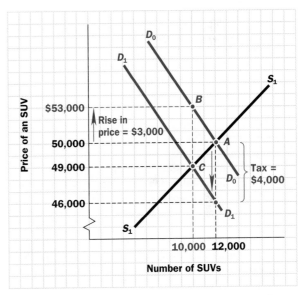

FIGURE 6

The Incidence of an Excise Tax Paid by Consumers

Tax shifting occurs when the economic reactions to a tax cause prices and outputs in the economy to change, thereby shifting part of the burden of the tax onto others.

Are There Any Benefits to High Taxation Rates? An Alternative View

In May 2007, a large majority of polled Quebeckers opposed the $1 billion tax cut that was being proposed in the budget of the newly elected minority Liberal provincial government led by Jean Charest. Quebeckers wanted instead the money to be spent to improve health care and education. The tax cut went through nonetheless, after some give and take, as none of the opposition parties wanted to go through another election campaign right away. The following excerpt, co-authored by Neil Brooks, a professor at Osgoode Law School—a school known for its anticonservative stance—reminds us that taxes, besides being a burden, help to provide worthy services.

It is often difficult to know precisely what taxcutters hope to achieve through more tax cuts and what evidence they think supports their claims. Their contention that Canadians would be better off if taxes were reduced is usually asserted as an article of faith. However, one way of attempting to answer the question of whether the Canadian government should be cutting taxes even more is to look across countries and compare the social and economic outcomes in high-taxed countries with the social and economic outcomes in low-taxed countries.

Is it really the case, as assumed by those who think taxes need to be further reduced in Canada, that the quality of life of the average citizen is higher in low-taxed countries than high-taxed countries? That is the question we undertake to answer in this study. As representative of low-tax countries, we study all six Anglo-American countries: the United Kingdom, the United States, Canada, Ireland, Australia, and New Zealand. As representative of high-tax countries, we study the four Nordic countries: Sweden, Norway, Denmark, and Finland.

Findings from this study show that high-tax countries have been more successful in achieving their social objectives than low-tax countries. Interestingly, they have done so with no economic penalty. On the majority of social measures we examine, high-tax countries rank significantly above low-tax countries. On a number of the economic indicators we examine, low-tax countries rank above high-tax countries, but the difference is almost never significant. We examine 50 indicators that are commonly used to measure a country's social progress. On over half of these indicators (29), the outcomes in high-tax Nordic countries are significantly better than those in low-tax Anglo-American countries, and on most of the remaining indicators (13), social outcomes are somewhat better in Nordic countries. In short:

- Nordic countries have significantly lower rates of poverty across almost all social groups;

- as an indicator of how well a country protects the vulnerable, the elderly have significantly higher pension income replacement rates in Nordic countries and the income received by those with disabilities relative to the population is much higher;

- income is distributed significantly more equally in Nordic countries;

- on every measure we examine there is significantly more gender equality in Nordic countries;

- Nordic workers have significantly more economic security;

- in terms of health outcomes, infant mortality rates are significantly lower and life expectancy is longer in Nordic countries;

- in terms of educational outcomes, a greater percentage of the population completed secondary school and university in Nordic countries and 15-year-old students score higher on math tests;

- as a measure of personal physical security, homicide rates are lower in Nordic countries;

- as indicators of the degree of community and social solidarity in a country and general happiness and life satisfaction, there is significantly more trust among individuals and for public institutions in Nordic countries;

- there is significantly less drug use in Nordic countries; individuals have significantly more leisure time; individuals have more freedom, according to a widely referred to index of economic freedom; individuals report more life satisfaction; and they are more likely to discuss politics with friends;

- Nordic countries rank much higher on an index of environmental performance, and the Nordic countries give significantly more in foreign aid than Anglo-American countries.

SOURCE: Excerpted from Neil Brooks and Thaddeus Hwong, *The Social Benefits and Economic Costs of Taxation: A Comparison of High- and Low-Tax Countries* (Ottawa: Canadian Centre for Policy Alternatives, December 2006). Retrieved from http://www.policyalternatives.ca. Reprinted with permission.

tax without shifting it to consumers. This naïve flypaper view of tax incidence stands little chance of being verified; Quebec drivers are likely to pay a substantial share of the new tax.

In some cases, however, the flypaper theory of incidence is roughly correct. So let us consider some specific examples of tax incidence.

■ The Incidence of Excise Taxes

Excise taxes have already been covered by our SUV example, because Figures 5 and 6 could represent any commodity that is taxed. Our basic finding is that *part* of the bur-

FIGURE 7   An Extreme Case of Tax Incidence

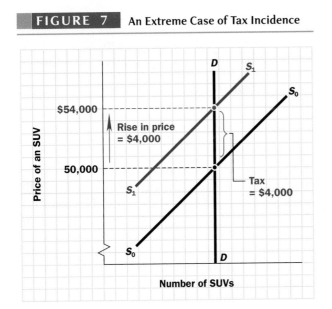

Number of SUVs

FIGURE 8   Another Extreme Case of Tax Incidence

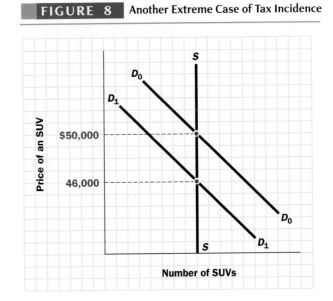

Number of SUVs

den will fall on consumers of the taxed commodity (including those who stop buying it because of the tax), and part will be borne by the firms and workers who produce the commodity.

How is the burden shared between buyers and sellers? It all depends on the slopes of the demand and supply curves. Intuitively speaking, if consumers are very loyal to the taxed commodity, they will continue to buy almost the same amount regardless of price. In that case, they will get stuck with most of the tax bill because they have left themselves vulnerable to it. Thus:

The more *inelastic* the demand for the product, the larger the share of the tax that consumers will pay.

Similarly, if suppliers are determined to offer the same amount of the product no matter how low the price, then they will wind up paying most of the tax. That is:

The more *inelastic* the supply curve, the larger the share of the tax that suppliers will pay.

One extreme case arises when no one stops buying SUVs when their prices rise. The demand curve becomes vertical, like the demand curve *DD* in Figure 7. Then no tax shifting can take place. When the supply curve shifts upward by the amount of the tax ($4,000), the price of an SUV (inclusive of tax) rises by the full $4,000—from $50,000 to $54,000. So consumers bear the entire burden.

The other extreme case arises when the supply curve is totally inelastic, as depicted by the vertical line *SS* in Figure 8. Because the number of SUVs supplied is the same at any price, the supply curve will not shift when a tax is imposed. Consequently, automakers must bear the full burden of any tax that is placed on their product. Figure 8 shows that the tax does not change the market price (including tax), which, of course, means that the price received by sellers must fall by the full amount of the tax, down to $46,000.

Demand and supply schedules for most goods and services are not as extreme as those depicted in Figures 7 and 8, so buyers and sellers share the burden. Precisely how it is shared depends on the elasticities of the supply and demand curves.[2]

---

[2] For concrete examples, see Test Yourself Questions 3 and 4 at the end of this chapter.

The Incidence of the Payroll Tax

Economists view the payroll tax as an excise tax on the employment of labour. As mentioned earlier, Canadian payroll taxes usually come in two parts: Half or less is levied on employees (via payroll deductions) and half or more on employers. A fundamental point, which people who have never studied economics often fail to grasp, is that:

> The ultimate incidence of a payroll tax is the same whether it is levied on employers or on employees.

A simple numerical example will illustrate why this must be so. Consider an employee earning $100 per day with a 10 percent payroll tax that is shared equally between the employer and the employee, as is the case with the current Canada Pension Plan. To hire this worker, a firm must pay $100 in wages to the worker plus $5 in taxes to the government—for a total daily cost of $105. But how much does the worker receive? He gets $100 in wages paid by the employer less $5 deducted and sent to the government, or $95 per day. The difference between wages *paid* and wages *received* is $105 − $95 = $10, the amount of the tax.

Now suppose members of Parliament try to "shift" the burden of the tax entirely onto firms by raising the employer's tax to $10 while lowering the employee's tax to zero. At first, with the daily wage fixed at $100, the firm's total labour costs (including tax) rise to $110 per day, and workers' net income rises to $100 per day. The MPs seem to have achieved their goal.

This achievement is fleeting, however, for what we have just described is not an equilibrium situation. With the daily cost of labour at $110 for firms, the quantity of labour *demanded* will be *less* than it was when labour cost only $105 per day. Similarly, with take-home pay up to $100 for workers, the quantity of labour *supplied* will be *more* than it was when the after-tax wage was only $95. Therefore, a *surplus of labour* on the market will develop (an excess of quantity supplied over quantity demanded), and this surplus will place downward pressure on wages.

How far will wages have to fall? We can easily see that an *after-tax* wage of $95 will restore equilibrium. If daily take-home pay is $95, the same as it was before the tax change, quantity supplied will be the same. From the firm's perspective, labour now costs $105 per day ($95 in wages plus $10 in taxes), just as it did before the tax change. Firms will, therefore, demand the same quantity of labour as they did when the payroll tax was shared. Thus, in the end, the market will completely frustrate the intent of the MPs.

The payroll tax is an excellent example of a case in which politicians, misled by the flypaper theory of incidence, think they are "taxing firms" when they raise the employer's share and "taxing workers" when they raise the employee's share. In truth, who really pays the tax in the long run depends on the incidence of the payroll tax. But no lasting difference results from a change in the employee's and the employer's shares.

So who, in fact, bears the burden? Like any excise tax, the incidence of the payroll tax depends on the elasticities of the supply and demand schedules. In the case of labour, a large body of empirical evidence points to the conclusion that the quantity of labour supplied is not very responsive to price for most population groups. The supply curve is almost vertical, like that shown in Figure 8. The result: Workers as a group can shift little of the burden of the payroll tax to employers.

But employers *can* shift it in most cases. To firms, their share of the payroll tax is an additional cost of using labour. When payroll taxes go up, firms try to substitute cheaper factors of production (such as capital) for labour wherever they can. This effort reduces the quantity of labour demanded, lowering the wage received by workers. Thus market forces shift part of the tax burden from firms to workers.

To the extent that the supply curve of labour has some positive slope, the quantity of labour supplied will fall when the wage goes down, allowing workers to shift some of the burden back onto firms. But firms, in turn, can shift that burden onto consumers by raising their prices. As we know from Part III, prices in competitive markets generally rise when costs (such as labour costs) increase. It is doubtful, therefore, that firms bear much of the payroll tax burden. The flypaper theory of incidence could not be farther from the truth. Even though the tax is collected by the firm, it is really borne by workers and consumers.

■ The Incidence of Corporate Income Tax

It is not always so easy to assess the incidence of a tax. In the case of the corporate income tax, there are widely different opinions, based on empirical research and theoretical models, as to whether the corporate tax is being shifted or not.

At first glance, it would seem that things are pretty straightforward, at least as long as the analysis remains within the short run. If a competitive firm is already producing at the output level that allows it to maximize profits at the given market price, there is nothing that it can do to shift the corporate income tax. The tax takes away part of the profits of the firm. If the profit-maximizing firm were to produce at any other output level, it would make less before-tax profits, and this would not be of any help. Monopoly firms, as examined in Chapter 11, are in a similar situation. Since they are assumed to maximize profits, any change in output and price that would be induced by a new corporate tax or a higher corporate tax rate would also lead to reduced before-tax profits. So, in contrast to what a noneconomist might expect, it is also impossible for monopoly firms to shift the corporate income tax.

But what if firms do not attempt to maximize short-run profits in the first place? As discussed in Chapter 12, this is quite possible, especially in oligopolistic industries. If firms there set prices on the basis of average cost pricing, the corporate income tax may be considered as a cost of production just like any other cost, including the GST and any other similar sales taxes. Since all firms face the introduction of or an increase in the corporate income tax, they will all be tempted to raise prices together. In this case, the average cost pricing firm will attempt to raise the price by the amount of the corporate income tax per unit of output, computed at the normal rate of capacity utilization. For instance, if the oligopoly assesses that when selling 10,000 units—its normal output—it will have to pay corporate income taxes of $500,000, then the price will have to be raised by at least $50.

We are thus back to an analysis that is very similar to that of an excise tax. Further, assuming constant average variable costs, as we did when discussing average cost pricing in Chapter 12, the supply curve will be flat and the tax will be entirely shifted to consumers (see Figure 9). Once again, the flypaper theory of taxation is not verified.

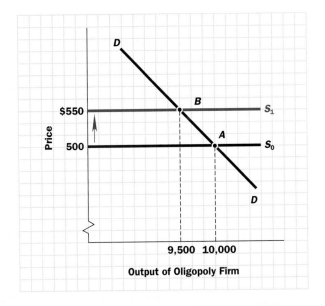

Output of Oligopoly Firm

FIGURE 9

Tax Incidence: Corporate Income Tax Assuming Average Cost Pricing with Constant Average Variable Costs

■ WHEN TAXATION CAN IMPROVE EFFICIENCY

We have spent much of this chapter discussing the inefficiencies and excess burdens that arise from taxation. Before we finish this discussion, we must point out two things.

First, economic efficiency is not society's only goal. For example, a tax on energy causes "inefficiencies" if it changes people's behaviour patterns. But these changes may be just what the government intends. The government wants people to conserve energy and is willing to tolerate some economic inefficiency to accomplish this goal. We can, of course, argue whether the conservation achieved is worth the efficiency loss. But the general point is that:

Some taxes that introduce economic inefficiencies may nonetheless be good social policy if they help to achieve some other goal.

We have already mentioned the excise tax on cigarettes, which aims to change behaviour. Another important example is the high tax on alcoholic beverages.

A second, and more fundamental, point is that:

> Some taxes that change economic behaviour may lead to efficiency *gains*, rather than to efficiency *losses*.

As you might suspect, this favourable outcome is possible only when the system has an inefficiency prior to the tax. In such a case, an appropriate tax may help set things right. One important example of this phenomenon was discussed at length in the previous chapter. Because firms and individuals who despoil clean air and water often do so without paying any price, these precious resources are used inefficiently. A corrective tax on pollution—the Pigovian tax—can remedy this problem.

■ EQUITY, EFFICIENCY, AND THE OPTIMAL TAX

In a perfect world, the ideal tax would raise the revenues the government needs, reflect society's views on equity in taxation, and induce no changes in economic behaviour—and so have no excess burden. Unfortunately, there is no such tax.

Sometimes, in fact, the taxes with the smallest excess burdens are the most regressive. For instance, a head tax, which charges every person the same number of dollars, is incredibly regressive. But it is also perfectly efficient. Because no change in economic behaviour will enable anyone to avoid it, no one has any reason to change behaviour.

Unfortunately, no tax is ideal, being both perfectly fair and totally efficient. A third element must be taken into consideration—administrative and compliance costs related to the taxes. This third element can be linked to the overall efficiency of a tax system. A tax may appear to create little excess burden, but what if the administrative and compliance costs are very high? In other words, what if the transaction costs, as defined on page 352 of Chapter 15, are overly high, costs such as bookkeeping, calculating, reporting, and remitting.

It may take an incredible amount of time for each taxpayer to complete all of the necessary tax forms and, as the old saying goes, time is money. In addition, specialized tax accountants may have to be hired by the government, at a high cost to the taxpayers. A little army of civil servants may also be needed to check that all of the paper work is done properly, and it may take an additional number of tax inspectors to make sure that all taxpayers are complying and that no one is evading the tax. Ideally, putting aside equity considerations, governments should use taxes that have low administrative and compliance costs relative to the amount of revenues that they generate.

ISSUE REVISITED: *The Pros and Cons of the GST Rate Reduction*

How does the GST stack up against the criteria of equity and efficiency, taking into account administrative and compliance costs? Should the GST rate be further reduced? Should the GST be eliminated, as the Liberals initially promised in 1993? Or is a GST rate reduction "bad economics" as argued by the same Liberals in 2006, and should the Canadian government rely even more on this value-added tax by raising the GST rate and reducing personal and corporate income taxes?

By now, you must have realized that there is no easy answer to these questions. All taxes, except for the head tax (although this may induce you to leave your country and live somewhere else), do create some excess burden, as they are likely to change some of your decisions with regard to leisure and work, saving and consumption, or the consumption of this or that good or service. In addition, different taxes have different implications in relation to equity. The personal income tax is usually regarded as the most progressive of all of the taxes, because higher income brackets are associated with higher marginal tax rates. But some studies show that this progressiveness is distorted by the many tax shelters that exist in the personal income taxation laws.

By contrast, value-added taxes such as the GST are usually considered as regressive taxes because the poor consume a greater fraction of their income than the rich, since rich people can afford to save and accumulate further wealth or just cannot find the time to spend everything they earn. However, with food being exempted and once the sales tax refund is taken into consideration, the GST is approximately proportional, at least for the lower- and medium-income earners.

Many studies show that the administrative costs of consumption taxes or value-added taxes, such as the GST, are much lower than those of the personal income tax.* This may explain why so many OECD countries rely more on consumption taxes than they do on income taxes, in contrast to what occurs in Canada. On the other hand, it has also been argued by some observers that the introduction of the GST led to substantial compliance problems. Small service providers sometimes offer their customers the option of omitting the GST if the customers pay in cash; the service providers thus are also able to avoid paying income tax on such transactions. But this tax evasion may fade in significance when the legal possibilities for the wealthy to avoid taxation are taken into account.

A huge overhaul of our tax system is unlikely. Some specialists argue that Canada should change its tax mix by putting in place higher GST rates and lower income tax rates. But in Canada, some pensioners spend nearly half of the year in Florida or in other warm areas of the globe, thus doing half of their consumption abroad. With the population aging and the number of pensioners rising, such a situation would reduce government revenues and would put a heavier burden on the shoulders of younger generations.

So where does this partial accounting of the pros and cons of the GST leave us? As usual, in a serious policy debate, there is plenty of room for reasonable people to argue both sides of the issue. As was said back in Chapter 1, economics is not supposed to give you all of the *answers*—it is supposed to help you ask the *right questions*. You now know what they are.

* See J. Clemens, N. Veldhuis, and M. Palacios, "Tax Efficiency: Not All Taxes are Created Equal," *Studies in Economic Prosperity* (Vancouver: The Fraser Institute, January 2007).

SUMMARY

1. The shares of GDP collected as taxes by the federal, provincial/territorial, and local governments in 2007 are not much different from the shares taken in 1970 or 1985. However, there was a clear increase in these shares in the early 1990s and a downward reversal in the late 1990s until now.

2. The Canadian federal government raises most of its revenue by **direct taxes,** such as the personal and corporate income taxes and the payroll tax. Of these taxes, the payroll tax is increasing most rapidly.

3. For decades, the Canada Pension Plan relied successfully on pay-as-you-go financing. In recent years, however, it has been accumulating large reserves to be used to pay benefits to the baby boom generation when it retires. After a major overhaul in 1998, experts now believe that the CPP is safe.

4. Personal income taxes and sales taxes are the major sources of revenue for provincial/territorial governments. Municipalities, as well as school boards, rely heavily on property taxes.

5. In our multilevel system of government, the federal government makes a variety of grants to provincial/territorial and local governments, and the provinces and territories in turn make grants to municipalities and school boards. This system of intergovernmental transfers is called **fiscal federalism.**

6. Fiscal federalism in Canada is mainly made up of two conditional programs—the Canada Health Transfer program and the Canada Social Transfer program—and one unconditional program—the Equalization Program, the purpose of which is to provide similar public services anywhere in Canada without tax rates being higher in regions with fewer resources and lower incomes.

7. The three concepts of fair, or "equitable," taxation occasionally conflict. **Horizontal equity** simply calls for equals to be treated equally. **Vertical equity,** which calls for unequals to be treated unequally, has often been translated into the **ability-to-pay principle**—namely, that people who are better able to pay taxes should be taxed more heavily. The **benefits principle** of tax equity ignores ability to pay and seeks to tax people according to the benefits they receive.

8. The **burden of a tax** is the amount of money an individual would have to be given to be as well off with the tax as without it. This burden normally exceeds the taxes that are paid, and the difference between the two amounts is called the **excess burden** of the tax.

9. Excess burden arises whenever a tax induces some people or firms to change their behaviour. Because excess burdens signal economic inefficiencies, the basic principle of efficient taxation is to utilize taxes that have small excess burdens.

10. When people change their behaviour on account of a tax, they often **shift** the burden of the tax onto someone else. For this reason, the "flypaper theory of **incidence**"—the belief that the burden of any tax sticks where lawmakers put it—is often incorrect.

11. The burden of a sales or excise tax normally is shared between suppliers and consumers. The manner in which it is shared depends on the elasticities of supply and demand.

12. The payroll tax works like an excise tax on labour services. Because the supply of labour is much less elastic than the demand for labour, workers bear most of the burden of the payroll tax—including both the employer's and the employee's shares.

13. Whether the corporate income tax is shifted onto consumers is a contentious issue. In the case of perfect competition and monopoly, where profits are already maximized, one would expect the owners of the firm to carry the burden of the tax; however, with oligopolistic firms using average cost pricing procedures, one would expect the corporate tax to be at least partly shifted onto consumers.

14. Sometimes "inefficient" taxes—that is, taxes that cause a good deal of excess burden—are nonetheless desirable because the changes in behaviour they induce further some other social goal.

15. When there are inefficiencies in the system for reasons other than the tax system (for example, externalities), taxation can conceivably improve efficiency.

KEY TERMS

Progressive, proportional, and regressive taxes   419

Average and marginal tax rates   419

Direct and indirect taxes   419

Tax shelter   421

Capital gain   421

Tax-exempt   421

Tax deductions   422

Tax credit   424

Fiscal federalism   428

Horizontal and vertical equity   429

Ability-to-pay principle   429

Benefits principle of taxation   430

Burden of a tax   430

Excess burden   431

Incidence of a tax   432

Tax shifting   433

TEST YOURSELF

1. Using the following hypothetical income tax table, compute the marginal and average tax rates. Is the tax progressive, proportional, or regressive?

Income	Income Tax
$20,000	$2,000
30,000	2,700
40,000	3,200
50,000	3,500

2. Which concept of tax equity, if any, seems to be served by each of the following?

   a. The progressive income tax
   b. The excise tax on cigarettes
   c. The gasoline tax

3. Suppose the supply and demand schedules for cigarettes are as follows:

Price per Carton	Quantity Demanded	Quantity Supplied
$3.00	360	160
3.25	330	180
3.50	300	200
3.75	270	220
4.00	240	240
4.25	210	260
4.50	180	280
4.75	150	300
5.00	120	320

NOTE: Quantity is in millions of cartons per year.

   a. What are the equilibrium price and equilibrium quantity?

b. Now the government levies a $1.25 per carton excise tax on cigarettes. What are the new equilibrium price paid by consumers, the price received by producers, and the quantity?

c. Explain why it makes no difference whether the government levies the $1.25 tax on the consumer or the producer. (Relate your answer to the discussion of the payroll tax in the text.)

d. Suppose the tax is levied on the producers. How much of the tax are producers able to shift onto consumers? Explain how they manage to do so.

e. Will there be any excess burden from this tax? Why? Who bears this excess burden?

f. By how much has cigarette consumption declined on account of the tax? Why might the government be happy about this outcome, despite the excess burden?

4. Now suppose the supply schedule is instead:

Price per Carton	Quantity Supplied
$3.00	60
3.25	105
3.50	150
3.75	195
4.00	240
4.25	285
4.50	330
4.75	375
5.00	420

NOTE: Quantity is in millions of cartons per year.

a. What are the equilibrium price and equilibrium quantity in the absence of a tax?

b. What are the equilibrium price and equilibrium quantity in the presence of a $1.25 per carton excise tax?

c. Explain why your answer to part (b) differs from your answer to part (b) in the previous question, and relate this difference to the discussion of the incidence of an excise tax in this chapter.

5. The country of Taxmania produces only two commodities: rice and caviar. The poor spend all their income on rice, while the rich purchase both goods. Both demand for and supply of rice are quite inelastic. In the caviar market, both supply and demand are quite elastic. Which good would be heavily taxed if Taxmanians cared mostly about efficiency? What if they cared mostly about vertical equity?

DISCUSSION QUESTIONS

1. "Canadians are overtaxed. The federal government should cut taxes." Comment.

2. If taxes need to be increased to finance more federal public expenditures, should the government increase the GST rate or the personal income tax? What are the principles on which you based your answer?

3. Should funds put into RRSPs and the CPP be deductible from taxable income, or should those tax shelters be eliminated? What is the basis for your answer?

4. Think of some tax that you personally pay. What steps have you taken or could you take to reduce your tax payments? Is there an excess burden on you? Why or why not?

5. Discuss the statement on taxes by Ludwig von Mises quoted on the first page of this chapter. Do you agree with him?

6. Use the criteria of equity and efficiency in taxation to evaluate the idea of taxing capital gains at a lower rate than other sources of income.

7. Should only poor and middle-class taxpayers have access to the Canada Child Tax Benefit, or should the program be universal?

THE DISTRIBUTION OF INCOME

V

I n Part V, we examine how a market economy distributes its income, using the price mechanism; that is, we investigate what determines the share of total output that goes to workers, to landowners, to investors, etc. Many economists would argue that the market assigns an important role to the marginal productivity of each of its recipients—how much of a marginal contribution each makes to the economy's total output.

In Chapter 19, we will study the payments made for the use of capital (interest), land (rent), and the reward to entrepreneurs (profit). Because most people earn their incomes primarily from wages and salaries, and because these payments constitute about two-thirds of Canada's national income, our analysis of the payments to labour (wages) merits a separate chapter (Chapter 20). In our bonus chapter (which can be downloaded from this book's website at http://www.baumolmicro1e.nelson.com), we turn to some important problems in the distribution of income—poverty, inequality, and discrimination. Another bonus chapter located on the text's website, International Trade and Competitive Advantage, introduces students to the principles of international trade and outlines the Ricardian doctrine of comparative advantage.

19

PRICING THE FACTORS OF PRODUCTION

*Rent is that portion of the produce of the earth which is paid to the landlord
for use of the original and indestructible powers of the soil.*

DAVID RICARDO (1772–1823)

I n Chapter 15, we noted that the market mechanism cannot be counted on to distribute income in accord with ethical notions of fairness, and we listed this as one of the market's shortcomings. There is much more to say about how income is distributed in a market economy, and we turn to that subject in this chapter.

The market mechanism distributes income through its payments to the **factors of production.** Everyone owns some potentially usable factors of production—which are simply the inputs used in the production process. Many of us have only our own labour; but some of us also have funds that we can lend, land that we can rent, or natural resources that we can sell. We sell these factors on markets at prices determined by supply and demand. So the distribution of income in a market economy is determined by the prices of the factors of production and by the amounts that are employed. For example, if wages are low and unequal and unemployment is high, then many people will be poor.

Factors of production are the broad categories—land, labour, capital, exhaustible natural resources, and entrepreneurship—into which we classify the economy's different productive inputs.

CONTENTS

PUZZLE: *Why Does a Higher Return to Savings Reduce the Amounts Some People Save?*

The rate of interest is the return you obtain by saving money from your income and holding it for a time as a financial asset—for example, by depositing the money into a bank interest-paying account or lending the money to a corporation by buying a bond. From the way the supply and demand mechanism works, we normally expect that a rise in the price of a loan will reduce the quantity demanded. Creditors would, therefore, have a higher inducement to lend and debtors would want to borrow fewer funds and get rid of more of their debts. But the evidence is that many people who save their money frequently do the opposite—they *reduce* their saving when the rate of interest goes up. Does that make sense?

Perhaps, even more paradoxical is the fact that many people borrow and lend simultaneously. At first glance, this would seem to be somewhat irrational. Why, for example, would you want to build up personal financial assets (with relatively low interest returns) while simultaneously accumulating debt on your credit card (at very high interest costs)? Studies of the behaviour of households in the United States conducted periodically by the Federal Reserve Board through its *Survey of Consumer Finances* have found that a significant majority of American households surveyed do actually engage in both borrowing and lending at the same time. Undoubtedly, a similar phenomenon exists in Canada.

Such puzzles affect other factors of production as well, in a way that may hint at an explanation. For example, wages are the price of labour, but when wages rise, workers often decide to work less, for example, taking longer vacations or a leave of absence. Why don't they work more when the pay is better? A little thought may give you the answer, but we will provide a fuller explanation of this behaviour later in the chapter.

Entrepreneurship is the act of starting new firms, introducing new products and technological innovations, and, in general, taking the risks that are necessary to seek out business opportunities.

It is useful to group the factors of production into five broad categories: land, labour, capital, exhaustible natural resources, and a rather mysterious input called **entrepreneurship.** In this chapter, we will look at three of them—the interest paid to capital, the rent of land, and the profits earned by entrepreneurs.

But first, because there is a great deal of misperception about the distribution of income among workers, suppliers of capital, and landlords, let's see how much these three groups actually earn.

Of all the gross payments made to the factors of production in Canada in 2007, interest and miscellaneous investment income accounted for about 6.2 percent; net income of nonfarm unincorporated business, including rent, were 8.1 percent (with rent being a very small proportion); and corporate profits before taxes (including those of government business enterprises) accounted for 20.4 percent.[1] In total, the payments to all of the factors of production that we deal with in this chapter amount to 34.6 percent of net domestic income. Where did the rest go? The answer is that the remaining 65.4 percent consisted mostly of wages, salaries and supplementary labour income, as well as the net income of farm operators (the latter being a minuscule amount).

There are many other serious misunderstandings about the nature of income distribution and about what government can do to influence it, and discussions of the subject are often emotional. That's because the distribution of income is the one area in economics in which any one individual's interests almost inevitably conflict with the interests of someone else. By definition, if I get a larger slice of the total income pie, then you end up with a smaller slice.

---

[1] Statistics Canada, *National Income and Expenditure Accounts* for 2007. Retrieved from http://www.statcan.ca

THE PRINCIPLE OF MARGINAL PRODUCTIVITY

By now it should not surprise you to learn that economists analyze factor prices in terms of supply and demand. The supply sides of the markets for the various factors differ enormously, so we must discuss each factor market separately. But we can use one basic principle, the *principle of marginal productivity*, to explain how much of any input a profit-maximizing firm will *demand*, given the price of that input. To review the principle, we must first recall two concepts from Chapter 7: **marginal physical product (MPP)** and **marginal revenue product (MRP).**

Table 1 helps us review these two concepts in terms of Naomi's Natural Farm, which has to decide how much organic corn priced at $10 per bag to feed its chickens. The *marginal physical product* (MPP) column tells us how many additional kilograms of chicken each additional bag of corn will yield. For example, according to the table, the fourth bag increases output by 34 kilograms. The *marginal revenue product* (MRP) column tells us how many dollars this marginal physical product is worth. In Table 1, we assume Naomi's prized, natural chickens sell at 75 cents per kilogram, so the MRP of the fourth bag of corn is $0.75 per kilogram times 34 kilograms, or $25.50 (last column of the table).

> The marginal productivity principle states that in competitive factor markets, the profit-maximizing firm will hire or buy the quantity of any input at which the marginal revenue product equals the price of the input.

The **marginal physical product (MPP)** of an input is the increase in output that results from a one-unit increase in the use of the input, holding the amounts of all other inputs constant.

The **marginal revenue product (MRP)** of an input is the money value of the additional sales that a firm obtains by selling the marginal physical product of that input.

The basic logic behind this principle is both simple and powerful. We know that the firm's profit from acquiring an additional unit of an input is the input's marginal revenue product minus its marginal cost (which is the price of the additional unit of input). If the input's marginal revenue product is greater than its price, it will pay the profit-seeking firm to acquire more of that input because an additional unit of input brings the firm revenue over and above its cost. The firm should purchase that input up to the amount at which diminishing returns reduce the MRP to the level of the input's price, so that further expansion yields zero further addition to profit. By similar reasoning, if MRP is less than price, then the firm is using too much of the input. We see in Table 1 that about seven bags is the optimal amount of corn for Naomi to use each week, because an eighth bag brings in a marginal revenue product of only $6.75, which is less than the $10 cost of buying the bag.

One corollary of the principle of marginal productivity is obvious: The quantity of any input demanded depends on its price. The lower the price of corn, the more it pays the farm to buy. In our example, it pays Naomi to use between seven and eight bags when the price per bag is $10. But if corn were more expensive—say, $20 per bag—that high price would exceed the value of the marginal product of either the sixth or seventh bag. It would, therefore, pay the firm to stop at five bags of corn. Thus, *marginal productivity analysis shows that the quantity demanded of an input normally declines as the input price rises.* The "law" of demand applies to inputs just as it applies to consumer goods.

	TABLE 1			
Naomi's Natural Farm Schedules for TPP, MPP, APP, and MRP of Corn				
(1)	(2)	(3)	(4)	(5)
Corn Input (Bags)	TPP: Total Physical Product (chicken, kg)	MPP: Marginal Physical Product per Bag	APP: Average Physical Product per Bag	MRP: Marginal Revenue Product per Bag
0	0.0 kg		0.0 kg	
1	14.0	14.0 kg	14.0	$10.50
2	36.0	22.0	18.0	16.50
3	66.0	30.0	22.0	22.50
4	100.0	34.0	25.0	**25.50**
5	130.0	30.0	26.0	22.50
6	156.0	26.0	26.0	19.50
7	175.0	19.0	25.0	14.25
8	184.0	9.0	23.0	6.75
9	185.4	1.4	20.6	1.05
10	180.0	-5.4	18.0	-4.05
11	165.0	-15.0	15.0	-11.25
12	144.0	-21.0	12.0	-15.75

INPUTS AND THEIR DERIVED DEMAND CURVES

We can, in fact, be much more specific about how much of each input a profit-maximizing firm will demand. That's because the marginal productivity principle tells

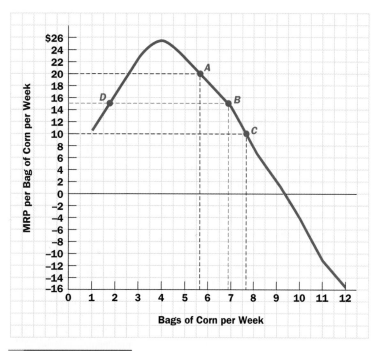

FIGURE 1

Marginal Revenue
Product Graph for
Naomi's Natural Farm

The **derived demand** for
an input is the demand for
the input by producers as
determined by the demand
for the final product that
the input is used to produce.

us precisely how to derive the demand curve
for any input from its marginal revenue
product (MRP) curve.

Figure 1 graphs the MRP schedule from
Table 1, showing the marginal revenue product for corn (MRP_c) rising and then declining as Naomi feeds more and more corn to
her chickens. In the figure, we focus on three
possible prices for a bag of corn: $20, $15,
and $10. As we have just seen, the optimal
purchase rule requires Naomi to keep
increasing her use of corn until her MRP
begins to fall and eventually is reduced to the
price of corn. At a price of $20 per bag, we
see that the quantity demanded is about 5.6
bags of corn per week (point *A*); at that
point, MRP equals price. Similarly, if the
price of corn is $15 per bag, quantity
demanded is about 6.8 bags per week (point
B). Finally, at a price of $10 per bag, the
quantity demanded would be about 7.7 bags
per week (point *C*). Points *A*, *B*, and *C* are
therefore three points on the demand curve for corn. By repeating this exercise for
any other price, we learn that, because the profit-maximizing purchase of an input
occurs at the point where the MRP has *fallen* down to the level of the input price:

> The demand curve for any input is the downward-sloping portion of its marginal revenue
> product curve.[2]

The demand for corn or labour (or for any other input) is called a **derived demand**
because it is derived from the underlying demand for the final product (poultry in this
case). For example, suppose that a surge in demand drives organic chicken prices to
$1.50 per pound. Then, at each level of corn usage, the marginal revenue product will
be twice as large as when poultry brought 75 cents per pound. This effect appears
in Figure 2 as an upward shift of the (derived)
demand curve for corn, from D_0D_0 to D_1D_1, even
though the marginal physical product curves have not
changed. Thus, an outward shift in demand for poultry leads to an outward shift in the demand for corn.[3]
We conclude that, in general:

> An outward shift in the demand curve for any commodity
> causes an outward shift of the derived demand curve for
> all factors utilized in the production of that commodity.

Similarly, an inward shift in the demand curve for a
commodity leads to inward shifts in the demand
curves for factors used in producing that commodity.

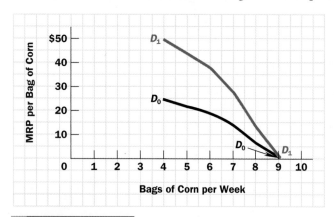

FIGURE 2

A Shift in the Demand
Curve for Corn

[2] Why is the demand curve restricted to only the *downward-sloping portion* of the MRP curve? The logic of the marginal productivity principle dictates this constraint. For example, if the price of corn were $15.00 per bag, Figure 1
shows that MRP = *P* at two input quantities: (approximately) 1.75 bags (point *D*) and 6.8 bags (point *B*). Point *D* cannot be the optimal stopping point, however, because the MRP of a second bag ($16.50) is greater than the cost of the
third bag ($15.00); that is, the firm makes more money by expanding its input use beyond 1.5 bags per week. A similar
profitable opportunity for expansion occurs any time the MRP curve slopes upward at the current price, because an
increase in the quantity of input used by the firm will raise MRP above the input's price. It follows that a profit-maximizing firm will always demand an input quantity that is in the range where MRP is diminishing.

[3] To make Figure 2 easier to read, the (irrelevant) upward-sloping portion and the negative portion of each curve have
been omitted.

This completes our discussion of the *demand* side of the analysis of input pricing. The most noteworthy feature of the discussion is the fact that the same marginal productivity principle serves as the foundation for the demand schedule for each and every type of input. In particular, as we will see in Chapter 20, the marginal productivity principle serves as the basis for the determination of the demand for *labour*—that crucial input whose financial reward plays so important a role in an economy's standard of living. On the demand side, one analysis fits all.

The supply side for each input, however, entails a very different story. Here we must deal with each of the main production factors individually. We must do so because, as we will see, the supply relationships of the different inputs vary considerably. We begin with *interest payments*, or the return on capital. First, we must define a few key terms.

INVESTMENT, CAPITAL, AND INTEREST

Although people sometimes use the words *investment* and *capital* as if they were interchangeable, it is important to distinguish between them. Economists define **capital** as the *inventory* (or stock) of plant, equipment, and other productive resources held by a business firm, an individual, or some other organization. **Investment** is the amount by which capital *grows*. A warehouse owned by a firm is part of its capital. Expansion of the warehouse by adding a new area to the building is an investment. So, when economists use the word *investment*, they do not mean just the transfer of money. The higher the level of investment, the *faster* the amount of capital that the investor possesses grows. The relation between investment and capital is often explained by analogy with filling a bathtub: The accumulated water in the tub is analogous to the *stock* of capital, whereas the flow of water from the faucet (which adds to the tub's water) is like the *flow* of investment. Just as the faucet must be turned on for more water to accumulate, the capital stock increases only when investment continues. If investment ceases, the capital stock stops growing (but does not disappear). In other words, if investment is zero, the capital stock does not fall to zero but remains constant (just as when you turn off the faucet the tub doesn't suddenly empty, but rather the level of the water stays the same).

The process of building up capital by investing and then using this capital in production can be divided into five steps, listed below and summarized in Figure 3:

Step 1. The firm decides to enlarge its stock of capital.

Step 2. The firm raises the funds to finance its expansion, either by tapping outside sources such as banks or by holding onto some of its own earnings rather than paying them out to company owners.

Step 3. The firm uses these funds to hire the inputs needed to build factories, warehouses, and the like. This step is the act of *investment*.

Step 4. After the investment is completed, the firm ends up with a larger stock of capital.

Capital refers to an inventory (*stock*) of plant, equipment, and other (generally durable) productive resources held by a business firm, an individual, or some other organization.

Investment is the *flow* of resources into the production of new capital. It is the labour, steel, and other inputs devoted to the *construction* of factories, warehouses, railroads, and other pieces of capital during some period of time.

| FIGURE 3 | The Investment Production Process |

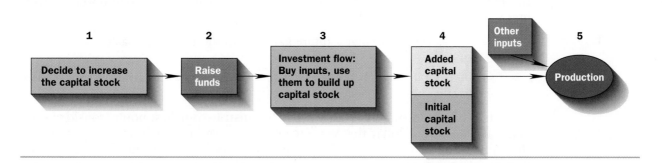

Step 5. The firm uses the capital (along with other inputs) either to expand production or to reduce costs. At this point, the firm starts earning *returns* on its investment.

Notice that investors put *money* into the investment process—either their own or funds they borrow from others. Then, through a series of steps, firms transform the funds into physical inputs suitable for production use. If investors borrow the funds, they must someday return those amounts to the lender with some payment for their use. This payment is called **interest,** and it is calculated as an annual percentage of the amount borrowed. For example, if an investor borrows $1,000 at an interest rate of 12 percent per year, the annual interest payment is $120.

The Demand for Funds

The rate of interest is the *price* at which funds can be rented (borrowed). Just like other factor prices, interest rates can be determined by supply and demand.

On the demand side of the market for loans are borrowers—people or institutions that, for one reason or another, wish to spend more than they currently have. Individuals or families borrow to buy homes or automobiles or other expensive products. Sometimes, as we know, they borrow because they want to consume more than they can afford, which can get them into financial trouble. But often, borrowing makes good sense as a way to manage their finances when they experience a temporary drop in income. It also makes sense to borrow money to buy an item such as a home that will be used for many years. This long product life makes it appropriate for people to pay for the item as it is used, rather than all at once when it is purchased.

Businesses use loans primarily to finance investment. To the business executive who borrows funds to finance an investment and pays interest in return, the funds really represent an intermediate step toward the acquisition of the machines, buildings, inventories, and other forms of physical capital that the firm will purchase.

The marginal productivity principle governs the quantity of funds demanded, just as it governs the quantity of corn demanded for chicken feed. Specifically:

> Firms will demand the quantity of borrowed funds that makes the marginal revenue product of the investment financed by the funds just equal to the interest payment charged for borrowing.

One noteworthy feature of capital distinguishes it from other inputs, such as corn. When Naomi feeds corn to her chickens, the input is used once and then it is gone. But a blast furnace, which is part of a steel company's capital, normally lasts many years. The furnace is a *durable* good; because it is durable, it contributes not only to today's production but also to future production. This fact makes calculation of the marginal revenue product more complex for a capital good than for other inputs.

To determine whether the MRP of a capital good is greater than the cost of financing it (that is, to decide whether an investment is profitable), we need a way to compare money values received at different times. To make such comparisons, economists and businesspeople use a calculation procedure called *discounting*. We will explain discounting in detail in the appendix to this chapter, but you need not master this technique in an introductory course. There are really only two important attributes of discounting to learn here:

- A sum of money received at a future date is worth less than the same sum of money received today.
- This difference in values between money today and money in the future is greater when the rate of interest is higher.

We can easily understand why this is so. To illustrate our first point, consider what you could do with a dollar that you received today rather than a year from today. If the annual rate of interest was 10 percent, you could lend it out (for example, by putting it into a savings account) and receive $1.10 in a year's time—your original

Interest is the payment for the use of funds employed in the production of capital; it is measured as the percent per year of the value of the funds tied up in the capital.

$1.00 plus 10 cents interest. For this reason, money received today is worth more than the same number of dollars received later.

Now for our second point. Suppose the annual rate of interest is 15 percent rather than the 10 percent in the previous example. In this case, $1.00 invested today would grow to $1.15 (rather than $1.10) in a year's time, which means that $1.15 received a year from today would be equivalent to $1.00 received today, and so, when the interest rate is 15 percent, $1.10 a year in the future must now be worth less than $1.00 today. In contrast, when the interest rate is only 10 percent per year, $1.10 to be received a year from today *is* equivalent to $1 of today's money, as we have seen. This illustrates the second of our two points.

The rate of interest is an important determinant of the economy's level of investment, and it could impact on the allocation of society's resources between present and future—an issue that we discussed in Chapter 15 (pages 349–350). Let us see, then, how the market sets interest rates.

■ The Downward-Sloping Demand Curve for Funds

A rise in the price of borrowed funds, like a rise in the price of any item, usually increases quantity demanded. But the two attributes of discounting discussed above also help to explain why the demand curve for funds has a negative slope.

Recall that the demand for borrowed funds, like the demand for all inputs, is a *derived demand*, derived from the desire to invest in capital goods. But firms will receive part—perhaps all—of a machine or factory's marginal revenue product in the future. Hence, the value of the MRP *in terms of today's money* shrinks as the interest rate rises. Why? Because future returns on investment in a machine or factory must be *discounted* more when the rate of interest rises, as our illustration of the second point about discounting showed. As a consequence of this shrinkage, a machine that appears to be a good investment when the interest rate is 10 percent may look like a terrible investment if interest rates rise to 15 percent. That is, the higher the interest rate, the fewer machines a firm will demand, because investing in the machines would use up money that could earn more interest in a savings account. Thus, the demand curve for machines and other forms of capital will have a negative slope—the higher the interest rate, the smaller the quantity that firms will demand.

> As the interest rate on borrowing rises, more and more investments that previously looked profitable start to look unprofitable. The demand for borrowing for investment purposes, therefore, is lower at higher rates of interest.

Note that, although this analysis clearly applies to a firm's purchase of capital goods such as plant and equipment, it may also apply to the company's land and labour purchases. Firms often finance both of these expenditures via borrowed funds, and these inputs' marginal revenue products may accrue only months or even years after the inputs have been bought and put to work. (For example, it may take quite some time before newly acquired agricultural land will yield a marketable crop.) Thus, just as in the case of capital investments, a rise in the interest rate will reduce the quantity demanded of investment goods such as land and labour, just as it cuts the derived demand for investment in plant and equipment.

Figure 4 depicts a derived demand schedule for loans, with the interest rate on the vertical axis as the loan's cost to a borrower. Its negative slope illustrates the conclusion we have just stated:

> The higher the interest rate, the less people and firms will want to borrow to finance their investments.

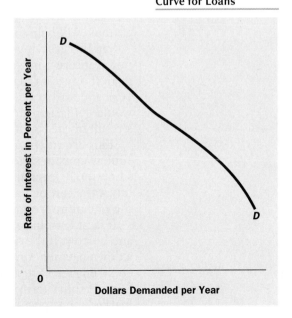

FIGURE 4

The Derived Demand Curve for Loans

FIGURE 5

Equilibrium in the
Market for Loans

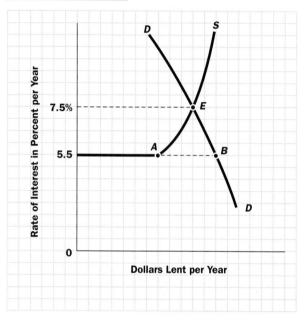

THE PUZZLE RESOLVED: *The Supply of Funds*

Somewhat different relationships arise on the supply side of the market for funds—where the suppliers or *lenders* are banks, households, and even other business firms. Such suppliers of funds cater to different segments of the financial markets: Banks traditionally provide short-term credit to borrowers, while households supply long-term financing to corporations through their purchases of corporate securities. Funds loaned out are usually returned to the owner (with interest) only over a period of time.

As it is discussed in Chapter 13 of *Macroeconomics: Principles and Policy*, for reasons having to do with the price leadership role of central banks in setting the level of interest rates in an economy, we can consider the supply schedule for funds facing an individual borrower to be horizontal for a significant range at a given level of the market rate of interest, where the latter is merely a markup on the central bank administered base rate of interest, such as the overnight rate in Canada. Hence, for analytical purposes, we can assume that, as the demand for funds increases, supply will be forthcoming at a set market rate of interest unless the central bank changes its monetary policy position (in which case, the whole *SS* curve shifts) or the borrower becomes less creditworthy as the individual agent's debt-to-income ratio rises (in which case *SS* begins to slope upward as demand moves outward along the curve).

Such a supply schedule appears as the relatively flat curve *SS* within the relevant range in Figure 5, where we also reproduce the demand curve, *DD*, from Figure 4. However, if demand shifts progressively outward, it will finally cross the upward-sloping portion of the *SS* curve. This is because lender's risk assessment of the borrower might eventually increase—a microeconomic outcome popularized by a renowned American economist Hyman P. Minsky (1919–1996). Hence, the rate of interest where the market demand curve crosses the more inelastic portion of the supply curve for funds is 7.5 percent.

This rate is the price of the funds advanced to creditworthy borrowers, such as a bona fide business enterprise, but it also represents a financial reward for those whose savings have been placed in corporate bonds. As was stated in the puzzle at the beginning of the chapter, sometimes a rise in interest rates (because of tightening of monetary policy by the central bank) will lead people to save *less*, rather than more. An example will help to explain the reason for this apparently curious behaviour.

Say Jim is saving to buy a $10,000 used tractor in three years. If he lends money out at interest in the interim, suppose Jim must save $3,100 per year to reach his goal. If interest rates were higher, he could get away with saving less than $3,100 per year and still reach his $10,000 goal because every year, with higher interest, he would get larger interest payments on his savings. Thus, Jim's saving may decline as a result of the rise in interest rate.

This argument applies fully only to savers with a fixed accumulation goal, but similar considerations affect the calculations of other savers who lump their consumption or capital expenditures over time (like Jim, who is putting money away to buy a tractor, or Jasmine, who is saving for an expensive digital camera). So when the rate of interest rises, some people could save more but some may save less.

It is, at least in part, for a similar reason that some people may simultaneously save and borrow. If the objective for a household is to accumulate enough money to make a down payment on a house or car, or save for a planned family vacation, individuals could engage in separate accounting, whereby they would choose to use a credit card to meet short-term, unforeseen eventualities while leaving untouched the funds earmarked for a specific planned expenditure.

Having examined the relevant demand and supply curves, we are now in a position to discuss the determination of the equilibrium rate of interest. This is summed up in Figure 5, in which the equilibrium is, as always, at point *E*, where quantity supplied equals quantity demanded. We conclude, again, that the equilibrium interest rate on loans is 7.5 percent in the example in the graph.

The Issue of Usury Laws: Are Interest Rates Too High?

People have often been dissatisfied with the market mechanism's determination of interest rates. Fears that interest rates, if left unregulated, would climb to exorbitant levels have made usury laws (which place upper limits on money-lending rates) quite popular in many times and places. Attempts to control interest payments date back to biblical days, and in the Middle Ages the influence of the church even led to total prohibition of interest payments in much of Europe. The same is generally true today in Muslim countries. Unlike the United States, where a patchwork of state usury laws was mostly dismantled during the 1980s when the banking system was deregulated, interest rates have historically remained largely unregulated in Canada. This could be due to the fact that the Canadian financial system evolved primarily after the repeal of English usury laws going back to the mid-nineteenth century in Great Britain; even today, some residual aspects of these usury laws still remain. For instance, the highest amount of interest legally allowable under Canada's Criminal Code is 60 percent annually, including fees and charges, thereby making interest rates in excess of 60 percent "criminal" rates.

Unscrupulous lenders often manage to evade usury laws, charging effective interest rates higher than established market equilibrium rates by adding various fees or charges. Recently in Canada, there has been much discussion over the need to introduce usury caps on credit cards and to assert greater control over various bank fees that have resulted in what appear to be ever-rising bank profits in local markets—the latter being broadly characterized by oligopoly with price leadership. The proliferation of Money Marts and other such institutions in many Canadian towns has further tapped into other substrata of the money market whose participants are more susceptible to abuse and has also raised public concern. But even when usury laws intended to protect borrowers are effective, they do interfere with the operation of supply and demand, and some economists argue that, if too restrictive, such laws may also harm economic efficiency.

Look at Figure 5 again, but this time assume it depicts the supply of bank loans to consumers. Consider what happens if a usury law prohibits interest rates higher than 5.5 percent per year on consumer loans. At 5.5 percent, the quantity supplied (point *A* in Figure 5) falls short of the quantity demanded (point *B*). This means that many applicants for consumer loans are being turned down even though banks consider them to be creditworthy.

Who gains and who loses from this usury law? The gainers are the lucky consumers who get loans at 5.5 percent even though they would have been willing to pay 7.5 percent. The losers come on both the supply side and the demand side: the consumers who would have been willing and able to get credit at 7.5 percent but who are turned down at 5.5 percent, and the banks that could have made profitable loans at rates of up to 7.5 percent if there were no interest-rate ceiling.

This analysis explains why usury laws can be politically popular. Few people sympathize with bank shareholders, and the consumers who get loans at lower rates are, naturally, pleased with the result of usury laws. Other consumers, who would like to borrow at 5.5 percent but cannot because quantity supplied is less than quantity demanded, are likely to blame the bank for refusing to lend, rather than blaming the government for outlawing mutually beneficial transactions.

Yet concern over high interest rates can be rational. It may, for example, be appropriate to combat homelessness by making financing of housing cheaper for poor people. Of course, it may be much more rational for the government to subsidize the interest on housing for the poor rather than to declare high interest rates illegal, in effect pretending that those costs can simply be legislated away, as a usury ceiling tries to do.[4]

THE DETERMINATION OF RENT

The second main factor of production is land. Rent, the payment for the use of land, is another price that, when left to the market, often seems to settle at politically unpopular levels. Rent controls are a popular solution. We discussed the effects of rent controls in Chapter 4 (page 78–80), and we will say a bit more about them later in this chapter. But our main focus here is the determination of rents by free markets.

The market for land is characterized by a special feature on the supply side. Land is a factor of production whose total quantity supplied is (roughly) unchanging and virtually unchangeable: The same quantity is available at every possible price. Indeed, classical economists used this notion as the working definition of land. And the definition seems to fit, at least approximately. Although people may drain swamps, clear forests, fertilize fields, build skyscrapers, or convert land from one use (a farm) to another (a housing development), human effort cannot change the total supply of land by very much.

What does this fact tell us about how the market determines land rents? Figure 6 helps to provide an answer. The vertical supply curve *SS* means that no matter what the level of rents, there are only 1,000 hectares of land in a small hamlet called Littleville. The demand curve *DD* slopes downward and is a typical marginal revenue product curve, predicated on the notion that the use of land, like everything else, is subject to diminishing returns. The free-market price is determined, as usual, by the intersection of the supply and demand curves at point *E*. In this example, each hectare of land in Littleville rents for $2,000 per year. The interesting feature of this diagram is that, because quantity supplied is rigidly fixed at 1,000 hectares whatever the price:

The market level of rent is entirely determined by the market's demand side.

If, for example, a major university relocates to Littleville, attracting more people who want to live there, the *DD* curve will shift outward, as depicted in Figure 7. Equilibrium in the market will shift from point *E* to point *A*. The same 1,000 hectares of land will be available, but now each hectare will command a rent of $2,500 per hectare. The landlords will collect more rent, even though society gets no more of the input—land—from the landlords in return for its additional payment.

The same process also works in reverse, however. If the university shuts its doors and the demand for land declines as a result, the landlords will suffer even though they did not contribute to the decline in the demand for land. (To see this simply reverse the logic of Figure 7. The demand curve begins at D_1D_1 and shifts to D_0D_0.)

FIGURE 6

Determination of Land
Rent in Littleville

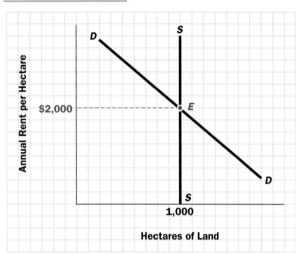

FIGURE 7

A Shift in Demand with
a Vertical Supply Curve

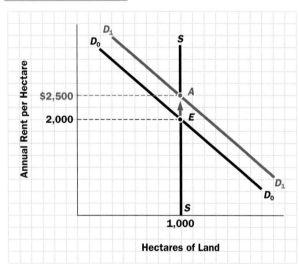

---

[4] The law also sometimes concerns itself with discrimination in lending against women or members of ethnic minority groups. Strong evidence suggests the existence of sex and race discrimination in lending. For example, married women have been denied loans without the explicit permission of their husbands, even where the women had substantial independent incomes.

This discussion shows the special feature of rent that leads economists to distinguish it from payments to other factors of production. An **economic rent** is an "extra" payment for a factor of production (such as land) that does not change the amount of the factor that is supplied. Society is not compensated for a rise in its rent payments by any increase in the quantity of land it obtains. Economic rent is thus the portion of the factor payment that exceeds the minimum payment necessary to induce that factor to be supplied.

As late as the end of the nineteenth century, the idea of economic rent exerted a powerful influence far beyond technical economic writings. An American journalist, Henry George (1839–1897), was nearly elected mayor of New York City in 1886, running on the platform that all government should be financed by a "single tax" levied on landlords who, he said, are the only ones who earn incomes without contributing to the productive process. George said that landlords reap the fruits of economic growth without contributing to economic progress. He based his logic on the notion that landowners do not increase the supply of their factor of production—the quantity of land—when rents increase.

> **Economic rent** is the portion of the earnings of a factor of production that exceeds the minimum amount necessary to induce that factor to be supplied.

Land Rents: Further Analysis

If all plots of land were identical, our previous discussion would be virtually all there is to the theory of land rent. But plots of land *do* differ—in geographical location, topography, nearness to marketplaces, soil quality, and so on. The classical economists took this disparity into account in their analysis of rent determination—a remarkable nineteenth-century piece of economic logic still considered valid today.

The basic notion is that capital invested in any piece of land must yield the same return as capital invested in any other piece that is actually in use. Why? If it were not so, capitalist renters would bid against one another for the more profitable pieces of land. This competition would go on until the rents they would have to pay for these parcels were driven up to a point that eliminated their advantages over other parcels.

Suppose that a farmer produces a crop on one piece of land for $160,000 per year in labour, fertilizer, fuel, and other nonland costs, while a neighbour who is no more efficient produces the same crop for $120,000 on a second piece of land. The rent on the second parcel must be *exactly* $40,000 per year higher than the rent on the first, because otherwise production on one plot would be cheaper than on the other. If, for example, the rent difference were only $30,000 per year, it would be $10,000 cheaper to produce on the second plot of land. No one would want to rent the first plot and every grower would instead bid for the second plot. Rent on the first plot would be forced down by the lack of customers, and rent on the second plot would be driven up by eager bidders. These pressures would come to an end only when the rent difference reached $40,000, so that both plots became equally profitable.

At any given time, some low-quality pieces of land are so inferior that it does not pay to use them at all—remote deserts are a prime example. Any land that is exactly on the borderline between being used and not being used is called **marginal land.** By this definition, marginal land earns no rent because if its owner charged any for it, no one would willingly pay to use it.

We combine these two observations—that the difference between the costs of producing on any two pieces of land must equal the difference between their rents and that zero rent is charged on marginal land—to conclude that:

> **Marginal land** is land that is just on the borderline of being used—that is, any land the use of which would be unprofitable if the farmer had to pay even a penny of rent.

> Rent on any piece of land will equal the difference between the cost of producing the output on that land and the cost of producing it on marginal land.

That is, competition for the superior plots of land will permit the landowners to charge prices that capture the full advantages of their superior parcels.

This analysis helps us to understand more completely the effects of an outward shift in the demand curve for land. Suppose population growth raises demand for land. Naturally, rents will rise. But we can be more specific than this statement. In response to an outward shift in the demand curve, two things will happen:

- *It will now pay to employ some land whose use was formerly unprofitable.* The land that was previously on the zero-rent margin will no longer be on the border-line, and some land that is so poor that it was formerly not even worth con-sidering will now just reach the borderline of profitability. The settling of the Canadian prairies illustrates this process strikingly. Land that once could not be given away is now quite valuable.
- *People will begin to exploit already-used land more intensively.* Farmers will use more labour and fertilizer to squeeze larger amounts of crops out of their land, as has happened in recent decades. Urban real estate that previously held two-storey buildings will now be used for high-rise buildings.

These two events will increase rents in a predictable fashion. Because the land that is considered marginal *after* the change must be inferior to the land that was considered marginal previously, rents must rise by the difference in yields between the old and new mar-ginal lands. Table 2 illustrates this point. In the table, we deal with three pieces of land: A, a very productive piece; B, a piece that was initially considered only marginal; and C, a piece that is inferior to B but nevertheless becomes marginal when the demand curve for land shifts upward and to the right.

TABLE 2			
Nonrent Costs and Rent on Three Pieces of Land			
Type of Land	Nonland Cost of Producing a Given Crop	Total Rent	
		Before	After
A. A tract that was better than marginal before and after	$120,000	$80,000	$92,000
B. A tract that was marginal before but is attractive now	200,000	0	12,000
C. A tract that was previously not worth using but is now marginal	212,000	0	0

The crop costs $80,000 more when produced on B than on A, and $12,000 more when produced on C than on B. Suppose, initially, that demand for the crop is so low that Farmer Jones does not plant crops in field C. Farmer Jones is on the fence about whether to plant crops in field B. Because field B is marginal, it is just on the margin between being used and being left idle—it will command no rent. We know that the rent on field A will be equal to the $80,000 cost advantage of A over B. Now suppose demand for the crop increases enough so that plot C becomes marginal land. Then field B com-mands a rent of $12,000, the cost advantage of B over C. Plot A's rent now must rise from $80,000 to $92,000, the size of its cost advantage over C, the newly marginal land.

In addition to the quality differences among pieces of land, a second influence pushes land rents up: increased intensity of use of land that is already under cultiva-tion. As farmers apply more fertilizer and labour to their land, the marginal produc-tivity of the land increases, just as factory workers become more productive when more is invested in their equipment. Once again, the landowner can capture this pro-ductivity increase in the form of higher rents. (If you do not understand why, refer back to Figure 7 and recall that the demand curves are marginal revenue product curves—that is, they indicate the amount that capitalists are willing to pay landlords to use their land.) Thus, we can summarize the theory of rent as follows:

As the use of land increases, landlords receive higher payments from two sources:

- Increased demand leads the community to employ land previously not good enough to use; the advantage of previously used land over the new marginal land increases, and rents go up correspondingly.

- Land is used more intensively; the marginal revenue product of land rises, thereby increasing the ability of the producer who uses the land to pay rent.

Generalization: Economic Rent Seeking

Economists refer to the payments for land as *rents*, but land is not the only scarce input with a fixed supply, at least in the short run. Toward the beginning of the twen-tieth century, some economists realized that the economic analysis of rent can be

Land Prices Around the World and Housing Prices Across Canada

Supply and demand do not equalize prices when the commodity, such as land, cannot be transferred from one geographic market to another. For instance, in the late 1980s, when property values in Japan hit their peak, the average price of residential land in Tokyo was $3,000 per square metre, compared to $110 in Toronto and $70 in Washington, DC. The world's highest rents on commercial property can be found in Hong Kong, where a square metre of office space will cost you more than $1,200, compared to $800 in New York, $400 in Stockholm, and $300 in Istanbul.

Such differences in land values obviously must filter down into differences in housing prices. Indeed, the wide dispersion in house prices across Canada mostly reflects differences in land values. As shown in the first accompanying chart, the average price of a standard house in Vancouver in 2006 was about 2.6 times that of a similar house in Halifax and 1.7 times the average price of a standard house in Toronto. While construction costs can account for some possible differences, the wide dispersion and the evolution of prices over time, even when adjusted for inflation (see the second chart), are primarily determined by the price of land—a demand-determined value that is, in turn, conditioned by demographics, the regional growth of household income, and mortgage rates. It is interesting to note that, when adjusted for inflation, house prices have been relatively stable over the last three decades in much of eastern Canada until recently (with the exception of Toronto), while there has been much higher growth in western Canada (with the exception of Winnipeg).

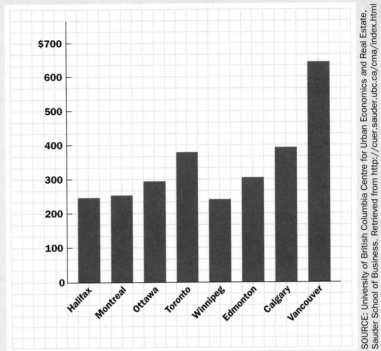

SOURCE: University of British Columbia Centre for Urban Economics and Real Estate, Sauder School of Business. Retrieved from http://cuer.sauder.ubc.ca/cma/index.html

Average Price of a House in Canada's Major Metropolitan Areas in 2006 (in thousands of dollars)

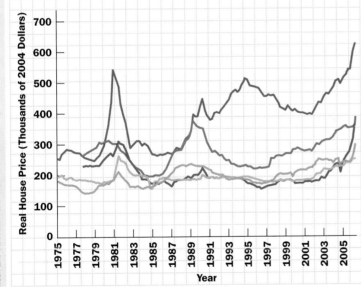

SOURCES: University of British Columbia Centre for Urban Economics and Real Estate, Sauder School of Business. Retrieved from http://cuer.sauder.ubc.ca. These numbers were calculated on the basis of the Royal LePage Housing Price Index and Statistics Canada CANSIM data.

Evolution of Housing Prices in Canada's Major Metropolitan Areas 1975–2006 (in thousands of constant 2004 dollars)

Note: House prices reflect the estimated average market value of single-storey three-bedroom houses and two-storey four-bedroom houses.

SOURCE: aliciahh/ Shutterstock

SOURCES: Steven K. Mayo, "Land Prices, Land Markets, and the Broader Economy," *Land Lines*, March 1998, Lincoln Institute of Land Policy, http://www.lincolninst.edu; and *The Economist*, September 12, 1998, p. 116.

applied to inputs *other* than land. As we will see, this extension yielded some noteworthy insights.

The concept of rent can be used to analyze such common phenomena as lobbying members of the House of Commons (attempts to influence the votes of members of Parliament) by industrial groups, lawsuits between rival firms, and battles over exclusive licences (as for a television station). Such interfirm battles can waste very valuable economic resources—for example, the time that executives, bureaucrats, judges, lawyers, and economists spend preparing and battling court trials. Because this valuable time could have been used in production, such activities entail large *opportunity costs*. Rent analysis offers insights into the reasons for these battles and provides a way to assess what *quantity* of resources people waste as they seek economic rents for scarce resources.

How is economic rent—which is a payment to a factor of production above and beyond the amount necessary to get the factor to make its contribution to production—relevant in such cases? Gordon Tullock, an economist also trained in legal matters, coined the phrase *rent seeking* to describe the search and battle for opportunities to charge or collect those payments above and beyond the amount necessary to create the source of the income.

An obvious source of such rents is a monopoly licence. For example, a licence to operate the only television station in town will yield enormous advertising profits, far above the amount needed for the station to operate. That's why rent seekers swoop down when such licences become available. Similarly, the powerful lobby effort of various primary producers in many countries, especially the United States and the European Union, to impede imports of agricultural produce and other primary products from the rest of the world could also be seen as an attempt to prevent a substantial cut in prices (and rents) in their domestic markets. Such activities do not increase the quantities of product supplied, just as higher rents do not increase the supply of land. That is why any resulting earnings are called *rent* and why the effort to obtain such earnings that contribute nothing to output is called *rent seeking*.

How much of society's resources will be wasted in such a process? Rent seeking theory can give us some idea. Consider a race for a monopoly cable TV licence that, once awarded, will keep competing stations from operating. *Nothing prevents anyone from entering the race* to grab the licence. Anyone can hire the lobbyists and lawyers or offer the bribes needed in the battle for such a lucrative licence. Thus, although the cable business itself may not be competitive, the process of fighting for the licence can be very competitive.

Of course, we know from the analysis of long-run equilibrium under perfect competition (Chapter 10, pages 222–223) that in such markets, economic profits approximate zero—in other words, revenues just cover costs. If owners expect a cable licence to yield, say, $900 million over its life in rent, then rent seekers (that is, the companies competing to gain the licence in the first place) are likely to waste something close to that amount as they fight for the licence.

Why? Suppose each of ten bidders has an equal chance at winning the licence. To each bidder, that chance should be worth about $90 million—one chance in ten of getting $900 million. If the average bidder spends only $70 million on the battle, each firm will still value the battle for the licence at $90 million minus $70 million. This fact will tempt an eleventh bidder to enter and raise the ante to, say, $80 million in lobbying fees, hoping to grab the rent. This process of attraction of additional bidders stops only when all of the excess rent available has been wasted on the rent seeking process, so there is no further motivation for still more people to bid.

▮ Rent as a Component of an Input's Compensation

We can use the concept of economic rent to divide the payment for any input into two parts. The first part is simply the minimum payment needed to acquire the input—for example, the cost of producing a ball bearing or the compensation people require in exchange for the unpleasantness, hard work, and loss of leisure involved in performing labour. The owner of the input must be offered this first part of the factor payment if she is to supply the input willingly. If workers do not receive at least this first part, they will not supply their labour.

The second part of the payment is a *bonus* that does not go to every input, but only to inputs of particularly high quality, like the payment to the owner of higher-quality land in our earlier example. Payments to workers with exceptional natural skills are a good illustration of the generalized rent concept. Because these bonuses are like the extra payment for a better piece of land, they are called *economic rents*. Indeed, like the rent of land, an increase in the amount of economic rent paid to an input may not increase the *quantity* of that input supplied. This second part of the payment—the economic rent—is pure gravy. The skillful worker is happy to have it as an extra, but it is not a deciding consideration in the choice of whether or not to work.

■ An Application of Rent Theory: Salaries of Professional Athletes

Professional athletes may seem to have little in common with plots of farmland. Yet to an economist, the same analysis—the theory of economic rent—explains how the market arrives at the amounts paid to each of these "factors of production." To understand why, let's look at a hypothetical basketball team, the Velociraptors, and its seven-foot star centre, Dapper Dan. First, we must note that there is only one Dapper Dan. That is, he is a scarce input whose supply is fixed just like the supply of land. Because he is in fixed supply, the price of his services is determined in a way similar to that of land rents.

A moment's thought shows how the general notion of economic rent applies both to land and to Dapper Dan. The total quantity of land available for use is the same whether rent is high, low, or zero; only limited payments to landlords are necessary to induce them to supply land to the market. By definition, then, a considerable proportion of the payments to landholders for their land is economic rent—payments above and beyond those necessary for landlords to provide land to the economy. Dapper Dan is (almost) similar to land in this respect. His athletic talents are unique and cannot be reproduced. What determines the payment to such a factor? Because the quantity supplied of such a unique, nonreproducible factor is absolutely fixed (there's only one Dapper Dan), and therefore unresponsive to price, the analysis of rent that we summarized in Figure 6 applies, and the position of the demand curve for Dapper Dan's services is determined by the superiority of his services over those of other players.

Suppose the Velociraptors team also includes a marginal player, Weary Willy, winner of last year's Least Valuable Player award. Willy earns just the $50,000 per year necessary to obtain his services. Suppose also that if no other option were available, Dapper Dan would be willing to play basketball for $50,000 per year, rather than working as a hamburger flipper, the only other job for which he is qualified. But Dan knows he can do better than that. He estimates, quite accurately, that his presence on the team brings in $10 million of added revenue over and above what the team would obtain if Dan were replaced by a player of Willy's calibre. In that case, Dan and his agent ought to be able to obtain $10 million *more* per year than is paid to Willy. As a result, Dan obtains a salary of $10,050,000, of which $10 million is economic rent—exactly analogous to the previous rent example involving different pieces of land of unequal quality. Note that the team gets no more of Dapper Dan's working time in return for the rent payment. (See "'David Beckham Inc.': Earning Lots of Economic Rent" on the next page for a real-world example.)

Almost all inputs, including employees, earn some economic rent. What sorts of inputs earn no rent? Only those inputs that can be provided by a number of suppliers at constant cost and with identical quality earn no rents. For instance, no ball-bearing supplier will ever receive any rent on a ball bearing, at least in the long run, because any desired number of them, *of equal quality*, can be produced at (roughly) constant costs and can contribute equal amounts to the profits of those who use them. If one

"David Beckham Inc.": Earning Lots of Economic Rent

In case you think that our discussion of economic rent is mere academic theorizing, there are numerous examples in the sports world of how individuals earn economic rents. One has only to consider how such Canadian superstar players in hockey, such as Nova Scotia's Sidney Crosby of the Pittsburgh Penguins in the NHL, or in basketball, such as British Columbia's Steve Nash of the Phoenix Suns in the NBA, earn their seven- or eight-figure annual salaries. However, let's check out these numbers from an increasingly popular sport in Canada and internationally—the world of soccer, where earnings appear to be literally going through the ceiling.

After leaving Manchester United in 2003 and subsequently turning down a two-year extension of his lucrative contract with Real Madrid, in Spain at the beginning of 2007, the then 31-year-old captain, England's David Beckham, was offered an estimated US$250 million (including income from sponsorship and other business deals) for five years to kick a soccer ball for the Los Angeles Galaxy in the United States—a deal that sent shock waves throughout the soccer establishment worldwide.

Beckham's earnings thus grew over six-fold from the US$7.7 million annually paid by Real Madrid (plus an estimated US$30 million for sponsorship deals with major multinational corporations such as Pepsi, Gillette, Motorola and Adidas) to the triple-digit millions, making him the highest-paid player in Major League Soccer (MLS) in the United States. However, of his estimated $250 million earnings, only 20 percent will be paid for him to actually play soccer for the Los Angeles Galaxy. The other $200 million over five years will be earned from commercial endorsements and sponsorship and other business deals.

SOURCE: © Bongarts/Getty Images

Until Beckham's landmark deal, the 13 MLS teams had a salary cap of $2.1 million. With the new "designated player rule"—the so-called "Beckham rule"—teams are now permitted to exceed the annual salary ceiling for one player and "strategically invest" in a soccer superstar to drive up team revenues and the economic rent accruing to their star player.

---

ball-bearing supplier tried to charge a price above their x-cent cost, another manufacturer would undercut the first supplier and take its customers away. Hence, the competitive price includes no economic rent.

■ Rent Controls: The Misplaced Analogy

Why is the analysis of economic rent important? Because only economic rent can be taxed away without reducing the quantity of the input supplied. Here, common English gets in the way of sound reasoning. Many people feel that the *rent* they pay to their landlord is economic rent. After all, their apartments will still be there if they pay $1,500 per month, or $500, or $100. This view, although true in the short run, is quite shortsighted.

Like the ball-bearing producer, the owner of a building cannot expect to earn *economic rent* because too many other potential owners whose costs of construction are roughly the same as her own will also offer apartments. If the market price temporarily included some economic rent—that is, if price exceeded production costs plus the opportunity cost of the required capital—other builders would start new construction that would drive the price down. Thus, far from being in perfectly *inelastic* (vertical) supply, like raw land, buildings come rather close to being in perfectly *elastic* (horizontal) supply, like ball bearings in the long run. As we have learned from the theory of rent, this means that builders and owners of buildings cannot collect economic rent in the long run.

Because apartment owners collect very little economic rent, payments by tenants in a freely competitive market must be just enough to keep those apartments on the market (the very definition of zero economic rent). If rent controls push these prices down, the apartments will start disappearing from the market.[5] The removal of apartments from the rental market could prove disastrous for those seeking shelter but you could hardly blame the growing number of homeless in major Canadian cities over the last decade on the existence of rent controls. For most economists, this distressing phenomenon is much too complex socially and has become a serious problem in some urban centres, regardless of whether rent controls are in place.

Rent controls provoke very strong reaction from supporters and opponents alike and have often led to acrimonious debates in Canada. While most provinces have no provisions related to the amount of rent that can be charged by landlords, provinces such as British Columbia, Manitoba, Ontario, and Prince Edward Island do have rent control regimes in place. For instance, in Ontario, the provincial rent increase guideline was 2.6 percent in 2007. Landlords could raise their rents above the mandated guidelines only if they convinced the Ontario Rental Housing Tribunal that they had incurred significant expenses in upgrading their rental units.

Numerous economists oppose rent controls because of the distorting effect that these controls could have on the long-run supply of rental housing. Because of the existing limited supply of affordable housing, however, many social activists see rent controls as an effective way to prevent the disappearance of local communities, because many low- and fixed-income tenants could not afford sharp rent increases and might be forced to move elsewhere. Since the 1944 National Housing Act, which established rent controls for the first time in Canada, successive provincial governments historically have pursued conflicting policy positions over the need for rent control, depending on the political pressures from various interest groups, particularly associations representing landlords and tenants.

PAYMENTS TO ENTREPRENEURSHIP: ARE PROFITS TOO HIGH OR TOO LOW?

We turn next to business profits, the discussion of which often seems to elicit more passion than logic. With the exception of some economists, almost no one thinks that profit rates are at about the right level. Critics point accusingly to some giant corporations' billion-dollar profits and argue that they are unconscionably high; they then call for much stiffer taxes on profits. On the other hand, the various national, provincial, and local Chambers of Commerce, the association of Canadian Manufacturers & Exporters, the Canadian Council of Chief Executives, the Canadian Federation of Independent Business, and other business groups complain that government regulations and high taxes keep profits too low, and they constantly lobby the federal government, the provincial legislatures, and even local municipalities for tax relief during pre-budget consultations.

As you have no doubt noticed by now, economists are reluctant to brand factor prices as "too low" or "too high" in some moral or ethical sense. Rather, they are likely to ask first: What is the market equilibrium price? Then they will ask whether there are any good reasons to interfere with the market solution. This analysis, however, is not as easily applied to the case of *profits*, because it is difficult to use supply and demand analysis when you do not know which factor of production earns profit.

In both a bookkeeping sense and an economic sense, *profits are the residual.* They are what remains from the selling price after all other factors have been paid.

---

[5] None of this is meant to imply that temporary rent controls in certain locations cannot have desirable effects in the short run. In the short run, the supply of apartments and houses really is fixed, and large shifts in demand can hand windfall gains to landlords—gains that are true, if temporary, economic rents. Controls that eliminate such windfalls should not cause serious problems. But knowing when the "short run" fades into the "long run" can be tricky. "Temporary" rent control laws have a way of becoming rather permanent.

But which production factor earns this reward? Which factor's marginal productivity constitutes the profit rate?

■ What Accounts for Profits?

Economic profit is the total revenue of a firm minus all of its costs, including the interest payments and opportunity costs of the capital it obtains from its investors.

Economic profit, as we learned in Chapter 10, is the amount a firm earns *over and above the payments for all inputs*, including the interest payments for the capital it uses and the opportunity cost of any capital provided by the owners of the firm. The payment that firm owners receive to compensate them for the opportunity cost of their capital (and that in common parlance *is* considered profit) is closely related to interest rates, but is not part of *economic profit*. In an imaginary (and dull) world in which everything was certain and unchanging, capitalists who invested money in firms would simply earn the market rate of interest on their funds. Profits beyond this level would be competed away. Payment for capital below this level could not persist, because capitalists would withdraw their funds from firms and deposit them in banks. Capitalists in such a world would be mere moneylenders.

But the real world is not at all like this. Some capitalists are much more dynamic than moneylenders, and the amounts they earn often exceed current interest rates by a huge margin. These active capitalists who seek out or even create earnings opportunities are called *entrepreneurs*. We can credit such creative individuals for the constant risk-taking change and innovations that prevent the operations of their firms from stagnating. Because entrepreneurs constantly seek to do something new, it is difficult to provide a general description of their activities. However, we can list three primary ways in which entrepreneurs can and do drive profits above "normal" interest rate levels.

1. Monopoly Power   If entrepreneurs can establish monopolies with some or all of their products, even for a short while, they can use that monopoly power to earn monopoly profits. We analyzed the nature of these monopoly earnings in Chapter 11.

2. Risk Bearing   Entrepreneurs often engage in financially risky activities. For example, when a firm prospects for oil, it must drill exploratory wells hoping to find petroleum at the bottom. Of course, many such exploratory wells end up as dry holes, and the costs then bring no return. Lucky investors, on the other hand, do find oil and are rewarded handsomely—more than the competitive return on the firm's capital. The extra income pays the firm for bearing risk.

A few lucky individuals make out well in this process, but many suffer heavy losses. How well can we expect risk takers to do, on the average? If one exploratory drilling out of ten typically pays off, do we expect its return to be exactly ten times as high as the interest rate, so that the *average* firm will earn exactly the normal rate of interest? The answer is that the payoff will be *more* than ten times the interest rate if investors dislike gambling—that is, if they prefer to avoid risk. Why? Because investors who are risk averse will not be willing to put their money into a business that faces such long odds—10 to 1—unless the market provides compensation for the financial peril.

In reality, nothing guarantees that things will always work out this way. Some people love to gamble and tend to be overly optimistic. They may plunge into projects to a degree unjustified by the odds. Average payoffs to such gamblers in risky undertakings may end up below the interest rate. The successful investor will still make a good profit, just like the lucky winner at the Windsor Casino. The average participant, however, will have to pay for the privilege of bearing risk.

Invention is the act of generating an idea for a new product or a new method for making an old product.

Innovation also includes the next step, the act of putting the new idea to practical use.

3. Returns to Innovation   The third major source of profits is perhaps the most important of all for social welfare. The first entrepreneur able to innovate and market a desirable new product or employ a new cost-saving machine will garner a higher profit than an uninnovative (but otherwise similar) business manager would earn. Innovation differs from invention. Whereas **invention** generates new ideas, **innovation** takes the next step by putting the new idea to practical use. Businesspeople are rarely inventors, but they are often innovators.

Entrepreneurial Versus Managerial Rewards

Famous Austrian–American economist Joseph A. Schumpeter once pointed out that, from the social point of view, the real measure of success of a firm is not so much based on how efficiently one administers existing business structures (whether privately or publicly owned) but on how well one innovates and creates new structures. Entrepreneurs are thus decision makers who take risk and use judgment to address novel problems in the context of overwhelming uncertainty. Their presence ensures a continued process of change that pushes outward an economy's production possibility frontier.

The reward for the successful management of an already established business enterprise is not necessarily the same as a reward for entrepreneurship. The administrative role of combining existing inputs so as to move closer to the firm's efficiency frontier is different from the entrepreneurial role of transforming existing structures by introducing innovations that increase the firm's productive potential. These two functions of management and entrepreneurship may reside in the same individual, but often they do not.

In Canada, we have many examples of very successful entrepreneurs who almost single-handedly built important companies. Frank Stronach, the founder of Magna International Inc., for instance, emigrated to Canada from Austria in 1954 with a mere $40 in his pocket and went from rags to riches by creating one of Canada's most important industrial enterprises. He undoubtedly would qualify as a successful entrepreneur. However, Magna's current chief executive officer (CEO), Donald Walker, could be considered primar-ily as an administrator who efficiently runs the business enterprise—if it wasn't for the fact that Stronach obviously feels differently about this. In line with Magna's philosophy to pay a relatively small salary to its CEO and to reward him or her on the basis of performance, Walker received a salary of slightly over $125,000 but bonuses of close to $5 million in 2006!

Canadian public opinion tends to be highly supportive of reward for successful entrepreneurship. However, in the wake of the scandals that have plagued the corporate world, especially in the United States, there has been a great deal of controversy over the financial rewards accruing to managers of large corporations, some of whom have shown more interest in their own short-term gain than in the long-term performance of the corporations that they managed.

Earnings of company administrators are mainly compensation for their management function, but a portion may also be for their entrepreneurial role. Each year, *The Globe and Mail*'s "Report on Business" publishes data from a survey of the top 100 CEOs' earnings in Canada. The top 12 CEOs arranged in descending order of their total compensation for 2006 are shown in the accompanying table. Do you think these levels of compensation reflect any reward for entrepreneurial achievements? (An Internet search of the companies represented in the table might reveal the accomplishments and innovations of each company in 2006 and help you to answer this question.) What are some other factors that might affect the compensation amounts paid to CEOs?

The Globe and Mail Executive Compensation Report, 2006

Rank	Company	Industry	CEO	Total Compensation*
1	Research in Motion Ltd.	Information technology	Balsillie, James	$54,709,465
2	Shoppers Drug Mart Corp.	Consumer staples	Murphy, Glenn	$34,441,947
3	Research in Motion Ltd.	Information technology	Lazaridis, Michael	$32,990,309
4	Power Corp. of Canada	Financial	Desmarais, Jr., Paul	$23,992,309
5	Loblaw Cos. Ltd.	Consumer staples	Lederer, John	$21,666,256
6	Manulife Financial Corp.	Financial	D'Alessandro, Dominic	$20,294,064
7	Gammon Lake Resources Inc.	Materials	Langille, Bradley	$19,946,318
8	Goldcorp Inc.	Materials	Telfer, Ian	$17,180,097
9	Rogers Communications Inc.	Telecom services	Rogers, Edward	$16,376,229
10	Power Corp. of Canada	Financial	Desmarais, André	$16,231,764
11	Suncor Energy Inc.	Energy	George, Richard	$15,505,012
12	Onex Corp.	Financial	Schwartz, Gerald	$13,685,678

* Total compensation includes salary, bonus, and stock option gains.
SOURCE: *The Globe and Mail*, "Report on Business," "Survey of Top 100 CEOs for 2006," June 4, 2007. Reprinted with permission from *The Globe and Mail*.

When an entrepreneur innovates, even if her new product or new process is not protected by patents, she will be one step ahead of her competitors. If the market likes her innovation, she will be able to capture most of the sales, either by offering customers a better product or by supplying the product more cheaply. In either case, she will temporarily find herself with some monopoly power as her competitors weaken, and she will receive monopoly profit for her initiative.

However, this monopoly profit—the reward for innovation—will be only temporary. As soon as the idea's success becomes evident to the world, other firms will find ways of imitating it. Even if they cannot turn out precisely the same product or the same process, they must find close substitutes in order to survive. In this way, new ideas spread through the economy, and in the process the innovator's special profits come to an end. The innovator can resume earning special profits only by finding still another promising idea.

> The market system forces entrepreneurs to keep searching for new ideas, to keep instituting innovations, and to keep imitating new ideas even if they did not originate those innovations or ideas. This process lies at the heart of the growth of the capitalist system. It is one of the secrets of the system's extraordinary dynamism.

We explored these issues of innovation and growth performance in free markets more fully in Chapter 16.

Taxing Profits

Thus, we can consider profits in excess of market interest rates to be the return on entrepreneurial talent. But this definition is not really very helpful, because no one can say exactly what entrepreneurial talent is. Certainly we cannot measure it; nor can we teach it in a college course, although business schools may try. We do not know whether the observed profit rate provides more than the minimum reward necessary to attract entrepreneurial talent into the market. This relationship between observed profit rates and minimum necessary rewards is crucial when we start to consider the policy ramifications of taxes on profits—a contentious issue, indeed.

Consider a profits tax levied on oil companies. If oil companies earn profits well above the minimum required to attract entrepreneurial talent, those profits contain a large element of economic rent. In that case, we could tax away these excess profits (rents) without fear of reducing oil production. In contrast, if oil company profits do not include economic rents, then a windfall profits tax can seriously curtail oil exploration and, hence, production.

The oil company example illustrates the general problem of deciding how heavily governments should tax profits. Critics of big business who call for high, if not confiscatory, tax on profits seem to believe that profits are mostly economic rent. If they are wrong—if, in fact, most of the observed profits are necessary to attract people into entrepreneurial roles—then a high tax on profits can have serious implications for the system's ability to expand productive capacity and to grow. If unable to shift the tax onto consumers in the form of higher prices because the industry is in a highly competitive environment, the capitalist system would soon lose its principal driving force and would quickly come to a halt. Business lobbying groups claim, predictably enough, that current tax policy creates exactly these disincentives to investment and growth and advocate cuts to taxes on corporations. However, these various advocacy groups are usually guided much more by the ideological position of those whom they represent, rather than by the meagre (if any) empirical evidence that they advance in support of their conclusions.

CRITICISMS OF MARGINAL PRODUCTIVITY THEORY

The theory of factor pricing described in this chapter once again uses supply–demand analysis. This theory also relies heavily on the principle of marginal productivity to derive the shape and position of the demand curve for various inputs. Indeed, many economists both historically and nowadays refer to the analysis as the *marginal productivity theory of distribution*. However, this is somewhat misleading. At best, it is only a theory of the demand side of the pertinent factor market.

Since its development in the late nineteenth century, factor pricing analysis based on marginal productivity theory has been the subject of criticism on many grounds. One of the most frequent and damaging accusations is the assertion that marginal productivity theory merely attempts to provide a justification for the income distribution that the capitalist system yields. Some of the early theorists of marginal productivity analysis were indeed strongly motivated by a desire to counter Marxist and other radical ideas on the exploitation of labour. There is, for instance, the well-known assertion by one of the early promoters of a theory of distribution of income based on marginal productivity analysis, the American economist John Bates Clark (1847–1938), who claimed that "What a social class gets is, under natural law, what it contributes to the general output of industry."[6]

On the basis of such claims, you can see why critics of marginal productivity theory rejected its normative implication. Critics have argued that what the theory is merely saying, in a somewhat complicated fashion, is that each factor is paid exactly what it supposedly deserves based on one's marginal productive contribution to output. The marginal productivity theory could thus easily serve to legitimize the gross inequities of the system—the poverty of many and the great wealth of a few.

The confounding of a positive theory of factor pricing with a normative statement about factor rewards was a problem that certainly characterized some of its most ardent supporters historically, but this very criticism from many of its detractors was itself considered somewhat problematic. First, some of its defenders have argued that payments are made not to factors of production, but rather to the people who happen to own them based on existing property rights. If a hectare of land earns $2,000 because that is its marginal revenue product, it does not mean, nor is it meant to imply, that the landlord *deserves* any particular payment, because he may even have acquired the land by fraud.

Second, an input's MRP does not depend only on "how hard it works" but also on how much of it happens to be employed—because, according to the principle of diminishing returns, the more the factor input is employed, the lower its MRP. Thus, a factor's MRP is not and cannot legitimately be interpreted as a measure of the intensity of its "productive effort," since the degree of utilization of a productive input would also have a bearing on its MRP. In any event, what an input "deserves," in some moral sense, may depend on more than what it does in the factory or the office where it may be employed. For example, workers who are sick or have many children may be considered more deserving, even if they are no more productive than their healthy or childless counterparts.

On these and other grounds, few economists today would claim that marginal productivity analysis shows that distribution of incomes under capitalism is either just or unjust. The marginal productivity principle is merely one important approach, among others, that offers some interesting insights into the determination of factor rewards. Consequently, some of its defenders would argue that it is as relevant to organizing production in a market-based socialist society as it is in a capitalist one.

Other critics have attacked marginal productivity theory for using rather complicated and unrealistic reasoning. This reasoning largely abstracts from the existing institutional structure of power and ownership in a society (as the famous American institutionalist economist Thorstein Veblen stated more than a century ago), and ultimately tells us very little about the really urgent problems of income distribution. In this view, it is all very well to say that everything depends on supply and demand and to express this idea in terms of complicated equations (many of which appear in more advanced books and articles). But these equations do not tell us what to do about such serious distribution problems as malnutrition among extremely poor populations living in diverse institutional environments in Africa, Asia, and Latin America or poverty among indigenous populations and other minority groups in Canada.

Admittedly, these are serious shortcomings. We have seen in this chapter that the theory provides some insights into real policy matters, although not as many as we would like. Later in the book, we will see that economists do have useful things to say about the problems of poverty and underdevelopment, but very little of what we can say about these issues arises out of marginal productivity analysis.

---

[6] John Bates Clark, "Distribution as Determined by a Law of Rent," *Quarterly Journal of Economics*, 5(3), April 1891, p. 312.

Perhaps, in the end, what should be said about marginal productivity theory is this: As an established model widely held in the economics profession, many economists would argue that marginal productivity theory offers at least some useful insights as to what could guide economic behaviour in the market for factor inputs. Until alternative models of the demand side of factor pricing are sufficiently robust, one should make the best use of all of the tools that we do have, including those offered by marginal productivity theory, while recognizing those tools' restricted domain of applicability.

SUMMARY

1. A profit-maximizing firm purchases the quantity of any input at which the price of the input equals its **marginal revenue product** (MRP). Consequently, the firm's demand curve for an input is (the downward-sloping portion of) that input's MRP curve.

2. **Investment** in a firm is the amount that is *added* to the firm's capital, which is its plant, equipment, inventory, and other productive inputs that tie up the company's money.

3. **Interest** rates are determined by the supply of and demand for funds. The demand for funds is a **derived demand**, because these funds are used to finance business investment whose profitability depends on the demand for the final products turned out with the aid of such investment. In this way, the demand for funds depends on the marginal revenue productivity of capital.

4. A dollar obtainable sooner is worth more than a dollar obtainable later because of the interest that can be earned on that dollar in the interim.

5. Increased demand for a good that needs land to produce it will drive up the price of land either because inferior land will be brought into use or because land will be used more intensively.

6. Rent controls do not significantly affect the supply of land, but they do tend to reduce the supply of buildings.

7. **Economic rent** is any payment to the supplier of a factor of production that is greater than the minimum amount needed to induce the factor to be supplied.

8. **Factors of production** that are unique in quality and difficult or impossible to reproduce will tend to be paid relatively high economic rents because of their scarcity.

9. Factors of production that are easy to produce at a constant cost and that are provided by many suppliers will earn little or no economic rent.

10. **Economic profits** over and above the cost of **capital** are earned (a) by exercise of monopoly power, (b) as payments for bearing risk, and (c) as the earnings of successful **innovation**.

11. The desirability of increased taxation of profits depends on the taxes' effects on the supply of entrepreneurial talent. If most profits are economic rents, then higher taxes on profits will have few undesirable effects. If most profits are necessary to attract entrepreneurs into the market, then higher profits taxes can weaken the capitalist economy.

KEY TERMS

Factors of production   445

Entrepreneurship   446

Marginal physical product (MPP)   447

Marginal revenue product (MRP)   447

Derived demand   448

Capital   449

Investment   449

Interest   450

Economic rent   455

Marginal land   455

Economic profit   462

Invention   462

Innovation   462

TEST YOURSELF

1. Which of the following inputs do you think include relatively large economic rents in their earnings?

   a. Nuts and bolts

   b. Petroleum

   c. A champion racehorse

   Use supply–demand analysis to explain your answer.

2. Three machines are employed in an isolated area. They each produce 2,000 units of output per month, the first requiring $20,000 in raw materials, the second $25,000, and the third $28,000. What would you expect to be the monthly charge for the first and second machines if the services of the third machine can be hired at a price of $9,000 per month? Which parts of the charges for the first two machines are economic rent?

3. Economists conclude that a tax on the revenues of firms will be shifted in part to consumers of the products of those firms in the form of higher prices. However, they believe that a tax on the rent of land usually cannot be shifted and must be paid entirely by the landlord. What explains the difference? (*Hint*: Draw the supply–demand graphs.)

4. Many economists argue that a tax on apartment buildings is likely to reduce the supply of apartments, but that a tax on all land, including the land on which apartment buildings stand, will not reduce the supply of apartments. Can you explain the difference? How is this answer related to your answer to Question 3?

5. Distinguish between investment and capital.

6. Explain the difference between an invention and an innovation. Give an example of each.

7. What is the difference between interest and profit? Who earns interest, in return for what contribution to production? Who earns economic profit, in return for what contribution to production?

DISCUSSION QUESTIONS

1. A profit-maximizing firm expands its purchase of any input up to the point where diminishing returns have reduced the marginal revenue product so that it equals the input price. Why does it not pay the firm to "quit while it is ahead," buying so small a quantity of the input that the input's MRP remains greater than its price?

2. If you have a contract under which you will be paid $10,000 two years from now, why do you become richer if the rate of interest falls?

3. Do you know any entrepreneurs? How do they earn a living? How do they differ from managers?

4. "Marginal productivity does not determine how much a worker will earn—it determines only how many workers will be hired at a given wage. Therefore, marginal productivity analysis is a theory of demand for labour, not a theory of distribution." What, then, do you think determines wages? Does marginal productivity affect their level? If so, how?

5. **(More difficult)** Canadian savings rates are among the lowest of any industrial country. This has caused concern about our ability to finance new plants and equipment for Canadian industry. Some politicians and others have advocated lower taxes on saving as a remedy. Do you expect such a program to be very effective? Why?

6. If rent constitutes less than 5 percent of the incomes of Canadians, why may the concept nevertheless be significant?

7. Litigation in which one company sues another often involves costs for lawyers and other court costs literally amounting to hundreds of millions of dollars per case. What does rent have to do with the matter?

APPENDIX *Discounting and Present Value*

Frequently, in business and economic problems, it is necessary to compare sums of money received (or paid) at different dates. Consider, for example, the purchase of a machine that costs $11,000 and will yield a marginal revenue product of $14,520 two years from today. If the machine can be financed by a two-year loan bearing 10 percent interest, it will cost the firm $1,100 in interest at the end of each year, plus $11,000 in repayment of the principal (the amount originally borrowed) at the end of the second year. (See the table that follows.) Is the machine a good investment?

Costs and Benefits of Investing in a Machine		
	End of Year 1	End of Year 2
Benefits		
Marginal revenue product of the machine	$ 0	$14,520
Costs		
Interest	1,100	1,100
Repayment of principal on loan	0	11,000
Total Cost	1,100	12,100

The total costs of owning the machine over the two-year period ($1,100 + $12,100 = $13,200) are less than the total benefits ($14,520). But this is clearly an invalid comparison, because the $14,520 in future benefits is not worth $14,520 in terms of today's money. Adding up dollars received (or paid) at different dates is a bit like adding apples and oranges.

The process that has been invented for making the magnitudes of payments at different dates comparable to one another is called **discounting**, or **computing the present value**.

To illustrate the concept of present value, let us ask how much $1 received a year from today is worth *in terms of today's money*. If the rate of interest is 10 percent, the answer is about 91 cents. Why? Because if we invest 91 cents today at 10 percent interest, it will grow to 91 cents plus 9.1 cents in interest = 100.1 cents in a year. That is, at the end of a year a payment of $100 will leave the recipient about as well off as he would have been if he had instead received $91 now. Similar considerations apply to any rate of interest. In general:

If the rate of interest is i, the present value of $1 to be received in a year is:

$$\frac{\$1.00}{(1 + i)}$$

This is so, because in a year

$$\frac{\$1.00}{(1 + i)}$$

will grow to the original amount plus the interest payment, that is,

$$\frac{\$1.00}{(1 + i)} + \frac{\$1.00}{1 + i} \times i = \frac{\$1.00}{(1 + i)} \times (1 + i) = \$1$$

What about money to be received two years from today? Using the same reasoning, and supposing the interest rate is 10 percent so that $1 + i = 1.1$, $1.00 invested today will grow to $1.00 times $(1.1) = \$1.10$ after one year and will grow to $1.00 times (1.1) times $(1.1) = \$1.00$ times $(1.1)^2 = \$1.21$ after two years. Consequently, the present value of $1.00 to be received two years from today is:

$$\frac{\$1.00}{(1 + i)^2} = \frac{\$1.00}{1.21} = 82.64 \text{ cents}$$

A similar analysis applies to money received three years from today, four years from today, and so on.

The general formula for the present value of $1.00 to be received N years from today when the rate of interest, i, is:

$$\frac{\$1.00}{(1 + i)^N}$$

The present value formula is based on the two variables that determine the present value of any future flow of money: the rate of interest (i) and the amount of time you have to wait before you get it (N).

Let us now apply this analysis to our example. The present value of the $14,520 revenue is easy to calculate because it all comes two years from today. Because the rate of interest is assumed to be 10 percent $(i = 0.1)$, we have:

$$\text{Present value of revenues} = \frac{\$14,520}{(1.1)^2}$$
$$= \frac{\$14,520}{1.21}$$
$$= \$12,000$$

The present value of the costs is a bit trickier in this example because costs occur at two different dates.

The present value of the first interest payment is:

$$\frac{\$1,100}{(1 + i)} = \frac{\$1,100}{1.1} = \$1,000$$

The present value of the final payment of interest plus principal is:

$$\frac{\$12,100}{(1 + i)^2} = \frac{\$12,100}{(1.1)^2} = \frac{\$12,100}{1.21} = \$10,000$$

Now that we have expressed each sum in terms of its present value, it is permissible to add them up. So the present value of all costs is:

$$\text{Present value of costs} = \$1,000 + \$10,000$$
$$= \$11,000$$

Comparing this figure to the $12,000 present value of the revenues clearly shows that the machine really is a good investment. We can use the same calculation procedure for all investment decisions.

SUMMARY

1. To determine whether a loss or a gain will result from a decision whose costs and returns will come at several different periods of time, we must discount all the figures represented by these gains and losses to obtain their present value.

2. For **discounting** purposes, we use the present value formula for X dollars receivable N years from now with an interest rate i:

$$\text{Present value} = \frac{X}{(1 + i)^N}$$

3. We then combine the present values of all the returns and all the costs. If the sum of the present values of the returns is greater than the sum of the present values of the costs, then the decision to invest will promise a net gain.

KEY TERM

Discounting, or computing the present value   467

TEST YOURSELF

1. Compute the present value of $1,000 to be received in three years if the rate of interest is 11 percent.

2. A government bond pays $100 in interest each year for three years and also returns the principal of $1,000 in the third year. How much is it worth in terms of today's money if the rate of interest is 8 percent? If the rate of interest is 12 percent?

20

LABOUR: THE HUMAN INPUT

Octavius (a wealthy young Englishman): "I believe most intensely in the dignity of labor."

The chauffeur: "That's because you never done any."

GEORGE BERNARD SHAW, *MAN AND SUPERMAN*, ACT II

L abour costs account for by far the largest share of gross domestic product (GDP). As noted in Chapter 19, the earnings of labour amount to about two-thirds of national income. Wages also represent the primary source of personal income for the vast majority of Canadians. For more than a century, wages were the centerpiece on which rested the Canadian dream of owning a home and living in relative affluence. In almost every decade, the purchasing power of a typical worker's earnings grew substantially, and the Canadian working class evolved into a comfortable middle class, with Canada attracting millions of immigrants. Then, in the 1970s, something changed fundamentally in much of North America in ways that economists do not yet fully understand.

Figure 1 shows that average real hourly earnings in the Canadian manufacturing sector (adjusted for changes in the purchasing power of the dollar) reached a plateau and then took a slight downward turn in the mid-1970s, only to recover by the late 1990s, almost a quarter of a century later. In contrast, hourly *compensation* (wages plus fringe benefits) did not fall. Fringe benefits include vacation, sick leave, disability and dental insurance, retirement payments, and even education subsidies that employers may provide for their employees. But compensation *growth* did slow markedly.[1] The graph also shows that average hours worked per week in manufacturing have declined by about 12 percent since 1946, even when wages and compensation were increasing. This would suggest that part of the benefits of rising productivity has been going toward reduced hours and to increases in nonwage benefits. But, since the mid-1970s, little has actually gone toward real wage growth.

CONTENTS

---

[1] The increases in compensation over the years reflect, at least in part, the rising cost of services such as dental and paramedical care, rather than an increase in the quantity and quality of benefits provided to workers. We explored the reasons for the rising costs of services in Chapter 15.

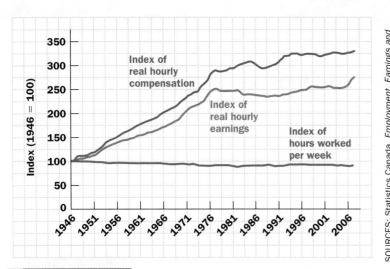

SOURCES: Statistics Canada, *Employment, Earnings and Hours, 1965–1985; Man-hours and Hourly Earnings, 1945–1965; Historical Statistics of Canada, 1983; CANSIM II Tables 281-0022, 281-0030, 281-0033, 281-0039, 281-0008, 281-0009, 383-0001, 383-0005, and 383-0012.*

FIGURE 1

Index of Trends in Real Wages, Real Compensation, and Work Hours in Canadian Manufacturing Industries, 1946–2007

Slowing wage growth has been accompanied by an expanding *income gap* between the rich and the poor. These days, the ratio between high-income and low-income families in Canada is nearly 4.0 and the disparity is slowly growing, although not as much as in the United States where this ratio has reached nearly 6.0.[2] Figure 2 shows that, in 1967, the richest one-fifth of Canadian households accounted for 42 percent of all household income generated in Canada, whereas the poorest one-fifth accounted for 4.2 percent. By 2006, the income share of the poorest fifth of households had fallen marginally to 4.1 percent, while the richest fifth's income share had risen to almost 47 percent, thereby suggesting that the share of the middle class of Canadian income earners is slowly being squeezed.[3]

In the Scandinavian countries, by contrast, the ratio between low-income and high-income families was less than 3.0. These cross-country differences in income notwithstanding, what is perhaps even more disturbing is that a trend toward growing inequality has been found in practically every industrialized country since the early 1980s. For instance, Canadian census data identify a mild, yet steady growth in earnings inequality, accompanied by rising poverty rates. In 2005, almost one in seven Canadian children lived in poverty, a rate that is well below that of the United States and Mexico on the North American continent but significantly higher than poverty rates in Western Europe.[4]

FIGURE 2

Income Inequality, 1967 vs. 2006: Shares of Aggregate Canadian Income Received by the Poorest and the Richest Households

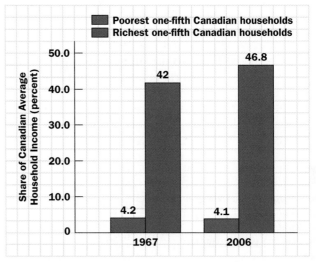

SOURCES: Statistics Canada, *Income Distribution by Size,* 1967 and 1969, and CANSIM II, Table 202-0402, Series V252731827.

---

[2] This ratio was calculated as the median of the top decile of the income groups divided by the median of the bottom decile. In the mid- to late-1990s, the ratio between high-income families (the 90th percentile) and low-income families (the 10th percentile) in Canada was 3.90 and that of the United States was 5.64, compared to 2.59 for Sweden and 3.18 for Germany. (Source: Timothy M. Smeeding, Director, Luxembourg Income Study, *The Gap Between Rich and Poor: A Cross-National Perspective for Why Inequality Matters and What Policy Can Do to Alleviate It*, March 21, 2001. Retrieved from http://www.sprc.unsw.edu.au/seminars/japan.pdf).

[3] Statistics Canada, *Income Distribution by Size* (1967 and 1969), and *Survey of Household Spending*, 2005.

[4] United Nations Children's Fund, *Child Poverty in Rich Countries 2005*, Report Card No. 6 (Florence: UNICEF Innocenti Research Centre, 2005). The percentage of children living in poverty was 14.9 in Canada, while it was 21.9 in the United States and 27.7 in Mexico. On the other hand, it was 10.2 percent in Germany, 7.5 percent in France, 4.2 percent in Sweden, and 2.4 percent in Denmark.

Along with this, the prospective gap between your income as a future university or college graduate and the incomes of your contemporaries who have not pursued a post-secondary education has been changing somewhat recently. Much like the trend in the United States, which has shown a sharp rise in the gap between the incomes of high school and college graduates during an era of unprecedented technological change (driven by the high-tech boom, which increased the demand for skilled workers), census data indicates there has been and continues to be a wide income gap in Canada throughout most of the last two decades of the twentieth century. On average, a university degree could fetch an individual as much as double the income of someone with a high school degree. However when controlling for such factors as age and gender, university education in Canada could earn you on average an income from at least 35 to 50 percent higher than the earnings of someone with only a high school degree.

This education premium has narrowed somewhat in recent years, perhaps reflecting the increasing growth of labour demand in this country since the late 1990s.[5] However, the education premium remains very important in Canada and it is likely to give you a significant financial advantage in terms of your living standard, leisure activities, and other fringe benefits connected with employment—in short, virtually every aspect of your existence.

These developments also have profound and distressing implications for the future of our society as a whole. We are not sure what is behind the trend in growing income inequality, nor do we quite know what can be done about it. But we will discuss some of the possible causes later in the chapter.

ISSUE: *Do Cheap Foreign Labour and Technological Progress Contribute to Lagging Wages?*

Throughout the history of the successful market economies, workers have usually identified two economic enemies: (1) the competition of underpaid foreign labourers and the underpriced exported products made by low-paid foreign workers, and (2) labour-saving technological progress that eliminates jobs. Either or both of these influences may be able to hold down wages in Canada and other industrial economies, and many economists believe that the peril is real (although they argue about which one poses the greater danger). Many workers worry about the future of their jobs and incomes, especially in light of trade legislation that seems to export jobs to other countries. But as obvious as these explanations of lagging wages may seem, as is often true in economics, things seem less straightforward when we dig beneath the surface.

For example, it is the much admired technical progress and labour-saving innovation that have raised productivity spectacularly—by definition, making it possible for fewer workers to produce a given amount of output. Is this change a great benefit or a major threat to jobs in Canada? These two issues—foreign competition and technological progress, and their effects on demand for labour—are among the most crucial that face economic analysis and policy. Although economists continue to gather valuable evidence, we are still a long way from having the complete answers to these questions. This chapter, however, will report some of the things we do know, or think we know, about the subject.

WAGE DETERMINATION IN COMPETITIVE LABOUR MARKETS

To begin to understand labour issues, we must first investigate how wages are determined in a market economy. In a completely free labour market, wages (the price of labour) would be determined by supply and demand, just like any other price. On the

---

[5] See Brahim Boudarbat, Thomas Lemieux, and W. Craig Riddell, *Recent Trends in Wage Inequality and the Wage Structure in Canada*, Working Paper No. 6, University of British Columbia, September 2003 (retrieved from http://www.econ.ubc.ca/ine/papers/wp006.pdf); and Lucy Chung, "Education and Earnings," *Perspectives on Labour and Income*, Statistics Canada, June 2006.

demand side, we would find that the demand curve for labour is derived like the demand curve for any other input—by labour's marginal revenue product, in the manner described in Chapter 19. But the labour market has a number of distinctive features on the supply side.

The labour market is also generally far from perfectly competitive. Nonetheless, we start our investigation by describing the theory of competitive labour markets in which the buyers are large numbers of tiny firms and the sellers are individual workers who act independently of one another. In this model, both buyers and sellers are too small to have any choice but to accept the wage rate determined by the impersonal forces of supply and demand.

The Demand for Labour and the Determination of Wages

The **marginal revenue product of labour** (MRP$_L$) is the increase in the employer's total revenue that results when it hires an additional unit of labour.

Much of what we can say about the demand for labour was already said about the demand for inputs in general in earlier chapters. Workers are hired (primarily) by profit-maximizing firms, which hire an input quantity at which the input's price (the market wage) equals its marginal revenue product (MRP). In this chapter, we will use the symbol **MRP$_L$** as an abbreviation for the **marginal revenue product of labour.** Recall that the marginal revenue product is the addition to the firm's revenue that it obtains by hiring one additional unit of input—in this case, one additional worker. So, MRP$_L$ is equal to the additional amount that worker produces (the worker's marginal physical product, or MPP) multiplied by the price of that product. In other words, to determine how much additional money that worker brings in, we multiply the amount she produces by the price of the commodity she produces.[6]

If the MRP$_L$ exceeds the price of labour (the wage), by the usual reasoning of marginal analysis, the firm can increase its profit by hiring at least one more worker either to produce more output or to substitute for some other input. The reverse is true when the MRP$_L$ is less than its wage. Thus, the derived demand and, consequently, the demand curve for labour are determined by labour's marginal revenue product. Such a demand curve is shown as the red curve *DD* in Figure 3. The figure also includes a blue supply curve, labelled SS. In a competitive labour market, equilibrium will be established at the wage that equates the quantity supplied with the quantity demanded. In this figure, equilibrium occurs at point *E*, where demand curve *DD* crosses supply curve SS. The equilibrium wage is $300 per week and equilibrium employment is 500,000 workers. In this example, because 500,000 workers will be employed at a wage of $300 per week, the total income of the workers will be $300 × 0.5 million = $150 million.

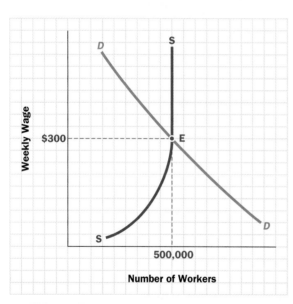

FIGURE 3

Equilibrium in a Competitive Labour Market

Influences on MRP$_L$: Shifts in the Demand for Labour

The conclusion that the demand curve for labour is one and the same as labour's MRP curve is merely the beginning of the story. The next question is: What influences affect MRP$_L$? The answers cast light on a number of important developments in the labour market.

Investment in human capital is any expenditure on an individual that increases that person's future earning power or productivity.

Some obvious influences can change labour's MRP. For example, increased education can improve the ability of the labour force to follow complex instructions and to master difficult technology, thus raising a worker's MRP. Economists use the term **investment in human capital** to refer to spending on increased education and on

[6] To review, see Chapter 7, page 145.

other means to increase the knowledge and skills of the labour force. Such spending is analogous to investment in the firm's plant and equipment because both of them are outlays today that lead to more production both now *and in the future*.

Workers can also improve their skills through experience, called *on-the-job training*, and in a variety of other ways that add to the information they possess and increase their mental and physical dexterity.

Because the demand for labour is a *derived demand*, anything that improves the market for the goods and services that labour produces can shift the labour demand curve upward. In particular, in a period of economic prosperity consumers will have more to spend; their demand for products will shift upward, which in turn will raise the price of the worker's product, thereby shifting the MRP curve upward. The result will be a rise in the demand for labour. That, of course, is why unemployment is always low when the economy is enjoying a period of prosperity.

Technical Change, Productivity Growth, and the Demand for Labour

Another critical influence on the MRP_L is the quality and quantity of the *other* inputs used in the workers' productive activity. Especially important is the technology of the workers' equipment. Innovation that improves machinery, power sources, and other productive instruments adds to the amount that can be produced by a given amount of labour. Thus, technical change that increases labour productivity plays a crucial role in determining the level of wages and the level of employment.

Technical change that increases the worker's productivity has two effects that work in opposite directions. First, increased productivity clearly implies an increase in the worker's marginal physical product—the quantity of widgets that an additional worker can produce will rise. Second, because of the resulting reduction in labour cost and the increased output of widgets, we can expect that when productivity rises, widget prices will fall. Now recall that:

Marginal revenue product of labour in widget production = price of widgets multiplied by the worker's marginal widget output:

$$MRP = P \text{ (of widgets)} \times MPP$$

Because an increase in productivity raises MPP but reduces *P*, we cannot be sure of the net effect on MRP—that is, the net effect on the demand curve for labour.

However, experience shows us how an increase in productivity will affect both wages and the demand for labour. In the very short run, an increase in labour productivity (that is, of labour-saving technology) often causes a downward shift in the demand for labour, which holds down wages. If firms can meet the current demand for their products with 10 percent fewer workers than they needed last year, they will be tempted to "downsize," which is a polite way of saying that they will fire some workers. This does not always happen, but it does sometimes occur. Thus, workers' widespread fear of labour-saving technology is, to some degree, justified.

Productivity Growth Is (Almost) Everything in the Long Run   In the long run, rising productivity has always improved the standard of living for both workers and the owners of other factors of production. In the long run, nothing contributes more to the economic well-being of the nation than rising productivity. Today workers enjoy far longer lives, better health, more education, and more luxury goods than they did a century ago or in any previous period in history. The fact that an hour of labour today can produce a large multiple of what our ancestors could create in an hour increases everyone's average income, including the workers who constitute so large a part of it. In the short run, labour-saving technological change sometimes cuts employment and holds down wages. Historically, however, in the long run it has not reduced employment. It has raised workers' incomes and increased real wages spectacularly since the Industrial Revolution. In Canada since 1946, productivity per hour of labour has increased approximately five-fold. The purchasing power of the wage a worker earns has also grown but not by nearly as much, largely because of the low growth of real wages since the 1970s.

■ The Service Economy and the Demand for Labour

Although productivity growth has not led to any strong long-term upward trend in unemployment, it *has* cut jobs drastically in some parts of the economy, sending the labour force to other economic sectors for employment. Agriculture is the prime example. At the time of Confederation in 1867, by far the preponderant share of the Canadian labour force held agricultural jobs and eked out what today would be considered a meagre standard of living. In parts of Europe, though, farm productivity was so low that famines and starvation were frequent occurrences, as was the case in Ireland just a couple a decades before Confederation.

Today, however, with a very small share of the nation's labour force working on farms, Canada produces such a surplus of farm products, particularly wheat and other grains, that we export them in large quantities to the rest of the world. This dramatic increase in farm productivity has forced agricultural employment to drop from over 50 percent of the labour force at the time of Confederation to no more than 2 percent today. At first, farm workers shifted to manufacturing, as growing incomes in Canada led to a sharp rise in demand for industrial products. Then, productivity in manufacturing took off, and workers again had to look elsewhere for their jobs.

Now, the increased productivity in manufacturing has moved workers into the service sector of the economy. Indeed, it has transformed Canada into a "service economy," meaning that almost three-quarters of the labour force is employed in services such as telecommunications, software design, health care, teaching, and restaurant services.

Some observers have argued that this trend has occurred in Canada because other countries are stealing away our manufacturing business base. Certain low-wage countries, especially in Asia, have seen a sharp expansion of their manufacturing sector, some of which has been at the expense of labour-intensive, low-productivity jobs in the industrial economies internationally. However, as was reported in Chapter 2 (Figure 10, page 34), the service sector has become dominant in *all* of the major industrial countries. No major industrial economy has been able to avoid this development by stealing manufacturing markets away from the other industrial countries.

A greater concern is whether the workers driven from manufacturing into the service sector of the economy have predominantly become low-paid dishwashers and hamburger flippers. This is true in some cases, but a large portion of new service jobs created in the past half-century are in the information sector of the economy, which includes computer technology, research, and teaching, among others; all of these knowledge-based occupations require both education and specialized skills. Many economists attribute the rising relative incomes of university-educated workers in North America to such developments.

■ THE SUPPLY OF LABOUR

Having discussed the demand for labour, we next turn to its supply. Several significant trends have characterized recent decades in Canada.

First, there has been a continuation of the expansion of the total labour force that has been going on throughout the country's history. Much of this expansion is ascribed to sheer growth of Canada's population through birth and immigration. More precisely, population growth is determined by the natural increase of the resident population (that is, the difference between the number of births and the number of deaths of Canadians) and net immigration (the difference between immigration and emigration). With a declining birth rate and a moderate rise in the death rate resulting from more and more post-World War II baby boomers entering old age, population dynamics in Canada has become ever more dependent on net immigration. With more people living in the country, the number of job seekers and jobholders has grown from about 5 million people in the Canadian labour force right after World War II to about 18 million today.

Second, the proportion of the working-age population that either holds a job or is seeking one has also grown from about 55 percent after World War II to 67 percent today. This increase is referred to as a rise in *labour force participation*.

Third, new groups of workers have entered the labour force. This is particularly true of women, who today hold proportionally more jobs (47 percent of the workforce) than they did in earlier decades (except perhaps during wartime).

Finally, in addition to the trends in sheer numbers of workers, the labour supply picture has been affected by institutional changes in the labour market, particularly the trend in trade union membership. Membership continues to rise in absolute terms and stands at over 4 million presently, even though this number has been growing less quickly in Canada than the labour force since the late 1970s. Indeed, unlike the trend in the United States which has seen a protracted and substantial relative decline in union membership, trade unions in Canada have been impacted far less dramatically by the structural changes in the North American labour market.

Since their peak share of the employed labour force in the 1970s, Canadian union ranks have grown by over 1 million members. This is not altogether surprising, since membership in a union offers several advantages, including higher wages and nonwage benefits and greater protection against unfair treatment. Because unions seek to bargain for all of the workers in a firm or an industry, thus eliminating competition among workers over jobs and wages, we will consider them later in this chapter after we have finished our discussion of wage determination in labour markets that are fully competitive. First, we discuss some other supply-side influences.

■ Rising Labour Force Participation

One of the most significant developments in the supply of labour in the industrial countries is the increase in the number of family members who hold jobs. For instance, in 1967, approximately one out of every three households in Canada was a dual-earner husband–wife family. Nowadays, this ratio has doubled to around two-thirds of Canadian households. It used to be that the (head of the household" (usually the husband) was ordinarily the only breadwinner. Today, however, the majority of married women also hold jobs. Interestingly, in a growing number of families, the wife earns more than the husband. In 1967, for example, the proportion of wives who were primary breadwinners constituted 11 percent of households. By 2003, this ratio had practically tripled to 29 percent, involving about 1.4 million Canadian couples.[7]

This phenomenon is in part attributable to lagging labour market wages, which means that both heads of the family are forced to seek gainful employment if the household's economic aspirations are to be realized. The rising cost of living, notably the ever-climbing costs of services such as education, has added further to these financial pressures on households. At the same time, declining employment in the traditionally male-dominated primary and secondary sectors of the economy and the concomitant growth of employment in the tertiary sector has increased occupational opportunities for women while reducing somewhat job availability for men.

But female participation in the labour force has increased for other reasons as well: The move toward the liberation of women from the traditional role in the family, along with women's increased educational achievements, has raised tremendously the range of jobs available outside the household. The broad acceptance of alternative work arrangements, such as flexible hours, parental leave, and greater accessibility to child daycare services, is also an important change that has further eliminated previous institutional barriers to female employment.

These major increases in female participation rates have affected the labour market in several ways that, some observers have suggested, may have held back wages, at

---

[7] Deborah Sussman and Stephanie Bonnell, "Wives as Primary Breadwinners," *Perspectives on Labour and Income*, August 2006, p. 10.

least for a time. First, labour demand did not keep pace with the increase in the supply of workers, which could have the effect of somewhat depressing overall wages. This is, of course, an implication of standard supply–demand analysis. Just draw the usual supply–demand graph for a labour market, and you will readily confirm that when the supply curve of labour shifts to the right and the demand curve remains unchanged, the price of labour (that is, the wage) can be expected to fall.

Second, it has been argued that a combination of discrimination and the initial lack of experience of these new entrants into the labour market (which temporarily reduced their MRP_L) had similar effects. Discrimination against women in the labour market means that, to get jobs, female workers must offer special incentives to prospective employers. This can force women with comparable ability to male co-workers to accept wages lower than those paid to male employees. Lack of experience can have a similar effect, but for a reason that is perhaps less objectionable: If workers acquire skill through experience on the job (on-the-job training), then, on average, inexperienced workers can be expected to have lower productivity than more experienced workers. Because their MRP_L is comparatively low, the demand curve for the inexperienced workers will also be low, and lower wages tend to follow. However, the persistence of a male–female earnings gap in the range of 20 to 40 percent, depending on the actual measurement techniques employed by researchers, would suggest that the lower wages for female workers in Canada cannot be easily explained away by productivity-related factors.[8]

■ An Important Labour Supply Conundrum

For most commodities, an increase in their prices leads to an increase in the quantities supplied, whereas a price decline reduces the amounts supplied; that is, supply curves slope upward. But the striking historical trends in labour supply tell a very different story. Supply has tended to fall when wages rose and to rise when wages fell. Throughout the first three-quarters of the twentieth century, real wages rose, as Figure 1 partly attests for the early post-World War II era in Canada. Yet labour asked for and received *reductions* in the length of the workday and workweek. At the beginning of the century, the standard workweek was 50 to 60 hours (with virtually no vacations). Since then, labour hours have generally declined to an average workweek of about 35 hours.

But in the two most recent decades, as real wages have fallen, the number of family members who leave the home each day to earn wages has increased. And, in recent years there has been a rise in overtime work—that is, workers labouring more than the standard number of hours in their firms. Thus, reduced real wages appear to have induced people to increase the quantity of labour they supply.

Where has the common-sense view of this matter gone wrong? Why, as hourly wages rose for 75 years, did workers not sell more of the hours they had available instead of pressing for a shorter and shorter workweek? And why, in recent years, have they sold relatively more of their labour time as real wage rates stopped rising?

To answer these questions it is helpful to follow the economic analysis of labour supply and make use of a simple observation: Given the fixed amount of time in a week, a person's decision to *supply labour* to firms is simultaneously a decision to *demand leisure* time for himself. The leisure time can be interpreted simply as the residue, what is left over after the time spent at work. Assuming that, after deducting the necessary time for eating and sleeping, a worker has 90 usable hours in a week, then a decision to spend 40 of those hours working is simultaneously a decision to demand 50 of them for other purposes.

The interpretation of the supply of labour as the opposite of the worker's demand for leisure offers us a very substantial insight into the relationship between wages and labour supply. Economists say that a rise in wages has two effects on the worker's demand for leisure: the substitution effect and the income effect. We will see that they tell us a good deal about the labour market.

---

[8] Marie Drolet, "The Male–Female Wage Gap," *Perspectives on Labour and Income*, Statistics Canada, December 2001, p. 5.

1. Substitution Effect   The **substitution effect** of an increase in the price of any good is the resulting switch of customers to a substitute product whose price has not risen. An increase in the price of fish, for example, can lead consumers to buy more meat. The same is true of wages and the demand for leisure. When the wage rate rises, leisure becomes more expensive relative to other commodities that consumers can buy. For instance, if you decide not to work overtime this weekend, the price you pay for that increase in leisure (the opportunity cost) is the wage you have to give up as a result of the decision. So an increase in wages makes leisure more expensive. This leads us to expect that a wage increase will induce workers to buy *less* leisure time (and *more* of other things). Thus:

> The substitution effect of higher wages leads most workers to want to work more.

The **substitution effect** of a wage increase is the resulting incentive to work more because of the higher relative reward to labour.

2. Income Effect   An increase in the price of any good, other things equal, clearly increases the real incomes of sellers of the good and reduces the real incomes of buyers of the good. That change in income affects the amount of the good (as well as the amounts of other items) that the individual demands. This *indirect* effect of a price change on demand, which is called the **income effect** of the price change, is especially important in the case of wages. Higher wages make consumers richer. We expect this increased wealth to raise the demand for most goods, *including leisure*. So:

> The income effect of higher wages leads most workers to want to work less (that is, demand more leisure), whereas the income effect of lower wages make them want to work more.

The **income effect** of a rise in wages is the resulting rise of workers' purchasing power that enables them to afford more leisure.

Putting these two effects together, we conclude that some workers may react to an increase in their wage rate by working more, whereas others may react by working less. Still others will have little or no discretion over their work hours. In terms of the market as a whole, therefore, higher wages can lead to either a larger or a smaller quantity of labour supplied.

FIGURE 4

A Typical Labour Supply Schedule

Statistical studies of this issue in countries such as the United States have arrived at the following conclusions:

- The response of labour supply to wage changes is not very strong for most workers.
- For low-wage workers, the substitution effect seems clearly dominant, so they work more when wages rise.
- For high-wage workers, the income effect just about offsets the substitution effect, so they do not work more when wages rise.

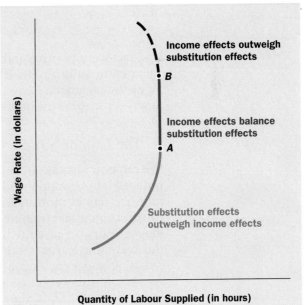

Figure 4 depicts these approximate "facts." It shows labour supply rising (slightly) as wages rise up to point *A, as substitution effects outweigh income effects*. Thereafter, labour supply is roughly constant as wages rise and income effects become just as important as substitution effects up to point *B*. At still higher wages, above point *B*, income effects may overwhelm substitution effects, so that rising wages can even cut the quantity of labour supplied.

Thus, it is even possible that when wages are raised high enough, further wage increases will lead workers to purchase more leisure and therefore to work less (see "The Income Effect: Is Time More Precious Than Money?" on the next page). The supply curve of labour is then said to be **backward-bending,** as illustrated by the broken portion of the curve above point *B* in Figure 4.

Does this theory of labour supply apply to college and university students? A study of the hours worked by students at Princeton University in the United States found that it does.[9] Estimated substitution effects of higher wages on the labour supply of Princeton

A supply curve of labour is **backward-bending** when a rise in an initially low wage leads to a rise in quantity of labour supplied, but a rise in a wage that was already high reduces the amount supplied.

The Income Effect: Is Time More Precious Than Money?

Since the early post-World War II years, both home and working life in Canada have undergone a radical shift. With the changing demographics and the dramatic rise of female participation in the labour market, we have witnessed the growth of the dual-earner family with the accompanying stresses and strains of trying to manage the work–family balance.

At the same time, the 1980s and 1990s brought with them employment instability together with a growing polarization of hours of work. Indeed, an increasing number of Canadians were working longer hours and, paradoxically, many more were also working fewer hours in the form of casual part-time employment, with an ever-shrinking number of workers benefiting from a relatively stable average workweek of about 35 hours. Because of these important structural changes affecting the Canadian labour market, the work–family conflict (that is, the allocation of time among competing wants—employment income, home activities, and leisure) has become a significant policy issue at the beginning of the twenty-first century. Instead of the promise of more leisure time made possible by increased productivity, the growing income of dual-earner households has created ever-greater stresses affecting the health and well-being of a significant number of workers, which is reflected in increased absenteeism and higher labour turnover.

According to studies done in 1994 and 2000 by Statistics Canada, one of the most commonly cited source of workplace stress was too many demands on hours, with its obvious ramifications on household activities.* Regardless of age, gender, duration of the workweek, day or night shift, white or blue collar, the most general complaint was the stress brought on by too many hours or too many demands in the work environment.

* Cara Williams "Sources of Workplace Stress," *Perspectives on Labour and Income*, Statistics Canada, June 2003, pp. 5–12.

students were positive and income effects were negative, just as the theory predicts. Apparently, substitution effects outweighed income effects by a slim margin, so that higher wages attracted a somewhat greater supply of labour. Specifically, a 10 percent rise in wages increased the hours of work of the Princeton student body by about 3 percent.

The Labour Supply Conundrum Resolved

We can now answer our earlier question: Why is it that, historically, rising wages have reduced labour supply and falling wages have increased it? We know that any wage increase sets in motion *both* a substitution effect *and* an income effect. If only the substitution effect operated, then rising wages would indeed cause people to work longer hours because the high price of leisure would make leisure less attractive. But this reasoning leaves out the income effect.

Rising wages enable the worker to provide for her family with fewer hours of work. As a result, the worker can afford to purchase more leisure without suffering a cut in living standard. Thus, the income effect of increasing wages induces workers to work fewer hours. Similarly, falling wages reduce the worker's income. To preserve the family's living standard, she must seek additional hours of work, and the worker's spouse may have to leave their children in daycare and take a job.

Thus, it is the strong income effect of rising wages that apparently accounts for the fact that labour supply has responded in the "wrong" direction, with workers working ever-shorter hours as real wages rose and longer hours as wages fell.

[9] Mary P. Hurley, *An Investigation of Employment among Princeton Undergraduates during the Academic Year*, senior thesis, Department of Economics, Princeton University, May 1975.

Consumption Norms and Labour Supply

Economics literature provides another explanation for the inverted-C shape of the labour supply function that has historically been supported by some economists on the basis of the notion of consumption norms for individuals and households. This view regarding household consumption habits formation was originally popularized in the late 1940s by James S. Duesenberry (1918–), an American economist at Harvard University.

To understand this alternative explanation of labour supply behaviour, let us imagine that either you (or your family) have decided that you would like to live in a certain size of dwelling in a particular area of town, equipped with cable, Internet services, and other amenities. Moreover, to further "keep up with the Jones," you would like to take at least one family vacation annually and own a sports utility vehicle. If this is a consumption norm that you and others in the labour market value highly and wish to attain but, unfortunately, your income level is much too low, a higher wage would be a clear incentive to increase your hours of work or to hold multiple jobs. In this case, as labour demand increases and wages rise, more labour will be forthcoming along the upward-sloping segment of the labour supply function in Figure 4.

However, attaining a high enough level of income that allows you to secure the desired consumption basket would now place you on the vertical or even backward-bending portion of the labour supply function. For instance, suppose that you are at the higher end of the wage scale in Figure 4 and your wage drops suddenly. Following this habit formation approach, you would now wish to work longer hours and hold extra jobs just to maintain the quality of your personal life that the targeted consumption basket confers.

In a sense, this behaviour is somewhat analogous to that of savers who have a fixed accumulation goal, as described in Chapter 19, which explained what otherwise seemed to be a counterintuitive observation. In this case, though, it has to do with attaining or maintaining a desired consumption level. Hence, in the North American context, where the trend of real wages has been somewhat flat or declining during a good portion of the last three decades, this analysis could offer at least a partial alternative explanation of the long-term rise in the labour force participation rate.

WHY DO WAGES DIFFER?

Earlier in the chapter, we saw how wages are determined in an unregulated market economy: In a competitive labour market, the equilibrium wage occurs where quantity supplied equals quantity demanded (refer back to Figure 3). In reality, of course, no single wage level applies to all workers. Some workers are paid very well, whereas others are forced to accept meagre earnings. We all know that certain groups in our society (the young, the disadvantaged, the uneducated) earn relatively low wages and that some of our most severe social ills (poverty, crime, drug addiction) are related to this fact. But why are some wages so low while others are so high? The explanation is important, because it can help us determine what to do to help poorly paid workers increase their earnings and move up toward the income levels of the more fortunate suppliers of labour. Because the issue is so significant, we will discuss it in some detail.

In the most general terms, the explanation of wage differences is the fact that there is not one labour market but many—each with its own supply and demand curves and its own equilibrium wage. Supply–demand analysis implies that wages are relatively high in markets where demand is high relative to supply, as in Figure 5(a). This can happen if qualified workers are scarce or if the demand for a product is great (because labour demand is a derived demand). In contrast, wages are comparatively low in markets where labour supply is high relative to demand, as in Figure 5(b). This also can be true if product demand is weak or if workers are not very productive. This is hardly startling news, however, and it doesn't tell us what we need to know about wage differentials. To make the analysis useful, we must breathe some life into the supply and demand curves.

Labour Demand in General

We start with demand. Why is the demand for labour greater in some markets than in others? Because the marginal revenue product of workers depends on their *marginal physical product* (MPP), the variables that influence MPP_L will also influence wages. Each worker's MPP depends, of course, on his or her own *abilities* and *degree of*

FIGURE 5   Wage Differentials

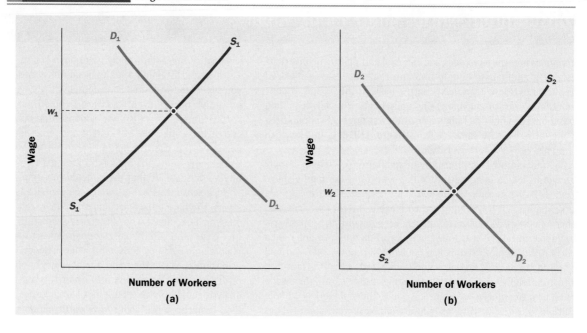

effort on the job. But, as we have seen, the influence of these characteristics is supplemented by the *other factors of production* that workers use to produce output. Workers in Canadian industry are more productive than workers in many other countries at least partly because they have generous supplies of machinery, natural resources, and technical know-how with which to work. As a consequence, they earn high wages. In other words, the marginal product of labour is raised by an abundance of efficient machinery and other inputs that increase the worker's effectiveness.

The marginal product of some workers can also be increased relative to that of others by superior education, training, and experience. We will go into greater detail later about the role of education in wage determination.

Labour Supply in General

Turning next to differences in the supply of labour to different areas, industries, or occupations, it is clear that the *size of the available working population relative to the magnitude of industrial activity* in a given area is of major importance. It helps explain why wages rose so high in Alberta, which was fuelled by a booming oil market, and why wages have been and remain so low in Newfoundland and Labrador, where industry is dormant.

The *nonmonetary* attractiveness of any job will also clearly influence the supply of workers to it. (The monetary attractiveness is the wage itself, which governs movements *along* the supply curve.) Jobs that people find pleasant and satisfying—such as teaching in suburban schools—will attract a large supply of labour and will consequently pay a relatively low wage. In contrast, a premium will have to be paid to attract workers to jobs that are onerous, disagreeable, or dangerous—such as washing the windows of skyscrapers.

Finally, the amount of ability and training needed to enter a particular job or profession is relevant to its supply of labour. Brain surgeons and professional ice skaters earn generous incomes because there are few people as highly skilled as they, and because it is time-consuming and expensive to acquire these skills even for those who have the ability.

■ Ability and Earnings: The Rent Component of Wages

In considering the effects of ability on earnings, it is useful to distinguish between skills that can be duplicated easily and skills that cannot. If Jill Jones has an ability that Sandra Smith cannot acquire, even if she undergoes extensive training, then the wages that Jones earns will contain an element of **economic rent.** We saw this to be true in the case of professional athletes in Chapter 19.[10]

Indeed, the salaries of professional athletes provide particularly clear examples of how economic rents can lead to huge wage differentials. Virtually anyone with moderate athletic ability can be taught to jump and shoot a basketball. But in most cases, no amount of training will teach the player to play basketball like Steve Nash, a star. His high salary is a reward for his unique ability.

But many of the abilities that the market rewards generously—such as those of doctors and lawyers—clearly can be duplicated. Here the theory of rent does not apply, and we need a different explanation of the high wages that these skilled professionals earn. Once again, however, part of our analysis from Chapter 19 finds an immediate application because the acquisition of skills, through formal education and other forms of training, has much in common with business investment decisions. Why? Because the decision to gain more education in the hope of increasing future earnings involves a sacrifice of *current* income for the sake of *future* gain—precisely the hallmark of an investment decision.

> **Economic rent** is any portion of the payment to labour or any other input that does not lead to an increase in the amount of labour supplied.

■ Investment in Human Capital

The idea that education is an investment is likely to be familiar even to students who have never thought explicitly about it. You made a conscious decision to go to college or university rather than to enter the labour market, and you are probably acutely aware that this decision is now costing you money—lots of money. Your tuition payments may be only a minor part of the total cost of going to school. Think of a high school friend who chose not to continue his or her education and is now working. The salary that he or she is earning could, perhaps, have been yours. You are deliberately giving up this possible income in order to acquire more education.

In this sense, your education is an *investment* in yourself—a *human investment.* Like a firm that devotes some of its money to build a plant that will yield profits at some future date, you are investing in your own future, hoping that your postsecondary education will help you earn more than your high school-educated friend or enable you to find a more pleasant or prestigious job when you graduate. Economists call activities such as going to college or university investments in human capital because such activities give the person many of the attributes of a capital investment.

Doctors and lawyers earn such high salaries partly because of their many years of training. That is, part of their wages can be construed as a *return on their (educational) investments*, rather than as economic rent. Unlike the case of a star athlete, any number of people conceivably *could* become surgeons if they found the job sufficiently attractive to endure the long years of training that are required. Few, however, are willing to make such large investments of their own time, money, and energy. Consequently, the few who do become surgeons earn very generous incomes.

Economists have devoted quite a bit of attention to the acquisition of skills through human investment. An entire branch of economic theory—called **human capital theory**—analyzes an individual's decisions about education and training in exactly the same way as we analyzed a firm's decision to buy a machine or build a factory in the previous chapter. Although educational decisions can be influenced by love of learning, desire for prestige, and a variety of other factors, human capital theorists find it useful to analyze a schooling decision as if it were made purely as a business plan. The

> **Human capital theory** focuses on the expenditures that have been made to increase the productive capacity of workers via education or other means. It is analogous to investment in better machines as a way to increase their productivity.

---

[10] See Chapter 19, pages 458–460

optimal length of education, from this point of view, is to stay in school until the marginal revenue (in the form of increased future income) of an additional year of schooling is exactly equal to the marginal cost.

One implication of human capital theory is that college or university graduates should earn substantially more than high school graduates to compensate them for their extra investments in schooling. Do they? Will your college or university investment pay off? Many generations of postsecondary students have supposed that it would, and recent data strongly confirm they were right. Indeed, as we noted earlier, the gap between the wages of workers with a postsecondary degree and those with a high school education has been widening. University graduates now earn as much as 50 percent more than their high school-educated peers.

> The large income differentials earned by college and university graduates provide an excellent "return" on the tuition payments and sacrificed earnings that they "invested" while in school.

Human capital theory emphasizes that jobs that require more education *must* pay higher wages if they are to attract enough workers, because people insist on a financial return on their human investments. But the theory does not address the other side of the question: What is it about more-educated people that makes firms willing to pay them higher wages? Put differently, the theory explains why the supply of educated people is limited, but does not explain why the *demand* is substantial even at high wages.

Most human capital theorists complete their analyses by assuming that students in high schools and universities and colleges acquire particular skills that are productive in the marketplace, thereby raising the marginal revenue products of those workers. In this view, educational institutions are factories that take less-productive workers as their raw materials, apply doses of training, and create more-productive workers as outputs. This view of what happens in schools makes educators happy and accords well with common sense. However, a number of social scientists doubt that this is quite how schooling raises earning power.

Education and Earnings: Dissenting Views

Just why do jobs with stiffer educational requirements typically pay higher wages? The common-sense view that educating people makes them more productive is not universally accepted.

Education as a Sorting Mechanism   One alternative view denies that the educational process teaches students anything directly relevant to their subsequent performance on jobs. In this view, people differ in ability when they enter the school system and differ in more or less the same ways when they leave. What the educational system does, according to this theory, is to *sort* individuals by ability. Skills such as intelligence and self-discipline that lead to success in schools, it is argued, are closely related to the skills that lead to success in jobs. As a result, the abler individuals stay in school longer and perform better. Prospective employers recognize this, and consequently seek to hire those whom the school system has suggested will be the most productive workers.

The Dual Labour Market Theory   Another view of the linkages among education, ability, and earnings is part of a much broader theory of how the labour market operates—the **theory of dual labour markets.** Proponents of this theory suggest that there are two very different types of labour markets, with relatively little mobility between them.

The theory of dual labour markets emphasizes that labour is supplied in two types of market, one with high wages and promising promotion opportunities and the other with low wages and dead-end jobs.

The "primary labour market" is where most of the economy's "good jobs" are found—jobs such as business management, computer programming, and skilled crafts that are interesting and offer considerable possibilities for career advancement. The educational system helps decide which individuals get assigned to the primary labour market and, for those who make it, greater educational achievement does indeed offer financial rewards.

The privileged workers who wind up in the primary labour market are offered opportunities for additional training on the job; they augment their skills by experience and by learning from their co-workers; and they progress in successive steps to more responsible, better-paying positions. Where jobs in the primary labour market are concerned, dual labour market theorists believe that education really is productive. But they also think that admission to the primary labour market depends in part on social position, and that firms probably care more about steady work habits and punctuality than they do about reading, writing, and arithmetic.

Everything is quite different in the "secondary labour market"—where we find all the "bad jobs." Jobs such as those in cleaning and fast-food services, which are often the only ones inner-city residents can find, offer low pay, few fringe benefits, and virtually no training to improve the workers' skills. They are dead-end jobs that offer little or no hope for promotion or advancement. As a result, lateness, absenteeism, and pilferage are expected as a matter of course, so that workers in the secondary labour market tend to develop the bad work habits that confirm the prejudices of those who assigned them to inferior jobs in the first place.

In the secondary labour market, increased education leads neither to higher wages nor to increased protection from unemployment—benefits generally offered elsewhere in the labour market. For this reason, workers in the secondary market have little incentive to invest in education.

In sum, we have a well-established fact—that people with more education generally earn higher wages—but little agreement on what accounts for this fact. Probably, there is some truth to all of the proposed explanations.

■ The Effects of Minimum Wage Legislation

As we have observed, the "labour market" is really composed of many submarkets for labour of different types, each with its own supply and demand curves. One particular labour market always seems to have higher unemployment than the labour force as a whole: the job market for teenagers.

Figure 6 shows that teenage unemployment rates (for persons aged 15 to 19) have consistently been much higher than the overall unemployment rate, and male teenagers have fared worse than female teenagers. For the most part, however, the

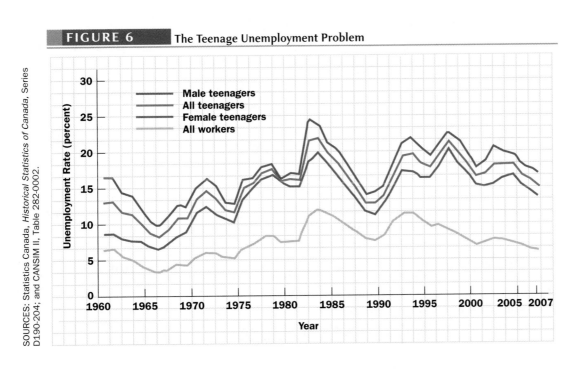

FIGURE 6   The Teenage Unemployment Problem

SOURCES: Statistics Canada, *Historical Statistics of Canada*, Series D190-204; and CANSIM II, Table 282-0002.

four unemployment series move in tandem, as the figure shows: Whenever the unemployment rate for all workers goes up or down, the teenage unemployment rate almost always moves in the same direction, but more dramatically. Thus, when things are generally bad, things are much worse for teenage workers and especially for male teenagers. Despite programs to encourage the hiring and training of young people, there has been no marked narrowing of these series over almost half a century in Canada.

One reason, to which economists frequently refer, is that teenagers generally have not completed their educations and have little job experience, so their marginal revenue products tend to be relatively low. This, however, would not explain the persistent unemployment gap between males and females. This latter phenomenon depends largely on the fact that the participation rate of males is higher than that of females within the 15–19 age group. Hence, for a given demand for teen labour, relatively more male teenagers would be queuing for these scarce jobs because of the higher male participation rates. Until recently, many economists argued that these facts, together with **minimum wage laws** that prevent teenagers from accepting wages commensurate with their low marginal revenue products, are the main causes of high teenage unemployment. The reasoning is that legally imposed high wages make it too expensive to hire teenagers. While evidence about the impact of the minimum wage law on teenage employment is somewhat conflicting, studies mainly in the United States during the 1990s suggest that a rise in the minimum wage produces little, if any, cut in the demand for teen labour. This would be indicative of a relatively inelastic labour–demand relationship that is much more sensitive to the level of overall product market demand than to any small changes in the relative price of labour.

We should also note that over the years, inflation has eaten into the real value of the minimum wage (the lowest hourly wage that provincial, territorial, and federal laws permit employers to pay). Figure 7 shows clearly that, after 40 years of sporadic increases in the nominal minimum wage rate, the real (inflation-adjusted) rate actually fell in the late 1970s and then more or less bottomed out around a real wage level that today barely exceeds the level reached in the late 1960s. In retrospect, it would be difficult to explain the upward trend in teenage unemployment on the evolution of real minimum wages in Canada over the last four decades.

A **minimum wage law** imposes a floor on wages and prohibits employers from paying their workers less than that amount.

| FIGURE 7 | The Minimum Wage, 1965–2007 |

SOURCES: Statistics Canada, CANSIM Tables 281-0005, 281-0015, 282-0012, 183-0003, and 183-0002; *Federal Government Employment, 1965–1980* (CPI, 1965 = 100). This minimum wage series is a weighted average of provincial, territorial, and federal minimum wages on the basis of their respective employment weights in Canada.

Note: 1965–1982 employment data for the Yukon and Northwest Territories are not available.

UNIONS AND COLLECTIVE BARGAINING

Our analysis of competitive labour markets has so far not dealt with one very important and distinctive feature of markets for labour in Canada: The supply of labour is not at all competitive in many labour markets in the sense in which we have depicted such markets in, for example, Figure 3. Instead, it is affected by **labour unions,** which some would argue hold a monopolistic position in a labour market because of their function as the exclusive legal representative of employees in a bargaining unit in negotiating the price of labour and other conditions of employment. Although it is individual employees who actually offer their services, the terms of employment are negotiated through the process of collective bargaining between the employer and the union, with market forces having some influence during negotiations but practically none during the duration of a collective agreement.

The news media is often filled with issues relating to labour relations in Canada. Strikes and lockouts in major Canadian industries; legal cases involving, say, gender equity considerations; issues over pensions rights because of industry downsizing and restructuring—all are matters that often pit employers and unions against each other. However, most Canadians would be surprised to learn that less than one in every three workers is unionized, with the vast majority of union members being in the public sector.

Figure 8 charts data series on **union density** in Canada since 1921, defined as the number of union members as a percentage of total nonagricultural employment. Union density rose significantly during and immediately after World War II, as industrial unionism took hold in Canada, which was then followed by a second wave connected with the growth of public sector unions during the 1960s and the first half of the 1970s. However, since the latter half of the 1970s, growth in union membership has not kept pace with overall employee growth—as it is reflected in the trend decline in union density rates, which have gravitated around 30 percent over the last decade.

One reason why unionization in Canada has been declining somewhat since the heyday of unionism during the first three decades after World War II is the shift of the Canadian labour force into service industries and out of manufacturing, where unions traditionally had their base. Indeed, but for the strong rates of unionization in the public service in Canada, union density would be in a percentage range not seen since the 1920s and 1930s, when unionism was largely limited to the building trades and craft unionism was dominant. In addition, deregulation has forced airlines, the telecommunications sector, and firms in other industries to compete more intensely, which may have further weakened unions in some of these sectors. Some theorize that the increasing number of women in the labour force could have contributed to this trend, because women are supposedly less prone than men to join unions, but this is completely contradicted by the evidence. There are no significant differences between male and female union density in Canada, with the rate for men at 29.4 percent and for women at 30.1 percent in 2006.[11]

A **labour union** comprises workers who constitute a certified bargaining unit that negotiates with employers on both financial and normative workplace matters in accordance with Canadian labour relations legislation enacted primarily at the provincial level.

Union density or unionization rate is the number of union members as a proportion of total employment or a subset of total employment, such as nonagricultural employment.

FIGURE 8

Unionization in Canada, 1921–2007

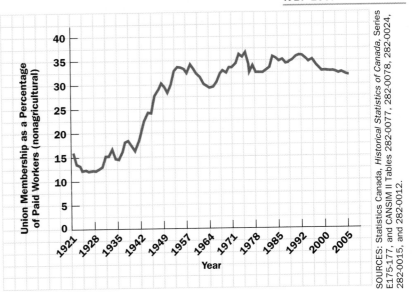

SOURCES: Statistics Canada, *Historical Statistics of Canada,* Series E175-177, and CANSIM II Tables 282-0077, 282-0078, 282-0024, 282-0015, and 282-0012.

[11] Statistics Canada, "Unionization," *Perspectives on Labour and Income,* April 2006, p. 21.

The Canadian Labour Movement: Its History and Challenges

During the mid-nineteenth century, Canada went through its earliest phase of the Industrial Revolution. The manufacturing industries that were emerging in the principal urban centres treated their employees very harshly, imposing very long hours of work, low pay, and dangerous working conditions. In reaction, the first workers to organize so as to improve their living standards were often members of a particular craft or trade, similar to the craft guilds in medieval Europe.

While some labour associations did set up on a cross-occupational basis, craft unionism was first to establish itself successfully in nineteenth century Canada for reasons that are now quite familiar to students of economics. Given the lack of substitutes for these highly skilled workers and the relatively small numbers of tradespeople as compared to unskilled workers, the elasticity of demand for the former was relatively low. This gave these workers greater bargaining power to negotiate collectively with their employers than could their unskilled confreres. Furthermore, since the uncertainties generated by mechanization and shifts in consumer demand threatened the very existence of their trades, certain craftsmen were often more vulnerable than manual workers and therefore were more eager to unionize. By 1883, a union central, the Trades and Labour Congress of Canada (TLC), was founded and eventually regrouped the various craft organizations on a Canada-wide basis. The TLC became the Canadian counterpart of a similar organization in the United States, the American Federation of Labor.

As industrial activity expanded to new levels and factories began to permeate Canada's industrial landscape, the need for organizing workers on an industrial basis rather than along craft lines became ever more pressing. By the late nineteenth and early twentieth century, opposed to unfettered capitalism and to "business unionism" of the craft organizations, new and more radical organizations began to take root, such as the American-based Knights of Labour, which formed industrial unions that cut across occupational lines and also stressed greater political activism. This was followed by the growth of widely based organizations more firmly guided by socialist principles, such as the International Workers of the World and, after World War I, the home-grown western-based One Big Union. In may be argued that the famous Winnipeg General Strike of 1919 was the culmination of this greater activism.

Despite the relative success of these radical industrial unions in appealing to a growing number of workers until immediately after World War I, these organizations had to cope with incredible repression. Further weakened by economic retrenchment associated with mass unemployment following World War I, and then even more profoundly during the Great Depression of the 1930s, this more radical model of industrial unionism faced political uncertainties. To fill the void, during the interwar years, "international unions" based on the industrial model of unionism (promoted in the United States by the Congress of Industrial Organizations), were slowly establishing roots in Canada. With the exception of the Canadian and Catholic Confederation of Labour, which was formed primarily at the instigation of the Catholic clergy and limited to Quebec (later to become the Confederation of National Trade Unions), by 1940 the establishment and proliferation of both national unions associated with the All Canadian Congress of Labour and the American-based industrial unions led to the founding of the Canadian Congress of

Trade unionists demonstrating

SOURCE: Library and Archives Canada, Duncan Cameron collection, FA-044

Labour, the Canadian counterpart of the Congress of Industrial Organizations in the United States.

Spurred on by major legislative changes that strengthened collective bargaining rights in Canada, the early post-World War II years witnessed a tremendous growth in union density. Modelled on the Wagner Act of 1935 in the United States, Privy Council Order 1003 (or simply PC 1003) in 1944 provided the legal framework to enforce collective bargaining between an employer and a legally certified union in Canada. The wording of PC 1003 came to be reflected in all provincial labour relations legislation across the country.

At about the same time, in settling a strike between the Ford Motor Company and the United Auto Workers in 1945, The Honourable Mr. Justice Ivan Rand established a legal principle that was to become critical to union security. The principle, nowadays referred to as the *Rand formula*, established that all employees of a bargaining unit had to pay union dues regardless of whether the worker chose to be a member of the union, since the benefits of the collective bargaining process would accrue to all employees. With growing membership and greater union security, the traditional rivalry that existed between the craft unions (represented by the Trades and Labour Congress) and the new industrial unions (in the Canadian Congress of Labour) came to an end with the merging of these two organizations to become the Canadian Labour Congress in 1956. This amalgamation mirrored a path earlier taken in the United States with the merging of the American Federation of Labor and the Congress of Industrial Organizations.

The Canadian economy grew at a remarkable pace during the early postwar years. With an increasing number of women entering the labour market and demand for government services (such as health care and education) rising ever more quickly, the trade union movement focused its attention more and more on the public sector to obtain new members. Collective bargaining rights were extended to public service employees, beginning in Saskatchewan after the election of a pro-labour government in the 1940s and then during the "Quiet Revolution" in Quebec in the early to mid-1960s. This culminated in 1967 with the federal government passage of the Public Service Staff Relations Act, which extended collective bargaining

The Canadian Labour Movement: Its History and Challenges (continued)

rights to federal public sector workers, whose ultimate impact was to then pressure the remaining provinces to enact similar legislation at the provincial level, which was accomplished by the mid-1970s. By the late 1970s, these broad legislative changes pushed union density rates in Canada to unprecedented historical levels and suddenly transformed a union movement that had previously been dominated by private sector workers into one in which its largest unions were now based in the public sector.

With the cresting of union density in Canada during the late 1970s, new challenges appeared both domestically and internationally. In an era of slower growth and increasing focus on government deficit fighting, the Canadian trade union movement has been struggling to look for other sources of expansion. As we have seen previously in this chapter, most of the growth of employment has been in the services sector. Yet, private sector services have been somewhat more impervious to union drives. Unlike the public sector services, private services are more fragmented and difficult to unionize. The experience with organizing bank workers during the 1990s and, more recently, the difficulties with McDonald(s and Wal-Mart, spell difficult times ahead for the Canadian trade union movement. Added to these problems domestically, growing trade liberalization internationally and increasing competition from the developing world for scarce jobs has exacerbated what was already a difficult situation. Without legislated changes to facilitate the unionization of private sector services, the most optimistic prospect is that union density will remain at a standstill in the coming years.

Finally, because of increasing trade liberalization, unions themselves have come to recognize the increasing pressure in the 1990s and 2000s of international competition. Indeed, Canada's major trade union federation, the Canadian Labour Congress, used to advertise a list of all plant closures and the number of jobs eliminated following the adoption of the North American Free Trade Agreement (NAFTA) in 1994. This downsizing trend, arising partly from the slow overall growth of the Canadian economy during the 1980s and 1990s and partly from the growing international competition affecting the Canadian manufacturing sector, has made it even more difficult for unions to win concessions that improve the economic positions of their members. That, in turn, may have reduced the attractiveness of union membership throughout this period of relative decline in union density.

When compared to the United States, which witnessed a sharp fall in unionization rates since the late 1950s, with current union density rates at a low of about 13 percent, Canadian unions have shown greater resilience in withstanding some of the common downward pressures affecting North American unions. However, when compared with the Nordic countries of Western Europe with union density rates at over 80 percent, the differences are striking and place Canada in the middle of the pack in terms of unionization rates internationally, between countries like the United States on the low end of the spectrum and the Scandinavian countries on the high end. Yet, the post-1970s period has been one that has seen a decline in unionization rates in practically every country, including some of the Scandinavian countries.

The underlying forces at work internationally because of growing trade liberalization and the general restructuring of domestic economies in favour of largely nonunionized service sector jobs would account for much of this downward trend in union density across countries. Other factors include the overall lower growth rates of output and employment experienced by most Western economies, which have established an economic environment that has been less favourable to union growth, especially with the threat by employers of **outsourcing** in the private manufacturing sector or **contracting-out** in the public sector.

Finally, unionism on the North American continent may have been further weakened by a political climate in the United States and to a lesser extent in Canada, favouring more conservative values that reject collective action and promote individualism, such as the right-to-work legislation that became prevalent in some U.S. states. On the other hand, the recent decision of the Supreme Court of Canada that reasserted the constitutional right to collective bargaining of British Columbia's

Outsourcing is the hiring of workers in foreign countries by Canadian firms to do work formerly carried out in Canada. The term is also used more generally to denote a process of contracting-out work to an external service provider.

Contracting-out, often associated with the phenomenon of public sector downsizing or privatization, is a process whereby an organization hires a private provider of a service that was previously done in-house.

health care employees does highlight the ability of the Canadian trade union movement to resist some of these downward pressures.

■ Unions as Labour "Monopolies"

Unions require that we alter our economic analysis of the labour market in much the same way that monopolies required us to alter our analysis of the goods market (see Chapter 11). Recall that a monopoly seller of goods selects the point on its demand curve that maximizes its profits. Much the same idea could apply to a union, which for analytical purposes can be considered a single seller of labour. It too faces a demand curve—derived this time from the marginal revenue product schedules of firms—and can, at least in theory, choose the point on the curve that suits it best.

The problem for the economist trying to analyze union behaviour—and perhaps also for the union leader trying to select a course of action—is how to decide which point on the demand curve is "best" for the union and its members. There is no obvious single goal analogous to profit maximization that clearly determines what a union should do. Instead, there are a number of *alternative* goals that sound plausible.

Alternative Union Goals   The union leadership may, for example, decide that the size of the union is more or less fixed and try to force employers to pay the highest wage they will pay without firing any of the union members. But this tactic is a high-risk strategy for a union. Firms forced to pay such high wages will be at a competitive disadvantage compared with firms that have nonunion labour, and they may even be forced to shut down. Alternatively, union leaders may assign priority to increasing the size of their union. They may even try to make employment as large as possible by accepting a wage just above the competitive level. One way, but certainly not the only way, to strike a balance between the conflicting goals of maximizing wages and maximizing employment is to maximize the total earnings of all workers taken together.

The basic conclusion of these alternative goals for unions is this: Even if unions, as monopoly sellers of labour, have the power to push wages above the competitive level, they can normally achieve such wage increases only by reducing the number of jobs, because the demand curve for labour is downward sloping. Just as monopolists must limit their outputs to push up their prices, so unions must restrict employment to push up wages.

In some exceptional cases, however, a union may be able to achieve wage gains without sacrificing employment. To do so, the union must be able to exercise effective control over the demand curve for labour. Figure 9 illustrates such a possibility. Union actions push the demand curve outward from D_0D_0 to D_1D_1, simultaneously raising both wages and employment. Typically, this is difficult to do. One possible approach involves *featherbedding*—forcing management to employ more workers than it really needs. Quite the opposite technique is to institute a campaign to raise worker productivity, which some unions seem to have been able to do. Alternatively, the union can try to raise the demand for the company's product either by flexing its political muscle (for example, by obtaining legislation to reduce foreign competition) or by appealing to the public to buy union products.

Have Unions Really Raised Wages?   To what extent do union members actually earn higher wages than nonmembers? The consensus would probably surprise most people. Economists estimate that most union members' wages are about 20 percent higher than those of nonmembers who are otherwise identical (in skills, geographical locations, and so on). Although certainly not negligible, we can hardly consider this gap to be a huge differential. Narrowing the gap

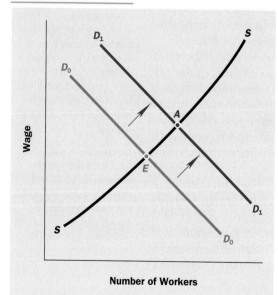

FIGURE 9

Union Control over the Demand Curve

even further is the fact that nonunion workers do not have to pay the dues that are required of union members.

This 20 percent differential does not mean, however, that unions have raised wages no more than 20 percent. Some observers believe that union activity has also raised the wages of nonunion workers by forcing nonunion employers to compete more fiercely for their workers. If so, the differential between union and nonunion workers will be less than the amount by which unions raised wages overall. A recent study of this issue found that unions raise compensation, including wages and benefits, by about 28 percent, that is, they raise total compensation more than they increase wages. The authors also reported that the impact of unions on total *nonunion* wages is almost as large as the impact on total *union* wages (with estimates ranging from 15 to 20 percent in the 1990s).[12]

■ Monopsony and Bilateral Monopoly

Our analysis thus far oversimplifies matters in several important respects. For one thing, it envisions a market situation in which one powerful union is dealing with many powerless employers: We have assumed that the labour market is monopolized on the selling side but is competitive on the buying side. Some industries more or less fit this model. For instance, many of the unions within the construction industry are much larger than the firms with which they bargain.

But many cases simply do not fit the model. The huge auto manufacturing corporations do not stand idly by while the Canadian Auto Workers (CAW) union picks its favourite point on the demand curve for autoworkers. Nor does the steelworkers' union sit across the bargaining table from representatives of a perfectly competitive industry. In these and other industries, although the union certainly has a good deal of monopoly power over labour supply, the firms also have some *monopsony* power over labour demand. (A **monopsony** is a buyer's monopoly—a case where sellers have only one purchaser for their products.) As a result, the firms may deliberately reduce the quantity of labour they demand as a way to force down the equilibrium level of wages. We can calculate the profit-maximizing restriction of the quantity of labour in the same way that we determined a monopolist's profit-maximizing restriction of output in Chapter 11.

Analysts find it difficult to predict the wage and employment decisions that will emerge when both the buying and selling sides of a market are monopolized—a situation called **bilateral monopoly**. The difficulties here are similar to those we encountered in considering the behaviour of oligopolistic industries in Chapter 12. Just as one oligopolist is acutely aware that its rivals are likely to react to anything the oligopolistic employer does, so a union dealing with a monopsony employer knows that any move it makes will elicit a countermove by the firm. This knowledge makes the first decision that much more complicated. In practice, the outcome of bilateral monopoly depends partly on economic logic, partly on the relative power of the union and management, partly on the skill and preparation of the negotiators, and partly on luck.

Still, we can be a bit more concrete about the outcome of the wage determination process under bilateral monopoly. A monopsonist employer unrestrained by a union will use its market power to force wages down below the competitive level, just as a monopoly seller uses its market power to force prices higher. It accomplishes this by reducing its demand for labour below what would otherwise be the profit-maximizing amount, thereby cutting both wages and the number of workers employed.

However, a union may be in a position to prevent this decline from happening. It can deliberately set a floor on wages, pledging its members not to work at all at any wage level below this floor. In this way, a union may force the monopsony employer to pay higher wages and, simultaneously, to hire more workers than the employer otherwise would.

Even though we can hardly find examples of industries that are pure monopsonists in their dealings with labour (with the possible exception of the public sector), these conclusions do have some important implications in reality. The fact is that

> A **monopsony** is a market situation in which there is only one buyer.

> A **bilateral monopoly** is a market situation in which there is both a monopoly on the selling side and a monopsony on the buying side.

---

[12]Source: Lawrence Mishel with Matthew Walters, "How Unions Help All Workers," Economic Policy Institute, EPI Briefing Paper, August 2003, pp. 1–18.

large, oligopolistic firms do often engage in one-on-one wage bargaining with the unions of their employees, and there is reason to believe that the resulting bargaining process closely resembles the workings of the bilateral monopoly model that we just described.

■ Collective Bargaining and Strikes

Collective bargaining is
the process of negotiation
of wages and working con-
ditions between a union and
the firms in the industry.

The process by which unions and management settle on the terms of a labour contract is called **collective bargaining.** Unfortunately, nothing as straightforward as a supply–demand diagram can tell us what wage level will emerge from a collective bargaining session.

Furthermore, actual collective bargaining sessions range over many more issues than just wages. For example, fringe benefits such as pensions, health and life insurance, overtime pay, seniority privileges, and work conditions are often crucial issues. Many labour contracts specify in great detail the rights of labour and management to set work conditions—and also provide elaborate procedures for resolving grievances and disputes. This list could go on and on. The final contract that emerges from collective bargaining may well run to many pages of fine print.

With the issues so varied and complex, and with the stakes so high, it is no wonder that both labour and management employ skilled professionals who specialize in preparing for and carrying out these negotiations. The bargaining in these sessions is often heated, with outcomes riding as much on the personalities and skills of the negotiators as on cool-headed logic and economic facts. Negotiations may last well into the night, with each side making threats and seeming to try to wear out the other side. Unions, for their part, generally threaten strikes or work slowdowns. Firms counter that they would rather face a strike than give in, or they may even threaten to close the plant without a strike (called a *lockout*).

The Playing Out of Bilateral Monopoly: NHL Owners Versus the NHL Players' Association

A much publicized example of bilateral monopoly is that of the National Hockey League (NHL). Although there are 30 teams in the league, the NHL owners can act as the single employer of major league hockey players, as they did when they ordered a lockout, suspending play for more than three months in 1994–1995 and, as they did again ten years later, when the entire 2004–2005 season was cancelled. As a monopsony employer, the NHL also faces a monopoly: the National Hockey League Players' Association (NHLPA), which acts as the unique seller of the services of the best hockey players of the world when it negotiates the collective bargaining agreement.

The outcomes of the 1994–1995 and the 2004–2005 labour conflicts were quite different. In 1995, despite the introduction of new rules in the collective agreement that were deemed to be favourable to owners, players managed to get an ever-rising portion of NHL revenues. By contrast, in 2005, an estimated US$400 million has been transferred from the wallets of the players to those of the owners (out of revenues of about US$2.2 billion). Obviously, the bargaining position and bargaining skills of NHL owners were much better in 2004–2005. Many team owners said they were losing less money during the lockout than if their team had played under the previous collective agreement, thus inducing the owners

to take a hard line. As to the players, several of them had not bothered trying to get a contract with some European team in the belief that the lockout would not last very long. Those who did were usually paid much less than in the NHL. The dice were loaded in the owners' favour.

Gary Bettman and Bob Goodenow shaking hands.

SOURCE: ADRIAN WYLD/Canadian Press

Mediation and Arbitration   When the public interest is seriously affected, or when the union and firm reach an impasse, government agencies may well send in a **mediator,** whose job is to try to speed up the negotiation process. As an impartial observer, the mediator sits down with both sides separately to discuss their problems and then tries to persuade each to make concessions. At some stage, when an agreement looks possible, she or he may call the parties back together for another bargaining session in the mediator's presence. Mediators, however, have no power to force a settlement. Their success hinges on their ability to smooth ruffled feathers and to find common ground.

Sometimes in cases in which unions and firms simply cannot agree but neither wants a strike, differences are finally settled by **arbitration**—the appointment of an impartial individual empowered to settle the issues that negotiation could not resolve. This happens often, for example, in wage negotiations in professional sports or for municipal jobs such as police and firefighters. In fact, in some vital sectors in which a strike is deemed too injurious to the public interest, the labour contract or the law may stipulate that there must be *compulsory arbitration* if the two parties cannot agree. However, both labour and management are normally reluctant to accept this procedure.

Mediation takes place during collective bargaining when a neutral individual is assigned the job of persuading the two parties to reach an agreement.

Arbitration occurs during collective bargaining when a neutral individual is appointed with the power to decide the issues and force both parties to accept his or her decisions.

Strikes   Most collective bargaining situations do not lead to strikes. But the right to strike, and to take a strike, remain fundamentally important tools in the bargaining process. Imagine, for example, a firm bargaining with a union that was prohibited from striking. The union's bargaining position would probably be quite weak. On the other hand, a firm that always capitulated rather than suffer a strike would be virtually at the mercy of the union. So strikes—or, more precisely, the possibility of strikes—serve an important economic purpose.

Fortunately, the incidence of strikes is not nearly as common as many people believe. Figure 10 reports the number of person-days not worked because of industrial dispute (strikes and lockouts) per 100,000 for all industries in Canada from 1901 to 2007. This value has varied from year to year and, in the peak years of the mid-1970s, it exceeded 10 million person-days lost. While these figures may appear large, even at its peak year in the mid-1970s it was just slightly over half of a percentage point per year of estimated total working time for all industries in Canada and, since the 1990s, it has been less than one-tenth of 1 percent. The chart also suggests that most periods of industrial dispute over the last century in Canada occurred during periods when inflation was high and labour markets were tight as immediately after World Wars I and II, during the late 1960s, and during much of the 1970s.

| **FIGURE 10** | Work Time Lost in Canada because of Strikes, 1901–2007 |

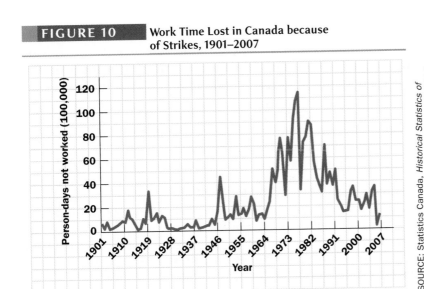

SOURCE: Statistics Canada, *Historical Statistics of Canada,* Series E190-197; CANSIM II, Table 278-0003. Statistics on work stoppage include all strikes and lockouts, whether legal or illegal, which lasted for one-half day or more and amount to 10 or more person-days of time lost. Time lost by workers indirectly affected, such as those laid off because of a work stoppage by other employees, is not included.

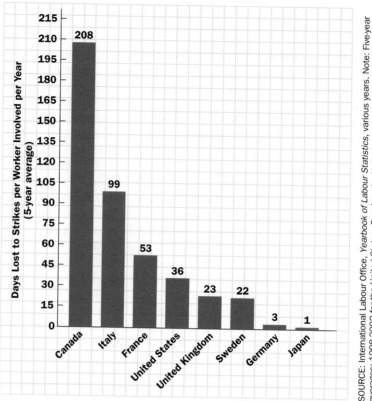

FIGURE 11

Incidence of Strikes in Eight Industrial Countries: Five-Year Averages, 1996–2005

SOURCE: International Labour Office, *Yearbook of Labour Statistics*, various years. Note: Five-year averages: 1998-2002 for the United States, Sweden, the United Kingdom, Germany, and Italy; 1997-2001 for Canada and Japan; 1996-2000 for France.

Despite the headline-grabbing nature of major national strikes, the total amount of work time lost to strikes is really quite small—far less, undoubtedly, than the time lost to illness or to coffee breaks! As an average, over the 1996-2005 period, each Canadian employee went on strike 0.2 day per year. Compared to other major countries, however, Canada has suffered substantially more from labour conflicts during that time period, as can be assessed from Figure 11.

ISSUE REVISITED: *Foreign Competition, Technology, and Canadian Jobs: Are Union Fears Justified?*

Canadian trade unions have actively taken up the issues we discussed at the beginning of this chapter. In the late 1980s and the early 1990s, trade agreements worldwide seemed to threaten jobs of Canadian workers—union jobs in particular. But historical evidence raises questions about whether these union fears were grounded in fact.

Careful analysis shows that there are two sides to the matter, and that overall Canadian living standards are sometimes hurt (but also sometimes improved) by practices such as outsourcing, that is, the hiring of workers in foreign countries by Canadian firms to do work formerly carried out in Canada and, more generally, by policies of increasing trade liberalization. We must first recognize that one effect of low-wage foreign employees would be to hold down Canadian *dollar* (or nominal) wages because of greater job loss domestically (as critics of trade liberalization have rightly pointed out). However, would this entail a fall in real wages?

Defenders of outsourcing and trade liberalization have argued that the availability of the inexpensive products imported from foreign countries could also help to protect or even raise *real* wages at home. Lower product prices of, say, Mexican or Chinese imports, mean that, all other things equal, Canadian wages command more goods per dollar. If cars, televisions, and foods become cheaper because of imports, a given wage can buy larger quantities of these items. Hence, the overall effect on real wages is less certain, since its deflationary impact on money wages may be offset by its accompanying negative effect on prices of consumer goods domestically resulting from lower prices of imported commodities.

Recent studies suggest that when controlling for other factors unrelated to trade liberalization, the overall deflationary effect of trade agreements on real wages was unfounded in Canada, at least for the 1990s. However, the results were not so positive on income distribution, since it was ascertained that the gap between the wages of the more-educated and the less-educated workers was very strongly impacted as a result of greater exposure to international trade.[13] Moreover, with unemployment rates in recent years at a 30-year low, it would be difficult to conclude that the initial job losses from trade liberalization had a permanent negative impact on overall labour market performance.

The second part of the story, related to technological progress, also raises questions. Labour-saving innovation has played a leading role in the economic history of Canada and the Western world. In a previous chapter, we saw how important both inventions and innovations were in pushing upward per-capita income via increases in productivity. In the course of the last four decades since 1961, the productivity of the Canadian labour force grew over twofold. This means that at least one out of every two Canadian workers could have been fired without any loss in measured production. Yet, as is evident from Figure 6 on page 483, current overall rates of unemployment are hovering ever more closely around the level that they were in 1961.

Evidently, technological progress, which has stimulated the demand for products, has not cut the demand for the workers who turn out those products. This is so for a couple of reasons. First, it is true that the introduction of a labour-saving machine, say, a new computer will necessarily lead to a reduction in the demand for labour that churns out the products jointly produced by the labour and the machine. However, one must not forget that the new machines themselves need to be built, as current users and others seek to replace their outdated computers over time. In fact, by making goods and services cheaper and better, technical progress has always stimulated the demand for improved commodities. Increased demand for goods and services, in turn, translates into a greater demand for labour.

Second, rising productivity has historically been accompanied by rising real incomes. To the extent that the rising incomes over time translate into increased consumer spending needed to purchase the greater number of goods that a given labour force can produce, then technological progress could take place without a cut in the overall demand for labour. Thus, in terms of demand for labour, there are always two sides to technical progress.

Still, if these compensating effects have occurred in the past, it cannot just be assumed that they will always happen in the future. For instance, if trade liberalization is not accompanied by a significant decline in the price of imports, say, because of monopolistic conditions at home, then the beneficial effect on real wages would not materialize. In much the same way, if technological progress is not accompanied over time by rising real wages, the compensating effects on the overall demand for labour would not arise and the long-term rate of unemployment would be growing, much as the famous nineteenth-century British economist, David Ricardo surmised almost two centuries ago. An economy's success would thus depend on its ability to avoid these undesirable outcomes.

---

[13] Omar Zakhilwal, "The Impact of International Trade on the Wages of Canadians," *Research Papers Series No. 2001156e*, Statistics Canada, Analytical Studies Branch, January 2001.

SUMMARY

1. In a free market, the wage rate and the level of employment are determined by the interaction of supply and demand. Workers in great demand or short supply command high wages. Similarly, low wages go to workers who are in abundant supply or who have skills that are not in great demand.

2. The demand curve for labour, like the demand curve for any factor of production, is derived from the **marginal revenue product curve**. It slopes downward because of the "law" of diminishing marginal returns.

3. The demand curve for labour can be shifted upward by an increase in education or on-the-job training that raises the workers' marginal physical products or by an increase in demand for those products that raises *product* price and therefore also increases labour's MRP.

4. Labour-saving innovations may either raise or lower workers' wages and available jobs in the short run. Because they are tantamount to increased productivity, in the long run they generally raise the incomes of workers along with those of other members of the community.

5. The supply of labour is determined by free choices made by individuals. The supply curve can be shifted so that more labour is supplied at any given wage level if there are developments such as increased labour force participation, as when women find it more desirable to hold jobs.

6. Because of conflicting **income and substitution effects**, the quantity of labour supplied may rise or fall as a result of an increase in wages. Historical data show that hours of work per week have fallen as wages have risen, suggesting that income effects may be dominant in the long run.

7. Some valuable skills are virtually impossible to duplicate. People who possess such skills will earn **economic rents** as part of their wages.

8. Most skills can be acquired by means of **investment in human capital,** such as education.

9. **Human capital theory** assumes that people make educational decisions in much the same way as businesses make investment decisions, and it tacitly assumes that people learn things in school that increase their productivity in jobs.

10. Other theories of the effects of education on earnings deny that schooling actually raises productivity. For example, one view is that the educational system primarily sorts people according to their abilities.

11. According to the theory of **dual labour markets**, there are two distinct types of labour markets, with very little mobility between them. The primary labour market contains the "good" jobs where wages are high, prospects for advancement are good, and higher education pays off. The secondary labour market contains the "bad" jobs, which are characterized by low wages, little opportunity for promotion, and little return on education.

12. Less than 30 percent of all Canadian workers belong to **unions**, which we can think of as monopoly sellers of labour. Compared with many other industrialized countries, unions in Canada have as members a share of the workforce that exceeds that of the United States but is well below that of the Northern European countries.

13. For the most part, unions probably force wages to be higher and employment to be lower than they would be in a competitive labour market.

14. **Collective bargaining** agreements between labour and management are complex documents covering much more than employment and wage rates.

15. Strikes play an important role in collective bargaining as a way of dividing the fruits of economic activity between big business and big labour. But strikes are not nearly as common as is often supposed.

16. For about three decades Canadians have experienced three noteworthy trends: (a) a moderate decline in union density, (b) a gentle decline, in real wages offset by rising fringe benefits, and (c) an increase in the income gap between well-paid and poorly paid workers.

KEY TERMS

Marginal revenue product of labour (MRP$_L$)   472

Investment in human capital   472

Substitution effect   477

Income effect   477

Backward–bending supply curve   477

Economic rent   481

Human capital theory   481

Theory of dual labour markets   482

Minimum wage law   484

Labour union   485

Union density   485

Outsourcing   487

Contracting–out   487

Monopsony   489

Bilateral monopoly   489

Collective bargaining   490

Mediation   491

Arbitration   491

TEST YOURSELF

1. The following table shows the number of pizzas that can be produced by a large pizza parlour employing various numbers of pizza chefs.

Number of Chefs	Number of Pizzas per Day
1	40
2	64
3	82
4	92
5	100
6	92

   a. Find the marginal physical product schedule of the pizza chefs.

   b. Assuming a price of $9 per pizza, find the marginal revenue product schedule.

   c. If chefs are paid $100 per day, how many chefs will this pizza parlour employ? How would your answer change if chefs' wages rose to $125 per day?

   d. Suppose the price of pizza increases from $9 to $12. Show what happens to the derived demand curve for chefs.

2. Discuss the concept of the financial rate of return on a postsecondary education. If this return is less than the return on a bank account, does that mean you should quit school? Why might you want to stay in school anyway? Are there circumstances under which it might be rational not to go to school, even when the financial returns for a postsecondary education are very high?

3. In which of the following industries is wage determination most plausibly explained by the model of perfect competition? The model of pure monopoly? The model of bilateral monopoly?

   a. Odd-job repairs in private homes

   b. Manufacture of low-priced clothing for children

   c. Auto manufacturing

4. Can you think of some types of workers whose marginal products probably were raised by computerization? Are there any whose marginal products were probably reduced? Can you characterize the difference between the two types of jobs in general terms?

DISCUSSION QUESTIONS

1. Colleges and universities are known to pay rather low wages for student labour. Can this trend be explained by the operation of supply and demand in the local labour markets? Is the concept of monopsony of any use? How might things differ if students formed a union?

2. College and university teaching staff are highly skilled (or at least highly educated!) labourers, yet their wages are not very high. Is this a refutation of the marginal productivity theory?

3. It seems to be a well-established fact that workers with more years of education typically receive higher wages. What are some possible reasons for this trend?

4. Approximately what fraction of the Canadian labour force belongs to unions? (Try asking this question of a person who has never studied economics.) Why do you think this fraction is so low?

5. What are some reasonable goals for a union? Use the tools of supply and demand to explain how a union might pursue its goals, whatever they are. Consider a union that has been in the news recently. What was it trying to accomplish?

6. "Strikes are simply intolerable and should be outlawed." Comment on this statement.

7. In a bitter strike battle in the United States between Eastern Airlines and several of its unions, it was clear from the beginning that the airline was in serious financial trouble. The airline was, indeed, eventually forced to close down at the cost of many jobs. Discuss what might nevertheless have led the unions to hold out so tenaciously.

8. European labour unions have traditionally had a strong socialistic orientation. How would you guess this tradition is likely to be affected by the movement of countries in Eastern Europe toward market economies?

9. What, if anything, do you think is the effect of long-term unemployment on crime rates? What about short-term unemployment?

10. Since the late 1970s, GDP per capita (that is, the average real income per person) in Canada has risen somewhat. Yet real wages have failed to rise. What do you think may explain this phenomenon?

GLOSSARY

Ability-to-pay principle The ability-to-pay principle of taxation refers to the idea that people with greater ability to pay taxes should pay higher taxes. (p. 429)

Absolute advantage One country is said to have an absolute advantage over another in the production of a particular good if it can produce that good using smaller quantities of resources than can the other country. (p. 22-7)

Absolute concept of poverty Falling short of a certain minimum standard of living. (p. 21-5)

Abstraction Abstraction means ignoring many details so as to focus on the most important elements of a problem. (p. 8)

Affirmative action Affirmative action refers to active efforts to locate and hire members of underrepresented groups. (p. 21-19)

Agents Agents are people hired to run a complex enterprise on behalf of the principals, those whose benefit the enterprise is supposed to serve. (p. 354)

Allocation of resources Allocation of resources refers to the society's decisions on how to divide up its scarce input resources among the different outputs produced in the economy and among the different firms or other organizations that produce those outputs. (p. 53)

Anti-combines policy The anti-combines policy refers to programs and laws that preclude the deliberate creation of a monopoly and prevent powerful firms from engaging in related anticompetitive acts. (p. 298)

Applied research Applied research is research whose goal is to invent or improve particular products or processes, often for profit. Note, however, that the military and government health-related agencies provide examples of not-for-profit applied research. (p. 385)

Arbitration Arbitration occurs during collective bargaining when a neutral individual is appointed with the power to decide the issues and force both parties to accept his or her decisions. (p. 491)

Average cost (AC) Average cost is total cost (TC) divided by output. (p. 153)

Average cost pricing Average cost pricing is a specific cost-plus pricing procedure whereby a normal average cost, which includes fixed costs, is assessed on the basis of normal output, to which a net costing margin is added. (p. 266)

Average physical product (APP) The average physical product (APP) is the total physical product (TPP) divided by the quantity of input. Thus, APP = TPP/X where X = the quantity of input. (p. 142)

Average revenue (AR) The average revenue (AR) is total revenue (TR) divided by quantity. (p. 172)

Average tax rate The average tax rate is the ratio of taxes to income. (p. 419)

Backward-bending supply curve A supply curve of labour is backward-bending when a rise in an initially low wage leads to a rise in quantity of labour supplied, but a rise in a wage that was already high reduces the amount supplied. (p. 477)

Barriers to entry Barriers to entry are attributes of a market that make it more difficult or expensive for a new firm to open for business than it was for the firms already present in that market. (p. 233)

Basic research Basic research refers to research that seeks to provide scientific knowledge and general principles rather than coming up with any specific marketable inventions. (p. 385)

Beneficial or detrimental externality An activity is said to generate a beneficial or detrimental externality if that activity causes incidental benefits or damages to others not directly involved in the activity and no corresponding compensation is provided to or paid by those who generate the externality. (p. 342)

Benefits principle of taxation The benefits principle of taxation holds that people who derive benefits from a service should pay the taxes that finance it. (p. 430)

Bilateral monopoly A bilateral monopoly is a market situation in which there is both a monopoly on the selling side and a monopsony on the buying side. (p. 489)

Bond A bond is simply an IOU sold by a corporation that promises to pay the holder of the bond a fixed sum of money at the specified *maturity* date and some other fixed amount of money (the *coupon* or *interest payment*) every year up to the date of maturity. (p. 192)

Budget line, household The budget line for a household graphically represents all possible combinations of two commodities that it can purchase, given the prices of the commodities and some fixed amount of money at its disposal. (p. 107)

Budget line, firm A firm's budget line is the locus of all points representing every input combination of inputs that the producer can afford to buy with a given amount of money and given input prices. (p. 162)

Bundling Bundling refers to a pricing arrangement under which the supplier offers substantial discounts to customers if they buy several of the firm's products, so that the price of the bundle of products is less than the sum of the prices of the products if they were bought separately. (p. 306)

Burden of a tax The burden of a tax to an individual is the amount one would have to be given to be just as well off with the tax as without it. (p. 430)

Capital A nation's capital is its available supply of plant, equipment, and software. It is the result of past decisions to make *investments* in these items. (p. 449)

Capital gain A capital gain is the profit made from the sale of an asset at a higher price than was paid for it. (p. 421)

Capitalism Capitalism is an economic system in which most of the production process is controlled by private firms operating in markets. The investors in these firms (called "capitalists") own the firms. (p. 368)

Cartel A cartel is a group of sellers of a product who have joined together to control its production, sale, and price in the hope of obtaining the advantages of monopoly. (p. 241)

Closed economy A closed economy is one that does not trade with other nations in either goods or assets. (p. 29)

Collective bargaining Collective bargaining is the process of negotiation of wages and working conditions between a union and the firms in the industry. (p. 491)

Common stock A common stock (also called a share) of a corporation is a piece of paper that gives the holder of the stock a share of the ownership of the company. (p. 191)

Comparative advantage One country is said to have a comparative advantage over another in the production of a particular good *relative to other goods* if it produces that good less inefficiently as compared with the other country. (p. 55, 22-7)

Complements Two goods are called complements if an increase in the quantity consumed of one increases the quantity demanded of the other, all other things remaining constant. (p. 128)

Concentration of an industry Concentration of an industry measures the share of the total sales or assets of the industry in the hands of its largest firms. (p. 299)

Concentration ratio A concentration ratio is the percentage of an industry's output produced by its four largest firms. It is intended to measure the degree to which the industry is dominated by large firms. (p. 299)

Consumer's surplus Consumer's surplus is the difference between the value to the consumer of the quantity of Commodity X purchased and the amount that the market requires the consumer to pay for that quantity of *X*. (pp. 101, 327)

Contracting-out Contracting-out, often associated with the phenomenon of public sector downsizing or privatization, is a process whereby an organization hires a private provider of a service that was previously done in-house. (p. 487)

Corporation A corporation is a firm that has the legal status of a fictional individual. This fictional individual is owned by a number of persons, called its *shareholders*, and is run by a set of elected officers and a board of directors, whose chairman is often also in a powerful position. (p. 190)

Correlated Two variables are said to be correlated if they tend to go up or down together. Correlation need not imply causation. (p. 10)

Cost disease of the personal services The cost disease of the personal services is the tendency of the costs and prices of these services to rise persistently faster than those of the average output in the economy. (p. 358)

Cost-plus pricing Cost-plus pricing procedures are an alternative to marginal cost pricing, whereby firms set prices by adding an arbitrary costing margin to some measure of unit costs. (p. 264)

Credible threat A credible threat is a threat that does not harm the threatener if it is carried out. (p. 277)

Cross elasticity of demand The cross elasticity of demand for product X to a change in the price of another product, Y, is the ratio of the percentage change in quantity demanded of X to the percentage change in the price of Y that brings about the change in quantity demanded. (p. 128)

Cross licensing Cross licensing of patents occurs when each of two firms agrees to let the other use some specified set of its patents, either at a price specified in their agreement or in return for access to the other firm's patents. (p. 378)

Cross-subsidization Cross-subsidization means selling one product of the firm at a loss, which is balanced by higher profits on another of the firm's products. (p. 289)

Deadweight loss The deadweight loss is the loss in economic surplus (consumer's surplus plus producer's surplus) that arises from conditions diverging from those of unhampered perfect competition. (p. 330)

Demand curve A demand curve is a graphical depiction of a demand schedule. It shows how the quantity demanded of some product will change as the price of that product changes during a specified period of time, holding all other determinants of quantity demanded constant. (p. 63)

Demand schedule A demand schedule is a table showing how the quantity demanded of some product during a specified period of time changes as the price of that product changes, holding all other determinants of quantity demanded constant. (p. 63)

Demogrant A demogrant is a lump-sum transfer (or grant) to an individual as a member of a specific demographic group, regardless of one's income or work effort. (p. 21-15)

Depletable A commodity is depletable if it is used up when someone consumes it. (p. 348)

Derived demand The derived demand for an input is the demand for the input by producers as determined by the demand for the final product that the input is used to produce. (p. 448)

Direct controls Direct controls are government rules that tell organizations or individuals what processes or raw materials they may use or what products they are permitted to supply or purchase. (p. 400)

Direct taxes Direct taxes are taxes imposed on the individual who is meant to bear the burden of the tax. (p. 419)

Discounting, or computing the present value The process that has been invented for making the magnitudes of payments at different dates comparable to one another is called *discounting*, or *computing the present value*. (p. 413)

Division of labour Division of labour means breaking up a task into a number of smaller, more *specialized* tasks so that each worker can become more adept at a particular job. (p. 54)

Dominant strategy A dominant strategy for one of the competitors in a game is a strategy that will yield a higher payoff than any of the other strategies that are possible for her, no matter what choice of strategy is made by her competitors. (p. 273)

Dumping Dumping means selling goods in a foreign market at lower prices than those charged in the home market. (p. 22-20)

Economic discrimination Economic discrimination occurs when equivalent factors of production receive different payments for equal contributions to output. (p. 21-11)

Economic model An economic model is a simplified, small-scale version of some aspect of the economy. Economic models are often expressed in equations, by graphs, or in words. (p. 12)

Economic profit Economic profit equals net earnings, in the accountant's sense, minus the *opportunity costs* of capital and of any other inputs supplied by the firm's owners. (pp. 171, 223, 462)

Economic rent Economic rent is any portion of the payment to labour or any other input that does not lead to an increase in the amount of labour supplied. (pp. 450, 481)

Economics Economics is a method of analyzing individual and social behaviour, especially as it relates to market phenomena. (p. 4)

Economies of scale Economies of scale are savings that are obtained through increases in quantities produced. Scale economies occur when an *X* percent increase in input use raises output by *more than X* percent, so that the more the firm produces, the lower its per-unit costs become. (pp. 154, 286)

Economies of scope Economies of scope are savings that are obtained through simultaneous production of many different products. They occur if a firm that produces many commodities can supply each good more cheaply than a firm that produces fewer commodities. (p. 289)

Efficiency A set of outputs is said to be produced efficiently if, given current technological knowledge, there is no way one can produce larger amounts of any output without using larger input amounts or giving up some quantity of another output. (p. 53)

Efficient allocation of resources An efficient allocation of resources is one that takes advantage of every opportunity to make some individuals better off in their own estimation while not worsening the lot of anyone else. (p. 315)

Elastic demand curve A demand curve is elastic when a given percentage price change leads to a larger percentage change in quantity demanded. (p. 122)

Emissions permits Emissions permits are licences issued by government specifying the maximum amount the licence holder is allowed to emit. The licences are restricted to permit a limited amount of emission in total. Often, they must be purchased from the government or on a special market. (p. 404)

Entrepreneur An entrepreneur is an individual who organizes a new business firm, particularly a firm that offers new products or new productive technology. (p. 371)

Entrepreneurship Entrepreneurship is the act of starting new firms, introducing new products and technological innovations, and, in general, taking the risks that are necessary to seek out business opportunities. (p. 446)

Equilibrium An equilibrium is a situation in which there are no inherent forces that produce change. Changes away from an equilibrium position will occur only as a result of "outside events" that disturb the status quo. (p. 71)

Excess burden The excess burden of a tax to an individual is the amount by which the burden of the tax exceeds the tax that is paid. (p. 431)

Excludable A commodity is excludable if someone who does not pay for it can be kept from enjoying it. (p. 348)

Expansion path The expansion path is the locus of the firm's cost-minimizing input combinations for all relevant output levels. (p. 163)

Export subsidy An export subsidy is a payment by the government to exporters to permit them to reduce the selling prices of their goods so they can compete more effectively in foreign markets. (p. 22-14)

External diseconomies External diseconomies are increases in the costs of an individual firm that are due to changes in the quantities being produced overall in the industry. Rising demand for high-rise apartments that leads to an increase in the price of steel, thus leading to an increase in the production cost of apartments, is an instance of external diseconomies that is unrelated to diminishing returns. (p. 270)

External economies External economies are decreases in the costs of an individual firm due to changes in the quantities being produced overall in the industry. (p 270)

Externality An activity is said to generate a **beneficial** or **detrimental externality** if that activity causes incidental benefits or damages to others not directly involved in the activity, and no corresponding compensation is provided to or paid by those who generate the externality. (pp. 342, 367, 390)

45° line Rays through the origin with a slope of 1 are called 45° lines because they form an angle of 45° with the horizontal axis. A 45° line marks off points where the variables measured on each axis have equal values. (p. 22)

Factors of production Inputs or factors of production are the labour, machinery, buildings, and natural resources used to make outputs. (pp. 26, 445)

Fiscal federalism Fiscal federalism refers to the system of grants from one level of government to the next. (p. 422)

Fixed cost A fixed cost is the cost of an input whose quantity does not rise when output goes up, one that the firm requires to produce any output at all. The total cost of such indivisible inputs does not change when the output changes. Any other cost of the firm's operation is called a *variable cost*. (p. 142)

Gross domestic product (GDP) Gross domestic product (GDP) is the sum of the money values of all final goods and services produced in the domestic economy and sold on organized markets during a specified period of time, usually a year. (pp. 28, 370)

Guaranteed annual income (GAI) A government-funded unconditional annual income floor below which no family or individual can fall. (p. 21-3)

Herfindahl Index (HI) The Herfindahl Index (HI) is an alternative and widely used measure of the degree of concentration of an industry. It is calculated, in essence, by adding together the squares of the market shares of the firms in the industry, although the smallest firms may be left out of the calculation because their small market share numbers have a negligible effect on the result. (p. 300)

High-tech (high-technology) A high-tech (high-technology) firm or industry is one whose products, equipment, and production methods utilize highly advanced technology that is constantly modified and improved. Examples are the aerospace, scientific instruments, computer, communications, and pharmaceutical industries. (p. 376)

Horizontal equity Horizontal equity is the notion that equally situated individuals should be taxed equally. (p. 429)

Human capital theory Human capital theory focuses on the expenditures that have been made to increase the productive capacity of workers via education or other means. It is analogous to investment in better machines as a way to increase their productivity. (p. 481)

Incidence of a tax The incidence of a tax is an allocation of the burden of the tax to specific individuals or groups. (p. 432)

Income effect The income effect of a rise in wages is the resulting rise of workers' purchasing power that enables them to afford more leisure. (p. 477)

Income elasticity of demand Income elasticity of demand is the ratio of the percentage change in quantity demanded to the percentage change in income. (p. 127)

Income trusts Income trusts are legal business entities that pay no tax on distributed dividends. (p. 190)

Increasing returns to scale Production is said to involve economies of scale, also referred to as *increasing returns to scale*, if, when all input quantities are increased by X percent, the quantity of output rises by more than X percent. (p. 154)

Index fund An index fund is a mutual fund that chooses a particular stock price index and then buys the stocks (or most of the stocks) that are included in the index. The value of an investment in an index fund depends on what happens to the prices of all stocks in that index. (p. 196)

Indifference curve An indifference curve is a line connecting all combinations of the commodities that are equally desirable to the consumer. (p. 109)

Indirect taxes Indirect taxes are taxes levied on specific economic activities. (p. 419)

Industrial Revolution The Industrial Revolution is the stream of new technology and the resulting growth of output that began in England toward the end of the eighteenth century. (p. 368)

Inelastic demand curve A demand curve is inelastic when a given percentage price change leads to a smaller percentage change in quantity demanded. (p. 122)

Inferior good An inferior good is a commodity whose quantity demanded falls when the purchaser's real income rises, all other things remaining equal. It is a good whose income elasticity is negative. (pp. 103, 128)

Inflation Inflation refers to a sustained increase in the general price level. Inflation occurs when prices in an economy rise rapidly. The rate of inflation is calculated by averaging the percentage growth rate of the prices of a selected sample of commodities. (p. 192)

Innovation Innovation is the process that begins with invention and includes im-

provement to prepare the invention for practical use and marketing of the invention or its products. (pp. 371, 462)

Input–output analysis Input–output analysis is a mathematical procedure that takes account of the interdependence among the economy's industries and determines the amount of output each industry must provide as inputs to the other industries in the economy. (p. 323)

Inputs Inputs or factors of production are the labour, machinery, buildings, and natural resources used to make outputs. (pp. 26, 48)

Interest Interest is the payment for the use of funds employed in the production of capital; it is measured as the percent per year of the value of the funds tied up in the capital. (p. 450)

Interest rate The interest rate is the amount that borrowers currently pay to lenders per dollar of the money borrowed—it is the current market price of a loan. (p. 192)

Invention Invention is the act of discovering new products or new ways of making products. (pp. 370, 462)

Investment Investment is the *flow* of resources into the production of new capital. It is the labour, steel, and other inputs devoted to the *construction* of factories, warehouses, railroads, and other pieces of capital during some period of time. (p. 449)

Investment in human capital Investment in human capital is any expenditure on an individual that increases that person's future earning power or productivity. (p. 472)

Invisible hand The invisible hand is a phrase used by Adam Smith to describe how, by pursuing their own self-interests, people in a market system are "led by an invisible hand" to promote the well-being of the community. (p. 62)

Isoquants Production indifference curves are also called isoquants. When these isoquants arise from fixed-coefficent techniques, they are called input-output isoquants or Leontief isoquants. (pp. 161, 165)

Kinked demand curve A kinked demand curve is a demand curve that changes its slope abruptly at some level of output. (p. 271)

Labour union A labour union comprises workers who constitute a certified bargaining unit that negotiates with employers on both financial and normative workplace matters in accordance with Canadian labour relations legislation enacted primarily at the provincial level. (p. 485)

Laissez faire Laissez faire refers to a situation in which there is minimal government interference with the workings of the market system. The term implies that people should be left alone in carrying out their economic affairs. (p. 320)

"Law" of demand The "law" of demand states that a lower price generally increases the amount of a commodity that people in a market are willing to buy. Therefore, for most goods, market demand curves have negative slopes. (p. 104)

Law of supply and demand The law of supply and demand states that in a free market the forces of supply and demand generally push the price toward the level at which quantity supplied and quantity demanded are equal. (p. 72)

Limited liability Limited liability is a legal obligation of a firm's owners to pay back company debts only with the money they have already invested in the firm. (p. 191)

Long run The long run is a period of time long enough for all of the firm's current commitments to come to an end. (p. 141)

Marginal analysis Marginal analysis is a method for calculating optimal choices—the choices that best promote the decision maker's objective. It works by testing whether, and by how much, a small change in a decision will move things toward or away from the goal. (p. 96)

Marginal cost (MC) Marginal cost is the addition to total cost (TC) resulting from the addition of one unit of output. (p. 152)

Marginal land Marginal land is land that is just on the borderline of being used—that is, any land the use of which would be unprofitable if the farmer had to pay even a penny of rent. (p. 455)

Marginal physical product (MPP) The marginal physical product (MPP) of an input is the increase in total output that results from a one-unit increase in the input quantity, holding the amounts of all other inputs constant. (pp. 143, 447)

Marginal private benefit (MPB) The marginal private benefit (MPB) is the share of an activity's marginal benefit that is received by the persons who carry out the activity. (p. 344)

Marginal private cost (MPC) The marginal private cost (MPC) is the share of an activity's marginal cost that is paid for by the persons who carry out the activity. (p. 343)

Marginal profit Marginal profit is the addition to total profit resulting from one more unit of output. (p. 175)

Marginal revenue (MR) Marginal revenue (MR) is the addition to total revenue resulting from the addition of one unit to total output. Geometrically, marginal revenue is the slope of the total revenue curve at the pertinent output quantity. Its formula is $MR_1 = TR_1 - TR_0$, and so on. (p. 172)

Marginal revenue product (MRP) The marginal revenue product (MRP) of an input is the money value of the additional sales that a firm obtains by selling the marginal physical product of that input. (pp. 145, 447)

Marginal revenue product of labour (MRP$_L$) The marginal revenue product of labour (MRP$_L$) is the increase in the employer's total revenue that results when it hires an additional unit of labour. (p. 472)

Marginal social benefit (MSB) The marginal social benefit (MSB) of an activity is the sum of its marginal private benefit (MPB) plus its incidental benefits (positive or negative) that are received by others, and for which those others do not pay. (p. 344)

Marginal social cost (MSC) The marginal social cost (MSC) of an activity is the sum of its marginal private cost (MPC) plus its incidental costs (positive or negative) that are borne by others who receive no compensation for the resulting damage to their well-being. (p. 343)

Marginal tax rate The marginal tax rate is the fraction of each *additional* dollar of income that is paid in taxes. (p. 419)

Marginal utility The marginal utility of a commodity to a consumer (measured in money terms) is the maximum amount of money that she or he is willing to pay for *one more unit* of that commodity. (p. 94)

Market A market comprises a set of sellers and buyers whose activities affect the price at which a particular commodity is sold. (p. 209)

Market demand curve A market demand curve shows how the total quantity of some product demanded by *all* consumers in the market during a specified period of time changes as the price of that product changes, holding all other things constant. (p. 103)

Market system A market system is a form of economic organization in which resource allocation decisions are left to individual producers and consumers acting in their own best interests without central direction. (p. 57)

Markup pricing Markup pricing is a specific cost-plus pricing procedure whereby the unit cost measure is the average variable cost, to which a gross costing margin is added. (p. 264)

Maximin criterion The maximin criterion requires you to select the strategy that yields the maximum payoff on the assumption that your opponent will do as much damage to you as he or she can. (p. 275)

Mediation Mediation takes place during collective bargaining when a neutral individual is assigned the job of persuading the two parties to reach an agreement. (p. 491)

Mercantilism Mercantilism is a doctrine that holds that exports are good for a country, whereas imports are harmful. (p. 22-11)

Minimum wage law A minimum wage law imposes a floor on wages and prohibits employers from paying their workers less than that amount. (p. 484)

Misallocated resources Resources are misallocated if it is possible to change the way they are used or the combination of goods and services they produce and thereby make consumers better off. (p. 342)

Mixed economy A mixed economy is one with some public influence over the workings of free markets. There may also be some public ownership mixed in with private property. (p. 42)

Monopolistic competition Monopolistic competition refers to a market in which products are heterogeneous but which is otherwise the same as a market that is perfectly competitive. (p. 253)

Monopoly power Monopoly power (or market power) is the ability of a business firm to earn high profits by raising the prices of its products above competitive levels and to keep those prices high for a substantial amount of time. (p. 286)

Monopoly profits Monopoly profits are any excess of the profits earned persistently by a monopoly firm over and above those that would be earned if the industry were perfectly competitive. (p. 238)

Monopsony A monopsony is a market situation in which there is only one buyer. (p. 489)

Moral hazard Moral hazard refers to the tendency of insurance to discourage policyholders from protecting themselves from risk. (pp. 353)

Mutual fund A mutual fund, in which individual investors can buy shares, is a private investment firm that holds a portfolio of securities. Investors can choose among a large variety of mutual funds, such as stock funds, bond funds, and so forth. (p. 196)

Nash equilibrium A Nash equilibrium results when each player adopts the strategy that gives her the highest possible payoff if her rival sticks to the strategy he has chosen. (p. 275)

Natural monopoly A natural monopoly is an industry in which advantages of large-scale production make it possible for a single firm to produce the entire output of the market at lower average cost than a number of firms, each producing a smaller quantity. (p. 234)

Negative income tax (NIT) A taxation system in which income subsidies are given to persons or families that are below the poverty line. (p. 21-15)

Normal good A normal good is the one whose income elasticity is positive. (p. 128)

Oligopoly An oligopoly is a market dominated by a few sellers, at least several of which are large enough relative to the total market to be able to influence the market price. (p. 256)

Open economy An open economy is one that trades with other nations in goods and services, and perhaps also trades in financial assets. (p. 29)

Opportunity cost The opportunity cost of some decision is the value of the next best alternative that must be given up because of that decision (for example, working instead of going to school). (p. 47)

Optimal decision An optimal decision is one that best serves the objectives of the decision maker, whatever those objectives may be. It is selected by explicit or implicit comparison with the possible alternative choices. The term *optimal* connotes neither approval nor disapproval of the objective itself. (pp. 48, 132, 168)

Origin (of a graph) The "0" point in the lower-left corner of a graph where the axes meet is called the *origin*. Both variables are equal to zero at the origin. (p. 19)

Outputs The outputs of a firm or an economy are the goods and services it produces. (pp. 26, 48)

Outsourcing Outsourcing is the hiring of workers in foreign counties by Canadian firms to do work formerly carried out in Canada (p. 487)

Paradox A paradox is a contradiction between two principles that operate at different levels; it often involves an outcome that is contrary to intuition. (p. 7)

Patent A patent is a privilege granted to an inventor, whether an individual or a firm, that for a specified period of time prohibits anyone else from producing or using that invention without the permission of the holder of the patent. (p. 233)

Payoff matrix A payoff matrix shows how much each of two competitors (players) can expect to earn, depending on the strategic choices each of them makes. (p. 273)

Per-capita income Per-capita income in an economy is the average income of all people in that economy. (p. 368)

Perfect competition Perfect competition occurs in an industry when that industry is made up of many small firms producing homogeneous products, when there is no impediment to the entry or exit of firms, and when full information is available. (p. 212)

Perfectly contestable market A market is perfectly contestable if entry and exit are costless and unimpeded. (p. 280)

Plowback Plowback (or retained earnings) is the portion of a corporation's profits that management decides to keep and reinvest in the firm's operations rather than paying out as dividends to shareholders. (p. 193)

Pollution charges Pollution charges (taxes on emissions) are taxes that polluters are required to pay. The amount they pay depends on what they emit and in what quantities. (p. 401)

Portfolio diversification Portfolio diversification means inclusion of a number and variety of stocks, bonds, and other such items in an individual's portfolio. If the individual owns airline stocks, for example, diversification requires the purchase of a stock or bond in a very different industry, such as breakfast cereal production. (p. 195)

***Post hoc, ergo propter hoc* fallacy** This is the error of assuming that if some event occurred before another, then the first one must have caused the second. (p. 11)

Poverty line The poverty line is an amount of income below which a family is considered "poor." (p. 21-4)

Predatory pricing Predatory pricing is pricing that threatens to keep a competitor out of the market. It is a price that is so low that it will be profitable for the firm that adopts it only if a rival is driven from the market. (p. 305)

Price cap A price cap is a ceiling above which regulators do not permit prices to rise. The cap is designed to provide an efficiency incentive to the firm by allowing it to keep part of any savings in costs it can achieve. (p. 292)

Price ceiling A price ceiling is a maximum that the price charged for a commodity cannot legally exceed. (p. 78)

Price discrimination Price discrimination is the sale of a given product at different prices to different customers of the firm, when there are no differences in the costs of supplying these customers. Prices are also discriminatory if it costs more to supply one customer than another, but they are charged the same price. (p. 242)

(Price) elasticity of demand The (price) elasticity of demand is the ratio of the *percentage* change in quantity demanded to the *percentage* change in price that brings about the change in quantity demanded. (p. 119)

Price floor A price floor is a legal minimum below which the price charged for a commodity is not permitted to fall. (p. 80)

Price leadership Under price leadership, one firm sets the price for the industry and the others follow. (p. 259)

Price taker Under perfect competition, the firm is a price taker. It has no choice but to accept the price that has been determined in the market. (p. 213)

Price war In a price war, each competing firm is determined to sell at a price that is lower than the prices of its rivals, usually regardless of whether that price covers the pertinent cost. Typically, in such a price war, Firm A cuts its price below Firm B's price; B retaliates by undercutting A; and so on and on until some of the competitor firms surrender and let themselves be undersold. (p. 260)

Principals Agents are people hired to run a complex enterprise on behalf of the principals, those whose benefit the enterprise is supposed to serve. (p. 354)

Principle of diminishing marginal returns Often called the *principle of diminishing returns*, this principle asserts that returns to a single input, all others being given, eventually diminish as more of the input is used. (p. 144)

Principle of diminishing marginal utility The principle of diminishing marginal utility asserts that additional units of a commodity are worth less and less to a consumer in money terms. As the individual's consumption increases, the marginal utility of each additional unit declines. (p. 95)

Principle of increasing costs The principle of increasing costs states that as the production of a good expands, the opportunity cost of producing another unit generally increases. (p. 50)

Private good A private good is a commodity characterized by both depletability and excludability. (p. 348)

Process innovation A process innovation is an innovation that changes the way in which a commodity is produced. (p. 383)

Producer's quota A producer's quota is the maximum amount that a producer is allowed to produce or the maximum area that a farmer is allowed to farm. (p. 81)

Producer's surplus The producer's surplus from a sale is the difference between the market price of the item sold and the lowest price at which the supplier would be willing to provide the item. (p. 327)

Product innovation A product innovation is the introduction of a good or service that is entirely new or involves major modifications of earlier products. (p. 383)

Production indifference curve A production indifference curve (sometimes called an *isoquant*) is a curve showing all the different quantities of two inputs that are just sufficient to produce a given quantity of output. (p. 161)

Production indifference map A production indifference map is a graph whose axes show the quantities of two inputs that are used to produce some output. A curve in the graph corresponds to some given quantity of that output, and the different points on that curve show the different quantities of the two inputs that are just enough to produce the given output. (p. 23)

Production possibilities frontier The production possibilities frontier is a curve that shows the maximum quantities of outputs it is possible to produce with the available resource quantities and the current state of technological knowledge. (pp. 49, 341)

Productivity Productivity is the amount of output produced by a unit of input. (p. 368)

Progressive tax A progressive tax is one in which the average tax rate paid by an individual rises as income rises. (pp. 42, 419)

Proportional tax A proportional tax is one in which the average tax rate is the same at all income levels. (p. 419)

Public good A public good is a commodity or service whose benefits are *not depleted* by an additional user and from which it is generally difficult or *impossible to exclude* people, even if the people are unwilling to pay for the benefits. (p. 348)

Pure competition Pure competition is a market structure that has all of the features of perfect competition except for perfect information. (p. 228)

Pure monopoly A pure monopoly is an industry in which there is only one supplier of a product for which there are no close substitutes and in which it is very difficult or impossible for another firm to coexist. (p. 232)

Quantity demanded The quantity demanded is the number of units of a good that consumers are willing and can afford to buy over a specified period of time. (p. 63)

Quantity supplied The quantity supplied is the number of units that sellers want to sell over a specified period of time. (p. 67)

Quota A quota specifies the maximum amount of a good that is permitted into the country from abroad per unit of time. (p. 22-14)

Random walk The time path of a variable such as the price of a stock is said to constitute a random walk if its magnitude in one period (say, May 2, 2009) is equal to its value in the preceding period (May 1, 2009) plus a completely random number. That is: Price on May 2, 2009 = Price on May 1, 2009 + Random number, where the random number (positive or negative) can be obtained by a roll of dice or some such procedure. (p. 205)

Ratchet A ratchet is an arrangement that permits some economic variable, such as investment or advertising, to increase, but prevents that variable from subsequently decreasing. (p. 382)

Ray through the origin (or ray) Lines whose Y-intercept is zero have so many special uses in economics and other disciplines that they have been given a special name: a ray through the origin, or a ray. (p. 22)

Recession A recession is a period of time during which the total output of the economy declines. (p. 31)

Regressive tax A regressive tax is one in which the average tax rate falls as income rises. (p. 419)

Regulation Regulation of industry is a process established by law that restricts or controls some specified decisions made by the affected firms; it is designed to protect the public from exploitation by firms with monopoly power. Regulation is usually carried out by a special government agency assigned the task of administering and interpreting the law. That agency also acts as a court in enforcing the regulatory laws. (p. 287)

Relative concept of poverty Earning significantly less than an average income. (p. 21-5)

Rent seeking Rent seeking refers to unproductive activity in the pursuit of economic profit—in other words, profit in excess of competitive earnings. (p. 353)

Repeated game A repeated game is one that is played over again a number of times. (p. 277)

Research and development (R&D) Research and development (R&D) is the activity of firms, universities, and government agencies that seeks to invent new products and processes and to improve those inventions so that they are ready for the market or other users. (p. 373)

Resource misallocation Resources are misallocated if it is possible to change the way they are used or the combination of goods and services they produce and thereby make consumers better off. (p. 342)

Resources Resources are the instruments provided by nature or by people that are used to create goods and services. Natural resources include minerals, soil, water, and air. Labour is a scarce resource because of time limitations and because skilled workers are rare. Factories and machines are man-made resources. These resources are often referred to as *land*, *labour*, and *capital*. They are also called *inputs* or *factors of production*. (p. 46)

Retained earnings Plowback (or retained earnings) is the portion of a corporation's profits that management decides to keep and reinvest in the firm's operations rather than paying out as dividends to shareholders. (p. 193)

Sales maximization A firm's objective is said to be sales maximization if it seeks to adopt prices and output quantities that make its total revenue (its "sales"), rather than its profits, as large as possible. (p. 261)

Shift in a demand curve A shift in a demand curve occurs when any relevant variable other than price changes. If consumers want to buy *more* at any and all given prices than they wanted previously, the demand curve shifts to the right (or outward). If they desire *less* at any given price, the demand curve shifts to the left (or inward). (p. 64)

Short run The short run is a period of time during which some of the firm's cost commitments will not have ended. (p. 141)

Shortage A shortage is an excess of quantity demanded over quantity supplied. When there is a shortage, buyers cannot purchase the quantities they desire at the current price. (p. 71)

Slope of a budget line The slope of a budget line is the amount of one commodity that the market requires an individual to give up to obtain one additional unit of another commodity without any change in the amount of money spent. (p. 110)

Slope of a curved line The slope of a curved line at a particular point is defined as the slope of the straight line that is tangent to the curve at that point. (p. 20)

Slope of an indifference curve The slope of an indifference curve, referred to as the marginal rate of substitution (MRS) between the commodities, represents the maximum amount of one commodity that the consumer is willing to give up in exchange for one more unit of another commodity. (p. 110)

Slope of a straight line The slope of a straight line is the ratio of the vertical change to the corresponding horizontal change as we move to the right along the line or, as it is often said, the ratio of the "rise" over the "run." (p. 20)

Specialization Specialization means that a country devotes its energies and resources to only a small proportion of the world's productive activities. (p. 22-5)

Speculation Individuals who engage in speculation deliberately invest in risky assets, hoping to obtain profits from future changes in the prices of these assets. (p. 203)

Statistical discrimination Statistical discrimination is said to occur when the productivity of a particular worker is estimated to be low just because that worker belongs to a particular group (such as women). (p. 21-22)

Sticky price A price is called *sticky* if it does not change often even when there is a moderate change in either demand or costs. (p. 268)

Stock option A stock option is a contract that permits its owner to buy a specified quantity of stocks of a corporation at a future date, but at the price specified in the contract rather than the stock's market price at the date of purchase. (p. 354)

Stock price index A stock price index, such as the S&P/TSX 60, is an average of the prices of a large set of stocks. These stocks are selected to represent the price movements of the entire stock market, or some specified segment of the market, and the chosen set is rarely changed. (p. 196)

Substitutes   Two goods are called substitutes if an increase in the quantity consumed of one cuts the quantity demanded of the other, all other things remaining constant. (p. 128)

Substitution effect   The substitution effect of a wage increase is the resulting incentive to work more because of the higher relative reward to labour. (p. 477)

Supply curve   A supply curve is a graphical depiction of a supply schedule. It shows how the quantity supplied of some product will change as the price of that product changes during a specified period of time, holding all other determinants of quantity supplied constant. (p. 68)

Supply curve of a firm   The supply curve of a firm shows the different quantities of output that the firm would be willing to supply at different possible prices during some given period of time. (p. 218)

Supply curve of an industry   The supply curve of an industry shows the different quantities of output that the industry would supply at different possible prices during some given period of time. (p. 219)

Supply–demand diagram   A supply–demand diagram graphs the supply and demand curves together. It also determines the equilibrium price and quantity. (p. 71)

Supply schedule   A supply schedule is a table showing how the quantity supplied of some product changes as the price of that product changes during a specified period of time, holding all other determinants of quantity supplied constant. (p. 68)

Surplus   A surplus is an excess of quantity supplied over quantity demanded. When there is a surplus, sellers cannot sell the quantities they desire to supply at the current price. (p. 71)

Takeover   A takeover is the acquisition by an outside group (the raiders) of a controlling proportion of a company's stock. When the old management opposes the takeover attempt, it is called a *hostile takeover attempt*. (p. 203)

Tangent to a curve   A tangent to a curve is a *straight* line that *touches*, but does not *cut*, the curve at a particular point. (p. 20)

Tariff   A tariff is a tax on imports. (p. 22-13)

Tax credit   A tax credit is a sum of money which can be subtracted from the amount of tax owed by a taxpayer. (p. 424)

Tax deduction   A tax deduction is a sum of money that may be subtracted before the taxpayer computes his or her taxable income. (p. 422)

Tax-exempt   A particular source of income is tax exempt if income from that source is not taxable. (p. 421)

Tax shelter   Tax shelter is a special provision of the Tax Act that reduces or defers taxation if certain conditions are met. (p. 421)

Tax shifting   Tax shifting occurs when the economic reactions to a tax cause prices and outputs in the economy to change, thereby shifting part of the burden of the tax onto others. (p. 433)

Technology trading   Technology trading is an arrangement in which a firm voluntarily makes its privately owned technology available to other firms either in exchange for access to the technology of the second company or for an agreed-upon fee. (p. 386)

Theory   A theory is a deliberate simplification of relationships used to explain how those relationships work. (p. 10)

Theory of dual labour markets   The theory of dual labour markets emphasizes that labour is supplied in two types of markets, one with high wages and promising promotion opportunities and the other with low wages and dead-end jobs. (p. 482)

Total physical product (TPP)   The firm's total physical product (TPP) is the amount of output it obtains in total from a given quantity of input. (p. 142)

Total profit   The total profit of a firm is its net earnings during some period of time. It is equal to the total amount of money the firm gets from sales of its products (the firm's total revenue) minus the total amount that it spends to make and market those products (total cost). (p. 170)

Total revenue   The total revenue of a supplier firm is the total amount of money it receives from the purchasers of its products, without any deduction of costs. (p. 171)

Total utility   The total utility of a quantity of a good to a consumer (measured in money terms) is the maximum amount of money that he or she is willing to give up in exchange for it. (p. 94)

Trade adjustment assistance   Trade adjustment assistance provides special unemployment benefits, loans, retraining programs, and other aid to workers and firms that are harmed by foreign competition. (p. 22-16)

Transaction costs   Transaction costs include the costs of obtaining necessary information costs and of the bargaining, implementation, and enforcement related to decision making. (p. 352)

Transfer payments   Transfer payments are sums of money that the government gives certain individuals as outright grants rather than as payments for services rendered to employers. Some common examples are social security and unemployment benefits. (p. 42)

Unit-elastic demand curve   A demand-curve is unit-elastic when a given percentage price change leads to the same percentage change in quantity demanded. (p. 122)

Union density   Union density or unionization rate is the number of union members as a proportion of total employment or a subset of total employment such as nonagricultural employment. (p. 485)

Variable   A variable is something measured by a number; it is used to analyze what happens to other things when the size of that number changes (varies). (p. 19)

Variable cost   A variable cost is a cost whose total amount changes when the quantity of output of the supplier changes. (pp. 142, 216)

Vertical equity   Vertical equity refers to the notion that differently situated individuals should be taxed differently in a way that society deems to be fair. (p. 429)

Workfare   A welfare transfer that requires recipients of social assistance to do work and/or acquire training in return for a welfare cheque. (p. 21-18)

Y-intercept   The *Y*-intercept of a line or a curve is the point at which it touches the vertical axis (the *Y*-axis). The *X*-intercept is defined similarly. (p. 22)

Zero-sum game   A zero-sum game is one in which exactly the amount one competitor gains must be lost by other competitors. (p. 276)

INDEX

Natural monopolies, 234–235, 241, 289
Natural resources, 350, 390, 397–399, 407–415
Necessities, 113–114, 122–123, 126
Negative slope, 20, 104–105, 109–113
Net costing margins, 267
New York Stock Exchange, 199–200
NHL (National Hockey League), 244, 348, 490
Normal goods, 103, 128
Nortel, 201

O

OECD (Organisation for Economic Co-operation and Development), 81
Oil industry, 407, 408, 411–412
Oil prices, 62, 75, 241–243, 406, 410–415
Oligopolies
  advertising and, 252, 257
  attributes of, 281
  average cost pricing and, 266–268
  behaviour models, 257–261
  capacity and, 263–268
  collusion and, 258, 259–261, 274–275, 277, 412
  definition of, 251–252, 256–257
  game-theory approach to, 272–279
  kinked demand curves and, 271–272
  marginal costs and, 261–264, 272
  markup pricing, 264–266
  price leadership and, 259–261, 267, 268
  prices and, 252, 261–262, 264–272, 411–412
  public welfare and, 278–280
  sales maximization and, 261–262
  sticky prices and, 268–271
  taxes and, 437
OPEC (Organization of Petroleum Exporting Countries), 241, 243, 412–413
Open economy, 29
Opinions, 15–17
Opportunity costs
  comparative advantage and, 55
  definition of, 6
  economic profit and, 170–174
  marginal utility and, 100–103
  perfect competition and, 223–224
  scarcity, choices and, 46–52
Optimal decisions
  definition of, 48, 168
  economic profit and, 171–174
  marginal analysis and, 95–98, 176
  time period and, 132
Optimal input quantities, 144–149
Optimal output, 331–335
Optimal purchase rule, 96–98, 101–103
Organisation for Economic Co-operation and Development (OECD), 81

Organization of Petroleum Exporting Countries (OPEC), 241, 243, 412–413
Origins (graphs), 19, 22
Outputs
  in Canada, 37
  cartels and, 241–242
  concentration ratio and, 299–303
  costs and, 149–154
  definition of, 26, 48
  economies of scale and, 154–159
  fixed costs and, 151–153, 179–180
  growth in, 335
  innovation and, 383
  inputs and, 142–149, 165, 323–325
  monopolies and, 238–242
  monopolistic competition and, 254–256
  oligopolies and, 252, 261–262, 264–272, 270, 411–412
  optimal, 331–335
  optimal input quantity and, 146–149
  perfect competition and, 214–215, 222–223, 331–335
  planned economy and, 323–325
  price and, 168–170, 173, 178, 321
  production indifference curves and, 161–165
  profit maximization and, 175–178
  supply and, 70
Outsourcing, 487, 492–493
Ownership
  foreign, 303–304, 384
  stocks and, 191–192

P

Paradox of savings/thrift, 7
Patents, 233, 372, 374, 378, 387
Payoff matrix, 273–276
Payroll taxes, 424–425, 436–437
Pension plans, 422, 424–426
Per-capita income, 368
Percentages, 120–121, 265
Perfect competition. *See also* Capitalist economy; Market economy
  attributes of, 281
  definition of, 212–213
  efficiency and, 225–228, 326–331
  individual firms and, 213–218
  industries and, 219–224
  marginal analysis of, 331–335
  monopolies, comparison of, 237–239, 329–331
  monopolistic competition *versus*, 253
  optimal outputs and, 331–335
  profits and, 214–216, 221–223
  surpluses and, 327–331
Perfectly contestable market, 280
Perfectly elastic demand curves, 121, 213–215

Perfectly inelastic demand curves, 122
Personal income tax, 419–423, 425–426, 429–430
Personal services, 356–362
Phillips, A. W. (Phillips curve), 12
Pigou, A. C. (Pigovian approach), 346–347, 390
Planned economy, 27, 165, 314, 319–325, 391–392
Plowback, 193–194
Point elasticity of demand, 135
Poland, 320
Politics, 58, 79, 83. *See also* Government; Government policies
Pollution
  costs of, 398–406
  as detrimental externality, 342–343, 345–347, 352–353, 390–406
  direct controls on, 400–403
  emission permits and, 404–406
  taxes/subsidies on, 212, 226–228, 401–403
  transaction costs and, 352–353
  voluntarism and, 400
Pollution charges, 401–403
Population, 64–66, 455–456, 474
Pork industry, 218
Portfolio diversification, 195–196
Positive slope, 20
Post hoc, ergo propter hoc **fallacy,** 11
Poverty rates, 470
Predatory pricing, 305–306
Preferences, consumer, 65–66, 109–114, 306, 322, 325–326
Present *versus* future expenditures, 349–351, 384–386
Present *versus* future value, 450–451, 467–468, 481–482
Price caps, 292–293
Price ceilings, 77–80, 292–293
Price discrimination, 242–246
Price elasticity of demand. *See* Elasticity of demand
Price floors, 77, 80–83
Price leadership, 259–261, 267, 268
Price makers, 236
Prices
  algebra and, 87
  break-even analysis and, 216–218
  budget lines and, 108–111
  cartels and, 241–246
  control of, 62, 77–84, 159, 360–362, 411–413, 460–461
  demand and, 63–64, 72–74, 318–319, 447–448
  demand curves and, 112–113, 169–170, 178
  deregulation and, 294